Zorach: *Child with Cat*, COLLECTION MUSEUM OF
MODERN ART, GIFT OF MR. AND MRS. SAM A. LEWISOHN

Aesthetics and Philosophy of

ART CRITICISM

A Critical Introduction

JEROME STOLNITZ
HERBERT H. LEHMAN COLLEGE
CITY UNIVERSITY OF NEW YORK

HOUGHTON MIFFLIN COMPANY · BOSTON
The Riverside Press Cambridge

Under the editorship of

LUCIUS GARVIN

MACALESTER COLLEGE

THE RIVERSIDE PRESS

CAMBRIDGE, MASSACHUSETTS

PRINTED IN THE U.S.A.

For

My Father and Mother

IRVING *and* JULIA STOLNITZ

Contents

Preface

Its subtitle, "A Critical Introduction," hits off the purpose and tone of this book.

The book is addressed to students in introductory courses in aesthetics, philosophy of art, or philosophy of art criticism. Many students enter such courses primarily because of their interest in one or more of the arts, and often with little or no previous training in philosophy. I have tried to bear this fact in mind. The text does not presuppose familiarity with logic, the history of philosophy, or any other field of philosophy which must be drawn upon in the study of aesthetics. All references to these fields are explained as they occur. More important, I have, throughout, attempted to relate the "critical" work of philosophy to the student's own concerns. If I have succeeded, he will feel the pertinence of bringing to light, analyzing, and assessing our foundational beliefs concerning art and the aesthetic. To this end, I have given particular attention to those concepts which, since they have great currency in aesthetic thought and discourse at the present time, dominate the thinking of many students, e.g., "expression," which is nowadays even used, without qualification, as a value-term ("How expressive!") or the genetic-biographical interpretation of fine art. The student must see for himself what is gained in clarity, consistency, and insight, by examining such beliefs. There is no point in trying to teach philosophy if our students come to think of the study as an exercise in futility or logic-chopping.

If the job of critical analysis is worth doing, then it must be done carefully and systematically. I have tried to avoid what seems to me the besetting sin of many elementary textbooks and courses, viz., "introducing" a major problem or doctrine so cursorily that it would be unrecognizable to the philosophers whose thought and interest were originally engaged by it, and then moving on to tip one's hat to another problem or "ism." The reader will find in what follows, especially in the chapters on theory of art and evaluation, detailed exposition of the major theories, much of it stated in the philosopher's own words. I try to explain the forces, sometimes historical but chiefly dialectical, which actuated the philosopher to develop his views. The analysis of each theory traces out its implications in some detail and seeks to disclose the tensions within it. Whatever my demurrers may be, I trust that I have shown that each theory has something to say that is worth saying. It need hardly be added that I have sought to expound and analyze these theories fairly and without bias, though whether or, more realistically, to what extent I have succeeded, must be left to others to judge.

It is my earnest hope that reading this book will help to make the student's thinking "critical" in several senses. He should be able to distinguish for himself what is illuminating and what is flawed in the major beliefs about the artistic and the aesthetic which vie for his allegiance at the present time. He should be able to turn the techniques of conceptual analysis upon theories other than those treated here and to test their logical consistency and empirical soundness. Most important of all, perhaps, he should come to develop the "critical" temper — forsaking credulity, refusing to suffer one-sidedness or unexamined assumptions, suspending judgment where need be. This frame of mind is especially to be prized in the study of aesthetics, a field in which edifying, but obscure phrases and eulogizing dressed up as "theory" have too often taken the place of analytic clarity and a catholic respect for fact.

But again, most students will not devote themselves to philosophical aesthetics unless they see its bearing upon the appreciation and criticism of concrete works of art. They will find copious, often detailed references to specific works both within the text and in the "Questions" which follow each chapter. Reproductions of many of these works will also be found herein. Students should, of course, be encouraged to cite, where relevant, other works with which they may be more familiar, though it is happily true that they do not usually need such encouragement. This is certainly not a book in "art appreciation," in the usual acceptation. Yet at a number of places it challenges the student to examine his own commerce with art-objects, how he approaches and tries to appreciate them. I have not thought it incompatible with the primarily "critical" function of the text to suggest ways in which aesthetic perception can become more discriminating and rewarding.

Prefaces to textbooks frequently offer the instructor an outline for organizing his course along the lines of the book. This seems to me fatuous and even faintly presumptuous. The instructor, who has his own interests and predilections, and who knows his students first-hand, can and will decide for himself. I therefore forbear. I should, however, note that the concept of "the aesthetic attitude" is logically central to the entire book, so that, however the course is organized, the student should read, fairly early, chap. 2, secs. 1, 2, and 5, and chap. 3, sec. 1.

It is also worth remarking that this text treats the issues of evaluation and art criticism at much greater length than do other texts in the field. Just these issues are often the most interesting of all to the beginning student. A semester course in philosophy of art criticism can be based upon parts V and VI. A semester course in aesthetics might sacrifice some of the earlier topics to one or both of these parts of the book. The number of topics treated in the entire book is, I believe, sufficiently great so that the instructor has considerable latitude for choice.

I am glad to record my considerable indebtedness to my own students, all of whom were guinea pigs and many of whom were — what is far better — gadflies. I am also indebted to those who read and criticized various parts of the manuscript: Henry D. Aiken, Frances Hamblin, Howard Merritt, Huntington Terrell. I am especially grateful to Professor Terrell for his meticulously careful reading and searching criticisms. It was at the suggestion of Professor Lucius Garvin that I began work on this book; his encouragement contributed to its completion; and his criticisms of the entire manuscript have improved it. However, the traditional *mea culpa* must be voiced at this point.

Dorothy N. helped too.

J. S.

Rochester, New York
January, 1959

P*lates*

❦

The following plates, with the exception of the frontispiece, are grouped together at the end of the text, following page 501.

Aesthetics and Philosophy of Art Criticism

The Study of Aesthetics

1. PHILOSOPHY — THE CRITICISM OF OUR BELIEFS

If I had to choose one single word to describe the function and "spirit" of philosophy, it would be *critical*. But the meaning of this word should not be misunderstood. In everyday speech it usually has a narrower meaning than the one I have in mind. When we say, in everyday discourse, that we are "critical of that person," we generally mean that we find fault with him. Philosophy is not "critical" in this sense. It is not peevish fault-finding; it is not "always belittlin'," like the bad-tempered people whom all of us know.

Rather, philosophy is "critical" in a broader sense. In this sense, it examines something in order to determine its strengths and weaknesses. On this meaning, critical inquiry is concerned with the virtues as well as the faults of what it studies. Now, *what* does philosophy study critically? It is not as easy to answer this question as might be thought. It can be said, however, that philosophy criticizes some of the most important and widespread beliefs held by human beings. An example would be the belief that God exists. Another example would be the belief that there are certain acts, such as keeping promises or being loyal to one's country, which we ought to perform, and others, such as telling lies or cheating on examinations, which are morally wrong. Still another example is the belief in certain goals or "values" of human existence for which we should strive, e.g., getting as much pleasure as we can, or, at the opposite pole, self-sacrificing Christian love.

I have described the beliefs which philosophy criticizes as being both "important and widespread." It will be obvious from the examples that such beliefs are indeed widespread. Virtually all adult human beings, in whatever culture or historical period they have lived, have held a belief of one kind or another concerning each of these issues. If the student will take a moment to think about it, he will find that this is true of himself as well, however vague or unsure his beliefs may be.

But we cannot understand the importance of the beliefs studied by philosophy until we consider the significance of beliefs in general. Beliefs are not so many items on the shelves of our intellectual stockrooms, generally unused, but occasionally dusted off and taken out — for a "bull session," for example. They are far more important than that. For they control and direct the course of our lives. We are always *acting* in the light of our beliefs. What we take to be true about the world and about ourselves is crucial to our decision to perform one act rather than another, to pursue some goal rather than its alternative. Your beliefs about yourself determine your choice of a field of concentration in college; your beliefs about others determine your choice of a date for the school dance.

Hence a great deal hinges on the soundness of our beliefs. Action will not generally be rewarding and successful unless it is based on reliable beliefs. Action which lacks the enlightenment of true belief is bound to be erratic and futile. It is the product of superstition, "hunch," or inertia.

The beliefs studied by philosophy are those which underlie our behavior in the central areas of human experience. In the case of ethics, philosophy is not so much concerned with a specific moral decision — Shall I tell a lie to make a profit in this business transaction? — as with the principles of right and wrong upon which the decision is based. A man whose moral principles are unsound will act in a shabby and reprehensible way. The situation is similar in the area of experience with which we shall be concerned — the creation and appreciation of art. Our enjoyment of art — if we have any — depends upon our beliefs concerning its nature and value. Here again, as we shall later see in detail, faulty beliefs lead to profitless behavior.

Now WHAT DOES IT MEAN, specifically, to say that philosophy is "critical" of our beliefs? To begin with, let us admit that most of our beliefs concerning such vital issues as religion and morality are conspicuously *un*critical. Stop again to consider your own beliefs in these matters, asking yourself why you have come to hold these beliefs. In most cases, it is safe to say, you will find that you have not "come by" these beliefs as a result of prolonged and serious thinking about them. Rather, you have accepted them on the strength of some authority, i.e., some individual or institution which urged these beliefs upon you. The authority might be your parents, your teachers, your church, or your friends. Many of our beliefs are taken over from what we vaguely call "society" or "public opinion." These authorities have not, as a general rule, forced their convictions upon you. Rather, you have assimilated these beliefs from the "climate of opinion" in which you have developed. Thus most of your beliefs concerning such questions as the existence of God or whether it is ever right to tell a lie, are intellectual "hand-me-downs."

But this does not mean, of course, that these beliefs are necessarily false or unsound. They may perfectly well be true. "Hand-me-downs" sometimes wear very well. The point is, rather, this: a belief is not true simply because some authority says that it is. Suppose I were to ask you about a certain belief, "How do you know that that is true?" It would certainly not be a satisfactory answer to say, "Because I was told so by my parents (teachers, friends, etc.)." This in itself does not guarantee the truth of the belief, because such authorities have frequently been wrong. Much that our forefathers believed about medicine and transmitted to later generations has been shown to be false. And since the very first schools, students have — thank Heaven — found errors in what their teachers were saying and have tried to work out sounder beliefs for themselves. In other words, the truth of a belief must rest upon its own merits. If your parents taught you that it is disastrous to overindulge in green apples, then their assertion is *true* not because they said so, but because certain (highly unpleasant) facts show that it is true. If you accept a "law" of science which you have read in a textbook, it ought to be accepted, not because it was written in a textbook, but because it rests upon experimental evidence and mathematical reasoning. We are *justified* in holding a belief only when it is supported by evidence and sound logic. But, as I have been urging, most of us never test our beliefs in this way.

Here is where the "critical" activity of philosophy comes in. Philosophy refuses to accept any belief which is not shown to be true by evidence and reasoning. A belief which cannot be established in this way is unworthy of our intellectual allegiance and is usually a hazardous guide to action. Philosophy dedicates itself, therefore, to the searching examination of beliefs which we have accepted uncritically from various authorities. We must rid ourselves of the prejudices and emotions which often becloud our beliefs. Philosophy will not permit any belief to pass inspection merely because it has been enshrined by tradition or because people find it emotionally satisfying to hold the belief. Philosophy will not accept a belief simply because it is thought to be "plain common sense" nor because it has been proclaimed by wise men. Philosophy tries to take nothing "for granted" or "on faith." It is devoted to persistent, open-minded inquiry, in order to learn whether, and to what extent, our beliefs are justified. In this way, philosophy keeps us from sinking into the mental complacency and dogmatism to which all human beings are prone.

AESTHETICS, or as it is sometimes called, *philosophy of art*, is a branch of philosophy. Hence, what has been said of philosophy in general is true of aesthetics as well. Aesthetics undertakes to examine critically our beliefs concerning such questions as these: What is the nature of "fine art"? What distinguishes the creative artist from the nonartist? What sort of experience is the "appreciation" of art? Why is this experience a valuable one? Can we settle disagreement concerning art, as when A says that jazz is "imaginative" and "exciting," and B says that it is "barbaric" and "nothing but noise"; or when you and a friend disagree about the merits of some particular artist, such as Tchaikovsky? What does it mean to say that a person has "good taste," or "better taste" than somebody else? Does it mean anything at all? What is the function of the critic? Is censorship of art ever justified? If so, under what circumstances? What is the importance of art in human experience?

These questions illustrate the kind of problem which we shall be studying. There is no need to try to tie them into any neat "definition" of "aesthetics," even if that were possible. Any such would-be definition would have little meaning or value for the student at this point. Later in this chapter the student will find a more systematic statement of the chief problems in aesthetics and the ways in which they are related to each other. There is, however, no way to learn what aesthetics is about except by seeing how it criticizes our beliefs concerning these questions.

But what exactly *are* our beliefs on these issues? Even if the student can give an answer to each of the above questions, can he state clearly what he means by it? Like our beliefs in ethics and religion, these beliefs are generally *un*-critical. Because we have not usually reflected upon them before accepting them, they are vague and largely inarticulate. Therefore, we must clarify what we *mean* when we use such terms as "art," "beautiful," and "good taste." This is an indispensable step in being "critical" of our beliefs. For we cannot adduce evidence for and against our beliefs until we know just exactly what it is that we believe.

Once we have spelled out our beliefs with some clarity, we may find that we believe not one, but several different things, about most or all of the above questions. We may be somewhat appalled by this, but it is not especially surprising. Most people's beliefs about these issues are an ill-assorted collection of catch phrases, undeveloped ideas, and emotions parading as ideas. It is part of the job of critical inquiry to set these forth in a systematic and orderly way. We may also learn something else about our beliefs which is more discouraging. And that is, not only do we have *different* beliefs about the same question, but these beliefs sometimes *contradict* each other. We hold two beliefs which are logically opposed to each other, in the sense that if one of them is true, the other cannot possibly be true. Thus a person may hold that anyone's opinion of the value of a work of art is as good as that of anybody else; yet, at another time he withdraws his own opinion in favor of the verdict of an "expert" or a professional critic, because he considers the latter especially qualified to pass judgment on art. This kind of self-contradiction is not especially surprising either, for "common sense" is full of such contradictions. They go unnoticed for the most part, precisely because what we call "common sense" never stops to take stock of its beliefs. To point out these logical inconsistencies, and to overcome them, is a further task of "critical" philosophy. Finally, aesthetics submits our beliefs to the acid test of evidence, to determine whether they are supported by fact. In view of the vagueness, diversity, and inconsistency of our beliefs, the student will begin to see that it is no trivially easy job to be "critical" of them.

2. WHY SHOULD WE STUDY AESTHETICS?

Before we proceed, however, there is a prior question which demands attention. I have been saying that philosophy is incessantly "critical." But if that is so, must not philosophy be critical *of itself* also? Indeed, throughout the history of philosophy, philosophers have asked searching questions about their objectives and methods, and about the *value* of engaging in philosophy. Let us also be "critical" from the very beginning and ask "Why should we study aesthetics?" Are there any good reasons why students should be concerned about such questions as those listed earlier? We would like to think that there are reasons for doing so which are better than those of the undergraduate in the old and cynical story, who chose his courses for the year with no regard for subject matter, but solely on the principle that none of them met before ten o'clock or above the second floor.

Probably the best way to meet this question is to consider certain arguments which try to show that we should *not* study aesthetics. As we shall see, these arguments attempt to prove that the study of aesthetics is superfluous or futile or even harmful. We must certainly try to answer these arguments successfully, if we can. No one, probably, expects that, if we fail to find the answers, we will close up shop before we have even begun our study. But this does not minimize these arguments, some of which are very strong indeed. Even if they do not prove their case, they are instructive because they keep us from falling into serious errors in our thinking about aesthetics. They help us to get clear about the purpose of studying aesthetics and the methods we must use in doing so.

What, then, are the arguments against studying aesthetics?

ARGUMENT 1. Other fields of study — such as psychology, sociology, art history, and the analysis of art techniques — can answer all of our questions concerning art. This is the argument that there is no need for aesthetics, because what we know about art comes, not from philosophy, but from other fields. Thus, to find out what goes on in the experience of appreciating art, we turn to the psychologist. For he is specially qualified to analyze and explain the psychological states of perception, emotion, imagination, etc., which make up the experience. Similarly, if we want to understand the psychological make-up of the creative artist, and how he differs from human beings who are not artists, then psychology alone can help us. The origins of art in society, its interrelations with other social institutions such as religion, economics, and morality, and its significance in human culture are explained by sociology and anthropology. To trace the evolution of artistic "styles" and periods, e.g., Romanticism, and the development of artistic "forms," such as the novel, is the task of the historians of each of the arts. Only those who are skilled in the particular arts can explain such things as harmony in music, or the workings of such devices as metaphor in literature. If we want interpretations and analyses of particular works of art, so that we may appreciate them more fully, we consult critics in each of the arts or the artists themselves. The chief sources of our knowledge of art have now been listed. In view of the overwhelming amount of information which they provide us, the argument runs, the study of aesthetics is superfluous and unnecessary.

How, if at all, can this argument be answered? In the first place, it is obvious that we *have* gained most of what we know about art from these fields of study. Aesthetics would be bankrupt from the start if it denied this and tried to set itself up as a substitute for these other studies. However, the conclusion of the argument — that aesthetics can add nothing — does not follow from this. For, as the following discussion will attempt to show, the other studies leave untouched certain crucial questions about art.

OF THE VARIOUS FIELDS mentioned above, it is noteworthy that none of them considers explicitly a question which is central to the study of art — why is fine art valuable? The belief that art ranks high among the "good things of life" is almost universal. There are even those who hold that art is the *most* valuable achievement in human experience. Aesthetics is "critical" of these beliefs: Is art really so admirable and worth while as we generally think? If so, what constitutes the value of art?

8

To these basic questions, the psychologist or the sociologist as such does not return an answer. He will frequently *presuppose* the value of works of art in his research. Thus a psychologist may examine the reactions of a large number of people to both "good" and "bad" art. Or the sociologist may say that a certain culture produced "great" art because of the organization of its society. But the meaning of "good" or "great" as applied to art, is not examined. The job of analyzing meaning is left to the aesthetician. Furthermore, psychology and sociology do not survey the knowledge gained by all approaches to art, including their own, art history, art criticism, etc. Aesthetics does just this, in order to gain a well-rounded and inclusive knowledge of art, as a basis for answering the questions of artistic value. Therefore, aesthetics differs from these other studies because it comes to grips with the problems of value and because it draws comprehensively upon all of the specialized fields of research into art.

Yet it might be argued, in rebuttal, that the psychologist *can* settle such questions. For whether a work of art is good or bad depends upon the kind of experience which a person has while looking at it. To take an elementary example for purposes of discussion, let us say that a work [1] is "valuable" only if it arouses intense emotion. (The example is not entirely hypothetical, for there are many people who seem to hold just this view.) If this is so, then we must turn to the psychologist to learn whether a given work has this effect. People are frequently confused and unreliable in describing their own "inner" experiences. The psychologist can determine whether and to what extent emotional excitation has occurred, why it was brought about by this particular work of art, and so on.

Now does this show that psychology can explain the value of art? Only on one condition, but that one is crucial: only if it can be shown that the arousal of intense emotion *is*, indeed, what makes art valuable. But this can never be established by means of psychology alone. Any such definition of artistic "value" in terms of psychological responses to art might be and often has been challenged. Those who oppose such a view believe that the value of art does not depend upon the response which it arouses in human beings. They hold that its value is inherent in art. Therefore they consider it a grotesque mistake to identify artistic value with the "twitches" and "tingles" which some human beings feel. Now we do not have to settle this conflict of opinions at the present time. We shall discuss the issue at some length later on. At this time the point is that psychology cannot itself resolve this disagreement. By contrast, aesthetics tries to set forth precisely the theories which have here been stated loosely, to think through their implications, and to determine their strengths and weaknesses.

Other specialized studies of art, such as sociology and history, also fail to elucidate its value. They are concerned with the importance of works of

[1] Here and elsewhere, this word is used in place of "work of art."

9

art in human society. But works can be "important" in social history whether or not they are valuable as works of art. A piece of literature or a musical composition can have significant influence on social change as a propaganda document or as a stimulus to revolution, but this does not mean necessarily that it is a *good* work of art. You may have heard the anecdote about Lincoln meeting Harriet Beecher Stowe, the author of *Uncle Tom's Cabin*, while the Civil War was going on, and saying to her, "So this is the little lady who made the great war." Assuming that it did help to crystallize antislavery feeling, it would not follow that *Uncle Tom's Cabin* is an especially good novel.

There is another question, one which is even more fundamental than that of the value of art, which the nonphilosophical approaches to art fail to consider. And that is the question, "What *is* art?" The fields of study cited earlier all use the term "art," for they are all concerned with art from one standpoint or another. But they fail to examine its meaning systematically. Hence this question too must be treated by aesthetics.

"But," it may be replied, "these other studies don't *have* to consider such questions. They can amass information about art, considered psychologically, sociologically, historically, technically, etc., without bothering about such 'high-level' questions as 'the nature of art.' " This is, to some extent, true. But notice that if you say this, then you are granting the point at issue — you are conceding that these studies do *not* answer all questions concerning art. Indeed, they fail to answer some of the most important and basic questions which can be asked about art. The first argument designed to show that we should not study aesthetics therefore proves to be inadequate.

However, it is not even true to say that the questions considered by aesthetics are of no importance to the nonphilosophical studies of art. In some cases, of course, the latter can get on without serious analysis of the nature and value of art. Thus, a man could write a "social history" of art, without entering into these questions. Even so, what he said would not be entirely clear if he never explained what he meant by "art," but simply took it "for granted." (If he did address himself to the question, then he would already be within the realm of aesthetics.)

But in other areas, failure to be philosophical about basic beliefs can have very damaging consequences. Consider, in this connection, criticism of the arts. It is sometimes said that the work of the critic is entirely different from, and even antithetical to, that of the aesthetician. The critic busies himself with particular works of art — *this* poem or *this* sculpture — trying to analyze and explain it, and to decide whether it is of value and to what extent. Hence the "abstract" questions of aesthetics are of no interest to him.

The critic, then, says of a work that it is "beautiful" or "great art" or "better than the artist's previous work." The critic's judgment is of little significance, however, unless we know his *reasons* for making it. His praise of the work is simply like shouting "Hurrah!"; it tells us nothing except that he likes the work, unless he can explain and defend his approval. He must be able to state clearly what he means by "beauty" or "greatness" in art. He must make explicit the criteria or yardsticks of value in the light of which he arrived at his judgment. If he fails to do so, his criticism is hopelessly vague and we literally do not know what he is talking about. To take a very simple analogy, it would be like saying that the temperature is 50 degrees, without specifying whether this is Centigrade or Fahrenheit. Therefore, if the critic is to do his job intelligently, he must reflect upon the nature of artistic value.

Most critics probably do make it clear which standards of value they are employing, though many do so only indirectly or by implication. However, they are often not philosophical enough in arriving at their beliefs about value, with the result that their criticism of art is trivial or worthless. For, as the history of art criticism shows, critics (like the rest of us) are prone to take over unquestioningly value-standards from tradition or some authority. These standards may be appropriate for judging works of a certain period or style. But the critic takes it for granted that they are valid universally, for all works of art. When he applies these standards to art of a quite different kind, he misjudges it entirely. It is like using the criteria of a good weight-lifter to estimate the virtues of a piano-player. Thus, if a critic believes that painting is good if it depicts faithfully objects and people in our everyday world, and applies this criterion to so-called "modern" art, which doesn't "look like" anything, he will come up with the conclusion which all of us have heard — that such art is "monstrous" or a "hoax" or something even more sinister than that. But the fault may be, not with the painting, but with the critic. His value-standards are too narrow and constricted. If he were to think more persistently and open-mindedly about the nature of artistic value, he might change his criteria. He might find more relevant value-criteria, in the light of which contemporary art can be seen to possess value, in its own way. So, like anyone else concerned with art, he must examine the underlying beliefs which govern his approach to art. The alternative is to shut himself up in unrepentant dogmatism.

Another instance of the vital importance of aesthetics to the nonphilosophical study of art will be given. Experimentation on the ways in which people respond to art has been going on in psychology since the last quarter of the nineteenth century. It has held out the hope of providing scientifically accurate and precise answers to many of the questions in aesthetics which have been debated for centuries. It has, in recent years especially, produced some valuable findings. For the most part, however, the results of psychological experimentation have been disappointing. Its conclusions have been trivial, sometimes even silly, even when presented in very elaborate mathematical and statistical terms. Why is this? Chiefly, as I now wish to show, because psychologists have so often failed to examine "critically" the beliefs concerning the nature and value of art which they "took for granted" in drawing up their experiments.

Psychologists have carried out innumerable experiments in which large groups of people were presented with elementary geometrical forms, such as rectangles of various shapes, or with patches of color. The "subjects" were then asked to express a preference among them. Which forms or colors do they find most pleasant? It is found in one experiment using 4,556 "subjects" that the color blue is preferred to violet, and the color orange is least popular of all; [2] in another experiment, that an arrangement of black-violet-gray is more pleasant than one of yellow-gray-red; [3] and so on.

Now, of what use are such findings? Those who performed these experiments were hopeful that, if the pleasantness of single colors could be determined, then the value of works of art could be explained. "Ultimately the complex effect of pictures, buildings, and landscapes could be reconstructed as an effect of colors of a certain degree of pleasantness, combined in relationships of . . . certain degrees of pleasantness." [4] But this enterprise is futile from the outset. The significance and value of a color taken in isolation are entirely different from what they are in a painting. Within the total work of art, the appearance, pleasantness, imaginative import, and emotional "tang" of the color are determined by its interrelationships with everything else in the painting. Its pleasantness is influenced by the texture of the paint, the way in which it is set off by other colors, the formal patterns of lines and masses in the painting, the people or events making up the "subject matter," the emotional expressiveness of the entire work, and a host of other factors. A yellow-green abstracted from one of the works of Toulouse-Lautrec might seem dull or inane, yet it is anything but that when we see it within the total painting. Therefore, any inference from experiments with color-patches to the value of works of art can only be grossly misleading. As Professor Morgan says, "Responding to an El Greco on a museum wall simply isn't much like comparing cardboard rectangles . . . and it is difficult to see . . . how any number of such cardboard comparisons will ever pile up, one on top of the

---

[2] Albert R. Chandler, *Beauty and Human Nature* (New York: Appleton-Century, 1934), pp. 72–73. Copyright, 1934, D. Appleton-Century Co., Inc. Reprinted by permission of Appleton-Century-Crofts, Inc.

[3] *Ibid.*, pp. 84–86.

[4] *Ibid.*, p. 71.

ing. Similarly, the experience alone can never explain what we mean when we speak of "fine art," and how it is different from nonartistic objects. Here again, reflection concerning a large group of objects must supervene upon immediate experience of one of them. Unless it did, human knowledge would be pitifully limited.

Yet, it may be said, conceptual knowledge is entirely irrelevant to the experience of perceiving art directly. Whatever we may think about "art" has nothing to do with our enjoyment of particular works of art. But this also is untrue, as I shall try to show in discussing the next argument.

ARGUMENT 3. The study of aesthetics is harmful, because it deadens our interest in art and destroys the vitality and excitement of works of art. The poet Keats wrote:

> Do not all charms fly
> At the mere touch of cold philosophy? . . .
> Philosophy will clip an Angel's wings,
> Conquer all mysteries by rule and line,
> Empty the haunted air, and gnomed mine —
> Unweave a rainbow.
>
> "Lamia"

Keats here speaks for many who are genuinely sensitive to and fond of art. If we analyze and pick at art, we make of it something dead and colorless; it is no longer a live being of imaginative excitement and emotional power; we "murder to dissect." If we stop to think about our experience of appreciating art, and try to understand the elements which make it up, we suffocate the experience. Let us, then, forego such analysis and simply enjoy art, spontaneously and to the full. Aesthetics is a kind of heresy which desecrates what is precious; if we allow it, it will "clip an angel's wings."

If this argument against studying aesthetics were sound, it would be the most powerful of all. Nothing more damning can be said about any activity than that it destroys human values. If aesthetics really does stultify our appreciation of art, so that art becomes no longer enjoyable and exciting, then that would be the strongest possible reason for not studying it. But does it have this effect?

It *may*, but if we are clear about what we are doing, it need not do so. The great danger to avoid is that of confusing the experience of direct appreciation with reflective knowledge about art, which we distinguished in discussing Argument 2. We fall into this confusion when, instead of responding to the charm and vigor of the work of art, we use the work to test some belief or theory about art with which we are concerned in aesthetics. To approach art with such an intellectual interest is not the way to appreciate it. Similarly, if we try to analyze the appreciative experience in order to gain understanding of it, we can no longer give our attention to the art-object. Like most experiences, it will collapse or change its character when subjected to self-conscious scrutiny. Then we lose out. For, as Professor Lee says, "It is probably more desirable to appreciate beauty than to understand it." [7] This is not only true, but should be made stronger by striking out the word "probably." It remains true even though the questions of aesthetics can be highly interesting and challenging in their own right.

However, the process of clarifying and justifying our beliefs is not entirely divorced from our appreciation of art. As was said earlier, our beliefs are important primarily because we act in the light of what we believe. Our beliefs about art and what makes it valuable determine how we approach works of art and what we try to "get out of" them. There is a great difference between believing that art is valuable because it is pleasingly "nice" to look at or listen to, and believing that its function is to create emotional excitement, and again between both of these and believing that what we should look for in the work is the personality of the artist. Now suppose for the moment that each or all of these beliefs is unsound. Suppose that art is not really what these beliefs take it to be, or that it is far richer and more worth while than these beliefs consider it to be. Then those who hold these beliefs are not really enjoying the true value of art, or they are missing a good deal of its value. Critical examination of their beliefs, and consideration of the beliefs of others, may lead to a more adequate conception of art. This, in turn, can make their experience of art more vivid and more satisfying. The analysis of art, against which Argument 3 protests, may disclose new values and new areas of interest in art. When this happens, as it often does, it gives the lie to the argument. For the best proof that the study of aesthetics does not deaden our appreciation of art is that it frequently makes our appreciation more perceptive and more rewarding.

Argument 3 has been directed not only against aesthetics, but also against other kinds of talking about and "dissection" of art. These include courses and lectures in art and "art appreciation." And indeed, courses in "art appreciation" frequently do anything but cultivate interest in art. Often, they destroy whatever interest the student has to begin with. This is why many people now say "art appreciation" with a sneer or a sour look. The chief reason, I believe, why such courses are frequently so deadly is that they blur the distinction between enjoying art and talking about it. Once we understand this distinction, we can apply it to the teaching of "art appreciation." Such teaching may then be able to avoid the chief mis-

[7] Harold N. Lee, *Perception and Aesthetic Value*, p. 9. Copyright 1938 by Prentice-Hall, Inc., Englewood Cliffs, N.J. Reprinted by permission of the publisher.

takes that have plagued it in the past. Thus this field, like those of psychology and art criticism, can profit from such discussions as we are now carrying on.

ARGUMENT 4. The study of aesthetics is futile because works of art are entirely unique, so that we can never find anything which is true of art in general. Aesthetics is concerned with the nature and value of art "in general." Therefore, it tries to decide what it is that particular works of art have in common. But works of art have little or nothing in common with each other. Each particular work of art is unique and unlike any other. Consider a poem by Wordsworth, an opera by Wagner, a painting by Picasso. We call them all "works of art." But how profoundly *different* they are from each other! They differ in certain obvious ways — one is made up of words, another is oils on canvas, and so on. More important, the experience which one of them arouses in us is not at all like that created by another. It is precisely this uniqueness which we cherish in a work of art. A work is just itself and unlike anything else in the world. If you try to tell someone in love that the object of his affection is "just like any other human being — a two-legged mammal with a complicated nervous system," he will become impatient with you. And with good reason. Though what you say is true enough, it ignores precisely those distinctive features of the lady which set off her adorable self from other human beings. The same is true of art. Think of some work of which you are especially fond, some novel or some melody. It is because of its distinctive quality, the special excitement of the novel or the "catchiness" of the melody, that you like it. Works of art are not like paper clips or assembly-line automobiles, all of which are alike and each of which is as good as the next. Therefore, this argument concludes, it is futile to try to arrive at any generalizations about "art," as aesthetics attempts to do.

This argument is very strong and must be given serious consideration.

In large measure, we know things by the characteristics or properties which they have in common with many other things. Take an elementary item of knowledge like "The table is green." To know that this object is a table, rather than a chair or a kangaroo, requires that we should recognize certain properties which are found in other tables — it has legs, is used to serve meals on, is sold by furniture stores, and so on. Similarly, to say that it is "green" presupposes that we recognize the similarity of its color to the color of other things — grass, flags, and clothing seen on St. Patrick's Day. We could not identify or classify things unless they were, in certain respects, similar to each other. If we were suddenly confronted by something different in every respect from anything that we had known before, we would be completely baffled. We would be like the savage seeing an airplane for the first time. But even the savage tries to overcome his ignorance by describing the strange object in terms of its resemblance to what he has already seen — he calls it a "large bird." Perhaps the best example of utter uniqueness is God. The Christian tradition has frequently insisted that we can never name or describe God, because He is completely unlike any other being. We use words, based upon our own experience, as when we say that God is loving or just. But these are only faint approximations, for God's "transcendent" nature is not really similar to anything that we have seen or known.

Now let us apply this reasoning in the case of art. Just as we say that certain objects are tables, we also say that some objects are works of art. This seems to imply that there *are* properties common to these objects, in virtue of which they resemble each other. The question for aesthetics is, "What are these properties which constitute an object a work of art?"

But those who uphold Argument 4 deny that there are any such properties, for, they say, works of art are unique. Yet this contention by no means clinches the argument. For *everything* is, in *some* respect, unique. This table resembles other tables; hence we can know it and speak of it as a table. Yet *this* table is unique, because it is located in just this room, has this odd-looking scratch on the top, is a precious heirloom of the family. All objects are unique in some respects, alike in others. Every human being has certain distinctive physical or psychological features. However, this does not prevent us from recognizing those characteristics which are common to all human beings. Uniqueness in certain respects does not preclude knowledge of a thing.

Now it may be that we shall find, in the course of our study, that the differences between works of art are far more important than the similarities. We may find that the respects in which works of art resemble each other are trivial. These common characteristics may not explain the value which we find in art, as the prosaic description quoted above does not explain the value of one's lady-love. If so, it would be more profitable to stop talking about "Art" in general, and to devote our time to the particular arts — poetry, music, architecture, etc., — and to particular works of art. But how are we to decide this unless we actually consider in detail the nature of art, by examining works of art and investigating the leading theories of art? In other words, the only way to find out whether there are significant resemblances among works of art is by the study of aesthetics. Argument 4 seems to provide an easy way out, because it short-circuits the study at the very start. But it has not proved its case and cannot possibly do so until we have completed our study. To say at the very outset that no important generalizations about art are possible is sheer dogmatism.

Though it is inconclusive, this argument is salutary. It makes us keep in mind the great differences between works of art. Thereby it keeps us from making hasty generalizations about "art" when we have made only a limited survey of works of art. We must take account of the art of many different media — literature, painting, the dance, motion pictures and so on, as well as art of many different periods and "styles." Only so can we be relatively sure that we have not ignored or glossed over salient differences among works of art. This is imperative if our beliefs about art are to be true to the facts of art. Further, if we do arrive at some generalizations about art, we should remember that works of art, like other things, are unique as well as similar. We should not allow our vision to be blinded, so that we see in works of art only those properties which they share with other works and fail to see what is distinctive about them. This is as disastrous in the appreciation of art as it is in love.

3. *HOW* SHOULD WE STUDY AESTHETICS?

Our discussion thus far has largely implied the answer to this question. But the question is an important one, and it warrants an explicit answer at this time.

First and foremost, we should study aesthetics *critically*. This means, as we have seen, that we should be prepared to challenge our beliefs concerning art, in order to determine their strengths and weaknesses. We should do so, whether the beliefs are our own or those of "common sense" or some "authority." We should demand that the meaning of these beliefs be made clear. We should investigate the reasoning by which these beliefs have been arrived at and decide whether it is sound. We should see whether these beliefs are logically consistent with other beliefs which have been shown to be true. If they are not, then they must be rejected. In addition to clarifying the meaning of our beliefs and analyzing their logical validity, we must test the truth of these beliefs by examining the relevant evidence. This includes, as we have seen, the evidence garnered by such fields of study as psychology, art history, and art criticism. Any belief which is not supported by evidence should be given up. Where the evidence is not conclusive, one way or the other, we should reserve judgment. We should never hold any belief with a degree of conviction greater than the available evidence warrants. In the words of the American philosopher William James, we should keep open "the windows of the mind," always searching for new evidence and changing our beliefs when we find it. We must resist the ever-present temptation to accept nice-sounding slogans or one-sided views of art, however attractive they may be, without examining them critically. Those who succumb to this temptation are losers many times over: they cannot know whether their beliefs are justified, they forego the real excitement and satisfaction which is to be found in the process of criticizing beliefs, and, perhaps most important, their experience of art is distorted or blind because of the weakness of the beliefs with which they approach art.

It follows from this that we should study aesthetics *empirically*. This means that we should gain as much factual knowledge about art as we can, and that our beliefs should be held accountable to this data. Whatever we say about art must be capable of being understood in terms of concrete experience. Any belief or theory must be stated with sufficient clarity so that we can put it to the test of empirical evidence. A belief which does not fail in this test only because it is stated so vaguely that we are unsure what evidence counts for and against it, or because it refers to what can never be observed in human experience, can never *pass* this test either. Of any such belief we must say "not proved."

To study aesthetics in this way means that we shall avoid two errors which have marred much previous thinking in aesthetics:

(1) Many traditional theories of art and beauty have not arrived at their conclusions by examining concrete works of art and the experience of appreciating art. Rather, they have formulated some grandiose conception of "Reality" and have then inferred from this what the nature of art must be like. Sometimes these "metaphysical" theories of art contain sound insights. More often, since their theories of "Reality" were highly questionable, and since they ignored the empirical data of art and its enjoyment, the conclusions which they drew were of little value. The German psychologist Fechner described such theories as proceeding "von Oben herab" — "from the top down." We shall study aesthetics "from the bottom up," basing our theories upon the empirical evidence so far as we can.

(2) Much talk and writing about art, under the guise of explaining its nature and value, has done something quite different — it has rhapsodized about art. Both traditionally and at the present time, aesthetics has been devoted largely to singing the praises of art. This is, of course, tribute to the great power and value of art, for men usually acclaim most profusely what is dearest to them. But it only leads to confusion and muddle-headedness if these eulogies are taken to be clear and empirically reliable explanations of the nature of art. Consider such would-be "definitions" as "Art is our only barrier against chaos" or "Art is the union of man and nature" or "Beauty is the supreme expression of the absolute reality uttering itself through man." What is wrong with them is not so much that they are false, as that they are so imprecise and tell us so very little. They are, indeed, so vague that it is difficult to know where to look for the evidence with which to test them. Let us try to steer clear of such rhapsodizing as we go on with our study.

Finally, we should study aesthetics with a sense of *curiosity*. We should try to maintain an interest in "finding out" — about art, about different theories of art and the sparks which they strike when they come into conflict with each other, about the relations of art to other areas of human experience. For those who are persistently inquisitive and "critical," the study of aesthetics can be richly challenging. Most students do have a great deal of spontaneous curiosity about such questions — unless or until it is destroyed by what they read in textbooks and listen to in the classroom. Let us hope that our study does not fall prey to this.

4. THE MAJOR AREAS OF STUDY

When we speak of art and its enjoyment, we use three words chiefly. They are "art," "aesthetic," and "beauty." It is an important part of our job to arrive at clear and precise meanings for words which people use loosely and unthinkingly. At this time, a preliminary analysis of the meaning of these terms, and the relations between them, will be given. This will provide a starting point for later analysis. Furthermore, each of these terms designates a different area of study in aesthetics. Hence the present discussion will help us to see what the major areas of our study are to be. It will also explain why we take up these areas in the order which is followed in this book.

People often use the terms "artistic," "aesthetic," and "beautiful" interchangeably. To express admiration of an object which is skilfully and cleverly designed, they will say that it is "highly artistic" or "very aesthetic" or "beautiful." Such usage is unfortunate, because it confuses three kinds of facts which are quite different from each other. Most of us are at least vaguely aware of these differences. "Art" refers to the production or creation of objects through some kind of human effort. Thus we speak of the "creative artist" and of the product of his activity, the "work of art." "Beauty" refers to the attractiveness or value of objects. "Aesthetic" is the least widely used of these terms. When it is used, it often retains the meaning of the Greek word (aisthēsis) from which it is derived, for it refers to perceiving or looking at interesting objects. The creation of objects, the value of objects, and the perception of them are clearly quite different. The distinctions between them will become better defined as we proceed.

Under the heading of "art," we wish to learn what distinguishes "works of art" from nonartistic objects, and more especially, what distinguishes "*fine* art." Now how is "art" related to what is "beautiful"?

To begin with, not all works of art are beautiful. We can all think of works which are dull and neutral or else downright ugly. Moreover, there are works which are attractive or exciting but which we would not be inclined to call "beautiful." When these works are small-scale and not of overwhelming value, we would say rather that they are "pretty" or "delightful." It would seem odd to call a slapstick comedy "beautiful," though we may find it uproariously funny. Again, there are works of art for which the term "beautiful" seems too limited. These are the surpassingly great and towering works of art, such as Shakespeare's *King Lear* and Beethoven's Ninth Symphony, which we speak of as "sublime." We may, then, justifiably conclude that the group or "class" of works of art is not the same as that of beautiful objects.

We come to the same conclusion if we go at the question from the other direction: not all beautiful objects are works of art. The class of beautiful objects also includes objects of nature, which are not created by human artistry. We say that massive cloud formations, landscapes, and flowers are "beautiful." Indeed, for many people, the beauties of nature are probably more easily appreciated than those of art.

We can now see that the study of "art" is quite different from that of "beauty." In seeking to learn what makes an object beautiful, we cannot restrict ourselves to examination of works of art. We must also consider what we mean by "beautiful" when we predicate it of scenes and events in nature. It is for this reason that "philosophy of art" is too narrow a name for our study. Though works of art are the most conspicuous and perhaps the most important of beautiful objects, it is not with art exclusively that we shall be concerned. Furthermore, we have now found that "beautiful" is itself too limited in meaning to describe all the objects, whether artistic or nonartistic, which we find valuable. Works of literature are sometimes "tragic" and the star-filled sky on a summer night is "sublime." In our discussion of value, we must consider these concepts in addition to "beauty." For this reason, similarly, our study is not properly called "theory of beauty" or "philosophy of beauty."

Now we turn to see how "aesthetic" is related to "art" and "beauty." Thus far I have said only that "aesthetic" refers to "looking" or perception. What particular kind of perception does it designate? We can begin to answer this question if we consider the many different ways in which a work of art can be perceived. The work can be considered as a propaganda document, like *Uncle Tom's Cabin*, which was referred to previously. In this case, we are concerned with its significance in molding public opinion. Or we may, like the historian or sociologist, study the work as a reflection of the period or culture in which it was produced. Thus the drawings of primitive peoples may help to explain their religious beliefs and myths, and the early writings of Hemingway can be used in studying the state of mind of America at the time of the First World War. In all these cases, the work is interesting because of something external to it, its origins or its consequences. But this is not the way in which we usually approach art. We usually read books and listen to music because they are interesting or enjoyable *in themselves*. We put out of mind any distracting concern with such things as history or social movements. This kind of experience is markedly different from being concerned with the work for some ulterior purpose. The term "aesthetic" distinguishes such perception of an object for its intrinsic interest.

We can appreciate the value which a work of art has in itself only if we apprehend it aesthetically. If we are concerned with the work solely as an instrument for achieving some further goal, we cannot relish it simply as a story or a painting. It is the intrinsic or aesthetic value of art which we have in mind when we speak of the "appreciation" or "enjoyment" of art. We can understand this most important kind of value in art only when we understand aesthetic perception, by means of which we apprehend it. Once we have done this, we will be able to avoid confusing the value of an art-object when it is enjoyed for itself with the value which it may have for other purposes. It is astonishing how often people confuse the two. They will often say that a work is "good" or "beautiful" simply because it makes men more righteous or encourages religious belief. But a work can have these consequences and yet be very mediocre in itself. In wartime, songs or posters which are effective in stimulating national loyalty are often inferior when considered as music or painting. Similarly, you may know people who profess admiration of works of art simply because they are fascinated by the life of the artist — he had a tragic love affair or suffered from some affliction or ran away from his native country. But surely an artist can have an exciting life and produce very dull art. Such people praise art for the wrong reasons. More important, they are so obsessed with these other matters that they never perceive the work itself. They fail to appreciate its intrinsic delightfulness. Any of us can become a victim of this sort of confusion. Therefore, we must study the distinctive nature of aesthetic "looking" to make sure that we are apprehending the work in a way that discloses its intrinsic value to us. Hence, in the next two chapters, we shall examine aesthetic experience to see in detail how it differs from other ways of approaching art.

It is obvious that we apprehend aesthetically not only works of art but also objects in nature. We look at huge, gnarled trees or the waves striking against the shore because they are interesting or dramatic in themselves. In other words, the objects of aesthetic perception are not art-objects solely. Furthermore, the objects which are perceived aesthetically are not all beautiful; they may also be "pretty" or "comic" or "sublime." Thus, of the three concepts with which we started — "art," "beauty," "aesthetic" — it is "aesthetic" which proves to be the most inclusive. For the objects which we apprehend for their intrinsic interest

— i.e., aesthetic objects — include both works of art and natural objects, both what is beautiful and what is valuable for aesthetic perception in other ways.

It has just been shown that we must understand aesthetic perception before we can distinguish the intrinsic values of art from its nonaesthetic uses. I now wish to show that the study of aesthetic perception must also precede the discussion of beauty.

We have been assuming that "beautiful" refers to what is aesthetically valuable in a certain way. This assumption is, on the whole, sound. However, "beautiful," like many terms of praise in our language, is often used loosely and imprecisely. Once we become "critical" of our ways of speaking and thinking, we are made aware of this. People often mean by the term "beautiful" not only that an object is attractive to look at aesthetically, but also that it is valuable for some further purpose — e.g., "the outfielder made a beautiful catch," or "what a beautiful day for the picnic," or even "a beautiful can-opener." Here the meaning of the term is partly aesthetic, partly nonaesthetic. But in many cases "beautiful" is used indiscriminately to express praise or approval, without any aesthetic significance at all. Thus an ardent baseball fan may exclaim "Beautiful!," if the catch saves the game for his team, even though the outfielder misjudged the ball at first, was clumsy in getting to it, and then almost let the ball pop out of his glove. Similarly, Clive Bell says of the phrase "a beautiful woman": "We live in a nice age. With the man-in-the-street 'beautiful' is more often than not synonymous with 'desirable'; the word does not necessarily connote any aesthetic reaction whatever." [8]

We must learn to distinguish the aesthetic from the nonaesthetic meanings of such terms if we are to achieve clarity in our thought and speech. Without such clarity our beliefs about art and aesthetic experience must necessarily remain confused and misleading. We must, therefore, try to understand the nature of aesthetic experience. With this we begin the study of aesthetics.

[8] Clive Bell, *Art* (London: Chatto and Windus, 1947), p. 15. Reprinted by permission of the publishers.

BIBLIOGRAPHY

In this and all succeeding bibliographies, references marked with an asterisk are especially recommended as collateral reading in the undergraduate course.

* Ducasse, C. J., "Aesthetics and the Aesthetic Activities," *Journal of Aesthetics and Art Criticism*, Vol. V (March, 1947), 165–176.
* Vivas, Eliseo, and Krieger, Murray, eds. *The Problems of Aesthetics*. New York: Rinehart, 1953. Part I.
  Chandler, Albert R. *Beauty and Human Nature*. New York: Appleton-Century, 1934. Chap. 5.

Gauss, Charles E., "On the Content of a Course in Introductory Aesthetics," *Journal of Aesthetics and Art Criticism*, Vol. VIII (Sept., 1949), 53–58.

Greene, Theodore M. *The Arts and the Art of Criticism*. Princeton University Press, 1947. Introduction.

Osborne, Harold. *Aesthetics and Criticism*. New York: Philosophical Library, 1955. Chap. II.

Prall, D. W. *Aesthetic Judgment*. New York: Crowell, 1929. Chap. XVI.

Stolnitz, Jerome, "On the Formal Structure of Esthetic Theory," *Philosophy and Phenomenological Research*, Vol. XII (March, 1952), 346–364.

QUESTIONS

1. Set down as clearly as possible the beliefs which you now hold concerning the meanings of "fine art" and "beauty." Have you encountered *other* meanings for these terms in books about art, courses in the various arts, etc.? How would you defend your own conceptions of "art" and "beauty" against these alternative conceptions?

2. Select some work of art with which you are closely familiar. What exactly do you "look for" in the work? Could the work be perceived in some other way, with attention being given to aspects of the work which you neglect or ignore? Is some theory of the nature of art presupposed in your way of looking at the work?

3. Do you think that an aesthetician must have the ability to create art? Do you think that an art critic must have such ability? Conversely, do you think that the creative artist must possess knowledge of aesthetics? Explain your answer in each case.

4. Which of the four arguments against studying aesthetics seems to you to be strongest? Why? Can you think of any other arguments to show that aesthetics is futile?

5. "People know very little about their own tastes, and are as often as not disappointed when they get what they thought they wanted. The chief purpose of aesthetics is to help us to clarify and to become conscious of our own tastes." — Kate Gordon, *Esthetics* (New York: Holt, 1909), p. 5.
   What do you think the author means by "becoming conscious of our own tastes"? Do you think that aesthetics is required for this purpose? Could we not "become conscious of our own tastes" simply by reflecting upon our likes and dislikes in art? Or would this lead into aesthetics?

25

PART I

The Aesthetic Experience

The Aesthetic Attitude

2

At the close of the previous chapter, I said that "aesthetic" stands for the most general and the most fundamental concept in our study. It refers to objects which are both works of art and objects of nature; it refers also to things which are beautiful and things which are valuable to perception in other ways, such as pretty, sublime, and comic objects. I suggested, tentatively, that an object is "aesthetic" whenever we perceive it in a certain way, that is, whenever we look at it for no other reason than simply to look at and enjoy it. We must now analyze and develop this suggestion.

We are defining the realm of the aesthetic in terms of a distinctive kind of "looking." This says nothing about the objects which are apprehended in this way. What they are like, and what characteristics, if any, they have in common with each other, are left open. But this approach is not used by many traditional theories in aesthetics. They do not begin, as we do, by asking, "What is aesthetic experience?" They take "aesthetic" to refer to certain properties which some objects have, by virtue of which they are beautiful, and which others lack. Then the theories set themselves to find out what these properties are specifically. Once these distinguishing characteristics are found, they make up the aesthetic area of experience.

But we are not going about it in this way. Why not? To be genuinely "critical," we must justify our approach. The justification is twofold.

Primarily, traditional attempts to explain the value of art and beauty by means of some distinctive "aesthetic" quality, have proven to be too limited. They have not done justice to the tremendous diversity of works of art and all of the other, very different things which men find interesting to look upon. The property taken to define "aesthetic," notably "harmony," [1] has been interpreted differently by various thinkers and eras. Generally it is the property of works of art which are found attractive or admirable by people of a certain historical period or a specific culture. It is put forth, however, as the characteristic common to *all* aesthetic objects. Any object which lacks it is excluded from the area of the aesthetic. Thus art of a particular style or the taste of a particular period is taken to be the model for all aesthetic value. But inevitably, art which is very dissimilar comes to be developed. And for this among other reasons, tastes change. (Specific examples of this will be cited later in this chapter.) [2] Then objects are found to be valuable for perception which do *not* possess the properties formerly taken to be "aesthetic." The original explanation of aesthetic value proves to be too circumscribed and narrow, or else it is found to misinterpret the nature of the aesthetic.

It is in order to avoid this crippling narrowness that we shall be defining "aesthetic" in terms of a particular sort of perception. It is extremely important, in beginning this study or any other, not to set too great limitations upon the field of study. At least this should not be done *a priori*, i.e., before the actual investigation of data has started. If you limit yourself too severely at first, you will very probably overlook facts of great importance. By defining "aesthetic" as perception of an object just for the sake of perceiving it, all objects, of whatever kinds, which men have found occasion to contemplate, are included in the field of study. This includes art of different forms, periods, and styles, and diverse objects and scenes in nature. We can then go on to analyze the structure of these objects and see to what extent there are similarities among them.

This brings us to the second reason for choosing this definition of "aesthetic." It has already been stated at the end of the first chapter. If we are to understand what is usually meant by "art" and "beauty," and our experience of them, we must understand the workings of aesthetic perception. We have seen that works of art can be studied and valued in many ways — morally, as a social document, and so on. When we approach the work as a sociologist or moralist, we do not grasp its intrinsic value. To do so we must look at the work without any pre-

[1] "Harmony, we know, has been the accepted synonym for beauty or for the artist's goal through all the ages of a philosophy of art." — Katherine E. Gilbert and Helmut Kuhn, *A History of Aesthetics*, rev. ed. (Indiana University Press, 1953), p. 186.
[2] Cf. below, pp. 39–41.

occupation with its origins and consequences. Therefore analysis of such perception is prerequisite to explanation of the *aesthetic* (not the historical, moral, etc.) value of art and the *aesthetic* senses of the term "beauty."

THIS IDEA OF THE UNIQUENESS of aesthetic perception, like all ideas, has its history. Although it is found at scattered places throughout aesthetic theory, it is not until the eighteenth century that it becomes central to the study of aesthetics. After that time the idea gains great currency. Let us see some of the historical causes of this.

Throughout all history and up to the present day, art has been explained and valued in nonaesthetic terms. It has been esteemed for its social utility, or because it inculcates religious beliefs, or because it makes men more moral, or because it is a source of knowledge. In all these cases, you see, art is valued for the consequences to which it gives rise, not for its intrinsic interest. In recent centuries, however, there has been much greater emphasis upon the aesthetic significance of art. One of the chief causes has been the great change in the position of the artist in society. Increasingly he has come to be dissociated from the rest of his society. He is no longer considered one among other craftsmen, as he was in Greek and medieval society. He comes to think of himself as being set apart by his distinctive creative abilities or "genius." Furthermore, his creative activity becomes divorced from other functions of society. The most striking example of this is probably music. Throughout social history music has been the handmaiden of other activities, e.g., work songs, ceremonial music, songs of war. It has been customarily enlisted in the service of religion, where it is used for purposes of worship and celebration. Thus the great German composer Johann Sebastian Bach (1685–1750) said that he wrote music to "sing the praises of God." But increasingly throughout the nineteenth century composers wrote music which was simply to be appreciated for itself. Music which serves no function other than to be heard is therefore a relatively recent development historically. Finally, there are a number of social and cultural forces which isolate the artist even further. For one thing, he is repelled by the ugliness of industrial society, with its squalid mill towns and teeming, dirty cities. At the same time, he rejects the pressures of "mass society" that compel conformity to the values and way of life of the "mass." Such uniformity stifles the individuality which the artist considers so precious. He attempts to express his individuality without restraint, but this aggravates the situation even further. He creates startlingly new and daring works for which there is little or no audience. Art and artistic activity become the object of scorn and derision, or, what is even worse, they are simply ignored. Consider, for example, the attitudes of most people at the present time toward "modern art" and contemporary music. Although

31

more and more people are finding value in such art, its appeal is still very limited. Thus art is forced out of the mainstream of society.

As a result of the causes sketched here, among others, a new conception of art gains prominence: art exists simply to be enjoyed for its own sake. It is valuable in itself, not because it promotes the goals of religion or morality or society generally. The best-known expression of this view is found in the so-called "Art for Art's Sake" movement, which flourished during the last half of the nineteenth century. This movement insisted that the only way to approach art is through aesthetic perception.

Philosophical interest in aesthetic perception thus arises from historical developments in the arts and in society.

BUT IT IS ONE THING to know about the historical origins of an idea and quite another thing to examine the idea itself and test its validity. To this we must now turn. Let us remember that the justification for making aesthetic perception central in our study has thus far been only partially explained. The significance of this concept, like that of the fundamental idea in any field of inquiry, will become clear as we go along. We shall find that the concept of aesthetic perception is enormously useful in solving many of the problems that we meet later on.

Finally, remember that since we shall be talking about a certain kind of human experience, what we say must be true to the facts of this experience. It should describe faithfully the way in which we apprehend literature, music, and painting, and help to explain the value of the experience. Unless it does so, our account will not be accepted by anyone who is philosophically critical.

1. HOW WE PERCEIVE THE WORLD

Aesthetic perception will be explained in terms of the aesthetic *attitude*.

It is the attitude we take which determines how we perceive the world. An attitude is a way of directing and controlling our perception. We never see or hear everything in our environment indiscriminately. Rather, we "pay attention" to some things, whereas we apprehend others only dimly or hardly at all. Thus attention is *selective* — it concentrates on some features of our surroundings and ignores others. Once we recognize this, we realize the inadequacy of the old notion that human beings are simply passive receptors for any and all external stimuli. Furthermore, what we single out for attention is dictated by the purposes we have at the time. Our actions are generally pointed toward some goal. In order to achieve its goal, the organism watches keenly to learn what in the environment will help and what will be detrimental. Obviously, when individuals have different purposes, they will perceive the world differently, one emphasizing certain things which another will ignore. The Indian scout gives close attention to markings and clues which the person who is simply strolling through the woods will pass over.

Thus an attitude or, as it is sometimes called, a "set," guides our attention in those directions relevant to our purposes. It gives direction to our behavior in still another way. It prepares us to *respond* to what we perceive, to act in a way we think will be most effective for achieving our goals. By the same token, we suppress or inhibit those responses which get in the way of our efforts. A man intent on winning a chess game readies himself to answer his opponent's moves and thinks ahead how best to do this. He also keeps his attention from being diverted by distractions.

Finally, to have an attitude is to be favorably or unfavorably oriented. One can welcome and rejoice in what he sees, or he can be hostile and cold toward it. The Anglophobe is a person whose attitude toward all things British is negative, so that when he meets someone with a British accent or hears "Rule Brittania," we expect him to say something disparaging or cynical. When one's attitude toward a thing is positive, he will try to sustain the object's existence and continue to perceive it; when negative, he will try to destroy it or avert his attention from it.

To sum up, an attitude organizes and directs our awareness of the world. Now the aesthetic attitude is not the attitude which people usually adopt. The attitude which we customarily take can be called the attitude of "practical" perception.

WE USUALLY SEE the things in our world in terms of their usefulness for promoting or hindering our purposes. If ever we put into words our ordinary attitude toward an object, it would take the form of the question, "What can I do with it, and what can it do to me?" I see the pen as something I can write with, I see the oncoming automobile as something to avoid; I do not concentrate my attention upon the object itself. Rather, it is of concern to me only so far as it can help me to achieve some future goal. Indeed, from the standpoint of fulfilling one's purposes, it would be stupid and wasteful to become absorbed in the object itself. The workman who never gets beyond looking at his tools, never gets his job done. Similarly, objects which function as "signs," such as the dinner bell or traffic light, are significant only as guides to future behavior. Thus, when our attitude is "practical," we perceive things only as means to some goal which lies beyond the experience of perceiving them.

Therefore our perception of a thing is usually limited and fragmentary. We see only those of its features which are relevant to our purposes, and as long as it is useful we pay little attention to it. Usually perception is merely a rapid and momentary identification of the kind of thing it is and its uses. Whereas the child has to learn laboriously what things are, what they are called, and what they can be used for, the adult does not. His perception has become economized by habit, so that he can recognize the thing and its usefulness almost at once. If I intend to write, I do not hesitate about picking up the pen rather than a paper clip or the cigarette lighter. It is only the pen's usefulness-for-writing-with, not its distinctive color or shape, that I care about. Is this not true of most of our perception of the "furniture of earth"? "In actual life the normal person really only reads the labels as it were on the objects around him and troubles no further." [3]

If we stop to think about it, it is astonishing how little of the world we really *see*. We "read the labels" on things to know how to act with regard to them, but we hardly see the things themselves. As I have said, it is indispensable to getting on with the "work of the world" that we should do this. However, we should not assume that perception is always habitually "practical," as it probably is in our culture. Other societies differ from our own, in this respect. [4]

But nowhere is perception exclusively "practical." On occasion we pay attention to a thing simply for the sake of enjoying the way it looks or sounds or feels. This is the "aesthetic" attitude of perception. It is found wherever people become interested in a play or a novel or listen closely to a piece of music. It occurs even in the midst of "practical" perception, in "casual truant glances at our surroundings, when the pressing occupations of practical effort either tire us or leave us for a moment to our own devices, as when in the absorbing business of driving at forty or fifty miles an hour along a highway to get to a destination, the tourist on his holiday glances at the trees or the hills or the ocean." [5]

2. THE AESTHETIC ATTITUDE

It will forward our discussion of the aesthetic attitude to have a definition of it. But you should remember that a definition, here or in any other study, is only a point of departure for further inquiry. Only the unwary or intellectually lazy student will rest content with the words of the definition alone, without seeing how it helps us to understand our experience and how it can be employed to carry on the study of aesthetics. With this word of caution, I will define "the aesthetic attitude"

[3] Roger Fry, *Vision and Design* (New York: Brentano's, n.d.), p. 25. Reprinted by permission of Chatto and Windus Ltd.

[4] Lester D. Longman, "The Concept of Psychical Distance," *Journal of Aesthetics and Art Criticism*, VI (1947), 32.

[5] D. W. Prall, *Aesthetic Judgment* (New York: Crowell, 1929), p. 31.

as "disinterested and sympathetic attention to and contemplation of any object of awareness whatever, for its own sake alone." Let us now take up in turn each of the ideas in this definition and see what they mean precisely. Since this will be a piecemeal analysis, the truth of the account must be found in the total analysis and not in any single part of it.

THE FIRST WORD, "disinterested," is a crucially important one. It means that we do not look at the object out of concern for any ulterior purpose which it may serve. We are not trying to use or manipulate the object. There is no purpose governing the experience other than the purpose of just *having* the experience. Our interest comes to rest upon the object alone, so that it is not taken as a sign of some future event, like the dinner bell, or as a cue to future activity, like the traffic light.

Many sorts of "interest" are excluded from the aesthetic. One of them is the interest in owning a work of art for the sake of pride or prestige. A book collector, upon seeing an old manuscript, is often interested only in its rarity or its purchase price, not its value as a work of literature. (There are some book collectors who have never *read* the books that they own!) Another nonaesthetic interest is the "cognitive," i.e., the interest in gaining knowledge about an object. A meteorologist is concerned, not with the visual appearance of a striking cloud formation, but with the causes which led to it. Similarly, the interest which the sociologist or historian takes in a work of art, referred to in the previous chapter, is cognitive. Further, where the person who perceives the object, the "percipient," [6] has the purpose of passing judgment upon it, his attitude is not aesthetic. This should be kept in mind, for, as we shall see later, the attitude of the art critic is significantly different from the aesthetic attitude.

We may say of all these nonaesthetic interests, and of "practical" perception generally, that the object is apprehended with an eye to its origins and consequences, its interrelations with other things. By contrast, the aesthetic attitude "isolates" the object and focuses upon it — the "look" of the rocks, the sound of the ocean, the colors in the painting. Hence the object is not seen in a fragmentary or passing manner, as it is in "practical" perception, e.g., in using a pen for writing. Its whole nature and character are dwelt upon. One who buys a painting merely to cover a stain on the wall paper does not see the painting as a delightful pattern of colors and forms.

For the aesthetic attitude, things are not to be classified or studied or judged. They are in themselves pleasant or exciting to look at. It should,

---

[6] This is a clumsy and largely outmoded word, but it is more convenient for our purposes than words of more limited meaning such as "spectator," "observer," "listener," and is accordingly used here and elsewhere in the text.

then, be clear that being "disinterested" is very far from being "*un*-interested." Rather, as all of us know, we can become intensely absorbed in a book or a moving picture, so that we become much more "interested" than we usually are in the course of our "practical" activity.

The word "sympathetic" in the definition of "aesthetic attitude" refers to the way in which we prepare ourselves to respond to the object. When we apprehend an object aesthetically, we do so in order to relish its individual quality, whether the object be charming, stirring, vivid, or all of these. If we are to appreciate it, we must accept the object "on its own terms." We must make ourselves receptive to the object and "set" ourselves to accept whatever it may offer to perception. We must therefore inhibit any responses which are "un-sympathetic" to the object, which alienate us from it or are hostile to it. A devout Mohammedan may not be able to bring himself to look for very long at a painting of the Holy Family, because of his animus against the Christian religion. Closer to home, any of us might reject a novel because it seems to conflict with our moral beliefs or our "way of thinking." When we do so, we should be clear as to what we are doing. We have *not* read the book aesthetically, for we have interposed moral or other responses of our own which are alien to it. This disrupts the aesthetic attitude. We cannot then say that the novel is *aesthetically* bad, for we have not permitted ourselves to consider it aesthetically. To maintain the aesthetic attitude, we must follow the lead of the object and respond in concert with it.

This is not always easy, for all of us have deep-seated values as well as prejudices. They may be ethical or religious, or they may involve some bias against the artist or even against his native country. (During the First World War, many American symphony orchestras refused to play the works of German composers.) The problem is especially acute in the case of contemporary works of art, which may treat of disputes and loyalties in which we are deeply engaged. When they do so, we might remind ourselves that works of art often lose their topical significance with the passing of time and then come to be esteemed as great works of art by later generations. Milton's sonnet "On the Late Massacre in Piedmont" is a ringing protest called forth by an event which occurred shortly before the writing of the poem. But the heated questions of religion and politics which enter into it seem very remote to us now. People sometimes remonstrate with a friend who seems to reject offhand works of art of which they are fond, "You don't even give it a chance." To be "sympathetic" in aesthetic experience means to give the object the "chance" to show how it can be interesting to perception.

We come now to the word "attention" in our definition of "aesthetic attitude." As has been pointed out, any attitude whatever directs attention to certain features of the world. But the element of attention must be especially underscored in speaking of aesthetic perception. For, as a former teacher of mine used to say, aesthetic perception is frequently thought to be a "blank, cow-like stare." It is easy to fall into this mistake when we find aesthetic perception described as "just looking," without any activity or practical interest. From this it is inferred that we simply expose ourselves to the work of art and permit it to inundate us in waves of sound or color.

But this is surely a distortion of the facts of experience. When we listen to a rhythmically exciting piece of music which absorbs us with its energy and movement, or when we read a novel which creates great suspense, we give our earnest attention to it to the exclusion of almost everything else in our surroundings. To be "sitting on the edge of the chair" is anything but passive. In taking the aesthetic attitude, we want to make the value of the object come fully alive in our experience. Therefore we focus our attention upon the object and "key up" our capacities of imagination and emotion to respond to it. As a psychologist says of the aesthetic experience, "Appreciation . . . is awareness, alertness, animation." [7] Attention is always a matter of *degree*, and in different instances of aesthetic perception, attention is more or less intense. A color, briefly seen, or a little melody, may be apprehended on the "fringe" of consciousness, whereas a drama will absorb us wholly. But to whatever extent it does so, experience is aesthetic only when an object "holds" our attention.

Furthermore, aesthetic attention is accompanied by activity. This is not the activity of practical experience, which seeks an ulterior goal. Rather it is activity which is either evoked by disinterested perception of the object, or else is required for it. The former includes all muscular, nervous, and "motor" responses such as feelings of tension or rhythmic movement. Contrary to what some snobs would have us believe, there is nothing inherently unaesthetic about tapping one's foot in time to the music. The theory of *empathy* points out that we "feel into" the object our muscular and bodily adjustments. We brace ourselves and our muscles become taut in the face of a sculptured figure which is tall, vigorous, and upright. [8] This does not occur in aesthetic experience alone, and it does not occur in all aesthetic experience, but when it does, it exemplifies the kind of activity which may be aroused in aesthetic perception. The direction of attention itself may not improperly be called "activity." But even overt bodily movement and effort may be required for aesthetic perception. We usually have to walk round all sides of a sculpture, or through a cathedral, before we can appreciate it. We would often reach out and touch

[7] Kate Hevner, "The Aesthetic Experience: A Psychological Description," *Psychological Review*, 44 (1937), 249.

[8] Cf. Herbert S. Langfeld, *The Aesthetic Attitude* (New York: Harcourt, Brace, 1920), chaps. V–VI; Vernon Lee, "Empathy," in Melvin Rader, ed., *A Modern Book of Esthetics*, rev. ed. (New York: Holt, 1952), pp. 460–465.

sculptured figures if only museum guards would permit us to do so.

But focusing upon the object and "acting" in regard to it, is not all that is meant by aesthetic "attention." To savor fully the distinctive value of the object, we must be attentive to its frequently complex and subtle details. Acute awareness of these details is *discrimination*. People often miss a good deal in the experience of art, not only because their attention lapses, but because they fail to "see" all that is of significance in the work. Indeed, their attention frequently lapses for just this reason. They miss the individuality of the work, so that one symphony sounds like any other piece of "long-hair" music, and one lyric poem is indistinguishable from another, and all are equally boring. If you have had the good fortune to study literature with an able teacher, you know how a play or novel can become vital and engaging when you learn to look for details to which you were previously insensitive. But awareness of this kind is not always easily come by. It often requires knowledge about allusions or symbols which occur in the work, repeated experience of the work, and even, sometimes, technical training in the art-form.

As we develop discriminating attention, the work comes alive to us. If we can keep in mind the chief themes in the movement of a symphony, see how they are developed and altered in the course of the movement, and appreciate how they are played off against each other, then there is a great gain in our experience. The experience has greater richness and unity. Without such discrimination it is thin, for the listener responds only to scattered passages or to a patch of striking orchestral color. And it is disorganized, for he is not aware of the structure which binds the work together. His experience may be said to be intermittently and to a limited degree aesthetic, but it is not nearly as rewarding as it might be. Everybody knows how easy it is to start thinking of other things while the music is playing, so that we are really aware of it only now and again. All the more reason, then, why we should develop the capacities for appreciating its richness and profundity. Only so can we keep our experience from becoming, in Santayana's famous phrase, "a drowsy revery relieved by nervous thrills." [9]

If you now understand how aesthetic attention is alert and vigorous, then it is safe to use a word which has often been applied to aesthetic experience — "contemplation." Otherwise, there is the great danger that this word will suggest an aloof, unexcited gaze which, we have seen, is untrue to the facts of aesthetic experience. Actually, "contemplation" does not so much add something new to our definition as it sums up ideas which we have already discussed. It means that perception is directed to the object in its own right and that the spectator is not concerned to analyze it or to ask questions about it. Also, the word con-

[9] George Santayana, *Reason in Art* (New York: Scribner's, 1946), p. 51.

notes thoroughgoing absorption and interest, as when we speak of being "lost in contemplation." Most things are hardly noticed by us, whereas the object of aesthetic perception stands out from its environment and rivets our interest.

THE AESTHETIC ATTITUDE can be adopted toward "any object of awareness whatever." This phrase need not, strictly speaking, be included in our definition. We could understand the aesthetic attitude as the kind of perceptual attention we have been talking about, without adding that "any object whatever" may be its object. But definitions are flexible to an extent. We can choose to include in them even what is not strictly necessary to identify the term being defined. The great and even limitless scope of aesthetic experience is one of the most interesting and important things about it.

The definition permits us to say that any object at all can be apprehended aesthetically, i.e., no object is inherently unaesthetic. But it might be thought odd, or even downright wrong, to say this. There are some objects which are conspicuously attractive, so that they "catch our eye" and draw attention to themselves — a bed of bright and many-colored flowers or a marching song, massive cloud formations, or a noble and stately cathedral. Certainly the same is not true of many, indeed most, other things in the world. Are we to say that a dirty, run-down slum section is to be called "aesthetic"? What about dull, unexciting things like supplies stacked row upon row in a warehouse or, if you please, the telephone directory? Indeed, the word "aesthetic" is often used in everyday speech to distinguish those objects which are delightful to look upon or listen to, from those which are not. As was pointed out at the beginning of this chapter, this is also the view of a good deal of traditional aesthetic theory.

This argument — that some objects do not qualify as "aesthetic" — certainly sounds plausible and convincing. I think that the best way to argue against it is to present evidence that human beings have contemplated disinterestedly objects which are enormously diverse. Among such objects are some which we might consider wholly uninviting. As was mentioned earlier, men have found perceptual enjoyment in things which people of earlier times or other cultures judged to be unaesthetic. The whole "history of taste" shows how the boundaries of aesthetic experience have been pushed back and have come to include a tremendous variety of things.

The best evidence of this broadening of vision is to be found in the arts. For here we have permanent records of the objects which have aroused aesthetic interest. It can also be found, however, in the appreciation of nature. The subjects chosen from nature for treatment by artists show the expansion of perceptual interest. "Social historians" can often trace changes in the appreciation of nature in other ways, e.g., memoirs and diaries, sites chosen for resort places, and so on. But let us for the moment speak solely of art. If we confine ourselves to the art of the last 150 years, we find an enormous amount of art devoted to the two sorts of objects which "common sense" considers intrinsically unaesthetic, viz., dull, commonplace objects and ugly or grotesque things and events. The poet Wordsworth, at the beginning of the nineteenth century, devoted much of his poetry to "humble and rustic life." One of van Gogh's paintings is of a perfectly prosaic yellow chair (see Plate 1), another is of the rude furniture in his bedroom.[10] In our own day, the painter Ben Shahn has chosen as the subject of one of his works city boys playing handball (see Plate 2). Instances of the depiction of ugly and macabre themes in recent art are even more obvious. The student may be able to think of some himself. I will cite Géricault's "The Raft of the *Medusa*" (see Plate 3), the harrowing treatment of a tortured and pathetic figure in Berg's opera *Wozzeck*, and such "realistic" literature as Gorki's *Lower Depths* and Farrell's *Studs Lonigan*.

To be sure, the artist apprehends such subjects with imagination and feeling. And when they emerge in the work of art, he has invested them with vividness and excitement. However, the very fact that his attention has been directed to these subjects shows how far-ranging aesthetic interest can be. Further, his use of them alters and expands the taste of the nonartist. The ordinary man now becomes newly sensitive to the perceptual interest of many different objects and events. Thus appreciation of the grandeur of mountain ranges, which is a relatively recent chapter in the history of taste, was stimulated by such works of art as Haller's poem *Die Alpen*. Less lofty objects and even scenes which are ugly become the objects of aesthetic attention. Here is the testimony of one who is not an artist:

[The] ugliest thing in nature that I can think of at the moment is a certain street of shabby houses where a street-market is held. If one passes through it, as I sometimes do, early on a Sunday morning, one finds it littered with straw, dirty paper and the other refuse of a market. My normal attitude is one of aversion. I wish to hold myself away from the scene. . . . But I sometimes find that . . . the scene suddenly gets jerked away from *me* and on to the aesthetic plane, so that I can survey it quite impersonally. When this happens, it does seem to me that what I am apprehending looks different; it has a form and coherence which it lacked before, and details are more clearly seen. But . . . it does not seem to me to have ceased to be ugly and

[10] The works here cited to illustrate the argument, but not found in the Plates, are readily accessible, and should be consulted by the student or made available to him by the instructor.

to have become beautiful. I can see the ugly aesthetically, but I cannot see it as beautiful. [11]

The student can probably think of things in his own experience — a face, a building, a landscape — which, though not conventionally "pretty" or "attractive," arouse aesthetic interest. Evidence of this kind cannot establish that *all* objects can be aesthetic objects. When such evidence is multiplied, however, it makes this assumption a reasonable one at the outset of aesthetic inquiry.

IN KEEPING WITH THIS ASSUMPTION, the word "awareness" is used in our definition of "aesthetic attitude." I have been using the word "perception" to describe aesthetic apprehension, but its meaning is too narrow. It refers to apprehension of sense-data, e.g., colors or sounds, which are interpreted or "judged" to be of a certain kind. Perception differs from sensation as the experience of an adult differs from that of the newborn infant, for whom the world is a succession of mysterious and unrelated sensory "explosions." In adult experience, we rarely apprehend sense-data without knowing something about them and interrelating them, so that they become meaningful. We see more than a color patch; we see a flag or a warning signal. Perception is the most usual sort of "awareness." But if sensation occurs, it too can be aesthetic.[12]

There is another kind of "awareness" that occurs, though relatively infrequently, in adult experience. This is "intellectual," nonsensuous knowing of "concepts" and "meanings," and their interrelations; such knowing takes place in abstract thinking, such as logic and mathematics. Even if images or "pictures" accompany such thinking, they are only secondary. When the mathematician thinks of the properties of triangles, his thought is not restricted to any particular triangle he may "see in his head" or draw on paper. A man who develops a system of mathematical logic is occupied with logical relationships which are neither sensed nor perceived. Now this kind of apprehension can also be aesthetic. If one's purpose is not, for the moment, problem solving, if he pauses to contemplate disinterestedly the logical structure before him, then his experience is aesthetic. Such experience has been attested to by many mathematicians, and it is evidenced by the use of such words as "elegance" and "grace," borrowed from the realm of the aesthetic, to describe a conceptual system. The poetess Edna St. Vincent Millay says, in a line that has become famous, "Euclid alone has looked on Beauty bare." The great Greek ge-

[11] E. M. Bartlett, *Types of Aesthetic Judgment* (London: George Allen & Unwin, 1937), pp. 211–212. Italics in original. Reprinted by permission of George Allen & Unwin Ltd.
[12] Cf. below, pp. 61–62.

ometrician discerned mathematical properties and relations which had no sensuous "dress" of sound or color.

To take account of such experience as well as sensation, I have used the broad term "awareness" rather than "perception." Anything at all, whether sensed or perceived, whether it is the product of imagination or conceptual thought, can become the object of aesthetic attention.

THIS COMPLETES THE ANALYSIS of the meaning of "aesthetic attitude," the central concept in our study. "Aesthetic," understood to mean "disinterested and sympathetic attention," marks out the field of our further investigation. All the concepts to be discussed later are defined by reference to this: "aesthetic experience" is the total experience had while this attitude is being taken; "aesthetic object" is the object toward which this attitude is adopted; "aesthetic value" is the value of this experience or of its object. It is therefore imperative that the student understand and think about the meaning of "aesthetic," before going on to further discussions.

3. THE SIGNIFICANCE OF AESTHETIC AWARENESS IN HUMAN EXPERIENCE

Essential to an attitude of any sort is a positive or negative orientation toward what is being perceived.[13] Either we look upon the object favorably or else we are hostile or averse to it. If the aesthetic attitude has been described accurately, it can now be said that aesthetic awareness is always oriented "positively" toward its object. We concentrate attention upon the object which, as we say, "holds our interest." The very fact that the utility of the object is not now in question proves that we welcome the existence of the object simply because it looks or sounds as it does. It is worth repeating that this does not mean that the object is necessarily "beautiful" or "pretty" or "charming." It can be aesthetically interesting in other ways — it can be "striking" or "moving" or "powerful," even if it is hideous or ugly.

Our description of the aesthetic attitude has therefore implied what is most significant about aesthetic experience — it is an experience which is good to have in itself. Or to say the same thing another way, the experience is *intrinsically valuable*. We are absorbed and find satisfaction in the very act of awareness. It is not like doing one's daily work or going to the dentist, which are valuable because of their consequences. The value of the aesthetic experience is felt in the very experience itself.

The intrinsic value of aesthetic experience has been recognized as often

13 Cf. above, p. 33.

as the existence of "disinterested contemplation" itself. It is noteworthy that both are attested to by philosophers who, in other phases of aesthetic theory, disagree profoundly. We find a clear intimation in the great medieval thinker, St. Thomas Aquinas, whose definition of "beauty" is *id cuius ipsa apprehensio placet* [14] — "that which gives pleasure when it is merely looked upon" or "that, the very apprehension of which pleases." The first systematic exposition in modern philosophy of the notion of aesthetic disinterestedness is presented late in the eighteenth century by Immanuel Kant. Kant also speaks of the "satisfaction" to be found in such experience.[15] One of the best brief descriptions of the aesthetic attitude to be found anywhere is in the writings of the nineteenth-century German philosopher Schopenhauer.[16] Although he was deeply pessimistic about the attainment of human happiness, Schopenhauer considered aesthetic experience supremely valuable. Examples could be multiplied from contemporary philosophers of very different persuasions from those just cited.

This belief shared by the philosophers is borne out by the experience had by almost all human beings, probably — being attracted by a color or the grace or elegance of a tree, or being engrossed in a story and continuing to give your attention to it, is a "moment" in life which is worth having in its own right. If, then, it should be demanded, "Of what value is such experience?" the answer is more obvious than it would be if the same question were asked about any other kind of experience. The value of aesthetic experience is palpable in the experience itself. Those of a "practical" turn of mind, those who want to get on with "the work of the world" are often skeptical of aesthetic experience; they consider it wasteful and unprofitable. It is true, as we have seen, that the aesthetic attitude inhibits practical perception and that, when it is sustained, it may stifle purposive activity which the world demands of us. But let us turn the question around. Of what value is human activity which only subserves some future goal? Is its purpose to make possible further experience that will be instrumental to still further experience which is not enjoyable in itself but is carried on for still another ulterior purpose? Is the model of human existence to be found in the lives of many urban workingmen in an industrial community, who perform work which is of no interest to them and in which they find no delight, so that they may keep alive to return to the same drudgery on the next day? The point is that there is no point to "practical" human effort unless somewhere it leads to experience which is interesting and joyous in itself. It is often said of contemporary Americans that they are so absorbed in the instrumentalities of life that they rarely savor the intrinsic values of experience. But I venture to say that this has always been true of many

[14] *Summa Theologica*, Ia, 2ae, quaest. 27, art. I.
[15] Cf. *Critique of Judgment*, trans. Bernard (New York: Hafner, 1951), pp. 37–45.
[16] Cf. *The World as Will and Idea*, Book III, Second Aspect.

people, in whatever age or society they may have lived. Yet the absence of aesthetic value from life is often the result of being-efficient-and-no-nonsense-about-it. Those who are committed to this way of life become so myopic that they never examine it critically and therefore never see its poverty. They must be reminded.

> A poor life this if, full of care,
> We have no time to stand and stare.[17]

This may not be first-rate poetry, but it is a fitting rejoinder to those who can see no value in aesthetic experience.

It would be easy at this point to fall into the rhapsodizing about aesthetic experience that I warned against in the opening chapter. But there is not even any need for it. Aesthetic perception is not something rare and exotic, unless life is so lived that it comes to be considered unnatural. In a sense there is nothing more "natural" than aesthetic awareness. What could be more natural than simply to look out upon the world and take interest in its sights and sounds, its movement and expressiveness? We all do this spontaneously on occasion, and the child does so constantly, so that the world is fresh and exciting to him.

But if we are to make our way in the world we must learn to recognize and name things and learn their uses and dangers. As was pointed out earlier, the development of habits of seeing is indispensable to effective and economical activity. When we know at once what things are and how we can use them, we need waste no time in perception. As a result, however, we suffer a loss in aesthetic value. For we see things only partially and hastily, with an eye to the future. Thus habit forms a crust of dullness and familiarity over our world and deadens its aesthetic excitement. So, as Professor Pepper says, "Were there no habit, all living would be in the highest degree aesthetic and we should need no art nor any technique to make it so." [18]

Yet I do not want to leave the impression that aesthetic and practical experience are necessarily fatal to each other. This belief is already too widespread in our civilization. We have shunted off art and aesthetic experience into a remote corner of our lives. We tip our hats to them when we go occasionally to the art gallery or concert hall or "read a good book." This way of thinking and acting is a needless impoverishment of our experience.

---

[17] "Leisure," in W. H. Davies, *Collected Poems* (London: Jonathan Cape, 1951), p. 141. The reference to aesthetic experience is made clear in the rest of the poem. Reprinted by permission of Jonathan Cape Limited, and Mrs. H. M. Davies.

[18] Stephen C. Pepper, *Aesthetic Quality* (New York: Scribner's, 1937), p. 55.

In this chapter, the aesthetic attitude has been distinguished from the attitude of practical perception. But when two things are distinguished in thinking about them, it does not follow that, in actual existence, they are always separate from each other. When we learn about the chemical structure of water, we distinguish the hydrogen within it from the oxygen. But in water itself, of course, they are indissolubly mingled. Now in concrete experience, practical and aesthetic interest can, and frequently do, coexist with each other. Our experience may be preponderantly practical, we may be chiefly concerned with the task at hand, and yet some of our attention, however slight, may be devoted to aesthetic enjoyment of the things about us. Even when our concern is almost wholly practical, the "casual truant glances" of aesthetic interest may obtrude. In the midst of a tense political struggle or some personal rivalry, in which a man's fortunes are at stake, he may be struck by what we call "the drama of the situation." It seems therefore to be an oversimplification psychologically to say that at any one time only a single attitude can be adopted.[19] To be sure, the aesthetic and practical attitudes are mutually opposed, in the sense that the focusing of attention characteristic of one inhibits the kind of attention proper to the other. But attention is always a matter of degree and it can be controlled simultaneously by different purposes. It is fortunate that this is so, for even a slim share of the aesthetic often makes bearable jobs which would otherwise be hopelessly dull and unedifying.

We need not trust wholly in good fortune to leaven the practical with the aesthetic. Human effort can increase the aesthetic value of experience. As we develop aesthetic responsiveness and make it more keen and alert, it creates "new interest in everything we do, in every object with which we come into contact, in every aspect of our world."[20] This will be especially true if, by means of art, we make the implements and furnishings of everyday life more attractive to perception. We should not write them off as "merely useful" and therefore without claim to aesthetic worth. Even primitive societies adorn the most commonplace objects so that they are a delight to sight and touch in addition to being useful. The anthropologist frequently finds that such ornamentation also served a social function, e.g., in hunting or war or in religious ceremonies, but this does not minimize the importance of the aesthetic. It shows rather how life can be enhanced when aesthetic and nonaesthetic interests are each served without excluding the other. There are heartening signs of such activity at the present time in our own society — in the production of such things as silverware and "modern" furniture, in our railroad engines and architecture.

The aesthetic value of everyday things need not be just mere gilding

[19] Cf. Langfeld, *op. cit.*, p. 73.
[20] John M. Warbeke, *The Power of Art* (New York: Philosophical Library, 1951), p. 19.

which is unrelated to the nature of the thing. Indeed, such adornment is frequently of relatively slight value. What an object such as an axe or a railroad locomotive is designed to do, is frequently integral to its aesthetic value. We can admire the way in which its construction is adapted to its function. When we look at such things aesthetically, we are not, like an engineer or the man who is going to use them, thinking ahead to their utility. But awareness of the object's utility is part of our perception, and it is indispensable to admiration of its fitness for its job. Aesthetic interest is enhanced when the total appearance of the object, its color, shape, and so on, bring out its usefulness. We see this in our airplanes and some recently constructed buildings, both residential and commercial. A pneumatic drill or a steel mill on which decorations were painted in a pale, feminine pink, might well operate efficiently and economically and be admired because of this utility. But there would be something grotesque about the disparity between its function and its total appearance.

THUS FAR WE HAVE DISCUSSED the aesthetic experience solely from the standpoint of its intrinsic value. This is its value as a self-contained experience. It is in the very nature of the aesthetic attitude that it gives up ongoing activity pointed toward the future. Considered nonaesthetically, however, the aesthetic experience, like any other, is not utterly isolated from life. It has consequences which go beyond the experience itself. Like any experience, our encounter with the aesthetic object changes us, perhaps only slightly, perhaps profoundly, and thereby alters our future experience. Thus, as all of us know, exposure to new works of art changes our taste. We no longer go back to the adventure stories which engrossed us in grade school and we begin to esteem other kinds of literature and other forms of art. In addition, we become more discriminating, so that we "see" values in art which formerly escaped us. But the influence of aesthetic perception is not simply confined to other aesthetic experiences. It also alters our character and experience in the nonaesthetic areas of life. A work of art may enlarge our insight into other human beings and ourselves, it may lead us to challenge the values to which we have been dedicated, it may broaden our sympathies. It is impossible to set limits to the psychological effects that it might have, or to try to specify them. We should remember, however, that if we deliberately set ourselves to gain these effects, we weaken or destroy aesthetic interest. For then the experience becomes forward-looking and utilitarian. The consequences of aesthetic experience come unbidden and unsought.

Now there is no guarantee that these consequences will always be beneficial. Ever since Plato it has been pointed out that art can have an unwholesome influence, particularly on young people. It can undermine character or impair morals. The danger of this is, probably, a good deal less at the present time, when the "fine arts" are relatively trivial in society. Nonetheless, the problem is still a real and important one. Consider the heated disputes over censorship of books and movies which have arisen in recent years, and the problems of censorship in wartime. We shall address ourselves to this difficult problem later in the book (Chapter 13).

4. THE AESTHETIC VALUE OF ART AND NATURE

I have already referred to the commonly recognized fact that we can and do perceive both art and nature aesthetically. I now submit twin questions for the student's consideration: (1) Do we "look for" different things when we contemplate works of art and when we contemplate nature? (2) Can we say that one of the two is, in some sense, more valuable or better than the other? Our discussion will center chiefly on Question 2 but it will touch upon Question 1 at several points.

Probably most people would say, in answer to Question 2, that art is more rewarding and more important in aesthetic experience than nature. Most traditional aesthetic theory has, certainly, held this view. When we speak of things aesthetic, we usually refer to works of art rather than natural objects. Notice, however, some of the causes of this. Art is a creative activity carried on by human beings, whereas nature, by definition, is not. Hence art has social significance which nature lacks. Furthermore, works of art are almost always stable and enduring, and they can be readily copied or reproduced. Hence they can usually be shared. As a general rule, we can all read the same books and hear the same recordings, whereas objects in nature such as seascapes and cloud formations are highly localized and transient. Both these considerations help to explain why we can *talk* more about art than we do about nature. But taken by themselves, they fail to prove that art is more *valuable* aesthetically than nature. Even though natural objects are not the products of human enterprise, it may still be true that they are objects of greater aesthetic value. In other words, given the distinction which we have drawn between artistic creation and aesthetic "looking," it does not follow logically from the fact that something is an art-object, that it is more enjoyable in aesthetic perception than a non-artistic object. Similarly, even if scenes in nature cannot be widely shared, it would not follow that they are of lesser value when they *are* experienced, than works of art. If we believe that art is, indeed, more valuable than nature, the belief must be justified by other arguments than these.

In opposition to those who hold this belief is the following statement, made late in life by an eminent philosopher for whom aesthetic enjoyment was one of the most important values in human existence:

. . . nor has my love of the beautiful ever found its chief sustenance in the arts. If art *transports*, if it liberates the mind and heart, I prize it; but nature and reflection do so more often and with greater authority. If ever I have been captivated it has been by beautiful places, beautiful manners, and beautiful institutions: whence my admiration for Greece and for England and my pleasure in youthful, sporting, ingenuous America.[21]

And E. F. Carritt says: "If we are put to the intolerable choice between 'natural' and 'artistic' beauty, weighing to the full the vast riches of music and poetry, I think our election must be for nature." [22]

IN THE FACE OF THIS TESTIMONY, how could it be argued that the aesthetic appreciation of art is more valuable than the appreciation of nature? First, by pointing to one of the most obvious differences between a work of art and a natural object, viz., the former has a "frame," the latter does not. The artist encloses and sets limits to his work; the book or the musical score begins and ends at a given point, the painting is bounded by its frame, the sculpture and building by their outer surfaces. But nature does not "frame" its landscapes, seascapes, and cloud formations so that they begin just here and end precisely there.

Now what follows from this concerning the relative *value* of artistic and natural objects? Does the presence of a "frame" in and of itself make art more valuable? We might say that the "frame" organizes and unifies the art-object and that this is valuable because it "holds together" our experience, which would otherwise be diffuse and shapeless. By contrast, the scene in nature lacks a frame and therefore cannot be grasped and comprehended by the eye and the mind. This argument, however, is not conclusive. For although nature lacks a frame when it simply exists, apart from human perception, this is not true when it is apprehended aesthetically. Then the spectator himself imposes a frame on the spectacle of nature. He selects what he is going to attend to aesthetically and himself sets boundaries to it. We all do so at one time or another. "A landscape to be seen has to be composed." [23] If one has keen perception and a fertile imagination, then he can "compose" a landscape of very great aesthetic value, one which may be of equal or even greater interest than many landscape paintings. But of course most of us do not have the capacities for doing so, something the artist possesses to a pre-eminent degree. Furthermore, since we cannot alter the scene in nature, it may contain disturbing

21 George Santayana, "Apologia pro Mente Sua," in *The Philosophy of George Santayana*, ed. Schilpp (Northwestern University Press, 1940), p. 501. Italics in original. Reprinted by permission of the publisher of the Second Edition, Tudor Publishing Co., New York.
22 E. F. Carritt, *The Theory of Beauty* (London: Methuen, 1928), p. 41.
23 George Santayana, *The Sense of Beauty* (New York: Scribner's, 1936), p. 101.

and superfluous elements, which could be removed in the work of art. We may therefore conclude that this argument proves only that works of art will *generally* be of greater value, by virtue of their unity, than natural scenes, not that they must *always* and *necessarily* be so.

Professor T. M. Greene, however, disagrees. He raises the question: "even if we impose a frame on nature and arbitrarily decide to include in our aesthetic apprehension this much and no more of what lies before us, is it ever possible to find a natural scene or object whose formal organization is as aesthetically satisfying as a work of art?" [24] Professor Greene thinks not. However, before deciding whether nature is ever "as aesthetically satisfying as a work of art," we must ask "*Which* work of art?" We should be careful not to speak of "art" in the ideal sense, as though all works of art were of great merit. It is, unfortunately, obvious, as all of us know, that many works are mediocre or poor, because of deficiencies in their "formal organization." If we compare works of this sort with some natural scenes, the verdict would unquestionably have to be on the side of nature. Thus we are again led to the conclusion that no answer to this question, on one side or the other, will be true in *all* cases. And there is something else which we should bear in mind, which has already been mentioned. Even if there were a scene in nature which possessed "formal organization" of very great value, most of us would never get to hear about it. For it would not be lasting and shareable as most works of art are.

But let us even suppose that Professor Greene's question should be answered in the negative. I would urge that nature sometimes possesses aesthetic value of a very important kind just *because* it lacks "formal organization" in the usual sense. I have in mind those natural spectacles of tremendous magnitude and power which seem to overwhelm and dwarf us. They seem to spill over any frame that we try to impose upon them. Think of an unobstructed view of the ocean during a storm and of your response as you look out upon it up to the horizon and then raise your sight to the vast, gray sky. The scene has that awe-inspiring "bigness" usually called "sublime." I doubt whether any work of art ever achieves such sublimity. Speaking from my own experience, I believe that the most sublime work of art I know is Shakespeare's *King Lear*. The great critic A. C. Bradley speaks of this work's "immense scope," its "interpenetration of sublime imagination, piercing pathos, and humour," "the vastness of the convulsion both of nature and of human passion." [25] Yet even this supremely great work probably never arouses the response created by some spectacles of nature. Hence, when we contrast the aesthetic value of art and

---

[24] Theodore M. Greene, *The Arts and the Art of Criticism*, rev. ed. (Princeton University Press, 1947), p. 9.
[25] A. C. Bradley, *Shakespearean Tragedy* (London: Macmillan, 1952), p. 247. Reprinted by permission of Macmillan & Company Ltd., St. Martin's Press.

nature, with respect to the presence or absence of a frame, or in any other connection, we should make it clear what *kind* of aesthetic value is at issue. Nature may be deficient in some kinds of value and yet superior in others.

Our discussion of the "frame" has emphasized the semicreative activity of the percipient in appreciating nature. But the argument should not deceive us into thinking that no similar activity is required for the appreciation of art.

That the art-object has a frame which is, so to speak, "built in," is not per se enough to give it structural organization. The frame and other devices are used to give order to the work, so that the percipient's attention is directed along a certain course. Thus in a novel or play, the characters are introduced, a conflict of wills develops, "the plot thickens," and finally is resolved in the climax. However the organization of the work is not something fixed and definite within it, so that the reader merely follows passively the order of events set out by the artist. Rather, novels and plays can frequently be interpreted in many different ways by the reader. Within each interpretation, the work has a different organization. Thus there may be major differences of opinion as to what parts of the work are most important. (The student has, perhaps, been in a literature course in which he was asked to decide where the climax occurred in the work being studied.) In other words, although the work has *some* order within its frame which controls and directs our perception, the reader must also contribute actively, by working out for himself the way in which the book is going to be organized in his own experience. This can be seen even more clearly in the other arts. It is well known that a piece of music can be interpreted very differently by different performers and conductors. One pianist will stress a passage that another will minimize; one conductor will "build" a climax by means of tempo, orchestral volume, and so on, where another will not. In painting and sculpture, the percipient must decide to which portion of the work he is first going to direct his attention, and what course his eye is going to take over the entire work. Here again, the artist sets up lines of interest within the work which may guide the beholder, but there is still plenty of room for different ways of "reading" the work.

To sum up, selective attention and interpretation are present in the experience of art as well as in the appreciation of nature. Insofar as the work of art indicates the lines along which perception and interpretation are to proceed, there is less latitude for the spectator's activity than in the appreciation of nature. But as I have tried to show, the difference between the two is a difference of *degree*, and it would be unsound to make it into a hard-and-fast dichotomy.

LET US NOW APPROACH THE PROBLEM of the relative value of art and nature from another angle. The most essential difference between them is that works of art are the products of skilled, deliberate human activity, whereas objects of nature are not. Does our knowledge of this fact enhance our appreciation of art? We might answer "yes" for at least two reasons. The first is that we feel a sense of kinship with the man who molded the work before us, which we cannot feel in the perception of nature. We may feel gratitude for the efforts which provided us with this enjoyable work, we may be impressed with the obstacles or discouragements which the artist had to overcome, or we may simply feel a bond with another human being who, through his art, is speaking to us directly and movingly. Secondly, we may admire the artist's skill. We may respect the expertness with which he has controlled and used his artistic medium or esteem the economy of line with which the painter has achieved a massive effect.

There can be little doubt that, because of these reasons, there is frequently an increment of value in the appreciation of art. However, we should also recognize that concern with the creative artist does not always enhance the aesthetic value of art. It can have just the opposite effect. This occurs when we approach the work of art for a revelation of or clues to the life and personality of the artist, or when we become exclusively preoccupied with the artist's technique. In both cases, the work is only of instrumental interest. In the first instance, it is being used as a biographical document. This frequently leads to romanticizing of the object, for the percipient reads into it what he already knows about the life of the artist. In the second case, the work is being used as a laboratory specimen for the study of technical problems. Hence interest in the creative artist must be exercised judiciously, lest it become aesthetically "irrelevant." [26] If it cannot augment the appreciation of nature, at least there it cannot arise to delude us and change our attitude from the aesthetic into something quite different.

However, when attention is directed to art-objects themselves, we frequently find values which are absent from nature. A work may possess great emotional expressiveness or it may have psychological overtones of other kinds which rivet our attention to it. Unlike most natural objects, it can have enormous cultural significance, embodying the aspirations and traditions of a society or its most revered religious doctrines. Such works as Dante's *Divine Comedy* set forth an overarching conception of the significance and purposes of human life. Now, as before, we cannot say that art possesses these values exclusively and that nature is entirely devoid of them. Such an "all-or-none" conclusion would be unjustified. Natural objects and scenes are often enough found "moving" and the mystic can "see a World in a Grain of Sand." But on the whole, nature is deficient in psychological and symbolic interest, compared to art.

THE QUESTION OF THE VALUE OF ART as compared to that of nature, like all the questions treated in this book, must be decided by the student for himself. He may be able to show that the reasoning I have used is logically unsound

[26] Cf. sec. 5, below, on aesthetic "relevance."

or he may adduce other facts than those which have been cited in this discussion. I believe, however, that my own analysis has shown this: no assertion that art is aesthetically superior to nature, or vice versa, is true universally and in all respects. In particular instances and in some respects, a work of art is more valuable than a nonartistic object; in other instances, the converse is true.

A dogmatic belief in this matter would be especially pernicious if it led to a loss of values in our own experience, i.e., if we thought that one of the pair, art and nature, had little or no value relative to the other and therefore ignored it. Satisfaction can be found in both. If we develop a keen eye for the aesthetic delights of nature, it can be a source of endless interest, sparing us, moreover, the necessity of going to theatres or sitting rigidly in a concert hall. Of course, most of our commerce with objects in nature is "practical" and this tends to drive out aesthetic attention. But as we saw in the previous section, there is always the possibility of aesthetic interest supervening upon the practical. Furthermore, we can learn from art to be more perceptive in the appreciation of nature and vice versa. It has been said that we come to appreciate nature only after we have had experience of art,[27] but this seems highly doubtful. Aesthetic attention can light on any object, man-made or not, and the development of discrimination which results from the encounter with any one object can increase the enjoyment of any other.

5. AESTHETIC "RELEVANCE"

The aesthetic experience, at its best, seems to isolate both us and the object from the flow of experience. The object, in being admired for itself, is divorced from its interrelations with other things. And we feel as though life had suddenly been arrested, for we are absorbed wholly in the object before us and abandon any thought of purposive activity looking toward the future.

This is how the experience feels. The foregoing account of the aesthetic attitude has sought to explain the distinctive nature of this experience. But we must not ignore an obvious and yet important fact: both the aesthetic percipient and the object have a history which extends beyond the duration of the aesthetic experience. Though the percipient has no concern for things past and future, he of course enters into the experience with the imprint of all of his past history upon him. He has a certain amount of knowledge, certain beliefs and values, and certain emotional predispositions. How he responds to the object is largely determined by what he has

[27] Cf. Vivas and Krieger, *op. cit.*, p. 12; Kate Gordon, *Esthetics* (New York: Holt, 1909), p. 2. For the opposite view, cf. Langfeld, *op. cit.*, p. 21.

experienced in the past. The object may, for example, arouse memories of his previous experience. He may "see" certain images while listening to a piece of music. Or he might have acquired some knowledge in the past which influences his perception. Most obviously, this can be knowledge about the work of art itself. One hears Stravinsky's "Rite of Spring" ("Le Sacre du Printemps") knowing that it created a scandal at its first performance, or Tchaikovsky's Fourth Symphony, knowing of the unusual love affair that Tchaikovsky had at the time of its composition. Or one reads Steinbeck's novel *Grapes of Wrath* after having learned that it created national interest in the plight of the "dust bowl" farmer.

Now notice a curious fact about these memories, images, and bits of knowledge which enter into the aesthetic experience — they are not embodied in the aesthetic object itself, but arise rather from the percipient's previous experience. The recollection of a past event in his life is stimulated by the music, but it is not something that is present within the music, like the notes and melodies which make it up. The memory is something superadded to the experience by the listener. Similarly, historical information about the works of Stravinsky or Steinbeck is obviously not found within the works themselves; it is learned from other sources.

But this creates an interesting and difficult problem. The aesthetic attitude, we have said, is concerned with the object alone, to experience whatever it may offer to awareness. Does it not follow that if we permit personal memories and images, and extraneous items of knowledge to enter into the experience, it thereby becomes unaesthetic? "Aesthetic attention is, above all, object-centered attention." [28] Do we not divert attention from the object when we dwell fondly on our recollections or when we think about the historical origins and influences of the work of art? What about the people who, in the "drowsy revery" which passes for their experience of music, weave the most ingenious and elaborate "stories" in their minds, or go off on a stream of memory? Can we say that their experience is genuinely aesthetic? Then there are the people who seem to know everything there is to know about a work of art — when it was created and under what circumstances, the biography of the artist, the technical names used in describing it, its position in the history of art, etc., etc., — and yet never seem actually to appreciate the work of art itself. Can it be that all of their knowledge *about* the work gets in the way of attending to it and enjoying it *aesthetically?*

This is the problem of aesthetic *relevance*. Is it ever "relevant" to the aesthetic experience to have thoughts or images or bits of knowledge which are not present within the object itself? If these are ever relevant, under what conditions are they so?

---

[28] Reprinted from *Art and the Social Order* by D. W. Gotshalk by permission of The University of Chicago Press. Copyright 1947 by The University of Chicago. P. 4.

LET US BEGIN BY CONSIDERING a psychological experiment involving a very simple aesthetic experience — the perception of single colors. This is not the sort of experiment which was criticized in the previous chapter.[29] Rather, the psychologist in this case, Edward Bullough, begins his report by repudiating the "barren question whether certain colours are *per se* and universally pleasing." [30] Bullough is concerned with the different ways in which people respond aesthetically. His results are highly illuminating, and we will consider them in detail in the next chapter. At the present time we will refer only to his findings concerning one type of response, the "associative."

In response of this kind, perception of the color was accompanied by a thought or image of some object experienced in the past. These associations were highly diverse. They included the sun, flowers, precious stones, blood and steel (pp. 428–429). Bullough raises the question whether all such associations are "illegitimate from the aesthetic point of view" (p. 432). He finds that there are two kinds of association. The first is that in which the association has a strong "emotional tone" of its own, which is distinct from the feeling-tone of the color itself. In such a case, the association absorbs virtually all of the spectator's attention, with the consequence that "the colour almost completely loses its already endangered position in the field of consciousness" (p. 454). That is, the spectator pays very little attention to the color, which merely stimulates the association or memory, and is then lost sight of. The second kind of association is quite different. It is that in which the association is not divorced from, but is "fused" with the perception of the color. Here, the feeling-tone of the color is augmented by that of the association, while the observer "[keeps] the colour attentively in the focus of consciousness" (p. 455).

Bullough argues that the first kind of association is aesthetically "illegitimate," because the color is simply being used as a stimulus to personal association, which calls attention to itself. The second kind, however, is not unaesthetic. Indeed, it can enhance the aesthetic value of the perception, for it may "impart life and significance to the colour, without endangering — thanks to the fusion — the self-contained character of the experience" (p. 456). Bullough therefore answers our original question by saying that "no hard and fast rule can be laid down concerning the aesthetic value of association in general" (p. 456).

Bullough's answer is, I believe, a sound one. If the aesthetic experience is as we have described it, then whether an association is aesthetic depends on whether it is compatible with the attitude of "disinterested attention." If

---

29 Cf. above, pp. 12–13.
30 Edward Bullough, "The 'Perceptive Problem' in the Aesthetic Appreciation of Single Colours," *British Journal of Psychology*, II (1908), 406.

the association re-enforces the focusing of attention upon the object, by "fusing" with the object and thereby giving it added "life and significance," it is genuinely aesthetic. If, however, it arrogates attention to itself and away from the object, it undermines the aesthetic attitude. The trouble with people who say, "Listen, darling, they're playing *our* song," is not simply that the music reminds them of something else. It is that generally they become engrossed in running through their memories, so that the music becomes simply a backdrop, heard dimly on the "fringe" of awareness.

HOWEVER, THE MEANING OF "FUSION" requires further elucidation. And we have thus far been speaking only of a fairly elementary aesthetic experience. We can throw further light on the problem of aesthetic relevance by turning to another sort of experiment.

Dr. I. A. Richards presented a series of unsigned poems to a number of British undergraduates and asked for their reactions.[31] The students' comments offer numerous examples of both "relevant" and "irrelevant" response. Let us consider some reactions to one poem which reads, in part, as follows:

> Between the erect and solemn trees
> I will go down upon my knees;
> I shall not find this day
> So meet a place to pray.
>
> . . .
>
> The worshipping trees arise and run,
> With never a swerve, towards the sun;
> So may my soul's desire,
> Turn to its central fire.
>
> . . .
>
> How strong each pillared trunk; the bark
> That covers them, how smooth; and hark,
> The sweet and gentle voice
> With which the leaves rejoice!
>
> May a like strength and sweetness fill
> Desire and thought and steadfast will,
> When I remember these
> Fair sacramental trees. [32]

One sort of irrelevant response is illustrated by the student who, speaking on behalf of what he calls "a sceptical age," says that "I don't like to hear

[31] I. A. Richards, *Practical Criticism* (New York: Harcourt, Brace, 1952). Reprinted by permission of Harcourt, Brace and Company and of Routledge & Kegan Paul Ltd., publishers.

[32] *Op. cit.,* p. 92.

people boast about praying" (p. 94). This student has not read the poem "sympathetically," as the aesthetic attitude demands. He has failed to inhibit his religious convictions, which interpose themselves between him and the poem. He has therefore failed to experience the imagery and emotions to be found in the poem when it is apprehended aesthetically, and, as a result, he has failed to appreciate its value.

But now let us consider the response of those who tried to read the poem sympathetically. One student describes an image which arose in his mind: "The 'erect and solemn trees' that rush upward to the sun, suggest the long aisle of a great cathedral, its stillness and sanctity" (p. 100). The poem, however, says nothing about a "cathedral." Is this image aesthetically relevant? There are a number of elements involved in the "suggestion" of a cathedral. Primarily, a cathedral is a building devoted specifically to prayer and worship; then there is the visual appearance of its "long aisle"; and finally there is the emotional quality of "stillness and sanctity." It is justifiable to say that each of these fits in with the poem. The poem speaks explicitly of prayer and adoration, e.g., "a place to pray." The religious motive is present in such words as "worshipping" and "sacramental." A number of other students emphasized this aspect of the poem in their comments (cf. pp. 93, 96, 100). We can also see how a "forest-aisle" of "erect and solemn trees" may suggest the image of the "aisle of a great cathedral." Finally, the mood of the poem is one of "stillness and sanctity"; thus, in a stanza which I have not quoted, the poet speaks of "the stillness of the air," and comparable allusions can be found readily in the above verses.

It may therefore be concluded that the "suggestion" of the cathedral *is* aesthetically relevant.[33] It is congruous with both the verbal meaning of the poem and the emotions and mood which it expresses. It does not divert attention away from the poem. Rather, it occurs in the course of attentive reading, and it makes vivid the meaning and quality of the poem.

But of course not *all* associations are relevant. I will cite two other comments on the same poem. The first is that of a student who reports an association which occurred to him while reading the second verse quoted above. The association is with the English game of Rugby, which resembles American football: "When I first read [this] verse, a vivid picture came into my mind of a forward breaking away with the ball, from a loose scrum [i.e., scrimmage] and 'with never a swerve' making straight for the line." The student then half-apologizes for this grotesquely irrelevant image: "I didn't try to think of the verse in a ridiculous light but the idea occurred to me spontaneously" (p. 96). The second comment praises the poem because "It creates the solemn peaceful reverent atmosphere of a pine wood for us" (p. 101). Solemnity, peacefulness, and reverence, we have already agreed, are certainly expressed within the poem. But what about *pine* trees? The

[33] *Ibid.*, p. 237.

next to the last stanza quoted above describes the trees: "the bark/That covers them, how *smooth*," and the trees have "leaves." Therefore Dr. Richards says of this student's response that it proves that a poem "can create enthusiasm without being read" (p. 101). This is probably a little too harsh. But we can say that the student has failed to read the poem with close and discriminating attention. He seems to be one of those people who get carried away by the prevailing "mood" of a work of art and fail to see the specific details which make it up.

People are especially prone to do this while listening to music. This is one reason why it is dangerous to imagine "stories" while hearing music, as some persons incorrigibly do. The "story" may be congruous in general with the emotional character of the work, e.g., the "story" of someone mourning the death of his beloved, when the music is slow and in a minor key, and expresses sorrow and melancholy. But the specific notes and melodies are incessantly changing. To "fuse" the association with the music, the "story" would have to be changed to conform with the continuous inflections and modulations in the work. Yet it would be almost impossible for any visualized "story" to do this. The consequence is that the variety and detail of the music become blurred for the listener. He does not discriminate the variety and nuances within the music, which give the work its distinctive character. This is seen in people who conjure up pretty much the same "story" for music of a certain kind, such as slow, mournful music, no matter what the specific composition may be. A related danger in visualization is that the "story" may develop a life of its own, so that the listener becomes absorbed in it, rather than the music. This, again, would be an instance of aesthetic irrelevance.

WE COME NOW to the most important area of our discussion — the relevance of knowledge concerning the aesthetic object. This is knowledge *about* the object, as opposed to what we learn of the object in direct, attentive perception of it alone. "Knowledge about" may be knowledge about the artist, the period in which the work was created, the society in which the artist lived; the resemblances and differences between this work and others; the "form" of the work, e.g., sonnet, symphony; the influence of the work upon the later development of art; how the work has been appraised by different critics and at different times; and so on. Mention has already been made of those who have enormous amounts of knowledge of this kind and yet seem to take pitifully little enjoyment in the work itself. Professor C. J. Ducasse therefore suggests that such knowledge is "more likely to be fatal than useful." [34] He goes on to say: "Anecdotes and other

---

[34] C. J. Ducasse, *The Philosophy of Art* (New York: Dial, 1929), p. 226. The phrase "knowledge about" is taken from Ducasse. Reprinted by permission of the publishers, The Dial Press.

biographical material of the great painters, musicians, and writers, make entertaining gossip, but have nothing directly to do with the aesthetic enjoyment of the works that such men have left behind." [35]

We need not, however, condemn all "knowledge about" as aesthetically irrelevant. Our previous discussion enables us to distinguish relevant from irrelevant knowledge. "Knowledge about" is relevant under three conditions: when it does not weaken or destroy aesthetic attention to the object, when it pertains to the meaning and expressiveness of the object, and when it enhances the quality and significance of one's immediate aesthetic response to the object.

Imagine someone looking at a painting of the Crucifixion who, unlike ourselves, does not know about the Christian interpretation of this event. He might respond partially, he might feel a sense of the pathos expressed by the painting, but it is not unlikely that he would be baffled by it. Why all this solemnity about the execution of this man? Then suppose he is told that the figure on the cross is the Son of God dying to redeem mankind. This by itself will not make the aesthetic experience more valuable for him. He will have to note carefully the placement of the figures in the painting, e.g., Christ, Mary, and their relations to each other, their facial expressions and bodily postures, the lighting which the painter has cast upon them, the colors in the painting and the contrasts between them, the appearance of the sky, and so on. And he must apprehend these, not piecemeal and analytically, as I have written them down, but by focusing aesthetic attention upon all of them in their interrelations with each other, as they present themselves immediately and directly to awareness. If, however, he does so, then the "knowledge about" which he has gained can make an enormous difference within his experience. For he now actually sees differently the expression on Christ's face and the lighting round his head, the reactions of those at the foot of the Cross, the ominously dark sky. The whole feeling of the picture is altered; it becomes more profound and more vivid. Thus the knowledge is absorbed into the spectator's perception and transforms the visual, imaginative, and emotional quality of his experience.

The importance of the third criterion of aesthetic relevance listed above can now be understood. The Christian interpretation of the life and passion of Christ is, in an obvious way, relevant to a painting of the Crucifixion. But knowledge of it is not *aesthetically* relevant unless it interacts with what we see and feel when we look at the painting aesthetically. It must be assimilated into the aesthetic experience. Merely to acquire this knowledge is not enough and may even be detrimental to aesthetic appreciation. For the spectator may be thinking of the story of Christ as he has heard it,

---

[35] *Op. cit.*, p. 230. Cf., similarly, Bertram Morris, *The Aesthetic Process* (Northestern University Press, 1943): "We need know nothing of the life of the artist in order to appreciate his work." P. 108.

and not as it is rendered uniquely by *this* particular painting. The proof of this would be that he responds in substantially the same way to extremely different treatments of the Crucifixion. Then he is simply putting a label on the painting — "Crucifixion" — like calling it a "landscape" or "still life," rather than perceiving it as a wholly individual object. (How differently this subject can be rendered may be seen by comparing the "Crucifixion" of Grünewald [see Plate 4] with that of Perugino [see Plate 5]).

This is the great danger in all "knowledge about" art — that it will remain external to the work, that it will not enter into one's immediate aesthetic response, that it will, indeed, divert attention away from the work. This is, precisely, aesthetic irrelevance. So much of the "knowledge about" art which is dispensed in "art appreciation" courses and books about art, and in "program notes" at concerts, is of just this kind. We are told the birth and death dates of the artist, that he had a bad temper, or what his political beliefs were. The student is taught to recognize a Petrarchan sonnet or the divisions of a movement in sonata form. He learns how to distinguish "baroque" art from "classical" and how some work of art influenced the creation of later works. But all this is worthless aesthetically (though it may be interesting historically or psychologically), unless it illuminates the work of art itself, unless it makes the student's aesthetic perception more acute and enriches the quality of his experience. The ability to tell a Petrarchan sonnet from a Spenserian is no more aesthetic in itself than the ability of a botanist to distinguish one species of flower from another; the structure of the society in which the artist lived may be important for the student of social history, but may cast no light whatever upon the work. Such knowledge may be, and often is, worse than worthless — it is downright harmful. For the student mistakenly believes that if he knows about the origins and history of the work, or can classify and analyze it, he is enjoying it aesthetically. In the light of our discussion in this chapter we can now see that this is mistaken. It is particularly unfortunate because all of the enjoyment which could have been had in genuine aesthetic experience is lost as a result.

Why are teachers in the arts so often responsible for this confusion? One reason is that it is very difficult to teach what the title of a course in "art appreciation" implies. It is by no means easy to cultivate discriminating interest and sensitivity. It is much easier to present *facts about* art to the student. But only a small minority of teachers choose, deliberately at least, this path of least resistance. A far greater number simply take it for granted that the student will be able to work such knowledge into his perception so that it becomes aesthetically relevant. This must not be assumed, however. The teacher should always select judiciously the "knowledge about" he is going to present, choosing only what can readily be made relevant, and he should then show *how* it is relevant to the aesthetic enjoyment of the work. What he says should be directed toward the difficulties which the student has had in his initial encounter with the work, and it should lead back into the work, enabling the student to "see what he had not seen before," making his experience not simply more informed — that is not an end in itself — but making it more intense and discriminating because it is more informed. When I first read Shakespeare, in high school, I was assigned the project of building a wooden model of the Globe Theatre, in which many of Shakespeare's plays were first presented. I did not at the time, and to this day, still do not know how this was relevant to the appreciation of *The Merchant of Venice*.

The cardinal rule in the teaching of art is the cardinal rule in aesthetic experience — focus attention solely on the object itself. Whatever else you say or do must be made subordinate to this, and it is worth doing aesthetically only if it gets absorbed into aesthetic perception and suffuses it with new significance.

There is one particular device in the teaching of art which invites irrelevance, and which should be mentioned because it is used so widely. Students are often asked to make a *comparison* between two or more works of art. There is certainly something to be said for this method. It is indispensable in studying the history of art. Moreover, it can be useful for strictly aesthetic purposes as well, for it often makes the student aware of the distinctive nature of each of the works in question. However, it also creates certain dangers. We can understand the first of these when we have understood the workings of the aesthetic attitude. This attitude concentrates on an object isolated from its interrelationships, in order to relish its individuality. If we are put in the position of having to relate the object to some other, it may be that attention can never be focused wholly upon just one of them. Rather it will shuttle between them. Thus attention is kept from being aesthetic. Comparative judgments are also employed in the psychological experiments described in the previous chapter. They were repudiated by Bullough in the article from which I have already quoted: "The method of comparison . . . destroys the pre-adaptation of the subject to aesthetic experiences. . . . It is precisely characteristic of the aesthetic appreciation to be non-comparative, individualising, isolating." [36] Since he cannot look at each work aesthetically, the student is compelled to analyze the works before him, to pick out the salient similarities and differences: this poem is "lyric," that one is "dramatic," this is an early work by the artist, the other is one of his mature works. But this is simply intellectual recognition, not aesthetic enjoyment, and taken by itself is of little or no aesthetic relevance.

[36] *Op. cit.*, p. 412. Cf., also, C. W. Valentine, *An Introduction to the Experimental Psychology of Beauty*, rev. ed. (London: Jack, 1919), pp. 107-108.

6. AESTHETIC "SURFACE" AND "MEANING"

Our definition of "aesthetic attitude" asserts that "any object of awareness whatever" can be perceived aesthetically. Thus we seek to recognize that men have contemplated disinterestedly an enormous variety of objects of all kinds, and that new areas of aesthetic interest are being constantly opened up. However, we must now consider the objection that this definition makes the scope of the aesthetic too broad.

The objection is that only what is apprehended directly and immediately by *sensation* is properly "aesthetic." Only sounds, colors, textures, and comparable objects of the senses can be aesthetic objects. These qualities constitute what D. W. Prall calls the sensuous "surface" [37] of the world.

We can appreciate the force of this view only when we understand the distinction which it draws between "surface" qualities and other objects of awareness.

When we apprehend a color, for example, its entire significance consists simply in the way it looks to us. It has no meaning beyond itself. No thinking or intellectual activity is required in order to enjoy it aesthetically. We need only sense it directly or, as Prall says, we "intuit" it. [38] Now consider, by contrast, our apprehension of a word. A word is not merely a certain shape on paper or, when spoken, a sound that we hear. It is that only to an infant or someone who does not know the language. For anyone else, the word has *meaning*, it refers to something beyond itself. The word "dog" refers to the four-footed creatures who are, it is said, man's noblest friends. It is only when we are laboriously learning a language that we have to stop and think about the meaning of a word. Once we know the language it comes to us effortlessly. But even so, the distinction remains between a color or sound, which presents to awareness only itself, and a word, whose significance is more than its mere appearance to sensation.

Now on the view we are considering, it is only qualitative "surface" which can be the object of aesthetic awareness. It is the whole nature of aesthetic experience that we take "delight in the object as directly apprehended, with no reference beyond this apprehended form or appearance" (p. 19). Anything which has such a reference is not really an aesthetic object: "as we leave [the] surface in our attention, to go deeper into meanings . . . we depart from the typically aesthetic attitude" (p. 20). Therefore, Prall believes, our appreciation of an art-form employing words, such as poetry, is not truly aesthetic (cf. pp. 189, 194).

Do you see how plausible this is as a theory of aesthetic experience? When we first stop to reflect on this experience and try to describe it in "common sense" terms, we say that it is looking at something "just for

[37] D. W. Prall, *Aesthetic Analysis* (New York: Crowell, 1936), p. 5.
[38] *Aesthetic Judgment*, p. 20. All further references are to this work.

itself." And sensory qualities are the most obvious objects of such experience. Colors, sounds, aromas, and textures are inviting or engaging in themselves; they are delightful in their sheer, immediate appearance. Attention comes to rest on them. It does not look beyond, as in "practical" perception.

BUT THOUGH IT IS PLAUSIBLE, does the theory of "surface" stand up under critical investigation? The theory holds that aesthetic perception is disinterested and lacking in ulterior purpose. In this it is surely right. But it also holds that only sensory qualities can be the objects of such perception. At this point the theory becomes questionable.

It is open to criticism because it is too limited. Only rarely in adult experience do we have an experience which is purely sensory, i.e., in which we do not interpret in some way the sense-data which we perceive. A red light induces the automobile driver to stop; a group of colors can symbolize the history and ideals of a nation. Even in aesthetic perception, when colors are more vivid and interesting than they are in ordinary experience, we usually "fill in" our perception, by relating them to past experience. Hence, as Prall admits (p. 182), sensory "intuition" almost never occurs.

But this is not the basic shortcoming of the theory. Sensation probably does occur at some time, and when it does, as was said earlier in this chapter, it can be aesthetic. Now, however, see how the area of the aesthetic is limited if we restrict it to sensation alone.

We must exclude from the aesthetic all experience which is other than sensory. *All* perceptual and intellectual awareness [39] must be lumped together as nonaesthetic. Not only are "practical" perception and thinking nonaesthetic, but so too are perception and thought when they are disinterested. We engage in such perception and thinking when we read a poem or a novel. We usually consider such experience aesthetic. But on Prall's theory it must fall outside the realm of the aesthetic.

The theory of "surface" thus blurs the important distinction between perception and thought which is disinterested and that which is not. It does so because it draws the distinction between the aesthetic and the nonaesthetic in the wrong place. Its definition of "aesthetic" is detrimental to the study of aesthetics. If we were to follow its lead, and deny that any experience other than sensory "intuition" is aesthetic, we would keep ourselves from studying a good deal, indeed most, of aesthetic experience, which is preponderantly perceptual and conceptual.[40]

[39] Cf. above, pp. 41–42.

[40] Prall himself hesitates to accept these conclusions. He attempts to avoid them by distinguishing between the "thinner surface" meaning of "aesthetic," which he takes to be the "strict" (p. vi) or "characteristic" (p. 28) sense of the term, and the "thicker" meaning, which is not restricted to sensuous awareness alone (cf. pp. 221–224; cf., also, pp. 181, 189).

There is, of course, no question that works of literature possess "meaning." At least they do for anyone who understands the language in which they are written. The Italian lady who knew no English thought that "cellar door" was the most beautiful word in our language, simply because of its sound. But just because words and sentences are meaningful, it does not follow that they cannot be apprehended aesthetically. We can attend to the words and their meanings disinterestedly. The words have a reference beyond themselves, but this does not mean that we must have some ulterior purpose in reading them. Prall says, in the sentence which I have already quoted, that in aesthetic experience we take "delight in the object as directly apprehended, with no reference beyond" it. This is true, if taken to mean that our interest is solely in the object and not in anything outside of the experience of perception. But for this to be true, it does not have to be true that the object itself, e.g., a word in a work of literature, must have no "reference beyond" itself. It is the failure to recognize this which is responsible for the inadequacy of "surface"-theory.

In reading much poetry, we appreciate both its "surface," e.g., the "music" of the words, and the "ideas" which it conveys. Our interest comes to rest in these. But when a mathematics student consults the logarithmic table or when one reads the dosages on the label of a medicine bottle, perception is not disinterested. Then the reader is concerned with meanings only for the sake of some purpose which outruns the experience of perception itself. To be sure, a "meaningful" word like "Fire!" is more likely to call forth practical activity than a nonsense word like "jabberwocky," but this does not imply that *all* perception of "meaning" must be nonaesthetic. Hence it is not the nature of the *object* that is crucial. Literature has "meaning," but this settles nothing. It is our *attitude* toward literature which can and does make it aesthetic.

IN THE AESTHETIC EXPERIENCE, any and every sort of awareness — sensory, perceptual, intellectual, imaginative, emotional — may occur. The definition of "aesthetic attitude" presented in this chapter does not exclude any of these *a priori*. It tries to do justice to the facts that men find aesthetic enjoyment in the smell of freshly cut hay, in novels and plays, in the mathematical-logical properties of "perfect" circles and trans-finite numbers. Thus we attempt to be faithful to the evidence and also avoid narrowing our investigation of aesthetic experience at the outset.

BIBLIOGRAPHY

* Gotshalk, D. W. *Art and the Social Order*. University of Chicago Press, 1947. Chap. I.
* Longman, Lester D., "The Concept of Psychical Distance," *Journal of Aesthetics and Art Criticism*, Vol. VI (Sept., 1947), 31–36.

* Rader, Melvin, ed. *A Modern Book of Esthetics,* rev. ed. New York: Holt, 1952. Pp. 387–428, 548–564.
* Vivas and Krieger, *The Problems of Aesthetics.* Pp. 315–325, 396–411.
* Weitz, Morris, ed. *Problems in Aesthetics.* New York: Macmillan, 1959. Pp. 621–625, 637–656.
Aiken, Henry D., "The Concept of Relevance in Aesthetics," *Journal of Aesthetics and Art Criticism,* Vol. VI (Dec., 1947), 152–161.
Copi, Irving M., "A Note on Representation in Art," *Journal of Philosophy,* Vol. LII (June 23, 1955), 346–349.
Dewey, John. *Art as Experience.* New York: Minton, Balch, 1934. Chaps. I, XI.
Edman, Irwin. *Philosopher's Quest.* New York: Viking, 1947. Pp. 231–250.
Langfeld, Herbert S. *The Aesthetic Attitude.* New York: Harcourt, Brace, 1920. Chap. III.
Prall, *Aesthetic Judgment.* Chaps. I–III, X.
Richards, I. A. *Practical Criticism.* New York: Harcourt, Brace, 1952. Part III, Chap. V.

QUESTIONS

1. "The aesthetic mode is generally supposed to be a peculiar way of regarding things. . . . [But] when we look at a picture, or read a poem, or listen to music, we are not doing something quite unlike what we were doing on our way to the Gallery or when we dressed in the morning." — I. A. Richards, *Principles of Literary Criticism* (New York: Harcourt, Brace, 1950), p. 16. Discuss. Read all of Chapter II in Richards, from which this passage is taken, entitled "The Phantom Aesthetic State."
2. One can become absorbed in a crossword puzzle, a mechanical problem, or the description of some historical episode. Is his experience then aesthetic? If not, what differentiates it from aesthetic experience?
3. The aesthetic attitude is described in this chapter as one of complete "sympathy" with the work of art. But if the percipient were always "sympathetic," would he not appreciate *every* work of art without exception? Could we, then, ever say that any work of art is *bad?* Is every instance of aesthetic disvalue due to a lack of "sympathy" on the part of the spectator?
    Can you cite any examples, from your own experience, of works of art which you failed to appreciate, at one time, because of a lack of aesthetic "sympathy"?
4. The word "disinterested" is often used outside of aesthetics, to describe, e.g., a judge, a man making a moral choice, a scientist seeking truth. What are the differences, if any, between this use of the word and its use in describing the aesthetic attitude?
5. Is *all* experience, to some degree, aesthetic? If so, in what sense of "aesthetic"?
6. Consider the analysis and discussion of a specific work of art, in some course which you have taken. How much of the discussion was aesthetically relevant, how much irrelevant? How can you tell the difference between the two?

3

The Aesthetic Experience

1. THE AESTHETIC EXPERIENCE IN TIME

We are now going to examine the aesthetic experience as a whole. This is the experience which we have while the aesthetic attitude is sustained. Thus far we have spoken only of the attitude with which we approach the object. In this and succeeding chapters, we shall consider the states of response, emotional, imaginative, intellectual, which enter into the total experience, and the nature of the aesthetic object.

As was pointed out in the opening chapter, there is a very great difference between having an experience and thinking about it. When we try to understand the experience, we must analyze it. This means that we must set out piecemeal, word by word, sentence by sentence, features of the experience which are all together while the experience is actually being had. In other words, one cannot say everything at once, in talking about the aesthetic experience or any other. Therefore we must now supplement in an important respect the account of aesthetic experience given in Chapter 2. Without this, our analysis would not give a true picture of aesthetic experience.

I HAVE EMPHASIZED THAT, in the aesthetic experience, the individual does not look ahead to some future goal. The aesthetic attitude is not like practical perception, which serves some ongoing purpose pointed toward the future. Aesthetic awareness comes to rest in the object. This might lead the student to think that the aesthetic spectator is concerned only with the enjoyment of the present moment, that he has no concern at all for the future.

Indeed, absorption in what is being "immediately" apprehended has often been emphasized in describing the aesthetic experience. The experience has therefore been said to be "timeless," i.e., there is no thought for past or future, but only for the present. This has been particularly stressed by those who have taken sensation to be the only avenue of true aesthetic experience. If you look at a color or listen to a sound, which has no "meaning" but simply looks or sounds delightful, there can be no preoccupation with the future. There is nothing about the sensory object which leads you to think ahead. Belief in the "timelessness" of aesthetic enjoyment has also been encouraged by another influential idea in the history of aesthetic thought. This is the distinction between "arts of time" and "arts of space." [1] The former are those in which the performance of the artist or the perception of the spectator takes place over a period of time, i.e., the arts of music, the drama, literature, the dance, and more recently, the motion picture. The time required for appreciation of works in these media can range from a few minutes devoted to reading a poem, to an hour or two in watching a moving picture, or even a number of days in the case of Wagner's operatic "Ring" cycle. (It can seem even longer to those who don't like Wagner.) The "spatial" or "nontemporal" arts are painting, sculpture, and architecture. Works in these media do not extend through time. They can be appreciated "all at once" or instantaneously.

I now wish to argue that this view is mistaken. I wish to argue that the aesthetic experience takes place in time and through time, no matter what kind of art-object is being appreciated. Indeed, this "temporal" character of aesthetic appreciation is one of the most important things about it. If it were not temporal, aesthetic experience would lack much of the vitality and excitement which, as a matter of fact, it possesses.

To BEGIN WITH, all experience occurs in time. This is true of any sort of experience whatever. This means that, as different things happen, we are aware of first this, then that, so that there is an irreversible sequence in our awareness. Thus we speak of "before" and "after" and calculate their relationships to each other by such devices as clocks. A man goes to his barber, then to the post office, then he has lunch, and later he reads the newspaper. Similarly, time elapses during aesthetic perception, which can also be measured by a clock.

But this is relatively unimportant. Aesthetic experience is temporal in a much more significant respect.

---

[1] This distinction is made prominent by Lessing's *Laocoön* (1766) and is found throughout 19th- and 20th-century aesthetics.

Practical experience is for the most part casual and humdrum. Something happens and then something else happens, in a loose, random way. Life is, as the phrase has it, "one darn thing after another" — the visit to the barber, followed by the trip to the post office, and so on. We are aware of the succession of events, but there is no particular interest or excitement in this awareness. In any particular task, such as mowing the lawn or washing the dishes, one moment simply follows another until the activity ceases. The activity does not generate increasing interest as it proceeds, and the final moment, when it comes, is of no particular significance, except possibly that now the job is over and done with.

But in some instances of practical experience, we have a much more acute sense of time. I do not mean by this a feeling of boredom, when all we want is that a period of time should elapse. I mean rather an experience in which our interest is engaged at each moment, and something more — when each moment creates forward-looking interest in the next, and when all of them are linked together by ever increasing interest in the "climax" of the experience. Each moment is felt to be integrally related to the next, each seems to require and point toward its successor, as it does not when experience is random and diffuse. The close of a tightly knit experience is not merely the terminating point in time. It has unusual significance. It is the climax of the interest which has developed throughout the experience, and it satisfies the expectations which have been built up in the foregoing moments. Thus it sums up all that has gone before and unifies and "rounds out" the experience.

The student will probably understand this better if I give some examples: A well-played chess game, in which each of the moves makes up a tightly knit pattern to force one's opponent into an untenable position, one move building upon the other, coming increasingly closer to success as each move narrows further the area in which the opponent can move freely, leading up finally to the decisive move which clinches the game. A doctor, treating a serious illness, who must counter any aggravation of the sickness, or weakness and discouragement in the patient, all the while bringing to bear means of cure which, taken together, prepare the patient for the moment of crisis. When he passes through the crisis successfully it is a consummation of all of the doctor's efforts and expectations.

BUT IT IS IN OUR APPRECIATION of the arts that the best examples are found. For in aesthetic enjoyment, more than in any other kind of experience, the moments of experience are tightly bound together. What we are apprehending at the "present" moment is intimately related to what has preceded it, and it arouses anticipation of what is to follow.

Thus the Greek philosopher Aristotle says that the plot of drama "has a beginning, a middle, and an end." [2] This does not, of course, mean merely that the play starts at a point in time and ends at a later time. Rather, Aristotle is saying that the events of the play are necessarily connected to each other. They do not follow each other any which way; instead, one causally brings about another, and yet another, and finally all of them together bring on the climax or dénouement. In this way, the significance and worth of a man's whole existence can be clearly displayed in a drama such as *Macbeth*. Life itself rarely does this. For the salient events in a man's biography occur over a period of years, and they are interspersed with many irrelevant and uninteresting occurrences. The latter are eliminated from drama, and only the crucial happenings and the causal interrelationships between them are presented, compactly and intensely.

At the "beginning" of a tragedy the persons of the play are introduced, and the character of each is exhibited. They are shown to have certain desires and aspirations, and also such traits as stubbornness and courage. Because of their character, they perform certain acts which have consequences that jeopardize themselves and others. A feeling of impending crisis develops, at first slowly, then at a quickened pace. Their well-being and even their lives are at stake. The tragic hero may try as he will to avert disaster. King Oedipus, whose country has been stricken, strives to free his subjects from the curse upon them. But the chain of events which has been forged cannot be broken. His actions lead relentlessly to his doom. The climax is brought about with "tragic inevitability." It brings to a head the emotions and fortunes of all concerned, and decides their destinies.

When we watch or read such a play, the temporal character of our experience is most pronounced. During the "middle" of the play, we are keenly aware of the events which have led up to this point, and we look ahead to climactic events. We feel the tension of "suspense." The issue is still in doubt, and yet it points toward the decisive moment. Our concern and anticipation are finally caught up in the dénouement. The "end" unifies the play by enabling us to understand the significance of all that has preceded it. Also, our emotional tension is resolved. For both these reasons, there is a sense of the integration and fulfillment of the total experience.

We can use less exalted art than Greek tragedy to illustrate this. Almost any "whodunit" mystery story will serve the purpose. Here too we must keep in mind, as the story unfolds, all the relevant clues — Lady Pemberton's jewels were last seen on Tuesday, and so on. And as the pace quickens, we look forward to the climactic solution. In a good story, all of the previous episodes then fall into place, the loose strings are tied up, and the mystery is dispelled. Here again we feel that our experience has "[run]

---

[2] From Aristotle: *On the Art of Poetry*, translated by S. H. Butcher and edited by Milton H. Nahm (The Library of Liberal Arts Series No. 6, New York, 1956), VII, p. 11. Reprinted by permission of the publishers, The Liberal Arts Press, Inc.

its course to fulfillment,"[3] and that it is now unified and "rounded out." It is not, as in much of ordinary life, a random succession of unrelated happenings. It is, as Dewey says, "*an* experience,"[4] set apart by its unity and vividness.

I SAID, in Chapter 2, that the aesthetic attitude, unlike the practical, does not anticipate the future realization of a purpose. Is this in contradiction with what has just been said? We can see that it is not. In the course of aesthetic experience, the percipient *does* anticipate what is to come next, e.g., the climax of a drama. Indeed, as we have seen, his expectation is more urgent and vivid than in most nonaesthetic experience. However — this is the crucial point — the "future" which he anticipates is part of the experience which is had just for the sake of having the experience. It is not something which is to be achieved as a consequence of the experience. He is looking ahead to that moment *within* aesthetic experience which will consummate and fulfill the experience. His concern with the object is disinterested throughout. The object's "beginning and end" set limits to the aesthetic experience. Within these limits there is recollection and expectation. Anticipation of the future is antiaesthetic only when it goes beyond the limits in time set up by the work of art, as when, while the music is playing, we think ahead to the work we have to do tomorrow, or what good conversation it will make to say that we have been to the concert and have heard this famous soloist.

Our awareness of "before" and "after" is integral to our appreciation of the work of art, as it unfolds in time. Without such awareness, our experience would be chaotic and disjointed. We would never see how the various parts of the art-object are related to each other. By virtue of memory and imagination, the work is unified in our experience. It "makes sense" and thereby holds our interest. Since memory and forward-looking expectation are aroused while the aesthetic attitude is being prolonged, and are, indeed, essential to maintaining this attitude, they are wholly aesthetic.

We can now understand aesthetic experience more fully. It includes both delight in what is currently apprehended and anticipation of a further part of the object still to be enjoyed. So a "moment" in aesthetic appreciation is, in Professor Morris' excellent phrase, "an elegant present having a future."[5]

BUT THE EXAMPLES THUS FAR have all been taken from literature. Can we say that painting, sculpture, and architecture are also "temporal"? That

---

[3] John Dewey, *Art as Experience* (New York: Minton, Balch, 1934), p. 35. Reprinted by permission of G. P. Putnam's Sons and George Allen & Unwin Ltd.
[4] *Ibid.*, p. 35. Italics in original.
[5] Morris, *op. cit.*, p. 28.

they are not is a recurrent doctrine in aesthetic thought, as I have pointed out. Further, this belief has entered into popular thought, and it has therefore affected the way in which people actually look at paintings and sculpture. The director of a leading American art gallery made a study of the amount of time spent by visitors in looking at paintings. It came to an average of *three seconds* per painting. Yet the same people will doubtless spend hours on a single work of music or literature.

If we do not take up the aesthetic attitude toward a painting or sculpture, we find nothing about it which indicates its temporal character. It is simply a collection of colors or a three-dimensional figure which occupies an area in space. This might lead us to think that it can be apprehended "instantaneously." By contrast, the externals of a piece of music or literature indicate duration through time, e.g., the successive numbering of movements or chapters, the sequence of notes or words. But what happens when we view painting or sculpture *aesthetically?*

Then we find that these works can only be apprehended in and through time. We must take time in moving our eyes over the painting and in walking round the sculpture, so that we can see it from many different positions. One of the most vital properties in the work is the "rhythm" which animates it. This is a pattern, which recurs in a number of places in the work, in which an element is stressed and is then followed by a pause or relative lack of emphasis. As we see the recurring "accents" of lines or shapes or colors in the painting, the work becomes dynamic. The same is true of the repetition of curves and arches in a cathedral. The eye is moved along [6] in anticipation of the future occurrence of the rhythmic pattern. However, the elements making up this pattern need not be precisely the same at each repetition. They can be altered somewhat, just as the "beat" in music can be syncopated or as subtle modifications can be made in the meter of a poem. Such slight variation adds variety and zest. Otherwise the pattern of repetition would be mechanical and dull.

Awareness of rhythm also helps to unify and "hold together" our experience. Remembering what has gone before, we can recognize recurrence in various areas of the work. If we did not, everything would seem radically novel and unrelated. Our attention would then be overwhelmed and distracted.

In music, a "rest" is not merely a dead silence. It is vital and pregnant, because the listener waits in suspense for resumption of the rhythm which was heard previously. Analogously, the "pauses" in works of painting, sculpture, and architecture — the "visual arts" — generate heightened interest in the future unfolding of the rhythmic pattern. "Not only the

---

[6] "Eye movement" is used elliptically to refer to the total process of perception. It has now been conclusively established that movement of the eyes bears little relation to the formal structuring of the work in the spectator's experience.

shape of objects is dynamic, but also that of the intervals between them.
. . . In baroque architecture, says Wölfflin, 'the quickening of the pulse
is clearly indicated in the changed proportions of the arches and the intervals between pilasters. The intervals keep getting narrower, the arches
slimmer, the speed of succession increases.' " [7]

But rhythm is by no means the only feature of the visual arts which is
temporal. Indeed, rhythmically ordered succession of like elements probably occurs less frequently in these arts than in music and poetry. It is
unfortunate that writers on painting and sculpture frequently use the
term "rhythm" loosely and vaguely. Their writing is salutary because
it shows that these arts are temporal. But the meaning of "rhythm" must
not be made so broad that the term loses its significance. When they use
it in a broader sense, they generally mean that there is *movement* within
the work. This aspect of painting and sculpture is enormously important.
It would seem best, however, to speak of "rhythm" only when a pattern of stress and hiatus, comprising identical or closely similar elements,
recurs in most or all of the work.

Consider this analysis of Correggio's "Jupiter and Antiope" (see Plate 6),
by the late Roger Fry, one of the greatest art critics of this century:

> . . . the figure is lying on the ground turned diagonally to the picture plane,
> so that the eye in following the sequence of its planes is carried forcibly back
> into the depths of the wood behind, whilst a counterbalancing diagonal move-
> ment of the figure of Jupiter brings us back again with a kind of spiral move-
> ment, thus closing and completing an asymmetrical but perfectly self-con-
> tained rhythmic phrase.[8]

Although "rhythmic" is used somewhat loosely, this passage is illuminating: it shows that, for aesthetic experience, it makes good sense to
speak of "movement within the picture." Those who object to this manner of speaking confuse the painting as a physical object with the painting
when it comes alive in aesthetic perception. It is with the latter that
we are, of course, concerned. Fry shows us too how movement contributes to the felt unity of the spectator's experience: the diagonal movement on the left "brings us back again," it "closes and completes" the
process of perception. The "Jupiter and Antiope" is also interesting because
it demonstrates that movement in painting is achieved by many different
means, e.g., the position of Antiope relative to the picture plane, the lighting
on her body in contrast to that of the forest, the gesture and facial expression of the god Jupiter, which express desire and suggest movement

[7] Rudolf Arnheim, *Art and Visual Perception* (University of California Press, 1954),
p. 347.
[8] Roger Fry, *Transformations* (New York: Brentano's, n.d.), p. 109. Reprinted by
permission of Chatto and Windus Ltd.

toward Antiope. The energy and direction of line is one of the most common instances of movement. Berenson defines a "contour" as "a line or curve with movement" [9] and then reports of his own experience 'that it is "as if there were nothing in me that was not living the life of the contour as it glides, turns, is swept on, smooth or rough, always animate and sentient, eager and zestful." [10] In sculpture, the interplay of thrust and recession, light and shadow, heaviness and buoyancy, can create a little drama in its own right.

We cannot and need not spell out the infinitely various instances of movement in the visual arts. That can be done only by empirical analysis of many specific works in these media. For our purposes, it is enough to emphasize that aesthetic experience of painting, sculpture, and architecture is significantly temporal. If this is, as I believe, true, it can be taken as a guiding principle for critical analysis and aesthetic perception. Neither can be fruitful if we conceive of the visual arts as "nontemporal."

It is important to emphasize that there are innumerably many kinds of rhythm and movement in the visual arts. Otherwise there is the danger that we may think that the sort of rhythm or movement which we find in the works of one artist or style, or in a single medium such as painting, is to be found in all works of the visual arts. Let us not ignore the salient differences between various artists and historical periods, and also the differences implicit in the use of such dissimilar media as oils, wood, and concrete. Furthermore, our discussion should not lead the student to infer that art is good only when it embodies vigorous, hurried movement. The paintings of Chaim Soutine are alive with writhing, contorted lines and vibrant, explosive colors. But paintings can also be of great value when our gaze moves over the surface and into the depths at a slow measured pace and when the experience is one of stability and composure. In Seurat's very great painting "Sunday Afternoon on the Island of La Grande Jatte" (see Plate 7), there is a good deal "going on" within the painting, but the relations between the stable, massed figures, and between the foreground and background are unhurried and majestic. This subtle fusion of movement and repose is perhaps best exemplified in the masterworks of Cézanne.

2. THE IMPORTANCE OF ARTISTIC FAMILIARITY

Because all art is temporal when viewed aesthetically, it makes great demands upon the spectator. Enjoyment of an isolated color or an ephem-

[9] Bernard Berenson, *Aesthetics and History* (Garden City: Doubleday, 1954), p. 78.
[10] *Op. cit.*, p. 79.

eral odor requires relatively little of the percipient. Momentary aware-ness, sympathetic and alert, will suffice. The "unity" of the experience is very rudimentary. The aesthetic object is extremely simple and our ex-perience is undifferentiated throughout its brief life. But works of art are not like this. They have a complex structure because, as aesthetic objects, they comprise a "beginning, middle, and end." Because they run through time, serious demands are made upon the percipient. He must be able to see how the "beginning, middle, and end" are interrelated in the work. At any given moment in the course of the work, he must see how it fol-lows from what has gone before and sense its push toward what is to come. Recollection of the past and imaginative anticipation of the future are therefore imperative. Otherwise, the work would simply be a kalei-doscopic succession of unrelated elements. We would never grasp its unity nor would we savor such values as the "suspense" of a drama or novel, or the "tension" in a sculpture.

In other words, we must "hold together" or synthesize the work in our experience, if we are to enjoy its value. But this is far easier said than done. When the work of art is complicated, we may not be able to see how all of its component parts are interrelated. When the work is very long, it may exceed our capacities of attention and memory. A person with little experience in music, listening to a large-scale symphony, frequently is unable to distinguish the chief themes. Or, if he can dis-tinguish them, he may be unable to "keep them in mind" after they have been set forth. This impairs his experience in a number of ways. He does not hear the recurrence of melody which helps to unify the work. Hence the music appears to be radically novel throughout. For this rea-son it seems "drawn out" and diffuse. Its impact and power are les-sened. For the more discriminating listener, whose experience takes exactly as much time by the clock, the music seems tightly knit and com-pressed. Isn't it true that music which we do not know well appears to us to "ramble" as though it does not "know where it is going"? More-over, inability to keep the theme in mind prevents the listener from en-joying the ways in which it is "developed." It can be altered harmonically or rhythmically, or the orchestration can be changed, or it can be brought into relation with new and different themes, and thereby take on an al-tered character. What a composer "does" with his themes is often the most exciting thing in music. But we cannot enjoy variation, unless we are able to remember what was heard originally, and is now being varied.

THIS POINTS UP the enormous significance of *familiarity* with the work of art. We are most likely to suffer from the difficulties just described when we are hearing the composition for the first time. This is partic-ularly true when the composition is by an artist or in a style which is radically unlike what we have heard before. It may even be music of a different culture, such as Balinese or Chinese music. When, however, a piece of music heard for the first time is very much like what we have encountered before — e.g., the latest juke-box favorite — we have little trouble listening to it. This shows that repeated exposure to music develops habits of attention and a sympathetic attitude which enable us to grasp and appreciate it. But when we are confronted with strikingly novel music, we cannot do this. And we are frequently so bored or disgusted by such music that we never venture to return to it. This is a mistake. It robs us of new delights and fresh enjoyments. With greater familiarity, we may very well come to "see" what the music is "saying" and find satisfaction in listening to it. If we do not reject it peremptorily and if we are patient and tolerant, we may, after repeated hearings, begin to feel at home with the music, and we may even come to think of it as an old and valued friend.

Now what, specifically, is gained by greater familiarity with a work of art?

Primarily, we become familiar with the work's formal organization or structure. This means that we come to see how the component parts of the work are interrelated with each other. We see how an element which occurs early in the work prepares the way for and leads into what comes later. We appreciate how the various parts or sections of the work illuminate each other. With familiarity, memory and anticipation are called into play.

One of the chief functions of form is that it emphasizes certain elements of the work and relegates others to a secondary status. In growing acquainted with form, we therefore come to see what is most important, what should be stressed in our reading or viewing. When, however, we view a strange work for the first time, *everything* seems equally important. Hence we have no sense of the dramatic interplay of stress and pause within the work. With familiarity, we can appreciate how the work "builds" to a climax, and thereby enjoy both the anticipation and the climax itself. When the work is unfamiliar, however, it seems to be throughout flat and unrelieved.

Consider our reading of Sophocles' tragedy of King Oedipus, once we have learned of the legend of Oedipus. We read of the king's attempts to discover the murderer who has brought a plague upon Thebes. But we know, as Oedipus does not, that he is himself that tragic evildoer. Hence the "end" of the play has great significance while we are reading the earlier sections. It invests all of the play preceding the point at which Oedipus finds out about himself, with heightened and poignant meaning. We are aware of the cruel paradox of his self-defeating efforts. For example, we feel the bitter irony of the scene in which Oedipus summons the blind prophet, Tiresias, and then grows angry when Tiresias' "dark words" suggest that Oedipus himself may be tainted with vileness and sin. We are painfully aware of Oedipus' profound ignorance when — blinder himself than Tiresias — he says to the prophet, "You being gone, our trouble goes with you." Moreover, we can feel how such episodes as the encounter with Tiresias and Oedipus' interrogation of Jocasta lead slowly and yet with ever heightening suspense to the fearful climax. Our experience is now animated by vivid and urgent expectation.

Familiarity with formal organization is also indispensable to one of the chief values of aesthetic experience — its unity. An important respect in which unity is achieved has just been referred to — when the suspense engendered in the course of a play is resolved, when its tensions work themselves out and are succeeded by repose. "Unity" then is not an abstract word of critical analysis. The percipient's experience *feels* unified — expectation has been intensified and then satisfied, there is a sense of "rounding out" and completeness. One also has this feeling at the close of a musical composition, when one has become sufficiently familiar with the theme to remember it throughout the course of the work, and then hears it return with a grand flourish at the end. In a jazz composition, such as a recording by the pianist George Shearing, improvisation can be so fanciful that it seems to take us thousands of light-years away from the original melody. But then the music simply turns a corner, and we are back at the melody. The experience has been rich and diverse, but it is tied together by this return. We can apprehend this unity more readily in jazz than in symphonic music, because the melody is generally a "popular" tune and therefore familiar to us at the very outset.

Discrimination of formal relationships is not the only benefit which accrues from familiarity. When we first encounter a radically new work, we are confused by its complexity and apparent formlessness. But there is another reason why we fail to respond to it and enjoy it: we don't "see the point" of it, we don't understand what the artist is "trying to say." In other words, we have no conception of the kind of effect that the work is supposed to have on us. Or, if we do try to conjecture what the intended effect is, we can be egregiously wrong. The history of so-called "modern art" is replete with examples of this. Works of the utmost seriousness were taken by those unfamiliar with them to be jokes or artistic exercises, and conversely, witty and rollicking works were apprehended humorlessly. You have probably read some of the hilarious poems of the comic poet Ogden Nash. Having this familiarity with his work, you will be surprised to learn that when his first book of verse was published, it was taken by the reviewer for the London *Times* to be in dead earnest, and Nash was criticized accordingly: his poetry was said to have "neat ideas marred by careless rhyming." But this is not any more surprising than the way in which all of us have probably mis-construed other works of art upon first acquaintance with them.

Here, then, is where familiarity is required. It is common experience that after the second or third or tenth encounter with a work, we "begin to see" what it is "saying." This enables us to become more sympathetic and discriminating in our approach to the work. We realize now what mental "set" is required for appreciation of the work, how we should prepare ourselves to respond to it. By the same token, we inhibit those responses which are alien to the "tone" and significance of the work. Moreover, we now know what to "look for" in the work. We can now see how the various elements of the work contribute to the total effect.

Our sense of the total import of the work and our awareness of its form are closely related to each other. Indeed, the latter depends upon the former. A musician or conductor, in trying to determine where the emphases should be placed in his performance of the work, how the tempos of different sections should be contrasted, and so on, cannot de-cide these questions until he decides what the total significance of the work is. What effect does he wish to achieve? Does he "read" the work as profound and sombre, or does he consider it essentially a charming and elegant pattern of sounds? We must all make comparable decisions in viewing painting and sculpture. What will we look at first on the can-vas, and what path will the eye traverse? This too can be decided only when we have some sense of the intended effect of the total work. There is somewhat less leeway for interpretation in music, literature, and the dance than in the visual arts, for works in the former media have a definite beginning point, e.g., Act I, and follow a fixed sequence. But this difference should not be exaggerated. As I pointed out in the pre-vious chapter, there can be many different interpretations of a piece of music or literature, and in each case the percipient will structure the work differently.

In coming to know a work of art, familiarity with its formal organ-ization and with its total effect develop hand in hand. Our interpretation or "reading" of the work as a whole guides our discrimination of its de-tails, what we "look for," where we place the emphases. On the other hand, awareness of the details influences our interpretation. As we re-turn to a work, we see new things in it. So Professor Pepper says of our experience of El Greco's famous "Toledo": "The first time we look at [it] we may notice principally the threatening clouds and the hills; the next time the dynamic movement of the forms; the next time details here and there that we had not noticed like the little figures down in the stream; the next time subtle repetitions of shapes; and so on." [11] Increas-ing knowledge makes our sense of the total effect of the work more con-

[11] Stephen C. Pepper, *The Basis of Criticism in the Arts* (Harvard University Press, 1946), p. 148.

crete and precise. There is always the possibility, of course, that grow-ing discrimination may lead us to abandon our original "reading" of the work. We may then interpret the work differently, in a way which does greater justice to it.

To REPEAT, it is because works of art, unlike isolated colors, are in-ternally complex and extend through time as aesthetic objects, that these problems of interpretation and discrimination are created. It is up to us whether these difficulties will discourage us, so that we abandon the work altogether, or stimulate us to gain greater familiarity with it. Very few works can be grasped and appreciated effortlessly at the first encounter. And it is questionable whether the value of these works is very great. Most works of any merit present a challenge to us. They make de-mands on our powers of attention, memory, imagination, and understand-ing. We must grow if we are to measure up to them. And we must be persistent in returning to them again and again. At first, our awareness of the work may be only fragmentary. But upon each return to the work, we sum up or "fund" [12] all that we have found in previous experiences of it, until its richness and coherence are progressively disclosed to us.

Thus the aesthetic enjoyment of a work of art is not something which is over and done with, once and for all. It is a growing, progressive, creative process. If we meet the challenge of the work, our reward is the felt value of our experience when we are capable of appreciating it. In the case of some works, notably those we call "great," the process of familiarization never ends. In these works we are always "seeing some-thing new," finding new formal relationships, discerning new significance. We can, of course, if we want to, remain comfortably at ease with works which lack complexity and subtlety. But there is something deadening and stagnant about this. If we shut ourselves up in this way, if we never venture out to encounter new and unfamiliar works, we impoverish our experience and rob ourselves of satisfaction and delight.

3. THE "TYPES" OF AESTHETIC PERCIPIENTS

We have spoken of the semicreative activity which the percipient must contribute to the aesthetic experience. He cannot be wholly passive and expect to enjoy the value of the art-object. He must interpret the work in one way or another, he must be alert to details and overtones which are not wholly obvious, he must structure the work in his awareness, so that it can be grasped as a unity. It is clear that different people find different values in art, or enjoy it for different reasons. This is largely because they approach art with greater or less familiarity with the work,

12 *Ibid.*, pp. 148 ff.

greater or less capacities for attention and emotional sensitivity, and so on.

The British psychologist Bullough, from whom I have already quoted, early in this century set up a classification of "perceptive types." Each of these types represents a different way of perceiving and responding to aesthetic objects. The classification is interesting because it shows how great the differences among aesthetic percipients can be. It will also probably be of interest to the student because he will almost certainly recognize himself in one or another of the types.

Bullough did not restrict himself to cataloguing the results of his experiments. He also "ranked" the types, according to whether they are more or less truly aesthetic, i.e., the extent to which the experience of each is "disinterested and sympathetic." He shows, as we shall see, that some people who are commonly thought to have intense aesthetic experience hardly have aesthetic experience at all.

It is worth noting that Bullough's types were also found among the "subjects" used in other experiments. Bullough himself arrived at his classification in experimenting with isolated colors [13] and color combinations.[14] His classification was taken over, with some slight modifications, in Myers' experiments with simple musical compositions,[15] in Feasey's experiments with rectangular forms,[16] and Valentine's experiments with pictures and musical compositions.[17]

BULLOUGH'S NAMES for the four types are "associative," "physiological," "objective," and "character." The "associative" type, with its subdivision into "fused" and "non-fused" has already been explained.[18]

The "physiological" type is aptly named. Persons of this class judge the object in terms of the personal effects which it arouses in them, notably bodily and organic reactions. A color makes one such subject feel "cold" (p. 453); another, listening to music, says "I had a lazy feeling";[19] another reports that a musical chord "gives a creepy feeling." [20] In all instances, the "physiological" spectator emphasizes the "feelings" which go on inside of him during the experience, and he then judges the object according to the nature and quality of the feeling.

The "objective" type offers just the opposite sort of judgment. These percipients make no reference to their personal reactions, but speak solely

13 *Op. cit.* (1908). All page references within the text are to this paper.
14 Edward Bullough, "The 'Perceptive Problem' in the Aesthetic Appreciation of Simple Colour-Combinations," *British Journal of Psychology,* III (1910), 406–447.
15 Charles S. Myers, "Individual Differences in Listening to Music," *British Journal of Psychology,* XIII (1922), 52–71.
16 L. Feasey, "Some Experiments on Aesthetics," *British Journal of Psychology,* XII (1921), 253–272.
17 Valentine, *op. cit.,* p. 34.
18 Cf. above, p. 54.
19 Myers, *op. cit.,* p. 55.
20 Valentine, *op. cit.,* p. 99.

of the nature of the object. They analyze its properties, e.g., the "purity" or brightness of colors, and then evaluate it in terms of some standard or criterion which they have set up for colors of this kind (pp. 450–451). Thus a color is condemned for being "washy" or "impure."

The last of the four classes, the "character" type, has a highly vivid and intense appreciation of the object. It is marked by strong emotional tone and also comprises the organic responses found in the "physiological" type. However, by contrast to the latter, the judgments of the "character" type do not call attention to the subject's personal feelings. His responses are "exteriorised," i.e., they are considered as qualities of the object. The object is then thought to possess a "life" and "character" of its own. The color red is found to be "frank" and "active"; blue, "reserved" and "contemplative" (p. 436). Or a piece of music is said to be "happy" or "bold." [21]

There are those who are skeptical of the responses of the "character" type. They consider such judgments to be mere romanticizing, indicating the failure of the percipient to view the object with discrimination and insight. Doubtless, those who make "character" judgments sometimes are merely speaking loosely. In some cases, further analysis of their experience will show that it has been one of "non-fused" association and therefore only slightly aesthetic. In general, however, Bullough found that percipients of the "character" type maintained a genuinely aesthetic attitude throughout their experience. He speaks of their "peculiarly sympathetic openness. There is much affective participation on the part of the subject in the special qualities of the individual colour, a readiness to sympathise with it, and the result is a strikingly vivid . . . appreciation" (p. 434). With this attitude of "sympathetic openness," the percipient accepts the object on its own terms, and makes himself receptive to experiencing its distinctive nature and value. This, as we have seen, is indispensable to aesthetic experience. Furthermore, the percipient's attention is so thoroughly "object-centered" that the responses aroused by the object do not call attention to his own body and mind. This distinguishes the "character" type from the "physiological" type. The object remains central in awareness; attention is not diverted to the spectator's organic and emotional processes. The "character" type therefore unites "impersonal objectivity and intense personal participation" (p. 458). In experience of this kind, aesthetic attention is most thoroughgoing, the object is most "absorbing." For now the percipient has lost all "sense of self." Just as we speak of "losing ourselves" in some engrossing task, so here the percipient "loses himself" in the aesthetic object, and "lives the life" of the object. This is, of course, a metaphoric way of speaking. And yet, I believe, it hits off the felt quality of our experience when it is most wholly aesthetic. Think of some time when you were absorbed in a story or a piece of music, and see whether you agree.

[21] *Ibid.*, p. 99.

The "objective" type is quite another matter. Their judgments *seem* to arise from a veritably aesthetic experience. They speak of the object rather than the spectator. And in referring to such properties of color as its brightness or hue, their judgments appear to be more concrete and reliable then such fanciful "character" type descriptions of color as "frank" or "contemplative." Bullough does not, however, rank the "objective" type highly. His conclusions concerning this type are among the most interesting results of his experiments.

He finds that these judgments, which analyze the object in a detached way, indicate a failure to achieve aesthetic sympathy with the object. "Members of this type give, in fact, generally the impression that they cannot get into any kind of intimate relation to colour, and that, in the absence of a more personal sympathy, they take refuge in a distant, almost hostile position" (p. 450). It is noteworthy that these percipients, who are more interested in analyzing and criticizing the object than they are in enjoying it, always bring with them to the experience some "type or standard" (p. 451) in the light of which they evaluate the object. If it conforms to this standard, it is praised; if it deviates from it, it is condemned. Thus one subject of this type says that the object is "unusual," [22] thereby revealing the importance in his mind of the standard from which the object deviates. But isn't "unusual" a lame thing to say about an aesthetic object? It simply means that the object is unlike what the spectator has seen before. One could say this without having taken aesthetic interest in the object. Unlike the "character" type, the "objective" type does not give itself over to enjoyment of the object in its own right. Instead these people merely calculate, rather mechanically, the extent to which it lives up to previously formulated criteria. If it is "unusual," they tend to reject it. Thus they fail to see the value which it might have in itself. It is small wonder that Bullough concludes that the "objective" type judgments "represent . . . the crudest form of aesthetic appreciation" (p. 451).

This conclusion is supported by Valentine's later experiments using pictures. Valentine found that those who had little interest in pictures gave judgments which "were almost entirely objective or associative." [23] One who does not maintain aesthetic interest in an object and take delight in its being will either begin to think about other things, so that the object is shunted on to the fringe of attention or else he will, as Bullough says, "take refuge" in analyzing and criticizing it. If ever we find ourselves doing either of these things, we might stop to inquire whether our experience is genuinely aesthetic.

[22] Bullough, *op. cit.* (1910), 414.
[23] *Op. cit.*, p. 87.

Myers, who submitted musical compositions to his subjects, disclosed another interesting feature of the "objective" type. He found that this type "occurs most frequently among those technically trained in music." [24] This somewhat paradoxical finding is noteworthy. It shows that technical training frequently does not enhance aesthetic appreciation, but has just the opposite effect. One who is so trained becomes more concerned with the problems of his craft than with aesthetic enjoyment. Myers' subjects say: "I noticed the second horn was too loud"; "As usual, the violinist uses too much *vibrato*." [25] Such concern with problems of technique and skill *can* coexist with aesthetic interest, but there is always the danger that the latter will be overwhelmed and lost sight of.

To conclude, here is Bullough's ranking of the perceptive types (pp. 461–463), proceeding from those that are least to those that are most aesthetic: "physiological" — lowest because attention is diverted to the percipient's bodily "feelings"; "non-fused associative" — here too the object is not central in awareness; "objective" — a failure to achieve sympathetic rapport with the object (in some cases, it might be added, members of this class can hardly be said to have aesthetic experience at all); "fused associative"; "character" — the most wholly aesthetic, for the reasons given earlier.

The student may disagree with Bullough's evaluation of these types. If so, on what grounds would you do so? The student might also wish to decide in which of these classes he himself is included. It should be remembered that the same person may, at different times, exemplify different types of perception. This will depend upon such variables as the particular art-form which he is apprehending, his familiarity with the work of art, whether the work of art is clear and straightforward, or vaguely suggestive like "impressionist" music, and so on.

4. AESTHETIC EXPERIENCE AND THE THEORY OF ART

Thus far, we have learned about the aesthetic attitude, the great range of aesthetic experience, which can include any object whatever, the temporal nature of aesthetic experience, and the importance of familiarity with the art-object. But what happens concretely during the aesthetic experience? What does the percipient feel in the face of the art-object? Is aesthetic experience always emotional? Questions of this kind remain to be answered.

[24] *Op. cit.*, p. 58.
[25] *Ibid.*, p. 58.

They will be taken up in Part Two of this book. There we will consider in detail some of the leading theories of the nature and value of aesthetic experience.

These theories are not, however, theories of aesthetic experience solely. They are also theories of fine art. They describe the process of artistic creation and its product, the "work of art." Thus they undertake to tell us how "fine" art is distinguished from the "useful" arts, and also from natural objects, i.e., objects which are not man-made.

The theory of art is closely related to the theory of aesthetic experience, in many of the thinkers we are going to study. The relation is this: what they believe about aesthetic experience is based upon their conception of fine art. Their reasoning generally proceeds in this way: a certain property (or number of properties) is taken to be crucial to fine art, i.e., it distinguishes works of fine art from all other objects. Let us say, for example, that this property is the "expression of emotion." It is then inferred that this property is also crucial to aesthetic experience. That is, it is inferred that all aesthetic experience must be emotional, since the percipient shares the emotion expressed by the artist.

Let us be on our guard when we find such reasoning. For even if the philosopher's conception of fine art is sound, his description of aesthetic appreciation may be inadequate or incomplete. Art is one thing, and the aesthetic experience is another thing, which must be studied in its own right. This can be shown quite readily. Aesthetic perception is not confined to works of art alone. As we have noted, objects and events in nature, like cloud formations, can also be apprehended aesthetically. Now, what is true of the appreciation of art need not be true of the enjoyment of nature. In our example, it may be that works of art "express emotion," but natural objects do not. Art-objects make up only part of the class of aesthetic objects. Hence, we must make sure that any theory of aesthetic experience is true of *all* cases of aesthetic perception, and not merely of some.

These are the two chief questions that we shall be talking about in the next section: (1) What is fine art? (2) What do we experience during aesthetic perception? Let us now see how these questions can be answered.

BIBLIOGRAPHY

* Vivas and Krieger, *The Problems of Aesthetics*. Pp. 277–304.
* Weitz, *Problems in Aesthetics*. Pp. 247–253.
  Chandler, *Beauty and Human Nature*. Pp. 97–103, 230–236.
  Dewey, *Art as Experience*. Chaps. II–III, VIII.
  Forster, E. M., "The *Raison d'Etre* of Criticism in the Arts," in *Music and Criticism*, ed. French. Harvard University Press, 1948.

Lessing, Gotthold. *Laocoön* (1766).

Morris, Bertram. *The Aesthetic Process.* Northwestern University Press, 1943. Chaps. I–IV.

Pepper, Stephen C. *Aesthetic Quality.* New York: Scribners, 1937. Chap. I.

————. *The Basis of Criticism in the Arts.* Harvard University Press, 1946. Supplementary Essay.

Souriau, Etienne, "Time in the Plastic Arts," *Journal of Aesthetics and Art Criticism*, Vol. VII (June, 1949), 294–307.

Stolnitz, Jerome, "On Artistic Familiarity and Aesthetic Value," *Journal of Philosophy*, Vol. LIII (April 12, 1956), 261–276.

Valentine, C. W. *An Introduction to the Experimental Psychology of Beauty*, rev. ed. London: Jack, 1919. Chaps. III, VII, VIII.

QUESTIONS

1. Read the chapters in Dewey, *Art as Experience*, cited in the Bibliography. What is the relation between aesthetic experience and "having *an* experience," according to Dewey? Are they identical? Is Dewey's conception of aesthetic experience the same as that presented in the previous chapter?
2. What do you take to be the salient differences, if any, between appreciating the "temporal" arts and the "spatial" arts? To help answer this question, read the article by Souriau, cited in the Bibliography.
3. Critics often speak of "rhythm" in painting, "drama" in architecture, "balance" in the novel. Do you think that such terms have the same meaning when applied to both the "spatial" and "temporal" arts? If not, why not? Are these terms being used metaphorically?
4. It is argued in this chapter that familiarity with the work is indispensable to aesthetic appreciation. But familiarity often deadens our interest in the work. Under which circumstances do you think this occurs?
5. Do you agree with Bullough's ranking of the aesthetic "types"? If not, what changes would you suggest?

PART II

The Nature of Art

4

The Creation of Art

1. THE WORK OF ART AND ITS ORIGINS

In the following chapters we shall be considering some of the most influential theories of the "nature of art." These theories single out certain properties which, they hold, distinguish "fine art." In doing this, they attempt to answer the question which is most commonly and simply stated as "What is art?" In this chapter we shall consider the way in which the work of art is created. This is the question, "How does art come into being?"

Now here, at the very outset, it is important to see how these questions are related to each other.

Primarily, it is important to see that these two questions are quite different from each other. Therefore they are to be answered in very different ways. This must be underscored because it is often thought that if you describe the origins of art then you are at the same time answering the question, "What is art?" Thus a common answer to the latter question is that the artist experiences intense emotions, and his desire to "express" them leads to the production of art-objects. Similarly, when people try to explain some specific work of art, they will describe what went on "in the mind of" the artist while he was creating the work. Or they will refer to the historical or social setting in which the work came to birth.

Historical accounts of this kind are often very informative. But I want to show that they are not identical with an explanation of the nature of the work of art. If we confuse the two, we are guilty of what is called "the genetic fallacy" or "the fallacy of origins."

It is easy to fall prey to this fallacy, not only in aesthetics but in other fields of study as well. For example, suppose that we are studying the nature of the state, in political theory. We might decide, like the philosopher Hobbes, that the origins of the state are in the incessant enmity and conflict of avaricious men, living outside of a social order, and that the state came into being in an effort to curb this hostility. But even if this is true, it does not necessarily explain the nature of the state at the present time. The state may outgrow its original function, and develop wholly different purposes and another sort of structure. We cannot then say that it is the very nature of the state to be regulatory and repressive. The justification for its authority may be completely different from what Hobbes, arguing from his genetic account, took it to be. Likewise, one might explain the psychological forces and social influences which led to the formulation of some theory, in economics, say, or in religion. But this by itself would not tell us about the truth and logical consistency of the theory.[1]

In short, the genesis of x is one thing, x itself is something else. Once x has been brought into being, it has, so to speak, a life of its own. Like a theory or like a human being, it will have a structure and value, and it will enter into relationships with other things, which cannot be understood wholly in terms of its origin. We must examine these characteristics in order to learn what it "is."

We can now begin to see that the simple-sounding question, "What is art?" is anything but simple. For once the art-object has been produced, it can be approached and understood from many different viewpoints. And these may have nothing to do with its origins. We can be interested in it morally, or financially, or practically, as well as aesthetically. Moreover, the ways in which we are concerned with it aesthetically can be highly varied. As the history of art makes clear, the significance and value of a work of art will be interpreted in diverse ways by different people at different times. The plays of Shakespeare have been chiefly valued by some for their poetic quality, by others for their melodramatic excitement, and by still others for their acute psychological treatment of human character. This is not to be regretted, for it testifies to the inexhaustible richness of these works. But we can see that, in some respect, each of these interpretations tells us what Shakespeare "is." And just as the works of this one artist wear many faces, so, of course, does fine art in general. We must therefore be on our guard against those who claim that only their theory tells us what art "*really*" is. It is always

[1] Cf. above, pp. 4–5.

possible that the nature of art can be construed in other ways which are sound and illuminating.

The danger of committing the "genetic fallacy" in aesthetics has been increased by certain trends in recent thought. For in modern times we have been far more preoccupied with the biography and personality of the individual artist than earlier periods have been. Thus nineteenth-century Romanticism places a premium on the uniqueness — often the eccentricity — of the artist. Such ideas, like all influential ideas in a period of thought, after a time filtered down from the high levels of artistic theory and literary criticism into popular thought and speech. As was pointed out a moment ago, we now often identify the work of art with the artist. This preoccupation with the artist also manifests itself in biographies of the artist that are sometimes little more than gossip, and in the formation of little cults devoted to the idolatry of some artist. This can readily lead us into the genetic fallacy. For example, we may misinterpret a work of art by reading into it what we know about the life of the artist.[2]

It was only natural that this preoccupation should lead to widespread speculation concerning the psychological make-up of the artist. This has been carried on by a great many psychologists, including the foremost pioneer in psychology of our time, Sigmund Freud. What Freud has to say about the artist is interesting in its own right. But more important for our purposes, it points up the necessity of distinguishing clearly between the artist and what he has created.

Freud's analysis of the creative artist rests upon his general psychological theory. We cannot, of course, take time for a full-dress exposition of that theory. It should first be said, however, that for Freud human beings have certain inherent drives and desires which cannot be wholly satisfied within society. Hence they are compelled to renounce or modify these urges or, as Freud puts it, they must accept "the reality-principle." But these desires will not down. They demand some kind of gratification, even if only in "phantasy." "In phantasy, therefore, man can continue to enjoy a freedom from the grip of the external world."[3] Fantasy is exemplified both by day-dreams and night-dreams, in which desires which are otherwise thwarted can enjoy imaginative satisfaction.

The artist, too, is in this universal human predicament. He seeks "honour, power, riches, fame, and the love of women; but he lacks the means of achieving these gratifications."[4] Hence he too has recourse to fan-

---

[2] Cf. above, chap. 2, sec. 5.

[3] Sigmund Freud, *A General Introduction to Psycho-Analysis*, trans. Rivière (New York: Liveright, 1935), pp. 324–325.

[4] *Op. cit.*, p. 327.

tasy. However, the fantasy which he creates is of a significantly different kind. The nonartist's fantasy incorporates images and thoughts which are personal, and therefore understandable only to the individual himself. The artist transforms his dreams, so that they can be communicated to others and enjoyed by them. They can be accepted publicly, however, only if he disguises their socially unacceptable sources. He does this chiefly by symbolism — using images and ideas which stand for and suggest, but are different from, the original contents of the fantasy, and ambiguity — using images which can be interpreted in various ways, and thereby blurring their original significance. Then both the artist and his audience can enjoy, without inhibition, his delightful "dream."

Freud himself, showing great personal modesty as well as intellectual clarity, insisted that this theory was speculative and unproved. But even if the theory is sound, we should see that, as Freud also recognized, it does not explain wholly the "nature of art."

It is not the history of the work, but the work itself, standing on its own feet, which is important to us aesthetically. When we want to explain its value, we point to elements which are internal to the work. We say that the symphony is good because the themes have been developed imaginatively, or that the drama is absorbing because of the tight construction of the plot. We make no reference to the artist's "phantasy" and we need not do so necessarily. Now, a Freudian may be able to show how the fantasy enters into the work itself. Freud himself attempted to do this in his study of Leonardo da Vinci.[5] But by itself, this would not explain the value of the work. The work is not *just* a fantasy. It is a fantasy which is shaped and worked out in an artistic structure, and by employing artistic devices. It has become part of a pattern of colors, tones, or words. We must never forget those elements of the work which make it what it is intrinsically.

If this is not yet clear, look at it this way: Two different artists could, presumably, be stimulated by very much the same kind of frustration, and they might imagine very much the same kind of vicarious gratification. Yet the works which they create may well be of very different merit, one mediocre, the other great. This would be due to such factors as the sensory attractiveness of the work, its imaginative excitement, its emotional eloquence. Aesthetic value can only be found in the work of art, not in its genesis.[6]

There is still another reason why the distinction between the work of art and its origins must be kept in mind if we are not to be misled by

[5] Sigmund Freud, *Leonardo da Vinci* (New York: Random House, 1947).

[6] It should be noted that a mediocre work may be of great interest to the psychologist, indeed of even more interest than one which is aesthetically excellent, as a clue to the psychological make-up of the artist. But then the work is a psychological document rather than an aesthetic object.

the Freudian theory. Let us again grant, for the sake of the argument, that a fantasy is embodied in the work. This is not a wholly subjective fantasy for, as we have seen, Freud asserts that the artist makes it communicable and shareable. However, both the fantasy and the work of art will be what they are, in large measure, because of the time and culture in which the artist lives. They will reflect the repressions imposed by that particular society, the symbols used by that society to disguise culturally unacceptable thoughts, and other such psychosocial factors. But once the work achieves a life of its own, it will be perceived by people living in other societies, whose psychological structure may be very different from that in which the artist lived. Hence they will interpret and value the work quite differently. Indeed, as Freudian theory has emphasized — and this is one of its great contributions — there is generally enough ambiguity in the work so that it lends itself to a plurality of interpretations. Therefore we cannot tie down the work to its genesis. We cannot say that the work "*is*" the public vehicle of just this particular "dream" of the artist or of his society. Within the limits of aesthetic relevance, a variety of "dreams" may be located in the work. Just as the artist's fantasy does not guarantee the aesthetic value of the work, so it cannot guarantee what the significance of the work will be to its changing audiences.

Once we understand the genetic fallacy, it makes our speech and thinking more wary and precise. It puts us on our guard against easy, uncritical inferences from the life of the artist to the nature of his work. We cannot lightly assume that because the artist was in a certain "mood" at the time of creation, the work will necessarily reflect that mood. As I have been urging, the work has a character all its own. As a matter of fact, there is often a tremendous difference between the mood of the work, and the frame of mind that the artist was in at the time of creating it. Two of Beethoven's most charming symphonies — the delightful Second and the candid, unaffected, captivating Eighth — were written at times of great personal pain or tragedy or both. Listen to these works. If you had no prior knowledge of the artist's biography, would you ever suppose that his life was anything but tranquil and happy? The composer Tchaikovsky is, as you probably know, one of the most unabashedly emotional of artists. We might be led to think that his music must necessarily be an outpouring of the emotions he felt in his personal experience. Yet Tchaikovsky's own testimony keeps us from this mistake: "a work composed under the happiest surroundings may be touched with dark and gloomy colors." [7] A distinguished contemporary American writer, Katherine Anne Porter, also differentiates the creative "mood"

[7] Quoted in Rosamond E. M. Harding, *An Anatomy of Inspiration*, 2nd ed. (Cambridge: Heffer, 1942), p. 78.

from the work of art: "I can't tell you what gives true intensity. . . . It is not a matter of how you feel, at any one moment, certainly not at the moment of writing. A calculated coldness is the best mood for that, most often." [8]

The fallacy of origins must also be avoided when the genetic factor is social rather than personal. For example, many objects of primitive art which we place in museums were used originally for practical purposes. These vases, jugs, spoons were once prosaic, everyday objects. Yet we cannot say that it distorts their "real nature" to treat them aesthetically, rather than practically. To say this is to confuse the object, which can be viewed in many different ways, with its genesis.

2. THE PROCESS OF ARTISTIC CREATION

But though the questions "What is art?" and "How does art come into being"? are quite different, they are not unrelated to each other. For an answer to the first question must, in part, take account of the way in which the object was created. To see why this is so, we must understand the meaning of the term "art."

To begin with, we should recognize that this term is ambiguous, i.e., it has two different meanings. "Art" can refer to a certain kind of *activity* and also to a certain kind of *object*. When we say that someone is "studying art" we usually mean that he is learning how to carry on a skilled activity; when we speak of a "museum of art," we refer to the objects that are found there. The "work of art" or "art-object" is the product of artistic activity. Let us now ask what we mean by "art" in the sense of an activity.

Let us think first of those human activities to which we would deny the name "art." What about breathing or sneezing, or the knee jerk when the doctor strikes you with the little rubber hammer? There is nothing artistic about that. What about tying one's shoelace? And how about aimless doodling or an unthinking gesture such as rubbing one's nose? In none of these cases would we speak of "art." So we can close in on the meaning of "art" by excluding from it those activities which are instinctive or reflex, habitual, or random.

To speak positively now, we can say first that art is "conscious of its aim." [9] It is undertaken with the deliberate thought of achieving some future goal. This sets it off from sneezing and doodling and also, very probably, from tying one's shoelace. Moreover, it must find a way to the

---

[8] Quoted in Brewster Ghiselin, *The Creative Process* (University of California Press, 1952), p. 206.
[9] Santayana, *Reason in Art*, p. 4.

attainment of its goal. There is no fixed, predetermined method, as in tying shoelaces, or switching on the light. Art must improvise, and when it produces alternative blueprints, it must decide which to select and which to reject. Third, art operates upon some "raw material," which it shapes or transforms in order to fulfill its purpose. This may be words, or marble, or tones. Finally, the artist possesses skill in the use of this medium.

We may sum this up in a definition of the activity of "art": "the skilled, deliberate manipulation of a medium for the achievement of some purpose."

You will see that this does not restrict "art" to what we call the "fine arts." But this is as it should be. For art is a far more pervasive activity than that of the composer, painter, or author:

> The realm of art is identical with the realm of man's deliberate control of that world of materials and movements among which he must make his home, of that inner world of random impulses and automatic processes which constitute his inner being. The breaking of a stick, the building of a hut, a skyscraper, or a cathedral, the use of language for communication, the sowing or the harvesting of a crop, the nurture and education of children, the framing of a code of law or morals, the weaving of a garment, or the digging of a mine — all these are alike examples of art no less than the molding of a relief or the composition of a symphony.[10]

"Art," in this broad sense, includes the "industrial arts" or the "arts of utility," such as the "art of cooking." Almost any activity can be performed artfully, if it is performed deliberately, skillfully, and purposefully. Think of the phrases, "the artful dodger" or "an artful liar." But what is it that sets off what we call the "*fine* arts?" The following chapters are devoted to this question. At present, we should see that art-objects of any sort are set off from nonartistic objects such as rocks, trees, and yawns because of the way in which they are created. Hence any definition of "art" as an *object* must make reference to its origins. However, as was urged in the previous section, the nature of the art-object cannot be understood *entirely* in terms of its origins.

LET US, AT THIS TIME, defer the question of art as an object, and consider the activity of art as it occurs in the "fine arts." To do this, we will listen to what the artists themselves have to say about artistic creation. They are, presumably, the only ones who can speak with first-hand knowledge.

However, one who begins this study of the artist's testimony should not do so with his hopes too high. Certainly he should not expect it to solve

[10] Irwin Edman, *Arts and the Man* (New York: Mentor, 1949), pp. 11–12.

the age-old "mystery" of the way in which artistic creation goes on. The literature, including recorded conversations, memoirs, and so on, in which artists describe their working methods is vast indeed. But it is often disappointing and, on the whole, quite inconclusive. There are a number of reasons for this.

For one thing, the artist's account of his creative activity is often extremely unclear and vague. This may be so even when the work of art which he has produced is itself extraordinarily clear and disciplined. This seems paradoxical and it is discouraging to one who is trying to learn about creativity. But is this really so odd? Is it odd that a man should do a job well without being able to explain *how* he does it? Especially when for many artists the creation of poems and songs is as natural and effortless as breathing is for the rest of us. When creative inspiration "comes easily," it is difficult to tell how or whence it comes. Moreover, creation seems to draw upon psychological processes which are complex and, as we shall see, often subterranean. Systematic study of creation by psychologists, such as that inaugurated by Freud, has made relatively little headway thus far. So it is not to be wondered at that the artists themselves have been baffled in trying to explain their gifts and the way in which they employ them.

Apart from its unclarity, what the artists report about their work is also notable for its lack of uniformity. They differ widely among themselves as to the techniques they use, the environment they find most favorable for creative activity, the amount of time required, and so on. This in itself would be enough to discourage anyone who might be so naïve as to think that he could become capable of artistic creation by reading what artists say about it. Furthermore, we must keep it in mind as we read the artists that they are not always presenting straightforward descriptions of the creative process. This is not to say that they are deliberately lying, though doubtless even that has crept into some of their testimony. Rather, they have been influenced, quite unconsciously, by the theories of art and aesthetics which prevailed in their time. So their account, instead of being unvarnished and factual, has been distorted by theoretical preconceptions. They report what, according to contemporary theory, they think they *ought* to be doing rather than what they *are* doing. Finally, the artists' evidence may be distorted for a host of other reasons. They may wish, consciously or not, to increase the layman's awe of the "mystery" of creation or they may wish to justify, after the fact, the works which they have produced. Hence we must be on guard against affectation, rationalization, and exaggeration.

After all this, you might think that there is little point in studying the artists' descriptions of creativity. But we must not forget that many artists *have* tried, honestly and earnestly, to give insight into the creative process.

What is more, they have, to a certain extent, succeeded. The preceding discussion has not been intended to show that we should ignore everything they say. Rather, it impresses upon us the importance of not expecting too much from the artists' testimony and of exercising a reasonable degree of prudence in reading it. Such prudence is imperative in reading historical documents of any kind.

WE TURN, AT LAST, to what the artists say. One of the first things that strikes us is that so many of them say that they do not control the creative growth of the work of art. Artistic activity was defined a moment ago as "deliberate." This implies that the artist is in conscious control of the process. But there is an old tradition which conceives of artistic creation as an irrational, or even frenzied process, in which the artist is "carried away." Plato, in his dialogue, the *Ion*, describes the artist as "inspired and possessed." In Plato's metaphor, the poet does not knowingly guide what he does, any more than the magnet in attracting iron: "For the poet is a light and winged and holy thing, and there is no invention in him until he has been inspired and is out of his senses, and the mind is no longer in him." [11] Shakespeare, in *A Midsummer Night's Dream* (V, i), follows Plato's lead closely in coupling "the lunatic, the lover, and the poet."

Many artists lend support to this belief. Primarily they describe, over and over again, what might be called the "involuntariness" or "selflessness" of creation. They do not feel that they guide the development of the work, consciously molding it into the form which they wish it to assume. They feel that they are being impelled by forces which they do not have the power to control. Creative power is not subject to the will of the artist; rather, it dominates his will. Nietzsche says that the artist is "merely the incarnation, merely the mouthpiece, merely the medium of higher forces. . . . One hears, one does not search; one receives, one does not ask who gives; like lightning an idea flashes out, appearing as something necessary. . . . —I never had a choice." [12] Many similar quotations could be adduced: The great German poet and dramatist Goethe: "The songs made me, not I them; the songs had me in their power"; [13] the novelist Thackeray: "It seems as if an occult Power was moving the pen"; [14] the contemporary American novelist Thomas Wolfe: "I cannot really say the book was written. It was something that took hold of me and possessed me." [15]

Creation is not described in this way by all artists. Moreover, those

[11] *Ion* 534, in *The Dialogues of Plato*, trans. Jowett (New York: Random House, 1937), I, 289.
[12] Quoted in Chandler, *op. cit.*, p. 329.
[13] Quoted in Harding, *op. cit.*, p. 14.
[14] *Ibid.*, p. 15.
[15] Quoted in Ghiselin, *op. cit.*, p. 194.

artists who report "involuntary" creation do not usually claim that it has produced all of their output, but only some of it. We should not, furthermore, overlook the possibility that this evidence has been influenced by certain theories of art and personality, e.g., "Romantic" theories which take the artist to be an intensely emotional and irrational person. But even after these qualifications have been made, testimony of the sort just quoted remains very impressive indeed. It comes from an enormously large number of artists, working in different media and employing different styles. We cannot simply dismiss such evidence. It forces us to give a second thought to the conception of artistic activity as deliberate and controlled.

This view of art is also called into question by something else that the artists report. They tell us that a good deal of artistic creation goes on unconsciously. They may have some idea or outline for a work of art without knowing how to develop it. They will then no longer attempt to work at it on the level of conscious awareness. At this point the artist will, as the poetess Amy Lowell puts it, "drop my subject into the subconscious, much as one drops a letter into the mailbox." [16] After a sometimes considerable period of time — in the case of the poem referred to by Amy Lowell, it was six months — the creative idea suddenly re-emerges into awareness. It may now have grown completely into the full-fledged work of art. If so, the artist need devote no further time to it. Or it may still be incomplete; but it has become developed and enriched during this period. As Henry James describes it, the idea now has "a firm iridescent surface and a notable increase of weight." [17] As a result, the artist can now see his way clear to the final stages of creative activity.

This process is sometimes called "incubation" or "gestation." Different artists use different figures of speech to describe it. The contemporary novelist Rosamond Lehmann does not speak of a "mailbox," but uses a much more suggestive image — the "jar of preserves" in which the idea ripens. J. L. Lowes, who made a careful study of this process in the poet Coleridge,[18] refers to the "storing of the Well." "Incubation," it should be noted, is not confined to creative activity in the arts. It has also been reported by thinkers in mathematics and the sciences, e.g., the mathematicians Hamilton and Poincaré. Indeed, it occurs among much more humble problem-solvers, as the student probably knows from his own experience.

The process is fascinating but bewildering. What actually goes on in the "jar of preserves"? This question must rank high on the agenda of future psychological investigations. But whatever its explanation, "gestation"

[16] Quoted in Marguerite Wilkinson, *The Way of the Makers* (New York: Macmillan, 1925), p. 263.
[17] Henry James, *The American*, Preface (New York: Scribner's, 1907), p. vii.
[18] John L. Lowes, *The Road to Xanadu* (Boston: Houghton Mifflin, 1927).

taken together with the "selflessness" of creation described earlier, casts doubt upon the definition of "art" as a "skilled, deliberate" activity. Art appears to become a matter of irrational, chance "inspiration" which defies human control. If this is so, then the creation of fine art is not like other skilled human activity; a poem is not "constructed deliberately as a watch-maker constructs a chronometer." [19]

AND YET WE MUST REMEMBER that neither "involuntariness" nor "gestation" is reported in *all* instances of creation. They are widespread, but not universal. Hence they cannot be used to define the activity of "art." Furthermore, "involuntariness," even when it does occur, is not sufficient to constitute artistic creation. It is often found, for example, in psychopathic personalities, whom we would not call "artists." Hence our question is this: to what extent do irrational and unconscious factors enter into the creative process?

I would caution against exaggerating their significance. That the artist *feels* as though he were "possessed" does not itself prove that his activity is not "skilled" and "deliberate." A highly skilled craftsman, who becomes absorbed in his task, will often have this feeling. If his work goes along effortlessly, if he encounters no obstacles, then he may well feel that he is not drawing upon his own capacities, but that the work is, so to speak, "doing itself." He will feel this, however, precisely because his skills are so highly developed that he can proceed without difficulty. In the second place, even when inspiration is most absorbing and impersonal, creation is still "deliberate." It is not true that the artist's mind "is no longer in him." For he must consider his work thoughtfully and make an all-important judgment upon it — the judgment, namely, that he considers it adequate or satisfactory. The proof that he has made this judgment rests in the fact that he expends no further effort upon the work; he considers it done. Or it may be that he will refuse to accept what inspiration has delivered to him. He then judges it critically and decides that it is, in some way, unworthy of his art. It is the responsibility of the artist himself to make this decision. In this very vital respect, he is exercising just as much "control" as his more plodding brother, who is not "possessed," and must laboriously piece out the work.

In this respect, furthermore, the "inspired" artist can go grievously astray. He may decide to use his inspiration, perhaps because it has come to him with such uncontrollable force, even when it is, actually, of little artistic merit. Then the work of art will be aesthetically mediocre, even though the artist was "inspired." Inspiration, when it occurs, is no guarantee of artistic value.

[19] J. M. Murry, quoted in Max Schoen, *Art and Beauty* (New York: Macmillan, 1932), p. 47.

Inspiration is, in point of fact, rarely if ever the whole story of artistic creation. Ribot, one of the most thoughtful students of creativity, goes so far as to say that inspiration "never delivers a finished work." [20] If this statement is too absolute, it does not miss the truth by much. The poet A. E. Housman does indeed tell how two stanzas of a poem "came into my head, just as they are printed, while I was crossing the corner of Hampstead Heath." [21] But another stanza of the same poem required over a year to write, till Housman was satisfied with it. In virtually all cases in which involuntary inspiration or incubation occur, what they give to the artist must be subjected to prolonged, conscious reworking. This will almost certainly be true when the work is on a large scale, such as a symphony or a novel. Let us also remember that in innumerable other instances creativity proceeds almost wholly at the level of conscious effort. Professor Gotshalk keeps us from being betrayed into error by the artists' testimony quoted earlier, when he says that "To describe creation as pure spontaneity is a romantic exaggeration." [22]

We do not understand the workings of inspiration, but we *do* know that it comes only to those who have already engaged in creative activity without benefit of inspiration. It comes to those who have devoted time and effort to achieving technical mastery of their medium. Also, they have given thought to the kind of problem which is clarified by inspiration when it strikes them. Inspiration generally presupposes "abundance of material, accumulated experience, knowledge." [23] Both Housman and Hamilton were "inspired." But notice that inspiration delivered poetry to the poet and the method of quaternions to the mathematician, not the other way around. Hamilton says that the solution when it burst upon him was "the result of fifteen years labor." So again we see that inspiration is not a wholly random, independent force — though it may appear so to the artist — but is, rather, largely dependent upon conscious, controlled activity.

I conclude that the existence of inspiration does not itself compel us to give up the definition of "art" on page 93. Further analysis of creative activity may demonstrate that the significance of irrational forces is far greater than we now believe. If that is shown, the definition may well have to be overhauled. Short of that, however, the evidence concerning inspiration is instructive. It keeps us from thinking that creative activity is as simple and straightforward as the definition makes it out to be. I now wish to show that another part of the definition does not wholly describe the creative process and it too must be supplemented by empirical evidence.

[20] T. Ribot, *Essay on the Creative Imagination*, trans. Baron (Chicago: Open Court, 1906), p. 58.

[21] A. E. Housman, *The Name and Nature of Poetry* (New York: Macmillan, 1933), p. 49.

[22] *Op. cit*, p. 66.   [23] Ribot, *op. cit.*, p. 163.

I SAID, quoting Santayana, that art is "conscious of its aim." This sounds as if the artist has, at the beginning of creative activity, a clear-cut notion of the goal he is trying to attain. But this is not true, unless you state the goal in very general terms, e.g., "to write a novel." Often even this cannot be said, unless, say, the artist has been commissioned to produce a certain kind of work. What the artist is after, exactly, is frequently very unclear to him at the outset. The form of the work, its expressive character, its specific details, become clarified only during the course of creation. He may have to make many false starts, try out and reject many alternatives, before his goal begins to fix itself in his mind. If, indeed, we identify the artist's purpose with the creation of the work in its final state, then we must say that characteristically the artist does not know his purpose until he at last puts down his tools and says "There! That's it!" As Charlie Chaplin's famous line has it, "Before I know where I am going, I must first get there."

Here again we must be careful not to generalize about *all* artists. One of the foremost artists of our time claims that the overall conception of the work is clear from the very first, and that creation consists essentially in working out the details. Picasso says: "there is one very odd thing — to notice that basically a picture doesn't change, that the first 'vision' remains almost intact, in spite of appearances." [24] But in the work of other artists even the outline of the end product is indeterminate at first and is sharpened only gradually and haltingly.

Examples of incessant revision and trial-and-error efforts among the artists are innumerable. I select the two following for a special reason — because these works are so thoroughly formed and unified that we might think that they were born full-blown in a single act of creative "vision." They were not. They were hammered out in a process of continuous reworking. Thus again we see the importance of distinguishing the nature of the art-object from its origins, and the danger of making inferences from one to the other. The first example is William Blake's well-known poem *The Tiger*. This fairly short poem is, as you may know, distinguished for its extraordinary intensity and unity. But the various drafts of the poem [25] reveal the complicated process of suggesting and rejecting numerous ideas which the artist went through, until he decided on the final version. Secondly, the composer Chopin. His piano pieces give the illusion of complete spontaneity and effortless creation. But George Sand tells us how Chopin would "shut himself up in his room for whole days, weeping, walking, breaking his pens, repeating and altering a bar a hundred times." [26]

[24] Alfred H. Barr, ed., *Picasso: Forty Years of His Art* (New York: Museum of Modern Art, 1939), p. 15.

[25] Cf. Wilkinson, *op. cit.*, pp. 246–250.   [26] Quoted in Harding, *op. cit.*, p. 18.

This passage is also of interest because it typifies a great many descriptions of the *painfulness* of the creative process. We speak of the artist's activity as "skilled" and "purposeful." This might lead us to picture him as a man who has easy mastery of the situation, deftly manipulating his tools and materials to overcome any and all obstacles, and taking delight in his powers. This too may be true of *some* artists, some of the time, but certainly not of all. The experience is often unbearably agonizing for those in whom the creative urge is strong, but who find themselves unable to "get it right." Thus Coleridge says of "Christabel" that "Every line has been produced by me with labor-pangs." [27] Similarly the contemporary poet Stephen Spender says that "I dread writing poetry," and gives as one of the reasons that "a poem is a terrible journey, a painful effort of concentrating the imagination." [28] If you should happen to have any artistic aspirations of your own, it might be somehow reassuring to see how even after an artist like Virginia Woolf has achieved considerable success, the old fears and trepidations surrounding creation will not down.[29] When we take special delight in a work of art, we often feel a sense of gratitude to the man who has given it to us. Our indebtedness would often be increased many times over if we knew the frightful personal expense of giving life to the work of art.

3. THE CREATIVE ARTIST

What distinguishes the creative artist from the nonartist? This question asks for empirical information about the artist. Specifically, when people ask this question — as they have for many centuries — they seek psychological knowledge. Does the artist have essentially the same psychological make-up as all other human beings, so that the only difference is that he has technical facility in a certain medium? If that is true, then all of us are, potentially, artists. Or is there something distinctive — something about his emotions, for example, or his imaginative capacities — which sets him off from the nonartist?

Modern thought has, on the whole, adopted the second of these views. This belief has developed at the same time that art was being set off from the rest of modern culture. Increasingly since the Renaissance, the creator of "fine art" has been distinguished from other craftsmen. As was pointed out earlier,[30] the work of the artist has become more and more an autonomous activity, one which is less related to other cultural institu-

27 Quoted in Chandler, *op. cit.*, p. 338.
28 Stephen Spender, "The Making of a Poem," in R. W. Stallman, ed., *Critiques and Essays in Criticism* (New York: Ronald, 1949), p. 28.
29 Cf. Virginia Woolf, *A Writer's Diary* (New York: Harcourt, Brace, 1954).
30 Cf. above, pp. 31–32.

tions and activities than in earlier times. So it is not surprising that the creative "gift" has been thought to be something wholly unique. The philosopher Kant, writing at the close of the eighteenth century, first popularized the term "genius" to describe this gift, and the term has since gained great currency.

But a word, by itself, never settles any question of fact. "Why do objects fall downwards?" is not answered by replying "Gravity," unless "Gravity" is used as shorthand for complicated empirical observations and mathematical calculations. Similarly, it will not do to say that artists create because they are blessed with "genius." This will be a genuine answer only if we can find out, empirically, the psychological capacities which constitute genius. But just here we must acknowledge our ignorance. Over the last century and a half there have been innumerable studies of creative genius. Many have been highly speculative, some have attempted to be experimental. Yet it is unfortunately true that they have not succeeded in their task. Indeed, contemporary workers in this field are not even certain which hypotheses will be the most useful avenues of approach to the problem. This does not mean that we must write off the problem as a "mystery" which will never be solved. We know only that at this stage in the development of knowledge our question must go unanswered.

Some researchers have attempted to find a relationship between genius and other psychological or even physiological traits. They are handicapped by their inability to examine artists of the past at first hand. They have had to rely on autobiographical and other accounts of artists, which are not always reliable and are sometimes conflicting. Nonetheless, they have attempted to show that creativity is found in people of a certain physical make-up, or in people who are insane, or in those who suffer from certain illnesses.[31] We should bear in mind that all studies of this kind do not analyze the nature of genius itself. They attempt to establish a correlation between genius and something else. But they use "genius" in the usual, uncritical sense in which it is applied to well-known artists, without telling us what it consists in. Furthermore, even if a correlation were to be found between artistic genius and, say, tuberculosis, we would want to know how, if at all, the ailment is a cause of creativity. Even though such studies fail to answer these vital questions, it would still be interesting to find a correlation between creativity and certain physical or mental characteristics. Often in the history of science the discovery simply that two events go together has been the point of departure for gaining systematic and detailed causal knowledge. Unfortunately, however, none of the above studies has succeeded in establishing a reliable correlation. For example, it is true that many artists, such as Beethoven, Keats, Robert Louis Stevenson,

[31] The first theory is exemplified by Galton, the second by Nordau and Lombroso, the third by Jeannette Marks.

have been gravely ill, but a great many others have enjoyed relatively good health. The failure of these studies should make us skeptical of those who claim, without a large amount of empirical evidence, that artistry is always found along with some other bodily or psychological factor.

ILLNESS AND INSANITY seem too far-fetched to help explain genius. Is there not some other feature of personality, more closely related to the nature of art as we know it, which will account for creativity? It is often thought that this must be the scope and intensity of the artist's *emotions*. G. E. Woodberry voices this belief: "The sign of the poet . . . is that by passion he enters into life more than other men. . . . Emotion is the condition of [the poets'] existence; passion is the element of their being. . . . The poet craves emotion, and feeds the fire that consumes him, and only under this condition is he baptized with creative power." [32] On this view, the artist has emotional "sympathy," which means literally that he "feels with" many different people and events. Thus he can people a novel with a rich assortment of characters, and imbue the work with emotional force. Furthermore, his intense emotions impel him to creation, and motivate him to persist even when the process is slow and painful.

How shall we assess the strength of this theory? Certainly it is an extremely popular one at the present time. This, per se, does not imply that it is either true or false. It should, perhaps, make us a little more cautious about accepting the theory, for it may be that we have taken it "for granted," simply because we have heard it and read it so often. Primarily, let us take note that this view has become most widespread at a time when a great deal of art has been highly emotional. Though the belief in emotional "inspiration" of the artist is, as we have already seen, an old one, it is prevalent chiefly during the so-called "Romantic" period of the last century and a half. This period produced such conspicuously "passionate" art as the music of Tchaikovsky, the painting of van Gogh, the poetry of Shelley:

> Oh, lift me as a wave, a leaf, a cloud!
> I fall upon the thorns of life! I bleed!
> > "Ode to the West Wind"

It is then a very real possibility that Woodberry's view reflects the art only of a certain period, or of a certain kind, and that it does not hold true of all artists, as it claims to do. Would it sound as plausible at a time when art showed great emotional restraint and discipline? If not, then the theory is a partial and limited one. It cannot be the whole truth about the psychology of the artist.

[32] Quoted in Wilkinson, *op. cit.*, pp. 13–14.

Furthermore, we must ask of this theory, "How do we know that it is true?" It purports to tell us about the psychology of the artist. Therefore it must rest upon evidence gained from psychological analysis. But this is not the way in which the theory is usually argued for. Rather its exponents point to works of art, find that they are markedly emotional, and then infer that the artist must be hyperemotional. But then the theory is really telling us nothing. For all that it means by "Artist A is hyperemotional" is "The work of art created by A is very emotional." However, the work of art is one thing, the psychology of the artist is another. The latter must be investigated independently, even if psychological clues are found in the work. This would require a large-scale study of the emotionality of the artist as compared to the nonartist. To take a short cut, by inferring from the art-object to the artist, is logically untenable. I have already cited evidence which shows that the emotional character of the object may be very different from the mood of its creator.[33] Finally, even if it were shown that all artists are intensely emotional, this would not, in itself, be a sufficient explanation of creativity. Hyperemotionality in its most extreme form is found among certain psychopathic personalities, who fail to create art. Something else is needed to make a man an artist.

The theory we have been discussing, like most theories of creativity, cannot be accepted as it stands. It must be tested by evidence to be gained in the future. The opposite view, stated by T. S. Eliot, may just as well be true: "It is not in his personal emotions, the emotions provoked by particular events in his life, that the poet is in any way remarkable or interesting. His particular emotions may be simple, or crude, or flat."[34]

BUT NOW, IS THERE ANYTHING that can be said about the creative artist with relative certainty? If anything, then it is probably this: the artist is one who "thinks" in terms of some artistic medium. A medium comprises certain sensory elements — colors, tones, etc., —which are ordered and interrelated. The medium of music consists of tones arranged on a scale, which can be related to each other in intervals, as well as rhythmically. Poetry employs words, whose meanings can be combined syntactically or grammatically, and which can be patterned metrically, by rhyme, and in other ways. Now whatever the emotions of the artist may be, whether they be intense or, as Eliot says, "flat," whatever his ideas, whether they be profound or superficial, they present themselves to the artist's mind embodied in his medium. Therefore the creative process is usually, even if not

[33] Cf. above, pp. 91–92.
[34] From *Selected Essays 1917–1932* by T. S. Eliot, copyright, 1932, by Harcourt, Brace and Company, Inc. "Tradition and the Individual Talent," p. 10. Reprinted by permission of Harcourt, Brace and Company, Inc., and of Faber and Faber Ltd.

always, one of elaborating a melody or working out a visual design which has suggested itself. It is not, characteristically, a process of having some "thought" or "mood" and then trying to find some artistic "dress" to put it in.[35]

The poet Stephen Spender illustrates the creative mind in his detailed and interesting account of "The Making of a Poem." He describes the way in which one line,

> A language of flesh and roses,

came to him: "I was standing in the corridor of a train passing through the Black Country. I saw a landscape of pits and pitheads, artificial mountains, jagged yellow wounds in the earth, everything transformed as though by the toil of an enormous animal or giant tearing up the earth in search of prey or treasure. Oddly enough a stranger next to me in the corridor echoed my inmost thought. He said: 'Everything there is man-made.' At this moment the line flashed into my head." [36] Spender goes on to say that he saw "the pitheads, slagheaps and ghastly disregard of anything but the pursuit of wealth" as a "symbol" or "language" of modern man. This language is "confused," an "irresponsible senile gibberish." [37] The sort of "language" of life that man really wants and needs is

> A language of flesh and roses.

There is nothing very startling about Spender's emotional response to the scene which he describes. Revulsion against the ugliness of a grubbing industrial civilization, and aspiration toward a more humane society, are common enough. They are experienced by many of us who are not artists. Spender's thought-and-feeling is in one sense, to use Eliot's adjective, "simple." Notice that the "stranger in the corridor" had very much the same thought at the same time. The difference between the artist and the nonartist is that "the stranger's" remark — "Everything there is man-made" — is wholly prosaic and prosy, whereas Spender's line is not. The line which "flashed into" the poet's head has poetic quality. Its sound, its cadence, its imagery show that Spender's response was formed within the poet's medium. The line is not itself a poem, but it might well develop into a poem, by tracing out the images and ideas implicit within it, by perpetuating the rhythm which it suggests, and so on.

The artist, then, is the man who is sensitive to and familiar with the medium in which the work of art is created. This, surely, is only a begin-

---

[35] That this does occur, however, is pointed out in Harding, *op. cit.*, pp. 64–65.
[36] Spender, *op. cit.*, p. 23.
[37] *Ibid.*, p. 23.

ning in learning about the psychology of the artist. It does not explain the difference between the great artist and the hack. We would still want to know whether the artist's sensory faculties such as hearing and sight are unusually acute, and therefore predispose him to creativity, how his imagination functions in creating new patterns within the medium, and so on. But at least this conception of the artist can be safely asserted. And it may serve as a guide for education in the arts. As the well-known contemporary poet W. H. Auden puts it: " 'Why do you want to write poetry?' If the young man answers: 'I have important things I want to say,' then he is not a poet. If he answers: 'I like hanging around words listening to what they say,' then maybe he is going to be a poet." [38]

THAT THE ARTIST'S CREATIVE GIFTS cannot be separated from the medium in which he works has been emphasized by the modern philosopher Benedetto Croce. We cannot enter into the details of his difficult theory. Within the present discussion, however, it is worth pointing out that for Croce it is senseless for a man to complain, "I have important things to say; I just can't find the words (or the notes, or the colors) to say them in." In Croce's terminology, there is no "intuition" without "expression." The composer's intuition is and can be nothing apart from a pattern of sounds. Nor can there be any poetic "idea" dissociated from the words of the poem, their rhymes and formal organization.[39]

And yet Croce has come under fire precisely because, it is charged, he neglects the importance of the artistic medium. Let us consider this criticism.

Croce asserts that artistic creation is wholly an "inner" process. That is, the act of artistic intuition occurs solely in imagination. It does not require any contact with or manipulation of physical objects such as a piano, a canvas, a block of marble. The artist *does* employ a medium; indeed, for Croce, as we have just seen, he *must* do so, to be an artist. But the medium is wholly internalized within his mind. Thus Croce would take Michelangelo's dictum, "One paints, not with the hand, but with the brain," to epitomize all artistic creation. Similarly, for Croce, the "work of art" does not exist as a physical object. The artist may, if he wishes, embody his imaginative intuition in some physical material. But this has nothing to do with the process of creation, which is already over and done with when this "external" activity is undertaken. Such activity serves only for the "reproduction" [40] of the artist's images, so that they may be preserved and

[38] W. H. Auden, "Squares and Oblongs," in *Poets at Work* (New York: Harcourt, Brace, 1948), p. 171.

[39] Cf. Benedetto Croce, *The Essence of Aesthetic*, trans. Ainslie (London: Heinemann, 1921), pp. 42–43, 44. This book was published in 1915 with the title *Breviary of Aesthetic*.

[40] *Op. cit.*, p. 45.

shared. When the percipient apprehends the physical object, it is only a "cue" to the re-creation of the real work of art — the artist's "vision" — in the spectator's own imagination.

This theory of art and artistic creation reflects Croce's overall position in philosophy, which is known as "Idealism." Briefly, this is the theory that only "mind" or "spirit," and its contents, are real; what is material is unreal. So Croce argues that since art is "supremely real," it must necessarily be nonphysical.[41] Leaving aside this metaphysical position, let us examine Croce's view of the "inwardness" of creation.

Certainly Michelangelo's statement describes a good deal of creation. Notice that Spender says that the line "flashed into my head." A better example, the best of all, probably, is the incomparable Mozart, reporting that he has "composed" a symphony, but has not yet "written it down." And yet, we must ask, could the artist employ the medium in imagination if he had not previously experienced its physical embodiment? Would Mozart have composed "in his mind" if he had not previously heard the distinctive timbre of the piano, the clarinet, the violin? The artist gains mastery of the technical processes involved in using the medium only by physical contact with it.

More important, the creative process is almost never brought to completion without overt manipulation of the physical medium. The artist's imagination is daring and far-reaching, but it is not enough. His "vision" of the imagined words or lines is incomplete or blurred until he attempts to give it material embodiment. Thus, when he is at the canvas or the piano, he comes to see previously neglected details. He can now understand how the "germ" of his imaginative vision can be developed into a total work of art.

One of the greatest artists of our time, the musician Pablo Casals, says:

> I think it is not enough for an artist to learn music only through his eyes: he needs to experience sound physically. Although sound by itself will not change your idea of the work, the transmission of sound to the ear communicates a sort of exaltation which is beneficial and fruitful. When experiencing sound, I find that its richness helps me to create my performance in a way unlike simply reading from a score.[42]

Croce speaks as though the work were entirely finished and complete within the artist's imagination and is then transferred whole to the physical medium. But this is not true to the facts of artistic creation. When the artist attempts to transpose his imaginative "idea" to the external medium, he may well find that it "won't go." What he had heard inwardly may not

[41] *Ibid.*, p. 9.
[42] J. Ma. Corredor, *Conversations with Casals*, trans. Mangeot (New York: Dutton, 1957), p. 194.

sound right when played upon an instrument; his plan for a sculpture may prove to be ill-adapted to the texture and massiveness of marble. This compels the artist to revise his conception of the work, and strike out in a new direction. In other words, the physical medium is not simply passive, like the wax which takes the imprint of a seal. It has a character of its own, which permits some things to be done with it, but not others.

But the importance of the physical medium is not simply negative. It also gives direction to the creative process by suggesting to the artist previously unthought-of ideas. Tones and colors are rich with associative and expressive values which the artist can exploit. Words, such as those in Spender's line, invite rhymes and suggest new thoughts. Professor Gotshalk quotes the sculptor, R. A. Baillie:

> As your carving progresses, the stone itself will suggest improvements over your first sketch. If you are sensitive to its messages, you will modify certain details as you work — leaving a bold plane where your sketch indicated a round or broken surface. . . . Many stones have veins, much as wood has a grain, and sometimes by following what these veins suggest you will get a finer effect than you had ever thought of when you were making your clay model.[43]

In innumerable ways, the medium is pregnant with leads which help to build the form of the growing work. This is, of course, also true of the imagined medium that Croce emphasizes. But to rule out the material medium, which is the "body" of the work of art, as "unreal" or inconsequential, leaves us with a distorted and one-sided conception of the creation of art.

[43] *Op. cit.*, p. 74.

BIBLIOGRAPHY

* Gotshalk, *Art and the Social Order*. Chap. III.
* Rader, *A Modern Book of Esthetics*. Pp. 94–113, 132–142, 235–244.
* Vivas and Krieger, *The Problems of Aesthetics*. Pp. 69–90, 118–179, 255–261.
* Weitz, *Problems in Aesthetics*. Pp. 93–107, 253–259, 344–351, 627–637.
  Alexander, S. *Beauty and Other Forms of Value*. London: Macmillan, 1933. Chaps. II–IV.
  Bosanquet, Bernard. *Three Lectures on Aesthetic*. London: Macmillan, 1923. Lect. II.
  Chandler, *Beauty and Human Nature*. Chaps. 15–16.
  Croce, Benedetto. *The Essence of Aesthetic*, trans. Ainslie. London: Heinemann, 1921.
  Ghiselin, Brewster. *The Creative Process*. University of California Press, 1952.

Harding, Rosamond E. M. *An Anatomy of Inspiration*, 2nd. ed. Cambridge: Heffer, 1942.

Schoen, Max. *Art and Beauty*. New York: Macmillan, 1932. Chaps. III–IV.

Wilson, Edmund. *The Wound and the Bow*. New York: Oxford University Press, 1947. Pp. 272–295.

QUESTIONS

1. It is argued in this chapter that the genesis of the work of art is distinct from the work itself. But can the origins of the work help to explain the nature of the work? Can you give specific examples of this? Will genetic factors *always* help to explain the work?

2. Aesthetic experience is often described as a "re-creation" of the work of art. In what sense, if any, do you think that this description is accurate? How does aesthetic perception differ from artistic creation?

3. This chapter describes the interaction between the artist's "idea" and his medium. Do you think that such interaction occurs to the same extent in all the arts? Compare sculpture with architecture in this regard.

4. "Let us suppose . . . that in the Samoan Islands there were born a child having the singular and extraordinary genius of Mozart. What could he accomplish? At the most, extend the gamut of three or four tones to seven, and create a few more complex melodies; but he would be as unable to compose symphonies as Archimedes would have been to invent an electric dynamo. How many creators have been wrecked because the conditions necessary for their invention were lacking?" — Ribot. *op. cit.*, p. 154. Discuss.

5

The "Imitation"-Theories

Our question now is, "What is fine art?" That is, how is "fine" art distinguished from art in the broad, generic sense, as defined in the previous chapter? The answers to be considered in this and the following chapters are among the most influential in the history of aesthetic thought. But they have not been important only among philosophers. These beliefs about fine art have dominated the thinking of all those concerned with it — artists, critics, teachers of art, and also the layman, whose interest is in looking at and enjoying works of art. As was pointed out in the opening chapter, these beliefs are important precisely because they guide behavior — how art is created, what the spectator looks for in the work, the methods used by critics in evaluating art-objects. Moreover, since all of the beliefs which we shall discuss are extremely widespread at the present time, they have almost certainly entered into the student's own thinking about art. As these theories of art are presented, the student will doubtless be moved to say, at one point or another, "Yes, I believe that." Indeed, you may well find that you hold *several* of these beliefs, even though you may never have put them into words.

Our job now is to state these beliefs clearly, and to distinguish them from each other. Then we must trace out the implications of each belief, seeing what other beliefs we must be committed to, if we are to hold the theory consistently. For example, each theory is concerned not only with the nature of art, but also its *value*. We must see what criteria the theory uses for judging the value of art, and whether these lead to evaluations that we are prepared to accept. Throughout, we must examine candidly the evidence and reasoning which are used in support of each theory. In this way, the student will have the opportunity to get clear about and test his own beliefs concerning art.

1. "SIMPLE" IMITATION

Now then, "What is fine art?" The first answer is, at once, the simplest, the oldest, and the most widely held of all. It says that art is *imitation*. "Fine art" is defined as "the faithful, literal duplication of the objects and events of ordinary experience." What is shown in the art-object resembles closely the model, outside of the work, which it "imitates." Thus a portrait "imitates" the person who sat for it by tracing the details of his appearance so carefully that his identity would be known at once to anyone who knew him "in the flesh." The most important thing about art, therefore, is its "verisimilitude" — it "looks like" and reminds us of what we know in reality apart from art. We will call this the theory of "simple imitation," to distinguish it from other forms of "imitation"-theory.

The theory is, as I have noted, the oldest theory of art. It is presented by the Greek philosopher, Plato, in the first systematic discussion of the nature of art in Western thought. And yet virtually no philosopher since Plato has wished to uphold "simple imitation." Even Plato, as we shall see, does not defend this theory as his own. To understand the enormous popularity of "simple imitation" we must look beyond philosophical aesthetics.

We need not look very far. Evidences of this belief are very close to hand. We have all heard people say — indeed, we ourselves have doubtless often said — about a novel, drama, or moving picture, that it is "true to life." On the other hand, we all know that so-called "modern painting" is roundly condemned either because the people and objects which it depicts do not "look like" those which we know in common experience or because it shows no recognizable object whatever. Painting which is, by contrast, popularly admired is like that done by "Fra Lippo Lippi" in Robert Browning's poem of that name:

> The monks closed in a circle and praised loud . . .
> Being simple bodies, — "That's the very man!
> Look at the boy who stoops to pat the dog!
> That woman's like the Prior's niece who comes
> To care about his asthma: it's the life!"

On the theory of "simple imitation," that phrase — "It's the life!" — sums up our response to painting and to all art. The people depicted in a painting or drama are obviously not precisely the people we know in "real life." In the painting, they are two-dimensional, and within a frame; in the drama, they appear on a stage. Yet the value of the art-object depends upon the degree of its resemblance to the model.

The prevalence of "simple imitation" in our own time is only one instance of its enduring historical influence. We find the great Renaissance figure, Leonardo da Vinci, describing painting as "the sole imitator of all visible works of nature,"[1] and saying "That painting is the most praiseworthy which is most like the thing represented."[2] Similarly, "simple imitation" is used to judge the value of art in this account of the well-known "Mona Lisa," written by the famous art critic and historian, Vasari (1550):

> Whoever shall desire to see how far art can imitate nature, may do so to perfection in this head, wherein every peculiarity that could be depicted by the utmost subtlety of the pencil has been faithfully reproduced. The eyes have the lustrous brightness and moisture which is seen in life, and around them are those pale, red, and slightly livid circles, also proper to nature, with the lashes, which can only be copied as they are with the greatest difficulty; the eyebrows also are represented with the closest exactitude, where fuller and where more thinly set, with the separate hairs delineated as they issue from the skin, every turn being followed, and all the pores being exhibited in a manner that could not be more natural than it is; the nose . . . might be easily believed to be alive.[3]

In the history of painting, great effort has been put forth to develop techniques which would increase verisimilitude. Thus a great deal of early Renaissance painting is devoted to conquering the problems of perspective, so that the appearance of three-dimensionality can be achieved on the two-dimensional canvas. By the nineteenth century, when these problems had very largely been met, the movement of "Impressionism" took pains to render faithfully the play of light upon colored surfaces.

This will suggest to the reader the historical scope of "simple imitation." The first statement of this theory is, as I have noted, in Plato. In his dialogue, the *Republic*, he says that the poet or painter, "besides producing any kind of artificial thing . . . can create all plants and animals, himself included, and earth and sky and gods and the heavenly bodies and all the things under the earth in Hades."[4] How is this done? Plato's answer

[1] Quoted in Elizabeth G. Holt, *Literary Sources of Art History* (Princeton University Press, 1947), p. 177.

[2] Quoted in Goldwater and Treves, eds., *Artists on Art* (New York: Pantheon, 1945), p. 54.

[3] Quoted in George Boas, "The Mona Lisa in the History of Taste," in *Wingless Pegasus* (Johns Hopkins Press, 1950), p. 215.

[4] *Republic* 596, trans. Cornford (New York: Oxford University Press, 1945), p. 325. All quotations from the *Republic* are in this translation, by permission of the publisher.

employs the metaphor which is at the heart of "simple imitation": all that the artist need do is "to take a mirror and turn it round in all directions." [5] Here too,[6] Shakespeare echoes Plato, for in Hamlet's speech to the players (III, ii), he says that the "end" of acting "was and is, to hold, as 'twere, the mirror up to nature."

"SIMPLE IMITATION" has been espoused by artists and critics, and by those whom Browning calls "simple bodies," but by virtually no philosophers. Why is this? I would suggest that this theory is one of those which seems obviously true when taken uncritically, but which are found to be anything but true upon critical reflection. When we look at a portrait, read a story, or watch a play, it seems obvious that the work is depicting what we know in "real life." Yet we should be especially skeptical of those beliefs which seem self-evident. Let us see why this belief about art is untenable.

Given an object which is a wholly literal recording of some "real life" happenings, or a straightforward pictorial representation of some natural scene: would we be prepared to call it a "work of fine art"? It is doubtful that we would, unless the object has some reason for being other than its literalness. An exact recording of a prosaic conversation, or a flat, literal photograph taken by an amateur photographer, does not epitomize "fine art." The "model" must somehow be organized and made significant, and there must be some enhancement of its interest, if the created object is to be one of "fine art." This is because "real life" is commonly so inane and formless, as A. A. Milne wittily shows:

> Imagine yourself putting your head in at the window of a strange house and listening to the conversation for three-quarters of an hour. There would be long silences; people would go in and out without explanation; there would be references to unknown Johns and Marys; private, unintelligible jokes; and even if the scene suddenly became intensely dramatic the cook would spoil it by putting her head into it, and asking . . . whether there were any orders for the butcher.[7]

We would all agree that Hemingway's short story, "The Killers," and van Gogh's famous painting, "The Starry Night" (see Plate 8), are works of "fine art," even if we were not yet clear as to the meaning of that phrase. But the talk of the American tough in the short story is not simply a stenographic recording. We fail to do justice to Hemingway's prose artistry if we think that. He has heard and drawn upon American speech, but he has vivified and intensified its sound and rhythm. Imitation is even

[5] *Ibid.*, 597, p. 326.
[6] Cf. above, p. 95.
[7] A. A. Milne, *Year In, Year Out* (New York: Dutton, 1952), p. 71.

less "literal" in the van Gogh. The swirling vortices in the sky do not occur in our ordinary experience. But this certainly does not disqualify the painting as "art."

The meaning of "fine art" in the theory of "simple imitation" does not embrace those objects which are widely considered artistic. Indeed, there are very few objects which are adequately described by this definition. This conclusion is underscored if we think of art-forms other than painting and literature. The arts of music and architecture have not even a vestige of "imitation" in them. Once we except a handful of passages in music, such as the bleating of the sheep in Strauss' "Don Quixote," we see that music does not imitate "literally" and "faithfully" the sounds of ordinary experience. Plato does speak of music "[imitating] the good or bad soul," [8] and the later Greek philosopher Aristotle says that music "imitates" feelings and moral virtues.[9] But it is clear that music cannot "imitate" states of character, in the sense in which a painting can "imitate" a tree. Some other word, with a different and more extended meaning, such as "expression," would have to be used.

"Simple imitation" is, then, too narrow as a theory of art. As I now wish to show, it misconceives the nature and value of art, both from the standpoint of the artist and of the aesthetic spectator.

The artist does not consider it his function to "turn a mirror in all directions." If he did, his job would be a great deal easier than it is. Whenever he does use a "model" in nature, he alters and modifies it for his creative purposes. The painter rearranges the masses in the natural landscape, omits a line here, adds a contour there. There is graphic evidence of this in a recent book on the painter Cézanne, [10] which juxtaposes photographs of the scenes observed by the artist with his paintings (see Plates 9 and 10). In the painting, the natural scenes appear wholly transformed. "Distortion," in this sense, appears throughout all artistic creation. Yet it would be incomprehensible if the artist were trying merely to "imitate." In some works all vestiges of the "real life" object are lost, and the artist depicts "the light that never was, on sea or land."

"Simple imitation" is correspondingly misleading if we want to understand aesthetic experience. If this theory were true, what would be the point of having works of art at all? Why should we bother with "copies," when, just by looking around us, we can see the "real thing"? Aristotle suggests an answer which would probably be accepted by many who believe in "simple imitation": "[It is] natural to delight in imitations. . . . The cause of this again is that to learn gives the liveliest pleasure to men

[8] *Laws* 812, in *The Dialogues of Plato*, trans. Jowett (New York: Random House, 1937), II, 566. Cf. *Laws* 655, 668; *Republic* 398–400.
[9] Cf. *Politics* VIII, v.
[10] Erle Loran, *Cézanne's Composition* (University of California Press, 1947).

in general. . . . Thus the reason why men enjoy seeing a likeness is that in contemplating it they find themselves learning or inferring, and saying perhaps, 'Ah, that is he.' " [11] Hence, like the admiring monks in Browning's poem, we are to recognize the model which the painting depicts. But even if it is true that recognition brings enjoyment, this is not *aesthetic* enjoyment. The painting is not then of intrinsic interest to the spectator. It is a "cue" for inferring to its model. "Recognition . . . is seeking a resting place in the past instead of being alive in the present." [12]

Because the percipient's interest is in "learning" or "inferring," he does not attend to the total work of art, but only to its "subject," i.e., the person or object which it depicts. If the subject is reasonably clear, the spectator is able to say "Ah, that is he." An inept though accurate photograph will serve just as well as a masterly portrait. But in genuinely aesthetic perception, everything that enters into the work of art is of interest. Not only the "subject," but also the appeal of the work to the senses, its formal structure, its emotional and imaginative significance, absorb the percipient. Aristotle seems to recognize this when he says: "For if you happen not to have seen the original, the pleasure will be due not to the imitation as such, but to the execution, the coloring, or some such other cause." [13] In other words, if the spectator's interest is not in recognition, it can be directed to the intrinsic properties of the work.

"Simple imitation" holds that a work of art is best when it is most "life-like." Plato himself shows the absurdity of this when he pokes fun at art which achieves such great verisimilitude that it deceives us into thinking that we are looking at the "real thing." Thus, Plato says, an artist may so paint a carpenter that "he might deceive a child or a simple-minded person into thinking his picture was a real carpenter, if he showed it them at some distance." [14] To judge aesthetic value by means of verisimilitude leads to evaluations that few of us could accept. We would have to say, for example, that the nakedly "lifelike" photographs of unsavory people found on postoffice bulletin boards are superior to the portraits of Modigliani, in which faces become elongated ovals (see Plate 11). One of the most unrelenting attempts at "literal imitation" in the history of art was made by the nineteenth-century novelist Champfleury, much of whose work is devoted to "stenographic reports of dialogue or catalogue inventories of furniture." [15] But "this makes for very boring reading," [16] and

[11] *Op. cit.,* IV, p. 6.
[12] Albert C. Barnes and Violette de Mazia, *The Art of Renoir* (New York: Minton, Balch, 1935), p. 10.
[13] *Op. cit.,* IV, p. 6.
[14] *Republic* 598, p. 328; cf. *Sophist* 234.
[15] George Boas, ed., *Courbet and the Naturalistic Movement* (Johns Hopkins Press, 1938), p. 101.
[16] *Ibid.,* p. 101.

the obscurity of his name testifies to the degree of aesthetic value which readers have found in his works. The student may be able to think of other works of so-called "realistic" or "naturalistic" art which suffer from the same defect.

WE HAVE NOW SEEN, in various ways, why it is a mistake to consider fine art nothing but "simple imitation." At several points in the analysis I have criticized the theory by showing that it is inconsistent with common facts of aesthetic experience and evaluation. And yet it is also a fact that we often say of a work of art that it is "real" or "true to life." Are we merely being "simple bodies" when we say things like this, or does it prove that there is more to "simple imitation" than we have yet discovered?

This way of speaking does have a place in our beliefs about art, but not, I would urge, in the way in which "simple imitation" interprets it. Let us note first that there are a great many works of painting and literature — the art-forms which, we have seen, are supposed to be the strongholds of imitation — which we do not condemn simply because they lack verisimilitude. Why not? For the same reason that we do not condemn a string quartet for its failure to "imitate" the sounds of ordinary experience — because, as we say colloquially, "That isn't what it's trying to do." We can use the criterion of being "true to life" only when speaking of *some* works of art, those that are trying to achieve fidelity to experience.

But such works are not necessarily those which depict ordinary people or trees or wars. Works which seem vastly "unreal" or "fantastic" are often justly described as revealing "truths" about experience. Think of satire, for example. Swift's *Gulliver's Travels* is replete with midgets, giants, and civilized horses. Yet this book lays bare personal and social follies of Swift's time and our own. The immortal "Mad Tea-Party" in *Alice in Wonderland* can be read as a take-off on English social customs, showing up their absurdity. These works attempt to be "true to life," but in a very subtle, indirect manner.

Hence, even when the intended aesthetic effect of the work is to be "true to life," the work is not just a "mirror." It seeks to depict something in our experience, but it does so in its own way, which may involve "distortion" or "fantasy." And when, as in Swift or Lewis Carroll, "lifelikeness" is achieved, it becomes part of the intrinsic interest of the work. The oblique caricature of life in these works enhances their vigor and charm. But our attention therefore remains upon the work; it is not led away from the work to the "real life" model.

This point can also be made if we consider painting. Specifically, let us turn to that style of painting which seems to fulfill the aims of "simple imitation" most thoroughly — so-called *trompe l'œil*. As its name says, such painting can "fool the eye" — i.e., it is so "lifelike" that the spectator may confuse the painted object with the real one. The work of the American artist William Harnett (d. 1892) is an excellent example of this style (see Plate 12). Among the stories which testify to his ability is one — which is historically true — that tells how he painted life-size American currency so faithfully that he was arrested by Treasury agents for counterfeiting.[17]

And yet we fail to do justice to Harnett if we praise him solely for verisimilitude. The objects which he depicts do, indeed, resemble their "models," but they do more than this. Harnett has heightened their color and texture so that they are extremely vivid and arresting to the eye. He has, through his art, enhanced the visual interest of pipes and books so that we "see" them as we rarely do in ordinary perception. Hence our attention is absorbed in the painting in which they appear. Furthermore, let us again remind ourselves that the "subject" is only one aspect of the work. The way in which the depicted objects are interrelated in the painting is another, and crucial aspect of the work. Harnett has studiedly placed these objects in such relations to each other that the painting takes on *formal* values. This too makes the work interesting in its own right. A contemporary of Harnett, whose "ability to render literal fact" is "equally remarkable," [18] is a far inferior artist, because his work lacks formal vigor and movement (see Plate 13). On the theory of "simple imitation," which concentrates on verisimilitude to the exclusion of everything else in the work, both artists would have to be ranked equally.

FOR THE REASONS we have discussed, "simple imitation" has been repudiated by most thinkers. Even those philosophers and critics who were cited earlier as exponents of this theory do not hold to it consistently. There is good reason to think that when Plato likened artistic creation to the turning of a "mirror," he was poking fun at some artistic trends which had developed in his own day, e.g., *trompe l'œil* or "illusionistic" painting and "realistic" drama. But he himself had no sympathy with such art. Also, he recognized that in other kinds of art, the artist will often "distort" for creative purposes.[19] Aristotle, as will be shown in the following section, rejects "simple imitation" in his theory of drama. And Vasari, despite his prolonged praise of the "Mona Lisa" for its verisimilitude, concludes by saying of the painting's subject that "while looking at it one thinks it rather divine than human." [20] In saying this, he unwittingly departs from "simple imitation" and introduces another criterion of aesthetic value.

And yet, "simple imitation" dies hard. It is still extremely widespread among those who have not examined critically their beliefs about art. It

[17] Alfred Frankenstein, *After the Hunt* (University of California Press, 1953), p. 56.
[18] *Ibid.*, p. 82.
[19] Cf. *Sophist* 235.
[20] *Op. cit.*, p. 215.

is manifested in prevailing attitudes toward "modern art." Two recent Presidents of the United States have given public expression to these attitudes: one spoke of modern painting as "ham and eggs painting," and the other said, "To be modern you don't have to be crazy." These harsh judgments might be retracted if it were considered that the function of art is not that of "simple imitation" at all.

Let us now go on to see how the nature of art is described by other, more plausible theories of "imitation."

2. IMITATION OF "ESSENCES"

We have seen that some, though not all art, attempts to be "true to life," though it does not do this by literal "copying" of ordinary experience. Of all the arts, drama is, in one sense, most "lifelike" for it depicts human beings speaking and performing actions. Yet its "truth" does not consist simply in this. The way in which it "imitates" life is analyzed by Aristotle in his *Poetics*, probably the single most important work ever written in the theory of drama and of literature in general.

Aristotle is chiefly concerned with tragedy, the supreme form of drama. He defines "tragedy" as "an imitation of an action that is serious, complete, and of a certain magnitude . . . with incidents arousing pity and fear." [21] But he does not mean by "imitation" what is meant by the theory of "simple imitation." He repudiates this theory in the famous passage in which he contrasts "poetry" (i.e., literature) with "history." He says that "it is not the function of the poet to relate what has happened," [22] that is, the poet does not record a sequence of events as they actually occurred. The significance of poetry is far greater than that: "[Poetry] is a more philosophical and a higher thing than history, for poetry tends to express the universal, history the particular." [23]

In this pregnant sentence, Aristotle formulates a wholly different version of the "imitation"-theory of art. The dramatist, Aristotle says, does not record the details of any and all events that take place within a certain period of time. If he were to record "the particular" in this way, the work of art would be full of random, trivial occurrences like those cited by Milne — "people would go in and out without explanation," [24] and so on. Therefore the work would be diffuse and meaningless. But the dramatist attempts to make sense of human experience and to explain it. The writer of tragedy, specifically, wishes to show that the events of a man's

[21] *Op. cit.*, VI, pp. 8–9.
[22] *Ibid.*, IX, p. 13.
[23] *Ibid.*, IX, p. 13.
[24] Cf. above, p. 112.

life are not random and disconnected, but rather are tightly interrelated with each other, in the sense that one brings about the next, and that causes another, and all together lead inevitably to the catastrophe of tragedy. Tragedy in human experience is due to the kind of character a man has, which leads him to perform deeds that result in disaster. As Aristotle puts it, the tragic figure is a man "whose misfortune is brought about not by vice or depravity, but by some error or frailty" [25] — the well-known "tragic flaw." It is in showing the effects of having such a character that drama is "philosophical." The drama exhibits the *reasons* for the events which it depicts.

It cannot do this, however, by turning a "mirror" upon life. For life is "just one darn thing after another," in which the crucial events in a man's existence are spread out over so long a period of time, and are obscured by so many unimportant occurrences, that we cannot generally see the causes of his joy or misery. Hence Aristotle recognizes that the tragic artist *selects* from the inchoate raw material of "real life" — he does not indiscriminately "copy" it. The tragedian does not relate everything which just happens to occur to a man. He relates only what is vital to understanding him. Thus in a play like *Oedipus Rex*, virtually every line of dialogue, every decision made by a character, every event, plays a part in the unfolding of Oedipus' fate. The artist is, to be sure, concerned with "real life." Remember that tragedy "imitates men in action." [26] However, it strips away the trivia and oddments of experience. Thus in the fairly brief time which elapses in a play like *Oedipus*, all of the hero's life is "telescoped," so that we come to know everything that is basic to his character, and all of the major events in his life, including his tragic destiny.

Thus "imitation" is selective and creative. As a result, tragedy has far greater significance than it would have if it were "simple imitation." Aristotle says that "poetry tends to express the universal, history the particular." He goes on: "By the universal I mean how a person *of a certain type* will on occasion speak or act." [27] In other words, tragedy does not simply show us what happens to the "particular" man Oedipus. It shows what would happen to anyone who possessed a character like his, placed in a situation like that in which he finds himself. The forces that bring about Oedipus' downfall also operate in the lives of other men, though they may live at other times and in other places. The particular circumstances may be different, but the cause-effect relationships which underlie a man's life are basically the same. Hence drama reveals a "truth" about life that is more general and profound than a day-to-day biography.

Indeed, insofar as all of us suffer from some "error" or "frailty" which

25 *Op. cit.*, XIII, p. 16.
26 *Ibid.*, II, p. 4.
27 *Ibid.*, IX, p. 13. Italics added.

is responsible for our misfortune, tragedy reveals what is truly "universal" in human experience. In this respect, the tragic figure is "a man like ourselves." [28] Thus Aristotle accounts for what we commonly refer to as "the universal appeal" of the tragic hero. What happens to him happens to many people, and for the same reasons. The tragic hero embodies Everyman, and so we can "see ourselves in him."

WITH HIS THEORY, Aristotle takes a giant step forward in clarifying the nature of fine art. We must not ask of art that it should be a "literal duplication" of the ordinary course of experience. That is not what it is trying to do. Whereas "simple imitation" trivializes art, Aristotle shows us its importance and profundity.

Since the work of art is not merely a servile "copy," it must not be judged as such. Thus, Aristotle says, if the poet commits a factual mistake, "he is guilty of an error; but the error may be justified if the end of the art be thereby attained . . . if, that is, the effect of this or any other part of the poem is thus rendered more striking." [29]

Although drama seeks to clarify "real life," it has an independent life of its own. We must therefore approach it sympathetically, meeting it on its own terms. Aristotle goes so far as to say: "The tragic plot must not be composed of irrational parts. . . . But once the irrational has been introduced and an air of likelihood imparted to it, we must accept it in spite of absurdity." [30]

In these passages, Aristotle suggests that the work should be judged in terms of its inherent, *aesthetic* effectiveness. It creates its "effect" only if it possesses internal *unity*. The various parts of the work must be so tightly interrelated that "if any one of them is displaced or removed, the whole will be disjointed and disturbed. For a thing whose presence or absence makes no visible difference is not an organic part of the whole." [31] In tragedy, such "organic" unity is achieved by scrupulous selection of only those events relevant to the tragic theme, as we saw earlier. A drama which merely depicts a random succession of events is a gross artistic failure — Aristotle calls it "the worst kind of plot." [32] The dénouement must arise "out of the Plot itself." [33] Therefore Aristotle criticizes the device of *Deus ex Machina*, i.e., the sudden, miraculous appearance of a god or superhuman figure, who intervenes to resolve all the problems created within the play, and to tie up all the loose ends of the plot.

Here again Aristotle re-directs our whole approach to the work of art.

[28] *Ibid.*, XIII, p. 16.
[29] *Ibid.*, XXV, p. 35.
[30] *Ibid.*, XXIV, p. 34.
[31] *Ibid.*, VIII, pp. 12–13.
[32] *Ibid.*, IX, p. 14.
[33] *Ibid.*, XV, p. 20.

The crucial metaphor is no longer the "mirror" — something which is important only because it reflects something else outside of it. Rather the work is an "organism" — something which is self-contained and autonomous, something which is valuable in its own right.

WE HAVE SEEN that Aristotle alters drastically the meaning of "imitation" and thereby makes it far more plausible and illuminating as applied to fine art. Further, we have just seen that Aristotle emphasizes the inherent significance and value of art, and the necessity of meeting it on its own terms. Yet Aristotle himself never uses the term "fine art." He is concerned with literature, chiefly tragedy. When, in the foregoing discussion, I spoke of "art," it was a generalization from what Aristotle says about tragedy. The term "fine art" is unknown to Aristotle and the Greeks. It is, indeed, a fairly recent term, for the French term *beaux arts* ("arts of beauty") came into being only in the seventeenth century, and the English term only in the following century.

Aristotle's discussion in the *Poetics* was, however, elaborated by later thinkers into a theory of "fine art" generally. We shall call this the theory of "imitation of essences."

We use the words "essence" and "essential" in ordinary speech to refer to what is "indispensable" or "most important." So we object to someone who is presenting us with superfluous details, "Never mind that. What is the *essence* of the matter?" This reflects the usage of the term in philosophy and theory of art. In philosophy, "essence" signifies those properties or characteristics which an object must possess if it is to be an object of a certain class or kind. Thus it is essential for a being to be "rational" if he is to be considered a man. Anything that is not-rational is not human. So we assert the essence of a kind of thing when we give a definition of, e.g., "man." By contrast, individual things possess properties which are not essential to their being of a certain kind. It is "accidental" whether a particular man is tall or short, dark or fair, Greek or American. Whichever he is, he is still human if he possesses the "essence" of man.

Therefore the "essence" is what is shared in common by all members of a certain class. Now we can understand how Aristotle's theory of tragedy serves as the basis for the "essence"-theory. You will remember that for Aristotle the tragic hero is not merely an individual, but a man "of a certain type" who embodies characteristics common to other men. Therefore tragedy "expresses" the "universal." On the "essence"-theory, art transcends the particular, to which "simple imitation" confines it, by ignoring the "accidental" properties of a thing. Hence all art has universal significance.

"Imitation of essences" is the central and seminal concept in thinking about art throughout much of modern times. Specifically, it dominates aesthetic thought and criticism during the so-called "neoclassical" period, from approximately 1550 to 1750.[34] Chiefly through the enormous influence of the *Poetics*, first translated from the Greek in 1498, it enters into Italian, French, and English thought. Although the theory has, in the last two centuries, largely receded, it still persists in contemporary ways of thinking and speaking about art.

We shall study it in two leading British critics of the mid-eighteenth century, Dr. Samuel Johnson (who is probably best known through Boswell's famous *Life*), and Sir Joshua Reynolds. These two men, who were close personal friends, were the pre-eminent spokesmen for literature and the visual arts in their time. A critical analysis of their writings will enable us to see the strengths and weaknesses of "essence"-theory.

AT TIMES DR. JOHNSON seems to expound "simple imitation." Thus he uses the Platonic metaphor which typifies this theory: "*Shakespeare is above all writers . . . the poet of nature; the poet that holds up to his readers a faithful mirror of manners and of life.*"[35] But like Aristotle, Johnson does not consider this the "mirror" of literal "copying." For he says of Shakespeare's dialogue that it "[seems] to have been gleaned *by diligent selection* out of common conversation."[36] So "real life" is only the starting-point for the artist, it is not all of art.

Having rejected "simple imitation," Johnson takes the "imitation of essences" to be the true function of art. It is his chief praise of Shakespeare that the artist depicts the "universal" in human experience: "His characters are not modified by the customs of particular places, unpractised by the rest of the world . . . or by the accidents of transient fashions or temporary opinions. . . . His persons act and speak by the influence of those general passions and principles by which all minds are agitated."[37] As was noted in our discussion of Aristotle, it is because the character of the tragic hero is shared by other men that his appeal is so widespread. So Johnson says that "As [Shakespeare's] personages act upon principles arising from genuine passion, very little modified by particular forms, their pleasures and vexations are communicable to all times and to all places; they are natural and therefore durable."[38] Thus the artist "imitates nature," but it is "*general* nature," the eighteenth-century counterpart of Aristotle's "universal."

[34] Authoritative historical accounts will be found in René Wellek, *A History of Modern Criticism*, Vol. I (Yale University Press, 1955), and George Saintsbury, *A History of Criticism*, Vol. II (New York: Dodd, Mead, 1902).

[35] "Preface to *Shakespeare*," in *Johnson: Prose and Poetry*, The Reynard Library, ed. Wilson (Harvard University Press, 1951), p. 491; cf., also, p. 493. By permission of the Harvard University Press and Rupert Hart-Davis, publishers.

[36] *Ibid.*, p. 492. Italics added.

[37] *Ibid.*, p. 491.   [38] *Ibid.*, p. 496.

In the visual arts, similarly, Reynolds repudiates the "vulgar idea of imitation," [39] i.e., "simple imitation": "nature herself is not to be too closely copied." [40] Rather, the artist, by observing many objects of a certain class or kind, can distinguish between the merely "accidental" properties and those which make up the "essence," what Reynolds calls "the invariable general form." [41] In this way, indeed, the artist achieves greater "lifelikeness" than he would through "simple imitation." Reynolds says that the artist who knows the "general character" of trees can produce "a more true resemblance of trees" [42] than one who paints trees with particular attention to specific details. If we can understand what Reynolds means by this, we can understand what is central to "essence"-theory. Think of the difference between a crude, though moderately well-lighted and "accurate" photograph of a single tree, which reproduces all of its details, and an artful sketch which leads us to say, "That captures the very essence of trees" — their height and grace and leafiness. The sketch need not represent any particular tree in the world; it may be only a few deft, economical lines. But that may be enough to "catch," as we say, "what trees are like." In using phrases of this sort, we are voicing the "imitation of essence"-theory.

We can sum up our exposition of this theory by quoting Reynolds' concise statement: "the whole beauty and grandeur of the art consists, in my opinion, in being able to get above all singular forms, local customs, particularities, and details of every kind." [43]

Now LET US GO DEEPER into this theory. To begin with, let me make explicit something that, perhaps, the reader has already thought of: a work of literature or painting cannot depict *nothing but* an "essence." An "essence" is, to repeat, a characteristic or property shared by all members of a certain class, by virtue of which they are members of that class. But when an essence is present in some particular object, it never exists by itself, but always along with some "accidental" properties. A particular man is never just the embodiment of "man-in-general"; he is also red-haired, or black-haired, or bald, he speaks with a certain accent, or perhaps he is an only child. These properties make him *just this* man. An essence exists by itself, without any accompanying characteristics, only when it is abstracted from the objects which share it. A definition does this. Thus the definition of "man" need make no reference to the color of hair, for example, whereas the description of a particular man does.

[39] Sir Joshua Reynolds, *The Discourses* (Oxford University Press, 1907), Disc. XIII, p. 198.
[40] *Ibid.*, Disc. III, p. 23; cf., also, p. 33.
[41] Letter to *The Idler*, no. 82, *op. cit.*, p. 256.
[42] *Ibid.*, Disc. XI, p. 169.
[43] *Ibid.*, Disc. III, p. 26.

Now let us apply this to the "imitation of essence"-theory. A drama or painting can show the essence of "man" or "tree" only by depicting some *particular* object of this kind. The tragic figure, we have said, is in some respect Everyman. But Hamlet is also a Danish prince, about thirty years old, "fat, and scant of breath," who as a child played with Yorick. However, it is not merely such biographical characteristics as these which are most important from the standpoint of art. All that the tragic figure thinks and says, his emotions, motives, and deeds, must unite to make him, in the eyes of the reader, a rounded, plausible *individual* human being. The essence which he embodies must be vitalized and given flesh and blood. Only so can he be interesting and credible aesthetically. The significance of the tragic hero can be "universal," he can seem to us, as Aristotle says, "a man like ourselves," only if he is *a* man.

Though Reynolds and Johnson emphasize the "general," they recognize that concrete details can, indeed must, enter into the work. Reynolds is "ready to allow" that "some circumstances of minuteness and particularity frequently tend to give an air of truth to a piece, and to interest the spectator in an extraordinary manner." [44] Again Reynolds says that "he that does not at all express particulars, expresses nothing." [45] And Johnson adds to his praise of Shakespeare that his characters are highly individual and "distinct from each other." [46]

That it is not enough to "imitate essences" is made painfully clear by those works which attempt to do only that. These are the works which attempt to depict human "types," without any of the particular details requisite to an individual human being. Many such works were written during the neoclassical period, in conformity to the "imitation of essence"-theory, but unhappily, they are also being produced today. Of such works we say that they are "cold" and "hollow." Their characters lack plausibility, or, as we commonly say, they do not "come to life." They are merely walking mouthpieces of timidity or avarice or virtue. It is for this reason that allegory is often so stultifyingly dull. Dr. Johnson states the "essence"-theory at its worst when, at one point, he says: "In the writings of other poets a character is too often an individual; in those of Shakespeare it is commonly a species." [47] But as Johnson himself recognizes, these characters are not *merely* species. If they were, then Lear, Macbeth, and Iago would not have retained their hold upon men's minds for so many centuries.

We may conclude that the definition of "fine art" in terms of "imita-

[44] *Ibid.*, Disc. IV, pp. 37–38.
[45] *Ibid.*, Disc. XI, p. 161.
[46] *Op. cit.*, p. 492.
[47] *Ibid.*, p. 491.

tion of essences" must be expanded if it is to do justice to the value of art. If, as Reynolds says, the goal of art is "to produce a pleasing effect upon the mind," [48] a view which is shared by Johnson, then the work must possess vitality, richness, and credibility. The imitation of essence alone will not suffice to achieve this.

Now WE TURN to an even more basic issue. We must examine further the meaning of "essence." Specifically, how do we *know* what the essence of a kind, such as "man," is? Reynolds, as we have noted, holds that "by the observation of [great] numbers" of particular things we can, "even without seeking after it," come to know "the invariable general form." [49] But if we examine the members of a class such as "man," in search of a property common to all of them, and to them alone, we shall find a great many such properties. Thus it is true of all men that they possess capacities for vision not found in other animals, they are "featherless bipeds," they are capable of laughter. And yet we would hesitate to say that any of these is the *essence* of "man." For as we have seen, "essence" usually has the connotation of what is "crucial" or "most important." The essence of man must be not merely a property which is distinctive of all men; it must also be a property which is "crucial" to man in the sense that it explains a good deal else about him. Thus if *reason* is the essence of man, we know that men are capable of using concepts and symbols in abstract thinking, that their actions need not be the product of momentary impulse but can be "thought out," that indeed all life can be organized thoughtfully and intelligently. Hence reason is much more crucial to man than the fact that he is a "featherless biped."

Now let us again ask — how do we know what the essence of a kind is? Reynolds is confident that we can all know and agree upon it. But, as you are probably aware, there are many different conceptions of the essence of "man." What is the most important thing about him? I have just mentioned the ancient view of man as the "rational animal." However, a number of influential theories have recently contended that reason is only a trivial human characteristic. More important is man's will or desire, according to voluntaristic theories such as Schopenhauer's, or unconscious, irrational forces, according to some recent psychologies. Then there is the Christian conception of man as the creature of God, and the mechanistic conception of him as a complicated physico-chemical structure. All of these theories purport to describe the essence of man, in the sense of "essence" stated above. But what we find in them is not *the* essence, but a multiplicity of "essences."

[48] *Op. cit.,* Disc. XIII, p. 206; cf., similarly, p. 137.
[49] *Ibid.,* p. 256.

Let us apply this analysis to art. We said, in our discussion of Aristotle and Dr. Johnson, that the tragic hero is a "universal" figure, that his dilemma is a microcosm of the "human predicament." And yet the great tragedies themselves present very different conceptions of the nature of man and human destiny. There are significant differences in the works of the two older Greek tragedians, Aeschylus and Sophocles, and enormous differences between these two and the later Euripides. In the modern treatment of Greek tragic characters by the contemporary existentialist J.-P. Sartre, e.g., *The Flies*, the interpretation of the "essence of man" is poles apart from that of Aeschylus. All these works cannot be said to be depicting *the* essence of human experience. Only if we dogmatically assume that the works of just one of these artists, e.g., Aeschylus, "imitates" the "invariable general form" of human destiny, could we speak of *the* essence. But then, to be consistent, we would also have to say that the other tragedies are devoid of artistic value, because they fail to "imitate the essence." This conclusion would certainly not be congruent with what we believe about these great works of art.

Let us take another example, this time from the visual arts. Look at Kollwitz' study of "Parents" (see Plate 14). It would be perfectly natural to say that this "captures the essence of grief." Look also at the Saint-Gaudens sculpture entitled "Grief" (see Plate 15). Again the same response would be in order. Notice that in both cases the work seems to "capture the essence" largely by minimizing "minuteness and particularity" of detail. They depict grief itself, in an elemental and uncomplicated way. Hence they illustrate clearly the "essence"-theory. And yet, if we compare these works among themselves, we can see how ambiguous the phrase "capture the essence of — " really is. For the "essences" are different in each case. In the Saint-Gaudens, grief is detached, stolid, and serene; in the Kollwitz, it overwhelms and crushes the sufferer. The essence is rendered differently because of the differences in the artists' emotional interpretations of the subject, the artistic "style" of each, and so on.

We can sum up this discussion by putting the following questions to the exponents of "imitation of essence"-theory: "Do you mean that art shows the universal significance of its subject, no matter how it construes that 'essence'? Or do you mean that there is just *the* one essence of, e.g., 'tragic destiny' or 'grief,' which can be known and 'imitated' by all artists? If the latter, then the range of art becomes severely limited."

Johnson and Reynolds, like the seventeenth and eighteenth centuries generally, give no consistent answer to these questions. At various places in his writings,[50] Johnson recognizes the limitless variety of "nature," so that, presumably, various essences of a class might be depicted. And

[50] Cf. *Rambler*, nos. 63, 70, 125.

Reynolds, in his judgments of specific artists, makes room for highly diverse works of art. Preponderantly, however, they believe that the "types" of things in the world have a well-defined essence. Hence works of art must, on the whole, depict very much the same essence. Johnson says that "though nature itself, philosophically considered, be inexhaustible, yet its general effects on the eye and on the ear are uniform, and incapable of much variety of description." [51] Specifically, Johnson thinks that human nature is fundamentally the same in all times and places: "the passions of men . . . are uniform." [52]

However, as we have seen, the nature of man has been interpreted, historically, in opposite ways. The eighteenth century was too prone to assume general agreement about human nature. Moreover, the thinkers of this period defined the essence of "man" by the attitudes and values of their own culture. "When the critics appealed to general human nature, to man in the abstract, they often had in mind only the man of their own time." [53] This man can be characterized by using some of the key words of this period —"taste," "decorum," "good sense." He is a man who dresses, speaks, and acts in the conventional manner of his society. But it is not difficult to see how this conception of man would fail to hold for other cultures, which are less simple, stable, and traditionalized. In other words, the eighteenth century's "universal man" is not truly universal. There is therefore unconscious irony in Reynolds' caution that "almost every one is apt to be guided by . . . local prejudices, who has not chastized his mind . . . by the eternal invariable idea of nature." [54] It is precisely because there is no general agreement concerning this "eternal idea" that we must be prepared to admit *many* essences into works of art. We may note, however, that Reynolds and his contemporaries are very far indeed from being the only thinkers who have confused the beliefs of their culture with "the eternal invariable idea of nature."

Now FINALLY, there is one other thing to see if we are to arrive at a balanced, critical understanding of the "imitation of essence"-theory.

This theory presumably offers a definition of "fine art," i.e., it attempts to tell us what fine art *is*. But it also functions as a theory which urges upon us what art *ought to be*. It is not so much a *description* as a *prescription*. Instead of describing the nature of all objects generally considered works of fine art, it excludes many such objects from the area of art. On the strength of our discussion thus far, we can tell which

51 Samuel Johnson, *The Rambler* (London: Bohn, 1850), no. 36, p. 65.
52 *Ibid.*, p. 66.
53 Wellek, *op. cit.*, p. 23.
54 *Op. cit.*, Disc. VII, pp. 106–107.

these are: (1) works which eschew the "universal" in favor of close attention to the particular features of the subject; (2) works which violate "general nature," as this was understood by the eighteenth century, by depicting the unusual, the fantastic, the bizarre, and even what is morbid and pathological.

The rejection of Class 1 is summed up in Johnson's famous dictum: "The business of a poet is to examine, not the individual, but the species; to remark general properties and large appearances. He does not number the streaks of the tulip, or describe the different shades in the verdure of the forest." [55] And yet many poets and painters have taken it to be their "business" to dwell upon the uniqueness of the person or event which they depict. Reynolds criticizes severely one instance of such art — the paintings of Rembrandt. This artist, he writes, gave "exact representations of individual objects." But "these particularities cannot be nature; for how can that be the nature of man, in which no two individuals are the same?" [56] Reynolds does not make it clear whether these works, because of their "particularity," are *bad* art, or not "art" at all. If "art" is defined as "imitation of essence or general nature," and if Reynolds' description of Rembrandt's works is accurate, then the second alternative follows — these paintings are just not "fine art." If this conclusion seems too drastic, then "essence"-theory must be given up as a complete theory of fine art. If, on the other hand, the theory holds that Rembrandt's paintings are art-objects, but that they are of little value, then the theory runs up against the consensus of critical opinion, which rates these masterly works very highly.

There are, indeed, many works which cannot be readily described by using the language of "essences" or "universals." Renoir's well-known "Girl with a Watering Can" depicts *this* pretty little girl, dressed in blue and white, with a ribbon in her hair. It is a charming and enormously popular work, but it is difficult to see what "essence" it "imitates." Reynolds' theory seems to be a plea against such art, in favor of art which treats of "universal" subjects.[57] Though the latter sort of art, e.g., tragedy, is clarified by the "essence"-theory, the theory does not encompass *all* art.

Art of Class 2 is ruled out by the "essence"-theory, because the theory insists that only what is conventional and familiar in experience is a "proper" subject for art. However, a great many objects which are commonly considered "works of art" depict the extraordinary and unfamiliar,

[55] Samuel Johnson, *History of Rasselas* (Clarendon Press, 1931), p. 62.
[56] *Op. cit.*, Disc. VII, p. 99.
[57] It is interesting that Reynolds has difficulty in deciding which subjects are genuinely "universal": "Strictly speaking, indeed, no subject can be of universal, hardly can it be of general, concern." He decides, however, that Greek, Roman and Biblical events are "sufficiently general for our purposes." — *Ibid.*, Disc. IV, p. 37.

and are, indeed, exciting to us precisely because of this. Some of the poetry of Coleridge, much of Surrealist art, and a great deal of recent literature and drama which treats of the abnormal, exemplify such art. Here again the "essence"-theory must decide whether such works are *bad*, or are not "works of art" at all, and here again the theory encounters grave difficulties, whichever alternative it accepts. Moreover, as we have seen, what the eighteenth-century thinkers consider "conventional" in human experience is largely what is conventional and familiar in the experience of their own time. Saintsbury caricatures their position wittily: "Just so the legendary King of Siam, had he written an *Art of Poetry*, would have said 'Follow nature, and do not talk about such unnatural things as ice and snow.' " [58]

LET US NOW SUM UP briefly our conclusions concerning the "imitation of essence"-theory: This theory makes clear the inadequacies of "simple imitation," for it shows us that the work of the artist is far more creative than mere "copying." He must select from, and give significance to, the events of ordinary experience. Furthermore, there are many works of art, including some of the greatest, of which we can and do justly say that they "capture the essence of — ." However, we have seen that this way of talking is ambiguous, for there are in the realm of art many different "essences" of, e.g., tragic destiny. Moreover, "imitation of essence" is not an adequate definition of all "fine art," nor is it, in itself, a sufficient condition of artistic value.

3. IMITATION OF THE "IDEAL"

Like "essence"-theory, this theory argues that the artist does not "copy" indiscriminately, but rather restricts himself to certain objects only. Dr. Johnson voices this theory: "It is justly considered as the greatest excellency of art, to imitate nature; but it is necessary to distinguish those parts of nature, which are *most proper* for imitation." [59]

By a "proper" subject, Johnson means one which is morally "decent," praiseworthy, and wholesome. The author and painter must either depict events which are, in themselves, praiseworthy, e.g., a classic episode of heroism, or else he should "idealize" the "real life" object, by removing its moral imperfections. In the seventeenth and eighteenth centuries this is known as the doctrine of *la belle nature* — "beautiful nature." This doctrine includes not only moral, but also aesthetic "idealization"; however, in the following discussion, we shall be concerned with "imitation of the *moral* ideal."

[58] *Op. cit.*, p. 456.
[59] *Rambler* no. 4, *op. cit.*, p. 7. Italics added.

One can hold consistently to both the "essence"-theory and the "ideal"-theory only if he makes a certain assumption, namely, that the essences of man and nature are always morally good. Otherwise these theories will not always agree as to which objects are "works of fine art." For a work may depict an essence which is evil or morally neutral, or, on the other hand, it may embody a moral ideal which is not found universally in nature. Dr. Johnson does not, however, make this optimistic assumption: "the real state of sublunary nature . . . partakes of good and evil, joy and sorrow, mingled with endless variety of proportion." [60] Again he says that "a play in which the wicked prosper, and the virtuous miscarry . . . is a just representation of the common events of human life." [61] And yet Johnson insists that a play should always depict the triumph of virtue. Here is the famous passage in which he castigates Shakespeare for violating "poetic justice," i.e., the doctrine that the good must be shown to be happy, the wicked unhappy: "[Shakespeare] sacrifices virtue to convenience, and is so much more careful to please than to instruct, that he seems to write without any moral purpose . . . [he] makes no just distribution of good or evil. . . . [He] carries his persons indifferently through right and wrong, and at the close dismisses them without further care." [62]

So the artist must be selective not merely in ignoring the "streaks of the tulip" in favor of "general properties." That is the difference between "simple imitation" and "imitation of essences." The artist must also, if need be, ignore or falsify "the common events of human life" on behalf of morality. Since Johnson does not hold that the world is essentially "good," this "ideal"-theory is wholly distinct from the "essence"-theory.

It is now even more imperative than before to distinguish a theory which asserts what art *is*, from one which urges what art *ought* to be. It is clear that the "ideal"-theory is of the latter sort. Johnson and Reynolds nowhere deny that works which use sordid or unwholesome subjects are works "of art." But they express the conviction that such works must be less than wholly good. In other words, the "ideal"-theory lays down a criterion of the *value* of art.

Now why, according to the "ideal"-theory, is art valuable when it depicts "proper" subjects? Is it because the morality of the work enhances its "pleasing effect upon the mind" [63] during the experience of aesthetic perception? Or is its wholesomeness valuable because it promotes virtuous feelings and character traits in the audience, and therefore makes them better men in their everyday lives? To put the question another way: is "imitation of the ideal" part of the *intrinsic* value of a work, when

---

[60] "Preface to *Shakespeare*," *op. cit.*, p. 494.
[61] "Notes on *King Lear*," *op. cit.*, p. 593.
[62] "Preface to *Shakespeare*," *op. cit.*, pp. 497–498.
[63] Reynolds, *op. cit.*, Disc. XIII, p. 206.

it is apprehended aesthetically, or is it *instrumentally* valuable, because of the beneficial consequences which it brings about?

Johnson gives no unequivocal answer. It is clear, however, that he is extremely sensitive to the moral influence of literature upon the reader. He insists that in all areas of life "the first requisite is the religious and moral knowledge of right and wrong . . . we are perpetually moralists." [64] Hence, he says, "it is always a writer's duty to make the world better." [65] "Those authors, therefore, are to be read at schools that supply most axioms of prudence, most principles of moral truth." [66] And yet, despite these passages, Johnson does not plead for "didactic" literature, i.e., literature which "preaches" to the reader, which obviously tries to inculcate "principles of moral truth" at the expense of providing aesthetic enjoyment. Johnson believes that "the end of poetry is to instruct by pleasing." [67] However, art cannot "please" unless it is moral.

Let us examine the truth of this view.[68] Let us ask whether there *are* any works which "please," even though their subject or their treatment of the subject is not "moral." For Dr. Johnson, a work, to be "moral," must depict "poetic justice." An obvious example of works which fail to do so are those which are criticized by Johnson, viz., the tragedies of Shakespeare. Most notably *King Lear* fails on this score. Yet *Lear* is usually considered one of the supremely great tragedies, and even one of the supreme works of art.

As Johnson himself reiterates, the plays of Shakespeare are extraordinarily plausible and convincing. He says that the characters in these plays "act and speak as the reader thinks that he should himself have spoken or acted on the same occasion." [69] And it is *Lear* which Johnson describes, in the passage already quoted, as "a just representation of the common events of human life." He says also that the reader's mind is "strongly seized" by Shakespeare. But if the characters and events in *Lear* are convincing, vivid, and dramatic, are we justified in demanding of it that virtue must triumph? If we are to read the work aesthetically, we must read it "sympathetically," i.e., we must meet it on its own terms, and then see whether it is a unified and moving work of art. The terms in which it describes human experience may differ from our own, but if the work is aesthetically persuasive, then, as Aristotle says, "we must accept it." [70] If we did not read literature "sympathetically"

---

[64] *Life of Milton, op. cit.,* p. 822.
[65] "Preface to *Shakespeare,*" *op. cit.,* p. 498.
[66] *Life of Milton, op. cit.,* p. 822.
[67] "Preface to *Shakespeare,*" *op. cit.,* p. 494.
[68] The problem of the moral effect of art upon its audience will be treated later (Chap. 13).
[69] "Preface to *Shakespeare,*" *op. cit.,* pp. 492–493; cf., also, p. 503.
[70] Cf. above, p. 119.

in this way, how could we read and enjoy works as diverse as those of the Greeks, Dante, Shakespeare, Thomas Hardy, and Sartre? If Johnson were to criticize *Lear* because its characters are implausible, or the play itself disjointed, his criticism would be on aesthetic grounds. But is he not criticizing the play for irrelevant reasons when he complains that the loyal and loving Cordelia dies at the end?

We can also look in the visual arts for works which are aesthetically valuable, though they fail to "imitate the ideal." Here an instructive example is the painter and engraver Hogarth. For Hogarth was a contemporary of Reynolds who, both in theory and in his art, poked fun at the "Grand Style" preached by Reynolds. As you may know, much of his work depicts corruption and debauchery among exceedingly unappetizing people. Yet his works are highly esteemed for their vividness and gusto (see Plate 16). Reynolds concedes that Hogarth shows "genius" in his portrayal of "low and confined objects." But Reynolds contends that "the praise which we give must be as limited as its object," [71] i.e., Hogarth's subjects being of a low order, his work must necessarily be inferior.

THUS REYNOLDS, although he recognizes the artist's power, tends to evaluate the work primarily in terms of the subject matter. When "ideal"-theory judges the work *solely* in terms of the subject, it falls into the error pointed out earlier,[72] i.e., it judges the *total* work of art in terms of only *one* component of the work. This mistake is committed by the neoclassical critic Félibien (1666), who sets up an "obsequious hierarchy" of subjects: "since the figure of man is the most perfect work of God, he who paints man is the most excellent among painters; next comes he who paints living animals rather than dead things without movement; then he who paints landscapes, and finally flowers and fruits." [73]

But the subject *alone* cannot determine the value of the work. One of Cézanne's paintings of "flowers and fruits," e.g., "The Blue Vase," is surely far superior to any number of portraits. Looked at the other way, a work of painting or literature which depicts a morally noble or edifying subject, may be dull or pompous or bombastic. This is true of a great deal of "didactic" art. The subject must be so treated by the artist that the total work possesses vitality and power. Therefore the "ideal"-theory is inadequate even as a theory of artistic value, if it concentrates solely on the morality of the subject. We must take account of all else that makes up the concrete work of art.

This inadequacy in the "ideal"-theory is found in all forms of "imita-

---

[71] *Op. cit.*, Disc. III, p. 34; cf., however, Disc. XI, p. 166.
[72] Cf. above, pp. 114, 116, 122–124.
[73] Lionello Venturi, *History of Art Criticism*, trans. Marriott (New York: Dutton, 1936), p. 127.

tion"-theory. For any theory of art which takes "imitation" to be central places the emphasis on what lies outside of the work of art, i.e., what is "imitated." This "model" may be "ordinary experience" or "essences" or "the ideal." The theory then focuses attention on the artistic representation of this model. But we can only understand the work of art when we take into consideration not only its subject, but also its sensory attractiveness, its imaginative overtones, its formal structure, and a great deal else. And these are not simply ornamentation added to the subject. All of these elements together are absorbed into the unity which *is* the work of art. It is the *whole* work of art that we are concerned with in aesthetic experience, and it is therefore the whole work of art that we must consider in explaining the value of art.

THE THEORIES OF "IMITATION" have persisted in the minds of men because they remind us of what is clearly true — that art draws upon human experience, and attempts to represent and clarify it. This is notably true of the "imitation of essence"-theory. If we recognize its tie to life, we judge art in terms of "verisimilitude" ("simple imitation"), universality ("essence"-theory), or morality ("ideal"-theory). On the other hand, we must recognize, as Aristotle did, that the work of art has a life of its own. When we appreciate it aesthetically, we are concerned with the work itself. If we want to do justice to the intrinsic significance of art, we judge it in terms of its inherent unity, vividness, and power. It is this tension between "life" and "art" that is at the heart of all "imitation"-theories.

Finally, we have seen that all three versions of "imitation"-theory are inadequate in a further respect. They do not describe accurately *all* works of art. Hence they cannot provide a sound foundation for art criticism. There are many works which cannot be said to "copy ordinary experience," many others which do not embody "essences," and yet others which do not "imitate the ideal." Indeed, there are many works of art which cannot be characterized by *any* of these theories. Works of art are so diverse and complicated that they elude the definitions of "imitation"-theory. This theory gives us *some* truths about *some* works of art, but not the *whole* truth about *all*.

BIBLIOGRAPHY

* Aristotle. *Poetics.*
* Johnson, Samuel. "Preface to *Shakespeare.*"
* Reynolds, Joshua. *The Discourses.*
* Weitz, *Problems in Aesthetics.* Pp. 5–49.

Butcher, S. H. *Aristotle's Theory of Poetry and Fine Art*, 3rd ed. London: Macmillan, 1902. Chaps. I–III.

Gilbert, Katherine E., "Aesthetic Imitation and Imitators in Aristotle," *Philosophical Review*, Vol. XLV (Nov., 1936), 558–573.

Lovejoy, Arthur O., " 'Nature' as Aesthetic Norm," *Modern Language Notes*, Vol. XLII (Nov., 1927), 444–450.

McKeon, Richard, "Literary Criticism and the Concept of Imitation in Antiquity," *Modern Philology*, Vol. XXXIV (Aug., 1936), 1–35.

Osborne, *Aesthetics and Criticism*. Chap. III.

Pepper, *The Basis of Criticism in the Arts*. Chap. 5.

Wellek, René. *A History of Modern Criticism*. Yale University Press, 1955. Vol. I, Chaps. 1, 5.

QUESTIONS

1. "[There] can be no such thing as pure sensation in the sense of absolutely passive reception of impressions from without." — Osborne, *Aesthetics and Criticism*, p. 60.
   What does this imply for the theory of "simple imitation"?
2. What is the meaning (or meanings) of "realism" in art? In what sense are the novels of Zola "realistic"? In what sense are Dutch *genre* paintings "realistic"? What is the relation between such realism and "simple imitation"?
3. Read in Plato, *Symposium* 210–212, *Phaedrus* 248, *Sophist* 234–235. Which school of "imitation"-theory does Plato belong to?
4. Find examples of neoclassical literature and painting which show the influence of "essence"-theory upon the artist. How do you decide that these works embody an "essence"? What are the most common formal and stylistic characteristics of neoclassical art? How are they related to the depiction of "essences"?
5. Oscar Wilde said, at the close of the nineteenth century: "We are no longer in art concerned with the type. It is with the exception that we have to do." What theory of art is Wilde rejecting? Can you give any examples from modern art which illustrate his contention? Are such works ever as great as those which depict the "type" in human nature?
6. Granting that moral "nobility" is not essential to *all* art, is it essential to all *great* art? Which works of art are commonly considered "great"? Is the subject matter of any of these works morally ignoble or crude?
7. Does music ever "imitate"? In what sense of "imitation"? Does music ever imitate "essences"? Compare Mendelssohn's "Hebrides" Overture with Debussy's "La Mer." Strauss' "Don Quixote" imitates everyday sounds. Does it also "imitate" human character? Discuss.
8. All of the "imitation"-theories are *cognitive* theories, i.e., they claim that art gives *knowledge*. Does a work's cognitive significance enhance its aesthetic value? Does it do so *always*?
   Which conceptions of art do you think would deny the cognitive function of art?

6

Formalism

1. MODERN ART — THE ORIGINS OF FORMALISM

The formalist theory of art is in many respects the antithesis of "imitation"-theory. Whereas "imitation"-theory is the oldest theory of art, formalism, in the version which we shall be studying, is one of the newest. Whereas "imitation"-theory has always been believed uncritically by the "ordinary" man, formalism is a direct challenge to the beliefs of "simple bodies." It tries to show that what "common sense" takes to be "art" is not really art at all, and that most people approach art in the wrong way and therefore are blind to its value. But the most important difference is this: "Imitation"-theory, as we have seen, emphasizes the close relation between art and human experience outside of art. Either art is a literal "mirror" of "life," or else it draws upon and tries to clarify "life." Formalism is completely opposed to this. Formalism argues that true art is wholly divorced from the doings and objects that make up ordinary experience. Art is a world of its own, with no responsibility to "copy" or borrow from "life." The values of art cannot be found in any other area of human experience. Art, if it is to be art, must be independent and self-sufficient.

Thus we can understand formalism as a vigorous challenge to "imitation"-

theory. Indeed, it is the most thorough challenge to that venerable theory in the history of aesthetics. But this is not simply a war between theorists of art. The war between imitationism and formalism began among the artists themselves. It has been fought in the "visual" arts, painting and sculpture, during the last hundred years. It was only after a radically new conception of the nature and value of art established itself in these arts that the theory of formalism arose.

Hence we can understand the theory only if we know something of the movements in painting and sculpture from which it developed. The historical discussion which follows is necessarily brief,[1] but it is indispensable. It may, moreover, introduce the student who is not familiar with painting to the most exciting and dramatic movement in recent art history — so-called "modern art."

This is the kind of art which is often identified, in the popular mind, with paintings that "don't look like anything," with portraits of girls in which the side and front views of their faces appear on the same plane, with pictures of disembodied feet and melting watches. It is little wonder that many people, steeped in "imitation"-theory, have considered such work to be a hoax, or the product of artistic clumsiness, or a stunt intended to "shock the bourgeoisie." One of the most famous pieces of modern sculpture, Brancusi's "Bird in Space" (see Plate 17), was the center of a *cause célèbre* during the twenties. Since, as one of the trial judges said, the piece "bears no resemblance to a bird," the customs officials ruled that it was not a work of art, and therefore could not enter the United States duty-free. At the trial at which this ruling was challenged, the government posed this question: "Mr. Brancusi claims that this object represents a bird. If you met such a bird out shooting, would you fire?" And yet the judges, in a classic decision, ruled on behalf of the sculptor. In their decision they recognized "the influence of modern schools of art" which have altered our conception of what "art" is.

What are these schools? Let us go back a century. Clive Bell, one of the leading formalists, writes: "About the middle of the nineteenth century art was as nearly dead as art can be."[2] A great deal of such art was "academic," in the bad sense, devoted to lifelike imitation of handsome people and attractive seascapes and landscapes. But the complacency of the period was jarred by a new and vital movement — the French "Impressionists."

---

[1] There are a number of excellent introductions to "modern art" which might be read along with this chapter. A very brief and elementary work is Alfred H. Barr, jr., *What Is Modern Painting?* 3rd. ed. (New York: Museum of Modern Art, 1946). More detailed treatments are Bernard S. Myers, *Modern Art in the Making* (New York: McGraw-Hill, 1950), Maurice Raynal, *Modern Painting* (Skira, n.d.), and Alfred H. Barr, jr., *Cubism and Abstract Art* (New York: Museum of Modern Art, 1936).

[2] Clive Bell, *Art* (London: Chatto and Windus, 1947), p. 177. All quotations from Clive Bell are used with the permission of the publishers.

These painters sought to capture the play of color, light, and shadow, on the objects of our visual experience. Since they were mainly concerned with such "impressions," they were less concerned than their contemporaries with the intrinsic dignity or importance of the "models" which they painted. They could depict atmospheric color by painting, indifferently, a haystack or Rouen Cathedral. (Monet used both.) Thus Impressionism anticipates one of the central tenets of "modern art" — that the "subject matter," i.e., the object or event shown in the painting, is of relatively slight importance. In another respect, too, the Impressionists exercise a great influence on later art. Here, however, their influence is indirect. Because of their interest in the appearance of light and color in the world, they concentrated their attention on the surfaces of things. Therefore they tended to slight the massiveness and solidity of the objects which they painted. Even so solid and monumental an object as Rouen Cathedral or the Doge's palace in Venice (see Plate 18) becomes, in Monet, shimmering and watery. For this reason, such painting seems often to be insubstantial and even flimsy. It lacks the massiveness which we find most obviously in sculpture and architecture, but which earlier painters had achieved in their own medium.

It is this deficiency which calls forth the work of the father of "modern art." In so far as one man can be said to give inspiration and direction to the chief artistic movements of the last seventy-five years, it is Cézanne. With him the term "form" takes on new prominence, as a result of which it is taken over as the name of the formalist theory.

Cézanne set himself to restore firmness and solidity to painting. The people and things which comprise the subject matter in his work have a real solidity and even dignity about them, as in the famous "The Card Players." (See Plate 19.) Color is used to render the "heaviness" or massiveness of objects. Equally important, Cézanne's paintings have great depth. Thus he can create a rhythmic interplay among the spatial relations which extend back from the picture plane. The spectator's eye passes over the overlapping planes of the painting, and he senses movement and tension as a result. These "plastic" relationships between the depicted masses constitute a large part of the meaning of "form" in Cézanne.

Thus the value of the work is to be found in the formal organization of the painterly devices of line, mass, plane, and color. The emphasis, then, falls on what is intrinsic and peculiar to painting, what cannot be shown or apprehended in any other way. There are two important corollaries. Primarily, in seeking to achieve these formal values, Cézanne resorts to pronounced "distortion" of what is given in nature. The human figure, the tree, the natural landscape which was Cézanne's model, are altered in order to satisfy the demands of the painting.[3] The artist foregoes "imitation." Moreover, Cézanne's work is a further step toward disparaging the impor-

[3] Cf. above, p. 113, n. 10.

tance of subject matter. Some of his greatest paintings depict objects which, in "real life," are of little importance — apples, oranges, and water tumblers. Similarly, we may be surprised to learn that his contemporary Degas, who is well known for his charming and affecting portrayal of ballet girls, considered his subject matter merely "a pretext for the design." Again, the sculptor Rodin said that, for the purposes of sculpture, "a woman, a mountain, a horse" are of precisely the same significance.

Thus, during the last quarter of the nineteenth century, painters and sculptors set up a ground swell of artistic autonomy. Art is not dependent upon or responsible to "life"; its purposes and values are uniquely its own. As the artist Léger was to say, in 1935, "During the past fifty years the entire effort of artists has consisted of a struggle to free themselves from . . . old bonds." [4] And yet the artists just mentioned still had this much "imitation" in their work — they depicted objects which were recognizably like the objects of our ordinary experience. After the turn of the century, artists move toward eliminating all vestiges of "representation." The plastic and color values of painting can be most fully exploited when the work does not have to be concerned with verisimilitude. The painter Kandinsky says that "The artist frees himself from the object, because it prevents him from expressing himself exclusively through purely pictorial means."

The art historian Maurice Raynal says of Picasso's "Les Demoiselles d'Avignon" (see Plate 20), which was completed in 1907: "It stood for nothing short of a revolution in the art of painting and a new vision of reality." [5] The preliminary studies made by the artist prior to the final work recapitulate the development of this "revolution." [6] At first, the work is intended to be representational, and even has some moral significance. In the later studies the formal structure of the work becomes more important, until finally the moral element is "eliminated in favor of a purely formal figure composition, which as it develops becomes more and more dehumanized and abstract." [7] In the finished product, faces and bodies have been broken up into designs of angles and planes. Similarly, the colors in the flesh tones are often wholly unlifelike. In the movement of Cubism, which follows from "Les Demoiselles," natural objects are treated even more "abstractly." They are "analyzed" into plane designs, often so drastically that it is only with the aid of the painting's title that we can tell what the model was. But that is not important. As Léger says, " 'What does that represent?' has no meaning." [8] What is important is the creation of an intrinsically arresting geometrical design. Finally, even a tenuous relation to "reality" is given up. In "nonobjective" art, such as that of Kandinsky,

[4] Quoted in Goldwater and Treves, *op. cit.*, p. 424.
[5] *Op. cit.*, p. 107.
[6] Cf. Alfred H. Barr, jr., *Picasso: Fifty Years of His Art* (New York: Museum of Modern Art, 1946), pp. 54–57.
[7] *Ibid.*, p. 57.
[8] *Op. cit.*, p. 424.

Mondrian, and the Suprematists, there is no subject matter at all, properly speaking. The painting is a configuration of colored lines, arcs, and other shapes. It does not depict objects or people. Therefore the artist uses such titles as "Diagonal Line," or "Composition in White, Black, and Red" (see Plate 21). As the art historian Venturi puts it, the traditional goal of Western art, "imitation," is repudiated in favor of "creation."

SINCE MODERN ART IS, even at the present day, the object of such great antipathy and scorn, we will not be surprised to learn that, throughout its history, it has lacked sympathetic and appreciative audiences. The human mind is as conservative in the area of art as in most other things. And because modern art, particularly in this century, has broken so profoundly with the past, it cannot be appreciated by those who approach it in the same way that they look at earlier art. If they look for the representation of interesting or pretty or heroic subjects, they will be disappointed. If they do not have the patience and tolerance to gain familiarity with the work,[9] they will reject it out of hand.

Thus the modern artist has had to make his way against the indifference, ignorance, misunderstanding, and, almost literally, the "blindness" of his potential audience. As far back as 1878, the painter Whistler protested that people refused to look at his work as an intrinsic color composition:

> The vast majority of English folk can not and will not consider a picture as a picture, apart from any story which it may be supposed to tell.
> My picture of a *Harmony in Grey and Gold* is an illustration of my meaning — a snow scene with a single black figure and a lighted tavern. I care nothing for the past, present, or future of the black figure, placed there because the black was wanted at that spot. All that I know is that my combination of grey and gold is the basis of the picture. Now this is precisely what my friends cannot grasp.[10]

The formalist theory of art came into being as a protest against such misunderstanding in the artistic public, and as an attempt to educate people to an appreciation of contemporary painting and sculpture. Formalism is the theoretical vindication of modern art.

2. FORMALISM — THE THEORY OF ARTISTIC AND AESTHETIC "PURITY"

The leading formalists, Clive Bell and Roger Fry, were practicing art critics who found themselves writing for a public which could not or would

[9] Cf. above, chap. 3, sec. 2.
[10] Quoted in Goldwater and Treves, *op. cit.*, pp. 346–347.

not appreciate the most important artistic movement of their time. They found that people were seeking in art a representation of "real life" objects, and responding to the painting as though it were "life": "Before a work of art people who feel little or no emotion for pure form find themselves at a loss. They are deaf men at a concert. . . . And so they read into the forms of the work those facts and ideas for which they are capable of feeling emotion, and feel for them the emotions that they can feel — the ordinary emotions of life. . . . They treat . . . a picture as though it were a photograph." [11] Thus they fail to experience the distinctive and precious values of art. Bell announces the campaign of the formalists: "Can we induce the multitude to seek in art, not edification, but exaltation?" [12]

The strategy of the formalists is daring. They try to "induce the multitude" by arguing that what it takes to be "art" is not really that at all, and what it considers aesthetic appreciation is only a corruption of true aesthetic perception. Paintings which merely depict "real life" things and events are not, properly speaking, "fine art." And when people see in paintings only a representation of "real life," they are not having a genuine aesthetic experience. The public had thought that modern art was artistically counterfeit or esoteric. Bell and Fry argue just the opposite: only modern art can truly be called "fine art."

BELL LABELS as "Descriptive Painting," i.e., not true art, "Portraits of psychological and historical value . . . pictures that tell stories and suggest situations, illustrations of all sorts." [13] In such works "it is not their forms but the ideas or information suggested or conveyed by their forms that affect us." [14] The interest of such work for us depends on the interest we take in the person or historical episode which it depicts. Hence our attention shifts from the painting to "real life," and the value of the painting is not then inherent within the work itself. Fry says that "in so far as the artist relies on the associated ideas of the objects which he represents, his work is not completely free and pure." [15] Neither Fry nor Bell deny that such works can have great "psychological" interest for the spectator. They hold, however, that such work is only superficially like true painting in that it uses paints and canvas. But it is not genuine painting, and our response to it must be "impure."

What then is true art? The preceding discussion prepares us for the answer. "Fine art" (speaking now only of the visual arts) is defined as "the elements distinctive of the media of painting and sculpture, organized into a formal pattern which is aesthetically valuable." Fry lists these

[11] Bell, *op. cit.*, p. 29. Cf., similarly, Roger Fry, *Vision and Design* (New York: Brentano's, n.d.), pp. 70–71.
[12] *Op. cit.*, p. 265; cf., similarly, p. 81.   [13] *Ibid.*, p. 17.
[14] *Ibid.*, p. 17.   [15] *Op. cit.*, p. 242.

"elements of design" as line, mass, light and shade, and color.[16] A painting or sculpture is a work of art when these are so interrelated that the work possesses what Bell calls, in a phrase that has become famous, "significant form." [17] Bell defines "significant form" by reference to the aesthetic experience. It is the formal relation which arouses in the disinterested spectator the "aesthetic emotion." [18] This emotion is "peculiar," wholly unlike the emotions of "life." To apprehend form, and therefore to feel this emotion, "we need bring with us nothing from life, no knowledge of its ideas and affairs, no familiarity with its emotions. . . . [We] need bring with us nothing but a sense of form and color and a knowledge of three-dimensional space." [19]

The best way, probably the only way, to understand the kind of aesthetic experience these men are talking about, is to read their formalist analyses of specific paintings, particularly those written by Fry, who is one of the ablest critics of our time. A specimen of his analysis of a painting into the "rhythmic movements" of lines and planes was quoted in an earlier chapter.[20] The student should read other critiques by Fry, notably those in *Transformations*.[21] Throughout his criticism Fry speaks of the "plastic drama" which is created by the interplay and tension between the lines and masses of the work. Thus he describes, in a work by Poussin, the rhythms which are set up by the arm movements of the depicted characters, which "play over and across" the heavy, solid "volumes." [22]

The most striking feature of such criticism is, of course, its total disregard of representational subject matter. But clearly very little Western art has been as highly abstract or as totally "nonobjective" as the later "Post-Impressionist" schools. In the past (and indeed, even at the present, e.g., Rouault), great painters have depicted landscapes, or religious events, or domestic scenes. Would the formalists deny the name "art" to the lion's share of Western painting? At times, they seem to want to restrict the area of art to the Post-Impressionists, Byzantine art of the sixth century, and primitive art, such as that of Africa or Polynesia, which is distinguished by its "absence of representation" and "sublimely impressive form." [23]

But the formalists do not go this far. They hold that a representational work *can* be a work "of art," if it *also* possesses formal and plastic values. To determine whether it possesses "significant form," we must ignore or "look through" the subject matter. Bell says of Epstein's figure of Christ,

[16] *Op. cit.*, pp. 33–34.
[17] *Op. cit.*, p. 8.
[18] *Ibid.*, pp. 6–7.
[19] *Ibid.*, pp. 25, 27.
[20] Cf. above, p. 71.
[21] Roger Fry, *Transformations* (New York: Brentano's, n.d.).
[22] *Ibid.*, p. 19.
[23] *Art*, p. 23; cf., also, p. 130.

"It [matters] not a straw whether this statue, considered as a work of art, represented Jesus Christ or John Smith." [24] Bell says elsewhere: "if a representative form has value, it is as form, not as representation. The representative element in a work of art may or may not be harmful; always it is irrelevant." [25] Thus when people or objects are depicted in a painting, "[we] shall treat them as though they were not representative of anything." [26] They are to be seen (notice again the affinity to modern art) as patterns of line, mass, and color.

But even this will seem too restrictive to most people. Must we abandon our interest in subject matter in order to appreciate form? Can we not respond to the emotional and imaginative significance of the Crucifixion, or a landscape, or a Dutch household, as well as to the work's design? At times, particularly in his earlier writings, Fry held that we could do so. Such an experience would be possible when the emotions aroused by the "dramatic idea" and those evoked by the "plastic design" re-enforce or "fuse" with each other, e.g., when the subject matter expresses solemnity and the form is massive. But increasingly in his later thought Fry held that such fusion did not occur.[27] In his most searching analysis of this question, Fry attempted to show that there is something like an inverse relationship between the "plastic" and "psychological" values of paintings. On the one hand, Breughel's "Christ Carrying the Cross" (the student should look at the reproduction in *Transformations*) is "a great psychological invention. [But] throughout this picture it is clear that Breughel has subordinated plastic to psychological considerations. It is indeed to my mind entirely trivial and inexpressive when judged as a plastic . . . creation." [28] On the other hand, Poussin's "Ulysses Discovering Achilles" is dull when considered as the "illustration" of an episode, but exciting when considered as a formal construction. And even in Rembrandt, "fusion" is rarely achieved: "How can we keep the attention equally fixed on the spaceless world of psychological entities and relations and upon the apprehension of spatial relations?" [29]

THUS FAR WE HAVE CONSIDERED formalism as a theory of the visual arts only. Can it be extended to embrace all of the arts?

Let us begin by noting that the formalists often use the term "literary" to describe narrative or historical painting, i.e., the sort of painting which is not true art. Literature does not use words as objects which are of interest in themselves like the lines in an abstract design. We do not read a novel

[24] Clive Bell, *Since Cézanne* (New York: Harcourt, Brace, 1922), p. 94.
[25] *Art*, p. 25.
[26] *Ibid.*, p. 225.
[27] *Vision and Design*, p. 301. Cf., however, pp. 35, 268.
[28] *Transformations*, p. 15.
[29] *Ibid.*, p. 23; cf., also, pp. 27 ff.

simply to see the shapes of words on the pages, or to hear their sounds when uttered. The words have "meaning," which is to say that they refer beyond themselves to episodes or things. It is what the words "stand for" that concerns us. Thus literature does not have an inherent, self-contained significance. Rather, it leads us off into "real life" situations of some sort, even when it is fictional — the tribulations of Oliver Twist, and so on.

Hence, as Bell says, "Literature is never pure art." [30] Our appreciation even of great poetry must be "impure" because "the form is burdened with an intellectual content, and that content is a mood that mingles with and reposes on the emotions of life." [31] Bell straightforwardly accepts the conclusion that formalism is not able to explain the value that people find in literature, which, he recognizes, is very great. Literature, he says, since it does not employ "abstract form," is "an art altogether different" [32] from painting. Aesthetic theory must therefore recognize the insuperable differences among the various arts.[33] Fry, however, suggests that his theory *can* hold for all the arts. For what is most important in *any* work of art is its formal structure. In painting, we do not respond to a color in isolation, but rather to the relationships among all the colors. Analogously, what is important in tragedy is not "the emotional intensity of the events portrayed, but the vivid sense of the inevitability of their unfolding." [34] This may sound odd, but consider for a moment what Fry is saying. Does not tragedy have what a later formalist calls "shape"?[35] Out of a welter of indeterminate events at first, a pattern of tensions emerges which propels us forward, and finally narrows down to the dénouement. Would the events portrayed be as vivid and moving as they are, apart from this formal patterning? It is worth noting that Fry's approach has been used in recent critical studies of form in the drama, the novel, and poetry. Nonetheless, it must be admitted that literature does not lend itself readily to analysis solely in terms of "form."

But whereas literature poses difficulties for the formalists, music does not. Bell and Fry repeatedly liken music to "pure" visual art, and it is no accident that Fry, in his criticism, so often uses words drawn from the vocabulary of music — "rhythm," "harmony," and so on. For the formalists take music to be the "pure" art *par excellence*. In this they carry forward the belief held throughout the nineteenth century, which is summed up in Walter Pater's famous dictum, "All art constantly aspires to the condition of music." Music does not "imitate" objects or "tell a story"; it cannot do so. Its medium, unlike that of painting or literature, does not permit it.

[30] *Art*, p. 153.
[31] *Ibid.*, p. 158.
[32] Clive Bell, "The 'Difference' of Literature," *New Republic*, 33 (1922), 18.
[33] *Ibid.*, p. 18.
[34] *Transformations*, p. 10.
[35] F. E. Halliday, *Five Arts* (London: Duckworth, 1946), p. 29.

Hence it must consist of formal patternings of the elements of its medium — tones, chords, etc. — just as the formalist definition of "art" has it. The aesthetic spectator responds to the formed sounds themselves, and is not distracted by representational significance. The "impure" listener may try to find "human emotions of terror and mystery, love and hate" in the music, but then he has, Bell says, "tumbled from the superb peaks of aesthetic exaltation to the snug foothills of warm humanity." [36]

Though music is ostensibly the "purest" of the arts, it is interesting to see how, half a century before Bell and Fry, the musical formalist Eduard Hanslick has to fight against the "impure" appreciation of music. He too challenges the prevailing taste of the artistic audience, and he does so by the use of arguments which are astonishingly parallel to those of Bell and Fry. Music, he says, is "a complete and self-subsistent whole," which is wholly unrelated to "the realities of the external world." [37] "[The] beauty of a composition is *specifically musical* — i.e., it inheres in the combinations of musical sounds and is independent of all alien, extra-musical notions." [38] Hence the listener must focus his attention exclusively on the formal development and working out of "sound and motion." In the visual arts, Bell points out, those who lack this discriminating awareness of form can at least take interest in the representational subject matter, what the painting is "about." Such people will, indeed, remember nothing of the picture after having seen it, except the subject matter.[39] (The student might wish to test himself on this score.) In music, since there is no such subject matter, no such way out is possible. But then, as Hanslick argues, there is another way in which the untutored listener can miss the point of music, and lose its value. This is to use music as a stimulus to diffuse and crude emotions. Instead of apprehending the precise, determinate structure of the music, he uses it to induce a pleasant, somewhat soporific state of being. (Think of the "background" or "mood" music sometimes heard in restaurants or factories, which are precisely places where attention is on something *other* than the music.) For such a listener, Hanslick says scornfully, "a good cigar . . . or a warm bath yields . . . the same enjoyment as a Symphony." [40] Since he has not "truly heard" the music, he will bring away from it not "a definite and lasting impression" of the specific composition, but only "the vague after-effect of his feelings." [41]

One (though not the only) test of the importance of a theory is its pertinence to one's own personal experience. Does it raise questions about your experience that you had not thought of previously, or that you had been aware of only slightly, or that you had brushed aside? Whether Hans-

[36] *Art*, p. 32. Cf. *Vision and Design*, p. 218; *Five Arts*, p. 25.
[37] Eduard Hanslick, *The Beautiful in Music*, trans. Cohen (London: Novello, 1891), pp. 68, 172.
[38] *Ibid.*, p. 12. Italics in original.
[40] *Op. cit.*, p. 125.
[39] *Art*, p. 30.
[41] *Ibid.*, p. 140.

lick's charge strikes home to the reader's own experience of music, will have to be decided by the reader, for himself.

3. CRITICAL ANALYSIS OF FORMALISM

I have described formalism as a campaign to educate taste. Perhaps the first thing to say, as we turn to a critical evaluation of this theory, is that the campaign succeeded. Because of the missionary work of Bell and Fry, many people came to understand the nature and value of modern art. They no longer considered it odd or ridiculous, they gave up the habits of perception which had been developed by looking at traditional art, and therefore they came to see and relish the vitality of the Post-Impressionist artists. Fry said, with a combination of personal modesty and British understatement, that because of his efforts and those of others "a rather more intelligent attitude exists in the educated public of today than obtained in the last century." [42] Doubtless much still remains to be done. But modern art, once the object of contempt and ridicule by all save a very few, has now established itself firmly. And even those who profess ignorance of it pay it the compliment of admiring advertisements, magazine designs, and household furniture which have borrowed heavily from modern painting and sculpture.

BUT THE *influence* of a theory is no proof of the *truth* of that theory. Cannot a theory be influential though it is false or logically inconsistent? Indeed, some critics of formalism have attributed its popularity to a combination of snob appeal — those who can appreciate or at least talk about modern art thereby prove that they are not "simple bodies" — and pretentious jargon like "significant form." Professor Ducasse calls the formalists "addicts" who are "genuinely incurable for they think of themselves as on the contrary connoisseurs or initiates equipped with the only true sort of aesthetic vision. Unfortunately they often are believed such also by the innocent, who are so bewildered and impressed by technical-sounding talk that they dare not call their aesthetic souls their own." [43]

But it would be harsh and mistaken to dismiss the formalists in this way. When you read Fry's criticism, with its incredibly sensitive and articulate accounts of the formal values of art, you cannot doubt that he is reporting a deeply felt personal experience. Sir Kenneth Clark, himself a distinguished critic, writes:

How often, in looking at a picture in [Fry's] company, I have been

[42] *Vision and Design*, p. 286.
[43] *Philosophy of Art*, p. 219.

delighted by a pretty face, a charming gesture, an agreeable association . . . and, turning to my companion, have found him groaning in despair at the lack of formal coherency.[44]

Moreover, we have the supporting evidence of those who listen to music as Fry looked at painting. Their experience is much like his. For they find in music "architecturally co-ordinated groups of sound-relations." [45] Appreciation of the formal patterning of the medium, without regard to non-painterly or extramusical matters, is a real and genuine aesthetic experience. Talk about such experience may seem obscure or pretentious to those who approach art in a radically different way. I remember one student who, during a discussion of formalism, asked with some heat, "But if you don't hear a story in the music, what is there to listen to?" For those who have such a view of art, it is especially imperative to try to understand and appreciate what the formalists are saying.

More important, Fry's approach is fruitful in art criticism. It brings out and illuminates what is in the work. If you read one of Fry's critiques of a specific painting, and then look at the painting, you will find that the plastic and design values which he describes are *there* in the work. Moreover, his critical technique is not restricted to Post-Impressionist art. It is noteworthy that formalist criticism has recently been turned upon traditional art as well, with good results, for it discloses values which "imitation"-theory and other modes of criticism had failed to see. The validity of a theory of art depends in large measure upon its usefulness in analyzing specific works. On this score, formalism ranks high.

WE NOW TURN from the positive to the negative criticism of formalism.

1. The first criticism is directed against the logical structure of the formalist theory. It points to inadequacies in the basic definitions of the theory, as they are presented by Bell. He says, you will remember, that "art" is defined by the presence in objects of "significant form." But if this definition is to be informative, the meaning of "significant form" must be explicated. Else the latter term is essentially empty, and therefore the entire definition is also empty. It sounds as though it were meaningful, when actually it has told us nothing.

Bell gives no satisfactory analysis of the meaning of "significant form." It is clear, however, that he does not think of significant form as a purely objective property of the work. Rather, he thinks of it in its relationship to the spectator — "significant form" is that pattern of lines and colors which arouses "aesthetic emotion." This is as close as Bell gets to a definition of

[44] Roger Fry, *Last Lectures*, Introduction (New York: Macmillan, 1939), pp. xvi–xvii.

[45] Vernon Lee, "Varieties of Musical Experience," in Vivas and Krieger, *op. cit.*, p. 302.

the term. But this moves our problem one step further back. What is "aesthetic emotion"? As we have seen, Bell holds that it is completely unlike the emotions of "real life." Yet this suffers from being purely negative. It is not enough to say about God that He is not human, or about a fish that it is not a mammal. Unless we have some clear empirical account of "aesthetic emotion," we cannot know how to use and test the theory, or even know what the theory is saying. But finally what we get from Bell is that "aesthetic emotion" is the emotion aroused by "significant form." Hence there is a logical circularity in the basic definitions of the theory — "significant form" is defined by reference to "aesthetic emotion" and conversely.

What is worse, the circle is, so to speak, a very small one. Both "significant form" and "aesthetic emotion" are unanalyzed, and no criteria are given for finding them empirically. One way out of circularity, which is open to some theories, is to define a term by means of concepts taken from other theories or other fields of inquiry. Thus the theory moves out of the circle of its own terms. For example, political science may define its central terms by means of concepts taken over from sociology, economics, psychology, and so on. But formalism cannot do this. It keeps itself from doing so by its insistence that the data which it treats are wholly peculiar to one area of experience — "pure" art and appreciation — and therefore cannot be understood in any terms other than its own. Doubtless the kind of art and aesthetic experience that the formalists are concerned with, exist, and are real and genuine phenomena. Yet the theory which seeks to explain their nature, at its crucial first step, runs into a dead end of obscurity.

Bell makes one attempt [46] to "widen" the circle by an explication of "significant form." He suggests, though only tentatively, that such form "expresses the emotion of its creator." [47] But this proves to be self-defeating. For he also holds that "significant form" can occur in nature, i.e., in nonartistic objects.[48] If this is true, then significant form can occur without "expressing the emotion of its creator," for there is no such creator in nature. Emotional expression cannot be part of the meaning of "significant form," for what is part of the meaning of a term must be present in whatever is denoted by the term. Thus the meaning of "significant form" remains unclear.

2. These logical difficulties create difficulties for formalism as a theory of art criticism. We have seen that Fry was largely successful in carrying out analyses of specific works. But more than this is required of a theory of

---

[46] Another will be considered presently; cf. below, p. 154.
[47] *Art*, p. 49; cf., also, pp. 61–62.
[48] *Ibid.*, p. 13; cf., also, p. 53.

criticism. It must set forth well-defined meanings for "good" and "bad" in the field of art — "beautiful" and "ugly" — so that these terms can be clearly and intelligibly applied. Otherwise we simply will not understand what the critic means when he uses these evaluative terms. Then the theory must tell us what *reasons* can be used by the critic to support his judgment that this work of art is "good," or that it is "better" than another work. In the absence of valid reasons, his criticism may be capricious or merely personal, simply an elaborate way of saying "I like it"; but then his value-judgment lacks authority and has no claim upon us.

On these counts, formalism fails.

"The function of the critic," for Bell, is to show how "qualities and relations of line and colour . . . excel or fall short." [49] But on Bell's own theory, how is the critic to do this? A painting will "excel" when it possesses "significant form." Yet as we have just seen, no clear meaning is assigned to this pivotal phrase. And Fry admits that he cannot explain its meaning.[50] Therefore the theory gives no workable criterion for distinguishing good art from bad. Surely not *all* formal relations of line and color are of artistic merit. Fry often denies "plastic" value to specific works, as in the specimens of his criticism cited earlier.[51] Yet formalism offers no workable method of analyzing works of art so that the presence or absence of value can be detected and described. There is a related difficulty here. Formalism defines "art" in terms of "significant form," and significant form is always aesthetically valuable. Therefore all works which are to be called "art" on this definition are *good*. There cannot be an object which is both "artistic" and "bad." If it lacks "form," then it just is not "art." This is somewhat paradoxical — do we not commonly speak of a "mediocre" or "inferior" work of art? But this paradox is not the major difficulty. Whether we want to call an object which lacks significant form "bad art" or "not-art" is a *verbal* question. The basic issue is the question of *fact* — what is there about the structure of the painting or sculpture which makes it good, and thereby sets it off from that other object which does not have "form"?

At many places in their writings, Bell and Fry hold that a work possesses significant form if it arouses "aesthetic emotion" in the disinterested spectator. Thus Bell writes: "When I say that drawing is bad, I mean that I am not moved by the contours of the forms that make up the work of art." [52] You will see the perplexing implications of this quite readily. If personal emotions are the test, and the only test, of value then we are in for a

---

[49] *Ibid.*, p. 169.
[50] *Vision and Design*, pp. 301–302.
[51] Cf. above, p. 141.
[52] *Art*, p. 232.

veritable Babel of value-judgments. Since different people are "moved" in very different ways by a work of art, and sometimes not at all, it will be a fortunate coincidence if ever they agree. But this is not the salient objection. Merely to reach agreement is not the goal of criticism. Whether we agree or disagree with each other, what is important is that we should be able to give reasons in defense of our judgments. It is not enough merely to give vent to autobiographical statements of how we feel. Then no judgment has any more or any less validity than any other, and when we exchange critical opinions we are like the little boys who repeat " 'tis!" — " 'tain't!" — " 'tis!" — " 'tain't!" endlessly. We can escape from this blind alley only if we can point to certain features of the work itself and show that these make the work genuinely good. Only thus can we show that our emotional response is justified and that the work is worthy of our approval and esteem. As we have seen, formalism does not show the critic how to do this.

So formalism, as a theory of criticism, leads to irrationality and futility. Given his theory, it is no accident that Bell says that "before a work of art the critic can do little more than jump for joy." [53] The critical *practice* of Bell and Fry, i.e., their critiques of Post-Impressionist art, was sound and helpful, because it called attention to features of the work which many had ignored or misunderstood, and because it described these properties skilfully and with enthusiasm. However, their critical *theory* is not on a par with their practice.[54] It does not clarify its basic terms, it offers no objective criteria of evaluation, and it leads into a predicament of critical anarchy. The crowning paradox is that, in this anarchy, anyone's critical opinion is as good as that of anyone else. This is an implication which Bell and Fry, who are often accused of snobbism, and who speak disparagingly of "the multitude" and "the average man" would certainly not wish to accept.

3. We have now seen both that formalism has genuine and important insights, but also that its development of these insights into what is supposed to be a coherent theory, leaves much to be desired. Formalism is by no means the only theory which has got hold of significant truths, but has found it very difficult to state these truths precisely and systematically in conceptual terms. As the philosopher William James noted, "insight" often outruns "argument."

Let us now set to one side the inadequacies of formalism as a theoretical system or as a basis for art criticism. Let us consider critically the twin

[53] *Since Cézanne*, p. 158; cf., also, p. 100.
[54] Fry writes in a letter: "My analyses of form-lines, sequences, rhythms, etc., are merely aids for the uninitiated to attain to the contemplation of form — they do not explain." — Quoted in Virginia Woolf, *Roger Fry: A Biography* (New York: Harcourt, Brace, 1940), p. 230. Italics in original.

doctrines which are at the heart of formalism — that fine art is essentially the formal patterning of the medium and that aesthetic experience is the disinterested appreciation solely of such forms. In general, I shall argue that formalism, as has been said of other philosophical theories, is "right in what it affirms, but wrong in what it denies." Its conception of art and aesthetic experience is, as far as it goes, a legitimate and important one. But it is limited. Formalism's "denial" — its exclusion of much that is usually considered artistic, and its severe restriction of aesthetic experience — is not justified.

LET US FIRST ASK *why* the formalists limit "pure" art and appreciation so severely. Why are they quite prepared to draw the conclusion that a great deal of Western painting and sculpture, and most of what passes for "aesthetic enjoyment," must be excluded on their definitions?

As we have seen more than once, their view rests ultimately on the experience of "aesthetic emotion." Whether an object possesses "form," indeed the very meaning of "form" in art, depends upon whether the percipient feels "pure aesthetic emotion." They hold that this experience, which is the only kind of experience that they consider truly aesthetic, can be had only if the spectator is apprehending abstract form. Why? Because if he apprehends a representational work, then he will "refer back its forms to the world from which they came." [55] He is then "using art as a means to the emotions of life." [56] Hence we must ignore representational subject matter, or treat it as if it "were not representative of anything," [57] on pain of losing the "pure" aesthetic experience.

The formalist argument, then, comes essentially to this: aesthetic experience can occur only when the work of art is formal; when the work is representational, we respond to it as though the subject matter were "real life," and therefore we feel "the ordinary emotions of life." It is this latter view that I now wish to challenge.

Is the subject matter — the object or event depicted in the work — just like the model in ordinary experience of which it is a replica? If it is not, then our response to it will not be the same response as that of "real life." And indeed, the subject matter of a work of art is *not* a mere duplicate of the corresponding object outside of art. Just as we had to point this out in criticizing "simple imitation," [58] so we must now remind ourselves of it in analyzing formalism.

Art can, and does, draw upon "real life" events — the Passion of Christ, Napoleon's invasion of Russia. But its representation of "life" is made part of a self-contained object which is set off from the rest of experience. The work of art, as Aristotle said, has a "beginning, middle, and

[55] *Art,* p. 29.
[57] Cf. above, p. 141.
[56] *Ibid.,* p. 32.
[58] Cf. above, pp. 112 ff.

end." Within the limits of the work, the subject matter takes on a significance of its own which is wholly different from that of the historical model. In the work, the subject matter is set forth within a total sensuous, formal, and imaginative structure. It is enmeshed in the rich "body" of the work. Thus it takes on vividness and "meaning" which its model does not possess in "real life." Indeed, the "meaning" of the subject, when it has been presented in painterly or literary terms, cannot be grasped or understood in any other way. It has the specific intensity and vividness which it gains when it is ingredient within the specific work of art, and which it loses when it is wrenched out of the total work and considered apart from it. To say that Renoir's "Girl with a Watering Can" "represents" a little girl in blue with a ribbon in her hair, may be true enough. But that is not the whole point of the painting. The significance of the painting's subject can be understood only when we consider the subject as it has been rendered by the artist, who has placed it within a certain color-structure, and has invested it with a distinctive charm and affection.

This important distinction between the "real life" object, and its representation in art, is marked by the critic A. C. Bradley, in his splendid essay "Poetry for Poetry's Sake." [59] Bradley (using different terms from those which I have employed) distinguishes between the "subject" and the "substance" of the work. (He is chiefly concerned with poetry). The "subject" is what the work is "about," and this can be stated in dissociation from the work itself. Thus one could learn from a manual of English literature, without having to read the poem, that, to use Bradley's example, the "subject" of *Paradise Lost* is the Fall of Man. Hence the subject "is not, as such, inside the poem, but outside it." [60] The subject as it is treated within the poem, when it is united with what Bradley calls "form," is the "substance." [61] What the "substance" is can be known only by reading the poem. Now, Bradley points out, the subject cannot guarantee the worth of the poem. A bad poem or drama could be written about the Fall of Man. However, this proves only that "the subject *settles* nothing, but not that it counts for nothing" [62] (as the formalists claim). There are some subjects, such as the Fall of Man, which can take on profundity and greatness when they become the substance of such a work as *Paradise Lost*. The same is not true of a subject which is trivial. We might note that Bradley is upheld by the consensus of critical opinion, which reserves its highest acclaim for works which are of large human import, notably tragedy. In any event, Bradley's analysis makes it clear that both the na-

---

[59] It is a tribute to the respective editors that this acute and sober treatment of one of the most vexing problems in aesthetics is reprinted in both Rader, *op. cit.*, pp. 335–356, and Vivas and Krieger, *op. cit.*, pp. 562–577.

[60] A. C. Bradley, *Oxford Lectures on Poetry* (London: Macmillan, 1909), p. 9.

[61] *Ibid.*, p. 12.

[62] *Ibid.*, p. 11. Italics in original.

ture and aesthetic value of what is represented in the work of art are quite different from what they are outside of art.

Now let us bring this conclusion around to formalism. If the representational subject matter (Bradley's "substance") resembles, but is quite distinct from "real life," because it is a component of the self-contained work of art, then we do not see it or respond to it, as we see and respond to the model in "real life." We apprehend the work aesthetically,[63] which is to say that we apprehend it disinterestedly, without any concern ulterior to the act of perception. Hence our interest is not "practical." The work of art discourages "real life" response. The episodes which it portrays are contained and, so to speak, immobilized within the "frame" of the work. Its events are thereby restrained from interacting with the events of ordinary experience.

However, art which employs subject matter *may* lead the spectator to adopt some attitude other than the aesthetic. Because such art presents people and episodes which remind one of "real life," the spectator may respond as though the subject matter *were* "real life." The formalists seem to hold that this *must always* happen, and therefore they hold that our experience can be aesthetic only if the work does not "look like" anything. Certainly there are many people who characteristically have the kind of experience that the formalists warn against. They respond *only* to the subject matter — a pretty girl, a patriotic or religious theme — divorced from the total work. Then their experience is nonaesthetic — they have religious feelings, or they are moved to practical action or reverie, and so on. The mark of such a person is that he has essentially the same experience no matter what the work of art is like, so long as it has a certain subject matter. Surely not all paintings of the Crucifixion are artistically good. But whether the painting be great or mediocre, he will feel precisely the same emotion. It is clear that he is responding to the historical event, to "life," and not to "art."

By contrast, when perception is truly aesthetic, the subject matter is seen, not dissociated from, but as absorbed within the sensory and formal structure of the work. Attention is then fixed upon the work of art, not the historical event. When the work is successful, the subject will take on significance, as was suggested earlier, which is peculiar to the work. Though Fry sometimes [64] thought that "dramatic idea" and "plastic design" were inherently opposed to each other, there are many places in his criticism in which he describes their "fusion." Thus he says that "when . . . we look at Michelangelo's 'Jeremiah,' and realise the irresistible momentum his movements would have, we experience powerful sentiments of reverence and awe." [65] Consider, similarly, this account of the Rembrandt portrait,

[63] Cf. above, chap. 2.
[64] Cf. above, p. 141.
[65] *Vision and Design*, p. 35. Cf., also, pp. 166–167, 268, 301.

"Old Woman": "The color scheme is worked out largely in restrained golden browns — colors of a type that we find in things old and seasoned. . . . The illumination is one suggestive of dusk. . . . [The representational] elements could stir only a portion of the response we feel before the . . . work. It is those elements backed by, echoed by, amplified by, the accompanying color, light, and breadth of surface, which . . . stir us so deeply." [66]

I have tried to show that our response to representational art is not the response of "real life." The subject matter in the work of art has a distinctive and intrinsic interest which its model lacks. Further, the detachment of the work from ongoing experience encourages disinterested perception. Moreover, the aesthetic attitude is "sympathetic," concerned to relish everything which makes up the individual work, and therefore it does not respond solely to the subject matter alone, but to the subject matter as it is embodied within the artistic medium. Representation *may* be antiaesthetic, for those who are concerned only with the subject matter. But it is not *necessarily* and *always* antiaesthetic.

If we can preserve the aesthetic attitude while looking at representational painting and sculpture, we can do so with literature as well. Literature draws its subjects from "life." As Professor Wimsatt has put it, "poetry deals with Frankie and Johnnie, who were lovers." But we can hear the story of Frankie and Johnnie without being moved to sentimental reverie or practical action. Nor is Bell correct in saying that our experience must be nonaesthetic if, to appreciate the work, we must "bring with us . . . from life" any "knowledge of its ideas and affairs." [67] All hinges on whether this knowledge enables us to contemplate, with understanding and discernment, what is found within the work, or whether we use the work as a "cue" or stimulus to dwell upon the "ideas and affairs of life" and thereby surrender interest in the work itself. What we "bring with us from life" can re-enforce the aesthetic attitude; it need not destroy it.

Thus there is an important similarity in the way in which we are interested in both literature and abstract art. We approach both art-forms with aesthetic detachment and sympathy. But on the formalist view, we must banish literature and representational painting from art and aesthetic perception, or else we must consider only the experience of literary "shape" and plastic form. The formalist definitions of "art" and "aesthetic experience" are too narrow. This theory is not an effective tool for analyzing the many different objects which are usually considered works of art, and the enjoyment of them. For that purpose we must take account of subject matter, which formalism simply dismisses, and all of the values related to it.

[66] Walter Abell, *Representation and Form* (New York: Scribner's, 1936), pp. 125, 128–129.
[67] Cf. above, p. 140.

Formalism fails in these crucial respects because it sets up the alternatives too sharply: either aesthetic experience of abstract, nonrepresentational art, or else no aesthetic experience at all. If the previous argument is sound, the alternatives are more complicated. There can be aesthetic experience of intrinsically interesting representational art. To be sure, the definitions of the formalists, like any definitions, cannot be said to be "true" or "false." Hence they cannot be "refuted." But if a definition can be shown to ignore salient empirical fact, and if it is not a fruitful guide to further investigation of the facts, then it is "disproved" as nearly as a definition can be.

Bell and Fry were moved to develop the formalist theory of art by their own experience of "aesthetic emotion," aroused solely by the formal aspects of art, which they wished to call to the attention of others. Let me repeat what I said earlier: such experience is a real and important kind of aesthetic experience which is had by many in the face of music and abstract art. Perhaps the present chapter will make the reader aware of such experience, and will help prepare him to have it, by pointing to features of art which he may have ignored previously. But the appreciation of formal relations is only *one* kind of aesthetic experience. The formalists have gone too far in contending that it is the *only* kind of aesthetic experience. Aesthetic experience can be "pure emotion," but it can also be a great deal else, and still be veritably aesthetic. Similarly, fine art *can* be wholly abstract, but it can also be a great deal else. It can borrow from, depict, and clarify "real life," and still preserve its own independence and value.

Perhaps the error of formalism is that, like some of the theories considered earlier,[68] it offers a definition of "art" which is used as a plea for what art *should* be. If formalism is such a plea, then it might be noted that some of its critics think that it has failed. They argue that it has failed in the crucial area — the actual practice of creative artists. These critics point out, rightly or wrongly (it may well be too early to say), that painters and sculptors are now abandoning abstract art, because they have found it to be too limited in what it can express. They are now returning to representational art which can alone attain the "human significance" which abstract art denies itself. It will be interesting to see what develops in the visual arts in the years ahead.

4. "ART" AND "LIFE"—AGAIN

Throughout our analysis of formalism, we have presupposed Bell's distinction between "art," with its unique and ineffable emotions, and "life,"

[68] Cf. above, pp. 126–127, 129.

with its "human business and passion." [69] We have seen how a representational work need not forfeit its claim to be a "work of art" or an "aesthetic object." But we have not discussed the formalists' claim that nonrepresentational art and its appreciation are wholly divorced from the doings and feelings of quotidian experience. It is this claim that we must now examine.

Let me begin by citing a doctrine set forth in the formalists' writings, which I have not thus far mentioned. It is one of the oddest and most paradoxical things that the formalists say. In the very midst of their writings, they seem to lapse into a kind of *"imitation"-theory* which is the very antithesis of formalism. They assert that abstract art reveals a "reality" which is ulterior to the work of art itself. At the very same time that they proclaim the complete divorce of "art" from "life," they also insist that art discloses truths, indeed important truths, about "life." Bell says that when we apprehend forms, we "become aware of [the] essential reality, of the God in everything, of the universal in the particular . . . that which lies behind the appearance of all things." [70] This is of course terribly vague, perhaps hopelessly vague, and Bell is properly apologetic about it.[71] But the other formalists make very much the same sort of claim. Fry speaks of the "peculiar quality of 'reality' " [72] in the aesthetic experience. The twentieth-century artists Kandinsky and Mondrian become almost mystical in describing the ability of abstract art to disclose the "objective spiritual force in the world." [73]

This creates a logical inconsistency with the doctrine of artistic "purity," and this must count against the formalist theory. However, a theorist's mistakes can sometimes be illuminating. The formalists may have given us a clue to deciding whether Post-Impressionist art is wholly unrelated to "life." Let us consider in turn "abstract" art, in which there is still some recognizable resemblance, even if it is only slight, to ordinary objects, and then "nonobjective" art, in which there is no such subject matter at all.

Abstract art "distorts" its model. This is most pronounced in modern styles, such as Cubism, in which faces and bodies are fragmented into a multitude of planes. But the use of "distortion" does not begin with Post-Impressionism. It is found throughout the long history of the visual arts. A good example, which may be familiar to you, would be the unusually elongated bodies painted by El Greco. Whether "distortion" occurs in traditional or modern art, it lends interest and vividness to the painting's subject matter. It is responsible for the emotional intensity of El Greco's saints,

[69] *Art*, p. 71.
[70] *Ibid.*, p. 69; cf., also, p. 54.
[71] *Ibid.*, p. 70; cf., also, p. 281.
[72] *Vision and Design*, p. 302.
[73] Frances B. Blanshard, *Retreat from Likeness in the Theory of Painting*, 2nd ed. (Columbia University Press, 1949), p. 135.

the humor of African masks, the charm of Modigliani's portraits (see Plate 11).

But now the important thing to see is this: we would not recognize that the subject matter is distorted, and therefore we would not enjoy the work as we do, unless we knew what the "real life" model looked like. We cannot know that a thing is "distorted," unless we have some norm of what it is like when it is *not* distorted. We can appreciate the work, therefore, only if we have ordinary perceptual knowledge of how people and trees normally look. Thus abstract art has a "hyphen with common reality." [74] Consider Brancusi's famous "Bird in Space" (see Plate 17). If we look at this work in the way suggested by the title, and not simply as a nonobjective form, we see its surprising and exciting affinity to what birds are like. To be sure, it does not "look like" any bird. And yet it has the economy and grace of a bird in flight. The sculpture is clear, incisive, unambiguous, like the path described by the bird as it cleaves the air. We can admire and enjoy it only if we reject Bell's contention that "we need bring with us nothing from life." Through the isolation and refinement of experience which it achieves by distortion, abstract art shows us "life," but with greater clarity and vividness than "life" usually exhibits.

I wish to advance a similar argument with regard to "nonobjective" art. But here we seem to encounter grave difficulties in establishing *any* relationship with "life." A purely geometrical construction of colored rectangles, as in Mondrian (see Plate 21), does not "look like" anything, nor can it be said to "distort" a natural object. Is it not wholly "pure"?

Here the formalists may guide us. Roger Fry, in describing mass as an "element of design," writes that when a work has the quality of "inertia," we feel the "power of resisting movement . . . and our imaginative reaction to such an image is governed by our experience of mass in actual life." [75] A nonobjective painting or sculpture does not show us mass as the property of some object, such as a mountain or a table. But when the work embodies mass, it presents us with a quality that is common to most of the objects with which we have commerce in ordinary experience. The same is true of "rhythm," "tension," and "movement," when these are set up by the contours and patterns of the work. These are qualities of a great many of the things and events with which we are acquainted, but now they have been isolated out of their usual settings — the rhythm of a specific activity, the tension of conflict — and considered by themselves. Perhaps (but this is only a tenuous speculation), this is what Bell means when he says that significant form depicts "the universal in the particular." [76] In any event,

[74] Leo Steinberg, "The Eye Is a Part of the Mind," *Partisan Review*, XX (1953), 207.
[75] *Vision and Design*, pp. 33–34.
[76] Cf. *Vision and Design*, pp. 295–296.

we could not respond to such art as we do, unless we had already experienced heaviness and lightness, buoyancy and inertia, rapidity and slowness, and all the other, immediately felt properties of our world. If this account is sound, then nonobjective art shows us what is at the core of all our experience. "We see what we never saw, and hear what we never heard, and yet, what we see and hear is flesh of our flesh and bones of our bones" (Lavater).

Moreover, this kind of analysis has also been applied to the other artform in the stronghold of formalism — music. Professor Pepper writes:

> On closer scrutiny, a Beethoven symphony is not after all simply a collection of tones. . . . There are contrasts and gradations, and tensions and resolutions of tonal patterns. Above all, there is tonality and the intricate interrelationship of demands of tones for one another and especially for the tonic. These set up human expectations and suspense, desires and frustrations. . . . Pure music has not freed itself from associations with human actions and desires.[77]

[77] Stephen C. Pepper, "Is Non-Objective Art Superficial?," *Journal of Aesthetics and Art Criticism*, XI (1953), 259.

BIBLIOGRAPHY

* Rader, *A Modern Book of Esthetics*. Pp. 44–61, 258–282, 317–356.
* Vivas and Krieger, *The Problems of Aesthetics*. Pp. 208–225, 296–304, 562–583.
* Weitz, *Problems in Aesthetics*. Pp. 49–61, 173–175, 351–360, 381–410.
  Blanshard, Frances B. *Retreat from Likeness in the Theory of Painting*, 2nd ed. Columbia University Press, 1949. Chaps. 5, 6.
  Ducasse, Curt J. *The Philosophy of Art*. New York: Dial, 1929. Appendix.
  Fry, Roger. *Transformations*. Garden City: Anchor, 1956.
  Halliday, F. E. *Five Arts*. London: Duckworth, 1946.
  Hanslick, Eduard. *The Beautiful in Music*, trans. Cohen, ed. Weitz. New York: Liberal Arts, 1957.
  Hospers, John. *Meaning and Truth in the Arts*. University of North Carolina Press, 1946. Chap. IV.
  Pepper, Stephen C., "Is Non-Objective Art Superficial?," *Journal of Aesthetics and Art Criticism*, Vol. XI (March, 1953), 255–261.
  Steinberg, Leo, "The Eye Is a Part of the Mind," *Partisan Review*, Vol. XX (March–April, 1953), 194–212.

QUESTIONS

1. Do you think that aesthetic "fusion" can be achieved between the "plastic" and "dramatic" values in painting? Compare the analyses of specific works in Fry, *Transformations*, and Abell, *Representation and Form*.
2. "[Unlike] the . . . media of music and architecture, the physical media of

painting and sculpture lend themselves so effectively to the representation of visible objects that the potentialities of these arts cannot be said to have been adequately exploited in pure 'abstractions'." — Greene, *op. cit.*, p. 37. Discuss. How do you think a formalist would reply to this argument? Cf., also, in Greene, pp. 410–413.

3. What are the major schools of Post-Impressionist art? In what ways do each of these schools exemplify the formalist theory of art?

4. Study the reading in Prall, *Aesthetic Judgment,* cited in the Bibliography of Chapter 2. What are the chief similarities between Prall's theory and formalism? What is the attitude of these theories toward literature as a fine art?

5. Can we have aesthetic experience of representational art? Is the experience of such art "less" aesthetic than perception of "pure" art? Explain your answer in each case.

6. Bradley says that subject matter "counts for something" (cf., above, p. 150). Does it follow that a "great" work of representational art will always be superior to a "great" work of abstract art? Can the value of these two kinds of art be compared with each other? If so, how? Discuss with regard to literature, music, and painting.

7. Study the paintings of Mondrian (e.g., Plate 21). How could it be argued that they embody "essences"? How, if at all, would such an analysis differ from a formalist analysis of these works?

8. "An *aesthetic* analysis can take no note of circumstances which lie outside the work itself." — Hanslick, *op. cit.,* p. 103. Italics in original. Discuss.

Emotionalist Theory

7

"Be guided by feeling alone. . . . [Follow] your own convictions. It is better to be nothing than an echo of other painters. . . . If you have really been touched, you will convey to others the sincerity of your emotion." [1]

These are the words of the painter Corot, in the middle of the nineteenth century. Note that he calls for three things in art: the artist should be under the influence of emotion; he should display his own individual character; and he should be sincere.

Thus Corot sets forth some of the leading ideas of a chief artistic movement of recent times — so-called "Romanticism." These ideas have also entered into the thinking of the nonartist. Indeed, for the last century and a half this conception of art has seemed to many who are not artists to be almost self-evidently true. This belief obviously has great influence upon the aesthetic experience of those who hold it. It determines what they will look for in the work of art and what they will try to "get out of" it. That this belief is widely shared at the present time — you may be among those who hold it — is demonstrated by the way in which we speak of art. We commonly say in praise of a work that it is "moving" or "expressive." On the other hand, we reject a work by saying that it "has no feeling," or that it "leaves us cold," or sometimes, that it is "merely intellectual." We speak of the artist in comparable terms: we describe van Gogh as "demonic" or "intense," or we say that Shelley is "passionate."

1 Quoted in Goldwater and Treves, *op. cit.*, p. 241.

Historically, this way of thinking about art does not originate with what is sometimes called "the Romantic Revolution" of the nineteenth century. It can be found as far back as Plato, who describes art as "watering the passions." It is present in Aristotle and Longinus, and elsewhere in classical thought. There are conspicuous examples of this way of thinking throughout the eighteenth century. And yet it is in the nineteenth century, for the first time, that the conception of art as a record of a man's emotion and a vehicle for communicating it to others, becomes widely influential. The creator in all fields of art comes to accept this view and carries on his work in accordance with it. You are doubtless familiar with some of the works produced in this way. Among the leaders of the Romantic movement at the beginning of the century are Wordsworth and Shelley in poetry, Victor Hugo in the drama, Beethoven and Schubert in music, Géricault and Delacroix in painting. These men not only created emotional art; many, — e.g., Wordworth, Hugo — wrote *about* art, offering vigorous, doctrinaire defenses of such art.

The intoxicating force of this movement among its contemporaries can only be appreciated if we understand what they were protesting *against*. Why, in other words, was this a *"Revolution"*? If I were to use a simple historical label (but these are always dangerous), I could say that the Romanticists were repudiating "neoclassicism." [2] They were fighting to throw off the restraints imposed by neoclassicism on the creative artist. Specifically, neoclassicism discouraged emotional effusiveness in art. An excessive show of emotion violated the ideals of "decorum" and "propriety." Moreover, the neoclassical thinkers considered emotion to be "subjective" and idiosyncratic to the individual, whereas they pleaded for art which would draw upon and reflect the common experience of all men of "good taste." Related to this, they urged that the artist must limit himself only to those subjects which are "proper" or "edifying." (We met this doctrine earlier, in the discussion of the "ideal"-theory).[3] Finally, neoclassical theory, particularly when it became institutionalized in the "Academies," held that the artist should emulate the art of Graeco-Roman antiquity.

When these precepts were put into practice, they led, at the worst, to art which suffered from emotional emptiness, conventionality and absence of originality, and inflexibility of form and style. Hence neoclassical art suffers often from just plain dullness. Such art is timid, prosy, and mechanical. So Keats writes derisively of his predecessors,

> They sway'd about upon a rocking horse,
> And thought it Pegasus.[4]

[2] Cf. above, pp. 120 ff.   [3] Cf. above, pp. 128 ff.
[4] "Sleep and Poetry." Pegasus is the mythological winged horse associated with the arts.

The Romantics sought to restore vitality and spontaneity to art. Their work was, by contrast to the later neoclassicists, markedly passionate and fervid. To give free rein to their creative desires, they rejected any limitations upon the subjects which they could use in their art. They boxed the compass, depicting commonplace or prosaic scenes, as in Wordsworth, or remote and exotic episodes, as in the novels of Scott, or what was aesthetically or morally ugly, as in "The Raft of the *Medusa*" (see Plate 3). The besetting concern of the artist is to express his personal feelings and responses, however individual or even eccentric these may be. "All imaginative thoughts, all caprices of the brain, are permitted to genius." [5] When traditional artistic forms and styles prove inadequate for self-expression, innovations must be resorted to. Hence the nineteenth century is replete with the development of new artistic forms and techniques, and a plethora of personal "styles." Thus in music new harmonies are employed to replace the "classical tonality" of the eighteenth century, and such expressive devices as the "tone poem" are introduced for the first time.

Out of this ferment of enthusiasm and innovation, much art that is good and even great emerges. Doubtless a great deal of Romantic art suffers from faults which are at the opposite pole from those of bad neoclassical art — sentimentality, morbidity, eccentricity and novelty for their own sake. But the influence of Romanticism, which extends even to our own day, has given us the lyrics of Keats, the *Lieder* of Schubert, the paintings of the twentieth-century "Expressionists."

It is precisely because Romanticism has been so widely influential, for so long a period of time, that its tenets are now taken for granted by many. To see exactly what is involved in this conception of art, we must turn to the aesthetic theories which grew out of Romanticism. In the Romantic artists, "theory of art" is often summed up in a slogan or a catch phrase. In the aestheticians, theory is presented systematically and in detail, drawing out the logical implications of the Romantic doctrines. By studying these philosophies of art, we may come to appreciate more fully the art of the Romantics. But also, by putting these ideas to the tests of evidence and logical reasoning, we want to see whether they constitute a satisfactory theory of art and aesthetic experience.

The aesthetic theory which speaks for Romanticism is the *emotionalist* theory. As we shall see, there are differences of opinion among the three emotionalist philosophers whom we shall be studying. But their theories are closely related, for in analyzing the phenomena of art, its appreciation and its value, they all take one factor to be uppermost — the individual emotional experience of the artist.

[5] Alfred Stevens, *Impressions on Painting*, trans. Adams (New York: Coombes, 1886), p. 4.

1. THE EXPRESSION OF "PERSONALITY"

The first emotionalist theory to be considered takes the work of art to be an expression of the artist's "personality." We have seen that a vigorous individualism is one of the basic credos of Romantic art. I quoted Corot's plea for artistic originality; at the beginning of the century, Goethe proclaimed: "In Art and Poetry, Personality is everything." [6] The artist could display his emotions and thoughts without inhibition, no matter how radical or unconventional they might be. (And not simply in his art; defiance of convention became a way of life for some Romantic artists.) From this there developed an interest in the life and character of the artist which is so conspicuous in books about artists and in program notes at concerts. We read of Byron's love life, and Beethoven's bad temper.

It is interesting to note that this is a comparatively recent phenomenon in the history of art. The medieval artist generally worked in complete anonymity. Often he did not sign his work, and we know little or nothing of the individual artists of that period. "In traditional arts it is never Who said? but only What was said? that concerns us." [7] Much the same is true of the art of Eastern cultures, which is a communal rather than an individual enterprise. "[The] art of the Orient is the direct opposite of Western individualism. The Oriental artist would be ashamed of thinking of his own ego and intending to manifest his own subjectivity in his work." [8]

Nevertheless, revelation of the artist's "subjectivity," which developed in the West during the Renaissance, became one of the cardinal features of nineteenth-century art. This is so far true, that when Eugène Véron published the first systematic exposition of emotionalist theory (1878), he wrote: "[The] influence of man's personality upon his work . . . is the unique and solid basis of all aesthetics." [9] For Véron, the work of art records the artist's personal response to some episode or object. This response is not simply emotional. It includes the artist's "ideas" and "thoughts" as well as his "sentiments." These, in a mediocre artist, will be commonplace.[10] Whereas "the greater [the artist's] genius, the greater

[6] Quoted in George Saintsbury, *A History of Criticism*, 4th ed. (Edinburgh: Blackwood, 1923), III, 370.

[7] Ananda K. Coomaraswamy, *The Christian and Oriental or True Philosophy of Art* (Newport: John Stevens, 1939), p. 19. Cf., also, Ananda K. Coomaraswamy, *The Transformation of Nature in Art* (Harvard University Press, 1935), p. 23.

[8] Jacques Maritain, *Creative Intuition in Art and Poetry* (New York: Meridian, 1955), p. 10.

[9] Eugène Véron, *Aesthetics*, trans. Armstrong (London: Chapman and Hall, 1879), p. 104, n. 1; cf., also, p. 139. [10] *Ibid.*, p. 73; cf., also, p. 106.

energy and individuality will such manifestation display." [11]

Now it is clear that "fine art" cannot be *defined* simply as "the expression of personality." Such a definition would be far too broad. A man "expresses his personality" whenever he performs an action which is characteristic of him, e.g., a moral act, such as helping those in need. Such acts lead his friends to say, "That's just like him." Or he can do so by some unthinking gesture, such as adjusting his eyeglasses in a certain way. No one would consider these actions "works of art."

Véron, as we shall see in the next section of this chapter, does not take "personality" to be definitive of "art." He does hold, however, that what is most important and valuable about the work is the distinctive personality which it reveals: "It is the manifestation of the faculties and qualities [the artist] possesses which attracts and fascinates us." [12] These "faculties and qualities" are of two kinds: first, the distinctive emotional and intellectual make-up of the artist noted above, and second, the skill with which he has expressed himself in the work, or as Véron puts it, "the power with which he depicts his impressions." [13] Therefore aesthetic experience is essentially what Véron calls "admiration" [14] of the artist. Our "admiration may be always summarised in the words 'What genius it must have required to execute such a work as this!' " [15]

LET US EXAMINE this view critically. A great deal of our talk about art describes the character and skill of the artist. We say that "Haydn is witty," "Edgar Guest is sentimental," "Melville sees the mystery in human existence," "Dali is an expert craftsman." What do we mean when we say things like this? There seem to be two possible interpretations.

Primarily, we may mean that the *works* created by these men have the characteristics which we attribute to the artist. Thus we say "Edgar Guest is sentimental" instead of "This poem by Guest is needlessly emotional"; "Haydn is witty" suggests the well-known *fortissimo* chord which is supposed to startle the audience in the "Surprise" Symphony. Such statements about the artist do not usually refer to a single one of his works, but to a number of them which resemble each other in the respect mentioned, e.g., Haydn playfully introduces the unexpected into several of his works, many of Guest's poems are sirupy. On this interpretation, "The artist is — " is an elliptical or shorthand way of speaking, in which we substitute the name of the artist for the titles of his works.

Thus we are speaking solely about the *works of art* and the characteristics which we find in them. Reference to the artist adds nothing.

11 *Ibid.*, p. 74; cf., also, pp. 118, 120.
12 *Ibid.*, p. 107.
13 *Ibid.*, p. 333.
14 *Ibid.*, p. 52; cf., also, pp. 54, 65.
15 *Ibid.*, p. 53.

But if this is true, then we come to this conclusion: the notion of "personality" adds nothing to our understanding of art. We will continue to analyze and evaluate works of art in the same way, i.e., by examining the works themselves. "Personality" gives us no clues as to how to go about this, nor does it explain anything about art. It is empty or redundant. Véron, anticipating this objection, writes at one place: "The critics may say that they are concerned with the work and not with the man: the two things are inseparable; and if the work be vile, so is the author, at least at the moment when he produced the poem or picture." [16] Does this argument help to support Véron's position? Does it not rather show up the weakness of that position? If "the man" and "the work" are "inseparable" and if, in all cases, we simply attribute to the former whatever we find to be true of the latter, then again, it is the work of art alone that we care about. And it is the work that we are really talking about.

This does not mean that we cannot feel and express our admiration of the creative artist. Because the work of art is just that — a work "of art" — and not a natural object, we recognize that it could come into being only because a man possessed certain "faculties and qualities." We honor and esteem these when the work is good. But we honor the man for what has been made manifest in the work.

This first interpretation of "The artist is —" trivializes the category of "personality." It is clear, however, throughout most of Véron's discussion, that he takes "personality" to be something quite distinct from the work itself. Thus he says that people speak of the work "but behind it they see perhaps unconsciously the worker. The picture or statue is but the starting point and first cause of their emotion." [17] "[A] work full of carelessness and other faults often extorts our admiration solely by the personality of its author which shines through it with powerful originality." [18] Véron gives a specific example of the distinction between the artist and his work: "[No] one can read Victor Hugo without adding, to their admiration of the work before them, a deep and inward joy at the discovery, in the poet himself, of a thinker devoted to all the problems which interest humanity." [19]

On the second interpretation, "The artist is —" really says something about the personality or skill of the artist, and not just about the work. The work is a starting point for inference to the character of the artist. "Haydn is witty" now means something more than that there are humorous passages in the "Surprise" Symphony and other compositions.

[16] *Ibid.*, p. 46; cf., also, p. 77.
[17] *Ibid.*, p. 53.
[18] *Ibid.*, p. 53.
[19] *Ibid.*, p. 351.

But now, we must ask, are we justified in making such inferences? We saw earlier, in the discussion of artistic creation,[20] that the state of mind of the artist may be very different from that which is embodied in the work. It is entirely possible that a man whose music is witty may himself be, *apart from his music,* wholly humorless. Another, whose poetry is profoundly emotional, may lead a placid, temperate existence. Many artists are uninteresting or inarticulate as people, though their work may be anything but that. In other words, it is highly perilous to attribute to the "man" what we find in the "work" unless we have *independent* evidence about the artist, that is, evidence gained in other ways than by examination of his works of art, e.g., from biographical data. Lacking such evidence, we invite the danger of confusing ourselves — we *think* that we are saying something about the artist, when in reality we are simply describing the work. All of us have had the experience of reading a tragedy by Shakespeare and concluding that Shakespeare possessed great human sympathy, or hearing the symphonies of Beethoven and deciding that he was a man of great emotional depth. But such assertions may be greatly misleading unless they mean only that the artist possessed the ability to display these characteristics *within his art.*

There is, however, a further difficulty. It is a commonplace that the same work of art may be interpreted in many different ways. Hence different spectators may not agree that "wit" or "profundity" or "sentimentality" is exhibited in the work. In the face of this, how could we use the work as a basis for inference to the mind and emotions of the artist? If we accept all of these interpretations, we would have to impute to the artist a whole host of diverse and contradictory traits of personality. Véron does not recognize this difficulty because he holds the view, to be criticized in the next section, that the audience always shares precisely the experience which was felt by the artist.[21]

When Véron emphasizes the importance of "personality," he does so in describing the experience of appreciating art. He considers such experience essentially "admirative" of the artist's "genius." However it is questionable whether he gives a fair account of what is generally considered "aesthetic experience." He says, in the sentence quoted earlier, that the work of art is "but the starting point and first cause" of aesthetic enjoyment. This implies that the spectator's attention is not fixed wholly upon the work itself. Interest does not come to rest in the work; it seeks "the worker." But then we are not so much enjoying the work for its own sake, as using it as a clue to something else. A psychologist or historian might do this. But this is not the way we apprehend art-objects

---

20 Cf. above, pp. 91–92.
21 The passage on p. 184 is an interesting exception.

when our interest is aesthetic. If we approached them in this way, we could never grasp their charm and vitality, for our attention would be dispersed. Véron says at one point: "[We] should preserve a sufficiently lively recollection of [the artist] to prevent . . . the subject of our contemplation from absorbing the whole of our attention." [22] Yet it is only when the work *does* "absorb the whole of our attention" that we can enjoy its intrinsic value, and only then is our experience truly aesthetic.

There certainly are instances of aesthetic perception in which we savor the artist's personality. This is particularly true when we are familiar with a number of works created by the same artist. Thus we feel Robert Frost's dry, subtle wit playing over the landscapes and episodes depicted in his poems. But in such cases "personality" is something ingredient within the work, tinging its emotional appeal and imaginative quality. We encounter and enjoy it by fixing aesthetic attention upon the work, not by taking the work to be a "starting point" to something else. In other cases, there simply is no concern with the artist's personality at all. We are interested in the "work" and oblivious to the "worker." Véron candidly admits this in discussing architecture. He calls this "the least personal of all the arts," and yet he says that "architecture in its own province has a power of expression which cannot be denied." [23] Since this is true of many works in other media as well, the scope of "personality" in art must be markedly limited.

To sum up: either admiration of the artist's personality is nothing but admiration of the work of art itself, so that the notion of "personality" can be dispensed with; or else, admiration as it is described by Véron (a) assumes wrongly that "the work" is an infallible clue to the total character of "the man," and (b) is not a faithful description of the aesthetic appreciation of art.

Historically, the concept of "personality" is important as a protest against the inhibitions and restraints of neoclassical art. It served as one of the rallying points of artistic freedom among the Romantics. It is still salutary as a reminder that we must appreciate each artist for what he is; we must not force him into pre-conceived molds. Philosophically, however, "personality" cannot serve as the basis of a sound theory of art or aesthetic experience. In addition to the shortcomings which we found in it just now, "personality" cannot by itself serve as a criterion for evaluating art. One critic, who takes it to be central to all art criticism, writes: "Personality is a law to itself. . . . For example, if I think that Delacroix is an artist, I must not seek the merits and defects of his painting. There are neither merits nor defects in the painting of Dela-

[22] *Ibid.*, p. 337.
[23] *Ibid.*, pp. 184, 186.

croix, there is only the style of Delacroix." [24] This impresses upon us the need for approaching the artist sympathetically. But it blocks the process of analysis and evaluation. Can we not sometimes say justifiably that a work of art is good in some respects and bad in others? And cannot an artist's personality be inane?

2. THE EXPRESSION AND COMMUNICATION OF EMOTION

Véron argues on behalf of emotionalist theory that it is superior both to the "simple" and "ideal"-imitation theories.[25] Specifically, he urges against the "ideal"-theory that it does not explain a great deal of art and artistic creation. The artist does not seek to picture "beautiful" things. He will often choose ugly subjects, and render them vividly without diminishing their ugliness. Véron cites from Greek literature "[the] corpse of Hector dragged round the tomb of Patroclus . . . Oedipus tearing out his eyes and coming in his blood to recount his woes . . . Medea cutting the throats of her sons to revenge herself upon a rival." [26] "Art," Véron concludes, "goes beyond mere beauty [for] it encloses what is terrible or sad, ugly or joyous." [27]

The distinguished Russian novelist, Count Leo Tolstoy, more than any other writer popularized emotionalist theory. In *What Is Art?* (1898), he too argued that art may arouse feelings which are unpleasant and portray "gloomy, heart-rending scenes." [28] More recently, Professor Ducasse has asserted as "psychological fact" that the artist does not seek to "create beauty." [29] Like Véron and Tolstoy he holds that "any subject may be treated by the artist." [30]

The indebtedness of these thinkers to the Romantic movement in art should be clear from our earlier discussion.[31] By reiterating this description of art, they were a powerful force in the decline of "ideal-imitation" in recent times. Therefore they are largely responsible for the fact that the concept of "beauty" no longer occupies such an important position in aesthetic thought. You will notice that in this book, like many recent books in aesthetics, there has been relatively little talk about "beau-

---

24 Venturi, *History of Art Criticism*, p. 36.
25 *Op. cit.*, pp. xiii, 98 ff.
26 *Ibid.*, p. 98.
27 *Ibid.*, p. 110.
28 Leo Tolstoy, *What Is Art?*, trans. Maude (Oxford University Press, 1955), p. 120.
29 Curt J. Ducasse, *The Philosophy of Art* (New York: Dial, 1929), p. 18; cf., also, p. 122. Reprinted by permission of the publishers.
30 *Ibid.*, p. 190.
31 Cf. above, p. 160.

ty." In previous centuries, by contrast, "beauty" was taken to be the single most important concept in aesthetics. Indeed "aesthetics" itself was often defined as "the theory of beauty." The emotionalists pointed out the narrowness of this view. They saw that the artist worked with the most diverse subjects, including those which were exotic, macabre, or repulsive. Hence the emotionalists have had a great influence on the way in which people approach art. The spectator no longer seeks beauty solely, or even at all, in the work of art. Roger Fry speaks for many contemporary minds when he salutes this liberating insight:

> In my youth all speculations on aesthetic had revolved with wearisome persistence around the question of the nature of beauty. . . . It was Tolstoy's genius that delivered us from this *impasse*. . . . [Most important] was the idea that a work of art was not the record of beauty already existent elsewhere, but the expression of an emotion felt by the artist and conveyed to the spectator.[32]

Here we have, I believe, one of the great strengths of emotionalist theory. If we examine the evidence of works of art themselves, we find a great many which incorporate ugly subjects. We find too that this ugliness has not been "prettified" or toned down. Rather, it has been accentuated and made vivid by the artist's treatment. In this way, as an emotionalist would say, the work becomes highly "expressive." If this were true simply of morbid or pathological art, it would not be worth talking about. On the contrary, it is found in work of unquestionable merit — Greek tragedy, as Véron points out, Goya's depiction of warfare, Berg's opera *Wozzeck*.

The emotionalists came to see this because of their conviction that the artist is motivated to create by some emotion that he feels, and that this emotion can be induced by any kind of situation whatever. This leads them to their basic theses: the work of art is an expression of the artist's emotion, and by contemplation of the work, the percipient shares this emotion. This theory we must now examine at some length.

HERE IS VÉRON's "general definition" of "fine art": "art is the manifestation of emotion, obtaining external interpretation, now by expressive arrangements of line, form, or colour, now by a series of gestures, sounds, or words." [33] To understand the activity of artistic "expression," we must first see what is wrong with describing it as "the manifestation of emotion." The mere "manifestation" of a person's emotion is not something artistic. Spontaneous laughing or crying, an unthinking yawn, or an angry gesture — all these reveal the presence of emotion. However, artistic ex-

[32] *Vision and Design*, pp. 292–293.
[33] *Op. cit.*, p. 89.

pression is not "purely impulsive, just a boiling over." [34] As Ducasse points out, "it is of the essence of art to be not blind like automatic action, but conscious and responsible." [35] This reminds us of our earlier definition of "art" in the generic sense as "skilled and deliberate." [36] Véron, it should be noted, is not unaware of this. For he frequently marks the distinction between spontaneous and artistic activity, as when he says that the art of the dance arose when spontaneous physical movements became regulated by the discipline of rhythm.[37]

Véron sees also that when emotion is uncontrolled, artistic expression cannot be carried on. "In its first outbreak, [emotion] is too vivacious, too tumultuous, too lost to all external considerations, ever to stop to relate or explain its sensations." [38] As Wordsworth's famous phrase has it, the artist can create only if his emotions are "recollected in tranquillity."

Artistic expression shows that it is "conscious and responsible" by its use of some objective medium. The emotion does not simply discharge itself upon the world, like the infuriated man kicking at a puppy. The artist molds and forms the medium in order to embody his emotions in it. He may use the musical scale, or the body, as in the dance or acting. But then he must subordinate his emotion to the demands and limitations of the medium. If the emotion simply spills over and beyond what the medium can accommodate and shape, nothing artistic is wrought. It would be like a man venting his emotion by pounding the piano keys at random — no musical composition would be produced.

Further, to express an emotion is not the same as *describing* it.[39] The artist does not announce, "I am angry" and give an account of his visceral disturbances. To label an emotion is to generalize it by bringing it under some inclusive term such as "anger." But this does not do justice to the distinctive quality of the *particular* emotion which the artist feels.

Thus far I have said that the process of artistic expression is controlled, not impulsive, it employs a medium, and it is not merely a description of emotion. Now what specifically *does* the artist attempt to do, in the course of expression? The most detailed answer in the writings of the emotionalists is given by Professor Ducasse.

HE DESCRIBES ARTISTIC ACTIVITY as the "conscious or critically controlled objectification . . . of one's feelings." [40] "Objectification" — an object is made. What kind of object? One that is "(1) capable of being contem-

---

[34] Dewey, *Art as Experience*, p. 61.   [35] *Op. cit.*, p. 114; cf., also, p. 125.
[36] Cf. above, p. 93.   [37] *Op. cit.*, p. 83; cf., also, p. 116.
[38] *Ibid.*, p. 331; cf., also, p. 75.
[39] This paragraph draws from R. G. Collingwood, *The Principles of Art* (Oxford University Press, 1938), pp. 111–115; reprinted in Vivas and Krieger, *op. cit.*, pp. 345–347.
[40] *Op. cit.*, pp. 111, 112.

plated by the artist at least, and (2) such that *in contemplation that thing yields back to him the feeling . . . of which it was the attempted expression.*" [41] In other words, the goal of the artist is to create a work, the aesthetic contemplation of which will enable him to say "Yes, that is what I felt." Only if the work "mirrors back" [42] his emotion is the activity of expression successful. It is in the light of this goal that the artist revises, omits, "edits," etc., as he goes along. The desire for self-expression distinguishes the artist from the mechanical copyist; the desire to express *emotion* distinguishes the artist from those — e.g., writers of expository prose — who seek to express *meanings*.

Thus does Ducasse spell out the conception of art which has been dominant among artists and laymen for the past century.

Now this view has, as Ducasse recognizes, an exceedingly odd implication. For it implies that the only one who can possibly tell whether an object is a "work of art" is the artist himself! This is the consequence of understanding the art-object in terms of its origins in the "inner" or "subjective" experience of the artist. The consequence follows because only the artist can know what his emotions are; hence "no one but the artist himself is in a position to say whether, or how far, he has succeeded in creating an object adequately embodying his feeling." [43] The conclusion is disconcerting, for we commonly think that whether an object is artistic is a matter of public knowledge.

A problem of much greater import than this, however, is involved in Ducasse's analysis of artistic creation. It centers around the meaning of the crucial term "expression." Let me pose the problem in this way: can even the *artist* tell whether the work "reflects" or "mirrors back" his emotion?

For consider: to say that the work "mirrors back" the emotion is as much as to say that the emotion can exist and be felt, *apart from* the work. Ducasse says that the "intrinsic nature" of the emotion is the same whether it is "objectified" or not.[44] But can the emotion which is expressed by the work be felt in any other way than by contemplation of the work? Can the-particular-emotion-expressed-by-the-particular-work exist outside the work or, as Ducasse has it, before the work is created? Emotions, in general, are individualized by the specific situations in which they occur. Love of mother, and love of sweetheart, and love of country, all *feel* differently. Now the emotion embodied in the work is individualized by that specific object. The emotion is part and parcel of a certain sensory structure, a distinctive construction of the artistic medium. This

[41] *Ibid.*, p. 113. Italics in original.
[42] *Ibid.*, p. 115.
[43] *Ibid.*, pp. 270–271. Cf., similarly, Curt J. Ducasse, "Some Questions in Aesthetics," *Monist*, XLII (1932), 47.
[44] *Ibid.*, p. 114.

is why we so often say that the only way to know what emotion is expressed in a certain piece of music, is just to listen to that music.

If what I have just said is true, then not even the *artist* can tell whether the process of expression has been successful. To do that, as we have seen, he must decide whether the emotion expressed by the work is the same as the emotion which he feels prior to its creation. But if the emotion expressed by the work does not exist apart from the work, then the artist can have no yardstick for testing. He cannot decide whether "the feeling he had intended to express was faithfully induced *again* in him"[45] by the work, for the feeling expressed by the work is something genuinely new and did not exist before the work came into being.

This argument urges that the expressed emotion is not an entity in its own right, something felt by the artist when in love or at war, and then incorporated bodily in the work. The argument urges that the emotion is transformed when it is taken from nonartistic experience and made ingredient within the work of art. It is therefore closely related to one of the commonest criticisms of emotionalist theory, viz., that this theory ignores the importance of the artistic medium and the skill with which the artist manipulates the medium.[46] Just these factors are distinctive of art and set it off from the rest of experience. Only when we recognize their importance can we distinguish the emotions of art from the other areas of life in which emotions are felt and, in other ways, expressed. Emotionalist theory, this criticism proceeds, reduces the medium and the artist's technique "to the status of mere means to the end of objectifying feeling."[47]

In one respect, Ducasse recognizes clearly that working with the medium may alter the artist's emotion. He points out that the emotion embodied in the work is not usually felt by the artist at the very beginning of the creative process. "The usual state of affairs is rather that the feeling which the work of art finally comes to embody is born in the artist only gradually, its growth preceding by but little the process of its objectification."[48] You may recall from our discussion of artistic creation that the medium is not simply passive, a "mere means." It resists the artist's attempts to mold it in some ways, but also it suggests to him new leads for developing the work in other directions.[49] Ducasse's view is far more tenable than that of the naïve emotionalists who think that the

---

[45] Curt J. Ducasse, *Art, the Critics, and You* (New York, 1944), p. 82. Italics added. Reprinted by permission of the publishers, The Liberal Arts Press, Inc.

[46] Cf., e.g., Henry D. Aiken, "Art as Expression and Surface," *Journal of Aesthetics and Art Criticism*, IV (1945), 89; Vincent Tomas, "Ducasse on Art and its Appreciation," *Philosophy and Phenomenological Research*, XIII (1952), 80.

[47] Tomas, *op. cit.*, p. 80.

[48] *Philosophy of Art*, p. 128.

[49] Cf. above, pp. 106–107.

artist's emotion is, in all cases, completely fixed and determinate before creative activity begins. However, even Ducasse, in holding that the emotion expressed by the work can be felt before the work is finished, is open to the above criticism.

And yet, how great is the force of this criticism? All of us, probably, share the conviction that somehow we *do* "express" something which we understood even before the expression was achieved. We "try to find the right word" and when we have found it we say, "*That's* what I meant (or felt.)" How could we know that the word is the "right" one, unless *somehow* we knew what we were trying to say even before we said it? How else could we, when groping for the word, reject some suggestion by saying, "No, that's not what I mean"? Similarly, there must be some congruence between what the artist feels, and the sensuous elements, the forms, the subject matter, etc., which he decides to make part of the work. When Picasso felt the indignation against warfare which moved him to create the "Guernica" mural, he did not paint a pretty countryside or an apple-cheeked child.

So we are left with a puzzle. On the one hand, the artist's emotion before the work is completed, gives direction to his creative activity, moving him in certain directions and not in others. He is trying to "say what he feels." On the other hand, the emotion which he feels cannot be the emotion which is expressed by the work in its final form, for that cannot properly be said to exist until the work is finished. Artistic creation seems to demand that a balance be struck between these two forces — the claims of the artist's emotion, and the inherent expressiveness of the object. Whether he will "accept" the object, and put down his tools, depends largely on what he has felt. But what he has felt cannot dictate *wholly* to the object, for the work cannot be simply a duplicate of previous emotion. It is not like a mirror which simply reflects whatever is brought to it. Rather it transforms and individualizes whatever it expresses.

Therefore the theory that art is "the expression of emotion" cannot be accepted just as it stands. There is a large element of truth in it, but the meaning of the crucial term "expression" must be clarified further. No theory of art is ever formulated unto eternity, and this is a problem which exponents of emotionalist theory must reckon with in the future. But since all of us, whether we are emotionalists or not, use the term "expression" so frequently, we should be aware of the ambiguity which is latent in it.

THUS FAR, in trying to learn the meaning of "expression of emotion," we have been assuming that this phrase accurately describes the creation of art and its products. Our assumption must now be examined. This is the second large question about expression: is it true that all artists carry on creative activity with the purpose of "objectifying" emotion and that the work of art itself is such an "objectification"?

Here the evidence is mixed. There is a great deal of evidence to be found in the testimony of the artists which upholds the emotionalist theory.[50] However, neither this nor any other single theory embraces *all* accounts of what the artist tries to do. In some cases, the artist seeks to create an object which will be attractive and gratifying to look upon — a "beautiful" object, let us say. In other cases, he addresses himself to some technical problem posed by his medium, and seeks to work it out to his satisfaction. In these instances, be it noted, the problem of "expression" which we have just discussed, simply does not arise. For now the test of successful artistry is not whether the art-object squares with something felt by the artist prior to its completion. The emphasis now is upon the object — whether it is beautiful, or well-constructed, and so on. The answer to such questions decides whether the artist will lay down his pen or his brush. Ducasse asserts that the artist may sometimes judge the work, not as an adequate expression of his original feeling, but as an expression of some *other* feeling "which on consideration he is willing to acknowledge as truly an aspect or part of himself." [51] This is a significant departure from the original theory of self-expression. The work is considered now, not as a suitable embodiment of something felt earlier, but as something of interest in its own right. Judging the work in this way is so widespread in artistic creation that we should be very cautious indeed about saying that all creativity is "expression of what the artist has felt."

But where the goal of the creative process is solely to create an object which the artist is "willing to acknowledge," then, on Ducasse's theory, it is not a "work of art." It can be that for Ducasse, you will remember, only if the artist sought "objectification of his feelings." This raises grave questions about the soundness of Ducasse's theory. Ducasse contends that his definition of "art" "does apply to whatever is acknowledgedly so called." [52] But does it?

If we apply Ducasse's definition to specific poems or paintings, we will be forced to say that objects which are commonly considered "works of art" really are not that at all. As we have just noted, the goal of the artist is not always emotional expression; in these instances, what he creates would not be, on emotionalist theory, a "work of art." In the face of such evidence, Ducasse must try to classify many objects usually called "artistic" in some other way. For example, he says that a lyrical poem

---

[50] Cf., e.g., Julius Portnoy, *A Psychology of Art Creation* (Philadelphia, 1942).
[51] *Philosophy of Art*, p. 269. All further references to Ducasse will be to this work unless otherwise indicated.
[52] *Ibid.*, p. 125.

written "to win the favor of a lady," in which the artist does not objectify himself, but rather presents "whatever sort of self one thinks the lady will like, — which self one passes off as one's own," — such a poem is not "fine art." Ducasse calls it "angling with spiritual bait, amatory engineering." [53] Similarly, the deliberate attempt to create an object of beauty is "skilled work," [54] not art.

But certainly in the vast area of love poetry, there are many works which, if we knew the inmost thoughts of the poet, would have to be described, following Ducasse, as "amatory engineering." The works addressed to their loves by the British poets of the Tudor-Stuart period often, doubtless, display the "sort of self one thinks the lady will like." Yet we do not hesitate to call these "works of art" and place them in anthologies of poetry. They resemble poems written with different motives more than they resemble, say, bringing candy and/or flowers, which is another sort of "amatory engineering." When a definition of "fine art" runs counter to commonly held belief, and relegates objects universally considered artistic to some limbo of nonart, we would do well to question the soundness of the definition. What is important is not the definition itself, but rather what can or can not be done with it. An excessively limited definition will lead us to ignore important similarities between various poems and it will handicap us in carrying out the job of analyzing and criticizing works of art.

The limitation of emotionalist theory is the result of defining the art-*object* in terms of the activity of artistic *creation*, and then restricting this activity to the fulfillment of a *single* motive, i.e., emotional expression. We have seen in various ways that the work of art has a life and significance of its own, which transcends the motives of the artist. Therefore emotionalist theory cannot be considered a wholly comprehensive theory of art.

UP TO THIS POINT we have treated all three emotionalist thinkers as exponents of a single theory. Tolstoy, however, differs from Véron and Ducasse on an important count.

He denies that the *expression* of emotion is enough to constitute art. Art must also *communicate* emotion to its audience. "Art begins when one person [has] the object of joining another . . . to himself in one and the same feeling." [55] Hence Tolstoy's definition of "art": "*To evoke in oneself a feeling one has once experienced and having evoked it in oneself then by means of movements, lines, colours, sounds, or forms expressed in words, so to transmit that feeling that others experience the same*

[53] *Ibid.*, pp. 118, 119.
[54] *Ibid.*, p. 122.
[55] *Op. cit.*, pp. 121–122.

feeling — this is the activity of art." [56] Art is profoundly important for Tolstoy, because it is a "language" which unites men in shared emotions. Art which "fails to move men" is "either bad or is not art at all." [57]

Ducasse, on the other hand, like Véron, rejects this "communicationist" theory. He recognizes that artists, sometimes at least, wish to transmit their emotions to others. But this, Ducasse says, is distinct from the "art-impulse" to express one's feeling. [58] Like the desire to make money from one's art, the desire to communicate is not essential to the creative process. Furthermore, "[that] products of art are capable of communicating feeling and are at times so used as to do it does not mean that they occurred as a result of the intention to do so." [59] Therefore, Ducasse concludes, the "deliberate plotting to move others" [60] should not be taken as part of the definition of "fine art."

There are two different questions involved in this controversy: (1) Is the artist, during creative activity, always concerned with communicating his emotions to a potential audience? (2) Apart from the artist's intentions, should "fine art" be defined in terms of expression only, or communication as well? (1) is a question about psychological facts, to be answered by learning about the thoughts and desires of the artist. (2) is a matter for the aesthetician to decide: is an "expressionist" definition more useful and workable for understanding art than a "communicationist" definition, or vice versa?

With regard to (1), it almost goes without saying that a great many, probably most, artists *have* been concerned with the communicative power of their work. The proof is that they have revised their work, during the creative process, in order to make it more readily understandable or more appealing to the prospective audience. In ancient and medieval society, and wherever art serves some communal function, the importance of communicating successfully to others is presupposed by the artist. Moreover, the medium used by the artist, such "forms" as the sonata or the novel, his symbolism, etc., are commonly taken from a cultural tradition. Hence he can employ them to make an object which is "public" and shareable.

It would be an error, however, to think that artists always seek to communicate. There are instances to the contrary. Artistic creation is often so intensely personal, or so absorbing, that the artist has no thought for those who may later apprehend the work. His engrossing and sole interest is to express himself fully, or to get the work "right," and so on. The poet Keats says: "I feel assured I should write from the mere

[56] *Ibid.*, p. 123. Italics in original.
[57] *Ibid.*, p. 178.
[58] *Op. cit.*, p. 36.
[59] "Some Questions in Aesthetics," p. 57.
[60] *Op. cit.*, p. 40; cf., also, pp. 37, n. 7, 39.

yearning and fondness I have for the Beautiful even if my night's labours should be burnt every morning, and no eye ever shine upon them." [61] Similarly, Gerard Manley Hopkins was impelled to create by the desire to express adoration of God and his own inadequacies in the eyes of God. His poems, as he knew, were "subtle and recondite" and consequently, for a long time, they had little or no audience. But it was not popularity that he was seeking in his poetry.

Hence if Tolstoy's "communicationist" theory is taken as a description of the facts of creative activity, it is invalidated by at least some of the relevant evidence. But Tolstoy insists that art must be a bond uniting all men. Therefore his definition of "art" should, perhaps, be interpreted as a plea for what artists *ought* to do. Now, we might ask, would conscious concern with the audience improve the value of the artist's work?

I do not see any simple "yes or no" answer to this. Much great art, e.g., the plays of Shakespeare, was created with "audience appeal" in mind. Yet excessive concern with what "the public" is going to think may lead the artist into vulgarity and mediocrity. He may try to make his work simple and palatable, and thereby destroy its quality. One can think of novelists and musicians in our own time who have succumbed to this. Thus attention to "communication" must be tempered by respect for the inherent value of the work and the artist's own integrity. But there are also dangers in being too introverted. The artist who has no regard for an audience thereby foregoes an important kind of critical control over his work. He does not have the basis for correcting and altering his work which is gained by asking "How will this sound (or look) to someone else?" As is true of so many amateurish artists, his own judgment may be inadequate. Therefore the work will be undisciplined or needlessly complicated or simply banal.

So much (though all too briefly — as you probably see, a great deal more might be said) on the "expressionist"-"communicationist" dispute over the *creation* of art. Now to consider (2), viz., should communication, as Tolstoy holds, be taken as part of the definition of "fine art," so that an object which fails to arouse emotion in the spectator is not a "work of art"?

Clearly an object which completely failed to communicate to *anybody* would be *ex hypothesi* valueless and therefore, perhaps, not even worth talking about. It would seem to make little difference whether we call it "art." Yet our question raises important questions about the meaning of "fine art."

Professor Ducasse gives strong and persuasive arguments against a "communicationist" definition. He points out that "to describe anything as a work of art is merely to say something as to the *sort of process* through

[61] *Letters of John Keats,* ed. Page (Oxford University Press, 1954), p. 173.

which it came into being." [62] As we saw in our earlier analysis of the generic meaning of "art," [63] it is the way in which it is produced that distinguishes art from natural objects and impulsive, habitual, and reflex actions. Now, Ducasse goes on, whether an object communicates has to do with its effects *after* it has been brought into being. The origin of an object is one thing; its history, following its creation, is quite another. To make "communication" part of the definition of "art" is to confuse the two. Hence the usual meaning of the term "art" is blurred. Furthermore, the "communicationist" theory leads to a paradoxical and even ridiculous conclusion. For suppose, what is often true, that the same object moves one person and not another, or one person at one time, but not at another time. Then we would have to say that the object both is and is not a work of art. But this, Ducasse says, "is absurd, for if a painting is in fact a product of the creative human activity called art, this fact remains forever and universally a fact." [64]

If we want to say of a work that it does or does not communicate, or if we wish to speak about what it communicates, we can perfectly well do so without making "communication" part of the definition of "fine art." Everything that the communicationist wishes to say about art can still be said. Moreover we can now say intelligibly, as we often wish to do, that one and the same work of art "moved" one generation but not another. Thus the *value* of art, when it is apprehended aesthetically, is kept apart from the *meaning* of "art," which refers solely to the object's mode of production.

THIS RAISES ANOTHER QUESTION: is the aesthetic value of the work the same as its capacity to communicate to the audience? Or have they nothing to do with each other? Tolstoy's answer is unequivocal. He says "not only is infection a sure sign of art" — we have seen that he considers "infection" part of the *meaning* of "art" — but also, he goes on, "the degree of infectiousness is also the sole measure of excellence in art." [65] "Degree of infectiousness" refers to a number of different things in Tolstoy's theory. At this point we will discuss it as it refers to the universality of the work's appeal. Thus a work is "infectious" when it can be understood by, and communicate emotion to, a great many people. Tolstoy says that "what distinguishes a work of art . . . is just the fact that its language is understood by all, and that it infects all without distinction." [66] He goes on: "The assertion that art may be good art and at the same time incomprehensible to a great number of people, is extremely unjust. . . . [Good] art always pleases every one." [67]

[62] *Op. cit.*, p. 20. Italics in original.
[64] *Art, the Critics, and You*, p. 46.
[66] *Ibid.*, p. 177.
[63] Cf. above, pp. 92–93.
[65] *Op. cit.*, p. 228.
[67] *Ibid.*, p. 176.

The reader will very likely anticipate the objection to this view. We all live in a "mass culture." That is, works of art in our society, like other commodities, are commonly designed to appeal to a vast audience. This is often a matter of economic necessity. If the movies do not find and reach a "mass market," they cannot be produced. But unless we are wholly submerged in the "mass culture" — and none of us is prepared to believe that about himself — we will not grant that popularity is a criterion of artistic value. Sometimes, indeed, we may even think that the worth of a work of art and its popularity are inversely related to each other. Often the most popular record in the juke boxes or the television program with the highest audience rating seem to be the most mediocre specimens of their kind. Such works "infect" untold numbers of people. But this does not prove that they are *good*. Of course, a specific moving picture or record *may* be both worth while and popular. Yet it remains true that there is no *necessary* relationship between "degree of infectiousness" and aesthetic value.

Again, there is much "good art" which, contrary to Tolstoy, does not "please every one." Many examples could be taken from the art of our own century. The writings of Joyce, Kafka, and Proust, or the schools of "modern art" discussed in the preceding chapter, make severe demands upon the percipient and therefore still have only limited audiences. We can come to appreciate such works only if we make the effort to familiarize ourselves with them and enlist the assistance of such critics as Fry. Tolstoy, however, denies that this is necessary for the appreciation of what he considers good art. He says that art can infect people "independently of their state of development and education." [68] The spectator need not "[exercise] effort" or "[alter] his standpoint." [69] But this flies in the face of what we know about aesthetic perception. We must often try deliberately to develop "sympathy" for works of art which are initially foreign to us. Only so can taste be developed. Works which can be enjoyed without effort are frequently trivial or mediocre.

Tolstoy's critics have often claimed that the clearest refutation of his theory of "infectiousness" is to be found in the evaluations of art which result when this theory is applied. Tolstoy condemns most of the classics of Western art, particularly those of the nineteenth century. Beethoven's Ninth Symphony is a poor work of art because it "does not unite all men." [70] Much the same is true of Brahms, Richard Strauss, and Wagner. On the other hand, Tolstoy claims that "The majority always have understood and still understand what we . . . recognize as being the very best art: the epic of Genesis, the Gospel parables, folk-legends, fairy-tales, and

[68] *Ibid.*, p. 178.
[69] *Ibid.*, p. 227.
[70] *Ibid.*, p. 249.

folk-songs." [71] We need not disparage the merit of these works if we hesitate to call them "the very best art," or if we deny that "infectiousness" is a criterion of value in art.

WE HAVE SET IN OPPOSITION the "expressionist" and "communicationist" schools of emotionalist theory. In one respect, however, they are not so sharply opposed as a comparison of Tolstoy's and Véron's definitions of "art" would suggest. Véron, the expressionist, does not define "art" in terms of communication. Yet for Véron, works which are expressive will also, as a matter of fact, communicate emotion to their audience. They will do so *if* one condition is satisfied — what Véron calls the "condition of absolute sincerity": "An artist of true feeling has but to abandon himself to his emotion and it will become contagious, and the praise that he deserves will be awarded to him." [72]

The "sincerity of the artist" is of fundamental importance in any emotionalist theory. Once art is thought of as a recording of emotion, then the demand is made that the artist must truly feel what he embodies in the work. We do not now seek verisimilitude, as in "imitation"-theory. As Véron puts it, "sincerity in art takes the place of truth." [73] Moreover, the emotionalists like Véron were protesting against the sort of art produced in the "Academies" — where students were taught the proper "rules" of painting, and developed technical ability, and studied Graeco-Roman art, and then produced works which were cold and lifeless. This was because they themselves felt no intimate and personal emotion as they created. Art can be infectious, Tolstoy says, only if "an author has in the manner peculiar to himself experienced the feeling which he transmits, and not when he passes on another man's feeling previously transmitted to him." [74] Another sort of insincerity occurs when the artist "does not himself feel what he wishes to express, but is doing it for him, the recipient." [75] Insincere art is "counterfeit" art. [76] Good art for Tolstoy, we have seen, is infectious art. Whether the work is infectious depends chiefly on the sincerity of the artist. [77] So Tolstoy speaks of "the chief and most precious quality of art — its sincerity." [78]

Like so much else in emotionalist theory, the notion of "sincerity" has entered into common thought and discourse about art. And there seem to be good grounds for it. We are ourselves impressed and moved when

[71] *Ibid.*, p. 177.
[72] *Op. cit.*, p. vii.
[73] *Ibid.*, p. 101.
[74] *Op. cit.*, p. 183.
[75] *Ibid.*, p. 229.
[76] *Ibid.*, pp. 190–192, 218–219, 230.
[77] *Ibid.*, pp. 228–229.
[78] *Ibid.*, p. 193.

we are persuaded that the artist is speaking "from his heart." His sincerity lends considerable earnestness to the work. But when we think that he is "faking," or "putting it on," we are correspondingly alienated. Similarly, when we think that the artist is trying to arouse and manipulate emotions which he has not himself experienced, we are also estranged. In general, works created by an insincere artist will often lack the warmth and conviction which is imparted to the work by the artist's emotion. So considered, "sincerity" is a notion of considerable importance and explanatory power.

It is only when we stop to analyze it critically that its limitations emerge.

In the first place, as a practical matter, how can we *know* whether the artist was sincere or insincere? "Sincerity" refers to certain episodes in the psychological biography of the artist, i.e., certain emotions which he felt. But we do not usually have access to such biographical data, particularly when they are as "private" as emotions generally are. What we *do* have is just the work of art itself. This is an object — in tones or stone or words — not a psychological state experienced apart from the work. As I tried to make clear earlier, to draw inferences from the work to the state of mind of the artist is, generally, extremely hazardous and often downright wrong. *Sometimes* we can draw such inferences with a fair degree of plausibility. It would be very difficult to believe that Milton did not himself feel indignation like that which is expressed in "On the Late Massacre in Piedmont" or that the display of emotion in Tchaikovsky's Fifth Symphony has no counterpart in the composer's emotional history. In such cases we can probably make the kind of judgment cited in the preceding paragraph. It is quite likely, however, that we go wrong far more often than we are aware. We fail to realize this only because we do not possess the evidence — of the artist's psychological states — which can alone determine whether our inference was right or wrong.

I have cited two instances in which biographical inference seems plausible. But it is only because of the deep-seated influence of the Romantic movement and emotionalist theory that we habitually think that such inference is *always* legitimate. Let us take another case. Consider Haydn, who wrote over a hundred symphonies as well as an enormous amount of music in other forms. Much of this music was written to order, at the request of his patron or on commission. Did he have to feel each of the infinite emotions which is embodied in his many works? Is it plausible to think that he did? Did he have to traverse the whole gamut of emotions every time he incorporated both a brisk, light-hearted *Allegro con spirito* and a pensive slow movement in a symphony? It is more realistic to think of Haydn as a craftsman, skilfully forming materials which are themselves vivid and evocative. The tones of the scale, the voices of the orchestra, the structure of the sonata form — these have a life and appeal of their own to the creative artist. They can be artfully contrived to produce an object of intrinsic delight. This is not to say that Haydn is a *mere* "technician." But his undoubted greatness will not be explained by dubious references to "sincerity." When a work is *expressive to* the spectator, we cannot always infer that it is an *expression of* the artist.

Even if the artist is sincere, it does not follow that the *work* will seem "sincere" to the aesthetic percipient. The emotionalist assumption to the contrary is unwarranted. The artist may feel his emotions earnestly and intensely. Yet, for a whole host of reasons, the work may fail to convey this. He may lack control of the medium, his technique may be inept, the structure of the work may be disorganized or opaque, and so on. Is this not often the tragedy of the amateur artist? Is it not true of the love poetry of the adolescent? What he feels he feels with desperate earnestness; yet what he creates is awkward, trivial, and cold. Given the work, nobody would ever dream that the artist was "sincere." Furthermore, as I have just suggested, the opposite state of affairs is quite conceivable: an artist who feels little or no emotion may create an object which is highly expressive emotionally. This may perhaps be unlikely — though if we want to say even this, we should do so with great caution — but it is by no means impossible. The insincerity of the artist does not, in and of itself, reduce or destroy the value of the work for the aesthetic spectator. It is the *work* that is the object of aesthetic perception, not the life of the artist. If the work speaks at all, it speaks for itself.

Some readers may find that these arguments grate on their firm belief in the importance of "sincerity" — perhaps they would wish to say that "the work *is* the man." Let me remind them that these arguments, like all those discussed in our study, are neither to be accepted nor rejected uncritically. The student should test them in the light of relevant evidence and reasoning, some of which I may well have overlooked. In this way he will rethink his belief in artistic "sincerity," even if, ultimately, he decides to keep this belief. Let me present for his consideration what I take to be the conclusions from the foregoing discussion: What is important is that the *work* should be animated by a feeling of sincerity; if it is not, then its value is diminished. In *some* instances, where the internal evidence of the work is strong, we can, with a degree of probability, infer to the feelings of the artist. However, although sincerity in the artist may *often* be one cause of the goodness of the work, it is never, in itself, *sufficient* to assure the work's value.

THE NOTION OF "SINCERITY" is closely related to another characteristic emotionalist doctrine, viz., if the artist is sincere, the percipient will share precisely the experience which was had originally by the artist. We have already encountered this view in the passages quoted from Tolstoy which set forth the communicationist theory.[79] Véron, similarly, says that a good work of art "brings to us the identical feeling of its author." [80] We often speak of aesthetic experience in just this way. Thus a critic discussing a painting by Pissarro writes: "One feels one's self penetrated little by little by a melancholy feeling which must have been itself experienced from the aspect of the natural scene." [81]

This view can be dealt with somewhat briefly, for it is much like other emotionalist doctrines which we have already considered. Here again the personal experience of the artist is taken to be central — this time as the norm for aesthetic experience — and here again problems arise as a result. How could we ever *know* that the spectator's experience is "identical" with that of the artist? I may be sure that *my* experience is just like the artist's, but since I usually have only the work of art to go by, and not the relevant biographical data, this is only a slim conjecture. Moreover, a work of art may arouse a whole host of different experiences in various people. Not *all* of these can be identical with the artist's own experience, and it is very likely that *none* of them is. Think of the profoundly different "readings" of Hamlet by the generations which have followed Shakespeare's, or the contrasting interpretations of one and the same composition by two different conductors. Furthermore, there is no reason to think that the aesthetic experience which most closely resembles the artist's is the most rewarding experience which could be had. The spectator may find values in the work to which the artist was oblivious. Departure from the artist's experience would then be a gain.

It is noteworthy that Ducasse, the most recent of the emotionalists, abandons the belief of his nineteenth-century predecessors in the identity of the artist's and spectator's emotions.[82] More important, Ducasse does not think that the spectator is under any obligation to pattern his experience on that of the artist: "*when a work of art is considered from the point of view of the [percipient], the values in terms of which it may legitimately be appraised by him are of the most diverse sorts.*" [83]

ONE CONCLUSION emerges clearly from our analysis of the emotionalist theory thus far: even if what the emotionalists say about the process of *creation* is right (and we have seen reason to question its universality), even if, that is to say, the artist seeks to "manifest his personality," or to "express his emotions sincerely," from this we cannot legitimately deduce the nature of the work of art, or the nature and value of the aesthetic experience. The creative process is the *genesis* of the art-object. But once

[79] Cf. above, pp. 173–174.
[80] *Op. cit.*, p. 105.
[81] Quoted in Venturi, *History of Art Criticism*, p. 266.
[82] *Op. cit.*, p. 274. Cf., similarly, *Art, the Critics, and You*, p. 125.
[83] *Art, the Critics, and You*, p. 126. Italics in original.

the work has been brought into being, it can be interpreted, enjoyed and evaluated by the aesthetic percipient in a variety of different ways which have nothing to do with the artist's personal experience. The work cannot be adequately understood merely as a replica of the artist's experience. The appreciative experience of the spectator cannot be "tied to" the artist's experience (even if we could know what that was). And the personal experience of the artist during creation cannot determine or legislate for the value of his work for contemplation. If you see how these conclusions arise out of the foregoing pages, then you will be able to see the force of Professor Lee's statement: "It is inevitable that confusion be introduced into any theory of aesthetics which goes to the creative experience of the artist for the solution of its problems." [84]

3. THE AESTHETIC EXPERIENCE

If the facts of artistic creation do not determine the nature of the aesthetic experience, then how, given the emotionalist theory of art, can we be sure that aesthetic experience always includes emotion? Moreover, aesthetic enjoyment can be had when its object is, not art, but nature. Since nature is not the product of artistic creation, nothing that we say about art will explain the perception of nature. Emotionalist theory can show that emotion is always crucial to aesthetic experience only by studying aesthetic experience in its own right.

DUCASSE CARRIES OUT the most detailed analysis. He holds that emotion is essential to aesthetic appreciation because he holds that it is precisely emotion that we are seeking when we view things aesthetically. The aesthetic attitude, we have seen, is one of "disinterestedness." Ducasse adds another element to its description — "receptivity" to the "feeling-import" of the object. "[One] throws oneself open in aesthetic contemplation . . . to the advent of *feeling*." [85] Our attention is fixed upon the object, but "our interest, our aim, is in feeling itself as such." [86] The feeling, when it is obtained, is "something to be tasted, and as it were, rolled under one's emotional tongue." [87] The feeling is "the completion, the success, of the contemplation." [88] Hence Ducasse's characterization of the aesthetic attitude as " *'listening,' or 'looking,' with our capacity for feeling.*" [89] The aesthetic attitude can be taken toward any object whatever,[90] and any emotion whatever can be felt during the aesthetic experience.[91]

---

[84] *Perception and Aesthetic Value*, p. 154.
[85] *Op. cit.*, p. 140. Italics in original.
[86] *Ibid.*, p. 141.
[87] *Ibid.*, p. 142.
[88] *Ibid.*, p. 142.
[89] *Ibid.*, p. 140. Italics in original.
[90] *Ibid.*, pp. 156, 223–224.
[91] *Ibid.*, pp. 189 ff.

Ducasse has put into words the nature of a great deal, at least, of aesthetic experience. Certainly many people do apprehend art and nonartistic objects in this way. If they are not "moved," then they would deny that aesthetic perception had achieved "completion" or "success." Moreover, in adding emotional "receptivity" to "disinterestedness," Ducasse seems to distinguish the aesthetic attitude more clearly from other modes of perception. One might find intrinsic interest in something which is not obviously an aesthetic object, e.g., some people read history or study mathematics in this way. Their experience is set off from the aesthetic, according to Ducasse, because they are concerned with the apprehension of "ideas" and not with the emotions which may accompany these ideas. If they *are* concerned with the "feeling-import" of, say, the mathematical proof, then their experience is aesthetic.

However, we may justifiably ask whether the aesthetic spectator is always concerned uniquely with the "feeling-import" of the object. There are many who would deny that they are. They give disinterested and sympathetic attention to the object and "throw themselves open" to *whatever* psychological states may be felt as a consequence. They focus upon the "sensory surface" of the object, the way it looks or sounds, and relish their sensations; or they grasp the formal organization of the object, and thereby experience its order and balance; or they become aware of the work's symbolic overtones. Those who deny the accuracy of Ducasse's account do not deny that emotion *may* be aroused during aesthetic experience. They deny however that there is anything privileged about it. They are interested in emotion no more and no less than any other state which makes up the total experience.

Some critics of emotionalist theory go further than this. They argue that if, as Ducasse says, "our interest, our aim, is in feeling itself as such," then our experience is not veritably aesthetic. For then we are merely *using* the work of art to induce a certain kind of experience. We are like the people who try to redeem the emotional poverty of their lives by reading romantic novels. Since interest is not being taken in the object intrinsically, the spectator's attitude is not aesthetic. Hanslick, the musical formalist cited in the last chapter, is one of the most forceful critics of emotionalist theory. He writes: "In the pure act of listening, we enjoy the music alone, and do not think of importing into it any extraneous matter. But the tendency to allow our feelings to be aroused, implies something extraneous to the music." [92] As a result, the distinctive nature and value of the music are not discerned. "Music may, undoubtedly, awaken feelings of great joy or intense sorrow; but might not the same or a still greater effect be produced by the news that we have won the first prize in the lottery, or by the dangerous illness of a friend?" [93]

[92] *The Beautiful in Music,* p. 21.   [93] *Ibid.,* p. 26.

When we consider Ducasse's theory of aesthetic experience in greater detail, the force of these criticisms is blunted. Hanslick contends that emotion is "something extraneous to the music." We can distinguish, in general, two kinds of situations in which emotion is "extraneous" to an object. First, when something is a *sign* or *symptom* of emotion. Tears, a frown, an angry gesture may lead us to believe that a person is experiencing emotion; a physiologist might infer this by measuring heartbeat or the secretion of adrenalin. In such cases, we could apprehend the sign and interpret it correctly without ourselves feeling emotion. Secondly, when an object is the *cause* or *stimulus* of emotion. Emotion can be induced by a pay check, a broken shoelace, or by the injection of nitrous oxide. When we are subjected to such stimuli we feel emotion. But the emotion is not then felt as being *intrinsic* to the object. The stimulus "sets off" the emotion, but the stimulus is not itself invested with emotion.

Now for Ducasse, the relation between the aesthetic object and its "feeling-import" is neither that of a sign or a cause. It is a much more intimate relation. Ducasse calls the aesthetic object the "immediate symbol" of an emotion. It is not something from which we infer an emotion, nor something which is itself, like nitrous oxide, nonemotional, but which stimulates emotion. Rather the aesthetic object "embodies" emotion so that we have only to apprehend it to get the "taste" of that emotion.[94] The "feeling-import" is, Ducasse says, "directly" apprehended as being intrinsically bound up with the nature of the object. Following Ducasse, we can ask how unrestrained exuberance can be dissociated from the dancing figures in Matisse's painting, "La Danse." Is not sadness felt to be part and parcel of the measures of Tchaikovsky's "None But the Lonely Heart"?

If this is true, then the aesthetic object's "feeling-import" is unique.[95] Since the emotion is inherent in the object, and since the object has its own distinctive nature, "no symbol . . . is ever completely interchangeable with any other." [96] Therefore, one can *not* get from the musical composition "the same effect" as is produced by good or bad news in everyday life. So we might say on behalf of Ducasse's view that the somberness of the Funeral March in Beethoven's "Eroica" is not like that of a personal disaster. We must add, however, that the distinctive "feeling-import" of the work will not be disclosed unless the spectator pays scrupulously close attention to the sounds and forms which make up the musical composition. If it is simply being heard dimly on the "fringe" of attention, then the music will be more like a *cause* of emotion than an *embodiment* of emotion. When this occurs, as it so often does, Hanslick's criticisms have great relevance and cogency.

---

94 *Op. cit.*, p. 179.
95 *Ibid.*, pp. 180–182.
96 *Ibid.*, p. 182.

Now Ducasse can take another step in defense of emotionalist theory. Hanslick, again speaking on behalf of many critics of this theory, charges that not even the emotionalists can describe *which* emotions are expressed by music. "Let those who, when listening to some instrumental composition, imagine the strings to quiver with a profusion of feeling, clearly show *what* feeling is the subject of the music. . . . Now, how can we talk of a definite feeling being *represented*, when nobody really knows *what* is represented?" [97] To this, Ducasse would reply that Hanslick is, in one respect, correct. Uusually we cannot say what the "feeling-import" is. Since it is "immediate" and "unique," it is "strictly speaking indescribable." [98] Any "immediate" quality of felt experience can only be known by being experienced; and insofar as it is unlike anything else, there are no general terms with which to describe it. But this cannot be used as a legitimate criticism of emotionalist theory. Because the expressed emotion is "indescribable," it does not follow that it does not *exist*. "[The] *feelings experienced by human beings are endlessly numerous and various, and . . . the immense majority of them cannot be referred to by name because they have received none.*" [99] Our emotions resist classification into "kinds" such as "love" or "anger," which are, at best, highly approximate. Ducasse puts great weight on this fact. He says that the failure to recognize it "is I believe the principal explanation of such opposition as there has been to 'emotionalist' theories of art." [100]

We can probably all agree that Ducasse's rebuttal is a strong one. How can mere descriptive words capture the subtle "tang" and nuances of our emotions? Indeed, we might almost wish to say that that is what poets, composers, and painters are *for* — to render the distinctive qualities of our emotional life. Yet we must be careful to see what Ducasse's argument does and does not prove. Ducasse has shown this: from the fact cited by Hanslick — that we cannot name the emotions expressed by music — it does not follow that music does not express emotion. On the other hand, of course, Ducasse's argument does not show that music *does* always express emotion, even if it is "indescribable." The stubborn critic of emotionalist theory might retort that Ducasse has taken refuge behind the namelessness of emotions. When he is presented with a work which, the critic claims, expresses no emotion, Ducasse can reply with impunity, "Oh, but it *does* express an emotion; unfortunately, however, I cannot tell you *what* that emotion is." But this leaves open the possibility that there may be *no* emotion there at all. Hence the critic might mutter sourly that Ducasse is "begging the question," i.e., he is simply reiterating the theory which he is supposed to defend, without actually defending it.

[97] *Op. cit.*, pp. 40, 44. Italics in original.
[98] *Op. cit.*, p. 175.
[99] *Ibid.*, p. 195. Italics in original. Cf. Véron, *op. cit.*, p. 326.
[100] *Ibid.*, pp. 197–198.

The only way out of this impasse is, as always in such cases, by appeal to empirical evidence. Is it, as a matter of fact, true that the aesthetic object always embodies an emotion which becomes part of the percipient's experience? Here it is important that both sides to the dispute should gather evidence and examine it candidly. They should not be more interested in saving their theories than in learning from the evidence. I do not wish to sound clever when I say that there has been too much emotion about emotionalist theory. Its proponents seem to think that only this theory does justice to the intensity and fervor of aesthetic experience; on any other theory, the experience becomes desiccated and "cold." The critics of emotionalist theory, like Hanslick, seem to think that it vulgarizes aesthetic experience, reducing it to a state of uncontrolled emotional indulgence which disregards or perverts the true value of art.

We do not have highly systematic evidence. But if we look at the kind of evidence urged by both sides, I think we find that it does not uphold universally the emotionalist theory. Ducasse, for his part, claims that even an isolated color has a distinctive emotional "flavor," and that this is perceptibly different from the "feeling-import" of a different shade.[101] This seems to be borne out in the experience of many of us when we are buying ties or dresses, or choosing the paint with which to do over the living room. Moreover, there is a great body of art criticism which speaks intelligently and revealingly about art in terms of emotional expression. But on the other hand, there are those who do not find such "feeling-import" in their aesthetic experience.[102] This is particularly true when they do not share Ducasse's belief that the aesthetic attitude is oriented especially to the arousal of emotion. Like Hanslick, they apprehend in music an objective structure of "sound and motion." And like Hanslick they find that "the beautiful is and remains beautiful though it arouse no emotion whatever." [103] As the American critic, John Crowe Ransom, has put it, "Art feels cool, not hot."

There are a number of related issues in the area of this evidence which I will mention briefly, and which the student is invited to reflect upon at greater length.

Primarily, even when emotion *is* aroused in aesthetic experience, the antiemotionalists contend that there is tremendous diversity and variability in the kind of emotion that different spectators feel. Hanslick points out that "[the] present generation often wonder how their forefathers could imagine that just *this* arrangement of sounds adequately represented just *this* feeling." [104] This argument is carried on by a later writer who urges that the variability of emotional reactions proves that "emotion is an accidental consequence of aesthetic apprehension," [105] and therefore cannot

---

[101] *Ibid.*, pp. 174–175, 199.   [102] Cf. H. N. Lee, *op. cit.*, p. 44, n. 20.
[103] *Op. cit.*, p. 19.   [104] *Ibid.*, p. 25. Italics in original.
[105] Eliseo Vivas, "A Definition of the Esthetic Experience," in Vivas and Krieger, *op. cit.*, p. 406.

be used to define "aesthetic experience." The emotionalist must explain, in rebuttal, how "feeling-import" can be "embodied" in the object, and yet fail to affect all percipients in the same way.[106] The evidence seems to show that emotion is not "internal" to the work, as Ducasse says it is, at least in the way in which the lines of a painting or the key change in a musical composition can be said to be inherent in the work. The emotionalist must carry out further his explanation of how a work can be *expressive to*, without being simply a cause or stimulus to emotion.

Further, it has been argued that when a great many different emotions are presented in the work of art, it is not even *possible* for the spectator to share in all of them.[107] Thus, in tragedy, which depicts the interplay of emotions between as many as half a dozen characters at once, it is out of the question for the percipient to try to feel each of these emotions. He is *aware* of the emotions but he does not *feel* them.

Finally, it may be that emotion is felt in the apprehension of *some* works of art, but not all. It is noteworthy that Véron, himself a leading emotionalist, holds just this view. Hence he does not espouse a thoroughgoing emotionalist theory of aesthetic experience. Véron believes that there are a number of schools and "styles" of art which do not express emotion in their work. Such art, which Véron calls "decorative" art, seeks only to please the senses through "grace, prettiness, and *beauty*." [108] This suggests that, e.g., "Classical" as opposed to "Romantic" art, and the arts of "ornamentation" can be enjoyed aesthetically though they lack "feeling-import." Does a Bach fugue express emotion or does a Greek vase or a Persian rug? It is up to emotionalist theory to show that and how it does.

For this purpose the theory may employ the notion of "mood." The emotions aroused by art, as well as by some natural scenes, are not always intense visceral disturbances. They may be subdued and fairly placid.[109] "Mood" refers to emotional states which are less intense and more enduring than emotional "seizures." Thus the tranquil music of a Mozart Divertimento might be found to express a mood, though it is not conspicuously emotional. By carrying out such analyses, emotionalist theory may be able to show its critics that it does not apply solely to the perception of tumultuous, breast-beating art.

To SUM UP, emotionalist theory has not yet demonstrated that its account is exhaustively true of all aesthetic experience. But though its scope may not be universal, the theory is, in an important respect, illuminating when compared with the theories of art discussed previously. Any aesthetic

---

[106] Ducasse addresses himself to this question, *op. cit.*, pp. 182–188.
[107] Cf. Morris Weitz, *Philosophy of the Arts* (Harvard University Press, 1950), pp. 174–175.
[108] *Op. cit.*, p. 111. Italics in original.
[109] Cf. Ducasse, *Art, the Critics, and You*, p. 55.

theory, we have seen, must show us how to carry out the analysis of specific works of art or at least give us important leads to doing so. We want such analyses to be revealing, to call to our attention elements of the work that help to explain its value. Thereby we hope to increase our appreciation of the work. Such analysis will not be possible when the theory leads us to disregard or minimize important features of the art-object. Both "imitation"-theory and formalism suffer from this. The former concentrates too much on what is represented in the work; the latter rejects the subject matter almost completely. Emotionalist theory, by contrast, does not limit itself in this way. It analyzes what Ducasse calls the "dramatic" significance of subject matter in order to show its emotional force; and it recognizes that "form is important in aesthetic objects for the very reason that it itself, in contemplation, is the source of certain aesthetic *emotions* which nothing else can objectify." [110] Emotionalist theory thus gives us a significant clue to analyzing anything whatever that enters into the totality of the aesthetic object: what is its significance for the "feeling-import" of the object? You have doubtless encountered this sort of analysis in the study of literature and the other arts, as when a well-known text-book of poetry asks about a poem by Blake, "How has the poet managed to give the sense of abrupt and impassioned utterance?" [111]

Emotionalist theory can do justice to the total work only when it considers emotional expressiveness to be "embodied" in the work. If it took emotion to be "extraneous" to the work, as Hanslick charges, then it would be vulnerable to the criticism that it neglects artistic medium and structure. Then the work would be reduced to a mere stimulus for inciting emotion; and then, as the antiemotionalists might say, picking a fight or having a love affair would be quite as effective as looking at a work of art. But when emotionalist theory recognizes what Ducasse calls the "internality" of the expressed emotion, it sees and it leads us to see that the emotion cannot be divorced from the work. Hence we must attend to the medium and its formal patterning if we are to feel the emotion which is peculiar to the work. The emotion has no existence except in and through its artistic embodiment.

WE ANALYZE WORKS OF ART not only in order to understand them better, but also to pass judgment on their *value*. This poses a final problem for emotionalist theory. If emotion is, in all cases, the centrally important element in art and its appreciation, how are we to discriminate good art from bad?

The facts of critical discourse show that emotion is often vital to the value of the work. We speak of the emotional profundity of a Greek

---

[110] *Op. cit.*, p. 198. Italics in original.
[111] Cleanth Brooks and Robert Penn Warren, *Understanding Poetry*, rev. ed. (New York: Holt, 1956), p. 429.

tragedy and the restrained ardor of a late Mozart symphony. And, as the emotionalists never tire of insisting, we reject a work which is "cold." Yet the value-criterion certainly cannot be "the *more* emotion the *better*." This would not be congruous with our commonly accepted evaluations of art. It would give the highest marks to works of uninhibited emotional frenzy, whereas we often rank these below works of composure and restraint. Indeed we use such terms as "sentimental" and "bathos" to condemn works in which there is *too much* emotion. But how can we tell when emotion becomes "too much" and therefore bad, if emotion is the only yardstick we have for measuring goodness and badness?

What then *is* an adequate emotionalist theory of aesthetic value? This too must be put on the agenda of work to be done in future by those who believe in emotionalist theory. Véron measures value by the manifestation of the artist's emotion. But suppose the emotion is banal or, at the other extreme, simply odd and eccentric, or too profuse, as in sentimentality? Tolstoy measures value by "infectiousness." This refers either to the universality of the work's appeal or to the degree to which the audience shares the artist's emotion. We have already seen the weakness of the first criterion.[112] The second is open to the same objection as Véron's, viz., what if the emotion with which we are "infected" is dull or overindulgent? Ducasse distinguishes good art from bad depending upon whether the expressed emotions are pleasurable or displeasing. Thus emotion itself is not used as the criterion of value, and Ducasse does not explain what there is about the emotion which makes it pleasant or unpleasant. This is significant, for it strengthens the conviction that emotion per se cannot serve as an adequate yardstick of value. There is more about the work of art and its appreciation which must be taken into account if we are to do the job of evaluation.

So WE SEE that important qualifications must be made about the validity of emotionalist theory — it may not hold true of all art and all aesthetic experience, it must explain more clearly the process of artistic creation, whereby an object becomes *expression of*, and also how the aesthetic object is *expressive to*, and it must provide us with a workable system for judging the value of works of art and other aesthetic objects. Nevertheless, emotionalist theory has proven indisputably that it is one of the most catholic and fruitful theories of art. It is, generally, close to the facts of experience of those who make and those who enjoy works of art. It may not be, it almost certainly is not, the *only* valid theory of art and aesthetic experience. But even those who will not accept the theory must meet its arguments and learn from its insights.

[112] Cf. above, pp. 176–178.

BIBLIOGRAPHY

* Ducasse, Curt J. *Art, the Critics, and You.* New York: The Liberal Arts Press, 1944.

* Rader, *A Modern Book of Esthetics.* Pp. 185–192, 258–282.

* Vivas and Krieger, *The Problems of Aesthetics.* Pp. 255–261, 343–386, 406–411.

* Weitz, *Problems in Aesthetics.* Pp. 410–417, 612–621.

Dewey, *Art as Experience.* Chap. IV.

Einstein, Alfred. *Music in the Romantic Era.* New York: Norton, 1947.

Garvin, Lucius, "An Emotionalist Critique of 'Artistic Truth'," *Journal of Philosophy,* Vol. XLIII (Aug. 1, 1946), 435–441.

Gotshalk, D. W., "Art and Beauty," *Monist,* Vol. XLI (Oct., 1931), 624–632.

Green, Peter. *The Problem of Art.* London: Longmans Green, 1937.

Hanslick, *The Beautiful in Music.*

Pepper, Stephen C., "Emotional Distance in Art," *Journal of Aesthetics and Art Criticism,* Vol. IV (June, 1946), 235–239.

Scott-James, R. A. *The Making of Literature.* New York: Holt, 1943.

Tomas, Vincent, "Ducasse on Art and its Appreciation," *Philosophy and Phenomenological Research,* Vol. XIII (Sept., 1952), 69–83.

QUESTIONS

1. Read some of the artistic credos of early Romanticism, e.g., Wordsworth's Preface to *Lyrical Ballads* (2nd ed.), Hugo's Preface to *Hernani.* In what respects do they repudiate the various schools of "imitation"-theory? In what respects do they resemble the emotionalist theory of art?

2. It is argued in this chapter that there is a crucial difference between the pre-artistic emotion and the emotion which is expressed in the work of art. Read Ducasse, *Philosophy of Art,* pp. 112–114, 68–71; Collingwood, *The Principles of Art.* How do these philosophers describe the differences between the pre-artistic and the expressed emotions?

3. The critic, John Crowe Ransom, is quoted (p. 186): "Art feels cool, not hot." Must a work "feel hot" if it is to express emotion? Does Ransom's aphorism apply to *all* art? Look at and compare the Plates, in answering these questions.

4. How does Ducasse's conception of the aesthetic attitude differ from that presented in Chapter 2? Which do you consider more adequate?
   Do you agree with Ducasse that emotion is "the completion, the success" of aesthetic contemplation?

5. What do you take to be the relation, if any, between the universality of a work's appeal and its aesthetic value? Is universality of appeal a sign of "greatness" in art? Consider specific works of art which are commonly considered great.

6. What do you take to be the relation between a work's emotional expressiveness and its aesthetic value? Are the two *identical?* Is expressiveness a *component* of value? Is it a *measure* of value? Explain your answer in each case.

7. What are the similarities and dissimilarities between emotionalism and formalism? Is formalism simply a subdivision of emotionalist theory?

8

The Theory of Aesthetic "Fineness"

1. THE "FINENESS" OF ART

"Art" in the broad sense refers to any human activity which is performed skilfully and with a purpose.[1] So we speak of the art of cookery, the art of stealing bases in baseball, the art of diplomacy, and even of artful murder. This is the *activity* of art. The *object* which is produced in this way is the "work of art." Such an object was not produced by the processes of nature or by accidental or haphazard human doing. Hence a great many of the objects which we see about us in our everyday lives can be described as "works of art." In a highly technological civilization, indeed, virtually all of the things with which we have anything to do are artistic. Our clothes and dishes, blackboards, automobiles, and newspapers are all works of art. Think of a man who spends his day in the business section of a large city. What does he see in his environment that is "natural" as opposed to "artistic"? Very little, unless it be the sky — assuming that he thinks to look up at it.

Thus the denotation of the term "art" is highly inclusive. But just here you may balk. Is this not using "art" *too* broadly? Much of the furniture

[1] Cf. above, p. 93.

of our quotidian lives is dull and prosaic. Must we call such things "works of art"? What of a crude water tumbler, which is little more than glass shaped to hold what is put into it? Or something simple like a matchbox? It offends us and it seems to strain language to call these "works of art."

Well, in one sense, these *are* "works of art." We need words to mark important distinctions in fact. "Art" distinguishes the way in which these objects came into being. Again, they are not "natural," like the sky, and they didn't "just happen."

Yet this does not meet the force of the objection. If something produced by deliberate human endeavor is not especially attractive or interesting to look at, if our attention simply notes it and passes over it, we would *still* hesitate to call it "artistic." What is at the heart of the objection now becomes clear. We often use the term "art" as shorthand for "*fine* art." And we reserve the title of "fine art" only for those products of human creation which are conspicuously gratifying or interesting or beautiful. What is more, we do not use "art" in this way simply to exclude prosaic water tumblers. We insist upon the importance of "fineness" in those activities which, unlike cookery or diplomacy, are generally called "the fine arts" — painting, music, literature, the dance, and so on. Thus a literary critic concludes his review of a book with the judgment, "This is a good enough novel, but it is not a work of art." What he means, clearly, is that the novel lacks those virtues which would make it an exemplary work of literature.

We now see this: the way in which we commonly talk and think about art emphasizes its value for aesthetic perception. Such value is the "fineness" of "fine art." An object is not a "work of fine art" unless it attracts us aesthetically. The theory of art which we are now to consider rests upon this belief of common sense.

"FINE ART is the production by man of objects intrinsically interesting to perceive; and any object so skilfully produced by man that it has intrinsic perceptual interest has fineness of art." [2] This is the basic definition of the theory expounded by Professor Gotshalk. "The construction of objects for aesthetic experience, then, will be the distinguishing property of fine art; . . . and human activities approach fine art in the degree that this type of construction is central or eminent in them." [3]

Artistic fineness is not found solely in the "fine arts." Many objects and actions which are intended to be useful — a locomotive, the movements of an athlete — also possess aesthetic merit. We place in "museums of fine art" objects from earlier cultures which served nonaesthetic purposes, e.g., vases, amulets, spears. On the "fineness"-theory, are these objects "works

[2] Gotshalk, *Art and the Social Order*, p. 29.
[3] *Ibid.*, p. 31.

of art"? The answer is, Gotshalk says, a matter of "degree." To the extent that useful objects have perceptual appeal, they are "fine art." But paintings, symphonies, poems, etc., have aesthetic excellence to a marked degree. In many cases, we might almost say that this is all that they are good for — to be contemplated and enjoyed. By contrast, those who create objects of utility do not seek *"primarily* to construct objects for their intrinsic perceptual appeal." [4] Here again common sense endorses Gotshalk's view. We admire craftsmen who give us clothes and silverware and furniture which are attractive to look at. But we would think a man absurd who made attractiveness his *chief* goal in designing such objects. A locomotive that did not run or a suit of clothes that was uncomfortable to wear would lead us to say that the workman was a failure, no matter how handsome these objects might be. The "centrality or eminence" of utility sets off the "crafts" from the "arts."

Hence the artist's *intention* is the distinguishing factor. It is what he is trying to do that makes the product one of "fine art." Thus Gotshalk points out that the artist may have many purposes in undertaking creation. He may seek money, fame, or social reform. But what sets off those who work in the fine arts is that they "strive to construct something splendid to perceive." [5]

As we saw in the last chapter,[6] a theory of the artist's intention can only be confirmed by checking the psychological evidence which we have about artists. It cannot be tested merely by examining the work of art. It is not enough for "fineness"-theory that the work should have "intrinsic perceptual appeal." The theory is saying that the artist *wanted* the object to have such appeal.

It is clearly common-sensical to say that composers, poets, etc., try to make something which will be "splendid to perceive." And there is testimony from the artists to endorse this view: "the desire to produce a favorable aesthetic effect has usually, and on the whole, been a characteristic aim" [7] of the artist. Yet the evidence is mixed. Hence, as in the case of emotionalist theory, we ought to be cautious about accepting any single account of artists' purposes. Different artists have different motives. We cannot say that they *always* intend to create something aesthetically enjoyable. That is not the goal of the artist who seeks the "poetic cure" of overpowering, sometimes painful emotions by expressing them. Nor is it the intention of the artist who sets himself to work out some technical problem in his medium. Although Professor Munro says that the desire to produce an aesthetic object is "a characteristic aim," he goes on to say that this is

[4] *Ibid.*, p. 31. Italics added.
[5] *Ibid.*, p. 30.
[6] Cf. above, pp. 169, 179–180.
[7] Thomas Munro, *The Arts and their Interrelations* (New York: Liberal Arts, 1951), p. 90.

"not the only aim, and often not the chief aim" [8] of the artist.

In the face of such evidence, the "fineness"-theory may withdraw its claim to describe the artist's intention. One theorist does just this: "It matters less what the [artist's] purpose is than whether [the work] actually conveys values." [9] However Gotshalk, whom we are studying as the chief proponent of "fineness"-theory, does not shorten his lines in this way. He holds that such purposes as the expression of emotion can be understood in terms of the "fineness"-theory: "may [the artist] not be described equally well as seeking to build an object which possesses a certain intrinsic perceptual characteristic, viz., a totality of expressed feeling?" [10] Gotshalk claims that whatever the goal of the artist may be, it can be made to fit into his theory. For "all such aims *qua* artistic can be translated into statements about intrinsic perceptual characteristics." [11] "Intrinsic perceptual characteristics" are, for Gotshalk, characteristics which arouse aesthetic interest. Thus he describes "intrinsic perception" as "the attentive submission of the [percipient] to the object for the sake of the . . . value offered by the object" [12] in other words, aesthetic contemplation.

Do you see what Gotshalk is trying to accomplish by this argument? He has presented an empirical theory about the intention of the artist. Any empirical theory must be tested by the evidence. There seems to be negative evidence against Gotshalk's theory — at least some artists, some of the time, do not make it their chief purpose to create an aesthetic object. Gotshalk is aware of these facts. Unlike the dogmatist or the propagandist, who wish only to preserve their beliefs or win their case, Gotshalk does not attempt to ignore what William James called "the nasty facts." He then has two alternatives. He can limit and qualify his theory, and concede that it holds only for *some* of the evidence. As we have seen, he does not choose to do this. Or else he can claim that his theory is, actually, sufficiently broad to hold for *all* of the evidence. This is what he is trying to do when he argues that any description whatever of an artist's aim "can be translated into statements about intrinsic perceptual characteristics." Thus he tries to show that the "fineness"-theory is richer and more inclusive than other theories of artistic creation.

However, when one statement is "translated" into another, they should both have the same meaning. Is this true of Gotshalk's "translation"? I would like to show that it is not, and therefore that his argument is untenable.

Suppose an artist seeks to "express emotion" without thinking about the potential appeal of his work to an audience. We have already noted that

[8] *Ibid.*, p. 90; cf., also, p. 92.
[9] H. N. Lee, *op. cit.*, p 148.
[10] *Op. cit.*, p. 40.
[11] *Ibid.*, p. 41.
[12] *Ibid.*, p. 44.

there are such artists.[13] Gotshalk says that the artist is trying to create an object with "intrinsic perceptual characteristics," i.e., characteristics which arouse aesthetic interest. Now, when the artist has created an object which expresses his emotion, it may well be that we will want to perceive the object aesthetically. The expressed emotion then becomes an "intrinsic perceptual characteristic" to us. But this does not mean that the artist *intended* the object to be enjoyed by us. We began by saying that he did *not*, as a matter of fact, have this intention. Therefore we cannot infer his intention from our aesthetic experience. *Any* object may be apprehended aesthetically, even a nonartistic object, such as a flower. But though any aesthetic object, by definition, has "intrinsic perceptual characteristics," it does not follow that the object was created *in order to* have these characteristics.

In other words, Gotshalk blurs the facts of artistic creation by his "translation." He interprets the activity of the artist in terms of the experience of the spectator. But the purposes of the artist are quite distinct from those of the spectator. The percipient may enjoy a work that the artist never intended for appreciation or he may find something of value in the work that the artist never dreamed of. It is a fatal mistake to "translate" the *effects* of the art-object into the *intention* of the artist.

A theory is genuinely empirical only when it makes some precise assertion about fact. It must say "the facts are so, and not otherwise." Only so can the theory be informative to us. But then the theory must run the risk of being falsified by negative facts. If, however, the theory claims that *no matter what* the facts may be, it can accommodate them, then it has become too broad.

"Fineness"-theory is clear and precise when it says that the intention of the artist is to create an aesthetic object. But when it tries to say that this is *always* the intention of the artist, no matter what his intention really is, then the theory becomes vague and misleading. It *seems* to be talking about artistic intention, but actually it is talking about something quite different — the aesthetic appeal of the art-object.

SUPPOSE, NOW, that the "fineness"-theory is *not* about the artist's intention. Intention has to do with the state of mind of the artist during creation. Therefore it is part of the *genesis* of the art-object. Suppose we set the genetic question aside, and consider "fineness"-theory as a theory of the work of art alone. As one "fineness"-theorist puts it, "It is the object, the thing, the work of art which is important . . . not the activity or process of constructing it." [14]

Then "fineness"-theory considers an object "a work of art" if (1) *it is*

---

[13] Cf. above, pp. 174–175.
[14] Lee, *op. cit.*, p. 150.

the product of skilled human making, and if (2) (irrespective of the artist's intention) *it has conspicuous aesthetic appeal.*

For Gotshalk, aesthetic appeal is not found solely in what is "conventionally beautiful." In common with the emotionalists,[15] he recognizes that art can be greatly valuable even when it is "bitter," "gloomy," "heart-rending."[16]

As we saw at the beginning of this chapter, the "fineness" conception of art is widely held by common sense. To the extent that things are graceful or attractive, they are said to possess "fineness." Furthermore, we reserve the term "*fine* arts" to those objects, such as paintings and symphonies, which have the power pre-eminently to arouse and reward aesthetic interest.

On the other hand, the definition does not square with *all* linguistic usage. It creates the same dilemmas as any "communicationist" theory.[17] To repeat these briefly: whether a thing is "art" for the "fineness"-theory, depends upon what it *does*, i.e., whether it arouses aesthetic interest in the spectator. If the object is appealing to one spectator and not to another, or to one generation and not another, then we seem to be forced to say that it both is and is not a work of art. Or we might have to say that the very same object was, at first, a work of art and then became nonartistic, when it was no longer enjoyed aesthetically. This sounds odd. We are always prepared to have disagreements about whether a thing is aesthetically *valuable.* We do not usually have too many qualms about saying that a work is beautiful to X but uninteresting to Y. Yet we hesitate to say that it can be a "work of art" to one person but not to another. We think that if an object is "art," then that is settled once for all. It has been settled by the way in which the object was produced. A proponent of "fineness"-theory suggests that even if we do not find the object valuable, we must call it "art" if it conveys values to others.[18] Some such way out must be resorted to when "aesthetic" is made part of the definition of "art."

THINGS IN NATURE as well as works of art can be aesthetic objects. "Fineness"-theory distinguishes the two kinds of objects by pointing out that works of art are man-made. Is this distinction important only for theoretical purposes, i.e., to define "art"? Or is it of importance also to the aesthetic spectator? Does it make a difference to the quality and value of his experience whether he knows that the object is artistic or, alternatively, natural?[19]

The philosopher Dewey poses the problem of an object which is pleasing

[15] Cf. above, pp. 166–167.
[16] *Op. cit.,* p. 46.
[17] Cf. above, pp. 175–176.
[18] Lee, *op. cit.,* p. 158.
[19] Cf. above, chap. 2, sec. 4.

aesthetically, and which is thought to be a product of human creativity. It is then learned that the object is an accidental product of nature. This leads us to withdraw the name "work of art." But something else happens. Dewey says that "[a] difference is made in appreciative perception and in a direct way." [20] When we appreciate a work of art aesthetically, we become aware of "qualities that depend upon reference to its source and its manner of production." [21] These qualities are necessarily absent when the object is a natural one.

Those who disagree with Dewey will contend that the origin of the object makes no difference to the percipient. Whether it be artistic or natural, he will respond to what is *there* in the thing before him. Doubtless works of art have, as a rule, greater social and symbolic significance, e.g., a novel about some social problem or the musical setting of a passage from the Bible. But such significance is not wholly absent from our appreciation of nature, as when we say that a natural scene reveals the grandeur of God. Moreover, if the spectator becomes concerned with the origins of the art-object, attention will be diverted from the work itself. He will think about the biography or personality of the artist, or the technical problems involved in creating the work.

On the other side of the fence, it will be argued that it *does* make a difference when we know that the object is artistic. Our knowledge can affect appreciation in a host of ways. We can feel a bond of kinship with the human being whose "precious lifeblood" animates the work. We can respond to his personality — the intense social concern of Zola or the carefree impudence of Prokofiev. We can admire his feeling for and mastery of the artistic medium. We can appreciate the skill and economy with which he has overcome technical problems. And such aspects of the work's "source and manner of production" are not irrelevant to aesthetic experience. They are qualities which permeate the work itself and thereby enhance our aesthetic enjoyment.

You will decide for yourself where the truth lies in this dispute. I now want to show that this controversy raises a larger question which is of great import for the criticism of "fineness"-theory — what should we look for in art?

PERHAPS YOU HAVE ALREADY NOTICED a curious difference between "fineness"-theory and the theories of art discussed in the previous chapters. The latter theories all call attention to some feature of art which they take to be crucial and which they would have us look for during appreciation. They stress either subject matter (in some version of "imitation"-theory) or "significant form" or "feeling-import." Each of these [22] is only one of

---

[20] *Art as Experience*, pp. 48–49.   [21] *Ibid.*, p. 49.
[22] With the exception of "significant form" in some instances.

the components which make up the total art-object. But "fineness"-theory does nothing like this. It takes the *total* work of art to be the aesthetic object. It does not single out any one characteristic of art. Hence it does not specify what we should look for in particular during aesthetic perception.

Gotshalk considers this perhaps the greatest strength of "fineness"-theory. He claims that the other theories, in concentrating upon a specific feature of art, are too narrow and limited. They fail to do justice to the richness and complexity of the art-object. The work has many "dimensions," as Gotshalk calls them — sensuous "material," form, expression, and the various "functions" which it can serve. Hence a theory which emphasizes form or expression is not so much "wrong" as it is "partial." Gotshalk holds that his theory is "sufficiently comprehensive to embrace and permit the several truths of these form and expression theories." 23

THE TECHNICAL NAME for a theory which attempts to synthesize diverse views is "eclectic." If, as the Bible says, "blessed are the peacemakers," then there is much to be said for an eclectic theory. It stills the dispute between one-sided theories, each grinding its own particular axe. It recognizes the truth in each of these theories but it shows us a larger truth than we can get from any of them alone. It points out that a work of art can include subject matter *and* form *and* expression, and that all of these are important. "Fineness"-theory reminds us of the complexity of the work of art. Thereby it keeps us from being limited and provincial in our approach to art. If we ask, "What should we look for in the work of art?" the theory replies, "Well, *everything* that is there." That is no mean answer. It voices the catholicity which is inherent in aesthetic "sympathy" and it cautions us against sacrificing any of the value of the aesthetic experience.

Because "fineness"-theory is catholic in this way, it is a sound basis for art criticism. It gives us a rich assortment of tools for analyzing the work of art. We are not limited to subject matter, as in "imitation"-theory, or formal structure, as in formalism. Emotionalism does, to be sure, take account of both subject and form, but only if they have "feeling-import." Gotshalk's concepts are broad enough to accommodate whatever we do, in fact, find in the specific work of art, and in using them we need not assume that what we find can be interesting or valuable in only one way. Art criticism has so often been doctrinaire and needlessly self-limiting that Gotshalk's approach is a welcome and refreshing change.

And yet, "fineness"-theory seems to be rather bland and unexciting, by contrast to the other theories of art. When particularistic theories such as

23 *Op. cit.,* p. 39; cf., also, p. xiii.

imitationism, formalism, and emotionalism fight among themselves, each theory has a cutting edge. Each may be too limited. But it throws light upon one salient feature at least of the realm of art and, in its very one-sidedness, provokes us. A theory tells us that art is "the language of emotion" or "the portrayal of what is universal in human experience." For one who is a beginner or amateur in the arts (and that describes most of us), such a doctrine gives focus and meaning to works of art. It gives art an importance which perhaps we did not see before. By contrast, the generality of "fineness"-theory is less obviously provoking. We are told that the work of art is whatever any aesthetic object is — a unity of the dimensions of matter, form, etc. Like any eclectic theory, this one lacks the bite and vigor of the particularistic theories. It does not tell us anything *distinctive* about "fine art" except that it is the product of human creativity (which is true of all art, in the generic sense), and that it is aesthetically valuable.

Moreover, an eclectic theory can synthesize what it considers "limited" views only after those views have been put forth. An eclectic theory, so to speak, "lives upon" monistic or one-dimensional theories. For the specific analysis of, e.g., plastic form in the visual arts, "fineness"-theory must turn to such theorists as Bell and Fry. The particularistic philosophers must do the spadework in explaining the dimension of art which each of them considers most important. Hence one can hold to "fineness"-theory only *after* he has studied theories which are less inclusive and more uncompromising.

2. THE THEORIES OF ART: CONCLUSIONS

We have now studied four theories of the nature of fine art (Chapters 5–8). I need hardly point out that these are not the *only* theories of art in aesthetic thought. It would, of course, be impossible to canvass them all. However, having seen how critical analysis of a theory is carried on, you should be able to apply the same methods to other theories which you may read about or study.

But those which you have learned about are among the most influential and recurrent conceptions of art. In the history of aesthetics and art criticism, they have largely dominated men's thinking about art and therefore they have given direction to creative and appreciative activity. These beliefs about art and its value have guided the hand of the artist, the perception of the spectator, the judgment of the critic. Such influence has not been less when it has been unconscious. Human beings are affected incalculably by the beliefs which they "take for granted" and which they do not therefore stop to think about. It is the job of aesthetic theory to articulate these beliefs and to determine whether they are reliable guides to action.

The theories which we have studied have not been of importance merely in the past. All of them are live and influential theories at the present time. ("Simple imitation" might appear to be an exception but it is still extremely widespread, in popular thought at least.) We can hear the voices of aestheticians and art critics speaking up for them. (Of the theories which are implicit in contemporary criticism, emotionalism seems to be more widely prevalent than any other.) You can doubtless find applications of all these theories in textbooks on the arts, reviews of concerts and books in the newspapers, and, closest to home, in the opinions of friends with whom you discuss specific works of art.

We have analyzed "imitation"-theory, formalism, emotionalism, and "fineness"-theory in order to learn their answers to two questions chiefly: (1) Which properties distinguish "works of fine art" from other objects and specifically from other art-objects? (2) What characteristics of aesthetic experience are most important to its value?

And now, at the conclusion of our study, one question will naturally arise: which one of the theories gives us the true answers to these questions?

In a very real sense, the reader can and must decide this for himself. Perhaps you have already done so. It may well be that you have decided that one theory presents a sound and adequate conception of art and aesthetic experience. If so, you should be prepared to justify your opinion. A belief is rational only when objective evidence can be adduced on its behalf. You should therefore be prepared to show how the chief concepts of the theory are grounded upon the facts of art, artistic creation, and aesthetic perception. And you should be in a position to meet the objections which were raised against the theory in our earlier discussion. On the other hand, however, it may be that you have made no decision among the various theories.

Whether the reader has or has not come to a conclusion, I now want to offer for his consideration a different kind of conclusion.

WE HAVE STUDIED FOUR THEORIES. (More accurately, the number has been greater, for we have seen that there are different versions of, e.g., "imitation"-theory and emotionalism.) Each theory has been subjected to critical analysis. No theory is to be swallowed hook, line, and sinker because it has been historically influential or merely because it has been expounded by distinguished thinkers. We asked of each theory: what is the meaning of its central concepts? is the reasoning which it employs valid? is it supported by empirical evidence?

Our judgments upon each theory, if they are to be truly philosophical, must be determined by the answers to these questions. Thus do we obey the precept of the first great philosopher, Socrates, that we must "follow the argument wherever it leads."

Now the first important conclusion to which, I think, the argument has led, is this: no single one of the theories of art and aesthetic experience is completely adequate and comprehensive.

No one of the theories has presented wholly satisfactory credentials to the challenge of critical analysis. Let me illustrate this by reminding you of some of the findings of our earlier discussion (you will probably be able to think of other examples): With regard to *meaning*, there is less clarity than we need to have for complete understanding, in some of the crucial concepts of "essence"-theory and emotionalism. What is the precise meaning of "essence" or "universal"? Specifically, can there be more than a single essence of a given class? What is the meaning of "expression"? Specifically, can the artist be said to express in the art-object precisely the emotion which he felt prior to creation? The problem is not, of course, that these terms are wholly devoid of meaning. The theorists who use these terms have explained them to a very large extent. But the concepts, when analyzed, are seen to be vague in critical respects.

With regard to the validity of *reasoning*, formalism has been found to be guilty of the logical error of circularity in its basic definitions. Tolstoy and Véron are guilty of invalid inference when they assume that if the experience of the creative artist is emotional, so also must be the experience of the aesthetic percipient.

Most important, the empirical validity of each of the theories is limited. No one of them is supported by all of the relevant evidence. If we take "fineness"-theory to be about the purposes of artistic creation, then there is negative evidence to be found in the testimony and practice of various artists. If a theory of art should set forth the properties which are commonly found among objects usually called "works of art," and which are not found in any other objects, then "imitation"-theory and formalism both fail to some extent. The former would include only those objects which have a representational subject matter; thus it does not take account of a great many works of art. The latter would deny the name "pure art" to all works lacking plastic value and therefore would exclude (in the case of Bell) virtually all of literature and a great deal else of fine art. Other examples could also be given.

Now if it be true that each of the four theories is empirically inadequate, it is appropriate to ask *why* this is so. It would be absurd to think that it is because the men who expounded these views were not sufficiently thoughtful or were ignorant about art. Each of the philosophers whom we have studied was greatly concerned with art and each devoted a great deal of his life to hard, systematic thinking about it. Some were themselves great artists (Reynolds, Tolstoy) and some were distinguished critics (Johnson, Fry). All of them knew more about art than most men do. Why then do they fall short of their goal of working out a theory which will be true and illuminating for *all* art?

There are a number of reasons. They all show how extensive and complex is the data with which the theorist of art works.

FIRST, HE DOES NOT start with a blank slate. The term "art" is used commonly in uncritical, everyday discourse. Hence it already has a meaning, even though those who use it may never have spelled out its meaning precisely. The theorist wishes to remain faithful to this common meaning so far as he can. He does not want a definition which will be totally at variance with the popular understanding of art. But now, when we examine ordinary usage, we do not find that "art" has only *one* meaning. It has *many* meanings. It is commonly agreed that a Beethoven symphony and a novel by Hemingway are "works of fine art." Yet it is not clear what properties are shared by such objects in virtue of which they are all "artistic." As a matter of fact, common sense harbors a great many different conceptions of the nature of art. These are not usually made clear, for the word "art" is generally used uncritically. It is only indirectly that we learn of the diversity of common meanings — when we find people disagreeing about what is important in a specific work of art and countering their opponent's suggestion by saying "*that* doesn't make it artistic," or in extreme cases, when they cannot agree whether a certain object is "art." A dictionary gives us evidence to the same effect. Dictionaries, which record standard usage, have a number of different entries under the heading "art." It seems clear that the conceptions of art in each of the theories we have studied — and by no means excluding "simple imitation," which is one of the most widespread of all — are to be found throughout everyday usage.

Could it be that we agree on the "denotation" of the term, i.e., which *objects* are "fine art," and disagree about the "connotation," i.e., the defining properties? In general, as I have just noted, we agree about the denotation. But even this is not always true. For whether we call a given object "artistic" depends upon the connotation of the term. And — this is the crucial point — the properties which are taken to be essential to art are often so radically different from each other that the same object cannot embody them all. Thus an object which on one meaning is "artistic" will be denied to be such by another meaning, and vice versa. For example, one common meaning of "art" is that of "simple imitation"; another is that of emotional expressiveness. A painting which is a faithful reproduction of "real life," but is emotionally hollow, would be a "work of art" according to the first usage but not according to the second. Conversely, the two meanings would be incompatible in the case of a painting employing extreme "distortion" which is emotionally powerful. Similarly, our discussion of "fineness"-theory showed that popular thought is of two minds about "fineness": on the one hand, a thing is "fine art" simply if it was produced in a certain way; on the other hand, a work of art can be "fine" only if it proves to be aesthetically attractive. Common sense, then, is not a single, unified body of belief. Within it there lurk many different beliefs about art, which not only differ from each other but are often at loggerheads with each other. No wonder that in everyday discourse people so often explode, "You call *that* art?!"

Now we see why no theory of art can ever be completely in accord with ordinary beliefs about art. Uncritical speech and thought is too sprawling, too complex, and too self-inconsistent to be brought under a single definition. The theorist tries to remain faithful to what people usually mean by "art." Yet his success can never be more than partial. His critic can always point to some *other* common meaning which the theory leaves out. Obviously, for example, the theory of formalism, which rejects all representation in art, can be brought under fire in this way.

But the complexity of ordinary beliefs is only a reflection of the more important complexity in the arts themselves. Stop to think of the vast array of objects generally considered "artistic." Think of the enormous differences among the artistic media — stone, words, sounds; the tremendous diversity of "styles" and schools and techniques in the history of the arts; the infinitely various circumstances — historical, social, and personal — under which works of art have been created. Such endlessly rich and various data must be brought together in a theory of art. Remember too that the arts are, in their very nature, incessantly adventurous and creative. The history of art makes it clear that traditional forms and methods are rejected when they do not meet the needs of the artist. The novelties that result give rise to profoundly new conceptions of the nature and value of art. We have seen this in our own study. Formalism came to birth with the development of Post-Impressionist art, and emotionalist theory spoke for nineteenth-century Romantic art. Revolt and innovation in the arts will cease only when men no longer create works of art.

Thus the realm of art is made up of very different sorts of objects and it is perennially changing and growing.

Finally, we cannot even suppose that the nature of a traditional work of art created centuries past is wholly and finally known to us. We might think that a traditional work, produced by an artistic movement which has run its course, would "stand still" for us to analyze its properties. But works of art often will not do so. This is part of their fascination. Long after their creation they can be understood and appreciated in a way which is wholly different from previous interpretations. The new interpretation will throw light upon features of the work which had formerly been ignored, and it will minimize those features which earlier generations had taken to be most important. Such re-evaluation can be the work of a single influential critic, like T. S. Eliot in our own time; more likely, it will be the product of a transformation in man's way of understanding his world, such as marks the great turning points in intellectual and social history. When a new vision is turned upon old works of art, we look for different things in the work and we value it for different reasons.

Hence art is fluid and changing not only as it grows into the future. In a very real sense, its *past*, so far from being "over and done with," is in constant flux. The "re-seeing" of the past, in bringing to light new values in art, will often make established theories of art seem inadequate or narrow.

For these reasons — the lack of uniformity in common speech and thinking about art, the innumerable differences among works of art, the constant re-interpretation of traditional art — the facts of art are almost incalculably varied. When the empirical phenomena are so diversified, it is not difficult to see why the question "What is art?" is such a vast one, and therefore why no single theory of art has given us a completely satisfactory answer.

AT THIS POINT some readers may wish to say that the theory of art is futile. We have found that each of the four theories studied earlier is inadequate in one or more respects and we have just seen that any theory of art sets itself to an almost impossible task. Should we not therefore abandon the theory of art altogether?

This is, I think, a counsel of despair. The reaction which it expresses is understandable enough. But like all counsels of despair it is too pessimistic and its recommendation is therefore short-sighted.

Let it be noted first that the various theories of art are not all equally and to the same extent inadequate. They do not fall on one level of error. Rather they possess truth about art in varying degrees. It is generally agreed that "simple imitation" is the least adequate. It does not describe faithfully the process of artistic creation, it takes account of relatively few works of art, and it misconstrues the nature of aesthetic appreciation and the sources of its value. A theory such as formalism, though it is also relatively limited in empirical scope, can nonetheless illuminate considerably the nature and value of the works to which it does apply. Emotionalism ranges widely, if not exhaustively, over the realm of art.

Now we can draw these comparisons justifiably because we have evidence in the light of which the theories can be appraised. We have a large fund of knowledge about art, its creation and appreciation, derived from the experience of artists, critics, and percipients. The difficulty for theory of art is not that we have no evidence. If anything, as we have seen, it may be the opposite — we may have almost too much evidence.

But where there are facts, there is a foundation upon which thought can build. Theory is impossible only where there are *no* facts nor any possibility of getting them. Only then is theory completely empty, for it lacks the sustenance of evidence and there is no way to estimate its truth. Only then would a counsel of despair be in order.

It would therefore be illegitimate to conclude that theory of art is destined to futility. And it would be absurd to turn our backs upon all that can be learned from the theorists of art. "[No] theory is ever held for long by serious men, or recurs again and again in the history of thought without some evidence in its favor."[24] Moreover, we would give up the increment of knowledge which is gained when facts are brought together and interrelated in a system of thought. A theory of art, which is, like all philosophy, "synoptic," brings together and thereby clarifies data from art criticism, the testimony of artists, psychology, history, and so forth. Such an organization of knowledge is itself a significant contribution to knowledge.

But our loss would not be intellectual only. We would lose the rich and acute insights into art which each of the theories discloses. It is just these insights which open up to us the meaning and value of works of art. Directly, and indirectly through their influence upon critics and teachers, these theories show us what to look for in art. If they did not, our experience would be vastly impoverished.

Each theory of art makes contact with *some* works of art. We must not forget this all-important fact merely because we decide that no theory has universal validity. Rather, even while recognizing its limitations, we can use each theory to clarify our understanding and appreciation of the works to which it applies. Each theory asks different questions about the art-object and throws light upon different aspects of it. In some cases, it will be appropriate to ask, as "essence"-theory would, "How much does this novel or drama reveal of the permanent and deep-seated forces in human destiny?" Looking at the work in this light, we may come to see more than the surface behavior of a few individual characters. We will find that they have significance beyond themselves. Our experience will therefore gain in depth and take on new overtones. Formalism can teach us to see what is important in "abstract" painting and music. It can keep us from asking the wrong questions — "What does this signify?" "What story does it tell?" — questions which are stultifying and self-defeating. The profound influence which formalism has had in our own time demonstrates the importance of a theory of art to popular appreciation and taste. Often two or more of these theories can be fruitfully combined. Thus, taking the "ideal"-theory and emotionalism together, we can ask whether the emotional flatness of a work is due to its failure to treat the subject with the moral elevation that it demands.

[24] De Witt H. Parker, "The Nature of Art," in Vivas and Krieger, *op. cit.*, p. 93.

Each theory lends itself readily to the analysis of a certain kind or style of art — "essence"- and "ideal"-theory to neoclassical art, formalism to abstract art, and emotionalism to Romantic art. But the explanatory power of these theories cannot be compartmentalized according to periods in the history of art. Often a theory can be turned upon art of an earlier epoch with fruitful results. Thus, formalism has been used in the analysis of Renaissance art, and in modern times Bach has been played "romantically." Moreover, one and the same art-object can be interpreted by two conflicting theories. They will, of course, point up different features of the work and they will "read" it differently. But most important works of art are so rich and wear so many different faces that both of these opposing interpretations can be legitimate and aesthetically rewarding.

How shall we know which theory applies to a given work of art? The only way to find out is by examination of the concrete and specific nature of each work. We may apply our theory and find that it fails. The questions which it poses to the work are largely irrelevant, and it ignores much that seems to be important in the work. Then we must cast about for a theory which will be more pertinent and illuminating. This sounds like a stilted and mechanical procedure. As a matter of fact, however, this is about how we usually proceed, albeit not so systematically, particularly when we meet new and unfamiliar works of art. At first we make the same demands upon the work that have been satisfied by the works which we have seen in the past. If these demands are not met by the work, we begin to look at it in another way. This shift in perception is implicitly a commitment to a different theory of the nature of the art-object. When we find that *no* extant theory of art leads us into the body and substance of the work — as has so often happened in the history of art — then a wholly new conception of art is called for. Think again of Post-Impressionist art and the theory of formalism.

Hence each theory of art possesses evidential strength, though it is in different areas of art or in regarding the same art-objects in different ways. I wish to urge that we should accept and indeed welcome the plurality of theories of art. In the house of art there are many mansions. We need all of the guidance and light that these theories can give us.

But still someone may protest, "How can we accept so many different theories? Is there not *one* theory which sums up the truth about art?"

All of the discussion thus far shows how I would try to go about answering these questions.

We have examined most of the leading theories of art carefully and in some detail. Then we traced the enormous complexity of the facts of art. On the strength of this, I would consider it untrue to the facts and, what is almost worse, an insult to the student's intelligence, to claim that there is any *one* theory which has the complete truth about all art. It is a characteristic tendency of the human mind to want an *answer*, and usually the quicker and simpler the better. But, as Aristotle says, we delude ourselves if we try to get an answer which is more "exact than the nature of the subject permits." We *do* have answers to our questions about art and aesthetic appreciation, but they are as diverse as the facts of our "subject." We should resist the urge to adopt some simple-sounding phrase like "Art is the record of human values" or "Art is significant form." The empirical phenomena are too complex and too fluid to be distilled into any simple formula. Only those who suffer from intellectual timidity will be discouraged by this.

Moreover, any attempt to add up the various theories of art into one all-embracing definition is doomed from the outset. Eclecticism, unlike the specific theories, gives us no factual knowledge of its own. And it can only create confusion. Each of the theories pulls in different directions. It tends toward certain styles or periods of art, or toward certain aspects of art. Sometimes the concepts of different theories can be brought together in the analysis of particular works. In general, however, they are more often incompatible than supplementary. Thus, "simple imitation" is diametrically opposed to the two other versions of "imitation"-theory, and formalism is incompatible with imitationism. We should use these theories when they are relevant to the work, as Gotshalk's "fineness"-theory does, but an all-inclusive synthesis into a single definition is out of the question.

Once again, the conclusion is impressed upon us that we must accept and work with a number of irreducible theories. As I have tried to show, this is no reason for dismay. The wealth of theories enhances our knowledge and enriches our appreciation.

The moral here, as elsewhere in human thought, is that we must "keep open the windows of the mind." The philosophers of art have taught us much that is of great importance. But open-mindedness is called for in several directions. Whether one decides to hold to a single theory, or whether he holds that each theory is true in some respect, he should be aware of the evidence and reasoning which supports these theories. He should be aware of competing theories and informed about their claims. He should be on the alert for new evidence, whether from new artistic movements or from the re-interpretation of traditional art. "What is concluded that we should conclude anything?" He should be prepared to modify or abandon his beliefs if the evidence demands it. If you do not decide to accept any one theory, then, as I have tried to show, there is a real and reasonable alternative to utter indecisiveness. That is to recognize the validity of each of the major theories in some areas of art and to apply them accordingly. Then open-mindedness takes another form. We should refuse to apply any preconceived theory until empirical analysis shows that the specific work is fruitfully explained by the concepts of that theory.

3. THE UNIQUENESS AND INTEGRITY OF THE WORK OF ART

The four theories can be grouped in a pattern which brings out interesting differences among them.

"Imitation"-theory and emotionalism fall together, in opposition to formalism and "fineness"-theory. The two former theories understand the art-object in terms of something which lies outside the work itself. "Imitation"-theory emphasizes the dependence of the work upon nonartistic reality, either the ordinary facts of existence ("simple imitation"), or what is universal in nature ("essence"-theory), or what is aesthetically or morally exalted ("ideal"-theory). In some sense, then, art is an "imitation" of "life" or "nature." Emotionalism, speaking for the Romantic artist, disavows the need for verisimilitude or idealization. But this theory also conceives of the work in relation to what lies outside of it, viz., the personal experience of the artist, notably his emotional experience. The work fulfills the artist's purpose to "express" what he felt prior to creative activity. Hence the work is understood genetically when it is said to be an "expression of emotion."

The two other theories, by contrast, focus upon what is found within the work itself. They are not concerned with its relations to anything else, the origins from which it arose or the "real life" which it depicts.[25] It is the intrinsic structure and value of the work that these theories speak of. Formalism vigorously repudiates any "real life" significance and confines itself to the elements of the medium which are included in the work and their formal organization. "Fineness"-theory sees the work as an aesthetic object and therefore stresses its "intrinsic perceptual characteristics," though Gotshalk does not restrict these in the manner of Bell and Fry.

This classification enables us to understand better the strengths and weaknesses of these theories.

Primarily, the two theories which bring in extra-artistic matters seem to tell us more about art than those which consider only the work itself. Perhaps this is a paradox, but I think that most of us get this impression when we study these theories. Take "imitation"-theory first. Once we see the relation of art to "life," there are a great many things to be

---

[25] Qualifications which were made in the foregoing chapters are omitted from the summarizing statements in this section.

talked about. Why has the artist chosen to depict these persons and events? How if at all has he distorted or idealized their "models"? What does the work show us about human experience? What "truths" does it reveal? If we take "imitation"-theory seriously, then nothing less than all of life and reality can become pertinent to the work. A great deal of the criticism of literature makes this clear. You have probably seen this in your own study of such works as the plays of Shakespeare or the novels of Melville or Dickens. Start to talk about these works and you are soon talking about the motivation of human behavior or the problems of social justice. Similarily, emotionalist theory tells us something about art which is highly provocative — that art is, uniquely, the area of human experience in which emotions are deliberately recorded and transmitted to others. This too stimulates many lines of thinking about the work. We want to see what has moved the artist to expression, we want to discover the methods which he used to achieve expression, most of all, perhaps, we want to share his emotions.

Formalism and "fineness"-theory seem, in comparison, relatively uninformative. Formalism does call our attention to "plastic" values in the visual arts, and this is a great contribution. But formalism becomes strangely inarticulate in talking about these values. It cannot define its basic term, "significant form." "Fineness"-theory tells us that the work is an aesthetic object. When the theory adds that the work possesses matter, form, and expression, it does not give us, in the manner of "imitation"- theory and emotionalism, any one way to take hold of the work. Hence, in different respects, formalism and "fineness"-theory are less explicit than the other two: formalism, because it lacks clarity, and "fineness"-theory, because it is not single-minded.

It would be a great mistake, however, to infer the superiority of "imitation"- and emotionalist theories on this account. There is another side to the coin.

Think of the pattern which has just been established: imitationism and emotionalism have much to say, and they are the theories which bring in extra-artistic data; formalism and "fineness"-theory are less explicit, and they are theories which are concerned solely with the work of art itself. This suggests, primarily, that what the first two theories say about art may take us *away from* the work to other matters. If so, then they are not seeing the work as a self-contained object which is of interest in its own right.

If you will think back to our earlier analyses, you will find that just this conclusion is true of these theories. "Imitation"-theory makes the value of the work dependent upon its relation to "life" — verisimilitude, and so on. Then the only aspect of the work that is important is the subject matter — the faithful duplication of ordinary objects, or the portrayal of "general form," or the representation of what is "proper" and "noble." Therefore the totality of the work is splintered apart. For the total work is *more*, a great deal more, than merely its subject matter. It is that subject matter presented in a particular sensuous embodiment, in a certain formal structure, shot through with emotional and imaginative overtones. To single out the subject matter exclusively is to disregard all else that is part of the work, and therefore to destroy the integrity or wholeness of the work. Such an approach is antithetical to the aesthetic attitude, which seeks to grasp the total concrete fullness of the work.

Véron and Tolstoy underestimate the inherent significance of the work in a somewhat different way. They hold that the work is nothing but the embodiment of emotions felt previously by the artist, and for the spectator it is just the vehicle for transmitting these emotions. But we have seen that this view is seriously mistaken. The elements of the medium, the form, the symbols which make up the work may have significance which far transcends the original state of mind of the artist. The work is not usually just a replica of his original thoughts and feelings. Consequently it can be interpreted and enjoyed by later audiences in a whole host of different ways which may have little or nothing in common with the artist's original experience. The work has a life and value of its own; it cannot be tied down to its origins.

So the first pair of theories, in different ways, destroy or misconstrue the intrinsic significance of the work. If we trace out their extra-artistic leads, we will be diverted from the work as an aesthetic object. We will abstract the subject matter and relate it to "real life." Or we will treat the work as a psychological document, using it as a clue to the artist's experience.

The second pair of theories is at the opposite extreme. They are concerned solely with the work as a self-contained object. But these are the theories, we said, which do not speak about the work so explicitly as imitationism and emotionalism. It is important to see why this is so.

The formalists can give no definition of "significant form." But this may be because the forms which make up the work cannot be described in words. They are peculiar to the painting or sculpture, and what they "say" cannot be said in any other way. To know "significant form," you must just see or — this word is often used — "intuit" it in a specific work. If the theory fails to describe the properties which it considers crucial to art, that can plausibly be attributed to the uniqueness and ineffability of works of art. If formalism is mute, it is because it wants to speak only about the work of art itself, and cannot do so. It does not wish to speak about something else, e.g., "real life," which is outside of the work of art and therefore *can* be talked about.

"Fineness"-theory takes no single line in discussing the work of art, e.g., its relation to "life" or the artist's experience. It encompasses all aspects of the work — its subject matter, form, expression, and so on. Consequently it may seem bland or unexciting by comparison to the other theories. But, like formalism, it is trying to respect what is *in* the work. Unlike formalism, it finds a great many different elements in art. "Fineness"-theory therefore considers it a mistake to emphasize any one "dimension" of art. Art, when considered aesthetically, is made up of many diverse elements and has many different values. A theory of art should be broad enough to encompass them all.

Thus the second pair of theories is trying to do justice to the work itself. They do not wish to obscure it with extra-artistic irrelevancies. It is for this reason that formalism can find no words for its crucial ideas and "fineness"-theory is so disarmingly catholic and inclusive.

THIS ANALYSIS gives rise to a conclusion which is, I think, of the first importance for anyone who is interested in art.

Whenever we are talking about works of art as aesthetic objects, we should make sure that we are talking about what is within the work itself. If we are not, then what we say is a gross confusion. What is said seems to be directed to the work, whereas it is really about irrelevant psychological or historical matters. This is the sort of thing that we find so frequently in books about artists, courses in "art appreciation," program notes at concerts, etc. Such talk can only have the effect of misleading or destroying aesthetic interest.

We can learn from formalism to respect the uniqueness of the work of art. We can learn from "fineness"-theory to respect the integrity or wholeness of the work. From both we can learn that the work of art, when considered as an aesthetic object, has a significance and value which is inherent in itself alone. Hence we can also learn from formalism that no words will ever be an adequate substitute for the work itself.

But this does not at all mean that "imitation"-theory and emotionalism have nothing to teach us. Far from it. Our original impression was that they tell us *more* than the other theories. They tell us "more," as we have seen, in the sense that they give us specific and pointed leads to the nature of art. We could hardly take a step forward in discussing literature, particularly drama and the novel, without examining its relation to "life." And often we find that a work can be interpreted and enjoyed as a personal emotional utterance of the artist.

But we can now see how these approaches to art must be disciplined if they are to be helpful rather than dangerous. They must tie in to what is ingredient within the work. They must not lead us away from the work. We shall consider subject matter as one among other dimensions of the work, when we are dealing with representational art. So we shall talk about "real life" only so far as it has a bearing upon the subject matter, e.g., the plausibility of the characters in a play, or the moral insight in a novel. Similarly, we shall talk of an artist's biography, including his emotions, only when it is relevant to what is *in* the work.

In other words, a balance must be struck between the extra-artistic approaches of imitationism and emotionalism, and the purely aesthetic approaches of formalism and "fineness"-theory. We do not wish to be simply mute in the face of art. That would leave us ignorant and aesthetically impoverished. But what we *do* say about art should be about *art*. What we say should, so far as words can, light up the inner richness of the work, its precious uniqueness and its goodness.

BIBLIOGRAPHY

* Gotshalk, *Art and the Social Order*. Chap. II.
* Vivas and Krieger, *The Problems of Aesthetics*. Pp. 90–105.
* Weitz, *Problems in Aesthetics*. Pp. 61–76, 107–139, 145–171.
  Thurston, Carl, "Major Hazards in Defining Art," *Journal of Philosophy*, Vol. XLIV (Feb. 27, 1947), 129–132.
  Weitz, Morris, "The Role of Theory in Aesthetics," *Journal of Aesthetics and Art Criticism*, Vol. XV (Sept., 1956), 27–35.

QUESTIONS

1. "To be truly artistic, a work must also be esthetic." — Dewey, *op. cit.*, p. 48. What meaning of "artistic" do you think is intended here? On which meanings of the term would this sentence *not* be true? Cf. Ducasse, *Philosophy of Art*, p. 20.
2. Which of the four major theories of art do you consider most adequate? How would you meet the criticisms of this theory, made in the previous chapters?
3. Show how two or more major theories of art can be used together in the analysis of some specific work with which you are familiar. Show how two theories of art would be *incompatible* with each other in the analysis of other works. Make use of the Plates in answering this question.
4. What, in your opinion, is the most valuable thing that can be learned from studying the theories of art?
5. "[All] the defects with which the method of definition may be charged when it is applied to aesthetics boil down to a single one, insufficient attention to the facts." — Thurston, *op. cit.*, p. 132.
   What do you think is meant by this? Do you agree? How does this view compare with that of Weitz, in the article cited in the Bibliography?

PART **III**

The Structure of Art

9

Matter and Form

1. THE STRUCTURE OF ART

Under this heading are included the parts or elements which together make up the work of art. We shall see what they are, how they are related to each other, and how they contribute to the aesthetic value of the work. No single theory of the nature of art will be presupposed. The discussion will draw upon each of the theories which we have studied. Each will be used where it helps to explain the structure of art. But we want to understand, in fullest measure, *all* of the elements which constitute the work. Hence no particularistic theory will do. For the same reason, the approach will be most like that of the eclectic "fineness"-theory.

Our inquiry will serve several purposes. As I have just said, we hope to learn what makes the work of art "tick." Moreover, we must understand the structure of art before we can *evaluate* art. To say that a work is "good" or "beautiful" or "inferior" is only the beginning of evaluation. If the judgment is to have any claims upon the opinions of others, we must be prepared to support it with reasons. These characteristically take the form of pointing to the elements which make up the work — "The rhythm of the poem is taut and exciting," "The colors of the painting are dull," "The composer has developed his themes ingeniously." Study of the structure of art enables us to single out these elements and estimate their importance. Furthermore, our study can enhance our own enjoyment of art. Once we understand the components of the work and their interrelations, we become more sensitive to all that is richly contained within the work. Aesthetic seeing is more acute and therefore aesthetic experience is more satisfying.

It may be helpful to list briefly, at this point, the "elements" which enter into the structure of art. This chapter deals with "matter" and "form"; the next chapter discusses "expression."

"Matter" refers to the sensory "building blocks" of which the work is composed — sounds, colors, words, etc. In the work these are arranged and organized in some way — "form." But the work is more than an arrangement of material elements. When we apprehend it aesthetically, we find that it embodies emotions, images, and ideas. We find "sadness" in the music and "pessimism" in the novel. This is, as we commonly say, what the work "expresses." There is another element which is found in some, though not all, works of art. We called this before "subject matter," i.e., the objects or events depicted in representational art such as the drama and traditional painting. Subject matter will be referred to when the structure of this kind of art is being discussed.

It should now be clear that study of artistic structure involves the *analysis* of art. We must "take apart" the total work of art in order to distinguish its elements. Just here someone will arise to protest. He will urge that this is a fatally wrong method where art is concerned.[1] The work of art is a *unity* and only so can it be understood theoretically and appreciated aesthetically. When we are enjoying a work, we are not aware of "form," "matter," and "expression" as independent entities. To break up the work into these parts is to destroy its meaning and value.

How can this charge be answered? As we have seen, we do commonly "analyze" the work when judging its value. We speak of its rhythm or color. And indeed we *must* do so. A work of art is very complex (the analysis of structure shows this, if we did not realize it before). If we are to speak of it at all, we must resolve complexity into its constituents. And we can only talk about one thing at a time. Analysis is therefore inevitable. The only alternative is to remain dumb in the face of the work — "dumb" in more than one sense, for then we can never learn about the work and enhance our appreciation of it.

But analysis *may* be grievously misleading, as our critic charges, if we misuse it. We do so when we commit the "fallacy of vicious abstraction": abstracting one element out of a total, concrete object and then thinking that it has the same properties, when thus considered in isolation, that it has when it is part of the object. Why is such thinking fallacious? Because when the element is part of the object, it has relationships to the other components of the object, and these relations affect it and make a difference

[1] Cf. above, pp. 15–17.

216

to its nature. Consider only the economic needs of a human being — the famous abstraction of the "economic man" — and you will decide how he will spend his money for certain objects. But when you examine the actual human being, who has personal, political, and emotional relationships to other people and to groups, you will see how far wrong your conclusions are. His economic behavior is influenced by all of these other factors. (Think of how many personal and household budgets go awry for just this reason.)

"Vicious abstraction" in the arts consists in trying to understand some element of the work such as form or expression as though it existed in isolation from the work. This leads into the error of thinking that the nature and value of the element can be wholly known apart from the rest of the work. Then follows the further error of thinking that once the value of each of the elements has been calculated, the value of the work is simply the sum of all these partial values. It is like those psychological experimenters who thought that if they could determine the aesthetic worth of each color in a painting, it would then be an easy step to determine the value of the whole painting.[2]

These mistakes are immeasurably serious. If we fall prey to them, they will lead us into absurdity. Equally bad, they will confuse and distort our aesthetic perception of art.

We must be on our guard against these errors throughout all of the following discussion of artistic structure. We should not for a single instant forget that the form, matter, and expression of a work exist only *within* that work. There they interact with and bear upon each other. They are what they are, and they have the value that they have, only because of their mutual interrelationships.

Thus although we must "analyze" — how else could we speak about art? — we must take care how we go about it. Our discussion of each element will be intelligent only if we keep in mind how it is related to the other elements. Indeed, at many places, we will be reminded of these interrelations. For we will find that we cannot even talk meaningfully about any one element unless we remember its place within the total being of the work.

To sum up:

> The ultimate fact in all aesthetic theory is the completed work of art in all its concreteness and organic unity. To analyze it we must tear it apart and so do violence to its living structure. . . . [But] to consider the work of art as a mere aggregate of ingredients and thus suggest that any ingredient . . . may be either present or absent without essential artistic gain or loss, is to commit the unpardonable sin in the study of art.[3]

[2] Cf. above, pp. 11–13.
[3] Greene, *op. cit.*, p. 126.

Now one further prefatory word before we begin: The analysis of structure is intended to be valid for *all* art. Necessarily, therefore, the analysis must be at a high level of generality. The very terms "matter," "form," and "expression" are highly inclusive. They are "categories," i.e., they classify the resemblances between elements of different art-objects. The notes of two different symphonies are the sensory elements of the works and therefore they fall into the category of "matter." Yet each material element as it occurs in a particular work is also specific and peculiar to that work. Similarly, a work never has just "expression." What it expresses is specific. It is poignant or joyful in a manner peculiar to the work.

Hence the three categories are no substitute for empirical study of the concrete work. They could not be. They are too abstract for that. They must be fleshed out by seeing what specific instances of matter, form, and expression are present in individual works. The categories are *guides* to artistic analysis. They show how to go about distinguishing the elements of the work. But they can only be used fruitfully in conjunction with the knowledge which we have of the particular arts. The analysis of structure, like aesthetic theory generally, is designed to clarify the concepts which we use in talking about art. It is therefore an invaluable help for the critic and the student of the arts. It makes no pretensions, however, to be more than the first step in the job of analyzing poems, symphonies, and paintings.

2. THE "MATTER" OF ART

Here at the very start we are impressed with the close interrelationship between the categories of art. We begin with the most rudimentary element — the sensuous "matter" of the work. Yet the very meaning of the term leads us to think of "form." The two terms go together. For we never find matter existing by itself; it always has *some* form. The sensory components of the work are always organized somehow, even if the form is irregular or unclear. Conversely, form is always *of* some matter. Thus Bell's "significant form" is the arrangement of lines, colors, and so forth.

The reciprocal relationship between matter and form is also clear when we look at matter in another way. When the artist undertakes creation, he does not construct the work out of a random assortment of sights and sounds. The sensory building blocks of the work are already organized within a stable pattern — the artistic *medium*. The most notable example of a medium is the musical scale. The composer does not choose from the infinite sounds of our experience. He works with tones which are systematically arranged in terms of their pitch. Such tones do not occur in our ordinary experience. There we have noises — the slamming of the door, the wail of the ambulance siren. Such noises are too random and unrelated to work with creatively.[4] But in the scale each note has a definite pitch-value assigned to it, and it is related in fixed, quantitative "intervals" to all the other notes. Thus, the scale — which, when you stop to think of it in this way, is one of the most extraordinary achievements of human devising — has inherent within it the means of forming the composer's matter. Because of the fixed relationships among the notes, he can calculate which notes "go together," how they can be contrasted with each other, what harmonic developments are possible when a certain note is taken as the "key" of the composition. (He will, of course, also draw upon historically established musical styles and theory of harmony, but these too would not be possible without the scale structure.) The medium of music, then, unites the sensory elements of tone with formal patterning.

None of the other arts can boast such a rigidly systematic and well-defined medium. Of all the arts, music has always had the closest affinity to mathematics and since Pythagoras (sixth century B.C.) it has been the subject of mathematical analysis. The medium of painting approximates it, however. Just as tones are distinguished by their pitch, colors are identified by their "hue." The hues are arranged on a "color circle" or "color scale," which brings out the relations of "complementary" colors to each other. Hue, along with the other aspects of color, "saturation" — the amount of grayness in a color, and "value" — its lightness or darkness, are mutually interrelated in the "color cone."[5] The painter is thereby enabled to predict, within limits, the results of color mixture and arrangement. However, this medium lacks the precision of the musical scale. Further, the painter and even more obviously, the literary artist, does not select from a restricted set of elements like the notes of the scale. Moreover, in literature least of all does the medium, words, have a built-in formal structure, unless we say that within the grammar of a language each word is a certain "part of speech" so that it can appropriately combine with some words and not with others.

The "matter" of a work of art, then, consists in the sensory elements, either visual or auditory, which have been chosen from the medium. In music, it will be notes and chords, and — this should not be forgotten — silence, for "rests" are, of course, one of the most effective musical devices; in painting, as we saw in the discussion of formalism, it is color, line, mass, plane, light and shade; in the dance or ballet, the sensory appearance of the human body; and so for the other arts.

Thus matter is the concrete substance and "body" of the work. Without

[4] The student might, however, wish to listen to Varèse' "Ionisation," which employs such sounds.

[5] Cf. Stephen C. Pepper, *Principles of Art Appreciation* (New York: Harcourt, Brace, 1949), chap. 8.

it, the work would be as thin and impoverished as those schematic outlines of the formal structure of a painting which reduce the work to a diagram of colorless areas and arrows designating "lines of force." "To say that one enjoys music just as fully by reading a score as by a performance of it upon instruments is either a mere affectation or else a very doubtful assertion." [6] The brilliance of the trumpets in Rimsky-Korsakov, the engaging orchestral sound of Richard Strauss and Stravinsky, the close-knit texture of the instruments in a Haydn quartet — these are among the chief values of music. Even when we cannot grasp the form or understand the "meaning" of a painting or musical composition, we can enjoy its color or sound. The matter of art revives the interest which all of us had as children in the "look" and "feel" of the world. Though the matter is of relatively small importance in some works of art, it is usually integral to the work's value. "There is no effect of form which an effect of material could not enhance. . . . The Parthenon not in marble, the king's crown not of gold, and the stars not of fire, would be feeble and prosaic things." [7]

As we have seen, the artist is distinguished by his sensitivity to some medium.[8] He particularly is aware of the quality of sounds, colors, or words. Because matter is not inert but vibrant and "alive," it directs the course of creative activity. "You cannot make the same things in clay as you can in wrought-iron, except by a *tour de force*. The feeling of the work is . . . altogether different. The metal challenges you, coaxes you . . . to do a particular kind of thing with it, where its tenacity and ductility make themselves felt." [9] Much of creative activity is devoted to exploiting the sensory appeal of matter and following out its "suggestions."

The value of matter is not found merely in its attractiveness to the senses. It is "good to look at" or "listen to," but it is more than that. Matter is *expressive*. Here again, talk about one "dimension" of the work leads us to talk about another.

The sensory elements of art can, in themselves, arouse images, moods, and thoughts. This is especially true of the matter of the visual arts. Innumerable psychological experiments as well as common experience show that colors and lines taken in isolation have pronounced emotional and imaginative quality. Red is "aggressive," or "brilliant," or "strident"; blue is "withdrawn" or "delicate." A broken, zigzag line seems "agitated" by contrast to a long, flowing curve. Because of such characteristics, painters can speak with a large degree of understanding and agreement about the "warmth" and "temperature" of colors. Moreover, colors can acquire conceptual meanings as when black (in Western countries, at least) stands for

[6] Prall, *Aesthetic Judgment*, p. 141.
[7] Santayana, *Sense of Beauty*, p. 60.
[8] Cf. above, pp. 103 ff.
[9] Bernard Bosanquet, *Three Lectures on Aesthetic* (London: Macmillan, 1923), pp. 59–60.

mourning. Though to a lesser extent, individual tones and chords can also be expressive. Play a note and then play the same note "flatted," or play the same note in two different registers — do they not "feel" different? Again individual words often have a "flavor" of their own. The poet Keats says that "There is a cool pleasure in the very sound of vale." Most of us, who lack the poet's ear and are intent only upon the meanings of words, do not usually detect these expressive overtones until they are pointed up within the poem.

It is not enough to appreciate the matter of art *solely*. Such aesthetic experience is needlessly limited. But even so, sensuous enjoyment is of value in its own right. When it accompanies the comprehension of form as well, so that the percipient can no longer distinguish them, aesthetic experience is fullest and most rewarding. People sometimes disparage a piece of music by saying, "It's nothing but sound," or of a painting, "It's simply decorative." They imply, of course, that the work is devoid of formal interest or expressive significance. This is doubtless an appropriate and important thing to say about some works of art. But neither should we forget that a work whose sensuous body is dull and lifeless fails us in a particularly crucial respect.

AND YET WE MUST NOT MAKE the mistake of thinking that all works must include only the most attractive materials. What we have just been saying might lead us to believe that the artist always selects elements which are, in themselves, sensuously glittering and emotionally stirring. This line of thinking results in the assertion that the material of art is "not any old material. . . . The great poet's words . . . are not the flat stereotypes of a business letter." [10] However, if this is taken literally, as a rule governing all poetry, it collapses. For at least one great poem (there are other examples) employs the language of business quite straightforwardly. It is probably the best-known poem of our time, Eliot's "The Waste Land," in which we find "C.i.f. London: documents at sight." [11]

The rule gets into trouble in this way because it commits a fundamental error in the analysis of art: it makes a universal generalization about the value of a single element, matter, without regard to the way in which it is used in a total work of art. Works of art are infinitely diversified and any such generalization is therefore hazardous. Whether matter is vivid and expressive can only be known by aesthetic experience and analysis of the work in which it appears. Words which *in isolation* are "flat stereotypes" can become forceful and arresting when they occur within the total poem.

[10] Gotshalk, *op. cit.*, p. 94. I doubt that Professor Gotshalk intends this as a hard and fast dictum; cf. pp. 95, 100.

[11] Cf. W. K. Wimsatt, jr., "The Domain of Criticism," *Journal of Aesthetics and Art Criticism*, VIII (1950), 217–218.

In Eliot, the business phrase hits off, quickly and effectively, the nature of "Mr. Eugenides, the Smyrna merchant" with whom it is associated. More broadly, it helps to characterize the banality of the "Unreal City" which in turn re-enforces the central theme of the emptiness of the modern world. The aesthetic value of matter is determined by all of its contextual interrelationships with everything else in the work.

The same criticism can be directed against the old doctrine of "poetic diction," which urged the poet to shun "common" words. This sometimes led to the widespread use of words which are generally found only in "poesy," e.g., "mead," "verdant," "sere," and so on. But there are innumerable poems of unquestionable worth each of whose several words is really quite ordinary:

> Brightness falls from the air;
> Queens have died young and fair;
> Dust hath closed Helen's eyes.[12]

With the exception of the now archaic "hath," every one of these words is commonplace enough in ordinary speech.

We can also see the one-sidedness of insisting that artistic matter must be "beautiful" if we look at it the other way: poems which use many nice-sounding and glittering words, but have little other merit, are generally ranked quite low. Much of A. C. Swinburne's poetry has suffered this fate. Again, matter must be evaluated in relation to all the other elements.

These considerations do not show that *any* generalization about matter is invalid. That the artist's words, sounds, colors are in themselves colorful and expressive is generally true. We can find many instances of works which use these attributes to good advantage. Yet our discussion has shown that these generalizations must always be tacitly qualified by "it is often true that" or some such phrase. Moreover, they should push beyond themselves to make reference to the formal and expressive elements of art. Then they can be helpful guides to artistic analysis.

WITH THIS CAUTION IN MIND, we can assess the contribution of matter to the total aesthetic effectiveness of the work. Buoyancy or heaviness, brilliance or dullness, warmth or coldness — all of the felt characteristics of sensory experience give flavor and expressiveness to art. In Zorach's sculpture, "Child with Cat," (see Frontispiece), the smoothness and charm of the marble are all of a piece with the affectionate charm of the subject matter. Yet the medium *is* marble, and so it is not merely "pretty." It has strength and firmness, and they are essential to the dignity which is a further characteristic of the child and cat. But notice that the influence of matter upon the other elements is reciprocal. The sensory and expressive qualities

12 Thos. Nashe, from "Summer's Last Will and Testament."

of the stone are brought out by the tenderness and poise of the subject matter, the delicacy of the lines, and the subtle combination of warmth and restraint expressed by the total work. The same piece of stone unworked,
though it would probably still be delightful to look at, would not be nearly
so ingratiating. Or if it were sculpted to depict a figure of a very different
sort from "girl with cat," the stone would look and "feel" differently to us.
Similarly, the renowned warmth and attractiveness of Renoir's colors are
due not only to the hues themselves, but also to their formal placement
within the painting, Renoir's endearing or good-natured subjects, and the
overall serenity of his works. These are instances of the successful integration of matter with the formal and expressive dimensions. Where there
is incongruity between these dimensions, we feel an inner disharmony
in the work. A subject which is physically massive and emotionally
lugubrious could not readily be rendered in a material as fragile as cello-
phane or as delicate as porcelain.

It would be impossible to catalogue the myriad ways in which matter
accentuates the form and expressiveness of art. These are as diversified
as works of art themselves. It can be left up to the student to analyze the
function and value of matter in those works with which he is most familiar.
Our discussion will have served its purpose if it shows the reader the
sensuous and expressive potentialities of matter and how its felt character
and value depend upon its mutual interrelationships with the other elements
of the work.

3. THE "HIGHER" AND "LOWER" SENSES

Matter is the sensory aspect of art. Notice, however, that what has been
said about matter was limited almost entirely to what is apprehended
through two senses only — sight and hearing. The major arts — literature,
music, painting, and sculpture — as well as the dance, architecture, the
moving picture, seem to be addressed to these senses only. But what of the
other senses — touch, smell, and taste? Does art ever employ matter which
appeals to them? More broadly, can these senses serve as avenues of aesthetic
enjoyment, whether the object be artistic or natural?

The most obvious answer to the last question appears to be that they *can*.
We relish odors, tastes, and textures for their own sake. We enjoy the smell
of flowers, the taste of foods, and the textures of various surfaces. By virtue
of this fact, they are genuinely aesthetic objects. Moreover, these sensations
are often called into play by works of art which are primarily visual or
auditory. Literature is probably richest in this regard. Because of the
limitless meanings of language, it can evoke sensations of taste, texture, and
aroma. Think of Keats' "jellies soother than the creamy curd," and Rupert

Brooke's "musty reek that lingers/ About dead leaves and last year's ferns," and "the rough male kiss/ Of blankets." Though painting and sculpture cannot exploit so many sense-modalities, they are even richer in their appeal to touch. The materials of sculpture especially invite us (if the museum guards would permit it) to stroke the surface of the work. To appreciate the sculptures of Henry Moore the spectator wishes not only to look, but to feel the texture of the material and trace out its swells and indentations (see Plate 22). Moreover, sculptures and buildings often arouse kinesthetic bodily sensations of reaching, lifting, and carrying. The contemporary critic Bernard Berenson has popularized the notion of "tactile values." He says that they "[stir] the imagination to feel [the works'] bulk, heft their weight, realize their potential resistance, span their distance from us, and encourage us, always imaginatively, to come into close touch with, to grasp, to embrace, or to walk around them." [13] Of the major arts, music is least adapted to stimulate sensations other than those proper to its medium. Yet it is not without reason that we speak of the "texture" of a string quartet, which can feel smooth or gritty or harsh.

Hence olfactory, gustatory, and tactile sensations can be aesthetically valuable in their own right, and they can add expressiveness to works of art. That is true enough. Yet there is this fact: there is no important art-form which addresses itself primarily to touch, taste, or smell. We speak of "the art of perfumery" and "the art of cooking," and doubtless a great deal of skill is involved in these pursuits. Yet no one would think of ranking them in importance with literature, music, or painting.

That touch, taste, and smell are inferior to the "higher" senses of sight and hearing is a belief that goes back to Greek thought. Socrates, engaged in one of the earliest attempts to define "beauty," says: "I do not mean to include all pleasures, but only what we enjoy through our senses of hearing and sight." [14] He goes on: "[Everyone] would laugh at us if we said that it is not pleasant to eat, but beautiful, or that a pleasant smell is not pleasant, but beautiful." [15] Plato holds that sight and hearing are closely related to the workings of the intellect, as the other senses are not, and this view is perpetuated in Aristotle, Plotinus, and Thomas Aquinas.[16] The Platonic-Christian tradition calls touch, taste, and smell the "lower" senses, a term which connotes that they are also morally ignoble, perhaps shameful. In part this is probably due to the association of touch with sexual activity.

[13] Cf. *Aesthetics and History*, pp. 69–73, 84–86.
[14] *Greater Hippias* 297 in *Dialogues of Plato*, trans. Jowett, 4th ed. (Oxford University Press, 1953) I, 586. Whether this dialogue is spurious is not here in question.
[15] *Ibid.*, 299, p. 587.
[16] Cf. Gilbert and Kuhn, *op. cit.*, pp. 79, 117, 140.

Setting aside moral and theological prepossessions, what are the reasons for the relative aesthetic inferiority of the lower senses? Here are the chief answers which have been given to the question.

(1) SIGHT AND HEARING are "distance receptors," i.e., the objects which they apprehend are not in immediate contact with the sense organ; taste, touch, and, though perhaps to a lesser extent, smell, call attention to the body. Since they do not permit of physical distance, "psychical distance" or disinterestedness is destroyed. The "lower" senses are therefore adapted to practical, not aesthetic, activity: There is doubtless some truth to this. But the evidence of common experience shows that this theory is not universally true. We can, and sometimes do, relish the objective properties of textures, odors, and tastes. Nor do we have to be wine-tasters or perfumers to do so. It is not always the case that when we eat "[the] important thing is the satisfaction of the bodily craving, not an interest in the taste or texture of the food." [17] The texture of shrimp and the odor of tea can be savored in their own right. Eating is perhaps the most widespread everyday activity in which aesthetic and other interests can be satisfied simultaneously. Moreover, the experience of blind persons, like that reported by Helen Keller, and of people in Eastern cultures,[18] shows how acute the aesthetic enjoyment of touch can be.

(2) The "higher" senses are more discriminating and sensitive than the lower. They can distinguish differences of quality more finely; further, when various auditory or visual stimuli are blended together, they can distinguish each of the components: This is a considerably stronger theory than the first. Sight and hearing are in man the most highly evolved senses (though in the human infant touch is the most important of the senses). They are *par excellence* the means whereby we learn about and adjust to our world. Because of their capacities for discrimination, we can apprehend a complex blending of colors, or a musical pattern like the close of the Prelude to *Die Meistersinger,* in which a number of different themes are heard simultaneously, and still distinguish each component. If this is true of the other senses, it is only to a much lesser extent. We can all distinguish readily enough between vinegar and chocolate fudge. But unless our palates are extremely sensitive, more subtle differences and gradations of taste are wasted upon us. So often a whole host of tastes and aromas in a salad will blur together and taste like nothing so much as wet blotting paper.

(3) D. W. Prall gives probably the most cogent explanation for the failure to develop major art-forms employing the "lower" senses. As we have seen, the media of music and painting have implicit within them

---

[17] Chandler, *op. cit.,* p. 11.
[18] Frances W. Herring, "Touch — The Neglected Sense," *Journal of Aesthetics and Art Criticism,* VII (1949), 204 ff.

formal relationships which place each element relative to all the others. One pitch is defined by relation to all other pitches in the scale. Prall points out that just this "intrinsic natural structure" is lacking in odors and tastes. Unlike notes and colors, "[one] smell does not suggest another related smell close to it in some objective and necessary order." [19] "Lower"-sense stimuli have gross differences among themselves, e.g., smooth-rough, sweet-bitter, and, to some extent, they are more or less compatible with each other. But these sensory elements "have neither intelligible structure nor apparently any discoverable order in variation." [20] "[What] could be said to lie exactly . . . as far from the odor of pine needles in one direction as some other given odor lies in another?" [21] Hence these sensations cannot be put together, contrasted, balanced, like the "higher"-sense stimuli. Cooks and perfumers can only proceed by relatively crude, trial and error methods. And their chances of creating large-scale formal constructions like a symphony are relatively slight.

Prall recognizes that we may yet discover principles which will define precisely an inherent order of smells and tastes.[22] Attempts are being made to construct a scale of degrees of tactile quality.[23] Whatever may be true in the future, however, at present there is no artistic medium for the "lower"-sense stimuli. Without it, and the potentialities which it provides for the development of complex forms, the "lower"-sense arts must remain rudimentary.

(4) The "lower"-sense stimuli lack symbolic and "spiritual" significance: This is certainly true. They do not have the meaning for us of, e.g., the Cross or certain songs. Yet here again, however, our own cultural traditions may mislead us. In India, "lower"-sense stimuli serve as religious and ethical symbols.[24]

IT IS IMPOSSIBLE TO CALCULATE the extent to which moral, philosophical, and religious prejudice have deadened the appreciation of aromas, textures, and tastes in Western man. It may well be that our cultural habituation has made us incapable of appreciating these sensations aesthetically and that we have then contrived theories to explain their "inferiority." It remains true, nonetheless, that significant artistic creations employing the "lower"-sense stimuli have not yet been achieved. This should not lead us to think, however, that future innovations are impossible, nor should it keep us from relishing the tang and quality of such stimuli, whether they occur in art or nature.

[19] *Aesthetic Judgment*, p. 62.
[20] *Ibid.*, p. 63.
[21] *Aesthetic Analysis*, p. 47.
[22] *Aesthetic Judgment*, p. 63.
[23] Cf. Herring, *op. cit.*, pp. 209–210.
[24] Cf. Munro, *op. cit.*, p. 138.

4. THE AESTHETIC FUNCTIONS OF FORM

The enjoyment of matter is the most simple and widespread mode of artistic appreciation. The look or sound or texture of the work can be the source of immediate, felt value. Matter is the "body" of the work and it is therefore indispensable. Yet philosophers and lovers of art, in all ages including our own, have felt that *form* is the distinctive and precious value of art.

Sensuous beauties are found in nature — the odor of flowers, the texture of stones. So are the people and situations which are the "models" of representational art. And in the gestures and movements of human beings, as in the symbols of institutions and nations, there can also be expressiveness. But "form" is found only when matter, subject matter, emotion, and imagery have been molded by an artist into an ordered and self-contained object of inherent importance.

Form clarifies. A novel or play borrows people and events from "real life," but the workings of character and circumstance and their interrelations are set into sharp outline and so delineated that we gain greater understanding of human nature than we ever could from "real life" itself.[25] Form enriches. The elements which the artist selects from his medium are so arranged within the work as to heighten their charm and vitality; the emotional overtones of the model are accentuated and deepened. Form organizes complexity. The structure of a piece of polyphonic music or a large-scale novel can be inexhaustibly rich. Yet it is also disciplined and ordered by form. And form unifies. It gives to a work of art that wholeness and self-completeness which makes it stand out from the rest of experience and seem to be a world of its own.

It is not to be wondered at that "form" is, nevertheless, probably the most ambiguous word in the language of art. Just because form serves varied functions in art and is the source of different values, the term resists any simple definition. Yet our discussion of form must necessarily begin with some definition. The definition will provide a starting point for the discussion to follow. There we will first see the various *kinds* of formal structure that occur in art and then, most important of all, we will examine the ways in which form *functions* to give value to the aesthetic experience.

There is a further reason for examining the meaning of "form." The term has, as I have noted, *many* meanings. If we can get clear about the differences between them, much would be gained. We could then become more careful and precise in our own use of the term, and we could understand more readily what is meant by teachers, critics, and others when they use the term without specifying its meaning.

25 Cf. above, chap. 5.

Here then are four of the most common meanings of the term:

(1) "The organization and interrelation of those elements of the medium included in the work." The medial elements are tones, line, etc. "Form" refers to the manner in which they are placed in the work relative to each other and how they interact upon each other. Thus it includes, among other modes of relation, the sequence of events which constitute a plot, the metrical scheme in a poem, the spatial arrangement of color areas in a painting, the balance or contrast between these areas, the progression of bodily movements in the dance. Form in this sense also refers to the kind of unity which is achieved by the organization of sensory matter and in representational art, subject matter.

This is a highly general definition and therefore it is necessarily thin. It is as little informative as Coleridge's comparable description of poetry as "the best words in their best order." The definition must be made more specific and therefore more informative at various levels — by showing first the various kinds of formal arrangement, then the devices of form peculiar to a single art such as music, and finally the formal structure of particular works. Yet meaning (1) is presupposed by such analysis. And it is worth our attention for another reason. It says that form is *of* the sensory elements and that it exists *in* their interrelations alone. The definition is therefore a salutary reminder that form is not some sort of independent container like a match box into which the artist places his materials. It is, rather, like a web which is made up of materials and organizes them. Meaning (1) therefore keeps our analysis from setting up an inner duality within the work — form and matter as independent entities — which is false to its nature. Let me repeat what can hardly be said too often: though the analysis of art requires that we distinguish the various dimensions, we must not think that such distinctions correspond to separations within the art-object. We can guard against this error if, as in meaning (1), the category makes reference beyond itself to the other dimensions as well.

(2) But though (1) is a very broad and general meaning, it is still not inclusive enough. The medial elements possess not only sensory attributes like hue or timbre, and in the case of words, sound quality and literal meaning. In isolation but, more especially, in conjunction with each other, they also have expressive significance. The "vigor" or "brashness" of a red color patch appears to be ingredient in the very color as perceived. Similarly the novels of Thomas Hardy are permeated by a forbidding sense of fatalism.

"Form," in sense (2), includes the meaning of (1), and also "the organization of expressive significance." This additional meaning is indispensable to artistic analysis. To understand the value of the work we must see how the imagery suggested by the sensory matter is developed and varied throughout the work, how such a "meaning" as Hardy's fatalism emerges from the episodes of the novel, how contrasting emotions are played off against each other. It is because of the formal organization of expression that a commentator (J. W. N. Sullivan) can describe the last movement of Beethoven's Quartet No. 14, Op. 131, in these terms: "a heroism which is also pathetic marches to its end attended by yearning and pain." The organization of expression not only heightens the conceptual and emotional import of the work; it also unifies the work. Thus a piece of Impressionist music or a play of Chekhov is held together by a prevalent mood.

In the ensuing discussion "form" will be used in sense (2), except where otherwise indicated.

(3) "Form" is often used to refer to some specific pattern of organization which is traditional and commonly known. Examples would be "the sonnet form" and such varieties of it as the Petrarchan sonnet, the "Spenserian stanza," the "sonata," the "fugue," and so on. This is obviously a much more limited sense of the term than either (1) or (2). It usually refers to formal organization only in sense (1), — e.g., a certain scheme of rhyme endings in the sonnet, an order of statement, development, and recapitulation of musical themes in the sonata, — without regard to expressive significance. Once again, however, the interrelations between the dimensions of art force themselves upon us. A comparison of the fugue and the sonata quickly leads one into a comparison of the expressive potentialities and limitations of each. The very names of other forms and *genres*, e.g., "epic," "comedy of manners," already suggest the emotional character of such works.

Traditional formal patterns, particularly when they are as detailed as the rhyme structure of a sonnet, can be of considerable aid both to the artist and the percipient. The artist has the form of his work, in one respect at least, ready to hand. For the percipient, the pattern provides a convenient means of organizing and interpreting the work. I need hardly add, however, that form in sense (3) is only a *partial* meaning of the term. For artistic analysis, it must be supplemented by meanings (1) and (2).

(4) All of the meanings of "form" thus far distinguished are *descriptive*. They say nothing of the goodness or badness of form in particular works. But as you listen to people speak about art, it soon becomes apparent that they very often use "form" in a *eulogistic* sense, i.e., as a term of praise or approval. They will say of a painting, "What form!" or, at the other extreme, "It has no form." Clearly "form" here connotes *good* form. Any work of art has *some* form; it is, if we take it literally, absurd to say of any painting that it has "no form." Still, human speech is no respecter of such niceties, and we should therefore be aware of sense (4).

This sense of "form" cannot be used by itself in artistic analysis. We want to be able to speak meaningfully of "*bad*" form as well. Hence a broader meaning is required. Moreover, we cannot decide whether form is good or bad unless we know what it *is* and how it differs from the other elements of the work. Hence we require meanings (1) and (2).

WE COME NOW to the second stage of our discussion — the *kinds* of formal organization which are most commonly found in works of art. It would be a mistake to think that this listing includes *all* of the common varieties of form. Art-objects and their formal structure are too diversified for that. However, most of the usual kinds of artistic organization are represented here. As we proceed, I will give brief examples of each. The discussion will be far more valuable to the student if he thinks of examples of his own, taken from those works of art with which he is most familiar. Remember too that the real point of such a listing is to make available concepts which, when they are made more specific, can be used for the detailed analysis of particular works of art.

TRADITIONALLY the most important kind of formal structure has been thought to be "unity in variety" or "organic unity." It occurs when, in Professor Parker's words, "each element in a work of art is necessary to its value. . . . it [the work] contains no elements that are not thus necessary, and . . . all that are needful are there." [26] There is diversity and complexity in the work. Yet each of the elements contributes something which is indispensable to the value of the whole. And the elements are so finely integrated with each other that their differences do not disrupt the unity of the work, but rather merge together to constitute it. From this integration there arises a value which cannot be found in the parts individually or taken together in another arrangement. What Browning says of music can be said of any work which possesses "unity in variety":

> And I know not if, save in this, such gift be allowed to man,
> That out of three sounds he frame, not a fourth sound, but a star.
>
> "Abt Vogler"

The elements of the work are "needful" to it because they are necessary to each other. Each re-enforces the significance and worth of the other, as in the Zorach sculpture,[27] in which the sensory matter, the subject matter, the quality and arrangement of line, and the emotional atmosphere of the work all sustain and coalesce with each other. In more complex works, where there is greater range of materials, subject, etc., unity is proportionately more difficult to achieve and, when attained, all the more rewarding. Then

---

[26] DeWitt H. Parker, *The Analysis of Art* (Yale University Press, 1926), p. 34. Like everybody else I am greatly indebted to chap. II of this work.
[27] Cf. above, pp. 222–223.

we have the works which make it understandable why men rhapsodize about art — those which have great profusion and wealth of interest, but all of it disciplined and harmonized, none of it superfluous or inimical to the rest of the work, all together making up a rich and integral being, a "star." What else in human experience gives us, at once, such richness and such order?

But now, as Robert Frost says, "Truth [breaks] in/ With all her matter-of-fact." Not that this account of "unity in variety" is untrue. But it would be untrue to say or imply that most, let alone all, works of art "contain no elements that are not necessary and all that are needful are there." It would rather be romantic exaggeration to say this. Would the value of most musical compositions be destroyed or significantly decreased if a single note or even a whole development section were omitted? Those conductors and instrumentalists who edit out whole passages for performance think that just the opposite is true. At least one listener, though he recognizes and admires the exotic orchestral color of Rimsky's "Scheherazade," yet believes (though you may, of course, wish to differ with me), that the work would be a better one if whole pages were dropped from the score. Similarly, plays are often abridged for performance, not merely because of limitations of time, but because it is thought that the passages which are eliminated add nothing to the dramatic impact of the work, but rather weaken it. You have probably heard of Ben Jonson's famous retort to the claim that Shakespeare had never "blotted" a line: "My answer hath been, would he had blotted a thousand." (Paintings and sculptures get off fairly easily because the physical canvas or sculpture is the only work of its kind. It cannot be literally reproduced like musical scores and the texts of plays. Hence whereas the original is still available when a score or text is altered, any change in the painting or sculpture would destroy the original work. But this is not to say that works of visual art do not often have "dead spots" and excrescences.)

Thus "unity in variety," interpreted literally, is found only in relatively few works. Generally these are small-scale works such as lyric poems. "Unity in variety" is like an ideal of form which is sometimes achieved but most of the time only approximated. Even those approximations, however, can be sources of very great aesthetic value.

"But," it may be protested, "if you change anything, if you omit a passage from the composer's score or a scene from the playwright's text, you then have a *different* work. Perhaps you have not 'destroyed' its value but you must necessarily have changed it. It is no longer the same work that it was previously and therefore its aesthetic value is no longer the same."

The criticism is a sound one as it stands. But it raises a further and even deeper question about the *meaning* of "unity in variety." Is it the distinguishing characteristic of such unity that when an element is omitted or revised, the whole object is altered? Why then *any* object whatever possesses "unity in variety." When a man grows bald, when an engine is reassembled, when a new idea is introduced into a theory and an old one eliminated, the total object is *different*. Change a part of anything and that thing is necessarily altered. We certainly do not wish to ascribe "unity in variety" to everything but only to works of art and only to good ones at that.

What, then, sets off "unity in variety" from the different sort of "unity" that other things possess? It is doubtful that any wholly clear answer has ever been given to this question. Those who have put forth the notion of "organic unity" have been impressed, as we must all be, by the blending of diversity and order in good works of art. Yet they have not been able to work out an unequivocal criterion of "organic unity."

We have just seen that it cannot be the hallmark of "unity in variety" merely that if a part is changed the whole is changed. Perhaps then the criterion is not that the change of a part simply makes the whole *different*, but that any change makes a *crucial* difference — it destroys the essential nature of the whole. The object can no longer perform the function for which it is intended if any of its parts is altered. For its functioning depends upon its internal coherence. This interpretation makes better sense than the one we have just rejected. And yet the concept is still too broad. For think of the many objects that are *not* works of art of which it can accurately be said that removing or changing a part will impair their functioning. What of a crossword puzzle? Or an automobile engine from which a vital part is taken, a good basketball team which loses a "key" player, a mathematical proof without one of its axioms or postulates?

Hence it is impossible to distinguish "organic unity" in art from such unity in other objects merely in terms of this part-whole relationship. How then is artistic unity to be distinguished? By understanding that the unity is of the work of art in its characteristic function — as an *aesthetic* object. This will set off art from crossword puzzles and automobile engines. A work of art possesses "unity in variety" when altering its elements reduces drastically or destroys its value for aesthetic experience.

To summarize thus far, we have concluded that artistic "unity in variety" involves (1) the change of a part will make, not just a difference, but a *significant* difference, and (2) the difference is in the aesthetic worth of the object.

This is better. But unfortunately we are not done yet. Does the change of *any* part undermine the work's value? The answer is clearly negative. Obviously indiscriminate slashing will ruin the work. But *some* elements, e.g., the lines that Ben Jonson wished to have "blotted," are less essential than others. The same is true of the living organism which first suggested to Plato and Aristotle [28] the metaphor of "organic unity." To remove the heart is fatal, but extraction of a tooth is not.

Except in relatively few works, therefore, the "necessity" of parts to the whole is a matter of degree. And the principle of "unity in variety" must be modified in another respect. The distinction between the "unity" of works of art and other objects is not absolute. Natural objects such as flowers, shells, and landscapes often have great formal coherence. We must again, therefore, be more modest about the claim for "unity in variety" in art and say that "in general" works of art are more integrated and harmonious than other aesthetic objects.

This whole analysis shows that the doctrine of "unity in variety" cannot be taken strictly and without qualification. If it means that the change of an element makes the work *different*, the doctrine is trivial. If it means that the change of *any* element will seriously reduce or destroy the work's aesthetic value, then it is usually false. Moreover, the doctrine is sound only if it says that the omission of "some" elements will reduce "considerably" the value of the work. Which elements are these? And how much will their omission affect the work? These questions cannot be answered merely by examining the objective structure of the work. Like any question of the aesthetic properties of things, they can only be settled by the evidence of aesthetic experience: what experience does the spectator have, in the face of the altered work?

With the necessary qualifications, the concept of "unity in variety" sums up exceedingly important truths about art. If it is interpreted as an ideal for art, it is not simply a single principle of value. Rather, it would have us look for a number of different things in the formal structure of art. Works which have these properties are, to that extent, good works of art. When we find these properties, we can understand better why these works are so absorbing to us, why they seem concentrated and intense, rather than diffuse and straggly. Here are the characteristics of form which are involved in "organic unity." We have spoken of them before but they bear repeating: an artistic element possesses aesthetic effectiveness within the work which it lacks in isolation; it acquires such significance because of its interaction with the other elements of the work; it contributes to the total aesthetic effectiveness of the work and in turn is enriched by its place within the work as a whole; a good work of art gives us the impression of having no aesthetically superfluous or irrelevant elements in it and it is therefore both various and one.

INTERPRETED IN THIS WAY, "unity in variety" is not so much a particular kind of formal structure as it is an ideal to be achieved by the use of specific formal devices. These will now be listed. They can be described much

28 For Plato, cf. *Phaedrus* 264c; for Aristotle, cf. *Poetics* VIII.

more briefly than "organic unity." Remember that their importance cannot be understood until we see later how they function in aesthetic experience.

Recurrence is the appearance of the same element at a number of different places in the work. Thus the same melodic theme is repeated in a musical composition, the refrain in a poem or song, an arch-form in a building, a bodily movement in a dance. I say the "same" element, but though this is true literally, it is not generally accurate *aesthetically*. The notes of a theme played at the close of a symphonic movement may be identical with those played at the beginning. But they have a wholly different significance for the listener. When they are heard again it is after the theme has been developed and elaborated, and set off against other themes. Hence the listener is now aware of its imaginative and expressive significance as he was not previously. Moreover, after the initial presentation of the theme gives way to a statement of it in another key, or when it is withdrawn altogether in favor of other melodies, the listener feels a sense of expectation, a desire to hear it again as it was originally. This is especially true, of course, when he is familiar with the style of the composer or the composition itself, and can therefore anticipate that a "recapitulation" is in the offing. The expectation creates a feeling of urgency and "suspense." When his expectation is fulfilled by the recurrence of the theme, the experience takes on added zest and satisfaction. A comparable account could be given of reading the refrain of a poem and for other instances of recurrence. The important thing to keep in mind is the general principle stated earlier in this chapter — that the aesthetic significance of an element depends upon the context in which it occurs and therefore upon its place in the work. What has just been said is an application of this principle to recurrence.

Simple recurrence is probably found less frequently in art than *recurrence with variation*, i.e., the repeated elements are recognizably like those which occur elsewhere in the work, but there is also some difference in them. In other words, not only is there the inevitable variation due to a difference of context, but also the repeated element is itself changed somewhat. A melody is heard again within a composition, but it is now with a different orchestration; in the ballad "Lord Randal," the last line of each stanza, "For I'm weary wi hunting, and fain wald lie down," changes dramatically at the close of the final stanza into "For I'm sick at the heart, and I fain wald lie down." The same hue can be employed at many places in a painting, as in Cézanne and the early works of Picasso, but there are slight changes in its "tonality."

Rhythm, which we discussed in an earlier chapter,[29] exemplifies either recurrence or recurrence with variation. It is a pattern of emphasis and

[29] Cf. above, pp. 70 ff.

pause, like the tempo in music or the metre in poetry, which is repeated throughout the work. Again, there will often be variations when these elements are repeated, as in musical "syncopation" which unexpectedly places emphasis on a beat which was previously unaccented.

As we saw in the previous discussion, rhythm in the strict sense is not so widespread in the visual arts (with the exception of architecture) as it is in poetry and music. You will remember, however, that painting and sculpture are not to be described as "nontemporal." When they are apprehended aesthetically, works in these media unfold in and through time and create a feeling of "movement." This is due, among other causes, to a formal device which is partially comparable to rhythm, i.e., emphasizing some elements relative to others, though not in the fixed and repeated pattern of rhythm proper. This distribution of emphasis Professor Parker calls "*hierarchy*" or "*dominance*." [30] Our earlier illustration [31] showed that dominance can be achieved in a painting by a number of different means, e.g., perspective, lighting, the importance of the subject matter. When there is a single element which dominates the work, like the face in a Rembrandt portrait which is brightly illuminated relative to the rest of the work, the formal organization is that of "*centrality*." [32] You will be able to think without too much difficulty of instances of hierarchy in novels and plays with which you are acquainted.

One of the most common kinds of formal organization is *balance*, i.e., the arrangement of elements so that they complement or "set off" each other. The term "*symmetry*" may be used to designate the balance of similar elements, as when, in a painting, like objects are placed in the same position on either side of the central axis. Here again, however, our enumeration of formal principles should not lose sight of what works of art are really like. In their use of balance, like rhythm and recurrence with variation, artists usually avoid mere mechanical repetition. Therefore balance is most often achieved by *contrast*, i.e., by setting against each other *unlike* elements, which nonetheless harmonize with each other. The distinctive character of each element calls attention to that of its opposite, e.g., a "warm" and a "cold" color. Yet together their dissimilarities become unified; so the juxtaposition of "warm" and "cold" colors constitutes a sensuously pleasing pattern. In many works, the balanced elements are alike in some respects, dissimilar in others. In *King Lear* there is a parallelism between the relationship of Lear to his daughters and Gloucester to his sons. In both cases, the father is treated outrageously by his children; in both cases, he is also aided by one of his children. The story of Lear is of course "dominant" over that of Gloucester, yet the latter echoes and par-

[30] *Op. cit.*, pp. 47–48.
[31] Cf. above, p. 71.
[32] Cf. Gotshalk, *op. cit.*, pp. 112–114.

tially duplicates the former. Much the same is true of Hamlet, Laertes, and Fortinbras.

Finally, *evolution* is "the unity of a process when the earlier parts determine the later, and all together create a total meaning." [33] The most obvious example is the development of a plot in literature, in which the interrelation of events and causes points toward and finally brings about the climax. Evolution is also found in some works of nonliterary art. Thus Professor Parker says of a painting by El Greco that in looking at it "we follow an intensely dramatic movement from the lower to the upper part of the picture." [34]

With these chief kinds of formal organization in mind,[35] we can now proceed to the most important question of all: What does form *do* in aesthetic experience? How does it contribute to the value of that experience?

I WILL BEGIN by stating briefly the three chief aesthetic functions of form which are to be discussed: (1) Form controls and directs the spectator's perception, guiding his attention along a certain course, so that the work will be clear, understandable, and unified. (2) Form arranges the elements of the work so as to point up and vivify their sensory and expressive value. (3) Formal organization itself possesses intrinsic aesthetic value.

(1) We have thus far discussed form chiefly as the structure inherent in the art-object. But whether a work is well-organized formally cannot be decided simply by examining its structure. It can be determined, ultimately, only by the experience of those who perceive it aesthetically. "For the unity of a work of art is the counterpart of a unity within the experience of the beholder." [36] How does form bring about this unity?

It was pointed out in an earlier chapter [37] that when a work of art is totally unfamiliar to us, e.g., a piece of "modern" music, we do not know what to "look for" and are therefore bewildered and put off by it. When we cannot distinguish what is important from what is unimportant, so that the composition seems to be nothing but a succession of sounds, then nothing is important and, what is worse, nothing is interesting. The work takes on significance for us only when we see which of its parts we must focus attention upon and how these are set off from the less important elements. One of the functions of form therefore is to call attention to certain selected elements and to have the percipient dwell upon them.

[33] Parker, *op. cit.*, p. 42.
[34] *Ibid.*, p. 43.
[35] For more detailed analyses of the principles of form and their interrelations, the reader should consult the references in the Bibliography.
[36] Parker, *op. cit.*, p. 35.
[37] Cf. above, pp. 73 ff. The student is urged to reread chap. 3, secs. 1–2, in conjunction with the present discussion.

The formal arrangement of the work is like a guide which announces at some points, "Now this is especially important; don't miss this," and at other places it comments, "Well, this is a 'bridge passage' or 'stage-setting' or 'comic relief'; attention can ease up here." Except, of course, that form "says" these things by what it *does* — how it places the elements relative to each other, e.g., a lull before the climax, developing some themes at great length, and so on.

Nor should we make the mistake of thinking that the "lesser" elements are of *no* significance. They set off the central passages or lead up to them and often they are of some interest in themselves. Therefore the formal structure of the work will be deficient in one of two instances: when the less important parts do not contribute at all to the organization of the work and are of no interest in themselves, like the "filler" in some professors' lectures which students do not take notes on, and even train themselves not to hear — these are the inert or "dead" spots in some works of art; or, at the other extreme, when some passage which should be subordinate relative to the total significance of the work instead has disproportionate interest and "swamps" the rest of the work. Those people who think that the best thing in *Macbeth* is the drunken Porter's speech offer an example of this. (We need not, however, share their opinion.)

Any of the principles of form can clarify the relative importance of the work's elements but hierarchy is the clearest example. By placing the elements in order of importance, it shows the percipient how attention should be distributed. Without this guidance, as we have noted, attention would be wholly dispersed and then experience could not have the intensity and vividness which is characteristic of aesthetic appreciation. Similarly, evolution toward a climax makes us attend to what is currently perceived in the light of its significance for future events. Attention is directed both toward the present and the future. "The writer makes a point and reserves it at the same time, creates an effect and holds it back, till in due course it is appropriated and used by the page for which it is intended." [38]

But it is not enough for the elements to be arranged in order of hierarchy. Their relative importance might be clear and yet if there were too *many* elements the work could not be an aesthetic object for us. Many elements become "*too* many" when they are more than the mind can grasp and hold together in attention. Aristotle says that an object of vast size cannot be beautiful, "for as the eye cannot take it all in at once, the unity and sense of the whole is lost for the spectator, as for instance if there were one a thousand miles long." [39] Nor can we "take the object all in at once" if its inner profusion is so great that we cannot distinguish the parts from each other. This breakdown in attention is accompanied by a breakdown in

[38] Percy Lubbock, *The Craft of Fiction* (New York: Scribners, n.d.), pp. 234–235.
[39] *Poetics* VII, *loc. cit.*, pp. 11–12.

memory. We must remember the earlier sections of a work if we are to appreciate their significance in later passages, when the consequences of an event are portrayed or when there is return to an earlier theme. Too great complexity will spill over the limits of what we can comprehend and remember. It will leave us bewildered and distracted.

That is why the discipline of form is needed. The complexity of the work must be moderated to the capacities of the spectator, and the elements must be presented clearly enough so that they can be retained in memory and anticipated in imagination. To this end the simplest formal device is recurrence. A succession of incessantly new elements would be more than attention could assimilate. Recognition of what has been met before, however, stabilizes the spectator's experience. Around this core of sameness further novelties are elaborated. Professor Gotshalk suggests that repetition occurs most often in those arts called "temporal," [40] such as literature and music. A symphony or a novel generally take so long a time to unfold that we could not possibly "take in the object" unless characters and themes recurred. In the "rondo" form, the music keeps returning to a single melody after contrasting passages are heard.

If, however, the work is excessively *simple*, the opposite situation arises — now there is not too much for the percipient to grasp, but too little to sustain his interest. The work has no zest or challenge to it. This may be due to factors other than form, e.g., a subject matter limited in range and interest, but poor form, which fails to "bring out" the subject, may be a contributing factor. An example of excessive simplicity is perhaps Malevich's painting "White on White."

In more complicated works, elements are made comprehensible not only by recurrence but by other modes of form as well. The persistence of a rhythm holds together a poem or a musical composition; when elements are played off against each other by the balance of contrast, we can more readily recognize and understand them. Where a work has the pattern of evolution, new elements, when they are first introduced, are not completely strange. For they take their place in the chain of events which has already been created and we see how they arise from what has gone before. Moreover, evolution arouses in the percipient expectations which look toward culmination later in the work. Their resolution unifies the aesthetic experience. When, however, the evolutionary climax does not "come off" the experience falls apart. There is a perceptible loss of values, as any of us can testify who have followed a novel or play through to the end only to find that the dénouement is implausible or contrived. Some of the paintings of Raphael suffer from a comparable failure. So Professor Greene says of the "Coronation of the Virgin" that "the upper and lower portions . . . are

[40] *Op. cit.*, p. 111.

hardly brought together by the upward gaze of the spectators" [41] depicted in the painting.

I have spoken of formal unification through the organization of matter and subject matter. It can also be achieved by organization of the work's expressive elements. A tone poem or a piece of Impressionist music may seem to lack the straightforward, lucid structure of eighteenth-century music. Yet these works are not simply diffuse and disorganized. They are often unified by some prevalent mood which hovers over the entire composition. What the listener hears at any one moment possesses the familiarity of sameness because of its emotional kinship with the rest of the work.

(2) WITHOUT FORM TO GUIDE and regulate our perception, appreciation would be impossible. But appreciation is worth while because of the vividness and excitement which the other elements acquire when they are organized by form. Form not only makes these elements understandable; it also dramatizes and heightens their appeal. What would be lackluster in isolation becomes absorbing when it is placed along with and played off against the other elements. Take the most primitive example: A color which is dull or only moderately attractive in itself becomes a gleaming and dramatic object when it is set into the pattern of a painting. Were it not for form, sensory matter would be uninteresting, subject matter would stir us as little as its "real life" model usually does, and expressed thoughts would be unclear, expressed emotions would be turgid. Form must live within each of the elements of the work, animating them and making them both sustain each other and dramatize each other.

All of the formal devices, singly or in combination, can be used to "bring out" what is in the work. Balance accentuates the sensory qualities of sound and color; the evolutionary climax of a play makes clear a certain conception of human character and destiny. Simple recurrence or recurrence with variation creates a cumulative emotional impact. The Shakespeare critic Granville-Barker calls attention to the repetition of the word-image "weed" in *Hamlet*. It occurs at the beginning of the play, in Hamlet's soliloquy. He expresses his disgust at the evil of the world by describing it as "an unweeded garden/ That grows to seed" (I, ii). Later, when he urges his mother to avoid Claudius, he uses the word to symbolize their sinfulness. He enjoins her not to "spread the compost on the weeds/ To make them ranker" (III, iv).[42] The reiteration of the word points up Hamlet's revulsion and adds further poignancy to his already desperate entreaty.

[41] *Op. cit.*, p. 218. The painting is reproduced on p. 606 of this work.
[42] Harley Granville-Barker, *Preface to Hamlet* (New York: Hill and Wang, 1957), pp. 187–188.

Which kinds of form are involved in the following instance?: "In Giotto's 'Death of St. Francis,' the organization of the figures surrounding the horizontal body so that they lead in slow, intense rhythms toward the haloed head of the saint serves to space and bring out more effectively the quietly intense sorrow that is variously expressed by each attendant figure and group."[43] (See Plate 23.)

It would be naïve and misleading, however, to look for mechanical application of the principles of form in each work of art. Let us remember that the categories of recurrence, hierarchy, balance, etc., are only guides to the analysis of specific works. We can use them only up to the point that they help reveal the formal structure of the work. This structure will generally illustrate the workings of one or more of the large-scale categories. But it will be as individual as the matter, subject, and expressiveness of which it is the form.

IF WE RESPECT the uniqueness of the work, we will also be wary of laying down *a priori* principles about what artists can or cannot do in the use of form. There is an even greater temptation to make such rules in discussing form than in discussing matter, but it is at least as dangerous as we have seen rules about matter to be.[44]

Consider the assertion: "For all forms of imaginative writing the constant requirement holds that, to attain unified effect, extraneous detail must be eliminated."[45] This sounds unexceptionable. It can, indeed, be considered simply a corollary of "unity in variety." Yet what in a work is "extraneous"? A large part of Sterne's *Tristram Shandy* consists of digressions from what is ostensibly the main theme — the biography of the hero. One irrelevancy leads to another and that to a third, and they develop into vast proportions. In fact, the narratives which lead away from the main theme not only obscure our interest in the life of Shandy but they are so lengthy and are so frequently interrupted that often we cannot even remember how they themselves started. If ever there were "extraneous detail" in a work, here it is. Does it follow that *Tristram Shandy* is a hopelessly bad piece of writing? Not for an instant. It is generally considered to be one of the supreme comic creations in English literature. (To test this judgment and — what is at least as important — to enjoy one of the funniest books ever written, you should read *Tristram Shandy* for yourself.) The point is that just these "extraneous" passages are vital to the uninhibited, fancy-free humor of the book. They are so infectiously playful that we surrender the demand for "unity" in the *usual* sense. (Sterne twits us about this as when he says sarcastically that he is taking great pains "to keep all tight

---

[43] Gotshalk, *op. cit.*, p. 127.
[44] Cf. above, pp. 221–222.
[45] Helen H. Parkhurst, *Beauty* (London: Douglas, 1931), p. 163.

together in the reader's fancy.") Then we can relish their absurdity and irreverence. This is not to say that works do not sometimes contain "extraneous detail" or that "extraneous detail" is a good thing. I am trying to show, rather, that what is "relevant" and what is "extraneous" depends upon the particular nature of the specific work. *Tristram Shandy*, like a great deal of humor, thrives on "irrelevance." Its apparently loose sprawling form is essential to its value.

Let me take a more solemn and, historically, a more important example. We have seen that Aristotle in the *Poetics* emphasizes that events in a tragedy are tightly interrelated "as cause and effect" so that they issue finally in the inevitable dénouement.[46] We have seen too the importance of formal evolution as a means of unifying the work of art and rounding off the spectator's experience. Aristotle goes on to say, however, that "the unravelling of the Plot . . . must arise out of the Plot itself; it must not be brought about by the *Deus ex Machina*."[47] As an instance of the latter sort of plot he cites Euripides' *Medea*. At the close of this play, the heroine, after having murdered her children, is rescued by a winged chariot which appears suddenly and inexplicably. Here again we must ask: does this apparently incoherent formal structure contribute anything to the expressive significance of the work? On one plausible interpretation, it does just that. It dramatizes vividly the central meaning of the play, that "the primitive things in the universe . . . are not reasonable."[48] "The magic chariot is a frightening glimpse of . . . the existence in the universe of forces that we can neither understand nor control."[49] Hence the climax gives the *Medea* its *own* kind of "unity." I will also cite a contemporary work, Sartre's short story, "The Wall," in which the hopelessly absurd and unpredictable ending is itself a microcosm of the irrationality of moral aspiration.

Now there is a further point to be made. In the examples which have just been discussed, the common principles of form are not simply ignored or rejected. In an important sense, these works presuppose such principles. For the whole force of these works depends upon some radical deviation from the usual kinds of form. Where an ordered narrative or a predictable dénouement is expected, we get instead a conglomeration of digressions or a winged chariot. These works trade upon the principles of form; they use them by defying them and thereby achieve their effect. Were it not for the standards of form of which we are implicitly aware, we would not see the absurdity in these works, whether comic or tragic. Indeed the author of *Shandy* takes care to remind us of these principles,

[46] Cf. above, pp. 117–120.
[47] *Poetics* XV, *loc. cit.*, p. 20.
[48] H. D. F. Kitto, *Greek Tragedy* (Garden City: Doubleday, 1954), p. 208.
[49] *Ibid.*, p. 209.

by speaking of "that necessary equipoise and balance . . . between chapter and chapter, from whence the just proportions and harmony of the whole work results" — but the narrative remains just as chaotic as before.

Similarly Goya's etching, "Accident in the Arena at Madrid" (see Plate 24), is radically asymmetrical, the focus of interest — the man impaled on the horn of the bull — being far over to the right-hand side, virtually nothing being shown on the left-hand side. This pronounced and startling imbalance underscores, however, the terrifying subject. Centrality is achieved, not by ignoring balance altogether, but by a violent deviation from balance. Again the effect depends upon the spectator's implicit acquaintance with the customary modes of form.

I cite one further work to show how form can accentuate the interest of subject matter and create great emotional impact. Here is the climactic passage from Graham Greene's *This Gun for Hire*, which describes the death of the central character, the criminal assassin Raven:

> He [Mather, a policeman] had no hand free for his revolver as Raven turned. He dangled outside the window . . . a defenceless mark for Raven's pistol. Raven watched him with bemused eyes, trying to take aim. It wasn't a difficult shot, but it was almost as if he had lost interest in killing. He was only aware of a pain and despair which was more like a complete weariness than anything else. He couldn't work up any sourness, any bitterness, at his betrayal. [He] had been marked from his birth for this end, to be betrayed in turn by everyone. [Further description of Raven's thoughts.] He took aim slowly, absent-mindedly, with a curious humility. . . . The only problem when you were once born was to get out of life more neatly and expeditiously than you had entered it. For the first time the idea of his mother's suicide came to him without bitterness, as he fixed his aim at the long reluctant last and Saunders shot him in the back through the opening door.[50]

The uses of form are infinitely subtle and various. We cannot spell them all out, nor should we expect that great works of art will disclose all of their formal patterns to us at once. But if we unite knowledge of the principles of form with sensitivity to their variations and combinations in specific works, we will come to appreciate more and more this most subtle dimension of art.

(3) It is NOT EASY to describe the aesthetic value of form in itself. That is why the theories of the formalists, like Fry in the visual arts and Hanslick in music, often seem so unsatisfactory. They talk a great deal of "formal relations" or "significant form" divorced from subject matter

---

[50] Graham Greene, *This Gun for Hire* (London: William Heinemann, Ltd., and New York: Viking, n.d.), p. 146. Reprinted by permission of Graham Greene.

but they cannot give us precise descriptions of these patterns. Thus Hanslick admits that "It is extremely difficult to define this self-subsistent and specifically musical beauty." [51] Moreover, if, as we have been saying, form is but one of the components of the concrete work, it is hardly possible to discuss the values of form considered in isolation.

And yet, *that* form possesses aesthetic value in itself can hardly be doubted. Balance not only facilitates perception and brings out sensory and expressive values; it is intrinsically delightful and satisfying. Our dissatisfaction when we see colors or masses *un*balanced (without some good aesthetic reason) is evidence enough of this. We can appreciate a pattern of interweaving themes and symbols, the economy and compactness of formal design, the tightly knit unity of the work. If you have ever tried to write a story or a piece of music you will know how difficult it is to effect graceful transitions between major sections of the work. Then you can appreciate all the more the deftness and ease with which such transitions are made in good works of art. Such fluency of organization is another sort of formal value.

When the composer chooses a traditional formal pattern such as the sonata, he employs certain well-known modes of musical organization and development. Because the listener can reliably predict the course that the music will take, he can attend to the music intelligently and synthesize it in imagination. We discussed this function of form under (1) above.[52] But in addition, when the music does *not* follow rigorously the line prescribed by tradition, form becomes inherently exciting. The temporary blocking or frustration of the listener's expectations creates surprise and interest. "The composer plays, as it were, with the listener's latent expectations." [53] The work may deviate unexpectedly from its established key or rhythm, or it may suddenly introduce dissonance to add variety. The eminent music critic, Sir Donald Tovey, in analyzing the start of the first movement of Beethoven's "Eroica" Symphony, writes: "[As] the violins enter with a palpitating high note, the harmony becomes clouded. . . . Whatever you may enjoy or miss in the Eroica Symphony, remember this cloud: it leads eventually to one of the most astonishing and subtle dramatic strokes in all music." [54] For when, later in the movement, the recapitulation seems about to occur in the "tonic," i.e., the basic key, the little harmonic "cloud" returns. "The cloud 'resolves' in a new direction, and the sun comes out in one of the two keys whose only characteristic is that of complete contradiction to the tonic which has been

[51] *Op. cit.*, p. 70.

[52] Cf. above, pp. 236–239.

[53] Leonard B. Meyer, *Emotion and Meaning in Music* (University of Chicago Press, 1957), p. 152.

[54] Donald F. Tovey, *Essays in Musical Analysis* (Oxford University Press, 1935), I, 30.

regained after all that suspense." [55] Then the other contradictory key is heard, and then finally the tonic, the music at last resuming its normal course. Do you see how, even if you do not know the music itself, this analysis suggests the doubt, suspense, and ultimately the satisfaction which can be aroused by the manipulation of form?

Formal dexterity and inventiveness are not enough, of course. The work must have strength in its other dimensions as well. If it does not, then we say of it that it is "empty" or "contrived," or perhaps, "merely intellectual." But the "Eroica" cannot be accused of this. It is an example of how the intrinsic interest of form can unite with the interest of the other dimensions, and how intrinsic interest can go along with the other aesthetic functions of form.

"Form . . . does not appeal to the unattentive; they get from objects only a vague sensation; . . . they do not stop to survey the parts or appreciate their relation. . . . Beauty of form, however, is what specifically appeals to an aesthetic nature; it is equally removed from the crudity of formless stimulation and from the emotional looseness of reverie." [56]

Why is it that, of all the dimensions of art, people are usually most insensitive to form? They will respond to and enjoy the sensory quality of the matter, the dramatic interest of the subject matter, and the more obvious emotions and thoughts expressed by the work. Why is form so often for many people little more than the "before-after" or "above-below" arrangement of the parts? I suggest two reasons.

(1) The passage just quoted implies the first reason, viz., the appreciation of form demands alert and intense *attention*. Formal relations extend throughout the entire work. If they are to be comprehended, which means literally "taken together," then what is apprehended at any one moment must be related to what has gone before and what is to come after. A chapter in a novel, a melody in a musical composition, a color-area in a painting must not be permitted to vanish from awareness after it has been perceived and enjoyed. It must be held in memory because of what it portends for the future life of the work. And at the same time we must attend to the future, the climax or the return to the tonic, which are not now being perceived, but which give significance to what *is* being seen or heard.

"[Unity] is an achievement. . . . The aesthetic object is no cheap unity." [57] It must be won by unflagging attention, capacious memory, vigilant anticipation. Else the aesthetic object will fall apart and our ex-

---

[55] *Ibid.*, p. 31.
[56] Santayana, *The Sense of Beauty*, p. 74.
[57] Morris, *The Aesthetic Process*, p. 21.

perience will become "a drowsy revery relieved by nervous thrills."[58]

Generally, if we are paying any attention to the work at all, we will recognize the same character at different places in the novel or the recurrence of a melody. But with only so much attention, the experience of the work will be loose and straggly, only thinly bound together. We may not be aware of this if only we find interest in each of the successive episodes in a novel. But the experience would gain enormously in value if it were more compact and closely woven. The critic Lubbock says of *Madame Bovary*: "The book is not a row of facts, it is a single image."[59] Awareness of that unity will cast new light on the "story" and characters, even though these may be of some interest in themselves without knowledge of the book's "image." Repeated allusions to the white whale in *Moby Dick* unfold the significance of this symbol, and each of them should be borne in mind to add to later evocations of its meaning. Ultimately the meaning is rich and varied. It is never wholly made clear, perhaps, but that in itself contributes to the air of imponderable mystery which hangs over the book.[60]

It is because form runs throughout the work, and is often so complex, that its values are frequently neglected. Indispensable to its appreciation is repeated experience of the work to develop *familiarity*.[61] Moreover the aid of critical analysis must often be enlisted. Tovey shows us the relation between two widely separated points in a long symphonic movement,[62] Granville-Barker explains the significance of the repetition of a single word which occurs more than two acts apart in one of the longest plays ever written.[63] Granville-Barker asks: "But will the ordinary attentive listener seize on this connection, spaced out, as it is, across more than half the play's length?"[64] The answer is that he probably will not, until discerning critics see for him and thereby enable him to see.

(2) Form is generally the most subtle aspect of art. Sensory elements often have an obvious charm. They are like what we see outside of art in sunsets and hats. And subject matter can be understood and enjoyed because it is like "real life," only usually more exciting — a voyage to Treasure Island and so on. Recurrence, balance, and the other kinds of form also occur outside of art but not with the complexity and richness which they have in major works of art. The intricate fabric of a piece of polyphonic music, the elaborate organization of Joyce's *Ulysses*,

---

[58] Cf. above, p. 38.
[59] *Op. cit.*, p. 62.
[60] Cf. E. K. Brown, *Rhythm in the Novel* (University of Toronto Press, 1950), pp. 55–57.
[61] Cf. above, chap. 3, sec. 2.
[62] Cf. above, pp. 243–244.
[63] Cf. above, p. 239.
[64] *Op. cit.*, p. 188.

the pattern of a "nonobjective" painting like "Composition" by Moholy-Nagy (see Plate 25) — these have no counterpart in nature. That is why the formalists in theory of art, like Bell, Fry, and Hanslick, have also been "purists": artistic form can only be understood and appreciated in its own terms; it cannot be translated into words or in any other way.

Hence to enjoy the values of form requires, as Santayana says, "specifically aesthetic" insight. The spectator must be able to respond though his nonaesthetic experience has not prepared him to do so. He must be able to discriminate and enjoy what is peculiar to art and therefore unlike anything else. To this end also, familiarity with the work, close attention, and the assistance of critical analysis in the various arts, are needed. But merely to schematize the work into "ABA" patterns and the like is not enough. The knowledge gained from such analysis must be absorbed into the very seeing and hearing of the work. If such knowledge remains external to aesthetic perception, if it does not make the work a richer and more meaningful object, then it defeats its own purpose. Similarly, the analysis of form must recognize its own limitations: it is never a substitute for the unique design of the work. Words can help, but they can never suffice.

Probably the first thing to do is to realize what form *is*, to understand that form in art involves a great deal more than just the succession of parts one after the other. Perhaps this discussion can contribute to such understanding.

BIBLIOGRAPHY

* Rader, *A Modern Book of Esthetics.* Pp. 62–88, 235–257, 357–378.
* Vivas and Krieger, *The Problems of Aesthetics.* Pp. 182–208, 262–276, 285–290.
* Weitz, *Problems in Aesthetics.* Pp. 175–184, 312–344, 419–454, 463–542.
  Dewey, *Art as Experience.* Chaps. VII–X.
  Gotshalk, *Art and the Social Order.* Chaps. IV–V.
  Greene, *The Arts and the Art of Criticism.* Chaps. I–XI.
  Herring, Frances W., "Touch — The Neglected Sense," *Journal of Aesthetics and Art Criticism,* Vol. VII (March, 1949), 199–215.
  Lubbock, Percy. *The Craft of Fiction.* New York: Viking, 1957.
  Meyer, Leonard B. *Emotion and Meaning in Music.* University of Chicago Press, 1957.
  Moore, Jared S., "The Work of Art and its Material," *Journal of Aesthetics and Art Criticism,* Vol. VI (June, 1948), 331–338.
  Muir, Edwin. *The Structure of the Novel.* London: Hogarth, 1928.
  Munro, Thomas. *The Arts and Their Interrelations.* New York: Liberal Arts, 1951. Chap. VII.
  ———. *Toward Science in Aesthetics.* New York: Liberal Arts, 1956. I, chap. 2, IV, V.

Parker, De Witt H. *The Analysis of Art.* Yale University Press, 1926. Chap. II.
Pepper, Stephen C. *Principles of Art Appreciation.* New York: Harcourt, Brace, 1949. Chaps. 3–5, 8.
Prall, *Aesthetic Judgment.* Chaps. V-IX.
Santayana, George. *The Sense of Beauty.* New York: Scribners, 1936. Parts 2–3.
Tovey, Donald F. *Essays in Musical Analysis.* New York: Oxford University Press, 1935, 1936, 1937.

QUESTIONS

1. Consider some specific works of art which are often said to be deficient in sensory attractiveness, e.g., the novels of Dreiser, the later music of Schönberg. Do you think that these judgments are sound? Is the "drabness" of the sensory matter indispensable to the aesthetic value of these works? If so, is material "drabness" a condemnation of the work? Or does the material element detract from the value of these works?

2. Do you think that the modes of form described in this chapter (pp. 234–236) can be of help in the analysis of specific works? Or are they too abstract for that?

3. Do you agree with Gotshalk's view (cf. above, p. 238), that repetition occurs most often in the "temporal" arts? Can you give examples? Can you give examples of repetition in the "spatial" arts?

4. Study the analyses of form in the novel, in the works by Lubbock and Muir, cited in the Bibliography. Do you think that form is as important in the novel as in poetry, music, and painting?

5. Study the critical analyses of musical compositions by Tovey, in the readings cited in the Bibliography (and listen to the music, too). Do you think that Tovey can be charged with "murdering to dissect"? If not, why not?

6. Do you find, in your own experience, that the appreciation of form is less important than the response to matter, subject matter, and expression? Do you find that you appreciate form only after you have gained familiarity with the work? Are there any works of art, in your experience, in which form is the most valuable of the elements?

10

E*xpression*

1. THE NATURE OF EXPRESSION

This is not the first time that we have spoken of "expression." This concept figured in several previous chapters. "Expression" is one of the words — perhaps it is *the* word — used most popularly in our age to talk about art. Think how often you have heard phrases like "The artist is expressing — " or "The work is highly expressive"; perhaps you have had teachers ask, "What does this work express to you?" "Express" and its cognates occurred in our analysis of artistic creation (Chapter 4), emotionalist theory (Chapter 7), and matter and form (Chapter 9). Let us remind ourselves what we have already established about "expression."

To begin with, the term is ambiguous. It can refer either to the process of artistic creation which leads up to the work, or to an intrinsic property of the work itself. The present chapter examines expression as a dimension of art like matter and form. In other words, it is the second meaning which is pertinent here. The ideas and emotions experienced by the artist in the course of expression (in the first sense), which he tells about in diaries, letters, etc., *may* help to explain the expressiveness of the *work*. They will do so only if they are found to be embodied in the work in one form or another. Whether they are present in the work cannot be learned merely by studying what the artist says about the causes of his creative activity or by reading some account of his life. The artist may have failed to incorporate in the art-object what he thought or felt, and historical studies may lead us to look for ideas and feelings which simply are not in the work.

We must therefore remind ourselves once again that the genesis of the work is one thing and the work itself another.[1] Consequently what a work expresses can only be known, in the first instance, by direct aesthetic awareness. Then critical analysis, based upon the findings of aesthetic experience, and perhaps drawing upon history, biography, and so on, can seek to describe the expressive significance of the work.

This leads to the further reminder that what the work expresses is peculiar to itself. We saw in the last chapter that matter, form, and expression are interdependent. They have no existence apart from each other. The expressive content of a work is as it is because of the material elements, the formal organization, and the subject matter which together with it make up the specific work. Hence no verbal account can duplicate or be a substitute for expression. Words can *describe*, as when we say, "The music is somber," or "The poem is thoughtful." Such statements may be meaningful and true enough. But they do not, and cannot, make us feel the specific quality of "somberness" which is expressed by the music. Only listening to the music can do that.

When a work is expressive, we have seen, it is neither a *sign* of what it expresses nor simply a *cause* of the thoughts and emotions which it induces in the percipient.[2] A cause, like a drug or a pin-prick, is something which leads to a certain kind of experience. But that experience is and is felt to be something different from its cause. A sign or symptom, like blushing or laughing, will lead us to infer that some emotion is being felt. However the sign is something distinct from what is being felt. We can apprehend the sign and make the appropriate inferences without ourselves feeling the emotion. The relationship between the work of art and what it expresses is not like that between a sign and what it stands for, or a cause and what it leads to.

But we have not yet said what expression *is*. We have to do so if we are to explain its role in the structure of art alongside of matter and form. And we must do so, too, because people nowadays so often demand that a work of art must "express" something. What do they mean when they say this? They do not always use the word "express." Perhaps they will protest, "I don't understand what the work is saying," or "I don't see what it all means." It is tolerably clear that these locutions refer to the expressive dimension of the work.

Yet it is not easy to explain the nature of expression. Whereas "form"

[1] Cf. above, pp. 87 ff.
[2] Cf. above, pp. 84.

suffers from having *many* meanings,[3] the trouble with "expression" is its vagueness — it is difficult to formulate a single clear meaning of the term. You may think this surprising since, as we have noted, "express" is one of the most common words in our artistic vocabulary. Often, however, just those words which are used most frequently by a certain society or in a certain age, are systematically vague. Perhaps they can be used so commonly precisely *because* their meaning has not been narrowed down and specified. Think of such words as "democracy" and "freedom" in political discourse or "relative" and "absolute" in modern ethical discussions.

Recently systematic attempts have been made to analyze the meaning of "expression." Perhaps none of these attempts has wholly succeeded. As we proceed, we will see the difficulties involved in using the concept. If those who speak of "expression" do not mention these problems, it may be not because they have solved them, but because they have ignored them.

LET US BEGIN by going back to the frustrated percipient who, having listened to or looked at the work, still asks, "But what does it express?" He says that there is something about the work which escapes him, something that he does not understand. But even so, *some* aspects of the work he *can* make out and understand. These are the properties which do *not* constitute the expressive content of the object. What are they?

Well, if the work is a piece of music, our friend can know the key in which it is written; he may be able to identify every single note in the score and to hear all of the notes when they are played; he can recognize the traditional formal pattern in which the work is written, e.g., sonata form. If the work is a painting, he will see the colors and recognize the subject matter, e.g., "Crucifixion." If it is a novel, he will understand the words and again, recognize the subject or what the book is "about."

Thus, the nonexpressive aspects of the work can be known merely by perceiving the work. We can sense the matter, identify the form, recognize the subject. Still the work is inert and lifeless. It does not "say anything" to us. How trivial to know that Mozart's Symphony No. 40 is in the key of G Minor, that Joyce's *Ulysses* tells what happens in the course of one day in a man's life.

What is lacking in the spectator's experience? He lacks awareness of those properties of the work which are *not* given directly to perception. Suppose that the music "expresses gayety" (though not to him). The "gayety" is not something that he can perceive directly like the sounds of the orchestra. He hears the sounds perfectly well. But "gayety" is

---

[3] Cf. above, pp. 227–230.

something else again. It is not like "loud" or "soft," or like the timbre of an instrument. "Gay" is not an auditory property at all. Or Keats' "La Belle Dame Sans Merci" expresses a poignant mood of the desolateness of lost love. But the poem nowhere speaks of "a poignant mood etc.," though it *does* say, "And no birds sing." What is expressed arises out of the sounds or pictures or words. It is something more than them. To appreciate expressive content we must do more than see or hear or read. We must experience those suggestions and "overtones" which are not "said," but which emerge from and characterize what *is* "said."

A work can express (1) images, (2) emotions, (3) ideas. The closing section of Respighi's musical tone poem, "The Pines of Rome," evokes an image of Roman soldiers marching along the Appian Way. The listener "sees" that which could not possibly be "shown," in the literal sense, by music. Again, music cannot be literally "sad" or "gay." Only sentient organisms like human beings can have and feel emotions. Yet a musical composition can seem to be permeated by a well-defined mood or emotion. And a novel can express, though it nowhere states, a thematic "idea." Thus Joyce's *Ulysses* is often taken to express the loneliness and alienation of modern man. It does so by describing the day of a Jew in Ireland, who has forgotten his key so that he cannot enter his own home. Often the images, emotions, and ideas expressed in a work will coalesce, as when an image symbolizes an expressed idea and also has a distinctive emotional quality of its own.

The work "comes alive" when it is expressive to us. It is charged with imaginative excitement by suggesting more than it explicitly depicts. It takes on depth and resonance from its emotional overtones. The G Minor Symphony is not now a sequence of tones; it is "lyrical" or "passionate," perhaps "tragic." The conceptual significance of the work helps to answer our original question, "What does it all 'mean'?" Whereas *Ulysses* often seems disjointed and rambling at first, it comes to "mean" something when read as a commentary on the plight of modern man.[4]

Santayana says, "In all expression we may thus distinguish two terms: the first is the object actually presented, the word, the image, the expressive thing; the second is the object suggested, the further thought, emotion, or image evoked, the thing expressed." [5] This makes it sound as though the percipient were aware of *two* different "objects." Our previous discussion seems to imply the same thing. I said that expression "arises out of" or is "suggested by" what is perceived, as though one heard the notes or looked at the colors and then, in addition, felt an emotion or thought of an idea.

[4] I am not, of course, suggesting that this is the only possible, or even the most legitimate interpretation of this novel.
[5] *The Sense of Beauty*, p. 147.

But this is untrue to the facts of aesthetic experience. In order to explain expression as a dimension of art, we distinguish analytically the "first term" from the "second." However, in the actual experiencing of the work, there is no such distinction. To the spectator, what is expressed is ingredient in what is directly given to perception. As Santayana puts it, the two "terms" "lie together in the mind." [6] That is why we so naturally and readily say, "The music is gay and lighthearted," although this is, strictly speaking, absurd. Our way of speaking is a report of our felt experience: when the music is expressive, "gayety" is as much inherent in the sounds as their pitch or the timbre of the instruments which are voicing them. We will not be confused by talk about "two terms" as long as we remember that such talk is for purposes of analysis, and that theoretical analysis is very different from concrete experience. [7]

If, however, the terms do *not* "lie together in the mind," then the work cannot be said to be expressive. "I may receive a letter full of the most joyous news, but neither the paper, nor the writing, nor the style, need seem beautiful to me. Not until I confound the impressions, and suffuse the symbols themselves with the emotions they arouse, and find joy and sweetness in the very words I hear, will the expressiveness constitute a beauty." [8] A man may know every note in a score, and he may know too, by means of stylistic conventions, and composer's markings such as *molto vivace*, that the work is supposed to express liveliness and gayety. But if the expressive content remains distinct from the heard sounds, the music cannot be said to be expressive to him. The "two terms" do not, for him, constitute a single being, an expressive object.

"The expressive thing" and what it expresses may be felt to be one, when experience is *not* aesthetic. An object can take up into itself imaginative and other significance without being an aesthetic object. When we say, "The ice looks cold," we are distorting literal meaning in a manner comparable to "The music is gay." The ice can, literally, look bright or scarred with figure eights, but it can only *feel* cold to our sense of touch and thermal sense. Yet the locution is perfectly meaningful and understandable. The imagined coldness has become part of the content of experience just as much as the seen brightness. Again, a house in which one has lived for a long time can become expressive of images and emotions. Each piece of furniture, each room can be "suffused" by a distinctive expressive quality.

Why are such experiences nonaesthetic? The answer here, as throughout this book, is in terms of the meaning of "aesthetic," i.e., the attitude

6 *Loc. cit.*
7 Cf. Vincent A. Tomas, "The Concept of Expression in Art," in *Science, Language, and Human Rights* (University of Pennsylvania Press, 1952), pp. 130 ff.
8 Santayana, *op. cit.*, p. 149.

of "disinterested and sympathetic attention." The perception of the ice or of the house *can* be aesthetic, if this attitude is adopted and sustained. We can, and indeed we often do, contemplate natural objects such as ice or trees, dwelling upon their expressive qualities. "Seeing" the texture of an object often occurs in the appreciation of sculpture, as it does in perceiving the ice. By the same token, however, our experience may *not* be aesthetic. "The house is sad," where this means that everything in it is imbued with certain moods and images, is not necessarily an aesthetic perception. It might be said after the death of a loved one, by somebody who does *not* wish to savor attentively the desolateness of the house. Then the statement voices a *practical*, rather than an aesthetic attitude, e.g., the decision to leave or move from the house. What is expressive is not always aesthetic.

And yet the expressiveness of things — what they suggest to imagination, emotion, and thought — is doubtless more pronounced in aesthetic experience than in other kinds of experience. This is due to the nature of aesthetic perception. When we are "practical," we want to apprehend things quickly and economically in order that we can act efficiently.[9] We do not then dwell upon things sufficiently to become aware of their expressiveness. Aesthetic perception rests upon the object so that its expressiveness can emerge and become palpable. This is, of course, especially true when the object is a work of art. For then the matter, form, and subject matter have been deliberately selected to exploit their expressive potentialities.

WE ARE NOW PREPARED to meet the charge that concern with expressive significance leads to neglect of the material, formal, and representational dimensions of the work. On this view, which is widely held, these aspects of art become, for one who is interested in expression, merely *means* of stimulating images and emotions: "the perceptual object, although doubtless a necessary condition of the aesthetic 'effect,' is simply a vehicle by which feeling is incited." [10]

If the work is only that, then our attitude is not genuinely aesthetic. And, on the meaning of "expressive" given above, the work cannot be said to be genuinely expressive. For if we use the work as a stimulus to feeling, we are not apprehending it for its own sake. Then, as Hanslick says, a "warm bath" will do just as well.[11] And if the work is used in this way, then it simply *causes* moods, etc.; it does not *express* them. The moods and images experienced by the percipient become dis-

[9] Cf. above, pp. 33 ff.
[10] Henry David Aiken, "Art as Expression and Surface," *Journal of Aesthetics and Art Criticism*, IV (1945), 87.
[11] Cf. above, p. 143.

sociated from the sounds or colors of the art-object. The great danger here is that the spectator will become absorbed in his own feeling states, so that the work gets shunted to the periphery of attention. In its most extreme and vulgar form, such experience becomes "sentimental," i.e., emotions are felt which are disproportionate to the expressive content of the work, for they have no basis in the work.

What is expressed by the work can only be known by unremitting attention to the formal organization of matter and subject matter. Expressiveness lives only in the lines and cadences, the words and events which the work presents to us. It is not, for aesthetic perception, an "effect" of them and it is coordinate in importance with them. As Professor Aiken has well said, "the relation between the object and [expressed] emotion is not one of means and end at all, but, rather, of mutually supporting components within a relational whole." [12] If you will think back again to the Zorach sculpture cited in the preceding chapter, you will remember that the work's sensory surface and formal devices point up its expressive significance, but also that the latter in turn heightens the work's sensuous charm and renders the subject appealing and "alive."

It follows that descriptions of what a work "means" — "Beethoven's Ninth Symphony expresses the brotherhood of man," "Thomas Hardy's novels show that man cannot control his destiny" — can be greatly misleading. They are suspect on two counts. Primarily, such statements suggest that expressive significance is the whole point of the work. Consequently they suggest that form, matter, and subject are simply means to its attainment. We have just seen the error in this. These brief lines by the contemporary poet Archibald MacLeish have become famous:

> A poem should not mean
> But be.[13]

It is the inherent being of the work that is important. What the work expresses or "means" resides in its very fibre and structure; "meaning" is not something divorced from the work. Secondly, it is worth repeating that no verbal summary of the work's expressive content is wholly adequate. That is why the composer who was asked the meaning of a piece he had just played, went back to the piano and played it over again.

2. EXPRESSION AND ASSOCIATION

How does it happen that things are expressive to us? How is it that they "mean" more to us than what we directly perceive? Why is a cer-

---

[12] *Op. cit.*, p. 89.
[13] "Ars Poetica," in Archibald MacLeish, *Collected Poems* (Boston: Houghton Mifflin, 1952), p. 41.

tain tone not only a sensed object of a certain pitch and timbre, but also something "blithe" or "mournful"?

These questions are directed to the origins of expressiveness. There is no doubt *that* things are expressive. *Why* are they so? As we shall now see, such questions force us to reconsider the meaning of "expression" which was worked out in the previous section.

SANTAYANA'S ANSWER is simple. All expression, he holds, is due to *associa-tion*. The "first term" takes on expression because it is associated, in the mind of the percipient, with previous experiences. The "meaning and tone" of these experiences accrue to the object and seem to be in-herent in it. So long as we are aware of the psychological gap between the object and its associations, it is not expressive. Then, as we say ex-plicitly, we value the object "for its associations." But when the suggested emotion or idea "escapes" from memory and "diffuses itself" over the thing perceived,[14] expression occurs.

Hence, although Santayana insists as much as anyone that the "two terms" are apprehended as one by the percipient, he holds that *causally* the "second term" is always superadded from memory and imagination.

Does this explain expression? Doubtless Santayana explains a great deal of it. Indeed, association is the most obvious and perhaps the most com-mon source of expressiveness. Our earlier example, "The house is sad," is an instance of the "fusion" of past and present experiences. The Ameri-can flag would not be as stirring as it is to us if it did not seem to sum up within itself the traditions and ideals of our country. We have seen that "fused association" can enhance the vigor of aesthetic perception.[15]

But association may not suffice to explain *all* expression. And even when association is one of the contributing causes, it may not be enough, in itself, to bring about expression.

On Santayana's theory, expression arises solely from past experience. Yet is there not something about the perceived object itself which is re-sponsible for its expressive significance? Does it not have *inherent* prop-erties which make it expressive, as opposed to the historical fact that it happens to be associated by the spectator with something else in his past experience? Santayana says that "things in themselves indifferent"[16] may become expressive. But the psychologist Rudolf Arnheim offers a vivid and telling example which casts doubt on Santayana's view. Pro-fessor Arnheim points to the photographs of athletes in action which we see every day in the sports pages of the newspaper — a football player leaping to catch a pass, a shortstop hurdling the runner who is sliding into second base. Often these photographs, as Arnheim says, "have the

---

[14] *Op. cit.*, p. 146.
[15] Cf. above, p. 54.
[16] *Op. cit.*, p. 146.

human figure awkwardly arrested in mid-air as though struck by sudden paralysis." Now, he continues, such photographs and those which, by contrast, show "vivid motion," "have equal chances of being associated by the observer with past experiences." And yet when the photograph seems to "freeze" the athlete in mid-air, "we understand that motion is represented; but not only do we not see it, we find it painfully absent." [17]

Do you see what Arnheim is arguing? A split-second photograph shows the athlete at a single moment; yet sometimes we say that it "expresses motion." Santayana explains this in terms of our past experience. We know that the athlete is in mid-air and is coming down to the ground; hence we imagine the motion. But if this explanation were sufficient, *all* such photographs would express motion whereas the truth is, as Arnheim says, that often they do not. Often the football or baseball player seems to be dangling in air like a puppet. The whole picture is static and non-expressive.

Therefore, there must be something which sets off those photographs which are "live" and vivid. Following Arnheim, we can suppose that the "force" of motion is inherent in the visual pattern itself. The vigor and direction of the lines, the bodily posture of the athlete, his position relative to other players and to the ground — these and other elements create tension and drive within the photograph. Hence it can "express motion." Then we can say either that (a) the picture is intrinsically expressive, or (b) association is required to give the sense of motion, but association is possible only because of the inherent pattern of the photograph. Whether we choose (a) or (b), we must reject a *purely* associationist theory.

Arnheim leans to (a). He says that "the rigid hardness of the circular line and the gentle flexibility of the parabola can be derived from the inherent make-up of the two curves." [18] Thus it could be argued that the associationists have put the cart before the horse. Lines, sounds, colors are expressive because of their inherent visual and auditory properties. Consequently they have become associated with certain ideas and emotions. They have not become expressive because of their associations. A bright, dazzling red has an expressive quality in virtue of which it becomes associated with brashness and absence of restraint. Its expressiveness is not something that we add to it after having seen wicked or, as we say (notice the word we use), "scarlet" ladies. Expressive content is not something that we learn from past experience; it is something that we find in current experience.

On the other hand, many philosophers find it difficult to say that an object is "inherently" expressive. We can say that the note is C sharp or that the color is blue. *These* are "intrinsic" properties, for notes, by

[17] Arnheim, *Art and Visual Perception*, p. 336.
[18] *Ibid.*, p. 364.

their very nature, must have a certain pitch, colors must be one shade or another. But a line cannot be "agitated" (though it can be jagged), a curve cannot be "tranquil" (though it can be long). It *appears* to the spectator as though such expressive properties were "inherent." However this is only a metaphoric way of speaking. We impute "tranquillity" to an object because it resembles like objects that we have seen in the past and these associations have entered into our subconscious.[19] Expressive properties "are resonances of a multitude of experiences."[20] This is, of course, an associationist theory and, so far, opposed to Arnheim's. However, it does not hold that expressiveness can be superadded to "things in themselves indifferent," as Santayana has it. Things are expressive only when they have certain properties.[21] The line seems "agitated" *because* it is jagged.

The argument just presented against Arnheim's view is a *linguistic* one. It rests upon analysis of the proper meanings of such words as "tranquil." His view is also subject to an *empirical* argument, one which the reader has very likely thought of already.

If what is expressed were really "intrinsic" to that which expresses, then all those who perceived the latter would also apprehend the former. Anyone who could hear the chord or see the line would also experience its emotional and imaginative quality. We could then expect general agreement concerning the expressive properties of objects. But, in point of fact, there is no such agreement. People disagree profoundly about the expressed "meaning" of a drama or in reporting what they hear "in" the music. The novelist E. M. Forster has given us an amusing example:

> It will be generally admitted that Beethoven's Fifth Symphony is the most sublime noise that has ever penetrated into the ear of man. All sorts and conditions are satisfied by it. Whether you are like Mrs. Munt, and tap surreptitiously when the tunes come . . . or like Helen, who can see heroes and shipwrecks in the music's flood; or like Margaret, who can only see the music; or like Tibby, who is profoundly versed in counterpoint, and holds the full score open on his knee; or like their cousin, Fräulein Mosebach, who remembers all the time that Beethoven is "echt Deutsch"; or like Fräulein Mosebach's young man, who can remember nothing but Fräulein Mosebach: in any case, the passion of your life becomes more vivid, and you are bound to admit that such a noise is cheap at two shillings.[22]

This passage is taken from fiction and it is, of course, intended to be entertaining. But does it exaggerate the diversity of aesthetic response?

[19] Cf. Dewey, *op. cit.*, p. 101, and John Hospers, *Meaning and Truth in the Arts* (University of North Carolina Press, 1946), p. 72.
[20] Dewey, *loc. cit.*
[21] Cf. above, pp. 153–156.
[22] E. M. Forster, *Howard's End* (New York: Knopf, 1943), p. 38.

Very likely not. Have you not sometimes discussed a work of art with friends only to learn that they "find" in it emotions and ideas which are completely different from and even opposed to those which you have "found"? The history of art interpretation and criticism is replete with comparable examples.

These facts seem to force us back to an associationist theory. The work has different expressive properties because each percipient comes to it and perceives it differently. Each has a different background, different interests, varying degrees of familiarity with the work, and so forth. The orchestra is playing just the one composition — Beethoven's Fifth Symphony — and the members of the audience hear just this piece of music; yet each one "reads into" the music his own particular expressive significance, depending upon his memories and imagination. Whereas the "first term" — what is heard — is the same for all, the "second term" — what is felt — is not.

But here we must raise a highly difficult question, though it is one which has not yet been satisfactorily solved: are the listeners hearing the "same" music, i.e., is the "first term" really the same for all of them? We could get an answer only if listeners could distinguish the content of hearing from what it expresses and then, further, compare what they hear among themselves. Neither of these conditions is readily satisfied.

We should not, however, take it for granted that the "first term" *is* always the same. "The assumption that persons whose sense of the meaning of a piece of music differs can yet have the very same sense perception of sounds is, so far as I know, devoid of all evidence." [23] In the absence of empirical data, one can only speculate on the answer to our question. So considered, it seems likely that the "first term" is *not* the same when the "second term" is different. "Same" and "different" refer to the actual felt experience of the percipient. Within his experience of the object, matter, form, subject, and expression are mutually interactive. Expression does not merely result from the other three dimensions of the work. In its turn it "colors" them. The mood of the Zorach sculpture mentioned in the last chapter determines in part how the marble looks to us. When the work of art has a different expressive significance for A and for B, then their *total* experiences are different from each other.

There is some, presumptive evidence for this view. And yet it is only presumptive, so that the view is only conjectural. Whether expression can vary independently of the "first term" has not yet been clearly ascertained, one way or the other. It is one of the problems that we must bear in mind when we speak of "expression." But now, even more important problems arise.

[23] Charles Hartshorne, *The Philosophy and Psychology of Sensation*, p. 186, as quoted in Tomas, *loc. cit.*, p. 140.

Just as the devices of form can only be understood in terms of aesthetic experience,[24] so "expression" must refer to the thoughts and feelings of the percipient. A work of art is expressive only when images, emotions, and ideas are found to be embodied in it by someone who takes the aesthetic attitude. This is a relativistic approach — expression is *to* a spectator — and it must pay the price of relativism. For it must address itself to the damaging implications which seem to follow from this view of "expression."

Consider what follows from the hypothesis that whenever in aesthetic experience the expressive properties are different, the "first term" is also different. A says, "This work is joyous"; B says, "Oh, I don't find it so. It seems to me to be somber." If the hypothesis is correct, then they are not talking about the "same" thing at all. They are merely reporting their personal feelings. When each says, "The work is — " the meaning of "the work" is different. It denotes colors seen differently, sounds heard differently, etc.

Suppose, however, that the "first term" remains the same for A and B, when the expressive properties are different for each of them. If what a work expresses is part of its total structure, the total work will still be different in each case.

The logical consequences are dismaying: What we generally call "the work of art" becomes shattered into many different objects of perception. A and B cannot communicate with each other, since they are not speaking about the same thing at all. Their talk about art is like those conversations in which one man describes *his* illness, and the other talks about *his* malady. No issue can be joined concerning *the work of art*. The aesthetic value-judgment, "This work is beautiful," has no "objective" validity, for it refers only to the work as it appears to the speaker. But when we evaluate and criticize works of art, we want to speak of something which is "public," something which is shared by many.[25]

Here, then, is the major dilemma of "expression": The images, moods, and thoughts expressed by a work animate and, as we commonly say, give "meaning" to it. For the aesthetic percipient, expressive significance seems to be as much "there" in the work as anything else. Yet analysis of the meaning of "expression" makes it out to be something *not* literally "there" in the work like the loudness of a *fortissimo* passage or the depiction of the Crucifixion. This seems to be borne out empirically by the enormous diversity among people reporting what the work "expresses to me." Expressiveness seems to be something superadded by each person. Therefore if it is taken to be part of the work, we can no longer

---

[24] Cf. above, pp. 236 ff.
[25] Cf. Douglas N. Morgan, "The Concept of Expression in Art," in *Science, Language, and Human Rights* (University of Pennsylvania Press, 1952), pp. 156 ff.

speak of *"the* work" but only of infinitely many. To be sure, we can go right on experiencing expression as we have experienced it before. The analysis cannot and will not stop *that.* But evaluation and criticism of *"the* work" seem no longer to be possible.

We must now begin to have serious reservations about the concept of "expression." Should we even go on using the concept at all, if this is what it leads to?

BUT PERHAPS THE IMPLICATIONS of "expression" are not quite so disastrous. It is a *fact* that people "see" and "feel" infinitely different things in a work of art. Beethoven's Fifth Symphony *does* "satisfy all sorts and condi- tions." This is simply an instance of the banal truth that people are not alike. And works of art offer a wide range for the exercise of their imagina- tion and feelings.

Yet we need not grant that any and every experience discloses equally the expressive content of the work. What the work expresses to the spec- tator seems to him to be embodied in the work. This is just the mean- ing of "expression." His experience is, however, only the starting point in finding out what the work expresses. The experience must be reflected upon and examined. We have seen that some associations are "irrelevant" to the work.[26] If "Fräulein Mosebach's young man" hears all of the sym- phony as one long love song to Fräulein Mosebach, we need not take this to be the truth about Beethoven's Fifth. Let us therefore distinguish between the expressiveness of the aesthetic object and the expressive con- tent of the work of art.

After all, there *is* a work of art which can be studied and known "publicly." The claim made by "The work expresses — to me" must be applied to that work. Has the percipient really grasped the expressive con- tent of the work? Expressive content is related to and depends upon the work's sensory matter, its organization, and what it represents. If the asser- tion about what the work expresses is to be valid, it must be shown to be grounded in the work. Analysis may show that the percipient's claim is not valid in this sense. Perhaps the formal structure has not been wholly compre- hended — recall from the last chapter how complex the form of a work can be; the spectator's ear may not be good, his eye may not be sharp, so that some feature of the sensory surface has escaped him; he may have misconstrued the representational subject matter, because of a lack of knowledge. We can often show a man that his "reading" of the work is distorted in some respect or that he has "missed" something. We do so by pointing to the objective properties of the work. If he experienced certain images, emotions, and thoughts while perceiving the work, then

[26] Cf. above, pp. 54 ff.

he experienced them, and that is the end of that. But these cannot be legitimately attributed to the work, as its expressive content, if it can be shown that he "mis-read" it.

We saw a little while back that the expression of motion in a photograph depends upon the "forces" which are set up by the visual pattern. Analysis of such a pattern is analysis of properties of the work which are "public." Art criticism proceeds in this way. Here is an analysis of Picasso's painting, "Glass of Beer" (see Plate 26), an early work of the "Blue Period," which depicts a single figure in "the specter of his solitude": "The spatial effect is subordinated to a purely two-dimensional order; the ascetic absence of all pictorial attractions, the economy of means [enhances] the expression of inwardness. As for the composition, particularly characteristic are . . . the deformations which are partly caused by the absence of spatial perspective. These deformations, however, serve expressive purposes, as in the flexible, wristless hand holding the beer-glass. The sober colors — the jacket is dark blue against a blue background, the hair is dull brown, the glass is gray — are entirely in keeping with the austere forms, and heighten the expression of genuine purity." [27] This analysis of expressive content proceeds by pointing to the commonly observable elements of the work — composition, color, etc.

Since expressive content is based upon the other elements of the work, it will be as unique as the work. "Fräulein Mosebach's young man," however, will very likely find that *any* piece of music expresses the loveliness of Fräulein Mosebach. Love has a way of diffusing itself over all the objects in one's neighborhood and gilding them. Probably, therefore, *Tchaikovsky's* Fifth Symphony, if he happened to be hearing it, would "express" to the young man pretty much what Beethoven's Fifth expresses. No one wishes to disparage love but this shows that the young man's experience is not a reliable clue to expressive content. Further if, as is not unlikely, he finds that all of Beethoven's Fifth — both the rhapsodic slow movement and the spirited last movement — expresses uniformly the loveliness of Fräulein Mosebach, then again his experience is suspect.

Wholly personal and private associations are therefore dangerous. They *can* become "embodied" in the work of art. As we saw earlier, this is not a phenomenon which is peculiar to aesthetic experience. But they very likely will distort our perception of the work. If we are to remain true to the work, it is safer to have only those objective associations which are indicated within it. These include such cultural symbols as Christ on the Cross, natural associations such as springtime and rebirth, and stylistic conventions such as the minor key or a descending cadence.

[27] Wilhelm Boeck and Jaime Sabartés, *Picasso* (New York: Abrams, 1955), p. 123.

Often the artist gives some distinctive meaning to a symbol which is elaborated within the work, e.g., the white whale in *Moby Dick*, keys (Keyes) in Joyce's *Ulysses*.

Thus expressiveness need not be a matter of "projecting" on to the work whatever associations I may happen to bring with me. It can be shown to have a basis in formed matter. Once again, the "first term" is not, as Santayana has it, a "thing in itself indifferent." Rather there is something about it, something public and demonstrable, in virtue of which it possesses expressive content. That is why we can speak meaningfully about the expressive content of *the work*, and not merely about the moods and ideas which we have experienced. Evaluation and criticism can get a purchase on what is not purely "personal." The important thing to see, therefore, is that the assertion, "This is what the work expresses *to me*" (often uttered in a proud "I-dare-you-to-disagree" tone of voice and with an air of finality) is not decisive and self-legitimating as a statement about the art-object.

I am not for a single instant suggesting that it is *easy* to carry out the analysis of expressive content. Quite the contrary is true. Nor would I have you take me to mean that there is only one, single expressive content to be found in any specific work. Works of art are too rich and "ambiguous" for that. A great deal more remains to be said on these matters when we come later on to the problems of evaluation and criticism.[28]

What I have tried to do is this: the concept of "expression" seemed to lead us, a few pages back, into a dead end. This was the result of both the linguistic argument — a work of art cannot literally be said to "embody" expressive properties — and the empirical argument — a work of art expresses different things to different people. From these twin arguments it seemed to follow that one could say almost anything about "expression" and get away with it. I have tried to indicate that we can avoid this dead end by appeal to the work of art which exists interpersonally or "objectively." Expressive properties are not "free floating"; they are grounded in the material, formal, and representational aspects of the work. The latter elements, when analyzed, provide evidence for the attribution of expressive content to the work. Such evidence often enables us to say that statements beginning, "The work expresses" are illfounded. Men have had, and doubtless will continue to have, infinitely various emotional and imaginative experiences in the face of art-objects. That is a fact, as the old song has it, "which nobody can deny." But the implications of this truth are not as sweeping as might be thought. They are not, if a distinction can be made out between the expressiveness of the aesthetic object and the expressive content of the work of art.

[28] Cf. below, chap. 15.

Perhaps, however, I have not made out the distinction successfully. Perhaps, even, there is *no* way out of the problems which arise from talking of "expression." These problems are subjects of lively concern in aesthetics at the present time. Never before have aestheticians given so much attention to a term which has been used widely and uncritically for so long. No one would claim that any generally accepted answer has been arrived at. Our discussion will have served its purpose if it makes the reader aware of the central issues in this area and if, also, it makes him somewhat more self-conscious about using the not-so-innocent term "expression."

ONE FINAL QUESTION, now, about "expression" which can be stated more quickly.

People often use the locution "The work expresses" — as though it were a *value*-judgment. If the work is "highly expressive," then it is aesthetically *good*. In this respect, "expression" resembles "form" which is also used as a value-term.[29] Here again, however, it seems best to use the concept *descriptively* and then to draw distinctions between "good" and "bad."

For are not both good and bad works of art aesthetically expressive? Do they all possess value because of this expressiveness? Why, if at all, is a piece of music good because it expresses, say, melancholy? Could it not be aesthetically *bad?*

Those who use "express" evaluatively — and that means most of us nowadays — should consider these questions if they are to become clear in their talking and thinking about art. Very likely there is some good reason for using "expressive" in this way, even though we are only dimly and half-consciously aware of it. When a work is expressive then, by definition, it is invested with significance greater than its sensory "look" and its form. The work thereby captures our interest. The imagery, mood, and ideas which it suggests are all the more absorbing because they are not presented straightforwardly. We sense the "something more" in what we perceive and this arouses imagination, emotion, and thought. We feel ourselves more thoroughly engaged in and alert to what we are experiencing than is usually true in nonaesthetic experience. There is a thick richness in the object when the "first term" is "suffused" by the "second," which is lacking when the object is only a sign of something distinct from it.

Something like this may be in the minds of those who use "expressive" as a value-term. But if so, then expression itself is not the criterion of aesthetic value. Expression is valuable because, let us say, it sustains our interest in the work. Then interest or absorption in the work is the

[29] Cf. above, pp. 229–230.

value-criterion. Or expression is valuable perhaps because it contributes to what Berenson calls "life-enhancement," by arousing our faculties of imagination and emotion. Thereby we "feel more hopefully, more zestfully alive, living more intense, more radiant a life not only physically but morally and spiritually as well, reaching out to the topmost peak of our capacities." [30]

Only if expression is not itself the criterion of value can we explain how a work can be both "expressive" and bad. Otherwise it would be self-contradictory to say this. The explanation would show, e.g., that though the work expresses, *what* it expresses does not sustain the percipient's interest. In other words, those who speak about "expression" *presuppose* a criterion of value which they must get clear about and spell out.

This conclusion rests upon another consideration. Let us not forget that expressive content is only *one* dimension of the work of art. It is the total work that is either aesthetically good or bad. When we ascribe value (in some sense) to it, we must speak of matter and form as well as expression. Expressive content is valuable only because it is disciplined and organized by form. If the form is lax, then the mere expression of images, emotions, and ideas will not be of interest to us but quite the opposite. Sensory matter and subject matter count too. Expression, then, is not the whole story. Therefore it cannot be the principle of value in art. To think that it is distorts profoundly the nature of the art-object. For if there is any one thing that we have learned from our study of the structure of art, it is that matter, form, and expression are coordinate and interdependent, and that each can be understood and appreciated only within the total and unified being which is the work of art.

[30] *Aesthetics and History*, p. 150.

BIBLIOGRAPHY

* Rader, *A Modern Book of Esthetics*. Pp. 258–282.
* Vivas and Krieger, *The Problems of Aesthetics*. Pp. 234–239, 368–386.
* Weitz, *Problems in Aesthetics*. Pp. 186–217, 410–417, 419–454.
  Arnheim, Rudolf. *Art and Visual Perception*. University of California Press, 1954. Chap. X.
  Bouwsma, O. K., "The Expression Theory of Art," in *Philosophical Analysis*, ed. Black. Cornell University Press, 1950. Pp. 75–101.
  Dewey, *Art as Experience*. Chap. V.
  Gotshalk, *Art and the Social Order*. Chap. VI.
  Hospers, *Meaning and Truth in the Arts*. Chap. 3.
  Reid, L. A. *A Study in Aesthetics*. New York: Macmillan, 1954. Chaps. II–IV.
  Santayana, *The Sense of Beauty*. Part 4.
  Tomas, Vincent A., and Morgan, Douglas N., "The Concept of Expression in Art," in *Science, Language, and Human Rights*. University of Pennsylvania Press, 1952. Pp. 127–165.

QUESTIONS

1. Do you think that a work of art can be aesthetically valuable without being expressive? Explain your answer.

2. It is argued in this chapter that speaking of "expression" may make it impossible for different people to talk about the "*same* work of art." Is this consequence necessarily fatal? Are you prepared to have all critics speak of what the work expresses "to me"? Discuss.

   This problem raises the further problem of "the locus of the work of art," i.e., whether the work is to be identified with the physical object, the response of a single percipient, a class of resembling responses, etc. Read Manuel Bilsky, "The Significance of Locating the Art Object," *Philosophy and Phenomenological Research*, XIII (1953), 531–536.

3. How are the problems of "expression" related to the problem of aesthetic "relevance" (Chapter 2, sec. 5)? Are the problems essentially the same? Discuss.

4. Study the painting of Picasso (Plate 26) referred to on p. 261. Do you agree with the critical analysis which is quoted there? If not, how would you alter it?

5. Read the article by Bouwsma cited in the Bibliography. Which aspects of the meaning of "expression" does it clarify? Are there any problems about the concept, discussed in this chapter, which Bouwsma fails to touch upon?

PART IV

Three Problems in Aesthetics

U*gliness in Art:*
Tragedy and Comedy

The problems we have thus far considered are foundational to all of aesthetic theory. The answers to "What is aesthetic perception?" and "What distinguishes fine art?" analyze the basic concepts and define the chief areas of our study. We must have these answers before we can consider the problems of this and the two following chapters, viz., whether art can be ugly and, if so, whether it can be aesthetically valuable, whether art is a source of "truth," and whether art can or ought to be judged morally.

1. THE CATEGORIES OF AESTHETIC VALUE

That works of art are, in some sense, "good" or "valuable" is agreed to on all hands. Like sunshine, good food, and love, they are among the things that make life worth living. When the work is an ordered unity and yet is charged with passion and zest, we evaluate it very highly indeed. Few things are more precious to us.

Many different words are used to ascribe value to art-objects. We can, of course, use the common words of ordinary value-discourse, e.g., "This work is good," "It is better than that one," etc. But most of the predicates we use are peculiar to the evaluation of art. These differ according to whether they connote value or disvalue, e.g., "beautiful" or "ugly"; or according to the degree of value, e.g., "great" or "superb" as opposed to "pretty" or "charming"; or according to the kind of value which they designate, e.g., "sublime," "comic," "expressive."

THE STAPLE WORDS in the vocabulary of aesthetic value are certainly "beautiful" and "ugly." Traditionally, these words have been taken to be opposites, which, between them, denote all aesthetic objects. On one common meaning, "beautiful" refers to things which are pleasant or attractive to awareness, "ugly" to things which are odious or distasteful. Those theories which conceive of the aesthetic in terms of formal properties such as "harmony" or "organic unity" (rather than an attitude of perception), use "beautiful" to mark the presence of such properties, and "ugly" to mark their absence. Often, when these two terms have been taken to include all the objects with which aesthetics is concerned, the study itself has been defined as "theory of beauty and ugliness."

But though much of ordinary speech continues to use the words in this way, they have, to a great extent, lost their traditional role in aesthetic vocabulary. Analysis shows critical vagueness and ambiguity in the meaning of "beautiful" and "ugly." And it shows that they cannot serve as the central and inclusive categories of aesthetic value. Indeed, as we shall see, some philosophers would almost go so far as to exclude these terms from aesthetics altogether.

The first great inadequacy of the term "beauty" is its ambiguity. Often "beauty" has been used, both by common sense and in aesthetic theory, to refer to all objects whatever which possess aesthetic value. Its connotative meaning is then identical with that of "aesthetic value." But the word has also been used in a less broad sense, so that "beauty" becomes ambiguous. The narrower sense is enforced upon us by objects which are found to possess aesthetic value, but which we hesitate to call "beautiful." Some things are too slight or small-scale to warrant so impressive an adjective as "beautiful." They are, rather, "pretty" or "charming," perhaps "exquisite." At the opposite pole are those objects which are "more than" beautiful, because of their magnificence and grandeur. Here we use the term "sublime," whose meaning I shall discuss in a moment. Again, a funny joke or a display of virtuosity may delight us aesthetically, but the predicate "beautiful" seems utterly inappropriate. And finally, it seems least appropriate when we find aesthetic value in things which are, in some sense, ugly. Does not aesthetic contemplation find goodness in Goya's "The Disasters of War" and Rodin's "The Old Courtesan," in literary studies of morbidity and degeneracy, in recent musical compositions which employ strident dissonances and cacophonies?

"Beauty," in the narrow sense, then, refers only to one of the many species of aesthetic value. Analysis of the term distinguishes between this meaning and the larger, generic meaning (= "aesthetic value"). The ambiguity latent in uncritical discourse has been exposed. But we now face the problem of vagueness: Given the narrow sense of "beauty," what precisely distinguishes this species of aesthetic value from the others?

The vagueness of "beauty," in the narrow sense, cannot be readily overcome. A hard and fast definition will not reflect the fluidity of the term's meaning in everyday usage. However, the term does seem to connote some or all of the following: sensory attractiveness or pleasantness, relatively great complexity in the object, conspicuous formal values, pleasing or edifying subject matter, conventionality of subject, form, and treatment. If this is correct, then the term connotes a large number of properties, not all of which are present in objects which are called "beautiful." And there may be considerable uncertainty whether these properties are present in a specific object. For example, when is an object "complex" rather than "simple," "conventional" rather than "unorthodox"?

We can now understand why "beauty" is no longer so prominent in aesthetic theory. In its generic meaning the term has been replaced by some such phrase as "aesthetic value." Since this category is vital to any system of aesthetics, it must be considered in some detail and defined as clearly as possible. Each of the theories of art studied previously attempts to do this. But the same is not true of "beauty" in the narrow sense. It is noteworthy that many contemporary aestheticians treat this category cursorily or not at all. Since it is only one among other categories, it is not of central importance. Many share the view of Professor Lee that "The term 'beauty' is best used to denote only a part of the general field of aesthetic value, and that part need not be carefully delimited, but can be left more or less vague." [1]

Thus the category of beauty has undergone a great sea change. The change in the meaning and importance of "ugliness" as an aesthetic category has been even more drastic.

THE TRANSFORMATION BEGINS, as I have already suggested, when men feel compelled to consider some objects both ugly and aesthetically valuable. They find that some things are not beautiful in any conventional sense and yet they are interesting or absorbing. The most striking and numerous examples are perhaps to be found in the art of the last two centuries, which has extended immeasurably the boundaries of aesthetic perception.[2] But it would be a historical mistake to speak only of this

[1] Lee, *Perception and Aesthetic Value*, p. 98.
[2] Cf. above, p. 40.

period. Aristotle, one of the earliest aesthetic philosophers, took ugliness to be essential to comedy.[3] And throughout the history of art there have been creators like the painter Hieronymus Bosch (c.1450-1516) who, in tracing out a compelling personal vision, have embodied the demoniacal and macabre in their art. The common conception of ugliness is that set forth by the aesthetician Solger: "The ugly is . . . positively opposed to the beautiful, and we can only regard them as absolutely exclusive of each other." [4] But if the denotation of "aesthetic value" includes ugly art, then ugliness is not "opposed to," but is rather a species of "beauty" in the broad sense. Nor is it "opposed to" "beauty" in the narrow sense, for they are coordinate as two among other species of aesthetic value.

The reader may, however, balk at this. Does it make sense to think of beauty and ugliness in this way? Are they not "absolutely exclusive" opposites like right and wrong, or true and false?

Granted, it sounds odd to speak of "ugliness" as a kind of beauty or as coordinate with beauty. But this is only to say that the proposed usage is inconsistent with the way in which we have been accustomed to use these words. Our linguistic habits are not fixed and incorrigible, however. They may have to change when there are good reasons for altering customary meanings. Let us examine more closely the reasons in this case.

HISTORICALLY, the change in meaning occurs, as we might expect, gradually. Indeed, it results in large measure from the development in aesthetic thought of another category, which has important resemblances to ugliness, viz., sublimity.

Although the sublime is discussed as far back as Roman antiquity, it first becomes important as an aesthetic category in the eighteenth century. It answers to the kind of personal experience described at the close of the preceding century by John Dennis, in speaking of his journey through the Alps. He says of the rocks and precipices that they produced in him "a delightful Horrour, a terrible Joy, and at the same time, that I was infinitely pleas'd, I trembled." [5]

The most striking feature of this experience is, of course, the mixture of positive and negative feelings toward the object — "delightful Horrour," and so on. Dennis does not feel unmixed, uninterrupted delight. Aversion and fear, which are usually unpleasant emotions, enter in. The latter element is emphasized by Burke, who developed one of the most important eighteenth-century theories of sublimity: "[Terror] is in all

[3] *Poetics* V, pp. 7–8.
[4] Quoted in Bernard Bosanquet, *A History of Aesthetic* (New York: Meridian, 1957), p. 397.
[5] Quoted in Samuel H. Monk, *The Sublime: A Study of Critical Theories in XVIII-Century England* (New York: Modern Language Association of America, 1935), p. 207.

cases whatsoever . . . the ruling principle of the sublime." [6] Clearly, however, if the experience is *solely* one of "terror," it cannot be aesthetic. The percipient would become wholly concerned with his personal well-being, and he would be motivated to practical action. Burke takes account of this: "When danger or pain pass too nearly, they are incapable of giving any delight, and are simply terrible; but at certain distances, and with certain modifications, they may be, and they are delightful, as we every day experience." [7] Burke's view is supported by the facts of our experience when we apprehend objects other than the sublime. When we read a suspenseful "murder mystery" — "a hand reached out slowly from behind the curtains of the darkened room and . . ." — or watch a "horror movie," we relish our fear and it becomes part of the experience. Even so, our trepidation makes us uneasy, and the total experience is an oddly mixed one.

The experience of sublimity is more complicated and more rewarding. It can perhaps be summed up in the twin words "awful" and "aweful." Our fear is accompanied by a sense of exaltation, as in religious reverence. The sublime object, unlike the "murder mystery," has a vastness and magnificence about it which overwhelms us. We are frightened of it and yet also ennobled by it. Kant, writing at the close of the eighteenth century, says that "[As] the mind is not merely attracted by the object but is ever being alternately repelled, the satisfaction in the sublime does not so much involve a positive pleasure as admiration and respect." [8]

Which objects induce such an experience? The eighteenth-century thinkers cite most commonly objects of vast size — the star-filled skies, a stormy sea, mountain ranges. However, they also take account of objects which are not of comparable size, but which possess vast power, e.g., volcanoes, hurricanes, waterfalls. [9] Burke very acutely suggests another class of sublime objects, viz., those which are "obscure"; the feeling of awe can be aroused by what is mysterious and shadowy. Since the eighteenth century the meaning of "sublime" has become broadened. A. C. Bradley points out that we speak of "sublime love" and "sublime courage." [10] Here the notion of "size" in the literal sense has been lost altogether.

In all cases the sublime overwhelms and defies us. It may be more than we can grasp in perception, like the heavens; or it escapes our understanding, like the "obscure"; or it transcends our usual conceptions of goodness and badness, like God. It is not enough for the object to be

[6] Quoted in Monk, *op cit.*, p. 93.
[7] *Ibid.*, p. 91.
[8] *Critique of Judgment*, p. 83
[9] These two classes correspond, respectively, to Kant's "mathematical sublime" and "dynamical sublime."
[10] "The Sublime," in *Oxford Lectures on Poetry*, p. 44.

merely big, like the size of our national debt, or merely incomprehensible, like a problem in geometry that the student cannot work out. The sublime is clearly more complicated than that. The object must create in us fear or bafflement and also a sense that we are "lifted out of ourselves" when we try to grasp its vastness or meaning. As a category of aesthetic experience, "sublime" designates a group of related but not identical experiences. In listening to the *Dies Irae* from Verdi's "Requiem," the feeling of "terror" may become so gripping that one would turn away from the music if the shattering sounds and ominous rhythm continued for much longer. In reading Kafka's "obscure" novel, *The Trial*, the feeling of fear is less acute but it diffuses itself over one's response to the nightmarish adventures of the protagonist. In thinking of Christ's self-sacrifice for man, one feels not so much fear as an emotion or attitude closely related to it — our own puniness and weakness in the face of such immeasurable love. In this instance, too, the sense of exaltation or what Bradley calls "self-expansion" [11] is more pronounced than in other experiences of sublimity.

When eighteenth-century thought turned its attention to the sublime, it demonstrated implicitly the narrowness of beauty as a value-category. A beautiful object is one which wins our affection and gives delight. An object which induces aversion or "terror" cannot be considered "beautiful" in the usual sense. Moreover, sublime objects often lack the formal ordering and unity generally associated with beauty. And yet there is value in the experience of sublimity. So, as we saw earlier, beauty cannot be taken as the sole category of aesthetic value. But furthermore, feelings of revulsion and pain were commonly considered the hallmarks of ugliness. If the sublime, which also arouses these feelings, is established as a value-category, why not ugliness itself? So it is noteworthy that Burke begins to make room among the aesthetic categories for ugliness.[12] This line of thinking is stimulated enormously by the addiction of many nineteenth- and twentieth-century artists to grotesque and abhorrent subjects, whether in literature or painting, and the use of such musical devices as chromaticism and dissonance on a large scale. Such works cannot simply be rejected out of hand. Since they are found to be aesthetically good, at least by some spectators, they must be accommodated within aesthetic theory. As one contemporary philosopher puts it: "Beauty for the aesthetician already includes the sublime, the terrible, the satirical, the comic. Why not the ugly as well?" [13]

BUT NOW, what becomes of ugliness in the traditional sense? Are there no

[11] *Ibid.*, p. 52.
[12] Cf. Monk, *op. cit.*, p. 208.
[13] W. T. Stace, *The Meaning of Beauty* (London: Richards and Toulmin, 1929), p. 82.

objects which are aesthetically *bad?* Is there no opposite to "aesthetic value"?

In the thought of many contemporary aestheticians, we find two kinds of answers returned to these questions. Both sorts of answers overhaul drastically the traditional antithesis of beauty and ugliness. The first narrows down the area of ugliness by attempting to show that what has often been taken to be ugliness is not that at all. The second, more extreme view denies the existence of ugliness altogether. We will consider each of these in turn.

THE WHOLE HISTORY OF TASTE, and not least in the present century, shows how works which are at first rejected because of their novelty, later come to be appreciated. Wagner's *Tannhäuser*, which created a scandal at its premiere, is now an accepted part of the repertory. So it has been said that the great artist must "create his own audience." In view of the apparently limitless expansion of taste, can we say that anything is inherently ugly?

Bosanquet, in his *Three Lectures*, argues that much of what is generally called "ugly" is really due to "the weakness of the spectator." [14] Things seem ugly to us only because we lack the capacities to appreciate their aesthetic value. Bosanquet says that objects of this kind possess "difficult beauty." "Difficulty" may be due to three different properties of objects: (1) "intricacy," i.e., complexity. The object "simply gives you too much, at one moment, of what you are perfectly prepared to enjoy if only you could take it all in"; [15] (2) "a high tension of feeling," [16] which many spectators cannot sustain; (3) "width," when the object defies the beliefs of conventional existence, e.g., satiric comedy.

Bosanquet is a foremost spokesman of the emotionalist theory which we studied earlier.[17] On this view, aesthetic experience consists essentially in feeling the emotion which is expressed by the object. As we have seen, the emotionalists sanction any artistic subject matter or technique so long as it is expressive. The grotesque or painful or heartrending can be intensely and poignantly expressive. Bosanquet defines "beauty" in the broad sense, i.e., "aesthetic excellence," in terms of expressiveness. Hence so far as the ugly is expressive, it is a kind of aesthetic value.[18]

Notice what Bosanquet has done thus far in his theory of the ugly. First, he has narrowed the denotation of "ugliness" enormously by transferring many of the things usually considered ugly to the category of "difficult beauty." Secondly, by virtue of his expressionist theory, he has estab-

---

[14] *Op. cit.*, p. 95.
[15] *Ibid.*, p. 89.
[16] *Ibid.*, p. 89.
[17] Cf. above, chap. 7.
[18] *Op. cit.*, pp. 97–99.

lished ugliness as a category of value. What becomes of ugliness in the traditional sense of "aesthetic disvalue"?

Bosanquet comes very close finally to the extreme view that ugliness in this sense just does not exist. For if something were wholly nonbeautiful (= nonexpressive), it would not be an *aesthetic* category at all. "Aesthetic" has been defined by reference to "expression." If x is nonexpressive then x falls outside the realm of aesthetics altogether. "[If] the ugly is the unaesthetic, well then it is not aesthetic at all, and we are not concerned with it." [19]

But though Bosanquet is "much inclined" to believe that "there is no such thing as invincible ugliness," [20] he qualifies this position somewhat. He holds that some things *are* "invincibly ugly." They are the expressive objects which "[arouse] the mind in a certain direction, and then [obstruct] it in that same direction." [21] The object, so to speak, "starts out" by being expressive and it seems to point toward other feelings which are yet to be had. Yet it frustrates our expectations. There is "the suggestion of expressiveness and its counteraction by a completion conflicting with it." [22] The object does not fulfill the emotional drives which it has set up. Thus if "insuperable ugliness" exists at all, it is in "insincere and affected art." [23]

So even that little of "invincible ugliness" which Bosanquet retains in his theory is not utter aesthetic disvalue. Even "invincibly ugly" objects are, as it were, "incipiently" aesthetic, for they are expressive to some extent. Do you see what a profound transformation the category of ugliness has undergone? In one sense, it is a species of aesthetic value; in another sense, it is simply irrelevant to aesthetics; and in that sense which most closely resembles the traditional meaning of "aesthetic disvalue," it is potentially and in some degree, valuable. In overhauling the beliefs of common sense (at least the common sense of tradition), Bosanquet must run counter to its linguistic usage. He shows first that the term "ugly" has no single, univocal meaning, as uncritical speech assumes, and then that its customary meaning must be modified. We must not reject his theory because he uses words "oddly," i.e., differently. We must understand his theory to see *why* he uses words as he does.

However Bosanquet is by no means the only contemporary aesthetician to reject traditional usage and belief. Other thinkers take the last step and deny ugliness altogether. Professor Stephen C. Pepper defines "aesthetic" in terms of the "intuition of quality." [24] The crucial word "quality" is not

[19] *Ibid.*, p. 103.
[20] *Ibid.*, p. 99.
[21] *Ibid.*, p. 104.
[22] *Ibid.*, p. 105.
[23] *Ibid.*, p. 106.
[24] *The Basis of Criticism in the Arts*, p. 56.

itself readily definable. But we can say that each of our experiences has some unique "quality." An experience is poignant or tense or "thin" or profound. We are immediately aware of, i.e., we "intuit" these characteristics of our experience. Here again, as in Bosanquet, the definition of "aesthetic" is extremely broad. Since "quality" occurs in all experience, "[aesthetic] value runs out into all life . . . . [There] is no negative aesthetic value." [25] Like Bosanquet again, Pepper relegates ugliness to the nonaesthetic, except that he does this with *all* ugliness. For when ugliness occurs at all, it is when the quality of experience is "drab or painful." "Ugliness is moral disapproval of the absence of aesthetic value in a situation. It is an ethical rather than an aesthetic evaluation." [26]

Still another conception of the aesthetic leads to comparable conclusions. In this book, I have construed "aesthetic" as a kind of attitude, that of "disinterested and sympathetic contemplation." This view is shared by a great deal of modern aesthetic thought. Now any attitude, I said earlier, involves either a positive or a negative orientation toward its object. [27] The aesthetic attitude is always favorably oriented in the sense that it directs attention upon the object and "accepts" it. Since, furthermore, there is no concern for utility or any other ulterior significance, attention is sustained solely because the object is found to be good in itself. Hence the very meaning of "aesthetic" involves positive value. Since the whole area of aesthetic experience is defined in terms of "the aesthetic attitude," all of aesthetic experience is [positive] value-experience. One of Bosanquet's conclusions can now be stated in these terms: If something is not the object of aesthetic attention, then it is just not aesthetic at all. If there were any thing which absolutely and "invincibly" resisted aesthetic perception, it would fall outside the area of aesthetic inquiry. "Ugliness," in that sense, would not be an aesthetic category.

This is a matter of the logical relationship between our concepts. What of the empirical facts? *Are* there any objects which are "insuperably ugly"? I urged earlier that "any object of awareness whatever" can be an aesthetic object, pointing to the history of art and taste in support of my view. [28] As Santayana puts it, "Everything is beautiful because everything is capable in some degree of interesting and charming our attention." [29] This probably sounds odd. Perhaps it sounds false or at least paradoxical. At this point in our discussion, the reader should have become accustomed to the oddness of many contemporary theories of ugliness. But consider the evidence which seems to bear against this view. Consider the objects and

[25] *Ibid.*, p. 58.
[26] *Loc. cit.*
[27] Cf. above, p. 33.
[28] Cf. above, pp. 39 ff.
[29] *The Sense of Beauty,* p. 98.

situations which are, presumably, "invincibly" antiaesthetic. Might it not be that our biasses and "blind spots" have kept us from taking the aesthetic attitude toward them? Perhaps these objects have associations with what we generally consider ignoble or unmentionable. Perhaps these objects arouse moral or religious hostility, like the animus of the Mohammedan against paintings of the Holy Family. Perhaps they are too much associated with practical, everyday life to be considered for their own sake. Perhaps they are simply unfamiliar to us, like Balinese music or the works of Wagner and Stravinsky at their first performance. Perhaps we are affected by snobbism or like prejudice, as in the attitudes of many people of "culture" toward American jazz.

If we could rid ourselves of such obstacles to "disinterested and sympathetic" awareness (which, since we are all too human, is not likely), we could see all objects for what they are aesthetically. And if aesthetically, then valuably. There is too much evidence of the cultivation and broadening of taste by new artistic movements and through aesthetic familiarization, too much evidence of the diversity of what is appreciated by people of different societies and by different people in our own, to dismiss this possibility lightly. Such evidence lends credibility to the view that "no object is essentially ugly." [30]

Yet I do not wish to claim that the case has been made out conclusively. It may be that I have been guilty of question-begging, if my argument comes to nothing more than that *if* everything could be apprehended "disinterestedly and sympathetically," then nothing would be "invincibly ugly." And, after all is said, there is something uncommonly strange about an aesthetic theory which leaves no room for disvalue. In other areas of value-experience, there is always a polarity of value-disvalue. Thus, morality involves right *and* wrong, not simply what is right, all else being irrelevant to morals.

You may decide, upon reflection, that you cannot accept the theories of ugliness just discussed. But you cannot come to this conclusion unless you first understand how these theories are led to *their* conclusions and why they are willing to diverge from traditional belief and linguistic usage.

BUT NOW WE MUST CONSIDER in greater detail a question which arises out of our discussion. Ugliness in one sense was said to be wholly nonaesthetic. In another sense, it was said to be a category of aesthetic value coordinate with beauty (in the narrow sense), prettiness, sublimity, etc. Let us define "ugliness" in the latter sense as "that, the aesthetic contemplation of which arouses displeasure or pain." The question now is, "How is it that we preserve the aesthetic attitude toward and find value in an object when our experience of it is painful?"

[30] *Ibid.*, p. 96.

2. THE "PARADOX" OF TRAGEDY

Throughout the history of aesthetics and criticism, this question has been posed most acutely by tragedy. The world's great tragedies, notably those of the Greeks, Aeschylus, Sophocles, and Euripides, and of Shakespeare, are universally considered to be among the very few supreme works of art. *Oedipus Rex*, the *Oresteia* trilogy, *Lear, Hamlet, Macbeth* — these are towering creations whose magnificence and power are hardly surpassed by anything else in literature or, indeed, in any of the other arts. "Tragic" need not be used as a term of value-appraisal; it can be used solely to describe a certain literary form. And yet connotations of profundity and dignity have become attached to the term. Thus it suggests value, as the purely neutral names of artistic "kinds" such as "symphony" and "landscape" do not, and a far higher degree of value than such semievaluative terms as "comic" or "melodramatic."

But on the face of it, tragedies should be to us almost the least valuable of works of art. For tragedy "is, in fact, essentially a tale of suffering and calamity conducting to death." [31] Even though Oedipus does not suffer death itself, he is shown to have committed the unspeakable acts of murdering his father and marrying his mother, he tears out his eyeballs in frenzied self-disgust, and he suffers anguish compared to which death itself might seem a blessing. Another king, Lear, is cruelly wronged by his daughters, he is reduced to ignominious despair and need, and he dies looking at the corpse of his only devoted child. Tragedy is shot through with grief, frustration and the blackest despair. "Tragedy is a spectacle of evil. Evil is precisely that which we do not enjoy. Yet we do enjoy tragedy." [32] This is the "paradox" of tragedy.

The problem is not peculiar to that kind of drama which we call "tragedy." "Tales of suffering and calamity" are obviously to be found in fiction as well, and there are many paintings whose subjects are horrid or repellent, e.g., Rouault's studies of prostitutes. The word "tragic" is even used in describing music, e.g., Brahms' "Tragic Overture." If works of this kind made up only a small "lunatic fringe" of art, the "paradox" would be a problem for psychopathology, to be explained away perhaps by saying that some people take masochistic delight in suffering. But tragedy is too pervasive in art to be dismissed casually. And the paradox of those works of dramatic literature which are, in the strict sense, "tragedies," will not down.

BUT NOW WHAT *is* the paradox exactly? Paradoxes have a way of collapsing when they are given a second look. Perhaps this one will too. We have

---

[31] Bradley, *Shakespearean Tragedy*, p. 7.
[32] Henry A. Myers, *Tragedy: A View of Life* (Cornell University Press, 1956), p. 6.

said that the depiction of frustration and despair is painful. Is this because frustration and despair arouse sympathetic pain in us when we encounter them in "real life"? Probably they do. But why should we infer that the same is true when evil is depicted in *art*? It is a vulgar error — that of "simple imitation" in its least plausible form [33] — to think that we respond to works of art precisely as we respond to their "models." If a friend or a member of my family suffered as the tragic figure suffers, then doubtless I would be pained. Let us, however, remind ourselves of the obvious truth that Oedipus and Lear are fictional characters. We approach them as imaginary beings and all that they do and undergo is, in a sense, "make-believe." Hence, in reading about them, we do not feel pain and despair.

This argument clearly has some force and it helps to set the paradox in truer perspective. If there is a paradox of tragedy at all, it has to do with art and not with "life." If someone we know meets with disappointment and defeat, and therefore experiences great unhappiness, our grief is probably far more intense than that which the aesthetic spectator feels. Think of our affliction when a member of our family dies. Is Lear's death nearly so moving? Moreover, if a friend or relative seemed to be heading toward disaster, we would doubtless take action in his behalf. The contemplation of art, however, rules out practical action. There was the hyperemotional young lady in the audience during the performance of *Othello*, watching as the villain Iago dupes the hero with his treacherous lies and leads on the Moor to his doom. In the middle of the performance, she suddenly rose from her seat and shouted toward the actors on the stage, "Can't you see that he's lying, you big black fool!" Perhaps this testifies to her good heart, but it is clear that she has forgotten that all of the events are "make-believe," and that she has, rather absurdly, permitted the practical attitude to usurp the aesthetic.

Thus the argument against the paradox insists that aesthetic response is not identical with "real life" response. Beyond this, however, if it proves anything, then it proves too much. For it stresses the "make-believe" of tragedy in order to prove that we do not feel any pain at all while watching tragedy. Here it comes into conflict with the facts of our experience. It is not likely that the paradox of tragedy would have engaged the minds of philosophers and critics throughout the centuries since Aristotle unless the audiences of tragedy felt and reported their sympathetic pain. If this were not a fact, the paradox would never arise. If this were not a fact, then the response to tragedy would be one of unmixed pleasure. In this respect, the response to tragedy would be like what we feel in watching an ordinary drama which ignores the tragic side of human existence and depicts small-scale events from which crushing frustration and anguish are absent. The language we use to describe the tragic experience — "almost

[33] Cf. above, chap. 5, sec. 1.

unbearably moving," "harrowing" (as Gilbert Murray says of *The Trojan Women*),[34] "unspeakable horror" (as another commentator says of *Oedipus Rex*) [35] — this is not the language we use to describe our response to other forms of drama. There are even some people who cannot bring themselves to see the tragedy through to its conclusion, because their feelings are too much edged with pain. There is something significantly different about tragedy, as there is about the sublime, which sets it off from the simply pleasurable, garden variety aesthetic object.

The argument against the paradox insists upon the difference between the suffering of "real life" and that depicted in art. The detachment and unreality of art save us from utter grief. We have seen that there is some force in this contention. And yet, the difference between art and "life" can be turned in the other direction. Precisely because art is *not* "life," it intensifies and accentuates sympathetic pain. Tragedy "dramatizes" the plight of the hero; the closely knit events which lead to his doom create in the spectator increasingly acute feelings of ominous fear; the hero's calamity is made vivid and overwhelming by literary eloquence, as when Lear repeats the memorable "never" five times in his last speech. Tragedy is compelling and insistent as "life" rarely is. Aristotle, you will remember, pointed out that tragedy foregoes the mere, indiscriminate chronicling of events.[36] The literary artist strips away the "accidents" and irrelevancies of ordinary existence and focuses solely upon the unfolding of tragic destiny. Thus he shows the tragedy of existence to which we are largely oblivious when it occurs in "life." This probably explains the Russian noblewoman, described by William James, who was moved to tears by a play but remained quite indifferent to the sufferings of her servants.

The implicit unreality of art keeps us, generally, from consuming grief and practical action. But the vividness and compactness of art accentuate the painfulness of tragedy. "It is a play, but it is not *only* a play." [37]

THERE IS ANOTHER SORT OF ARGUMENT which might be used to destroy the paradox. It too denies the fact upon which the paradox rests, viz., that the response to tragedy is painful. This, the argument holds, is shown to be false by the very fact that we continue to watch or read tragedy. "Pleasure [is] the affective accompaniment of the tendency to keep or con-

---

[34] *The Trojan Women*, in *Five Plays of Euripides*, trans. Gilbert Murray (New York: Oxford University Press, 1934), p. 6. All quotations later in the chapter are from this translation.

[35] *Sophocles: The Seven Plays*, trans. Lewis Campbell (London: Oxford University Press, 1930), p. xv. All quotations later in the chapter are from this translation.

[36] Cf. above, pp. 117 ff.

[37] L. A. Reid, *A Study in Aesthetics* (New York: Macmillan, 1954), p. 343. Italics in original.

tinue." [38] The prolongation of aesthetic interest in the tragedy therefore shows that the experience is pleasurable rather than painful. Only if we stopped looking could the experience be said to be painful.

What is at issue here is the meaning of "pleasure." Like other terms which refer to the immediacies of felt experience, "pleasure" is not easily defined. It is sometimes said that such words cannot be defined at all, strictly, and that we can only point to examples of what they denote. To say that pleasure always accompanies "the tendency to keep" does not tell us what pleasure "feels like." Rather, it describes the circumstances in which pleasure arises. But should "pleasure" be construed in this way? A great deal of aesthetic, as well as moral and other kinds of experience, shows that we often "keep or continue" in an activity *despite* painfulness. Tragic experience is a striking instance of this. To say that the experience must be pleasurable because it is prolonged, is merely to apply a definition which obscures the salient facts. The argument is a verbal one only.

The argument reflects the viewpoint of *hedonism,* the theory that pleasure and pleasure alone is intrinsically good. "To a hedonist [tragedy] is a mystery. Why in the temple of pleasure do we set up a god of sorrow?" [39] If we reject hedonism, we can say without inconsistency that the tragic experience is both painful and valuable. The paradox of tragedy now becomes essentially a question of fact: what forces within the tragic experience induce us to keep up our interest in the play, interest which is so keen and absorbing that we consider the experience supremely valuable?

MANY ANSWERS have been given in the vast literature of theory of tragedy, and only some of them can be considered here. From these, however, we can gain insight into the tragic experience.

The paradox arises because of the suffering of the characters in a tragedy. This puts the emphasis on the *plot.* In explaining the paradox a few pages back, I cited the kinds of events which occur typically in tragedy. But certainly the literary work, like any work of art, is more than just its subject matter. It also possesses great sensory refinement and formal order. Santayana may exaggerate in saying that "The treatment and not the subject is what makes a tragedy," [40] but the exaggeration can be illuminating.

What else, besides plot, is found in a tragedy? Most obviously, perhaps, there is great poetry. Excerpts from the tragedies have been admired for their sensory charm and imaginative vividness. The best-known examples are probably the soliloquies of Hamlet. So, it has been argued, we retain our interest in tragedy because of its poetic quality, which is not at all painful to us. We enjoy it as we enjoy all great poetry. Professor Parker,

[38] Lee, *Perception and Aesthetic Value,* pp. 78–79.
[39] Pepper, *The Basis of Criticism in the Arts,* p. 67.
[40] *The Sense of Beauty,* p. 169.

speaking not only of tragedy but of all works whose subject is evil, holds that "Engaging lines, winsome colors and tones, and compelling rhythms can overcome almost any repugnance that we might otherwise feel for the subject-matter." [41]

The difficulty in this theory, which tries to show that the tragic experience is pleasurable, is exactly similar to that of the theory which emphasizes plot, in trying to show that the tragic experience is painful. Both views consider only one aspect of the total work of art, taken in isolation. The "poetry" of tragedy is employed in unfolding "a tale of suffering and calamity." The poetry must be understood in its interaction with the development of character and plot. It makes vivid and eloquent the dilemma of the tragic figure, his sufferings, and the inevitability of catastrophe. When we identify ourselves sympathetically with the tragic figure and become absorbed in his destiny, we feel sympathetic pain not *despite* the poetry, but because of it. A prosaic or a poetically inept recital of his woes would not move us. Consider such a passage as:

> Ah, me! and is it come, the end of all,
> The very crest and summit of my days?
> I go forth from my land, and all its ways
> Are filled with fire.[42]

This is distinguished poetry, but it is spoken by the aged queen Hecuba, in *The Trojan Women,* as she laments the destruction of her homeland, and prepares to kill herself:

> O, in thine agony,
> My Troy, mine own, take me to die with thee!

Or, similarly, the passage which begins:

> Blow, winds, and crack your cheeks! rage! blow!
> You cataracts and hurricanoes, spout
> Till you have drench'd our steeples, drown'd the cocks!

This is Lear, at the beginning of his agony in the storm-scene upon the heath (III, ii).

These speeches are the outpourings of personal grief. Perhaps, therefore, it is not fair to use them against the current argument, which may be valid for the rest of tragic poetry. Consider, then, Othello's speeches while he is still successful and in love, before disaster descends upon him. Othello

---

[41] De Witt H. Parker, *The Principles of Aesthetics,* 2nd ed. (New York: Crofts, 1947), p. 85. Cf., however, pp. 85–86.
[42] *The Trojan Women, loc. cit.,* p. 74.

is perhaps the most "poetic" of tragic heroes.[43] All of his utterances are marked by their sensory charm and imagery. But his metaphors and images are not poetic gilding. They hit off the character of the man — romantic, charming, imaginative, somewhat addicted to self-dramatization. And his character must be set within the total context of the play. Othello is the kind of man who can be played upon and duped by the villainous Iago.[44] His character is thus integral to the unfolding of the plot, as in all tragedy. Further, his personal charm and attractiveness only accentuate the pathos of his downfall. Our sense of loss is so much the greater because of the kind of man who is lost. Othello probably lacks the depth and complexity of other tragic heroes, but he is as personable and winning as any. So Othello's poetry, for all its unquestioned loveliness, is edged with the pain and horror of the tragedy of which it is a part.

We can, assuredly, enjoy the poetry which occurs in tragedy in divorce from character and plot, just as we can view a representational painting in the manner of Bell and Fry, as a pattern of lines and masses. Works of art are complex enough so that we can pick and choose if we like. But then we must be clear that a great deal has been left out of our experience. Professor Parker, who argues that painfulness of subject can be overcome by the sensory material, grants that the material "[diverts] the attention to itself." [45] If this be so, then the total work — the tragedy — is not the object of attention. It would then follow that the argument which we have been discussing is not a theory "of tragedy" at all. It has, rather, to do with dramatic poetry in general. If the poetry of tragedy is not taken in isolation, then it is suffused by the painful emotions of the tragedy. We cannot then accept the theory which holds that "the spectator can bear up nobly under the sorrows of others if they are accompanied by soft music and fitting words." [46]

THE PARADOX OF TRAGEDY, like almost everything else in the theory of tragedy, goes back to Aristotle's *Poetics*. At the beginning of the *Poetics*, he asks, concerning art in general, why we take delight in the imitation of objects "which in themselves we view with pain." He answers in terms of our delight in "learning." [47] In speaking of tragedy itself, Aristotle implies the paradox by saying both that tragedy characteristically arouses emotions of pity and fear [48] (sometimes translated "terror") and that the tragic experience is one of pleasure, though "only that" kind of pleasure "which is proper to" tragedy.[49]

---

[43] Cf. Bradley, *Shakespearean Tragedy*, p. 188.
[44] But on "the Othello question" cf. Bradley, *op. cit.*, Lects. V–VI; F. R. Leavis, *The Common Pursuit* (New York: George Stewart, 1952), pp. 136–159.
[45] *Loc. cit.*
[46] Myers, *op. cit.*, p. 8.   [47] Cf. above, pp. 113–114.
[48] *Poetics* VI, p. 9.   [49] *Ibid.*, XIV, p. 18.

Yet Aristotle offers no clear solution to the paradox. Historically it has been thought that his answer is found in the concept of *catharsis*. Aristotle says that pity and fear are aroused and yet "purged," [50] i.e., eliminated from or driven out of the spectator. However, as the vast literature devoted to interpreting this notion shows, Aristotle does not make it at all clear what *catharsis* means or how it functions. He speaks of it only briefly and he fails to explain what the causes of *catharsis* are or why *catharsis* is pleasurable. Perhaps Aristotle meant that we feel relief after great emotional agitation, or that it is morally wholesome to eliminate these emotions, but this again is only conjectural.

A more fruitful clue is that of "learning," though here too we must develop and go beyond Aristotle's brief suggestion. "Learning" can be taken to involve two different things: (1) recognizing, through the imitation, the "model" which it depicts, so that we say, as Aristotle puts it, " 'Ah, that is he' "; [51] (2) gaining wisdom. Both help to explain our interest in tragedy.

Without diverting interest from the work to "life," we recognize that tragedy depicts the people and concerns of shared human experience. It does not simply "imitate" nonartistic experience. It strips away the irrelevancies and superfluities which obscure the causal interrelation of events in "life." [52] We feel that this is what life is like when seen with rational clarity. Tragedy's "reality" absorbs our interest as "escapist" fiction and fantasy cannot. Burke, whose theory of sublimity was quoted in the previous section, says of tragedy:

> I imagine we shall be much mistaken if we attribute any considerable part of our satisfaction in tragedy to a consideration that tragedy is a deceit. . . . The nearer it approaches the reality, and the further it removes us from all idea of fiction, the more perfect is its power.[53]

Of crucial importance, too, is the *kind* of reality which we "recognize" in tragedy. Tragedy treats of the most deep-seated concerns and involvements which we have as human beings. It treats of what in "life" is most intimate and important to us. How many of the great tragedies, both Greek and Shakespearean, center upon family relationships — *Oedipus*, the *Oresteia, Antigone, Medea, Hamlet, Lear*. Tragedy thus acquires both universality of meaning and emotional force. What Matthew Arnold called "high seriousness" is also present in tragedy because of its preoccupation with moral and religious issues. Tragic conflict occurs because of the protagonist's attempt to fulfill his highest ideals. What is at stake is not

[50] *Ibid.*, VI, p. 9.
[51] Cf. above, p. 114.
[52] Cf. above, chap. 5, sec. 2.
[53] Quoted in Earl R. Wasserman, "The Pleasures of Tragedy," *ELH, A Journal of English Literary History*, XIV (1947), 303.

anything trivial. What is at stake are the values which give purpose and dignity to life.

The tragic hero, moreover, is "lifelike." Aristotle, as we have seen,[54] says that he is "a man like ourselves." Tragedy is not melodrama. Its personages are not virtue incarnate or deep-dyed villains. The tragic hero is "a man who is not eminently good and just, yet whose misfortune is not brought about by vice or depravity." [55] Good and evil interact subtly in his character, making him a rich and complex figure. His credibility to us increases our kinship with him.

Since our sympathetic absorption in tragedy is focused upon the hero, let us consider his character somewhat further. The morally evil man alienates us. The morally good man, such as the tragic hero, enlists our sympathy and evokes our pity when he suffers. A good man is one who performs actions which he believes to be right. When Orestes kills his mother or when Othello kills Desdemona, each thinks that the action is justifiable. Of all tragic figures, Macbeth might seem to be the clearest instance of a villain — one who deliberately chooses to perform wicked acts. But though he attempts to will evil to be his good, it is painfully clear that he cannot transform himself into a ruthless and unscrupulous being: "To know my deed, 'twere best not know myself" (II, i). He is assailed by the most acute feelings of remorse both before and after the slaying of Duncan. His deeds rise up as vivid, perceptual images to plague him. And his sense of guilt keeps him from enjoying the fruits of his wrongdoing. Life loses its savor and value: "All is but toys: renown and grace is dead" (II, i). Moreover, a great number of dramatic devices preserve our sympathy for Macbeth.[56]

The "reality" of tragedy, its "high seriousness," the spectator's sympathetic identification with the hero — all of which are pointed out in the *Poetics* — sustain our interest in the unfolding tragedy. We "cannot choose but hear" although the experience be painful. Precisely because of the evil and suffering which are endemic to tragedy, and our sympathy for the protagonist, the experience must be painful to some extent. Intense aesthetic interest persists in spite of this.

We come now to "learning" in the second sense — that of gaining "wisdom." Professor Ducasse says that tragedy gives us "wisdom which is our most useful equipment in dealing with, or warding off, tragic events. This gain in wisdom is felt in a quite direct and immediate way, and is pleasant. This pleasure is I believe the essential constituent of the tragic pleasure." [57]

It is not easy to describe precisely the content of such wisdom. Only

[54] Cf. above, p. 119.

[55] *Op. cit.*, XIII, p. 16.

[56] Cf. Wayne C. Booth, "Macbeth as Tragic Hero," *Journal of General Education,* VI (1951), 17–25.

[57] *Philosophy of Art,* p 253.

rarely is it asserted straightforwardly, as when the Greek chorus comments upon the significance of the play's events or when Edgar, in *Lear,* says that

> Men must endure
> Their going hence, even as their coming hither:
> Ripeness is all (V, ii).

The wisdom which we most cherish in tragedy is not usually set out as in a treatise on ethics or human values. It is implicit within the concrete doings and sayings of the characters. As Ducasse says, the "gain in wisdom is felt in a quite direct and immediate way." And tragic wisdom has emotional and imaginative power such as a purely discursive statement lacks. Hence any prose paraphrase can only be approximate at best. Moreover, it would be difficult to find any single view of human destiny common to all tragedies. The Greek playwrights differ among themselves and they in turn from Shakespeare concerning, e.g., the relative significance of human character and impersonal "fate" in bringing about tragic ruin. We should be careful not to blur these differences in speaking of "tragedy" in general. Finally, as we might expect where rich and profound works of art are concerned, many different interpretations of the "meaning" of a tragedy are possible.

With these necessary cautions in mind, we can turn to look for the "wisdom" traditionally attributed to tragedy. Tragedy, we have noted, deals with man's most deep-seated and important commitments. It depicts the fate of those who try to attain their most cherished values. Wisdom is, therefore, necessarily implicated in tragedy. For "wisdom" has generally been taken to be a peculiar kind of knowledge — knowledge of the values of life. To be wise is to be able to discriminate what is genuinely and lastingly good from what is only speciously good. It is to look at the world with detachment and perspective, and not to be carried away by intemperate enthusiasms. It involves the just discernment of one's own capacities and limitations. Wisdom is not simply factual knowledge. It is the most important kind of knowledge that human beings can possess. We gain it from tragedy by seeing the dramatic depiction of the consequences of unwisdom.

A common characteristic of the hero in Greek tragedy is his *hybris* — presumptuous, overbearing "self-will" and pride. It cannot be said that this, in itself, is the cause of his downfall. Tragedy is far more complicated than that. Yet *hybris* enters into the character of many heroes who are, let us remember, essentially *good* men, morally, and it therefore affects and distorts their behavior. Even though the hero acts in defense of his values, his action is corrupted by "self-will." This is true of Prometheus in

Prometheus Bound and of the hero of *Ajax*, who is driven to madness by the gods because he possesses courage without wisdom.

The best-known Greek tragic figure, Oedipus, can hardly be said to be "responsible" for his sufferings, because he is foredoomed by prophecy to kill his father and marry his mother. Moreover, he initiates the chain of events which terminate in the disclosure of his sins, in an effort to fulfill his duty as king. For he must find the murderer of his father in order to lift the plague from Thebes. And yet his own arrogance is instrumental in hastening the fatal revelation. He goads the blind prophet Tiresias into revealing the truth, and yet he obdurately refuses to accept it. Oedipus says to Tiresias,

> You being gone, our trouble goes with you.

He suspects all about him, save only himself. That Oedipus the king is himself the sinner shows how unfounded is complacent self-assurance, and how limited and precarious is man's wisdom. There is no facile copybook "moral" here. But the play confronts us with a grave caution, and with the challenge to persistent re-examination of ourselves and our "tragic limitations."

Comparable truths emerge from the fate of Creon, Oedipus' successor as king, in the *Antigone*. Creon, too, wishes only to defend his kingdom when he orders that the traitor who has fallen in battle should go unburied as an object lesson. This brings him into conflict with Antigone, who has both a divine and a family obligation to bury her brother. Creon argues plausibly on behalf of his edict. Yet he, like Oedipus, is warned against obsessive self-assurance:

> Nurse not one changeless humour in thy breast,
> That nothing can be right but as thou sayest.

Creon's action — the action of a tragic hero — leads ultimately to the death of his wife and son. At the close of the play he bewails the "bitter consequence of seeming-wise decree" and he decries his "folly." Again, this is not to say that Creon's action was "wrong." That is a debatable question. Yet we see that the actions of a "good man" can be corrupted by "self-will," and that actions in the name of one's ideals can be catastrophic in their consequences. The content of "learning" here is moral humility.

Shakespeare's Lear also believes that he acts rightly in disowning his daughter Cordelia and dividing the kingdom between her sisters, Regan and Goneril. For he has invited the three of them to speak of their love for him and, whereas Regan and Goneril protest their love fulsomely,

Cordelia says only, "Nothing, my lord" (I, i). Lear's action is not plainly and clearly villainous. Let us again remind ourselves that tragedy does not deal with deep-dyed villainy. *King Lear* treats of the more complicated and far more important moral experience in which an essentially good man is undone by his lack of wisdom. Lear sets the privileges of kingship — flattery and pomp — over the enduring value of love. The trumped-up rhetorical contest and his decision show this. When Cordelia cannot bring herself to cater to his royal vanity, he acts with "hideous rashness" (I, i). He is unwise in cherishing specious values more than true ones, and in acting without forethought and discrimination. He betrays himself as much as he does Cordelia, for he says of her that

> I lov'd her most, and thought to set my rest
> On her kind nursery (I, i).

From Lear's action there follows his long and almost unbearable agony, and the death of the innocent Cordelia.

We are speaking of the wisdom which we gain, as spectators, in seeing the consequences of the hero's unwisdom. We must also speak of the wisdom which is gained by the hero himself, in which we share. The tragic figure is not, like so many of us, a man who passes through crisis relatively unchanged and, as we say, "no wiser for it." If he were, there would be little to redeem the suffering which he undergoes and which causes us sympathetic pain. The bleakness of tragedy would then be almost unendurable. And the tragic hero would lack the greatness and nobility which we sense in our response to him. Rather, as has many times been said, he "learns through suffering." He learns, to a greater or less degree, what it is most profoundly important for him and all human beings to know — the nature and importance of wisdom.

Let us return to *Lear* to illustrate this. When Regan and Goneril, having gained the kingdom, begin to show their true colors, and treat Lear with contempt, his reaction is a combination of impotent rage and self-pity:

> I will have such revenges on you both
> That all the world shall, — I will do such things, —
> What they are yet I know not . . .
> I have full cause of weeping; but this heart
> Shall break into a hundred thousand flaws
> Or ere I'll weep (II, iv).

But as he passes through the awful crucible of his suffering, he develops deep compassion and wisdom. His heart goes out to

> Poor naked wretches, wheresoe'er you are

and he berates himself:

> O, I have ta'en
> Too little care of this! Take physic, pomp (III, iv).

Now he cannot speak too bitterly of the hollow pretensions of kingship — "a dog's obeyed in office" (IV, vi) — and the fawning adulation on which he once set so much stock: ". . . they told me I was everything; 'tis a lie, — I am not agueproof" (IV, vi).

Most significantly of all, his blind self-importance is replaced by the detachment which enables him to recognize his earlier folly. He can now see how cruelly he has wronged Cordelia and so he says to her,

> If you have poison for me I will drink it (IV, vii).

And once again, in a speech of ineffable beauty, he begs her forgiveness (V, iii). His last thought as he dies is for her.

Even those tragic figures who are most nearly men of action, like Ajax and Othello, seek to reflect upon and "make sense of" their downfall. When we last see Oedipus, in the *Oedipus at Colonos*, he is a man of impressive dignity, full of the maturity and balance of wisdom.

The suffering of the tragic hero is immense, but so is his greatness. He is a figure drawn to a large scale — in his emotional responses, in his proud assertion of his values, in his capacity for "learning." He is, indeed, tragic rather than pathetic, as a man would be who was struck down by calamity or illness which was unrelated to his actions, and which did not transform his character. Our response to the tragic hero is not one of unalloyed pity. His nobility is in large part responsible for the proud exaltation which we feel at the same time that we share in his sorrows.

Finally, we must look to the formal structure of tragedy to help resolve the paradox. Again we follow the lead of the *Poetics*. Aristotle, you will remember, emphasizes the "causal necessity" which binds together the events of the plot into a tightly-knit sequence. The plot of tragedy is not "episodic," i.e., the events do not "succeed one another without probable or necessary sequence." [58] All the actions lead to the dénouement with inexorable force. This formal unity is responsible for an aesthetic experience of great suspense and coherence. The percipient is caught up irresistibly in the movement of the play and looks forward keenly to its climax. His absorption is so thorough and his anticipation is so vivid that he accommodates the pain which is ingredient in tragedy. "Struggle and conflict may be themselves enjoyed, although they are painful, when they are experienced as means of developing an experience." [59] Tragedy, for

---

[58] *Op. cit.*, IX, p. 14.   [59] Dewey, *Art as Experience*, p. 41.

all its pain, exercises rigorous control over the interest of the spectator like few other art-forms.

WE HAVE NOW CONSIDERED several of the most important answers to "the paradox of tragedy." Each has some force, for each rests upon the observable facts of tragic literature, particularly its subject matter, form, and expressive significance, and of the aesthetic response to tragedy. Since these theories are not logically incompatible with each other, they can be used together to explain the value of tragedy. It may or may not be the case that the felt pain of tragic response is exceeded in intensity by pleasure. Perhaps this varies from person to person. In any event, it is an important question only for a hedonistic theory of value. The important thing for the rest of us to see is that, and how, the tragic experience can be immensely valuable despite its painfulness. We should not try to ignore or explain away painfulness for it is inherent in the tragic aspect of human existence. *Oedipus* and *Lear* are "tales of suffering and calamity." They are not drawing-room comedies or melodramas. With all their painfulness, they are among the very greatest works of art which we possess.

They remain enduring challenges to the intellectual vision and emotional catholicity of each of us. The student cannot begin too soon to know these works. The process of developing familiarity with and appreciation of the tragedies is endless. Yet one grows aesthetically and emotionally in the process, which is, in this way, endlessly rewarding.

3. THE "COMIC MASK"

But why should *comedy*, of all things, be considered in a chapter on "ugliness in art"? Comedy thrives on "innocent merriment." Here, if anywhere, we cast off those sober concerns upon which tragedy thrives and abandon ourselves to playfulness. Everything is funny and therefore everything is pleasurable. Nothing could be more different from tragedy.

And yet, the paradoxical affinities between comedy and tragedy have been noted almost from the beginning of aesthetic thought. The first great philosopher, Socrates, drops a cryptic hint about their similarity.[60] In our own time the distinguished humorist James Thurber has commented that "The closest thing to humor is tragedy." [61] It is noteworthy how many characterizations of one of these literary forms can apply equally well to the other, e.g., "Eager human aspirations being continually impeded by . . . the limitations of human foresight: this is perhaps the essence of

---

[60] Cf. Plato, *Symposium* 223.
[61] Max Eastman, *The Enjoyment of Laughter* (New York: Simon and Schuster, 1936), p. 342.

the human comedy." [62]   On the strength of the previous section of this chapter, one might also be tempted to take this as the "essence" of tragedy.

It is Aristotle, in the *Poetics*, who sets comedy squarely into the problem of artistic ugliness: "Comedy is . . . an imitation of persons inferior — not, however, in the full sense of the word bad, the Ludicrous being merely a subdivision of the ugly. It consists in some defect or ugliness which is not painful or destructive. . . . [The] comic mask is ugly and distorted, but does not imply pain." [63]

If Aristotle ever wrote his treatise on comedy, it has not been preserved. It is not difficult, however, to find instances of comic ugliness as he describes it in the literature of his own and later times. Aristotle is speaking of a defect of character "which is not painful or destructive." It must be some kind of aberration or folly which, unlike tragic folly, has relatively innocuous consequences. We find this in the "stock" figures of comedy — the braggart, the liar, the buffoon, the coward. They suffer from "defects" of personality and they are morally odious. When they occur in "life," they cause us pain or at least embarrassment. Few people make us so uncomfortable as those whom we know to be confirmed liars, and we feel anger or indignation toward the coward. Why do we not have these feelings, why indeed do we *laugh*, when we meet these people in comedy? Comic ugliness can also be physical. Bodily deformity is found frequently in comic figures. Think of Falstaff's belly, Durante's nose, Ben Turpin's crossed eyes. How is it that we laugh at such grotesqueries, and even at such normally pitiable afflictions as stammering, in the case of the late comedian, Joe Frisco?

Moreover, the comic figure, like the tragic protagonist, often finds himself involved in situations of defeat and frustration. He sets in motion events which he cannot control and he is overwhelmed by them. His agonies are not those of the tragic hero, but he suffers bewilderment and distress. Often he endures bodily indignities, which range from the incessant knockabout of the traditional Punch and Judy shows, to Falstaff being dumped in the river, to Chaplin being caught up in the machines in the motion picture *Modern Times*. You can doubtless think of many other examples. Physical abuse distresses us when it occurs in "real life," particularly if we consider the victim blameless, as the comic figure usually is. Again our question presents itself: Why is it that "the comic mask does not imply pain?"

What we are after is a "theory of comedy." Let us first note that this is not the same as a "theory of laughter." For there is a great deal of laughter which is not aroused by comedy. People often laugh when they

---

[62] D. H. Monro, *Argument of Laughter* (Melbourne University Press, 1951), p. 131.
[63] *Op. cit.*, V, pp. 7–8.

are embarrassed, or when they are hysterical, or when they are being tickled, or as a result of "laughing gas." The causes of such laughter we can leave to the psychologist and the physiologist. Our job is to analyze comic literature as an aesthetic object, in order to answer our question.

"But," some readers may protest, "the question hardly needs answering. It is an artificial question which almost answers itself. Of course we don't get worked up about the comic coward or Chaplin's distress. That is because we never take them seriously. It's all 'in fun,' [64] so we can afford to laugh."

This would be an appropriate retort. It does not dispose of our question but, what is even better, it begins to answer it. For, as in the comparable case of tragedy, we must remind ourselves that the representational subject matter — personality defect or physical abuse — is not all of the work of art. There is all else which enters into and distinguishes the work of art, which thereby sets it off from "life." Hence the practical response is discouraged. The young lady referred to earlier, who responded practically to *Othello*, is perhaps sufficiently absurd. How much more absurd it would be to try to rescue the comic figure from his predicament.

So much on behalf of the view which I have attributed to the hypothetical reader. Yet we cannot stop here. *Why* is it that comedy encourages aesthetic detachment to such a pronounced degree? What is there about comic character and comic situation which keeps us from taking them seriously? What exactly is the "set" or attitude of the aesthetic spectator toward comedy? To these questions, which develop the original question, we must now address ourselves.

THE LITERATURE of theory of comedy is almost as vast as that of theory of tragedy, and again we can speak of only a few of the leading theories. Let us begin with the theory which has dominated reflection on comedy throughout the present century, that of the philosopher Bergson, in *Laughter (Le Rire)*.

Bergson accepts and expands upon our common sense conclusion of a moment ago, viz., comedy is not "taken seriously" by the spectator. We do not laugh at a person for whom we feel affection or pity. Hence in comedy, unlike tragedy, sympathetic emotion must be suppressed. "[The] comic demands something like a momentary anesthesia of the heart. Its appeal is to intelligence, pure and simple." [65] Bergson's view calls to mind the aphorism, "Life is a tragedy to those who feel, a comedy to those who think." His view is supported by the evidence, which probably all of us can cite, that we generally laugh *at* a person only when we feel detached

---

[64] Cf. Eastman, *op. cit.*, pp. 3, 15–17.

[65] Henri Bergson, *Laughter*, in *Comedy*, trans. Brereton and Rothwell (New York: Macmillan, 1911), p. 5. Reprinted by permission of Doubleday & Company, Inc.

or even aloof from him. Start to "feel sorry" for him and your laughter will stop.

Bergson analyzes further the attitude of the spectator toward the comic figure. It is the attitude of a judge. We decide that the behavior of the comic figure is wrong because it is antisocial, and we punish him for it by "humiliating" him with our laughter.[66] What is there about the comic figure's behavior which warrants such judgment? Now we come to the heart of Bergson's theory.

Life is made up of incessantly changing situations. We meet its demands successfully by adapting our thought and behavior to novel circumstances. We must be flexible and resourceful. We must not persist in fixed patterns of behavior when, as is always the case, our changing environment has rendered them outmoded. But this is precisely what the comic figure does. Instead of being adaptive and flexible, he is guilty of *"mechanical inelasticity."* [67] He behaves in a fixed, rigid, machine-like way. Comedy is to be found in "automatism established in life." [68] Society cannot tolerate automatism. It can survive only if men are sufficiently flexible to adjust to each other. Hence laughter is a social corrective, which condemns and seeks to reform the comic figure.[69]

Bergson develops this theory with extraordinary ingenuity. It is astonishing how many aspects of comedy can be brought under his hypothesis and clarified by it. First of all, *repetition*, which is one of the most common comic devices. That repeating a phrase or a line of dialogue can be funny follows almost immediately from Bergson's view. (The comedian Jack Benny is past master of the art of repetitive dialogue.) Repetition displays the automatism of the speaker, who clings to an idea though the circumstances have changed. Moreover, since the comic figure is an ineffectual person who cannot meet the demands of life, we should expect him to lapse into dreams or other ways of "adjusting things to [his] own way of thinking." [70] The classic example is Don Quixote, but there are many others, such as Chaplin in *The Gold Rush*.

Because he lacks the creative adaptiveness which marks the "living" human being, the comic figure is often more like a "thing" [71] than a person. We see him tossed about or buffeted or hurled through the air or rolled up like a ball. This too helps to explain the spectator's estrangement from him. How can we be concerned about a "thing"?

Finally, Bergson makes an extremely acute observation concerning the character of the comic figure as compared to that of the tragic hero. The

---

[66] *Ibid.*, p. 197.
[67] *Ibid.*, p. 10. Italics in original.
[68] *Ibid.*, p. 32.
[69] *Ibid.*, p. 134.
[70] *Ibid.*, p. 185.
[71] *Ibid.*, p. 58.

comic personality suffers from a "defect," as Aristotle said. But, Bergson points out, it is not a defect which corrupts his total character. Bergson cites a comic figure who is "thoroughly honest" but "unsociable." [72] The fault is "trifling" because it does not infect his basic honesty. Or we may cite the example of Charlie, in the early Chaplin comedies, who remains essentially good though he acts stupidly and blunderingly. In other words, the various elements of comic character do not affect and interact with each other. In tragedy, by contrast, we find the character defect "attracting and absorbing, transforming and assimilating the divers energies of the man." [73] Think of Oedipus' pride, Macbeth's ambition, Lear's vanity.

Here again Bergson helps to explain our detachment from the comic figure. Precisely because the tragic hero's character displays clearly the interplay of his motives and desires, he is a complex and "real" human being. The comic figure is much less complex and he is therefore less absorbing. This is most obvious when the comic figure is nothing but a "general type," [74] rather than a distinctive individual like Hamlet. Such comic "stock characters" are often, in Monro's phrase, "animated mannerisms" [75] solely. They are walking embodiments of only a *single* trait of personality. They are cowards and nothing else, or hypocrites and nothing else, and so on. Every speech and action is the manifestation of just this one characteristic. Since he lacks a rich and flexible character, the comic figure never becomes aware of his own shortcomings.[76] He is, to use one of Bergson's favorite words, "absentminded" to the last. Compare this utter lack of development of character and "learning" with the tragic hero, as we described him earlier.

I HAVE ATTEMPTED to set out the essentials of Bergson's theory. It would be impossible to take note of all the many insights in *Laughter*. I commend the book itself to the student's attention.

How adequate is Bergson's theory? It is, unquestionably, rich and fertile. However it must be supplemented and, at certain points, it must give way to other theories, if we are to take account of the whole range of comic literature.

To begin with, the nature of comic situation discourages the spectator's involvement. We spoke of the "reality" and "high seriousness" of tragic situation. Comic situations are notoriously improbable by "real life" standards, particularly as they shade off into farce and fantasy. They teem with extravagant coincidences. Molière's farce, *Les Fourberies de Scapin*, consists essentially of one implausible occurrence after another. We must take such

[72] *Ibid.*, p. 138.
[73] *Ibid.*, p. 142.
[74] *Ibid.*, pp. 149, 163.
[75] *Op. cit.*, p. 116.
[76] *Op. cit.*, p. 146.

comedy "in fun" because it is so far removed from the world in which we take things seriously. This can be seen most clearly in those comedies whose subject matter involves important human issues, like taking a life. In the play *Arsenic and Old Lace*, two benighted old ladies benevolently kill off a large number of men. In Thurber's classic cartoon, "Touché," a swordsman decapitates his opponent with one deft stroke. But again, the situation is so vastly improbable, and the whole "tone" or atmosphere of the work is so obviously light-hearted, that a moral response has no chance to assert itself.

Moreover, the closely knit unity of tragic plot is absent from a great deal of comedy. The structure of much comedy, even when its component events are not fantastic, is of the sort that Aristotle would call "episodic." [77] It is a strung-along succession of predicaments with little internal connection among them. Lacking the structural tension and unity of tragedy, the "climax" of comedy is often contrived. It is a wholly fortuitous "happy ending" or a larger or more riotous escapade than any that has gone before. The diffuseness of comic plot keeps us from intense absorption.

These remarks are all of a piece with Bergson's view that sympathy is alien to the appreciation of comedy. That view, however, has been challenged from opposite directions by other theories of comedy. On the one hand, it is held that we are even more aloof than Bergson would have it. When we laugh, we are not concerned with the values of society nor are we reproving the comic figure. Rather, when we see the weakness and folly of the comic figure, we enjoy a pleasing sense of our own superiority to him. In Hobbes' famous phrase, we experience "sudden glory," which expresses itself in laughter.

On the other hand, many thinkers have argued that Bergson and Hobbes are too narrow in their conception of comedy. For though both may explain, in somewhat different ways, why it is that we laugh *at* the comic figure, neither can explain — what is certainly a fact — why we often laugh *with* the comic figure. We do so if we do not have the "anesthesia of the heart" that Bergson speaks of. Think of the "lovable rogue" or scamp, who occurs so often in comedy, e.g., the legendary figure of German folklore, Till Eulenspiegel. He flouts social and moral conventions with a vengeance. In appreciating his antics we are not, as Bergson has it, upholding the ideals of society, but just the opposite. We can laugh only if we suspend our usual moral preconceptions. We are quite prepared to do so, however, because of the comic figure's gusto and vivacity. His good nature wins us over and along with him we enjoy a "moral holiday." Laughter, then, is caused by our exhilaration, a sense of being freed from everyday restraints. The proponents of this theory hold that it accounts for a great deal of "off-color" or "dirty" humor.

[77] Cf. above, p. 290.

The comic rascal just described also presents another difficulty for Bergson's theory. So far from acting "rigidly" and "mechanically," he displays great ingenuity. He is extremely inventive in contriving how to get into mischief and how to get away from long-faced magistrates. In this way, too, he wins our sympathy and he keeps us from being condescending.

Grant that we are sometimes sympathetic to the comic figure, and then we can and must give up the view that he is always a one-dimensional "stock character." Our sympathy will be greatest when he is a complex and "real" human being. Then he becomes an individual in his own right and thereby defies Bergson's dictum that the comic figure is a "type." Falstaff, in Shakespeare's *King Henry IV, Part I,* is probably the supreme example. He is a well-rounded (this is not a pun) and enormously endearing character. He is, to be sure, a liar, a braggart, a coward, and a thief. But he is not *just* any of these. And though he has "defects," they are not, for a number of reasons, "painful or destructive." The consummate rogue, he wins us over by his irrepressible zest and cheerfulness. He preserves a naïvely idealized image of his own character (II, iv). For all of his vices, he has no wickedness or cruelty in him. We do not pass moral judgment for he persuades us that he is beyond good and evil. Finally, there is a somewhat pathetic, childish ineffectuality about him, so that we can say, as Prince Henry does, "Were't not for laughing, I should pity him" (II, ii). We are therefore moved to enormous sympathy with Falstaff.

How deep our sympathy runs can be measured by our response to one of the most curious episodes in all literature — the famous "rejection" of Falstaff at the close of *Part II.* Falstaff goes to Westminster Abbey to greet his long-time friend, Prince Hal, who has just been crowned Henry V. Whereupon the king spurns him with cruel and lacerating words,

> I know thee not, old man: fall to thy prayers;
> How ill white hairs become a fool and jester. . . .

Falstaff is reduced to ineffectual bumbling — "my lord, my lord" — and he dies shortly thereafter of a broken heart. The rejection scene is, for many readers, immeasurably painful.[78] It demonstrates not that comedy is painful — there is "nothing funny" about the scene — but rather that some comic figures win our sympathies.

OUR DISCUSSION OF COMEDY has been addressed to the question, "Why does the 'comic mask' not 'imply pain'?" We have been concerned with comedy of character primarily, and only incidentally with other kinds of comedy.

---

[78] Cf. "The Rejection of Falstaff," in Bradley, *Oxford Lectures on Poetry,* pp. 247–273.

We have not, of course, spoken of such varieties of humor as word play, "sheer nonsense," irony, etc. Nor have we by any means canvassed all of the theories of comedy. One of the most important, which should at least be mentioned, takes "incongruity" to be central to humor. Incongruity occurs when the response to a situation is wildly inappropriate to it, or when attitudes and values of radically different kinds, e.g., the monumental and the trivial, are juxtaposed. There is the cartoon in which the suburban matron, on Halloween Eve, says to the little man from another planet who has just landed on earth, "I'm sorry, sonny, I'm all out of treats."

Faced with the bewildering diversity of theories of comedy, one might be tempted to say that there are "too many" of them. But if you stop to ask *why* there are so many, the answer is clear enough. Comedy is an enormously complex affair. It takes many different forms. Consider just the different *genres* of literary comedy — "comedy of manners," "farce," "satire," "high comedy," even "tragicomedy." Consider then the many other different kinds of humor — word play, wit, and so on — and it becomes clear why no single theory has been able to accommodate all instances of humor and why theorists have had to use "wrong-headed ingenuity" [79] when they have attempted to do so. The Hobbesian theory may explain at least some malicious laughter but it breaks down when laughter is affectionate and when we feel no self-glory. Bergson's theory is inadequate when the comic figure is sympathetic and "human," and so on.

We cannot, however, simply stake out different areas in the domain of comedy, assigning each to the appropriate theory. These theories conceive of comedy in such different ways that, if we take them all together, "comedy" will no longer have a single, unitary meaning. There will be no property or characteristic common to all instances of comedy. We would have to define "comedy" at a very high level of abstraction, e.g., "that literary form which induces laughter in the spectator." This, of course, tells us very little and, what is worse, it is misleading, for there are people who laugh at tragedy. Can we retain "comedy" as a meaningful term and still respect the differences between the many kinds of comedy?

The notion of "family resemblances," put forth by the contemporary philosopher Wittgenstein, may provide the answer. To begin with an example used by Wittgenstein, not all the many kinds of "games" possess the same common properties. In the range of games, "similarities crop up and disappear." [80] One kind of game shares certain characteristics with another; the latter has certain similarities to a third kind, but they are not the same as the similarities to the first kind. These are "family resem-

[79] Monro, *op. cit.*, p. 16.
[80] Ludwig Wittgenstein, *Philosophical Investigations*, trans. Anscombe (New York: Macmillan, 1953), p. 32e.

blances" since "the various resemblances between members of a family: build, features, colour of eyes, gait, temperament, etc., etc., overlap and criss-cross in the same way." [81] Though the notion of "family resemblances" first occurs in recent philosophy, it is noteworthy that Bergson had very much the same idea. He rejected any attempt to "imprison" the nature of comedy in a definition, for it "[passes] by imperceptible gradations from one form to another." [82] Each of these forms is a "[model] round which new effects resembling them take their places." [83]

So it may be that there is no set of properties common to all instances of comedy which is sufficient to define "comedy." And yet there may be "family resemblances" among the different kinds of comedy. One "model" includes the traits of a playful attitude toward life, a comic "type" with an obsessive fault such as hypocrisy, repetition of dialogue; a second includes a playful attitude, an affectionate rogue who affords the spectator vicarious release from conventional restraints, repetition of dialogue, improbable situations; a third includes a playful attitude, improbable situations, slapstick buffeting about of characterless personages who are more like "things" than human beings; a fourth includes little more than fantastic situations and word nonsense; a fifth includes a half-serious attitude toward social values and a sympathetic protagonist who gets himself involved in fantastic situations which show up the silliness of social conventions; a final "model" includes a largely, though never wholly, serious attitude toward social ideals, penetrating criticism of them which affords the spectator a sense of release, sympathetic characters, plausible situations.

You will see how complicated the "family tree" of comedy can become. But where the facts are as complicated as those of comedy are, it is unwise to ignore them for the sake of a specious simplicity. Let us remember Bergson's wise words: "[It] would be idle to attempt to derive every comic effect from one simple formula." [84]

There is a further reason why we should tolerate and indeed welcome the complexity of "family resemblances." No one of the traits which have been traditionally identified with the comic is, in itself, funny. "Incongruity" is sometimes embarrassing rather than laughable; "repetition" can be downright boring and sometimes it is solemn, as in the Old Testament and the refrain of a poem; "defects" of character like cowardice can be abhorrent. Moreover, would-be writers of comedy often employ devices such as "repetition" in an attempt to be funny, but the effect upon the spectator is anything but that. What distinguishes *comic* vice or repetition or incongruity from that which is noncomic?

[81] *Ibid.*, p. 32e.
[82] *Op. cit*, p. 2.
[83] *Ibid.*, p. 37.
[84] *Ibid.*, p. 36.

Some theorists have been forced to the lame conclusion that these are comic precisely when they are *funny*. It may be that this is the best that can be done. The "theory of comedy" would then consist of a classification and analysis of those things which are usually found to be funny. But if the analysis is to be at all fruitful, it cannot focus on a single trait such as "incongruity." In all art, any single element of the work must be considered in its interrelations with all of the other elements. So in the case of comic literature. We must take account of plot structure, comic character, dialogue, and the overall expressive "tone" which encourages the spectator to take the work "in fun." All of these help to make the incongruity or repetition "funny." Thus we are led almost inevitably to speak of "clusters" of comic properties. And if we wish to preserve the unity of comedy, as a category inclusive of many, diverse works of literature, we will be led to speak of "family resemblances." Further, the "family resemblances" of comedy can give us significant leads for the analysis of new and unfamiliar works.

This may be as much as we can do, but this much is by no means trivial. We can learn a great deal that is true and important about comedy even if the question, "Oh! But what makes it *funny?*" proves to be difficult or, at worst, unanswerable. The analysis goes on. The nature of comedy remains, in the words of one of its most acute students, "this little problem, which has a knack of baffling every effort, of slipping away and escaping only to bob up again." [85]

[85] Bergson, *op. cit.*, p. 1.

BIBLIOGRAPHY

* Rader, *A Modern Book of Esthetics*. Pp. 114–126, 223–226.
* Weitz, *Problems in Aesthetics*. Pp. 548–607.
Aristotle, *Poetics*.
Bergson, Henri. *Laughter*, trans. Brereton and Rothwell. New York: Macmillan, 1911.
Bosanquet, *Three Lectures on Aesthetic*. Lect. III.
Bradley, A. C. *Oxford Lectures on Poetry*. London: Macmillan, 1926. Pp. 37–65, 247–275.
Garvin, Lucius, "The Problem of Ugliness in Art," *Philosophical Review*, Vol. LVII (July, 1948), 404–409.
Lee, H. N. *Perception and Aesthetic Value*. New York: Prentice-Hall, 1938. Chap. X.
Parker, *The Analysis of Art*. Chap. IV.
Reid, *A Study in Aesthetics*. Chap. XIII.
Stolnitz, Jerome, "On Ugliness in Art," *Philosophy and Phenomenological Research*, Vol. XI (Sept., 1950), 1–24.

———, "Notes on Comedy and Tragedy," *Philosophy and Phenomenological Research*, Vol. XVI (Sept., 1955), 45–60.

QUESTIONS

1. Must any adequate aesthetic theory have a category of ugliness? In what sense(s) of "ugliness"? Explain your answer.
2. Are there any objects which you consider "invincibly ugly?" Is your judgment due to any of the causes listed on p. 278? If not, why, in your opinion, are these objects ugly?
3. Which of the four theories of art studied previously (Chapters 5–8) can be applied most fruitfully to the analysis of tragedy, in your opinion? Defend your answer.
4. Is aesthetic "sympathy" required for the appreciation of farce or comedy in which the leading figure is a one-dimensional character? In what sense of "sympathy" (cf. above, p. 36)?
5. Do you think that the notion of "family resemblances" can be applied to the concept, "fine art"? If so, how?

12

Truth and Belief in Art

1. ARTISTIC "TRUTH"

Joseph Conrad, in the eloquent Preface to his novel, *The Nigger of the Narcissus*, describes the function of the artist:

He makes "a single-minded attempt to render the highest kind of justice to the visible universe, by bringing to light the *truth*, manifold and one, underlying its every aspect. It is an attempt to find . . . what is enduring and essential. . . . The artist, then, like the thinker or the scientist, seeks the *truth*." [1] Art takes a fragment of life to "reveal the substance of its *truth* — disclose its inspiring secret." [2]

This is a revealing statement by a great writer who was also a thoughtful student of his craft. Conrad claims *truth* for the arts. This claim is a perennial one in the history of art. As far back as Plato, that philosopher speaks of "the ancient quarrel between poetry and philosophy." The "quarrel" was over the contention of poetry that it could compete with philosophy in bringing truth to man. Conrad, too, likens the artist to the "thinker." Among the critics, Coleridge is only one of many who hold

[1] Joseph Conrad, Preface to *The Nigger of the Narcissus* (New York: Doubleday, Page, 1924), p. xi. Reprinted by permission of J. M. Dent & Sons Ltd., Doubleday & Company, Inc., and the Trustees of the Joseph Conrad Estate. Italics added.
[2] *Ibid.*, p. xiv. Italics added.

that "poetry relies for its power on truthfulness." Why has this claim been made so insistently?

There are, I think, two chief reasons.

Primarily, those who take art seriously and respond to it deeply testify that they *learn* from works of art. Over the centuries, they report that they come away from their encounter with the work, not only delighted or moved or invigorated, but also with greater knowledge than they had before. All of us, probably, have felt this. We learn about human nature from Molière, Dostoevski, or Thomas Mann. Indeed, the truths which we gain from these artists are not readily come by in ordinary experience or even in treatises in psychology. Such truths seem to be distinguished by their acuteness and profundity. Similarly, tragedy, as we saw in the previous chapter, is often esteemed for the "wisdom" which it discloses. But literature is not the only source of artistic truth. It is a commonplace to say of Rembrandt's paintings that they reveal the depths of human character. And the musical compositions of Bach and the later Beethoven are said to give rich insights into life. The aesthetic spectator has found this in his experience. His belief in artistic truth will not down. Conrad's account of art gives voice to this belief.

Moreover, the sort of claim that Conrad makes for art has been used traditionally to save art from the charge of triviality. What would art be, what would be the use of it, if it did not reveal truths? It would have no relation to "life." It would be simply imaginative "make-believe." And the appreciation of art would be idle and insignificant. Art might still give pleasure to the senses; it might arouse emotion or imagination. But then it becomes something like a plaything or a stimulant. It gains enormously in dignity and in cultural importance when it is taken to be a revelation of truth. Art lays claim to truth as a reason for its being.

This can be illustrated throughout the history of aesthetics. Plato charged that "the artist knows nothing worth mentioning about the subjects he represents, and that art is a form of play, not to be taken seriously." [3] Whereupon Aristotle attempted to uphold the importance of art by arguing, as we have seen, that poetry is a "high" and "philosophical" enterprise, because it expresses the "universal." [4] When the sixteenth-century English Puritans claimed that literature was false and corrupting, and therefore morally unjustifiable, Sir Philip Sidney wrote his *Defence of Poesy*. In it, he invokes Aristotle's doctrine of the "universal" to support his view that poetry "[furnishes] the mind with knowledge" [5] and he argues throughout that poetry is "an art of true doctrine." [6] In the

---

[3] *Republic* 601.
[4] Cf. above, p. 117.
[5] Sir Philip Sidney, *The Defence of Poesy*, ed. Cook (Boston: Ginn, 1890), p. 22.
[6] *Ibid.*, p. 44.

nineteenth century, when, with the rise of science, literature was attacked as a useless and outmoded relic of "the infancy of civil society," [7] Shelley, Matthew Arnold, and others pointed to the "truth" and "knowledge" which poetry imparts.

But now, when we look into these accounts of artistic truth, we find something odd. Truth is claimed for art. And yet, it is not "truth" in the usual sense. "Truth" in this sense is the property of straight-out factual assertions about the world. Those who speak for artistic truth, however, speak of a peculiar *kind* of truth. Or they use "truth" in some sense other than the usual one.

Conrad says that the artist resembles "the thinker" and "the scientist." Yet Conrad calls attention to a significant difference between these seekers after truth and the artist. For the latter, he says, is not so much concerned with facts and theories as with "our capacity for delight and wonder . . . the sense of mystery surrounding our lives." [8] The artist must compel men to see "the surrounding vision of form and colour, of sunshine and shadows, to make them pause for a look." [9] To do this, according to Conrad, is to disclose "all the truth of life." [10] At this point, we think twice about the word "truth." How is the word relevant to Conrad's description of the artist? To say that art stimulates "our capacity for wonder" and gives us a vivid sense of the texture of our world, is one thing. This is probably unexceptionable. But where does "truth" come in here? If, as Conrad concedes, the artist does not provide us with facts and theories, what "truth" *does* he give us? And where are we to find it in art?

Comparable questions must be raised in reading Sidney. He also recognizes that the poet does not make straightforward factual statements. There may be untrue assertions in the poet's work, but this does not count against him, for "he telleth them not for true." [11] If, however, this is Sidney's rebuttal to the Puritan charge that the poet "lies," is it not self-defeating? For now, how can he speak of the "true doctrine" in poetry? Only by showing that the poet "affirmeth," not in the manner of a scientist or philosopher writing a treatise made up of true statements, but in some other way. Thus Sidney says that the poet writes "not affirmatively but allegorically and figuratively." [12] The truth of poetry,

---

[7] *Peacock's Four Ages of Poetry*, etc., ed. H. Brett-Smith (Oxford: Blackwell, 1923), p. 18.
[8] *Op. cit.*, p. xii.
[9] *Ibid.*, p. xvi.
[10] *Ibid.*, p. xvi.
[11] *Op. cit.*, p. 36.
[12] *Ibid.*, p. 36.

then, is not presented explicitly and factually. This marks an important difference between artistic "truth" and garden variety truth.

Furthermore, Sidney says that we gain knowledge of human emotions when we see them embodied in the concreteness of poetry. To "know the force love of our country hath in us," we should read of Ulysses; to gain "insight into anger," we should see Ajax mad.[13] But again, it might be asked: "Why call this 'knowledge' or 'insight'? What *truths* are we learning? Do Sidney's examples show anything more than that the poet dramatizes and makes evocative the emotions of his characters? Everybody grants that. But why speak of 'truth' at all?"

These can be rhetorical questions, of course. They are, when they are asked by philosophers who wish to exclude "truth" from all talk about art. To do so would be clear gain, according to these thinkers. For it would rid aesthetics and criticism of one of the most vague and misleading words in their vocabularies.

Even in our brief quotations from Conrad and Sidney, we have already seen the vagueness of "artistic truth." Each insists upon the presence of "truth" in literature, yet each grants that it is not the mode of truth found in science or philosophy. When we ask what they mean by "truth," it turns out to be something like "imaginative vividness" or "symbolic meaning" or "emotional power." And it is not even wholly clear that these are the intended meanings. Hence, "artistic truth," as it is used by its champions, is both vague and ambiguous. The ambiguity of the expression becomes all the more painfully clear when we consider some other ways in which it is used.

Sometimes it designates the formal and expressive unity of the work. The parts are then "organically" related to each other and there is a coherent mood or "tone" to the work. That which disrupts the formal organization or is discordant with the prevailing mood is said to have "a *false* ring" to it. Sometimes "truth" is used synonymously with "sincerity." "That has a false ring to it" would then refer to affectation or pretense. Sometimes "true" has the sense of the theory of "simple imitation," i.e., "lifelike," and sometimes that of "essence"-theory, i.e., expressing some common or universal feature of existence through the depiction of a particular. Sometimes "truth" refers to the "greatness" or depth of a work. "The 'truest' work of art in this sense is that which is most profound, in the experience of which as a whole we are aware of a deep sense of 'reality'." [14] And doubtless this list could be extended indefinitely, if we were to try to distinguish the various nuances of meaning which the term has in different critics and aestheticians.

So "artistic truth" is ambiguous with a vengeance. It would be worth

13 *Ibid.*, p. 16.
14 Reid, *A Study in Aesthetics*, p. 251.

the student's effort to try to make clear what is meant by the expression when he finds it in textbooks, art criticism, etc. (and not least, perhaps, when he uses it himself). If the ambiguity is not overcome, clarity is lost and conversation and argument are futile, for the speakers are simply not talking about the same thing. The remedy of those philosophers who are skeptical of "artistic truth" is a simple one: let us give up this needlessly confusing expression when we already have other terms which enable us to say what we mean. If we want to say that the work possesses formal coherence, then let us say just that; if we want to praise it for its profundity, we have the term "profound," and so on.[15]

But finally, these philosophers insist, after we have distinguished all the various meanings which attach to "artistic truth," we must recognize that, in many instances of its usage, the expression just does not mean anything at all. It is empty. It does not denote any property of the art-object, either factual or evaluative. It is not like "sonnet" or "comic" or "expressive." "True" is used simply to voice admiration or praise of the work. It gains eulogistic force by trading upon the commonly accepted value and importance of "truth" in the usual sense. Those who use the word uncritically confuse themselves and others by seeming to attribute some property to the work. Actually, "true" is, in these instances, simply a high-sounding way of saying "How nice" or even just "I like it." In this respect, it resembles another word which is often empty, but which seems to lend authority to an opinion or preference — "real" or "really." (Can you think of any examples of such usage?)

Confusion is worse confounded when "true" dresses itself up with pretentious adjectives, as in "higher truth" or "ultimate truth" or, if you please, "real truth." Such expressions have been used to bolster the view that art discloses a superior kind of truth which cannot be gained by the usual methods of knowledge. Then recourse is had to such vehicles of knowledge as "revelation," "insight," and "intuition." The critics of artistic truth have, of course, equally little patience with these expressions. It is their contention that all truths are on the same level; no truth can meaningfully be said to be "higher" than any other. "Truths about the human heart are no *truer* . . . than truths about the human pancreas."[16] Moreover, the history of knowledge shows clearly that "revelation," "intuition," and the rest are highly subjective and notoriously fallible methods of knowing.

"Artistic truth," the argument therefore concludes, is responsible for endless confusion and obscurity. But furthermore, why should we even

---

[15] Cf. Bernard C. Heyl, *New Bearings in Esthetics and Art Criticism* (Yale University Press, 1943), pp. 57 ff.; Hospers, *op. cit.*, pp. 141 ff.

[16] Arnold Isenberg, "The Problem of Belief," *Journal of Aesthetics and Art Criticism,* XIII (1955), 399. Italics in original.

want to retain the notion as a "defence of poesy"? To claim truth for literature and the other arts is to fight for them on the weakest grounds imaginable. For truth is not the salient value of the art-object. By contrast to science, history, and the other enterprises which are devoted to furthering human knowledge, there is little or no truth to be found in art. "[The] ideas in poetry are usually stale and often false and no one older than sixteen would find it worth his while to read poetry merely for what it says." [17] We do not exalt art, we degrade it, when we use truth as a criterion of its value. All the talk about "truth," moreover, blinds us to what is genuinely good in art. The value of art is peculiar to it, whether such value be taken to be the capacity to give aesthetic satisfaction, express emotion, or whatever. It is on these grounds that we should proclaim the importance of art. Fine art may not be able to compete with science, etc., in terms of truth, but that is not its function. It exists for other reasons and it gives us other and at least equally important values.

THUS FAR I have sketched the two opposite theories of "artistic truth." At one pole are those who insist upon the presence of truth in art and insist, too, that without it art would be trivial; at the other are those who object to the vagueness and ambiguity of "artistic truth" and contend, moreover, that to impute truth to art misreads its function.

Our discussion has merely drawn the battle lines. The philosophical battle — between those who expound and defend opposing theories of "artistic truth" — this battle remains to be fought. We can now see, however, what we must ask of these theories: (1) In what precise sense of the term "truth" does truth occur in art, if it occurs at all? (2) Is it the function of art to disclose truth? (3) If truth is found in a work of art, does it contribute to that work's aesthetic value?

BEFORE WE BEGIN, let me set out a few assertions that would be assented to by most parties to the dispute. Like most assertions that all or nearly all philosophers can agree on, these are pretty dull. But they will clear the way for the more important and more controversial statements which follow.

To begin with, let me telescope a large area of logic and say that "truth," in the usual sense of the term, can be a property only of *propositions*. A proposition is always verbal and it always describes some state of affairs in the world. "Canada is north of the United States" is a proposition, whereas "Open the window!" is not.[18] Neither is a smile or a

---

[17] George Boas, *Philosophy and Poetry* (Wheaton College, 1932), p. 9.
[18] I ignore, among other things, *a priori* propositions, and the distinction between a proposition and a sentence.

frown. Propositions, indeed, are often *defined* as "statements which are either true or false." Let me now telescope a large area of epistemology and say that a proposition is, by definition, "true" when what it asserts "corresponds" to the facts which it purports to describe. This is both the most common philosophical theory of truth and the most widespread common sense meaning.

Now apply this conception of truth to the arts and see what happens. First off, all the nonliterary arts — music, painting, architecture, the dance, etc. — drop out of the picture. They do not make verbal assertions. Hence they cannot possibly be said to contain either truths or falsehoods. What of literature, the only art in which truth could conceivably occur? That large share of it which is made up of nonpropositional verbal utterances also drops out. Thus we exclude expressions of desire, e.g., "Then sing, ye Birds, sing, sing a joyous song!" (Wordsworth, *Ode: Intimations of Immortality*), and of attitude, e.g., Hamlet's "O, from this time forth/ My thoughts be bloody or be nothing worth!" (IV, iv). Moreover, those sentences which are, grammatically, declarative but which employ metaphor or comparable devices, are generally either absurd or false. Straightforward factual assertions, e.g., that Oliver Twist asked for "more," or that Hurstwood sank into poverty (Dreiser, *Sister Carrie*), are false, simply because no such human beings ever existed. There remain those propositions, chiefly in the novel, which are empirically true, e.g., that Napoleon invaded Russia (Tolstoy, *War and Peace*), or that the Okies migrated (Steinbeck, *The Grapes of Wrath*), but these make up only a small fraction of literature.

Truth in the usual sense, therefore, occurs only in a minute proportion of works of art. In the same sense, furthermore, it is trivial as a criterion of aesthetic value. We do not condemn aesthetically all works which are devoid of propositions. Nor do we condemn those, all or almost all of whose propositions are false. Probably the best-known factual howler in all of literature is Keats' ascription of the discovery of the Pacific Ocean to Cortez ("On First Looking Into Chapman's Homer"). By a pointed coincidence, this blunder occurs in a work by one of the most quintessentially "poetic" of all poets. Is he any less the poet for it? Do we read the poem in order to gain knowledge of maritime history? And finally, of course, there are many bad novels which are replete with accurate references to historical or topical events.

The point is now amply clear to the reader. If we take the ordinary meaning of "truth" and apply it literally to art, then the problem of "artistic truth" turns out to be, not only easy, but also more than faintly absurd. This "solution" is, clearly, *too* simple. Those critics and philosophers who have claimed truth for art will not be put off so easily. When they insist that truth is an important and even essential source of the value of art, they are reporting their own deeply felt aesthetic experience. The community of their experience is impressive. They are aware of the ordinary meaning of "truth," but they find art to be cognitively superior to "the dreary formulae of mathematics, the sciences and philosophy." [19] They must be using "truth" in some sense other than the ordinary one. Can we find a meaning of "truth" which will make sense of their claim and do justice to their experience?

But there is another kind of theory which can be developed, after we find that "truth" in the ordinary sense has little or nothing to do with the fine arts. This is, as I suggested earlier, to abandon the quest for "artistic truth" altogether and to try to understand the value of art in some other way.

We will study first a theory of this kind, as presented by I. A. Richards. Then we will study the theories of "artistic truth" developed by T. M. Greene and John Hospers.

I. A. RICHARDS is one of the most distinguished men of letters of our time. He has been a creative and fertile worker in the humane studies of language and literature. *The Meaning of Meaning*, of which he is co-author, was a pioneer study which has greatly stimulated recent interest in semantics.

This eminent humanist, like Matthew Arnold before him, is sensitive to the decline of poetry and the other arts in modern culture. The chief threat, according to Richards, comes from the rise of science in the modern world. Scientific thinking, with the mastery of nature which it has made possible, has undermined the imaginative and mythic way of looking at the world on which poetry has thrived in the past. "It is," he says, "a possibility seriously to be considered that Poetry may pass away." [20] But poetry must be preserved if we are not to become culturally impoverished. Science is not enough. Richards speaks of "the vain attempt to orient the mind by belief of the scientific kind alone." [21] Poetry must complement science.[22] Poetry can survive, however, only if we make clear its justification and value. Richards set himself to this task in a number of his early writings.

Oddly enough, however, Richards has been considered by many a prime mover in the denigration of poetry in our time. He has recently admitted that his early works have been used in support of "scientism," though, he insists, they were not so intended.[23] How has this come about?

[19] Philip Leon, "Aesthetic Knowledge," in Vivas and Krieger, *op. cit.*, p. 619.
[20] "Science and Poetry," in Rader, *A Modern Book of Esthetics*, p. 286.
[21] I. A. Richards, *Principles of Literary Criticism* (New York: Harcourt, Brace, 1950), p. 280. Quotations from Richards' books are used by permission of the publishers, Harcourt, Brace and Company and Routledge & Kegan Paul Ltd.
[22] "Science and Poetry," *loc. cit.*, p. 299.
[23] I. A. Richards, "Emotive Meaning Again," *Philosophical Review*, LVII (1948), 151, n. 11.

Richards' conception of poetry rests upon his theory of language. In *The Meaning of Meaning* he set forth a view which has since become so much of a commonplace that we must remind ourselves of Richards' originality. He shows in detail that we use linguistic symbols not only to talk about the facts of the world, but for other purposes as well. The use of words to record matters of fact is their "referential" use. It is found in the everyday communication of information — "The book is on the top shelf" — and, most clearly and systematically, in science. But there is another great category of language — the "emotive," i.e., "the use of words to express or excite feelings and attitudes." [24] The language of poetry is characteristically emotive.

This sharp antithesis between science and poetry keeps them from competing with each other. If they were to fight over truth, science would win a quick and decisive victory. But poetry is not to be scorned because of this.[25] For "it is *not* the poet's business to make true statements." [26] Thus Richards' "defence of poesy" consists in denying that "the functions of science and poetry are identical . . . or that they conflict." [27]

But, it has been thought, Richards' vindication of poetry is self-defeating. For he "saves" poetry only by evacuating it of all meaning and truth. If poetic language is purely emotive, then either the poem is a manifestation of emotion, like a laugh, or a stimulant to emotion, like a tickle. Richards seems to have robbed poetry of its traditional significance. He does so because he has succumbed unwittingly to the very forces — the growth and influence of science — which he was attempting to curb. Science pre-empts all claims to knowledge and poetry is thereby trivialized.

We must examine Richards' theory further to assess the strength of this criticism.

Primarily, Richards does *not* deny that the words of poetry, sometimes at least, have "referents" in the empirical world. Nor does he deny that poems sometimes include statements which are true in the sense of "correspondence." "Very much poetry consists of statements, symbolic arrangements capable of truth or falsity." [28] What he *does* insist is that such statements are not "*used* . . . for the sake of their truth or falsity." [29] Again, it is not the function or "business" of the poet to give us truth. "Provided that the attitude or feeling is evoked the most important func-

---

[24] C. K. Ogden and I. A. Richards, *The Meaning of Meaning*, 4th ed. (London: Kegan Paul, 1936), p. 149.
[25] *Ibid.*, p. 148.
[26] "Science and Poetry," *loc. cit.*, p. 290. Italics in original.
[27] *Ibid.*, p. 294.
[28] *The Meaning of Meaning*, p. 150.
[29] *Ibid.*, p. 150. Italics added.

tion of [emotive] language is fulfilled, and any symbolic [i.e., referential] function that the words may have is instrumental only and subsidiary to the evocative function." [30] In other words, the distinction between "referential" and "emotive" language is a distinction in the *purpose* or *function* of language. To say that poetic language is emotive is not to reduce it to "meaninglessness." Poetry may contain very "precise" and "elaborate" references.[31] As a later author puts it, "No law prohibits statements found in poems from correctly describing an existing state of affairs." [32] But it is not in order to give knowledge about the world that the poet writes, nor in order to gain such knowledge that we read.

Richards says:

> The best test of whether our use of words is essentially symbolic or emotive is the question — "Is this true or false in the ordinary strict scientific sense?" If this question is relevant then the use is symbolic, if it is clearly irrelevant then we have an emotive utterance.[33]

Take the line of poetry cited by Richards, "O Rose, thou art sick!" [34] Would it be "relevant" to ask, "Is that true? Is the rose really sick? What seems to be the trouble?" Is it any more "relevant" to ask, when we are concerned with the *poem*, and not with maritime history, "Is it true that Cortez discovered the Pacific?" For Richards, the scientific truth of a poetic utterance has no more to do with its poetic value than the emotional effects of a scientific theory have to do with the truth of that theory.[35]

That is why Richards calls the assertions of poetry "pseudo-statements." One of Richards' sternest critics says that "pseudo-statements" are "false statements, or just plain lies." [36] It would follow that all of poetry is a gigantic fraud or error. But this is simply to ignore Richards' straightforward definition: "A pseudo-statement, as I use the term, is not necessarily false in any sense. It is merely a form of words whose scientific truth or falsity is irrelevant to the purpose at hand." [37] The "purpose at hand" is to arouse and organize the feelings and attitudes of the reader of poetry.

Hence much of the criticism brought against Richards seems to be misdirected. His theory of "emotive language" does not automatically expel meaning and truth from poetry. There are passages in which he speaks incautiously, as when he says that "[Poetry] tells us, or should tell us,

---

30 *Ibid.*, p. 150.   31 *Ibid.*, p. 124.
32 Sidney Zink, "Poetry and Truth," *Philosophical Review*, LIV (1945), 148.
33 *The Meaning of Meaning*, p. 150. Cf. *Principles of Literary Criticism*, p. 267.
34 "Science and Poetry," *loc. cit.*, p. 291.
35 Cf. *The Meaning of Meaning*, pp. 124, 235.
36 Allen Tate, *Reason in Madness* (New York: Putnams, 1941), p. 12.
37 "Science and Poetry," *loc. cit.*, p. 292, n. 5.

nothing." [38] This passage can be seized upon by a critic who wishes to show that Richards robs poetry of all significance. But what Richards is saying here is clear from the rest of his writings: it is not the purpose of poetry to impart truths; poetry is not to be condemned for failing to do so; scientific truths *may* occur in poetry, but they do not affect its aesthetic value; poetry is valuable because it creates an ordered emotional experience in the reader; its characteristic use of language is to achieve this end. All these theses are involved when Richards writes: "The people who say 'How True!' at intervals while reading Shakespeare are misusing his work, and, comparatively speaking, wasting their time." [39]

I have suggested that the more extreme criticism of Richards' theory is not justified. Let me note, however, those features of his writings which have given rise to such criticism. Richards introduced the category of "emotive language" in order to call attention to the noncognitive uses of words. These had been too much overlooked in earlier conceptions of language. The model of linguistic usage had been thought to be the use of words to describe the facts of the world and to communicate this information. Richards forced us to see how widespread is the use of language for other purposes. Later thinkers, following his lead, have shown that emotive language is prominent, and is sometimes, indeed, the chief type of language in such areas as propaganda, ethics, and so on.[40] Because Richards emphasized so strongly the distinction between the "referential" and the "emotive," it was thought that descriptively meaningful assertions could not occur in emotive discourse, such as poetry. This conclusion seemed to be re-enforced by another aspect of Richards' theory.

"Emotive" and "referential," we have seen, refer to the *uses* or *functions* of language. How is the referential function — that of giving scientific truth — to be carried out? Only by employing descriptively meaningful language. The facts of the world cannot be described by words which lack factual "referents." If the referential *purpose* of language demands referential *meaning*, it seemed to follow that the *emotive* function of language demands *nonreferential* meaning. This would reduce poetry to factual "meaninglessness." But the parallelism is false and misleading. As we have noted more than once, Richards is quite prepared to admit descriptive meaning into the emotive use of language.

This brings us, however, to a salient criticism of Richards' theory. If descriptive meanings can be used for emotive purposes, then how, precisely, do they achieve their emotive effect? How is it that referential symbols can arouse emotions and attitudes in the reader of poetry? It is one thing to draw the distinction between "sense" and "feeling"; it is

---

[38] *The Meaning of Meaning*, p. 158.
[39] *Principles of Literary Criticism*, pp. 272–273.
[40] Cf., e.g., C. L. Stevenson, *Ethics and Language* (Yale University Press, 1943).

another thing, and probably more important, to show how they mutually influence each other. Had Richards done this,[41] he would have prevented a great deal of criticism of his views. Moreover, he would then have provided the tools for linguistic analysis of specific poems. Only by such analysis can we explain the distinctive aesthetic values of poetry which Richards was insisting upon and wished to preserve.

Moreover, may not "truth," in the sense of factual "correspondence," be more important in poetry than Richards makes it out to be? He grants that descriptive meanings and therefore truths *can* and sometimes *do* occur in emotive utterances. He thinks, however, that neither truth nor falsehood affects the aesthetic merit of the poem, and he holds that this is the case in *all* poetry. Just here, however, some questions arise. Let us grant that it is not the *function* of poetry to impart truth. And yet, may not its aesthetic value depend, in part at least, upon its truth? Keats' howler, we will all probably agree, is no blemish upon the poem. But in other instances, if a poetic assertion is false "in the ordinary strict scientific sense," may this not detract from or damage our aesthetic experience? We are not reading the poem, as we would a scientific treatise, *for the sake of* gaining truth primarily. However, descriptive references to the world are a component of the work like its meter or imagery. Cannot the falsehood of these references, in *some* poems, be antiaesthetic, like faulty meter or diffuse imagery? We often speak as though it were. This is a possibility that we shall have to consider. If truth can occur in poetry at all, then perhaps it occurs in some significant way, so that it is not simply "irrelevant," as Richards has it.

Finally, if the question of "poetic truth" is still open, then we must consider meanings for "truth" other than "the ordinary strict scientific sense." Richards recognizes that the term is often used to mean something other than "correspondence" with fact; indeed, he was one of the first to call attention to this use (or abuse) of the term. However, Richards holds that when "true" is used to mean something like "genuine," it has no descriptive reference, and for this reason he is suspicious of such usage.[42] But there is another possibility, viz., a poem, or a work of art generally, may disclose truth in the "ordinary" sense that it describes some aspect of the world accurately, and yet it may not make straightforward factual assertions. Truth, in something like the "strict" sense, may be conveyed to the reader in an indirect, oblique manner and, what is more, enhance the value of his aesthetic experience as a result.

This is another direction that we can take if we wish to reinstate truth

---

[41] The job is not done in the earliest works. It is undertaken in *Principles*, pp. 124 ff., and carried out much further in *Practical Criticism*, Part III, chap. III.

[42] Cf. *The Meaning of Meaning*, p. 241; "Science and Poetry," *loc. cit.*, p. 292; *Principles of Literary Criticism*, p. 269.

as a significant, and not merely an accidental and trivial property of the art-object.

Professor T. M. Greene, like most philosophers who contend for "artistic truth," is encouraged by the fact that we *do* inveterately use "truth" and "falsehood" in evaluating works of art.[43] Critics commonly say of novels that they "ring true," that the author shows knowledge of the locale in which the story is set or of his characters, and so on. Professor Greene also believes firmly that the significance of art can only be understood by taking account of its truth. Only so can we understand the efforts of the creative artist and the value of the aesthetic experience:

> In attempting to apprehend reality in his own way the artist resembles the scientist and the philosopher, the moralist and the theologian. . . . To ignore this basic characteristic of art is to do violence to its historical character and to rob it of much of its human import.[44]

Let us notice at once how Greene differs from Richards in his conception of the function of art. Greene, like the thinkers cited earlier in this chapter, brings art round to a cognitive enterprise, such as science and philosophy. He holds that the artist discloses some interpretation of human experience which is supposed to be true. Art supplements science, by revealing truths which science can never achieve. "Each gets what the other misses." [45]

Greene says that "A work of art . . . may be *as* true or false as a scientifically expressed proposition." [46] Unlike many who use "artistic truth," he carries out a detailed analysis of its meaning. Further, Greene recognizes the salient differences between artistic and scientific truth. "The artist resembles the scientist," and yet the *kind* of truth which the artist gains, and the way in which he expresses it, differ in important respects from science.

Some of the dissimilarities between artistic and scientific discourse are obvious enough. The work of art is charged with emotion, the scientific treatise is not; the work of art manifests the individuality of the artist, the scientific theory is deliberately impersonal, etc. However, the crucial differences for Greene are these: (1) Science always employs concepts in order to describe the uniformities of the physical world; art is not primarily conceptual. (Concepts are used in literature, but even there they are not the chief means of expressing truth.) The work of art does

[43] *The Arts and the Art of Criticism*, p. 424.
[44] *Ibid.*, p. 229.
[45] *Ibid.*, p. 438.
[46] *Ibid.*, p. 425, n. 1. Italics in original.

not assert, "The world is essentially good." This may be expressed, however, by the artist's treatment of an individual and concrete subject matter. Similarly, the painter depicts particular human beings "in such a way as to emphasize . . . those generic human traits which interest him." [47] These psychological "universals" are set forth in concrete painterly terms, not by means of concepts.[48] (2) Art, unlike science, always gives an interpretation of reality which relates it to "man as a normative and purposive agent." [49] Art, that is to say, is *evaluative* as well as factual.[50] It is concerned with the significance of its subject matter for the goals and ideals of human beings. Hence art makes some normative judgment on what it depicts. Science, by contrast, so far as it treats human values at all, considers them as objective facts only.

Now what does it mean to say that "art expresses truth"?

It may seem odd at first, but Greene begins by accepting two definitions which are usually insisted upon by the other side to this dispute, viz., only propositions can be true or false, and a proposition is true only when it "accurately describes what it purports to describe." [51] But how then can Greene say that truth occurs in all the arts, including the non-verbal arts? And if truth consists in "correspondence," is not art, so far, exactly like science?

Greene answers these questions when he goes on to explain "proposition" and "correspondence." Propositions convey meanings and truths in some medium which permits "inter-subjective communication." [52] However, the medium need not be verbal and conceptual. Propositions, i.e., what the artist claims to be true about his subject matter, are found in the media of painting, music, and so on. We must say, then, if we are to follow Greene, that propositions are "expressed" by art, rather than "stated" in art. Greene admits that he is "conceiving of propositions much more broadly than they are commonly conceived of." [53] But he insists that expressed propositions are not simply vague approximations to what could be said better by linguistic statements using concepts. What can be expressed by art cannot be said by science.[54]

As we might expect, Greene has come under fire for this extremely broad use of "proposition." As one of his critics puts it, "a work of art cannot reasonably be called a proposition." [55] Propositions, if they are to be meaningful, must include symbols whose meanings have been fixed

47 *Ibid.*, p. 263.
48 *Ibid.*, pp. 445–446.
49 *Ibid.*, p. 230.
50 *Ibid.*, p. 443.
51 *Ibid.*, p. 425.
52 *Ibid.*, p. 427.
53 *Ibid.*, p. 427.
54 *Ibid.*, p. 438.
55 Heyl, *op. cit.*, p. 63.

by convention. A dictionary is a compilation of such conventions; a theorist, introducing a new term or symbol for some purpose, inaugurates a linguistic convention. However, there are no comparable conventions in the case of colors and tones. Hence we cannot say what the "propositions" in music and painting *are*. "In propositions, something is always *asserted* to be the case; but what, in the case of colors and sounds, is being asserted? How can they be said to be making assertions at all?" [56]

Comparable objections have been brought against Greene's use of "truth." "Consistency" is, along with "correspondence," one of the necessary conditions of truth, for Greene. The work is "consistent" when it satisfies several conditions. It must exploit the potentialities of its medium and respect the principles of treatment appropriate to such forms as the lyric, the sonnet, etc. It is, further, consistent only "if the expressed propositions, or interpretations of the subject matter, do not contradict one another." [57] Greene gives as an example of "contradiction" the arbitrary mingling of such diverse styles as those of Bach and Debussy. Finally, all that the artist has to say about his subject matter must be integrated "so that the work of art as a whole expresses a complex and coherent commentary on the nature and import of the entire subject matter." [58] Greene's critics are quite prepared to accept all of these as criteria for evaluation of the art-object. They are not prepared to concede, however, that "truth," as it is generally understood, has anything to do with "consistency," as this has been defined by Greene. [59]

The second criterion, "correspondence," is much closer to the usual meaning of "truth." Greene writes: "Artistic truth, like truth in the other universes of discourse, must satisfy the criterion of correspondence." [60] But the correspondence is of a sort peculiar to art. "[A] proposition can be directly tested for correspondence only by the immediate application to it of data which are strictly relevant to it, and not by data relevant to a radically different universe of discourse." [61] We cannot generally test the propositions expressed in art by appealing to the facts of common sense and science. To do so would be self-defeating, and it would give too easy a victory to those who claim that "scientific truth" is the only authentic mode of truth. Each artist adopts a certain "frame of reference" or way of looking at the world. If we are to understand his "insights," as Greene calls them, we must adopt the same frame of reference and then see whether the world, as thus interpreted, contains the facts to which he points.

56 Hospers, *op. cit.*, p. 160. Italics in original.
57 *Op. cit.*, p. 449.
58 *Ibid.*, p. 450.
59 Cf. Heyl, *op. cit.*, p. 63; Hospers, *op. cit.*, p. 144.
60 *Op. cit.*, p. 452.
61 *Ibid.*, p. 434.

Greene cites a fairly elementary example — Cézanne's depiction of trees. His treatment emphasizes certain features which other artists ignore. Cézanne stresses their "three-dimensional solidity." [62] "We can then go directly to nature . . . and test the accuracy of his recorded observations in terms of Cézanne's own cognitive preoccupation. . . . And if he tests Cézanne's observations in this manner, the critic cannot but be impressed by the objectivity of Cézanne's vision, or fail to realize that what Cézanne saw we too can see." [63] Or, to take an example from our previous chapter, we can say that the "frame of reference" of tragedy is significantly different from that of comedy. What we find in human beings when we look at them "in fun" is not at all what we find when we see them as tragic protagonists. We can test the truth or falsity of each work only when we examine the "artistically relevant" [64] data.

On the other hand, we can accept the artist's "frame of reference," go to the world to "test for correspondence," and find that he has ignored certain data or has failed to make clear the significance of the data which he has selected. Hence, for Greene, we are really invoking the criterion of "falsehood" when we say of a work that it is "shallow." [65] Critics seem to accept Greene's view implicitly when they say, as they often do, that the artist has "failed to do justice to his subject." Thus, W. K. Wimsatt, jr., says of a contemporary poem which treats of the evil in human existence: "What is wrong with this poem is that it is simply not enough. The poem does not do justice to the occasions and concrete character of bad feelings." [66] It is noteworthy that Wimsatt uses cognitive terms in evaluating similar works. He says that they are "too naïvely *mistaken* to have [poetic] interest." [67] Confused, myopic, or superficial perception of the "relevant" data — these constitute the "falsehood" of the work, for Greene.

PROFESSOR JOHN HOSPERS is among those who object, on logical and linguistic grounds, to Greene's use of "proposition" and "true." [68] Yet Hospers, like Greene, holds that truth, in some sense (again I must use that saving phrase — at this point you should understand why) often enhances the aesthetic value of works of art.[69] Like Greene, too, he follows the Aristotelian line that the artist depicts the "universal," e.g., some recurring type of human character is hit off by the delineation of a single

[62] *Ibid.*, p. 277.
[63] *Ibid.*, p. 454.
[64] *Ibid.*, p. 452.
[65] *Ibid.*, p. 424.
[66] W. K. Wimsatt, jr., "Poetry and Morals: A Relation Reargued," in Vivas and Krieger, *op. cit.*, p. 543.
[67] *Ibid.*, p. 543. Italics added.
[68] Cf. above, n. 56, n. 59.
[69] *Op. cit.*, p. 213.

personage.[70] Like Greene once again, Hospers says that "we can verify [the artist's] insights in our own further observations of people and actions."[71] But Hospers departs from Greene in refusing to speak of "propositions." Propositions affirm "truths about" the work's subject. "The novel does not *state* truths about human nature; but it presents them indirectly by simply *being* true-to human nature."[72] A "truth-to" is not a propositional description. It is a rendering of personality within the work itself, by showing concrete actions and traits of character. But such a personality can be found to resemble what exists outside the work. Such "true" characterization in Rembrandt makes his portraits more valuable aesthetically.

Even more common in art than "truth-to" character is "truth-to" "the felt qualities of experience in general."[73] Such art hits off the perceptual "tang" and "feel" of things, which cannot be readily described by "truths-about." There is "truth-to" our visual experience when a painter "captures the freshness of the morning landscape." Hospers also applies the concept to music, which gives "truth-to" our inner experience: "[When] the hearing of music evokes in us a certain emotion, we can often recognize, even though we have not experienced just this emotion before, that it is a deep and human emotion, and true-to some feeling we have had or might have."[74]

Hospers' concept of "truth-to" can be seen as an attempt to preserve the aesthetic character of fine art. It is not the function of art to make discursive assertions "about"; artistic truths are immanent in the work, in what the work *is;* they contribute to the work's aesthetic value. And yet, as a critic of Hospers points out,[75] "truth-to" should not lead us to a distorted or one-sided interpretation of the aesthetic object.

Primarily, we must not insist upon its presence in *all* works of art. "Truth-to" character is found in some portraits, but not in others. The portraits of Cézanne and Matisse are not concerned to disclose the "universals" of human nature, but are rather formal and plastic designs. "Artistic truth" is not relevant to the appreciation or evaluation of such works.[76] Moreover, even when "truth-to" is present, it is often less important than the formal and expressive values. It is neither the sole nor, often, the chief criterion of aesthetic value.

The latter criticism suggests, implicitly, a further problem. "Truth-to"

[70] *Ibid.*, p. 163.
[71] *Ibid.*, p. 173.
[72] *Ibid.*, p. 206. Italics in original.
[73] *Ibid.*, p. 175.
[74] *Ibid.*, p. 195.
[75] Bernard C. Heyl, " 'Artistic Truth' Reconsidered," *Journal of Aesthetics and Art Criticism*, VIII (1950), 251–258.
[76] *Ibid.*, p. 252; cf. Hospers, *op. cit.*, p. 213.

is being opposed to form and expression. The latter elements of the work, such as "emotional intensity and fervor," are "intrinsic" to the work. By contrast, "revelation of character" is always "true-to something *outside* the work of art." [77] But if there is a reference to "something outside," is not "truth-to" subject to even stronger criticisms than those just given? Is it not inimical to aesthetic experience? Hospers claims that "truth-to" contributes to aesthetic value, but how can it do so, if it diverts attention away from the work?

Look again at the phrase which generates our questions: "true-to something *outside* the work of art." "Outside" — that is a spatial term. What is "outside" lies beyond the "frame" of the work. Certainly, what art is "true-to" is "outside," in this sense. Human beings and their character, or the felt qualities of experience, are "outside." We must go beyond the work if we take Hospers' view that we can "verify [the artist's] insights in our further observations of people." [78] If the verification requires "further observations," then clearly we cannot know "truth-to" during the aesthetic experience. Again, is "truth-to" an *aesthetic* category?

It is not, if we treat the work as a psychological document, whose analysis of character is taken as a hypothesis to be tested by observation. Professional psychologists might do this. (They have often drawn upon literature in this way.) The rest of us might do so, less systematically, when we are jarred by the artistic portraiture into asking, "Are people really like that?" This would be a disruption of aesthetic interest. But suppose we then carry out "further observations" (remembering Greene's admonition that we must adopt the artist's "frame of reference"). Then suppose we find the type of human personality depicted in the work. We conclude that the work possesses "truth-to."

This sounds formal and stilted, and nobody probably ever does it this way. Yet in less formal ways, simply by "living and learning," we can come to see the "truth" expressed in the work. Do we not speak of "growing up" to a work? Novels and dramas which perplex us and, therefore, usually, bore us, when we are too immature to "understand" them, we acclaim for their "revelation of character" and "insight," when we have learned more of how the world wags.

When we return to the work, there is no longer any question of "testing." We bring with us the funded knowledge that we need to recognize "truth" when we meet it. We may not have encountered the specific trait of character of the fictional protagonist; yet we know enough about the human animal generally so that we can appreciate the plausibility and truth of the characterization. If there is "confirmation" at all, it is more like an immediate awareness of truth than a process of testing. Per-

[77] *Ibid.*, p. 253. Italics in original.
[78] Cf. above, p. 319.

haps this is the point of the idiom when we say that a character in fiction *"rings* true." Doubtless this locution can mean a great many things, e.g., "sincerity," and sometimes, perhaps, it means nothing at all beyond an expression of approval. In some instances, however, it certainly suggests our clear and direct recognition of psychological authenticity.

So the work is always "true-to something outside." But the spectator's attention need not go "outside" to know the truth. "Outside" has to do with the meaning of "correspondence" and therefore of "truth." It does not have to do with the direction of aesthetic perception.

The criticism of Hospers was that "truth-to" is less important than the "intrinsic" values of form and expression. The last few paragraphs qualify the criticism by making "truth-to" as intrinsic as other kinds of expression. The criticism proceeds, however, by challenging Hospers' view of music, in the passage quoted above,[79] viz., that we recognize that the expressed emotion is "true-to some feeling we have had or might have." Hospers' critic concedes that there is such resemblance between the two emotions. "But once again," he goes on, "the emphasis for artistic appreciation and analysis is wrong. It is the intrinsic quality of the emotions communicated — for example, the incomparable delicacy, subtlety, warmth and poignancy of much of Mozart — that is of artistic value, not their congruence with emotional states that have been or may be experienced." [80]

Our question a moment ago was whether "truth-to" could be apprehended aesthetically. Our question now is that of the aesthetic *value* of "truth-to" immediate experience.

We will probably all agree that there is some force in the argument just quoted. It is not *enough* for the emotion expressed by a piece of music to be "congruent" with one that we have experienced. Suppose the expressed emotion is "thin" or vapid; suppose it is "sentimental," i.e., the music is putting on a greater show of emotion than it seems to warrant. So far as we have felt "thin" or sentimental emotions before, we will be aware of "truth-to." But that will not redeem the music. It will remain bad music despite its "truth-to." Once again, then, "truth-to" cannot be a *sufficient* condition of aesthetic value.

But Professor Hospers would very likely grant this. (Note that, in the passage quoted from him, he speaks of a *"deep* and human emotion".) Assume, then, that the expressed emotion is one of "profundity" or "delicacy." We must still ask whether anything is gained from the congruence of the music with our previous emotional states. I do not, however, see that any answer can be readily got at, largely because of the vagueness of the language which we have at our disposal. I can only suggest, with no very great conviction, that the music's "truth-to" gives us a sense of the

[79] Cf. above, p. 319.
[80] Heyl, *op. cit.*, p. 258.

community or universality of emotional experience. If the expressed emotion is "unnatural," as some have said of Strauss' opera, *Salome*, we may be estranged from the work. In other works, however, the composer seems to be "speaking for us." The poet Baudelaire thus describes his response to the music of Wagner, in a letter to the composer: "[It] seemed to me that I already knew that music; then, when I'd reflected on it later, I discovered whence came this illusion, for it seemed to me that the music was my own, and that I was recognising it. . . . I've found in your work the solemn majesty of . . . the great passions of man." [81] When some common human chord seems to be sounded in the music, the work's expressive import is enhanced.

But Hospers' critic speaks of the *"incomparable"* emotions in Mozart. Take the adjective literally and we must be skeptical of what I have just said. The emotions expressed in music, so far from being "common," are not identical with anything that human beings have ever experienced before. I argued in a previous chapter that what is expressed by art is distinctive of the specific work.[82] Do we not cherish a composer like Mozart precisely because of the *uniqueness* of the emotions which we find in his work, emotions which are uniquely lucid and poignant because of the "incomparably" ordered sensory "body" in which they are expressed? When we listen to Mozart, are we concerned with "emotional states that have been or may be experienced"? Are we not concerned precisely with the emotions that *are* being experienced?

WE HAVE NOW CONSIDERED several of the leading theories of "artistic truth." You should see that each is trying to do justice to certain facts of art and aesthetic experience. You should also feel the intellectual tension between them, as each pulls in a different direction, in order to emphasize and explain different facts.

In which of these theories is the truth about "artistic truth" to be found?

Each reader will decide this for himself. I myself am inclined to think that it is in the area marked out by Greene and Hospers. I shall, presently, cite and analyze concrete examples of truths which enhance the aesthetic value of the works in which they occur. Even short of that discussion, however, can we agree that we often esteem works for what they disclose about the world and about ourselves? Think of the analysis of character in comedy and tragedy in the previous chapter. The tragedian depicts the interplay of motives in a complex human being, and the relationship between character and destiny. The comic artist exposes personal folly and social pretense. We cannot ignore these elements of

[81] Quoted in Enid Starkie, *Baudelaire* (London: Faber and Faber, 1957), p. 419.
[82] Cf. above, pp. 169–171.

the work. They are vital to the work and they impress themselves upon us. Are we "misusing" the work, as Richards has it, when we say, "How true"?

Those who speak against "artistic truth" do so largely because they want clarity and preciseness in our talk about art. All of us must share this concern. If we do, we must admit that it is not at all easy to give a satisfactory analysis of the concept, "artistic truth." We have seen that such "truth" has to be hedged about in various ways — it is not propositional (in the usual sense), it is not tested experimentally, it occurs only within the artist's "frame of reference," and so on. We are forced to use odd-sounding locutions like "truth-to." Perhaps, indeed, no wholly adequate analysis of "artistic truth" has yet been carried out. But it is not reasonable to give up the concept altogether, and the large and important facts for which it stands, because we cannot be as clear as we could wish. The logical and linguistic objections to Professor Greene's use of "truth" and "proposition" are, in some degree, clearly and even obviously sound. Yet I cannot but think that, in emphasizing the artist's endeavor to illuminate human existence, Professor Greene has got hold of a significant fact about art. Indeed, is not this account of art almost a commonplace? It seems to be accepted tacitly by most people in their talk about art. Who would even want to deny it, except on the grounds that the meaning of "artistic truth" is not wholly clear? *That* "artistic truth" exists seems to be far more certain than *what* it consists in exactly.

In what follows, I will use "artistic truth" to refer either, as in Greene, to a coherent evaluative interpretation of subject matter, or, as in Hospers, to "truth-to" human nature or the quality of felt experience. I want to propose several theses concerning "artistic truth." To ignore or deny them, I wish to urge, leads to a distorted or inadequate conception of "artistic truth":

(1) TRUTH DOES NOT OCCUR in *all* works of art. Much theorizing about "truth in art" has been unsound because it failed to remember this. We should not take as a model for all fine art certain selected works in which truth can plausibly be said to occur. This leads to exaggeration; often it has led to the untenable view that it is the principal function of the artist to impart truth. As the history of our problem shows, those who reject this view can justly appeal to *other* works of art of which it makes little sense to predicate either "truth" or "falsehood."

Professor Greene, who speaks up for "artistic truth" as strongly as anyone in recent aesthetics, recognizes this. He holds that truths are present only in "genuine works of art, i.e., works which are artistically expressive and are not *merely* decorative or aesthetically agreeable." [83] But the word

[83] *Op. cit.*, pp. 443–444. Italics in original.

323

"genuine" here is bothersome. Does it mean that works which are lacking in truth are not "real" works of art, i.e., not works of art at all? It is difficult to accept this conclusion, for then the realm of art would be narrowed excessively. Or does it mean that works which lack truth are always of lesser value aesthetically? This is equally untenable. Matisse is commonly considered the "decorative" painter par excellence of this century, and yet he is ranked among the greats. (Greene himself speaks of Matisse as a "decorative" artist, but it is noteworthy that he qualifies this somewhat.[84] His qualifications may indicate either the difficulties involved in applying "artistic truth" to specific works and therefore the vagueness of the concept; or else they may show Greene's embarrassment in trying to reconcile his demand for "artistic truth" with commonly accepted evaluations of art.) Similarly, the poet A. E. Housman quotes Shakespeare's

> Take O take those lips away
> That so sweetly were forsworn . . .

and he says of it, "That is nonsense; but it is ravishing poetry." [85] Hence (2) truth is not indispensable to aesthetic value.

We have seen that truth cannot *guarantee* the goodness of the work. It is only *one* of the several components of the work. Throughout this book I have tried to caution against one-sided views of art and aesthetic value by reminding you of the internal complexity of the work of art — its sensory appeal, its subtleties of form, its imaginative overtones, and so on. I must now do so again.

The case is clearest in so-called "didactic" or propagandistic literature, in which straightforward propositional assertions are made. It is precisely because of the badness of much literature of this sort that "didactic" has taken on a pejorative meaning. Consider

> It was in fourteen-ninety-two,
> Columbus sailed the ocean blue.

Truths in art are not usually asserted so baldly. When they are not, they are part of the expressive significance of the work.[86] But there is expression and expression. Works of art are often bad because we feel the disparity between the truths which they suggest and the rest of the work. Our attention is disrupted when these truths are incongruous with the subject matter in which they are supposed to be embodied. The artist seems

---

[84] *Ibid.*, pp. 278, 312, 464.
[85] *The Name and Nature of Poetry*, p. 40.
[86] Cf. above, chap. 10.

to be claiming too much. The concrete situations and personages of his work are not adequate vehicles of the "universal." The contemporary novelist, Graham Greene, has been criticized in this way. It is clear that he wishes to express truths about the large and solemn questions of religious faith and sin. Yet his characters are too ill-defined and trivial for this task.[87] Or we may find that the sensuous material, "tone" or formal structure of the work are incongruous with the truths which it suggests. Hence, even when these truths are acute, original, or profound, we will judge the work to be inferior *aesthetically*, whatever we may think of it on philosophical, psychological, or other grounds. Truth, like all else that is expressed in art, must be tightly bound up in the sensory body and formal development of the work.

Indeed, when the expressed truth is thus enmeshed in the work, we cannot even know what the truth *is*, except by discriminating perception of everything in the work. We can, to be sure, paraphrase the truth in expository prose. Much of the discussion of tragedy and comedy in the previous chapter did just this. But such paraphrase will be, as Cleanth Brooks has said, a "heresy," if we take it to be "the essential core of the poem itself."[88] What the poem "says" has nuances and qualifications within the work which are lost when the truth is abstracted. "Indeed, whatever statement we may seize upon as incorporating the 'meaning' of the poem, immediately the imagery and the rhythm seem to set up tensions with it, warping and twisting it, qualifying and revising it. . . . Perhaps this is why the poet, to people interested in hard-and-fast generalizations, must always seem to be continually engaged in blurring out distinctions [or] coming to his conclusion only after provoking and unnecessary delays."[89] Brooks likens the poem to a drama. It is "*an action* rather than . . . a statement about action."[90] (Notice the similarity of this to Hospers' distinction between "truth about" and "truth-to.") Unless we see that poetic truth is "enacted," we will make the mistake of thinking of a poem as "an idea 'wrapped in emotion.' "[91]

Hence (3) the truth of a work of art cannot be understood, and its contribution to the value of the work cannot be estimated, unless we examine the total work of which it is an element. And (4), because of the distinctive way in which it is "said," artistic truth is significantly different from scientific and common sense truth. However, as we saw earlier, whether the expressed truth is indeed a *truth* depends upon its correspond-

---

[87] This criticism is used as an example, for our present purpose. Its soundness must be debated elsewhere.

[88] Cleanth Brooks, *The Well Wrought Urn* (New York: Harcourt, Brace, 1947), p. 199.

[89] *Ibid.*, pp. 197, 208.

[90] *Ibid.*, p. 204. Italics in original.

[91] *Loc. cit.*

ence with commonly observable facts.

All four of these theses limit the claims that can be made for "truth in art." Those theories which repudiate one or more of the theses seem to me to have claimed too much. The first thesis establishes that "artistic truth" is not universal in art; the second, that it is not essential to aesthetic value; the third, that it cannot be the sole criterion of value; the fourth, that it is neither a competitor of science nor — an even more extravagant claim — that it is, in some vague sense, "higher" than scientific truth.

So MUCH BEING SAID, we must go on to say that truth *does* occur in some art, and that when it does, it *sometimes* contributes to aesthetic value. Our questions now are: How can we know whether truth is being expressed by the work? And how does truth make the work better?

Let us examine some specific works of art. First, a short poem. Santayana says in his own way that truth is not present in all art by distinguishing poets as "musicians" and "psychologists." The "musicians" "know what notes to sound together and in succession." [92] Our poem is by a "psychologist."

The opening lines of "Loss" by Babette Deutsch [93] are an evocative account of the emotion of grief:

> The mouth speechless,
> The heart so squeezed and wrenched, . . .

Here, there is "truth-to" the felt quality of our emotional experience. But the most striking truth in the poem is found in its closing lines:

> Here's further pain, to know
> That smart so sharp
> Can find release;
> That not alone the loved body and self
> Must die, but this pang too,
> And love that mourns its dead will learn to be at peace.

The poem depicts the universal experience of mourning. People often try to dispel the grief of mourning by reflecting that "this too will pass." But in the lines just quoted, the poet gives an unexpected turn to this banal truth, and in so doing she expresses what I believe to be an acute and fairly subtle truth. The appropriate paraphrase is easily formulated: the realization that present grief will in future pass away itself accentuates

---

[92] *The Sense of Beauty*, p. 128.
[93] Babette Deutsch, *Take Them, Stranger* (New York: Holt, 1944), p. 41. Reprinted by permission of the author.

the present grief. Or, alternatively: the mechanism that we use to reduce pain is self-defeating, for it forces us to realize that memory of the loved one will lapse and grow dim.

Do you agree with me that this is both a "psychological" truth and, what is more, a subtle one? Is it a new idea to you? Here is an instance of Hospers' "truth-to" human nature. This truth is expressed feelingly, though not, perhaps, with great sensory richness, by the words and rhythms of the poem, e.g., the hush surrounding the last line as it trails off into "at peace." Contrast the poem with my dry-as-dust paraphrases. A truth has been expressed poetically, and the originality of the truth enhances our interest in the poem.

How do we know that "truth" is relevant to the appreciation and analysis of "Loss"? The answer can only be that we must have some sense of what the poem is setting itself to do — or be. It is not simply a "sounding together of notes." It might, of course, be read in that way, e.g., by someone who, because he did not understand English, was reading the poem simply for its "music." To the rest of us, however, the poem is claiming to describe human experience — "Here's further pain," etc. The poem therefore implicitly involves itself in "truth-to." We are not making an irrelevant or gratuitous demand upon it when we look for "truth-to," nor is it irrelevant to praise the poem for the "truth-to" when we find it. We are accepting the artist's "frame of reference," as Greene would say. We invoke the criterion of correspondence with psychological fact because the poem does so. Its "truth" is one of the essential constituents of the poem.

Does this imply that we should use the same criterion in evaluating *all* poetry? Of course not. May I urge once again that the surest way to go wrong in discussing "artistic truth" is to generalize from one kind of art to *all* art. A poem by a "musician" does not purport to reveal "truth-to" human nature, any more than farce does. "Comedy of character" *is* concerned with such truth, but in an indirect and oblique manner. Unlike "Loss," such comedy expresses truth by pronounced exaggeration, comic "types," etc. We must examine the subject matter of the work, its form, its "tone" or mood, and much else, to decide whether "truth" is relevant to it. Is this not how we decide that Keats' famous historical howler is not relevant to the evaluation of his sonnet?

Now suppose that we are justified in thinking that some work *does* claim "truth-to" human nature. Then we find that it is false to psychological fact. It distorts or misconstrues human beings, not as in comedy or fantasy, but because the artist lacks psychological understanding. Here we have novels whose characters, as we say, do not "ring true," or do not "come to life," or are "implausible." Again we have adopted the artist's "frame of reference," but now the work is found wanting. The characters are one-dimensional or they act inconsistently without explanation. In speaking of such novels, critics report that they "cannot get interested" in the characters. "Falsehood" is then an aesthetic blemish.

Consider another example of "truth-to" human nature, this one of extraordinary acuteness and profundity. The character is Iago in Shakespeare's *Othello*. Iago is, by common consent, one of the most diabolical villains in literature. Ask, however, *why* he perpetrates the evil deeds which doom Othello and Desdemona, and the answer is startling: nobody knows, Iago himself least of all. This is not an example of the sort of unmotivated behavior which is a flaw in dramatic literature. Iago is irresistibly motivated to do evil. He tries to explain his motives to himself, but fails. He proposes *too many* motives — professional jealousy, personal jealousy, misogyny, etc. His soliloquies show, in Coleridge's famous phrase, "the motive-hunting of a motiveless malignity." The "truth-to" human nature which Shakespeare hits off has not been treated systematically by psychology until our own century, viz., that a man may fail to understand his own most compelling motives.

Othello is a tragedy. It therefore claims to be, in Aristotle's phrase, an "imitation of men in action." The trenchant analysis of Iago makes good this claim and contributes to the depth and intensity of the work. Truths of this order of psychological subtlety vivify the "reality" of the works in which they appear and increase our aesthetic interest accordingly. The truth which is "enacted" by Iago makes him profoundly human. Moreover, as those who have read the play will testify, it makes him all the more ominous.

The two examples that I have chosen are doubtless not typical of literature in general. Far more often the artist's interpretation of his subject matter expresses such truths as "death comes to all men," or "people must give up the hopes which they had when they were young." These propositions are true enough, but are they worth shouting from the housetops? They document Boas' claim that the ideas in poetry are "stale." [94] Why, then, do we say "How true!" so often, even when the truth lacks originality? Again we must consider the *total* work. The truth, when it is paraphrased and therefore abstracted from the work, sounds hackneyed. Within the work, however, it is invested with great vividness and power. The truth is, as we say, "brought home to us" movingly. We have never before felt the cutting edge of "death comes to all men." The truth is ingredient in the poem, and it contributes to its value, but much of what we probably mean by "How true!" could be rendered by "How eloquent!" or "How moving!" Even in these cases, however, the truths deal with universal human concerns and they therefore add "reality" and interest to the work. Perhaps it is because such truths touch the nerve of common

[94] Cf. above, p. 308.

values and fears that people so often say that art discloses a "higher" truth than science. In any event, we will condemn poetry of this kind for its "staleness" only if we forget that it is not the function of poetry to impart "truths about," and that "truth-to" is only one of the components of the art-object.

A case in point is Rouault's painting, "Three Judges." It is less easy to frame a linguistic paraphrase of what this work expresses. But it would be something like "[Some] judges are corrupt and inhuman." This is "enacted" in the gross and coarse features of the judges. The work is intended as a social commentary and we approach it as such. It is concerned with a major social institution and it expresses at least a partial truth about it. The work does not "reveal" anything that we could not learn, and in greater detail, from a history of the judicial system. Yet the painting is a "revelation" in the sense that it impresses the truth upon us with overpowering force. Rouault has seen through pretense and power, and he has made corruption palpable. This explains in part, but again, not altogether — there is more to the work — the authority and impact of "Three Judges."

2. AESTHETIC "BELIEF"

Once you admit truth into art, you have further problems on your hands. If we use "truth" in anything like its ordinary sense, i.e., if we do not use it simply as a vague expression of praise, we are establishing a relation between art and "life." This follows from the very meaning of "correspondence." The "purists," such as the formalists, who repudiate any connection between art and "life," need not get involved in the problems with which we have just wrestled. Those who insist upon "artistic truth" think that this is too easy a way out. They hold that we cannot have rounded knowledge of the nature and value of art unless we see that truth is part of its expressive significance. But then they must face up to further problems.

A formalist denies that art is an "imitation." This is, of course, what baptizes him a "formalist." [95] Formalists, and other thinkers of like persuasion, never tire of insisting that the work of art is "complete, self-sufficient, isolated." [96] Those who do not go to the extremes of Bell and Fry, and recognize that the artist expresses beliefs concerning his subject matter, nevertheless contend that we must accept these beliefs just as they stand. We must not criticize or question them in terms of our *own* beliefs. To do so is to commit the error of letting our extra-artistic experience legislate for art. This error vitiates aesthetic appreciation.

[95] Cf. above, pp. 134 ff.　　[96] Leon, *op. cit.*, p. 621.

In support of this argument, the following fact is cited: painters and authors frequently express beliefs in different works of art which, compared among themselves, are logically contradictory. Some artists are Christians, like Giotto and Dante; others are atheists, like the poet Swinburne and the "naturalists" in contemporary fiction. Other artists espouse still other world-views. Now they cannot all be right, as a matter of logic. And yet we can and do appreciate all of these works. What does this show? It shows that we do not have to *believe* what the artist believes, for purposes of aesthetic appreciation. We leave behind the beliefs of the everyday world. The devout Christian who is also aesthetically mature will often evaluate more highly a work which expresses atheism than one which voices his faith.

I will assume common agreement that this *is* a fact. Why does it create difficulties for those who believe in "artistic truth"?

We can use "truth" meaningfully only if we can speak meaningfully of its opposite, "falsehood." These concepts are "cognitive," i.e., they have to do with human knowledge; specifically, they distinguish those knowledge-claims which are well-founded from those which are not. "Belief" and "disbelief" are also cognitive terms. They refer, however, not to the properties of propositions but to psychological states of mind. They distinguish respectively our acceptance or rejection of knowledge-claims.

Now it is, of course, unhappily true that we can believe what is false. But this is an imperfection in human knowing. We *ought* to believe only what we know to be true. We should not be guilty of "wishful thinking," stubborn ignorance, or their ilk. For a wholly rational being, the soundness of knowledge-claims, and that alone, should dictate the commitments of belief.

Moreover, we believe what is false only when we "don't know any better," i.e., when, because of ignorance or misapprehension, we fail to realize that it is false. Can a man say, "*x* is false but I believe it"? Not likely. Such an assertion is absurd or very nearly so. We can believe only what we take to be true.

This brings us to the problem of belief for those who insist upon "truth in art": If belief should be coupled only with truth and disbelief only with falsehood, how is it that we can appreciate works whose cognitive claims are mutually contradictory? There seem to be two alternatives: Either, when we appreciate such works, we are guilty of the wildest inconsistency. But nobody thinks this. We accuse a man of being "irrational" when he asserts two propositions, both of which cannot be true. But we do not charge a man with irrationality because he enjoys both Giotto and Swinburne. Or else — what seems to follow — the notions of "truth" and "falsehood" are simply out of place when it is art, rather than science or philosophy, that is in question. If a Christian can appreciate Swinburne, then he is not concerned with the poem's "truth" at all. If he believes in his religion, he cannot believe in atheism, for he takes it to be false. Yet he reads the poem. Belief — an attitude toward truth-claims — is not part of the aesthetic experience, because truth is not aesthetically significant in art. The proponent of "artistic truth" must then concede to the purist and admit a complete divorce between art and "life." But then he seems to be giving up his whole theory.

We saw earlier that "artistic truth" differs in important respects from truth in "the ordinary strict scientific sense." We will now see how the meaning of "belief" must be modified if there is to be any escape from the above dilemma.

THE MOST RADICAL noncognitivist theory was advanced by Richards during one period of his thought. He was defending the view, cited earlier, that the poet creates and the audience reads poetry in order to induce an experience of harmoniously organized emotions and attitudes. The reader does not, therefore, raise any questions about the truth of the poet's statements. They are "pseudo-statements." The reader is concerned with what he feels, not what he believes. Richards then goes on to say, in a passage which has become famous (or notorious), that "poetry conclusively shows that even the most important among our attitudes can be aroused and maintained without any belief entering in at all. Those of Tragedy, for example. We need no beliefs, and indeed we must have none, if we are to read *King Lear*." [97]

T. S. Eliot reports that he found the view set forth in this passage "incomprehensible." [98] Others found it comprehensible enough but completely mistaken. Richards himself gave up this view. Why is it unacceptable?

Richards has divorced belief from attitude. Consider this as a matter of psychology. Can we have attitudes — of enthusiasm, indifference, or revulsion — unless we have certain beliefs about that to which the attitude is taken? Even when our attitudes are most irrational, as in racial prejudice, they are generally accompanied by beliefs about the "inherent inferiority" or "dirtiness" or "laziness" of the "inferior" race. We have one sort of attitude toward the heroes in *Lear*, e.g., Edgar, Kent, and quite another toward the villains, e.g., Edmund, Goneril. We would not have these attitudes unless we had certain beliefs about these characters and their actions. Moreover, we must bring with us beliefs from ordinary experience, for example, concerning the obligations which children have to

---

[97] "Science and Poetry," *loc. cit.*, p. 293.
[98] "Dante" in *Selected Essays: New Edition* (New York: Harcourt, Brace, 1950), p. 230.

their parents. Without these beliefs, the conflicts and tensions which animate the play would evaporate.

That "Edmund is villainous" is true, and we all believe it. This belief is shared by the artist and his audience. Shakespeare could presuppose and capitalize upon such beliefs. In this case, there is and must be some relation between art and "life." However the problem of "aesthetic belief" centers upon the situation in which the percipient does *not* share the artist's beliefs. How can he believe what he takes to be false?

THE PROPONENT of "artistic truth" is now caught between two convictions which face in opposite directions: the first, that truth *does* occur in art, so that art is related to and is, in a sense, responsible to what is actually the case in "life"; the second, that art must be approached "sympathetically," if we are to appreciate it aesthetically, and it must therefore be considered "complete, self-sufficient, isolated." (You will see that this is a restatement of the "imitationist"-"formalist" controversy.) To overcome this conflict, we must move in the second direction, i.e., toward the aesthetic "autonomy" of the work. If we do not, if we hold that we can believe in a work only if what it asserts or expresses is true, then we reduce art to science or history. Then truth, in the usual sense, becomes the decisive criterion of value, and we lose sight of what is distinctive and precious in the work, both at the level of theory and of aesthetic appreciation. Any theory of "artistic truth" will cost us more than it is worth if it leads us into the fatal error of ignoring the intrinsic significance of art.

Greene knows this, for he says that the "work of art . . . is far more self-sufficient than any scientific theory; it is, to a notable degree, a self-contained universe with an autonomy of outlook not to be paralleled in science." [99] Hence, the "insights" expressed in works of art are not subject to "correction" and "falsification" by other works, in the same way that scientific theories can be refuted by further empirical observations.[100] Modern medicine disproves ancient theories of disease, but nobody says that a modern play "disproves" Aeschylus or Shakespeare. To respect the "self-containedness" of the work, we must, as we have seen,[101] adopt the artist's "frame of reference." With regard to the problem of belief, therefore, Greene insists that we must not approach the work or judge it in terms of our own world-view. We can only "demand of an artist . . . that he deal with *some* significant subject in *some* significant way." [102] It is then possible for "a Christian critic [to] assert the greatness of a pagan

[99] *Op. cit.*, p. 455
[100] *Ibid.*, p. 457.
[101] Cf. above, pp. 317–318.
[102] *Op. cit.*, p. 471. Italics in original.

masterpiece." [103]

Thus Greene weakens the parallelism between "truth"-"belief" and "falsehood"-"disbelief." So does Aristotle when he says that if the poet makes a factual mistake "he is guilty of an error; but the error may be justified if the end of art be thereby attained." If the error contributes to the aesthetic "effect" of the work, "we must accept it." [104] The usual criteria of rational belief, which distinguish well-founded and ill-founded beliefs, must be relaxed. We must recognize the differences between our cognitive interests and our aesthetic interests. Truth is not the sole component of art nor is it the function of art merely to impart truth. Therefore "aesthetic belief" must be distinguished from the cognitively ideal belief which accepts only what is true and rejects whatever is false.

WE MUST NOW EXAMINE FURTHER the nature of "aesthetic belief."

We find a fruitful lead in Richards, after he gave up the view discussed a moment ago. He distinguishes belief in a scientific assertion from "emotive belief." The former involves a readiness to act in a certain way. If a man does not act upon his beliefs, we say that he does not *really* believe what he professes. In the appreciation of art, however, there is little or no room for action. Here our beliefs are, Richards says, "provisional acceptances . . . made for the sake of the 'imaginative experience' which they make possible." [105]

T. S. Eliot takes over this view in his famous essay on "Dante." Eliot recognizes the importance of the cognitive element in art. He says that "you cannot afford to *ignore* Dante's philosophical and theological beliefs." [106] However, he marks the distinction between aesthetic and nonaesthetic belief: "[On] the other hand you are not called upon to believe them yourself. . . . For there is a difference between philosophical *belief* and poetic *assent*." [107] Dante's world-view is derived from the philosopher Aquinas, but "[we] are not to take Dante for Aquinas or Aquinas for Dante. . . . The *belief attitude* of a man reading [Aquinas] must be different from that of a man reading Dante, even when it is the same man, and that man a Catholic." [108] Eliot adds the observation that "one probably has more pleasure in poetry when one shares the beliefs of the poet," but he considers this aesthetically "irrelevant." [109]

"Aesthetic belief," then, is "provisional acceptance" for the sake of aesthetic experience. The purist is right in claiming that we must not oppose

[103] *Ibid.*, p. 473.
[104] Cf. above, p. 119.
[105] *Principles of Literary Criticism*, p. 278.
[106] *Op. cit.*, p. 218. Italics in original.
[107] *Ibid.*, p. 218. Italics in original.
[108] *Ibid.*, pp. 219–220. Italics in original.
[109] *Ibid.*, p. 231.

333

our own beliefs to those of the artist. But where, if at all, does "acceptance" stop? Do we "assent" to *everything* in the work, and in all works? If so, then it hardly makes sense to speak of "belief" at all, for the term is meaningful only where there is a possibility of *dis*belief. Suppose a percipient does *not* "accept" the beliefs expressed in the work. Would that be what Bosanquet calls a "weakness of the spectator"? Would it show that he has let his beliefs — or biasses — get in the way of aesthetic "sympathy"?

Now we come up against a fact of aesthetic experience quite different from that of our tolerant appreciation of "contradictory" works. It is the fact that our response to the work is, on occasion, something like "Don't ask me to believe *that!* That's asking too much." We will believe (= "accept") that Circe turned men into swine (Homer) or that horses are blue (Franz Marc). Yet there are some things that we refuse to believe. And this is not because of any "weakness" in us, but because of an imperfection in the work of art.

We have seen that the usual relations between "truth"-"belief" and "falsehood"-"disbelief" must be modified somewhat in the case of art. But they must not be given up altogether. If "purism" does so, then it cannot take account of the fact just cited. We want to be able to say that some works are "false" and therefore justifiably disbelieved.

Greene, as we have already noted, holds that we must adopt the artist's "frame of reference," even if it is not our own during nonaesthetic experience. He holds, however, that even after we have done so, we may charge the artist with "falsehood" if he has ignored relevant data or has treated his subject matter superficially or inadequately. Thus, to use our earlier example, if the work claims to be a serious treatment of "men in action," then the actions and motives of the characters must be explained consistently and plausibly. But if one of the characters should suddenly and inexplicably begin to act in a way completely opposed to his earlier behavior, or if he should in some other manner go counter to ordinary human behavior, we would balk. This would "ring false" and it would therefore be "unbelievable." We know how often inferior "whodunits" have to resort to some such device in order to tie up the otherwise hopelessly loose ends of the plot. Aesthetic "acceptance" stops here.

It is the work of art which defines what is "probable" and "possible" within its bounds. We do not impose upon it the cognitive criteria of everyday existence. That is why we can and do "assent" to myth and fantasy. But if we are to accept the criteria of credibility which are relevant to the work, so must the artist who implicitly enunciates them. Given his "frame of reference," the work must be coherent and credible. In the now famous words of the poet, Marianne Moore, the "imaginary gardens" must have "real toads in them." If we are to dwell within the artist's "world," then he must not depart from it precipitously because his imagination has faltered or because he cannot sustain dramatic interest or mood. "Sympathetic" belief in the work involves expectations of what is going to come next as the work unfolds. Unless our expectations are thwarted for some good reason, as in comedy, their frustration will disrupt aesthetic interest. To adopt the aesthetic attitude at all is to commit our belief to the work. But our faith must be respected and rewarded.

Do you remember when, in *Through the Looking-Glass*, Alice expresses her incredulity upon seeing a unicorn for the first time, whereupon the Unicorn proposes a "bargain" — "if you'll believe in me, I'll believe in you"? Well, take Alice to be the aesthetic spectator and the Unicorn to stand for the "make-believe" work of art, and the "bargain" between the two of them is something like that.

BIBLIOGRAPHY

* Rader, *A Modern Book of Esthetics*. Pp. 283–311, 335–356.
* Vivas and Krieger, *The Problems of Aesthetics*. Pp. 562–577, 583–625.
* Weitz, *Problems in Aesthetics*. Pp. 219–242, 455–461.
  Bilsky, Manuel, "Truth, Belief, and the Value of Art," *Philosophy and Phenomenological Research*, Vol. XVI (June, 1956), 488–495.
  Eliot, T. S. "Dante" in *Selected Essays: New Edition*. New York: Harcourt, Brace, 1950.
  Greene, *The Arts and the Art of Criticism*. Chaps. XXIII–XXIV.
  Heyl, Bernard C., " 'Artistic Truth' Reconsidered," *Journal of Aesthetics and Art Criticism*, Vol. VIII (June, 1950), 251–258.
  ———. *New Bearings in Esthetics and Art Criticism*. Yale University Press, 1943. Chap. III.
  Hospers, *Meaning and Truth in Arts*. Chaps. 5–7.
  Jessup, Bertram E., "Meaning Range in the Work of Art," *Journal of Aesthetics and Art Criticism*, Vol. XII (March, 1954), 378–385.
  ———, "Truth as Material in Art," *Journal of Aesthetics and Art Criticism*, Vol. IV (Dec., 1945), 110–114.
  Ogden, C. K., and Richards, I. A. *The Meaning of Meaning*, 4th ed. London: Kegan Paul, 1936. Chap. VII.
  Weitz, Morris. *Philosophy of the Arts*. Harvard University Press, 1950. Chap. 8.
  Zink, Sidney, "Poetry and Truth," *Philosophical Review*, Vol. LIV (March, 1945), 132–154.

QUESTIONS

1. The critic Allen Tate speaks of "the special, unique, and complete knowledge which the great forms of literature afford us." — *Op. cit.*, p. 9.
   But Professor Krieger asks: "How can poetry tell us something about our world that we can learn nowhere else when . . . it is not in any obvious sense

referential?" — Murray Krieger, *The New Apologists for Poetry* (University of Minnesota Press, 1956), p. 192.
Compare and discuss these two passages.

2. Cite, from your own experience, works of art which contain (a) truths which enhance their aesthetic value, (b) truths which make no difference to their aesthetic value, (c) falsehoods which detract from their aesthetic value, (d) falsehoods which make no difference to their aesthetic value, (e) neither truths nor falsehoods. What meanings do you give to "truth" and "falsehood"? Can you make any generalizations concerning the relative aesthetic value of these classes of art?

3. Study the theories of "artistic truth" in the readings by Greene and Hospers, cited in the Bibliography. How, if at all, do these theories differ from each other? Are the differences purely verbal?

4. Why is it that the "truth" of one work of art is not "refuted" by another work, which expresses a contradictory "truth," whereas one scientific theory is disproved by another which is contradictory to it? What does this show about the meaning of "artistic truth"?

5. Do you find that you appreciate a work more when you happen to share the philosophical, moral, etc., beliefs of the artist? Do you agree with Eliot that this is aesthetically "irrelevant" (cf. above, p. 333)? Discuss with reference to aesthetic "sympathy."

13

Art and Morality

This chapter does not deal with a question in aesthetics. It is, rather, concerned with a question or, more accurately, a cluster of questions in moral philosophy or ethics: Do works of art alter the percipient's character for good or ill, and thereby influence his moral behavior? If they do, can we therefore judge works on moral grounds, just as we praise or condemn people — moral saints or moral villains — or institutions and social conditions — democracy or slums? Specifically, are we justified in regulating, by political and legal means, the creation and distribution of works of art, even to the point of suppressing certain works? Or is art, both in its creation and its appreciation, exempt from moral judgment and control?

The aesthetic attitude trains attention upon the work "for its own sake alone." Here we are concerned with the intrinsic properties of the work and with its values for intrinsic perception. Ethics, by contrast, is concerned with the relations of the work to other things. Therefore it stresses the consequences of art — its effect on behavior, on other institutions in society, and on the conditions of human existence generally. Ethics sets the work back into the interrelationships out of which aesthetic interest has taken it.

Aesthetics and ethics are therefore concerned with different properties of the art-object. So it is not too much to say that they are talking about different things. That is why we can speak, without inconsistency or absurdity,

337

of "a beautiful case of cancer" or "an artful thief." These locutions refer both to extrinsic and intrinsic properties.

As we shall see, those who have fought the age-old battle over "art and morality" also insist upon the distinction between aesthetic and moral properties. For each party to the dispute claims that those on the other side ignore salient features of fine art. Those who insist that art is not subject to moral discipline contend that stern-faced, blue-nosed moralizers are either incapable of appreciating art aesthetically or else wilfully ignore its values for contemplation; the moralists consider their opponents either too flighty and unrealistic to recognize the palpable effects of art on human existence or else irresponsible in refusing to regulate these effects for social well-being.

THIS ISSUE DOES NOT SEEM to be so live a question in our own time as it has been in the past. The problem of censorship has not died out, of course. We have seen the workings of rigid censorship in modern totalitarianism. And in our society there have recently been a number of important legal cases involving the censorship of books and movies. The problem is of some importance in both kinds of society for opposite reasons — in totalitarianism, because the preservation of the regime depends upon vigilant control of thought and expression, in democracy, because we place a premium upon individual rights and wish to resist any encroachments upon them. Nevertheless, art is not nearly so important morally, at the present time, as other social institutions and practices. Our society gets far more agitated about the moral aspects of economic activity — "unfair restraint of trade," wages and working conditions, and so on. We hear a great deal about the "ethical codes" of the professions and about such issues as birth control and euthanasia. Politics and the law are hotly debated in moral terms.

If what I have just said is true, *why* is it that "art and morality" has become a relatively secondary issue? This is a very large question in social history, and I can only mention a few of the possible answers.

The first is somewhat discouraging but it probably has a great deal of truth in it, viz., fine art has become a fairly trivial and peripheral activity in contemporary society. It can safely be ignored because it has comparatively little influence on our lives. Political, economic, religious, and national affiliations are infinitely more important. Many therefore share the popular conception of artists and "art lovers" as harmless and eccentric creatures woefully in need of a haircut. The decline in the social importance of art has gone hand in hand with the development of "the compartmental conception of fine art," [1] i.e., art has become dissociated from other im-

---

[1] Dewey, *Art as Experience*, p. 8. All of chap. I of this work can be read with profit in the present connection.

portant social activities such as religion and work. This is not completely true, of course, as hymns, work songs, and national anthems show. But these are not what we generally have in mind when we think of the art of music. We think, rather, of individual composers working on their own (who are rarely able to support themselves by their music alone). And we think of their compositions as objects which do not subserve any social functions, but exist only to be heard.

What of the second term in our problem — "morality"? Two possible considerations can be suggested. The first is that moral standards in our society may have become so relaxed — or lax — that they cannot be harmed by art, even if it were more influential than it is. Depicting illicit sexual behavior or unscrupulous business practices in moving pictures will not greatly disturb a society which tacitly condones or accepts such practices. There is a second hypothesis, which may not be closer to the truth but which is certainly more edifying, viz., our moral standards have not become looser, but rather more tolerant and humane. We are not so inflexible as our Puritan forebears, because we are no longer so certain of the indubitable rightness of our beliefs. We have come to understand the moral systems of other cultures and the reasons why people hold them. And we understand better the causes of crime and delinquency in our own culture. We are therefore not so prone to use the epithet, "immoral," and to take action in the name of morality. Finally, American society is "pluralistic." It embraces a great variety of moral beliefs and practices, and even of whole ways of life. Compare the Greenwich Village bohemian with the members of a mid-Western farm community or with an upper-class suburbanite. A small, tightly knit society will have in common a well-defined moral code. But a complex, heterogeneous culture like our own must embrace a great many different codes. "Morality" means too many things to too many people. It cannot be used to enlist popular interest in criticizing and censoring art.

For these and doubtless other reasons, "art and morality" is not a dominant issue for our times. Yet the problem is a perennial one and it is still of some importance. Our analysis of those earlier thinkers who were hotly absorbed in the problem can further our understanding of the present. It will also help us to appreciate more fully the place that art has had in human existence and the role that it might have in future if society were ordered differently.

Although our discussion will be in the area of ethics, it will draw heavily upon our study of aesthetics. We cannot speak intelligently of the relation of art to morality unless we know something of the nature of fine art, of aesthetic perception and how it differs from ordinary experience, and of the value of aesthetic contemplation. Only so can we decide what morality can and cannot justifiably demand of the creative artist and the aesthetic spectator.

339

1. THE ROLE OF ART IN THE GOOD SOCIETY

Plato's *Republic* is the first systematic account of a Utopia in Western thought, but it is still the most important. The *Republic* stands at the head of almost every list of "great books" in our cultural tradition. Written over three hundred years before the Christian era, it has exercised a profound influence to the present day. It has captured men's imaginations and enlisted their allegiance because it sets out in detail a vision which is usually vague and diffuse — the vision of the best possible life for man.

The *Republic* depicts a society in which the conduct of life is not left to chance or caprice. The good life for the individual can only be achieved in the well-ordered society. Hence society is not to be ruled by those who gain power in the usual ways — demagoguery, armed might, etc. Such men do not have the abilities which are indispensable to the guidance of society. Plato's thesis is, in one respect, a simple and even obvious one — only those should rule who are qualified to do so. Man has within himself the capacity to direct life so that his basic ends will be achieved. This is the capacity of reason. The knowledge which it gives of what is genuinely good for man can rescue us from the blind, short-sighted, and ultimately self-defeating choices which we make in our quest for happiness. Hence, let those rule the state who have rational knowledge of what is best for it. Plato's Republic is a society ruled by the wise — the famous "philosopher-kings" — in the interest of the well-being of all its members. The *Republic* spells out the vision of "the life of reason." At the same time, it reiterates the grave reminder that only the rational life can, ultimately, be the happy life.

The *Republic* is, at a number of places, extremely abstract, sometimes even mystical. A great deal of the book, however, is devoted to concrete, everyday concerns such as education and marriage. Plato shows in detail how the rule of the philosopher-kings is to be exercised. Some of his specific proposals do not sit well with many modern readers. For example, political power is vested solely in the philosophical rulers, who make up the smallest class in the Republic; they are not permitted to have families or own property; the program of education is rigidly planned and enforced; those who are physically or mentally incapacitated are to be put to death. Socrates, who is Plato's spokesman, meets objections to such proposals by pointing out that "our aim in founding the commonwealth [is] to secure the greatest possible happiness for the community as a whole." [2] This must always be kept in mind: if it is indeed the case that life in the Republic is the best possible life for man, then we must accept what seems to us to be distasteful

[2] 420 (p. 110). All quotations from the *Republic* in this chapter will be identified by the standard pagination followed, in parentheses, by the page reference in the Cornford translation (New York: Oxford University Press, 1950).

in it. For, if Plato is right, consider how much more we lose, in futility and unhappiness, when life is not guided by reason.

Plato's proposals for the arts are especially unpalatable to the modern reader. For he advocates a program of regulation of art which is as stern and rigid as any in Western thought. There is a famous passage in the *Republic* in which Plato tells what he would do with any artist who refused to submit to social regulation:

> [We] shall tell him that we are not allowed to have any such person in our commonwealth; we shall crown him with fillets of wool, anoint his head with myrrh, and conduct him to the borders of some other country.[3]

Not only does Plato banish these artists from the Republic (note that he does not ban *all* artists, as is sometimes said of him); he speaks of such artists with lacerating scorn. His sarcasm in the passage just quoted is obvious; just prior to this passage he calls the artists "clever" and "miraculous." Plato, in his passionate defense of the life of reason, inveighs against many sorts of folly and wickedness. But he reserves his most bitter satire for the artists.

Those readers who are not repelled by this are puzzled by it. Why does Plato get so excited about the artists, of all people? Are there not far more serious threats to the Republic? And there is another reason for puzzlement. If the artists were banished by some dry-as-dust philosopher, by some thinker who had no aesthetic sensitivity, we could understand even if we did not approve. But Plato is not only a great philosopher; he is also, by common consent, a great artist. His dialogues, particularly those of the early and middle periods, are literary masterworks of a high order. They have great charm, imagination, dramatic power, and clarity of form. How could a great artist, living moreover in one of the most creative epochs in history, condemn his fellow artists so unremittingly?

THE FIRST THING TO SEE is that Plato takes the arts very seriously. We spoke a moment ago of the relative unimportance of the arts in contemporary society and I mentioned the dissociation of art from other social functions. In Athenian society, however, at the time that Plato lived, the arts were a major social force. Their influence was so pervasive, indeed, that the Greeks did not draw the modern distinction between the "fine arts" and the arts of utility. Moreover, literature, music, and the dance were closely allied to religion and education. The classic poets, Homer and Hesiod, were important sources of moral and religious belief. It was because the arts had very great influence, and because Plato thought that their influence was mostly for the bad, that he proposed such stern measures in the *Republic*.

[3] 397 (p. 85).

341

Crucial to the ideal state is the education of the young. During childhood character is formed which will determine a man's behavior throughout his life. If the young are to grow up to be worthy members of the commonwealth, the earliest influences upon them must be wholesome ones. Hence their education must be carefully supervised. But in Plato's Athens the children were exposed to Homer and Hesiod, who depicted all manner of evil behavior in the gods and in the heroes of antiquity. The effects upon the impressionable child are bound to be corrupting. If his character and therefore his whole future well-being are at stake, must there not be some controls over what he is permitted to read? "[Shall] we simply allow our children to listen to any stories that anyone happens to make up, and to receive into their minds ideas often the very opposite of those we shall think they ought to have when they are grown up?" [4] Platonic censorship is often criticized as an abridgment of freedom. It obviously does limit choice. But what sort of "freedom" is it which leads to corruption of character and undermines the well-being of society? That is Plato's rejoinder. Even the most ardent lover of "freedom" must take it seriously.

Plato would not have adults, any more than children, exposed to works of art whose subject matter is ignoble.[5] Ultimately, the range of permissible subject matter is severely limited: "[We] can admit into our commonwealth only the poetry which celebrates the praises of the gods and of good men." [6]

The moral criticism of art can be directed most readily against subject matter. The most obvious way in which art can be immoral is just by showing us immoral behavior. But Plato's strictures do not stop with subject matter. Every other dimension of art — sensory material, form, and expression — falls under his critique.

Plato recognizes that the materials of art can be the source of great sensuous pleasure. Again, he is not unaware of the power of art. But sensory pleasure is not enough to justify art. We must consider the role of art in the total pattern of existence. Those who would defend poetry must show that "she is no mere source of pleasure but a benefit to society and to human life." [7] Indeed its very capacity to give pleasure only increases the dangerousness of art. For men will be more likely to respond to art and therefore to be influenced by it when the work charms them.

Musical rhythms and other modes of form leave their imprint upon the soul. Forms which are slack and undisciplined are therefore justifiably censored. Plato will admit only "rhythms appropriate to a life of courage and self-control." [8] He bars those musical compositions which are expressive of

[4] 377 (p. 69).
[5] 379 (p. 72).
[6] 606 (p. 339); cf. *Laws* 829.
[7] 607 (p. 340); cf. *Laws* 655.
[8] 400 (p. 88).

"drunkenness, effeminacy, and inactivity." [9]

It is not just certain kinds of expressive effect that are morally important. If the work is expressive at all, it will arouse emotion. The popular artist of Plato's day, like those of our own, sought to play upon the audience's emotions. Their work enabled the spectator to enjoy what we now call "a good cry." But the life of reason requires that emotions should be kept under rational control. Emotions are not to be suppressed altogether; Plato is not an ascetic. But they should not be immoderate or uncontrollable. If they are, then they destroy the rule of reason and therefore undermine human happiness. Just here the arts come under moral judgment. Poetry "waters the growth of the passions which should be allowed to wither away and sets them up in control." [10] Once again, it is the carry-over from aesthetic experience to the rest of life that troubles Plato. If we indulge our emotions while watching a play, our total character is influenced for the worse. "[The] emotions of pity our sympathy has strengthened will not be easy to restrain when we are suffering ourselves." [11]

The artists cannot be trusted to discipline their own works. They are oblivious to the larger issues of social well-being, for they are generally interested only in "audience appeal." Even if they are not, they are irrational beings. Their creative activity is a kind of "madness." [12] Hence their works are not to be made available to the public until they have been examined and approved by those who are responsible for the community. [13] Nor can artists have the freedom to experiment with new forms and styles. Once certain artistic forms have been found to be morally beneficial, no innovations will be permitted. [14]

Taking all these proposals together, you will see how narrowly Plato limits artistic and aesthetic freedom. But though he takes away a great deal, he does not replace it merely with a small number of morally "wholesome" works. You will not understand his theory if you think that. For Plato holds up the ideal of a whole way of life which will possess aesthetic quality. The citizens of the Republic will dwell in an environment which is suffused with grace and harmony. There aesthetic properties are not to be confined to what we call the "fine arts." They can be instilled everywhere — "in every sort of workmanship, such as painting, weaving, embroidery, architecture, the making of furniture." [15] The rulers of the state will not permit "baseness, licence, meanness, unseemliness" [16] in any product of

[9] 398 (p. 86).
[10] 605 (pp. 338–339).
[11] 605 (p. 338).
[12] *Phaedrus* 245, *Ion* 533–534.
[13] *Laws* 801.
[14] *Republic* 424 (p. 115), *Laws* 798–799.
[15] 400 (p. 89).
[16] 401 (p. 90).

human skill. Before we pass judgment on Plato, we should stop to think of all that is tawdry and "phony" in the "commercial" art and the everyday implements of our society.

Just as artistic baseness corrupts the soul, so order and charm refine the soul. The young people will live and move in an environment in which they "may drink in good from every quarter, whence . . . some influence from noble works constantly falls upon eye and ear." [17] When Plato speaks of "good" here, he does not mean *aesthetic* value solely. Like the Greeks generally, he did not have the modern conception of "the aesthetic" as a distinct category. Rather, he tends to identify moral and aesthetic values for they have in common order and harmony.[18] So when the young "drink in good" from all of the objects with which they have commerce, their moral character is being improved. They are developing within themselves the psychological balance which is essential to the virtuous and happy life. "[Rhythm] and harmony sink deep into the recesses of the soul and take the strongest hold there, bringing . . . grace of body and mind." [19]

YET THIS WILL PROBABLY NOT SATISFY the modern reader. He will probably say, "It is all very well to talk about 'noble works' and how they improve the soul. But what about all the rest of Plato's theory? He has handcuffed the artist and has placed severe restrictions on aesthetic appreciation. In the name of 'morality' and 'the interests of the state' (that has an ominous ring to modern ears), he has robbed us of some of our most precious values."

If this is the criticism, then there is one thing above all that we must get clear about. What precisely is being objected to? There are two possibilities: (1) Is the objection to *any* moral criticism and social control of art? Or (2) is it to the *particular* program of social regulation that Plato sets forth?

(1) We live in an age and in a society which put a premium on individual liberty. The reader may therefore be expected to bridle at Plato's theory. But here as elsewhere in philosophy, we must examine our beliefs critically; those which we hold with the greatest conviction must probably be examined with the greatest care. Does our belief in artistic and aesthetic liberty commit us to the view that there should be *no* limitations on art? How can we defend this view against Plato?

What Plato is saying comes to this: The good life can be achieved only if we act in the light of reason. It will not come by chance or as the result of irrational choices. All of our activities must therefore be subjected to rational control. Any activities which destroy "the health of the soul," in Plato's metaphor, can and ought to be censured morally. They create indi-

[17] 401 (p. 90).
[18] *Philebus* 64, *Lysis* 216.
[19] *Republic* 401 (p. 90).

vidual unhappiness and social instability. Such an activity obstructs the fulfillment of man's ideals. This is enough to condemn it.

The moral supervision of life embraces all major social institutions. Do we not, in our own time, think that marriage and family life, working conditions, the educational system, are subject to at least some degree of social control? Then why not art also? Why should art have special privilege like no other institution? As Plato puts it, at the close of the *Republic:* "[Much] is at stake, more than most people suppose: it is a choice between becoming a good man or a bad; and poetry, no more than wealth or power or honours, should tempt us to be careless of justice and virtue." [20]

If we could seal off poetry and the other arts from the rest of life, then Plato would probably withdraw his objections. But the whole force of his argument rests on the fact that we cannot do so. Reading a poem or listening to music influences character, particularly in the young. Even in our own age, which has "compartmentalized" art to a great extent, we recognize this fact. Do we not keep children from reading certain books and seeing certain moving pictures? It is crucial to the aesthetic attitude that it is concerned only with the present object of awareness. But the effects of aesthetic perception go beyond the aesthetic experience itself. A man who wishes a blueprint of the ideal society is not an aesthetic percipient. He must take account of the personal and social consequences of art even if the percipient does not.

(2) However, even if we accept the need for *some* regulation of art, we may still reject the specific program presented by Plato. *If* it could be demonstrated, as Plato attempted to do, that the Republic was indeed the best possible life for man, then presumably we would have to abide by the censorship and all the rest. Is this too great a price to pay for the ideal? We would say, with Will Rogers, "The best is good enough for me."

Many critics, however, think that Plato has failed to make out his case. In general, they contend either that the Republic could not be achieved in actual practice or that, even if it were established, it would be a less than ideal social order. It would take us too far afield to go into their arguments. We must therefore consider Plato's proposals for art in themselves.

The proposal for rigid censorship is one of the things that make Plato's critics skeptical about life in the Republic. We have had more than our share of totalitarianisms in the twentieth century. Everyday life in these societies is often reported to be dismally gray and drab. This pervasive dullness is almost as frightening as the persecutions and loss of liberty. The Republic is not likely to be immune to it. The subject matter, forms, and styles of art are severely circumscribed. How much of the felt quality of living must be lost as a result! The artist's far-ranging imagination, when it is permitted to go free, brings zest and novelty into our lives. Art in the

[20] 607 (p. 340).

Republic is highly traditionalized. Would it not become dull and stuffy? We know how often this is true of patriotic and didactic art. We can point to recent painting in the Soviet Union, which is largely devoted to celebrating the heroes and historic events of the revolution, and the sterile art produced in Nazi Germany. A vigorous and enriching poetry can hardly arise if it is limited to "praises of the gods and of good men."

So there would almost certainly be a great, indeed, an incalculable loss in the felt values of aesthetic enjoyment. This is on the side of the aesthetic spectator. Platonic censorship is, if anything, even more deadening to the artist. He has both the capacities and the desire for creative activity. The working out and fulfillment of his abilities is vital to him. His personality must necessarily be stunted if he cannot give free play to his creative ideas. To thwart creative desires is to arrest human development. For some artists, it would be like depriving them of air or food. Moreover, he is kept from a fruitful relationship with one of the most important influences upon his development — his audience. Discriminating response and criticism are often invaluable aids to artistic self-criticism and therefore to artistic improvement. The audience enables the artist to measure his successes and failures. In the Republic, however, we could not expect the audience to serve this function. Its tastes would necessarily be narrow. For taste can be catholic only when the percipient is exposed to a variety of art-objects. It is not unlikely that, as a result of censorship, taste would become crude and undiscriminating. And if the artist must submit his work to censors before it can be publicized, his most daring inventions will probably not be put to the test of audience response.

Plato's ban on innovation is one of his most crippling restrictions on art. Fine art thrives upon experimentation. The artist's restless dissatisfaction with tradition leads to the development of new forms, such as the novel and tone poem, and new styles. Think of how much would have been lost to human culture if Plato's proposal had been put into effect at any point in the history of art. We must grant that some of our greatest art has been created by using traditionalized forms and styles. We must also concede that in our own time there has been too much artistic indulgence in novelty-for-novelty's-sake. It remains true, however, that a perennially static art would paralyze the artist and impoverish the spectator.

Plato is so much concerned about the long-range consequences of art that he seems to have lost sight of its power to enrich immediate experience. He certainly recognizes that art can stimulate emotion and imagination, but he writes this off as "pleasure" or the "watering of the passions." He ignores the intrinsic value of aesthetic response.

The clearest indication of this, perhaps, is not found in Plato's proposals themselves, but in the spirit in which he advances them. Even on the most charitable interpretation of his theory, even assuming that the censors will be surpassingly humane and rational, we have seen that art will suffer a great loss. Yet Plato never seems to be grieved by the loss. He turns aside this objection on the few occasions in the dialogue when it is brought up. A man who would deprive life of so much of its richness must show us that he understands how much is being given up. He must show regret and compunction. I do not think, however, that Plato does so. It must therefore be asked whether he sees with what right art can demand its place in the sun. There is no question that Plato is aware of the claims of morality to order human life for the sake of human happiness. But the whole problem of "art and morality" is to consider the claims of morality *and* those of art, to set them against each other and to give each their due, not to let the one simply override the other. Plato's attitude toward the arts, which is sometimes casual and sometimes callous, shows the lack of balance and fairness in his theory.

Later in this chapter (sec. 3), we will see whether a more viable theory of moral regulation can be worked out.

THE PARADOX OF A GREAT ARTIST passing severe and even harsh judgment on the arts confronts us again in the eminent novelist, Leo Tolstoy. At the close of *What Is Art?* he asks whether it would be better to have all of modern art, both good and bad, or no art at all. He answers: "I think that every reasonable and moral man would again decide the question as Plato decided it for his *Republic.* . . . Rather let there be no art at all." [21]

Some of Tolstoy's strictures on art parallel those of Plato. From these two influential thinkers we can learn how the moralistic indictment of art has usually been carried out. Tolstoy condemns art whose subject matter is unworthy or ignoble, and which therefore arouses emotions which ought to be suppressed. Thus he finds that a great deal of modern art feeds upon the feelings of "pride, sexual desire, and weariness of life." [22] Moreover, the nineteenth century, like the period in which Plato lived, was a time of great ferment and innovation in the arts. Tolstoy, like Plato, strongly condemns the development of new artistic forms.[23] Like Plato again, Tolstoy rejects the idea that art exists to give pleasure. He considers it the basic error of all art since the Renaissance that it has dedicated itself to this alone.[24] The modern world calls "beautiful" whatever gives disinterested pleasure, but beauty does not justify itself. It must be measured against the demands of morality. "The more utterly we surrender ourselves to beauty the farther we depart from goodness." [25] We shall see in a moment the grounds on which Tolstoy rests these criticisms.

[21] *Op. cit.*, pp. 261, 262.
[22] *Ibid.*, p. 152.
[23] *Ibid.*, chap. X.
[24] *Ibid.*, p. 235.
[25] *Ibid.*, p. 141 n.

However, one of Tolstoy's criticisms, the one which he probably felt most deeply of all, is not to be found in Plato. It reflects a deep concern for and a profound love of "the common man," an attitude which is more characteristic of the modern world than of antiquity. Tolstoy over and over again denounces "the waste of priceless human lives" [26] in artistic pursuits. First, the artists themselves fritter away their lives in trying to gain mastery over their medium and in creation. Students of all the arts must spend endless hours in practice and rehearsal. They become "so demoralized that they are no longer fit for anything but to blow trumpets and walk about with halberds and in yellow shoes." [27] But more important, the performance and display of works of art necessitates endless labor by those who are not themselves artists. Some of these people work in allied crafts — stage setting, printing, etc. Far more, however, do not have even an indirect relation to the arts. They are the working people who provide the economic base on which art rests. They produce the necessities of living. The artist, who is not productive as they are, is therefore socially parasitic: "[Fine] art can arise only on the slavery of the masses of the people." [28]

This criticism may strike some readers as inept or unintelligent. "Of course," they will say, "artists must work hard at their jobs. But this is no argument. Think of what they produce, of how much they contribute to culture. Certainly their labor justifies itself many times over. And as to the charge that art is an economic luxury, what would be gained by diverting artists to 'productive' work? Art is the sort of 'luxury' without which life would hardly be worth living."

This rebuttal to Tolstoy presupposes the value and dignity of fine art. But that assumption is just the point at issue. Tolstoy, like all major social critics, refuses to accept what the society of his time takes for granted. He insists upon raising "the question whether it is true that art is so good and so important an affair." [29] He answers in terms of his conception of the proper function of art. On his view, most of modern art stands condemned. Hence, if his view is tenable, the rebuttal loses its force.

WE HAVE ALREADY STUDIED one aspect of Tolstoy's theory of art.[30] We have seen that art is, for him, the deliberate communication of emotion from the artist to the spectator, and that the degree of "infectiousness" measures the value of art. This says nothing as to the particular emotions which are transmitted by art. Tolstoy, as we have found, recognizes that these emotions can be highly diverse. All of this is consistent with the

[26] *Ibid.*, p. 252.
[27] *Ibid.*, p. 77.
[28] *Ibid.*, p. 146.
[29] *Ibid.*, p. 81.
[30] Cf. above, pp. 173 ff.

aesthetic conception of art, i.e., considering the work as an object of disinterested attention and evaluating it by what is felt during the aesthetic transaction. But when we turn to Tolstoy's moral conception of art, the aesthetic significance of the work recedes or even disappears.

Like all moral critics, Tolstoy sees art in its social setting. He holds that the greatest art has always been that which reflects the "religious perception" [31] of its time. Tolstoy uses "religious" to refer to a sense of "the meaning of life" [32] and its ideals. Art can play a vital role in disseminating religion. Since it is, uniquely, the "language of the emotions," it can communicate those emotions which are bound up with the ideals of an age. "[Feelings] less kind and less necessary for the well-being of mankind [must be] replaced by others kinder and more needful for that end. That," Tolstoy says, "is the purpose of art." [33] Now art is taken to be a vehicle of social and moral improvement.

But most of modern art has failed on this score. Instead of transmitting "the highest and best feelings," [34] it has devoted itself simply to giving pleasure. To achieve this goal, it has capitalized on such emotions as those associated with sex. Modern art has turned its back on what Tolstoy takes to be the central "religious perception" of our time — the brotherhood of all men united in love and equal before the God of Christianity. "The task for art to accomplish," according to Tolstoy, is to make the feeling of mutual love "the customary feeling and the instinct of all men." [35] Therefore only two kinds of emotion can be admitted into art — those of Christianity and "the simple feelings of common life accessible to every one without exception." [36] As we saw in our earlier discussion, Tolstoy holds that such art can be appreciated by all without training or familiarization, and without the help of art criticism. Such art can bring men together.

The moral or "religious" influence of art is the measure of its goodness. Tolstoy applies this criterion unremittingly, and with consequences that have dismayed most of his readers. Baudelaire in poetry, the Impressionists in painting, Wagner, Brahms, and Richard Strauss in music, are condemned,[37] chiefly because the novelty or obscurity of their work make them emotionally inaccessible to the common man. Tolstoy rejects such masterworks as *Don Quixote* and *Pickwick*, but he would keep *Uncle Tom's Cabin*.[38] The one judgment which has probably caused more howling than any other is that which Tolstoy passes on Beethoven's Ninth Symphony — he holds "indubitably" that it "is not a good work of art." [39] I SAID, in criticizing Plato, that the claims of morality and those of art must

---

[31] *Op. cit.*, p. 125.
[33] *Ibid.*, p. 231.
[35] *Ibid.*, p. 288.
[37] *Ibid.*, chap. X.
[39] *Ibid.*, p. 248.

[32] *Ibid.*, pp. 127 ff.
[34] *Ibid.*, p. 143.
[36] *Ibid.*, p. 240.
[38] *Ibid.*, p. 242.

both be respected, and that one should not lead us simply to ignore the other. I want to take the same line in criticizing Tolstoy. Because of the similarities between the two theories, the analysis of Tolstoy can proceed more rapidly.

Here, as with Plato, we need not disparage the moral claim. We will probably all agree that the brotherhood of man is no mean ideal. Perhaps it has even more pertinence now than when Tolstoy wrote, half a century ago. If we accept it as an ideal, then we are constrained to accept all means to this end. Therefore we must approve and encourage all art which brings men together in common loyalty and love.

But then we are approving such works on *moral* grounds. Art can, however, be evaluated on *other* grounds, and one of the most important of these is *aesthetic* value. There is no contradiction in saying that one and the same work is both morally beneficial and aesthetically trivial or inferior. Indeed, many of the simple and sentimental works for which Tolstoy contends are like this.

At the close of *What Is Art?* Tolstoy says: "All that I have written I have written with the sole purpose of finding a clear and reasonable criterion by which to judge the merits of works of art." [40] But *which* "merits"? Certainly not the merits of the work as an object of disinterested contemplation. Tolstoy thinks of nothing but the *effects* of the work in inculcating certain emotions. Even more than Plato, he is oblivious to the *intrinsic* significance of art. That is the basic reason why we are so dismayed by Tolstoy's condemnation of specific works — Beethoven's "Ninth," *Don Quixote,* and also, be it noted, his own great novels. Even if we happen not to share the usual opinion of these works, we feel that Tolstoy is rejecting them for wrong or gratuitous reasons.

If Tolstoy is one-sided in his neglect of the aesthetic value of art, he is equally one-sided, at the other extreme, in exaggerating the moral influence of art. He says, in the sentence which I have already quoted, that art must make brotherly love "the customary feeling and the instinct of all men." Thereby art will break down the barriers which keep men apart. Tolstoy therefore proposes, as we have seen, two kinds of art — that which expresses the emotions of Christianity and that which expresses "the simple feelings of common life."

But how will such art work its influence upon the spectator? Suppose he feels these emotions during the aesthetic experience. Does it follow necessarily that these emotions will be uppermost when he makes moral choices and, in general, lives a certain kind of life in his nonaesthetic experience? Merely to be *exposed* to the emotions of Christianity and "common life" does not guarantee that they will become "the instinct" upon which we act. Here we must remind ourselves of the nature of the aesthetic attitude,

[40] *Ibid.,* p. 248.

even if Tolstoy has forgotten it. Implicit in this attitude is a sense of detachment from practical concerns. Hence it is not likely that art will have such a direct impact upon character as moral or religious exhortation. The latter are professedly concerned with "life," with specific deeds and traits of character. Since morality, politics, and religion are of practical importance to the spectator, he can be impelled by their propaganda to storm the barricades or transform his way of life. But there is no such involvement in art. And if the work seems clearly to be moralizing or propagandizing, we will lose our aesthetic interest in it.

Our "belief" in the work was described in the previous chapter as "provisional acceptance." [41] That is why we can appreciate both Christian and atheistic works, or those which express "common" emotions and those which express rare and exotic emotions. Works of art express an enormous diversity of ideals and emotions which we could not possibly carry over into our moral lives. We act upon what we "really" believe, not what we have "accepted" for the sake of aesthetic perception. Tolstoy's case might be stronger if he advocated the public display of *only* those works which communicated the "highest and best feelings." Repeated exposure to such works would probably have much greater psychological effect upon the audience, as Plato believed. However Tolstoy, unlike Plato, rejected censorship, which he calls "an immoral and irrational institution." [42] (It is worth noting that Tolstoy himself, like most of the great Russian writers of the nineteenth century, suffered from the severe censorship practiced at that time.)

Finally, Tolstoy overestimates the power of art because he neglects all of the other forces which make for social solidarity or hostility in the modern world. For good or ill, it certainly seems to be true that art has far less influence on the affairs of men than economic, political, racial, and religious factors. A man steeped in one of the Eastern religions may well appreciate a work expressing the Christian faith. But it is quite another thing for him to abandon his traditional faith as a result. Similarly, the racial hatreds and economic rivalries which divide men are ignored by Tolstoy. Such symbols as flags, slogans, and national stereotypes are carriers of emotion far more potent than art-objects. A realistic program for realizing Tolstoy's ideal would have to take account of all of the factors which Tolstoy simply leaves out.

What Is Art? remains one of the oddest books in the literature of aesthetics and ethics. It is magnificently wrong-headed, in its exclusion of the aesthetic values of art and in its exaggeration of art's moral import. Yet it is the testament of a visionary and saint-like old man, proclaiming the good society for all.

[41] Cf. above, p. 333.
[42] *Op. cit.*, p. 65.

2. "LIFE FOR ART'S SAKE"

You have undoubtedly heard the phrase "Art for art's sake." This phrase was first used at the beginning of the nineteenth century. It summed up epigrammatically the concept which has dominated a great deal of modern aesthetics — that of aesthetic disinterestedness.[43] "Art for art's sake" says that the work exists to be appreciated for its own sake and for no other purpose. Hence it is a protest against those who would make art subservient to some other goal. It is directed against the moralist, like Plato and Tolstoy, who emphasizes the psychological and social consequences of art. It announces the liberation of art from didacticism and propaganda: "There is no such thing as a moral or an immoral book. Books are well written, or badly written. That is all." [44] "Art for art's sake" is also a rejoinder to those who charge that art is "useless." Why should art be good *for* something when it is good *in itself?* Particularly when those who insist upon "usefulness" speak for a gadget-minded culture which is essentially ugly and barren. "Art for art's sake" was a rallying cry for artists and critics who were rebelling against the commercialism of their times. They opposed to the endless round of money-grubbing and practical ambition the only activity which seemed to them to make sense — the direct, self-sufficient enjoyment of aesthetic value. Hence they flaunted the "uselessness" of art: "Art is freedom, luxury, flowering, the blooming of the soul in indolence. Painting, sculpture, and music serve absolutely nothing." [45]

"Art for art's sake" helps to restore the balance which was upset by Plato and Tolstoy. To insist that the arts "serve absolutely nothing" is a corrective to thinking of art as a *useful* device of moral betterment. Our attention is returned to the intrinsic worth of fine art.

So far, "Art for art's sake" is a defence of the aesthetic experiencing of art. But "Art for art's sake" came to mean more than this. It came to stand for a whole way of life. At this point, it becomes one of the theories of "art and morality."

PLATO AND TOLSTOY have their own conceptions of the good life for man. They subordinate the aesthetic value of art to this ideal. "Art for art's sake" in its broader meaning also sets up an ideal for life. It is an ideal of almost childlike simplicity — the good life is one in which each moment of experience is lived richly and intensely, and is therefore good in the very having. Hence the model of the good life is the aesthetic experience.

[43] John Wilcox, "The Beginnings of L'Art pour L'Art," *Journal of Aesthetics and Art Criticism,* XI (1953), 360-361.

[44] Oscar Wilde, Preface to *The Picture of Dorian Gray,* in *The Portable Oscar Wilde,* ed. Aldington (New York: Viking, 1957), p. 138.

[45] Gautier (1832), quoted in Wilcox, *op. cit.,* p. 371.

"Art for art's sake" has now become "life for art's sake,"or, more specifically, life devoted to intrinsic enjoyment.

When life is practical, the present is subordinated to the future. One looks forward, hopefully or covetously. Each day is lived with an eye to what it may yield later on. But then the whole day can go by with "no measure danced." And all one's days can be consumed in the endless pursuit of what is yet to come. Or, what is even worse, the present can be sacrificed, not to the future, but to dull and zestless routine. We move about unseeingly in a world which has become habitual and overly familiar.[46] The sights and sounds and forms which surround us lose their excitement.

Then it is time to be reminded that life should be good in the very living of it. This is what the movement of "Art for art's sake" announced to the industrial culture of the nineteenth century. We must see and hear zestfully, we must *live* vitally and feelingly.

The most eloquent statement of this credo appears at the close of the century, in the famous "Conclusion" to Walter Pater's *The Renaissance*. How many generations of young people have been moved by this essay! It is the sort of thing that is best when discovered by oneself. However I will quote the best-known passages, leaving it to the student to read the entire essay if he finds this sampling attractive:

> "Not the fruit of experience, but experience itself, is the end. . . . To burn always with this hard, gemlike flame, to maintain this ecstasy, is success in life. . . . While all melts under our feet, we may well grasp at any exquisite passion . . . that seems by a lifted horizon to set the spirit free for a moment, or any stirring of the senses. [Our] one chance lies . . . in getting as many pulsations as possible into the given time." The finest source of such experience is "the love of art for its own sake. . . . For art comes to you proposing frankly to give nothing but the highest quality to your moments as they pass, and simply for those moments' sake." [47]

This, on the theory of "Life for art's sake," is the rejoinder to Plato's charge that art corrupts and Tolstoy's charge that art is wasteful. Art justifies its existence as nothing else can. "[If] aesthetic activity is itself directly satisfactory, instead of seeking ulterior justification, it is in the clear position of needing none. It is in fact the very type of the only sort of thing that ever justifies anything else." [48]

In these terms the formalist, Clive Bell, returns a firm answer to the problem of "art and morality": "Art is above morals, or, rather, all art is moral because . . . works of art are immediate means to good. Once we have

---

[46] Cf. above, chap. 2, sec. 3.

[47] Walter Pater, *The Renaissance* (New York: Modern Library, n.d.), pp. 197, 198, 199.

[48] Prall, *Aesthetic Judgment*, p. 13.

judged a thing a work of art, we have judged it ethically of the first importance and put it beyond the reach of the moralist. . . . Art is good because it exalts to a state of ecstasy better far than anything a benumbed moralist can even guess at; so shut up." [49]

IN DISCUSSING PLATO AND TOLSTOY, I granted the validity of their moral ideals, but I tried to argue that they neglect the intrinsic values of aesthetic experience. In the present theory, just these values become the moral ideal itself. Can this view be argued against without contradicting the earlier criticism?

Note first that Pater, in his famous last sentence, speaks of the "moments" of living. His view of life stresses the goodness of each individual "moment"; he wishes to crowd "as many pulsations as possible" into life. Since the model of life is aesthetic, each moment is taken to be self-contained and independent. If it is rich and vital, then it justifies itself.

But now we must call Plato to mind. We must remind ourselves that each moment interacts with and has consequences for the next, and indeed, for all the rest of life. So far as each moment has causal influences, it is *not* self-contained, even though the aesthetic spectator may forget this. What is experienced in a moment is passing or, precisely, "momentary." But there is all the rest of a man's life to be lived. And there are the interrelations between any given moment and the lives of others who are affected by it. Then a moment can be good in the very having and bad or even disastrous in its consequences.

"Life for art's sake" is fixated upon the present and therefore sees life as a series of unrelated experiences. Yet if it is a fact that our experiences bear upon each other, then it is simple prudence to take thought for the morrow. A man could dwell upon the quality of the present while the whole structure of his life was disintegrating. Shakespeare's Richard II does just this. Aesthetic absorption could lead to the neglect of family duties or obligations to one's country or the development of oneself as an informed and responsible human being. Bell says that art is so good in itself that "we need not trouble ourselves about any other of its possible consequences." [50] But I find it difficult to believe that wisdom speaks here. As we have all learned to our distress, if we do not "trouble ourselves" about the consequences of an experience, they will often arise to trouble us when it is too late to do anything about them.

Santayana puts it this way:

Every impulse, not the aesthetic mood alone, is innocent and irresponsible in its origin and precious in its own eyes; but every impulse or indulgence,

[49] *Art*, pp. 20, 106.
[50] *Ibid.*, p. 115.

including the aesthetic, is evil in its effect, when it renders harmony impossible in the general tenor of life, or produces in the soul division and ruin.[51]

Morality, in the sense of thoughtful concern for long-range consequences, is needed to avert such evil effects. It is idle to attempt to shake off morality. In saying this, I am not denying the intrinsic goodness of aesthetic experience. I have insisted upon this goodness over and over again in the course of this book. But it does not follow, as Bell has it, that art is "beyond the reach of the moralist." Plato and Tolstoy may emphasize too much the moral supervision of life and thereby deprive experience of its richness and zest. It is, however, simply trading one monomania for another to try to exempt art and aesthetic experience from all moral control.

The view that all experience should be approached and evaluated aesthetically I would call "the fallacy of aestheticism." There are many times — in a world where human values are often so precarious, all too many times — when other and more important issues than aesthetic quality are at stake. It is almost as irrational to exalt the aesthetic above all else as it is to exalt money-making or inherited traditions above all else.

Ibsen's dramatic heroine, Hedda Gabler, is a diseased and disordered personality. When she urges the promising young scholar, Lövborg, to kill himself, she says: ". . . listen to me. — Will you not try to — to do it beautifully?" [52] And her first thought, when she learns of his suicide, is to ask whether he shot himself "in the temple," i.e., "beautifully." [53] You may find this absurd or pathetic or disgusting. But no matter which, it is clear that the demand for "beauty" above all is not always self-justifying or good. Nor need we go to fiction to illustrate the argument. We have the testimony of the consummate end-of-the-century aesthete, Oscar Wilde. After he had been humbled by his trial and while in prison, he wrote an acute critique of his earlier way of life. In his former life, he says, he "treated art as the supreme reality and life as a mere mode of fiction." [54] The hollowness and disorganization of aestheticism as a way of life have never been more powerfully exhibited.

"Life for art's sake" reminds us of what we too often forget — that life is not worth living unless it issues in intrinsic delight. As the philosopher Spinoza puts it, in a wonderful sentence, "There cannot be too much joy." But the theory is self-defeating when it repudiates all concern for the consequences of our experience. Only with more good luck than any man has a right to expect could the aesthete achieve his values without thoughtful planning. But then he will have to become concerned with instrumentali-

[51] "A General Confession," in *The Philosophy of George Santayana*, pp. 20-21.
[52] Henrik Ibsen, *Hedda Gabler*, trans. Gosse and Archer (New York: Scribners, 1907), p. 150.
[53] *Ibid.*, p. 169.
[54] *De Profundis*, in *The Portable Oscar Wilde*, p. 515.

ties as well as immediacies or, in Pater's terms, with "the fruits of experience" as well as "experience." And even if the gods should smile upon him, the aesthete would be vulnerable to Tolstoy's earnest charge, viz., that he is a parasite on those whose labor make his way of life possible.

We cannot face toward the future while our interest is aesthetic. The moral is not, as the sour moralist has it, that we should never adopt the aesthetic attitude, but rather that the aesthetic attitude is not the *only* one with which we should meet the world.

WE HAVE SEEN THE TENSION between the moral and aesthetic ways of judging the work of art. I now want to show the workings of this conflict in judging one element of the work — its representational subject matter.

Plato, you will remember, criticized the classic poets for describing the vices of the gods. Comparable charges have been made over the centuries to our own day. In the eighteenth century, Hogarth was criticized for painting libertines and prostitutes; [55] in the nineteenth, Flaubert was brought to trial because *Madame Bovary* showed the heroine in adulterous relationships; in the twentieth, moving pictures have been condemned for their licentious or sacrilegious subjects. Morality looks anxiously toward consequences. The argument here is that of Plato — the consequences of seeing such works are harmful, for the moral standards of the percipient are weakened and therefore his behavior will become evil.

There are several possible rejoinders to this argument.

Primarily, it can be pointed out that subject matter is only one element of the work and that it is the *whole* work which must be appreciated and judged aesthetically. If we consider the subject matter alone, we might just as well be talking about the real life "model," for we ignore all that makes the work a distinctive aesthetic object. It is like saying that *Macbeth* is simply a story about a lot of murders. Evil may be depicted in both an inferior and a great work.

This kind of answer does not move the moralist very much. For although Plato criticized sensory matter and form in moral terms and Tolstoy did the same with emotional expression, it is subject matter that the moralist is chiefly concerned with. The sensory elements may be morally innocent; the form may be as "purely" aesthetic as any formalist could wish. But the subject matter is made up of the character and behavior of human beings. And these are things that we describe as "good" and "bad," "right" and "wrong." They therefore have an obvious relevance to our non-aesthetic lives. If we grant that art can be judged morally at all, then we must grant that subject matter is fair game for moral criticism, no matter what may be true of the rest of the work.[56]

[55] Cf. above, p. 131.
[56] Cf. below, p. 363.

The next rejoinder to the moralist also insists that you cannot judge by subject *alone*. But it meets the moralist's charge more directly. For it proceeds to point out that the moral import of the work is also in the moral *attitude* which the artist takes toward evil. Unless the work is obviously didactic, this attitude will be implicit in the work, like artistic "truth." Yet the artist's attitude is usually clear enough. Is there any question that Goya ("The Disasters of War") or Picasso ("Guernica") are *condemning* the brutalities of warfare which they depict? Or that the painter George Grosz is passing bitter judgment on the corruption and debauchery of Germany during the twenties? The artist shows us the face of evil, but only so that he can show us how hateful it is. If we do not abstract the subject matter, and if we consider also the expressed attitude toward it, we can realize how truly *moral* the work is.

This is true even of the most shocking or revolting works. Perhaps the most notorious work of modern literature is Baudelaire's collection of poems, *The Flowers of Evil* (*Les Fleurs du Mal*). It abounds with descriptions of usually unmentionable sexual behavior and of objects which are commonly found to be repulsive. Baudelaire was brought to trial in 1857 and convicted as a result. But his stature as a poet has grown steadily over the last hundred years. We can now see better than his contemporaries that "All he had wanted was . . . to express his loathing of the sin and vice to which man is prone, and his compassion for the misery of his degradation." [57] As Baudelaire had cried, "The book must be judged as a whole, and then there follows a terrifying morality!" [58]

There are, however, two other classes of art-objects: those in which the artist tacitly *approves* evil, and those in which he neither condemns nor approves.

It is difficult to find examples of the former. Works which seem to be examples, like those of Baudelaire or the French novelist, Huysmans, upon analysis turn out to be subtle condemnations of evil. Such works shock the audience out of moral lethargy and thereby strengthen its sensitivity to evil. If there are any works in which the artist condones what both he and his audience believe to be evil, then we are probably forced to say that aesthetic perception demands the "provisional acceptance" of his beliefs. The distinction between aesthetic experiencing and moral judgment must again be applied, however. In judging such art the case for the moralist would seem to be strongest.

A more interesting problem is posed by those works in which the artist depicts vice but withholds judgment upon it. To the moralist such art is incomprehensible or worse. He insists that wickedness must be reproved wherever it arises. Otherwise evil is tolerated and therefore, inevitably,

57 Starkie, *Baudelaire*, p. 320.
58 Quoted, *op. cit.*, p. 320.

encouraged.

At this point the aesthetic mentality is roused to anger. To its way of thinking, the moralist does not understand the function of art. It is not the artist's purpose to pass judgment. Leave that to the judge and the church-man. The artist is trying to catch hold of experience and to render it evocatively, movingly, authentically. Corruption and vice are part of the world. They are of interest in their own right. The artist becomes ab-sorbed by the character of the villain, his dark-hued motives, perhaps the sublime enormity of his malice. He tries to identify himself with villainy and to express what it must feel like.

> As to the poetical Character itself . . . it is not itself — it has no self — it is everything and nothing — It has no character — it enjoys light and shade; it lives in gusto, be it foul or fair, high or low, rich or poor, mean or ele-vated — It has as much delight in conceiving an Iago as an Imogen. What shocks the virtuous philosopher, delights the camelion Poet.[59]

Once again then, the theme of "Art for art's sake" is sounded. The artist-aesthete is "beyond good and evil." He relishes the imaginative and emotional "gusto" of experience, *all* experience. Moral considerations are simply irrelevant.

Shortly before Baudelaire was brought to trial, Flaubert was prosecuted on the grounds of the immorality of *Madame Bovary*. (1857 was obviously a red-letter year for the French descendants of Plato.) Some said, in de-fence of the novel, that the adulterous heroine does, after all, come to a premature and painful death. But for the "Art for art's sake" movement, this is beside the point. Comparable works might show the wrongdoer living happily ever after. The point is that Flaubert was trying to trace the work-ings of a hyperromantic and frustrated personality, confined in a dreary middle-class community. It is difficult to find evidence in the novel that he is either condemning or approving the actions of his heroine. It is as though he were saying, "Emma Bovary is like this," and getting us to under-stand and share her feelings.

3. THE CLAIMS OF ART AND THE CLAIMS OF MORALITY

The second of our concepts, "morality," has many meanings. An ade-quate analysis would require at least as much time as we devoted earlier to the analysis of "art." We must, however, recognize the ambiguity of the term. For the solution which we give to the problem of this chapter will depend upon our understanding of "moral."

[59] Keats, *Letters, loc. cit.,* p. 172.

"Moral" is often used to refer to certain obligations and prohibitions which are of particularly great force, e.g., "Be loyal to your country," "Do not tell lies," and so on. Foreigners sometimes comment that Americans have narrowed down the meaning of the term to sexual behavior, so that "immoral" connotes sexual license. In any event, this first meaning of "moral" restricts its application to only certain areas of human activity. These usually include family relationships, contractual commitments in business, promise-keeping, etc., as well as sexual behavior. Other kinds of activity, which are of less importance, are not subject to moral commandments. Thus the distinction between "manners" and "morals."

Art and aesthetic experience also seem to fall outside the moral domain. We do not usually speak of artistic and aesthetic duties as we speak of the duties involved in being a member of a family, a church, or a nation. If we say that the artist "ought to have used a different medium" or that "you ought to see the play," we do not think that this is a *moral* use of "ought." "Ought" in these sentences lacks the stern and thundering quality of the moral "ought," as in "You ought to tell the truth." Common speech therefore seems to sanction the divorce of art from morality. It seems to imply that in the realm of art and aesthetic enjoyment, we can take a "moral holiday." Some exponents of the "Art for art's sake" movement have used this sort of argument. "Morality," they say, "applies to those who are involved in the workaday activities of family and business life. It does not apply to those who want nothing to do with such activities."

Another meaning of "moral," closely related to the first, identifies it with what society approves. The evidence of social approval is found in the rewards and punishments which are assigned for various actions and traits of character. Given this meaning, too, those who speak for art claim exemption from morality. They claim that the artist is not to be bound by what is conventional or customary. He has vision and daring. Art is liberating, not static. Indeed the artist may deflate traditional morality on behalf of morality in a different and higher sense — an ideal which is not yet commonly accepted in society but which is superior to custom. The novels of Dickens and Thomas Hardy challenge the legal and social practices of their day. More recent novelists have called into question our whole way of life. Morality, in the sense of "social approval," cannot legislate for art.

BUT THERE IS ANOTHER and more catholic meaning of "morality." The late Ralph Barton Perry explicates this meaning and then attempts to show how the moral regulation of art can be justified. Perry notes that his view is closely similar to Plato's in the *Republic*.[60] However the reader who is alienated by Plato's harsh censoriousness will probably find Perry more palatable.

To begin with, anything whatever is "good" for Perry if "interest" is

[60] Ralph Barton Perry, *The Moral Economy* (New York: Scribners, 1909), p. 191.

taken in it, i.e., if it is an object of striving or desire. Any one interest, taken in isolation, is as morally innocent as a baby's curiosity or hunger. But our desires do *not* exist in isolation. They interact with each other. Most important, they often *conflict* with each other. Having one desire may involve the frustration of another. Thus what is good, taken by itself, may be bad in its interrelations. "[The] goodness of action cannot be judged without reference to all the interests affected, whether directly or indirectly." [61] If our interests were left to work themselves out without control or moderation, the results would be ruinous. The strongest desire is often the most destructive.

At this point, morality arises. "Morality is simply the forced choice between suicide and abundant life. When interests war against one another they render the project of life, at best a hard adventure, futile and abortive." [62]

It is the function of morality to minimize (it is never possible to eliminate wholly) the "war" of interests "against one another." Morality organizes interests so that they become "coherent and united." [63] It restrains those desires which threaten other desires. Moreover, it establishes a "community" of interests, within which they mutually support and reinforce each other. Thus the fulfillment of one interest not only does not impede, but actually contributes to the fulfillment of another. Therefore an object of interest is "*morally* good" only "when the interest is endorsed by other interests." [64]

Morality in Perry's sense is not restricted to certain areas of activity, as on the meaning discussed at the beginning of this section. It is not one interest among others. Rather it is the overarching interest which legislates for *all* of life. But it is not stone-faced traditionalism or dyspeptic Puritanism. (H. L. Mencken once "defined" Puritanism as "the haunting fear that someone, somewhere, may be happy.") Morality does not repress desires simply because it considers any and all desires sinful. Morality is in the service of a rich and happy life. Its supervision is inescapable because of the inescapable fact of conflict among our interests. "[No] man can exempt himself from moral liability." [65]

Now apply Perry's theory to our problem in this chapter, and you should be able to anticipate his answer:

"Art is subject to moral criticism, because morality is nothing more nor less than the law which determines the whole order of interests, within which art and every other good thing is possible." [66]

[61] *Ibid.*, pp. 112–113.
[62] *Ibid.*, p. 14.
[63] *Ibid.*, p. 14.
[64] Ralph Barton Perry, *Realms of Value* (Harvard University Press, 1954), p. 104.
[65] *The Moral Economy*, p. 8.
[66] *Ibid.*, p. 174.

Morality regulates all of man's interests and art is one of those interests. No more than any other interest can it claim immunity from moral supervision. Moreover, as Tolstoy insisted, art can be carried on only when nonartistic social and economic needs are attended to. Since these activities require morality, art is in its debt. Art profits from morality and therefore has obligations to it.

Perry is as clear as any "art for art's sake" theorist that aesthetic judgment cannot be reduced to moral judgment and that the two should not be confused. However, there is no such confusion when the moralist judges art "*on moral grounds.*" [67] His verdict always overrules that of the aesthetic critic, not because he is more astute aesthetically, but because he speaks for the whole of life, rather than just a part of it.

You see how Platonic this is. Yet Perry's theory is a good deal more humane and, in its application, more flexible than Plato's. Though he upholds the claims of morality, Perry gives full recognition to the claims of art. He says that the aesthetic interest, the "interest simply in looking at things, in just the perceiving, feeling, thinking, or imagining them," [68] can be indefinitely satisfying. Art gives us a "continuous return of good." [69] It would follow that any prohibition on art, no matter how justifiable morally, involves a regrettable loss of values. Moreover, Perry is not so stringent as Plato in his application of moral controls. He does not set up a few permissible subjects for art, he does not prohibit novelty in art, and he certainly does not advocate expulsion of the nonconforming artist from society.

Perry's approach is flexible because his moral theory is relativistic. The overarching criterion is the harmonious integration of interests. But how this is to be achieved will depend upon the particular situation in which a decision is to be made. When situations differ, different courses of action are called for. No absolutes of conduct for *all* situations can be laid down. In some societies, at some periods of history, a censorship as rigorous as that of Plato might be called for. At other times, when art does not imperil nonaesthetic interests, no censorship whatever would be required. Hence Perry's proposals are not so rigidly drawn as Plato's. I would say that Perry is not so *afraid* as Plato. He does not feel the need for rigid controls which are supposed to guard against all future evils. Perry would grant the aesthetic interest as much freedom as possible to begin with, and would impose controls only when it became a clear threat to the "good life" of "harmonious happiness." [70]

Using perry's theory as a basis, I would like to conclude with some observations concerning censorship.

[67] *Ibid.*, p. 176. Italics in original.   [68] *Ibid.*, p. 180.
[69] *Ibid.*, p. 192.   [70] *Realms of Value*, p. 104. Italics omitted.

The arguments given by Plato and Perry, and the inadequacies of "life for art's sake" show quite conclusively, in my opinion, that art can *not* claim privileged status for itself. Like every other human activity, it must be judged and supervised in the light of its effects upon life generally. When these effects are so deleterious that they outweigh the goodness of aesthetic enjoyment, social control in the form of censorship is called for. This seems to me to be simply an instance of a principle which need not be argued for — that greater values should not be sacrificed to lesser.

This conclusion is easily enough established and even more easily said. The really painful problems of censorship are those involved in the doing — when censorship should be applied, to what extent it should be used, what specific modes of regulation should be employed.

In a democratic society such as ours, the presumption must be in favor of art and against censorship. The creation of art is one vital kind of self-expression. For some people it is indispensable to a happy life. Our belief in freedom must embrace artistic activity as much as it does political or religious activity. Any act of censorship is an abridgment of freedom and therefore runs counter to one of our highest ideals. And censorship may have harmful after-effects. It may create an atmosphere of timidity among artists which will deaden their efforts. Even more important, it may pave the way for political control in other areas of life.

Nor can we remind ourselves too often that any act of censorship entails a loss, perhaps a great loss, in aesthetic enjoyment. The aesthetic experience is good in itself, if anything is. To prohibit the public display or performance of a work of art deprives us of the occasion for intrinsic value.

Further, with all our talk about the harmful consequences of art, we should not forget that the effects of aesthetic experience are often *beneficial*. Such experience almost never has a direct moral effect so that we rush out to perform a virtuous action. The moral influence of art is more subtle and pervasive. Art can alter our character in many ways so that when the time to act does come, we will be wiser and more perceptive. Art can enlarge our understanding of human motives, our own and those of others. (We spoke of tragedy in this regard.) [71] It can deepen our sympathy for other human beings. By setting out all of the complex forces which enter into a moral situation, it can illuminate moral perplexity and help us to overcome it. More than this, however, works of art can make us thoughtful and critical of our moral beliefs. Comedy, as we saw, often shows up the absurdities and inconsistencies of accepted morality.[72] Such art induces us to seek more rational and valid ideals. In this sense, art offers "moral questions" rather than "answers." [73] It is therefore a catalyst to moral enlightenment.

[71] Cf. above, pp. 286 ff. [72] Cf. above, pp. 296 ff.
[73] Sidney Zink, "The Moral Effect of Art," in Vivas and Krieger, *op. cit.*, p. 556.

From these considerations it follows that censorship in a society like ours should be invoked sparingly, cautiously, reluctantly. It does *not* follow that censorship should *never* be invoked.

For the influence of art can be baneful as well as wholesome. There are countless ways in which it might work to undermine personal and social well-being. It may corrupt character, particularly in the young, by re-enforcing the motives to illegal and antisocial behavior; it may call into question traditional ideals which are indispensable to social order; during times of political or military crisis, art may be seditious or subversive.

The chief offender will probably be the subject matter of the work. We have heard the plea of the art lover that this is only one element of the art-object and that it must not be dissociated from the whole. But this is an argument on behalf of intelligent *aesthetic* appreciation and criticism. We are now, however, concerned with the *moral* aspect of the work. It may be that the work's audience pays attention to the subject matter only and is affected adversely by it. After all, a great many people seem to be unconscious adherents of "imitation"-theory. If the effects of seeing the subject matter are conspicuously harmful, then it does no good to say that the audience has not seen the work for what it really is. The effects are there, and if the work continues to be publicized they will multiply. It would be especially painful to censor the work under these circumstances, for the audience is more at fault than it is. But we have seen that all censorship is painful. And yet it must act on behalf of the goodness of life as a whole.

The aesthetic sophistication of the audience is only one of the factors to be taken into account. If one's approach is relativistic, then whether censorship is applied must depend upon the facts of the particular situation. And these facts are almost always highly complex. It is not likely that a work of art, in and of itself, will have seditious or corrupting effects. It must be viewed in the light of the whole climate of moral, political, and social opinion at the time. Thus works which could be permitted to go unregulated at one period in our history might be legitimately censored at another time.

Censorship ought not to be invoked until the facts of the situation make it reasonably clear that the effects of the work are preponderantly bad. Therefore it is probably a good working rule that censorship should not be applied until *after* the work has already been displayed to the public. Only then can we gain empirical evidence of the work's harmfulness. Only with such evidence can we justify limiting the freedom of the artist and the spectator. Applying this rule, of course, creates the danger that censorship will come too late, after the damage has been done. But this is a risk that we probably have to take, though we should do so knowingly. The alternative is what the law sometimes calls "prior restraint," i.e., censorship *before* the work is publicized. The risks here are even greater. The censor has to judge the work before it has been put to the test of aesthetic response and moral influence. He may well underestimate the aesthetic value of the work and overestimate its moral disvalue. The chance of error will be particularly great when the work is in a new and unfamiliar style or form. Censorship would then rest on conjecture rather than fact, and it would require incalculable foresight and imagination in the censor.

Which brings us finally to the question which puzzled the mice who wished to bell the cat — "*Who* will do the job?" The ideal censor would combine a deep respect for freedom, acute sensitivity to the aesthetic values of art, and intelligent regard for the well-being of society. But though I have argued for censorship, I confess that those who have historically acted as censors, do not, as a class, impress me greatly. They have often, perhaps usually, been men of small vision and narrow minds. Such men have not understood the claims of art; some of them disdained aesthetic value altogether. What is worse, they have not understood the claims of morality any better. Morality to them was something parochial and ultraconservative. They did not understand the importance of re-examining and challenging traditional morality. They often confused their own prejudices with moral rightness. A censor in one of our large southern cities who, in the years before his recent death became known for his irrational and high-handed decisions, refused to permit the showing of movies which depicted train robberies, because he himself had been a railroad worker in his youth. Earlier in this chapter, I cited other well-known follies of censorship, viz., the prosecution of two of the greatest works of art of the last century, *Madame Bovary* and *Flowers of Evil*. But censorship is probably silliest of all when it calls attention to works which would go unnoticed if the censors did not make a fuss about them. Censorship then becomes self-defeating, for it creates popular interest in morally harmful works and when such interest is sufficiently great it can usually find ways to circumvent the law.

The problem of choosing the censors is a difficult and important one, but it is not insuperable. It is not greatly different in principle from that of choosing our judges. They too must combine impartiality, vision, and sympathy. But there *are* such men and we know who they are. Their names stand out in the history of our judicial system. There have also been judges whose decisions were biassed or worse, and we know *them* for what they are. So there is not much point in the argument that we could never find anyone good enough to serve as a censor. The job of the censor is a difficult one, and it can be abused for the sake of personal power or gain. Yet a well-functioning democracy is bound to produce men capable of doing the job well. If ever a democratic society gets to the point where it fails to turn out such men, it will be facing far graver problems than that of the censorship of art.

As AN EXAMPLE of the social evaluation of art at its best, let me cite what is probably the most famous censorship decision of this century, viz., the decision by Judge Woolsey, on Dec. 6, 1933, in the case of Joyce's *Ulysses*. At the trial, the United States Government contended that the novel was obscene and therefore could not be brought into the country.

Judge Woolsey first takes account of the aesthetic claims of the novel. He recognizes the literary novelty of the work and, indeed, describes Joyce's methods with great perceptiveness and clarity.[74] He discusses such features of the book as its "dirty words" in reference to the artist's intent — again, he considers the *whole* work of art — and finds that they are justified by Joyce's "honest effort to show exactly how the minds of his characters operate." [75] He passes judgment on the overall aesthetic success of the work.

But Judge Woolsey does not stop here. He also recognizes the claims of morality. In order to decide whether the American public should be kept from reading the book,

> it is not sufficient merely to find, as I have found above, that Joyce did not write "Ulysses" with what is commonly called pornographic intent, I must endeavor to apply a more objective standard to his book in order to determine its effect in the result, irrespective of the intent with which it was written.[76]

Here there is as much concern with consequences as any moralist could wish. The intent of the artist is one thing and Judge Woolsey does not ignore it. But the "effect in the result" is yet another thing and, considering Judge Woolsey's role and function, even less can this be ignored.

On the pivotal legal question — whether *Ulysses* is obscene — Judge Woolsey takes care that his judgment should not mirror "his own idiosyncrasies." [77] He decides that the novel, when read by the normal man, does not "tend to excite sexual impulses or lustful thoughts." [78] And "[it] is only with the normal person that the law is concerned." [79]

I quote the famous last sentence of the decision: " 'Ulysses' may, therefore, be admitted into the United States." [80]

As you probably know, *Ulysses* is now widely read in colleges and by the educated public.

The problem of reconciling the claims of art and of morality is, at best, enormously difficult and at times it seems to be little less than insoluble. But I think that if all of our censors were of the caliber of Judge Woolsey, it would be solved as fairly and reasonably as we could hope for.

[74] James Joyce, *Ulysses* (New York: Modern Library, 1934), pp. xi–xii.
[75] *Ibid.*, p. xi. All quotations reprinted by permission of Random House, Inc.
[76] *Ibid.*, p. xii.
[77] *Ibid.*, p. xiii.   [78] *Ibid.*, p. xiii.
[79] *Ibid.*, p. xiv.   [80] *Ibid.*, p. xiv.

BIBLIOGRAPHY

* Rader, *A Modern Book of Esthetics*. Pp. 335–356, 527–571.
* Vivas and Krieger, *The Problems of Aesthetics*. Pp. 483–583.
  Gotshalk, *Art and the Social Order*. Chaps. IX–X.
  Murray, J. Courtney, "Literature and Censorship," *Commonweal*, Vol. LXIV
  (July 6, 1956), 349–351.
  Perry, Ralph Barton. *The Moral Economy*. New York: Scribners, 1909. Chaps.
  I, V.
  Plato. *The Republic*. Books II–IV, X.
  Rader, Melvin, "The Artist as Outsider," *Journal of Aesthetics and Art Criticism*, Vol. XVI (March, 1958), 306–318.
  Reid, *A Study in Aesthetics*. Chap. XI.
  Tolstoy, Leo. *What Is Art?*, trans. Maude. New York: Oxford University
  Press, 1955.

QUESTIONS

1. Assuming that you accept the principle that censorship can sometimes be justified morally: Can you find any *specific* instances of censorship in the history of art which you think were justified in their particular circumstances? (Consider in detail the cases mentioned in this chapter, or any others.) If you can find *none*, would it follow that we should give up censorship even *in principle?*
2. Do you think that *the artist* has a right to suppress his work once it has been offered for public consumption? What reasons do you think would justify such an action? Are these reasons still valid if the work has been found to be highly valuable by its audience? In general, are there any significant differences between suppression of the work by the artist and by a censor acting on behalf of society?
3. Can you find any examples of works of art in which the artist expresses *approval* of what he believes to be evil? Are such works always inferior *aesthetically?* If so, is this because of what Bosanquet calls a "weakness of the spectator," i.e., our inability to perceive these works with aesthetic "sympathy"?
4. Compare the following propositions:
"Jones is immoral."
"This action is immoral."
"This work of art is immoral."
How do these propositions differ in meaning? Does the third proposition use "immoral" metaphorically?
5. "The one good thing Society can do for the artist is to leave him alone. Give him liberty." — Bell, *Art*, p. 252.
Is there something more that society "can do for the artist"? Discuss.

PART V

The Evaluation of Art

14

Aesthetic Experience, Evaluation, and Criticism

1. AESTHETIC VALUING AND EVALUATION

The aesthetic experience is pre-eminently one in which we accept and enjoy an object — and "no questions asked." We embrace the object "for its own sake alone." We do not use it as a sign, for practical purposes; we do not seek to extract knowledge from it; we are not concerned with its influence for good and evil. We meet the object on its own terms and we try to live its life. If our attitude is truly "sympathetic," we forego criticizing or challenging the object. In this, aesthetic experience is like love — at least until love becomes demanding and querulous.

I say that, in the aesthetic attitude, we "ask no questions." But it is as obvious as anything can be that we *do* "ask questions" about works of art and other aesthetic objects. How *many* questions we ask! How much we *talk* about art! The analysis of a short lyric poem can run to many pages of discursive prose. All of the commentaries on *Hamlet* taken together would fill a fair-sized library. The work of art is no longer something to be accepted, gratefully and submissively. After we give up the aesthetic attitude, it becomes something to be probed, analyzed, and wrangled over. Indeed, there are some people who, if the truth be told, get more fun out of this sort of thing than from aesthetic perception itself.

WHAT EXACTLY ARE WE TRYING TO DO when we analyze the work? And *why* do we want to analyze? The *philosophy of art criticism*, to which the remainder of this book is devoted, addresses itself to these questions. It is concerned with two activities, *evaluation* and *criticism*. Evaluation estimates the aesthetic goodness or badness of the work. It judges that "this work is beautiful," or "this work is better than that one." There are, as we shall see, several different kinds and functions of criticism. At present, I will define "judicial criticism" as "finding reasons to support or verify the value-judgment." On this definition, "That's ugly!" or "Ah! how nice!" are not themselves criticisms of the object. Criticism begins when the speaker is asked, "Why do you say that?" or "Is the work *really* ugly?"

Philosophy of art criticism, like all branches of philosophy, examines the beliefs and concepts which underlie our thinking and doing. It does not argue for or against specific judgments like *"Oedipus* is a great play". But it calls our attention to what such judgments take for granted. It raises such questions as these:

What do we mean when we say that the work is "aesthetically valuable" (or some less pedantic term like "good")? Are we talking about the work itself or are we merely reporting our own response to it? If we are talking about ourselves, then there is unconscious deception in saying *"the work is —."* We assert the value-judgment as though it were a truth, and sometimes we defend it with so much heat that we evidently consider it an important truth. But how can the judgment be verified? Can it be verified at all? Can we ever prove to someone who disagrees with us about art that he is wrong? If we are not clear about the answers to these questions, there is no point in carrying on arguments about the merits of a work of art. Unless all sides to the argument agree upon the meaning of the value-judgment, and the methods of confirming it, i.e., showing that it is true, their debate will lack direction and purpose. Furthermore, debates about art usually get involved in talk about "good taste" and "bad taste." Most of us presumably believe that some people have better taste than others. But, once again, what do we *mean* by "good taste" and how can we justify our belief in it if, indeed, it can be justified at all?

Comparable questions can be raised about criticism: What is the function of the art critic? What should we expect to learn from him? Can criticism enhance aesthetic enjoyment? How should the analysis of art be carried on? Or is the whole business of art criticism needless or even harmful, a torrent of talk which destroys the spontaneity of aesthetic interest?

There are some students, however, who do not have to be persuaded of the worth of philosophy of art criticism. Indeed, they are so interested in the questions just mentioned that they become impatient with the problems treated earlier in this book. The nature of the aesthetic attitude, the definition of "fine art," the relation of art to "life," cognitively and morally — such topics seem less urgent and interesting than art criticism. Why then do we come to criticism only at the end of our study?

Even if the reader happens to be one of the students just described, he should be able to anticipate at least part of the answer. He should see that we cannot discuss art criticism intelligently until we have first gotten clear about the concepts, "artistic" and "aesthetic." These concepts are central to criticism. We cannot simply assume that their meanings are clear and universally shared. As we have seen, "fine art" has many meanings and "aesthetic" is a highly vague term in common discourse. Without the earlier analyses of these terms, the discussion of criticism would be confused from the outset.

This can be shown specifically. One of the most common errors in critical writings is that of confusing the aesthetic and nonaesthetic values of art. When a critic calls some work "ugly" because he does not share the artist's moral beliefs, but fails to make clear the reason for his judgment (perhaps he does not realize it himself), his criticism is endlessly misleading. The value-predicate, "ugly," leads us to think that he is talking about the work *aesthetically*, when, in point of fact, he is not. Only if we understand the aesthetic attitude and the nature of aesthetic "belief," can we unravel this confusion. To be aware of this confusion of values also furthers our understanding of "taste." For now we know how to treat the value-judgments of the snob or the man who appraises works solely in terms of their scarcity or market value. Santayana said that such people are guilty of "aesthetic vulgarity." But they do not lack taste because they have set fashionableness or money above aesthetic value. Rather, they have lost sight of the aesthetic altogether. The aesthetic attitude is itself the first requirement for "good taste."

Yet it is not wholly accurate to say that the earlier chapters merely cleared the ground. The student should also see that much in those chapters was already philosophy of criticism itself or came very close to it. Each of the major theories of art, we saw, told us what to "look for" in the work of art. Each thereby established criteria for judging art. Moreover, the various theories of art gave at least suggestions of an answer to the important question stated earlier, viz., is the aesthetic value-judgment an assertion about the work or a report of our feelings? The "imitation"-theories take the judgment to mean that certain commonly discernible properties, e.g., "universals," are present in the object. Formalism pays greater attention to the spectator; emotionalist theory goes still further in this direction. These are latent theories of evaluation which will be developed systematically in the next chapter.

Finally, the theories of "artistic truth" laid down certain criteria for judging art. And our discussion of ugliness and other aesthetic categories revealed the wide scope of critical vocabulary and the meanings of some of its most common terms. Here again, while talking "aesthetics," we were also talking "philosophy of criticism."

What are the real differences between these two studies? It might be said that aesthetics deals with the *facts* of artistic and aesthetic experience, e.g., what art is, what aesthetic perception is like, whether truth occurs in art, and so on. Philosophy of criticism might then be said to deal with the *value*-aspects of artistic and aesthetic activity. But we have just seen how weak this distinction would be. Our discussions under the heading of "aesthetics" were involved continuously with values. This is because the "facts" treated by aesthetics either are, or are closely related to, values. Artistic creation and aesthetic appreciation are charged with values, as the data of geology, say, are not. The artistic and aesthetic are intimately bound up with human enjoyment. Our language shows this, e.g., the evaluative term, "*fine* art," and the common use of "aesthetic" to mean "beautiful" or "aesthetically satisfying."

So we were involved in values from the very start. Hence the distinction between aesthetics and philosophy of criticism must be drawn in another way. The former deals with the experience of *valuing* — taking interest in an object and finding it delightful. Aesthetics studies the distinctive attitude which governs this experience, the objects toward which this attitude is taken, and their structure. Philosophy of criticism deals with the process of *evaluation* — analysis and judgment of the aesthetic goodness of the object. The discussion of aesthetics has important implications for philosophy of criticism. Still judgment and criticism are not the same activities as artistic creation and aesthetic perception. Philosophy of criticism treats systematically the problems of judgment and criticism.

BUT THE FIRST QUESTION OF ALL IS, "Why *do* we judge and criticize?" Why do we not accept the work of art or natural landscape for what it is and simply enjoy it to the utmost? Why must we jabber about it and pick at it and measure its precise value?

Probably we do this, in part, just because we enjoy talking about works of art. This is a harmless pastime, and it can be carried on with great sophistication. Having enjoyed the virtues of art in aesthetic experience, we like to dwell upon them during evaluation. We relish the impudence of Prokofiev and the exuberance of Matisse in aesthetic experience. Then we think back fondly to them during evaluation.

Moreover, there is a social aspect to our value-judgments. We share with others our likes and dislikes in art, as in food. Offering an evaluation is like giving a recipe; it invites others to enjoy what we have enjoyed. We are like the speaker in Frost's little poem, who is going out

> . . . to rake the leaves away
> (And wait to watch the water clear, I may):
> I shan't be gone long. — You come too.
> "The Pasture"

More important, we invite others to "come too" so that we can test our own responses to art. We want to have our judgments confirmed. We are not quite sure that the work is as good as we have found it to be until others find it so too. "[The] value that I attach to the picture is somehow strengthened by agreement and . . . diminished by disagreement." [1] This intersubjective testing may lead us to withdraw our original opinion and it may even persuade us that the work is not worthy of further attention. (There may be, and doubtless there often is, snobbery and authoritarianism at work here. How, if at all, the aesthetic dogmatist can be distinguished from the man of good taste is a problem for the next chapter.)

But the most important reason for evaluation has not yet been given.

Let us generalize our question and ask why we judge *any* values whatever, not only the aesthetic. Why do we evaluate foods, or a moral act, or even a whole way of life? Each of these may be enjoyable at the time that we choose it. And yet sober reflection, or the force of painful experience, or both, may lead us to say later that the object was not *"really good."* We say that "I *thought* it was good" or that "I was fooled by it." The food endangered my health; I now consider the moral act wrong and unworthy of me; after the social prophet has shown me a new way of life, abandoning the old one is like waking from a nightmare. Here is the most elementary and probably the most important distinction in values, viz., between what is seemingly or momentarily good, and what is genuinely and enduringly good. Here too is the beginning of wisdom. For wisdom is the capacity to tell the difference between the two in specific cases.[2]

Reflection upon the earlier valuing can condemn it for any one of a host of reasons. Most obviously, as in the case of the harmful food, the object may have painful consequences. The badness of the "morning after" (in the broadest sense) may far exceed the goodness of the "night before." We have seen how the appeal to consequences may lead to the moral regulation of art.[3] In another kind of value-situation, one may devote all of his efforts, perhaps all of his life, to achieve some object and then, upon attaining it, find that it turns to ashes. The object, he may say, looking up from the ruins, was not *worthy* of his striving. Or, before we reach for an object which tempts us, we may analyze its properties. Then we may find

---

[1] De Witt H. Parker, in Ray Lepley, ed., *Value: A Cooperative Inquiry* (Columbia University Press, 1949), p. 427.
[2] Cf. above, pp. 287–290.
[3] Cf. above, chap. 13.

blemishes and flaws which we did not see at first. Or, with greater knowledge, we may learn that something which is good is not *as* good as a comparable object which is available to us.

Reflective evaluation is a guide to future action. Our value-experience, in all areas of life, involves *choice*. Our judgment that an object is genuinely worthwhile or better than another enables us to choose with a greater chance of success than when we choose ignorantly. We can reasonably hope that we will not "make the same mistake again" — nor pay the price for the mistake twice over. Wisdom is especially vital when it is, in one way or another, expensive to attain our heart's desire. We can calculate both whether the object is worth the cost, and how to choose the most economical means. Wisdom is also demanded when there are a great number of objects from which to choose.

Now, these problems are not usually so grave in the area of aesthetic experience as they are in other areas of life. The risks and costs of action do not have to be calculated so carefully. The realm of the aesthetic is that of intrinsic and self-contained experience. No thought need be given to the causes of or means to the production of the art-object, though the *moralist*, like Tolstoy, may, of course, argue that the means are too expensive. The consequences of aesthetic perception are generally too slight to warrant worrying about them. Moreover, aesthetic appreciation is not usually institutionalized, like economic or religious activity. Hence it is not surrounded by rules and prohibitions, as they are. Finally, aesthetic activity is usually noncompetitive, because works of art are ordinarily available to all, unlike food or the pretty girl for whom two swains are vying. When I listen to Beethoven's Fifth, I do not appropriate the work to myself alone. I do not deprive you of the opportunity of hearing it.

For all these reasons, cautious judgment and prudent calculation are not so imperative in the area of the aesthetic. We need not worry so much about our choices because there is less at stake. That is why aesthetic enjoyment is sometimes described as an escape from the workaday world. Santayana says that the arts are "employments of our freedom, after the work of life is done and the terror of it is allayed." [4]

AND YET AESTHETIC EVALUATION *does* have a role to play, and not a small one either.

For aesthetic values, like other values, have to be chosen. What is more, we can make mistakes in choosing them. The realm of the aesthetic is not completely different from the other areas of value in these respects. We probably exaggerate the difference because the aesthetic attitude itself has no thought for causes and consequences. It is fixed solely on its object. *Before* we take the aesthetic attitude, however, we must make choices.

[4] *The Sense of Beauty*, p. 166.

Which book shall we read? Which of these phonograph records shall we buy? Fruitful choice requires knowledge of the work, its relative goodness, how well it will "wear." Well-founded evaluations enable us to increase our enjoyments and ward off disappointment. This may not be as important as selecting wholesome food or the right moral act, but there is nothing trivial about it either.

In our dealings with aesthetic objects, as with other value-objects, we can be disappointed and deceived. A work which delights at first encounter may seem dull and mediocre when we return to it later. What seemed to be finely wrought and deeply felt turns out to be jerry-built and sentimental. Then we feel as though we had been "taken in." We might alter a well-known phrase and say "What did I ever see in *that?*" Again, disappointments in art may not be as cataclysmic as in marriage. But that does not prove that we should choose blindly in our aesthetic lives.

Something else is involved in making evaluations. It might be called our "aesthetic integrity." Reflective evaluation makes our felt aesthetic preferences conscious and deliberate. Our likings become *standards*. We do not wish to betray our standards by giving approval to what is cheap and tawdry. We would not compromise them any more than we would water down the demands which we make upon a man if he is to be our friend. We may condemn trashy "popular" music and literature, not so much because it displeases us aesthetically — it may bounce off us — but because it demeans the standards of taste.

So evaluation is a guide to choice and it is essential to our own integrity. But by far the most important reason for evaluation is this: It can make a difference within the aesthetic experience itself and thereby magnify the felt value of the experience.

Most works of art worth talking about are enormously complex. Our study of aesthetics impressed this upon us more than once. Very few works reveal all that is within them to us at first. Lacking familiarity, and the requisite capacities of memory, imagination, emotion, and knowledge, good and even great works — indeed great works especially — will seem dull or obscure to us.[5] Criticism, which works in behalf of evaluation, can help us to master the work's complexity. Critical analysis can show us formal interrelationships which bind the work together, meanings which make up its truth, expressive significance which gives it resonance and depth. Such knowledge enables us to see more when we go back to the work. We can then "set" ourselves to respond to all that is in the work.

Some thinkers, like Tolstoy, reject the whole enterprise of criticism. They consider it unnecessary. "What is there . . . to explain?"[6] Very little, perhaps, in the folk songs and legends esteemed by Tolstoy.[7] How-

[5] Cf. above, chap. 3, sec. 2.
[6] Tolstoy, *op. cit.,* p. 194.   [7] Cf. above, pp. 177–178.

ever, those who extend this argument to all art hold that we have only to look at the work with spontaneous and genuine interest to capture its value. But this view has little foundation in fact. "Is not the work of art self-sufficient? Yes. But it may not be self-explanatory." [8] We should not be misled by the apparent simplicity of the aesthetic attitude. It is all very well to say that aesthetic perception just grasps what is *there* in the work, what is "immediately given." The point is that we do not know *what* is "there" until perception has been instructed and enlightened by criticism.

So evaluation and criticism are the indispensable auxiliaries of our aesthetic lives. Without them our perception would be blind or distorted, and our value-experience would be impoverished. This fact is their reason for being. How, specifically, they do their work is on the agenda for succeeding chapters.

HOWEVER, ONE RESERVATION MUST BE MADE. It does not prove the case of those who would do away with criticism altogether, but we must note that criticism sometimes leads to a *loss* in aesthetic valuing. Analysis may show us faults in the work that we do not see while we are simply attending to it aesthetically. This may very likely keep us from enjoying the work again as we might have done otherwise. A source of satisfaction is given up. It is then cold comfort to think that at least now we know the work for what it really is.

We do not mind outgrowing the stories which we read as children. That seems "natural," somehow. But there may seem to be something wrong about criticism coming along and ruining a work for us. Indeed, we might do something about our resentment. We might persist in valuing what evaluation has condemned. Let the critics go hang.

Such stubborn liking does not come easily, however. So great is the authority and force of thoughtful evaluation. We have qualms about rejecting its conclusions. In our very protest, we acknowledge that we "know better." We have to turn our back upon rationality in order to like what we believe to be unworthy of liking.

We protest against criticism because we want to preserve spontaneous enjoyments. Why must we give up these pristine delights? This is the perennial demand of innocence. The question arises in all areas of experience, not simply the aesthetic. It is the usual response to any admonition to stop doing what we want to do. But the question is probably most pointed in the area of the aesthetic. Aesthetic experience is unselfish; it is not concerned with consequences; it calls into play feeling and imagination for their own sakes. It is found in the child's pure delight in sights and sounds. Here, if anywhere, valuing is innocent. Far less than moral or

[8] Donald A. Stauffer, "Introduction," *The Intent of The Critic,* ed. Stauffer (Princeton University Press, 1941), p. 12.

religious or economic activity, if at all, should it be subject to critical judgment.

Probably no reply will still this protest competely. Criticism *does* sometimes deprive us of values. If we no longer like what we have liked before, then — this is just a tautology — values are lost. This is the risk we take in all areas of value when we begin to reflect upon our unthinking desires and joys. As the philosopher, John Dewey, has said: "Let us admit [that] if we once start thinking no one can guarantee where we shall come out, except that many objects, ends, and institutions are doomed." We can justifiably hope, however, that what is lost will be more than made up for. Innocence cannot sustain itself for very long and, even if it could, its values, however "pure" they are, would be relatively thin and simple ones. Innocence, by definition, can never know the values which come only with knowledge and reflection. In the area of the aesthetic, criticism can reveal complexity and profundity in the work which we had never dreamed of. For every work which it condemns, there are many more which it makes meaningful to us. The net gain in our value-experience is incalculable. As we grow in discrimination and sensitivity, there will be little regret for the likings that we have left behind.

2. THE AESTHETIC AND CRITICAL ATTITUDES

I have argued that aesthetic valuing and critical evaluation are different from each other, but that the latter can enhance appreciation. I will now try to show that appreciation and criticism are distinct in another way, viz., they are psychologically opposed to each other. The aesthetic and critical attitudes are such radically different ways of approaching an object that when one is uppermost in the mind, it drives the other out. The two do not readily coexist. If we can see why, we will understand better why artists and "art lovers" have so often been suspicious of or hostile to the critics of art. We will be able to understand their feeling that criticism lacks the vitality and warmth of appreciation.

To BEGIN WITH, think of how we use the phrase, "to be critical." In its sternest sense, it connotes fault-finding. In a broader sense, it refers to assessing the strengths as well as the weaknesses of some object. In any sense, however, it suggests a certain frame of mind — that of being detached, cautious, on guard against being taken in. To be critical is to refuse approval until, like the man from Missouri, one has been "shown." The object must come forward and show its credentials; it does not pass until it has proved itself worthy.

The aesthetic attitude is not like this at all. It is just the opposite. It commits our allegiance to the object freely and unquestioningly. The figure of speech is a little flowery, but it is sometimes said that the spectator "surrenders" himself to the work of art. He wishes to live the life of the object, but he cannot do so if he is aloof and quizzical. He accepts the object on its own terms and foregoes any challenges to it. When aesthetic interest is most intense, the percipient "loses himself" in the object.[9]

Thus the very temper or "spirit" of criticism is inimical to the aesthetic attitude. If the critical attitude dominates our attention it will destroy aesthetic perception. We all know people in whom this occurs. They are always so intent on picking out flaws in the work. We are often tempted to say to them, "Why don't you just relax and enjoy the music?"

Furthermore, criticism is analytic. The foes of criticism have long known this. Their rallying cry has been "We murder to dissect."[10] But the critic cannot get along without analysis. To show that the work is good, he must show what there is in it that contributes to its value. He may speak of its sensory charm, the clarity of its formal structure, the profundity of the emotion, and the acuteness of the truth which it expresses. He must consider the components of the work both in isolation and in their relation to each other.

But this is not the way that aesthetic perception proceeds. It does not chop up the work; it grasps it as a whole. The sensory qualities which criticism talks about are felt immediacies to the spectator; the formal relations which are analyzed out by criticism are, for aesthetic perception, vital linkages in the expectations and tensions which animate the experience and tie it together; the truth which is paraphrased by the critic is felt by the percipient to be enmeshed in and "enacted" throughout the work. It is the total "body" of the work that the spectator wishes to grasp. He is interested in what Dewey calls "having *an* experience";[11] he does not want an inventory.

Finally, the *purpose* of criticism is not that of aesthetic perception. The critic wishes to defend his value-judgment. Hence he seeks knowledge about the work. He has an interest ulterior to the act of criticism. The aesthetic attitude, however, has no interest beyond that of just perceiving. "Esthetic satisfaction . . . can be at its height only when it is unself-conscious, and is an absorption unqualified by the cognitive intent of objective appraisal and analysis."[12]

In these three respects, the aesthetic attitude and the critical attitude are opposed to each other. They are different "sets"; they approach the work with different purposes; the experiences which accompany these attitudes

[9] Cf. above, pp. 79–81.
[10] Cf. above, pp. 15–17.
[11] Cf. above, p. 69.
[12] C. I. Lewis, *An Analysis of Knowledge and Valuation* (La Salle, Illinois: Open Court, 1946), p. 442.

are correspondingly different. When attention, perception, and our capacities for feeling are organized critically, they cannot be "thrown open," as Ducasse says, to aesthetic response. The two attitudes are inherently antithetical.

IT WILL PROBABLY BE AGREED that criticism and aesthetic perception are different. But not all will agree that the opposition between these attitudes is as great as I have made it out to be. Two objections must be considered:

(1) The two attitudes are different; yet they usually, perhaps always, occur simultaneously in the percipient. Wholly "sympathetic" and "unselfconscious" perception is an ideal or limiting case, which is never achieved in fact. When we appreciate, we also judge: This is pretty clearly true. We all know how often, while listening to the music or watching the play, we whisper critical comments for the benefit of our companions. For most people part of the time, and for some people most of the time, "aesthetic experience" is really a mixture of the aesthetic and critical attitudes.

This is a fact, but one which does not destroy the distinction between the two attitudes. Like many other things, they can be distinguished analytically, though they coexist concretely. Objection (1), in saying that there are *two* attitudes, presupposes the distinction. Furthermore, however, the fact just cited is an unfortunate one. For just because the two attitudes are inimical, whenever criticism obtrudes, it reduces aesthetic interest. Therefore it reduces aesthetic value.

Criticism, for some thinkers, as we shall see,[13] consists in describing the personal responses of the spectator to the work. He must ask himself, "Do I find this pleasing?," "What emotions does this arouse in me?," and so on. Criticism of this kind is clearly incompatible with aesthetic interest in the work. "Aesthetic attention is, above all, object-centered attention." [14] Attention cannot be wholly "object-centered" when the percipient directs it to his own psychological states. (It might be added that this kind of percipient is almost as much a nuisance to his friends and companions as he is to himself, with his incessant question, "Am I *really* enjoying this?" The answer is that he will never find out until he stops posing the question. He should apply to aesthetic experience the old rule for all value-experience, "The way to *get* happiness is to *forget* happiness.")

But criticism which looks out toward the object is also antiaesthetic, for the reasons given above. Sometimes, when the spectator punctuates the experience with judgments upon the niceties of the work or the performance, the motive is a kind of snobbism or social exhibitionism. Sometimes he is a professional artist interested in technique and the tricks of his trade. Sometimes — most unhappily of all — criticism is a last resort for those

---

13 Cf. below, chap. 16, sec. 3.
14 Gotshalk, *Art and the Social Order*, p. 4.

who cannot become absorbed in and respond to the work. Always it inhibits aesthetic interest. That is why Bullough decides that the "objective"-type spectator "represents . . . the crudest form of aesthetic appreciation." [15] As Lewis puts it, criticism "must always dilute a little . . . immediately realized value. [The] fullest glory of the aesthetic is open only to the innocent or to those who approach it with humility and for whom it is a gift of the gods." [16]

Objection (1) says that the critical attitude "usually, perhaps always" accompanies the aesthetic. What about that "always"? Is our state of mind *never* completely aesthetic? Obviously it is not easy to answer this. It is difficult to get clear about the immediacies of experience; "object-centered attention" tends to lapse; and there is always the possibility of self-deception. Yet sometimes, at least, we "give ourselves over" wholly to the object. This probably occurs most often when the work is as familiar to us as an old friend. We can anticipate the course it will take and our responses come readily and freely. Most of all, we have "accepted" the work; there are "no questions asked." Bullough's "character"-type [17] exemplifies such experience.

But perhaps the objection should be changed to say that the critical attitude *ought* to accompany the aesthetic. Otherwise our perception will be naïve and undiscriminating. I think, however, that there is a serious ambiguity in saying that we ought to "read critically" or "listen critically." Does this mean that we must analyze, measure in terms of value-criteria, etc., *during* the supposedly aesthetic experience? If so, the experience will no longer be aesthetic. Rather, it should be taken to mean that we ought to read or listen perceptively and acutely. We should be aware of all that is richly contained in the work. But this must come from the criticism which occurs *prior* to the aesthetic encounter. What is gained from the process of learning about the work must become absorbed into our knowledge and guide our attention and expectations as the work unfolds. "Not criticism, but the fruits of criticism — greater knowledge, more acute discrimination, more sensitive receptiveness — are ingredient in experience which is veritably aesthetic. Having done its work, the best thing criticism can do is die." [18]

(2) This objection to the "aesthetic"-"critical" distinction is more subtle. Whereas (1) accepts the distinction, (2) challenges it. The argument rests partly on the definition of "aesthetic attitude" and partly on a psychological fact about aesthetic experience.

The aesthetic attitude, like any attitude, refers, by definition, to a certain

[15] Cf. above, p. 80.
[16] *Op. cit.*, pp. 442, 443.
[17] Cf. above, p. 79.
[18] Jerome Stolnitz, "On Esthetic Valuing and Evaluation," *Philosophy and Phenomenological Research*, XIII (1953), 472.

way of controlling and directing attention. Now attention is always selective. We do not see everything at once. Nor do we consider everything that we see of equal importance. Thus we find contrasts and emphases within works of art. Here the psychological fact enters: how we direct attention to the work depends upon our previous aesthetic experiences, particularly of similar works. Our earlier conditioning has instilled in us standards of what is valuable in such art. Professor Parker says that "The first poem we read sets the standard for all readings of poetry." [19] These implicit criteria determine what we will "look for" in the work. Hence "in every act of appreciation norms of judgment are latent." [20] Therefore the sharp distinction between "critical" and "aesthetic" is unsound. Evaluation and judgment are present in every act of aesthetic contemplation. The aesthetic attitude is not properly understood if it is said to be wholly noncritical. It is always critical to some extent.

Now, the fact upon which (2) rests is incontestable. Who can deny that our selection of what is important in art is the outgrowth of our earlier aesthetic education? Critics, teachers, our previous experience and our reflective evaluation of that experience — all of these influence aesthetic interest and discrimination. This is just an instance of the larger, somewhat banal truth that everything that we have encountered in the past has left its mark upon us.

Aesthetic attention *is* selective. We concentrate upon some things in the work and not on others. But this only means that we meet the object with certain ways of perceiving which are part of our aesthetic "equipment." It does *not* mean that we are "critical" during aesthetic experience in the sense that we are trying to appraise and analyze the work. We do not have "the deliberate intent" [21] of criticism.

Let me cite the testimony of one of the most distinguished critics of our time, F. R. Leavis:

> Words in poetry invite us, not to "think about" and judge but to "feel into" or "become" — to realize a complete experience that is given in the words. They demand . . . responsiveness — a kind of responsiveness that is incompatible with the judicial, one-eye-on-the-standard approach. . . . The critic — the reader of poetry — is indeed concerned with evaluation, but to figure him as measuring with a norm which he brings up to the object and applies from the outside is to misrepresent the process. . . . His first concern is to enter into possession of the given poem . . . in its concrete fulness.[22]

Of course, norms are "latent" in Leavis' reading. We can say the same

---

[19] In Lepley, *op. cit.*, p. 228.

[20] Harold Osborne, *Aesthetics and Criticism* (New York: Philosophical Library, 1955), p. 31.

[21] Lewis, *op. cit.*, p. 442.

[22] "Literary Criticism and Philosophy," in *The Common Pursuit*, pp. 212–213.

thing less misleadingly by saying that Leavis has developed a certain taste and therefore "looks for" certain things in the work. But he does not try to read the work with "one-eye-on-the-standard." You will notice that Leavis puts "the reader of poetry" in apposition to "the critic," thereby showing that he is describing aesthetic perception itself. Only if we use "critical" in a misleading way, can aesthetic perception be said to be "critical."

I quoted Professor Parker, who emphasizes the influence of aesthetic conditioning upon aesthetic experience. He, too, makes the point that "the standard for all readings of poetry" is something inherent in our perceptual apparatus; it is not used for conscious evaluation: "[This standard] is not a mere instrument of intellectual judgment, of classing and serializing satisfactions; but as fulfilled, surpassed, or fallen short of, determines the very quality and intensity of the satisfaction itself." [23]

WE HAVE GONE FAR toward divorcing criticism and contemplation. Some thinkers would take one further and final step in this direction. They hold that criticism and aesthetic enjoyment are so utterly different that criticism has nothing whatever to do with appreciation. It is simply futile. With its approach to the work and its methods, criticism cannot possibly explain the aesthetic value of the work of art.

Here is their argument: The subject of the value-judgment is the work of art. We judge the whole work because it is the whole work that we have enjoyed aesthetically. We say that it is "beautiful," or "great," or whatever, but that is only the beginning of evaluation. How can we defend our judgment? We must talk about the total work. But what can we say about it? It itself, as a distinctively valuable object, is unique. Its specific nature cannot be described in general terms or concepts, which always apply to many things. What we relish in the work is its precious individuality. That is why we will not trade one poem for another. Works of art are not synonyms. Therefore the philosopher Croce insists upon the work as an "inviolable individual — the individual which must not be touched by conceptual abstraction if it is to retain its aesthetic validity." [24]

If we cannot describe the work, still less can we judge it. Evaluation uses criteria or standards of judgment. These standards define the various ways in which the work can excel or fail, and measure its success in these respects. Examples would be "formal unity," "expressive power," the rules for a "well-constructed" sonnet or sonata. But these are always *general,* i.e., they are supposed to hold for many objects of a certain kind. The specific work, however, is just itself. Its form is peculiar to it. We can judge automobiles as they come off the assembly line, or paper clips, or

[23] *Op. cit.,* p. 229.
[24] W. K. Wimsatt, jr., and Cleanth Brooks, *Literary Criticism: A Short History* (New York: Knopf, 1957), p. 512.

apples. They are all of a kind and we can set up specifications for what is a good example of that kind. But the work of art is, so to speak, "its own kind" of sonnet or sonata. It can violate the textbook "rules" and still be of great aesthetic value. How then can we expect critical judgments to do justice to the felt value of our experience?

The rules of "good form" and so on apply to certain *parts* or *elements* of the work. Multiply these rules as much as you like. Use criteria for "representational fidelity," "composition," "harmony," or anything else. Still you are only grasping at partial characteristics of the work. What these characteristics are like and how they are valuable depends upon their interaction with everything else in the work. That is why the work can violate the rules for goodness or badness in one of its parts and still be a good work of art. It is just the "organic" quality of the total work which you can never catch — at least, not by criticism. If you cannot evaluate the whole, you cannot evaluate the parts. And you will certainly not understand the value of the whole by just adding up the values of the parts.

The paradox for criticism is this: the unique, "organic" quality of the work, i.e., what the whole work feels like to aesthetic perception, leads us to assert the value-judgment; yet it is just the uniqueness of the whole work which keeps us from proving the judgment. According to the foes of criticism, this paradox is fatal to all critical activity.

The art-object is "ineffable," i.e., it cannot be talked about. We can, of course, say, "There! Look!" But that is enthusiasm, not criticism. Art being what it is, criticism is inherently impossible.

How CAN CRITICISM DEFEND ITSELF against its foes? It takes two ways out of the impasse into which it has been led.

The first is, despite the critics of criticism, just to go ahead and analyze the parts of the work and the interrelations between them. Granted, the total work is "unique" and "incomparable." But, after all, it is not an undifferentiated blur. It is not like the world to the mystic, when he sees the "all in all" without any parts or internal distinctions, simply as a seamless, homogeneous One. Most works of art have a highly differentiated and therefore complex internal structure. Think of the differences of color, light, and subject matter in a painting, of the contrasts and balances between them. Think of the differences within a classical symphony — between the first movement and the *scherzo*, between various rhythms and instrumentation, and so on. The discriminating spectator is sensitive to these differences. They make the "organic" whole what it is. Then, in our critical moments, we can, and do, evaluate the elements of the work. Since these *are* parts of the work, surely we are talking about "the work" and supporting the judgment, "The work is aesthetically valuable."

Yet we are still talking only about the *parts* of the work. The foes of criticism insist that the goodness of the whole is not a total of the values of its parts. Here we run into a large question in "the logic of criticism": How can we infer from a number of judgments about the parts to the value of the whole? If we evaluate the plastic relationships, color values, and balance in a painting, and yet the painting is something more than all of these, how can our analysis support the evaluation of the *total* work?

There is no simple and obvious answer to this difficult question. It is a question which is central to all criticism. Yet we need not conclude that criticism is futile.

To begin with — though this is not the chief consideration — the elements of *some* works of art can be evaluated apart from the total work. It is not always true that the value of a part depends upon its place in the whole. We may appreciate the sound and rhythm of a poem, ignoring deliberately its intellectual significance. We must remind ourselves that not all works are perfect exemplifications of "organic unity." The thoroughgoing interdependence of parts and whole is more like an ideal for art than a descriptive fact about works of art.[25] In some works, particularly small works, the ideal may be achieved. In many works, however, the sensuous matter is incongruous with what is supposed to be expressed.[26] Large-scale works often have "dead spots" which are not related vitally to other passages or areas of the work and to the whole. The argument of the foes of criticism probably sounds stronger than it really is because they forget these facts.

Still their argument cannot be refuted on this point alone. For one thing, if you consider a sufficiently large "part" of the work, such as the structure of line, mass, and depth in a representational painting, then that becomes an aesthetic "whole" in its own right. For another thing, there *are* many works in which parts and whole are tightly knit into an "organic unity."

Art criticism must therefore give a stronger answer to its foes. It must show that it recognizes the importance of the part-whole relation and that the critic can take account of this relation in doing his job.

Again let us begin by granting that the quality of the whole work is "unique" and therefore, strictly speaking, "ineffable." This simply means the critic cannot capture in words just what the work "feels like" during rapt aesthetic attention. (If he could, we might just as well read critics as look at works of art.) It does not follow, however, that the critic can say *nothing* about the value of the whole work. He does not have to put his hands upon his mouth. We *can* and do say things about the total work which are meaningful and, within limits, accurate.

Think of the differences in the value-predicates. We describe some

[25] Cf. above, pp. 230–233.
[26] Cf. above, pp. 324–325.

works as "beautiful," others as "pretty," others as "ugly," and still others as "sublime." [27] Each of these terms suggests the kind of value which the work possesses and how it differs from other works. We can justify our use of any of these terms in a specific case by pointing to the structure of the work and the kind of aesthetic response which it arouses. In other cases, by using the same methods, we can show that the term has been used inappropriately. The "organic" quality of the work is not an utter mystery, about which we cannot speak meaningfully. Nor is it destroyed or distorted by applying general terms to it.

What is more, we can describe the work's total quality in much greater detail. "Beautiful," "pretty," and so on, are, of course, only approximate descriptions. The critic can do more. Once he has relished the quality of the work in his own experience, he can, if he is sufficiently adept with words, give us at least some sense of what the work "feels like" in aesthetic perception. You have probably read such evocative accounts of the work's quality. The name which is usually given to this kind of criticism is especially interesting. It is "appreciation." Such criticism moves away from mere analysis, with its handing-out of grades to the parts of the work, and toward aesthetic perception itself. It tries to render the immediacy and wholeness of the aesthetic experience.

Thus the quality of the whole is not completely ineffable. But what is most important, the critic can take account of the whole work while he analyzes the parts. He does not have to be guilty of that dissociation of parts and whole that his foes accuse him of.

As we have seen, understanding of the whole work's aesthetic import develops slowly. [28] It is imperative, however, that the critic should understand what the work is "trying to do," aesthetically. Only then can he judge the parts of the work intelligently. For, as the foes of criticism rightly insist, the values of the parts depend upon their contextual interrelationships within the whole. "Without a unifying point of view . . . criticism ends in enumeration of details [which] is as boring as it is irrelevant." [29] With the "unifying point of view," however, the critic will not be talking simply of isolated parts. He will, in all cases, study the part as it functions within the whole. Hence, he will avoid the mechanical application of "general rules," which, as the foes of criticism contend, is so often misleading. When the critic speaks of "distortion," or "balance," or "truth," he will speak of it as it occurs in *this* work. He will respect the uniqueness of the work.

Thus criticism should not simply ignore the arguments of its foes, even though it refuses to accept their conclusion and commit suicide. It should

[27] Cf. above, chap. 11, sec. 1.
[28] Cf. above, pp. 75–77.
[29] Dewey, *Art as Experience*, p. 314.

learn from their arguments. Criticism should never forget that it is the *whole* work that is being judged ultimately and that all that is said by the critic must be disciplined by this fact.

To sum up, the defence of criticism is, first, that we *can* talk meaningfully about the whole. And second, and more important, what we say about the parts need not be futile and misleading. These arguments may not satisfy those who insist that the work is "just itself" and therefore ineffable (but what will?). And they, after all, have the last word. No matter how discriminating and acute critical analysis may be, and no matter how much it may be governed by a sense of the whole, still criticism can never be a substitute for aesthetic perception of the individual work. The work of art is one thing and talk about it is another, just as the aesthetic attitude is one thing and the critical attitude is another. When criticism forgets this and tries, somehow, to replace aesthetic perception, it is bankrupt. For then it misconstrues its function. And it cannot but be harmful to those who read it, for it deludes them into thinking that there is no need for their own aesthetic experience. Criticism of this kind we must denounce as roundly as the foes of criticism condemn *all* criticism.

BIBLIOGRAPHY

* Rader, *A Modern Book of Esthetics.* Pp. 470–479.
* Vivas and Krieger, *The Problems of Aesthetics.* Pp. 414–418, 430–436.
 Boas, George. *Wingless Pegasus.* Johns Hopkins Press, 1950. Chap. VII.
 Gilbert, Katharine. *Aesthetic Studies.* Duke University Press, 1952. Pp. 115–124.
 Leavis, F. R. *The Common Pursuit.* New York: George W. Stewart, 1952. Pp. 211–222.
 Lepley, Ray, ed. *Value: A Cooperative Inquiry.* Columbia University Press, 1949.
 Lewis, C. I. *An Analysis of Knowledge and Valuation.* La Salle, Illinois: Open Court, 1946. Chap. XIV.
 Osborne, *Aesthetics and Criticism.* Chaps. I–II.
 Stolnitz, Jerome, "On Esthetic Valuing and Evaluation," *Philosophy and Phenomenological Research,* Vol. XIII (June, 1953), 467–476.

QUESTIONS

1. The philosopher John Dewey has said that after we examine and reflect upon a spontaneous liking ("valuing"), and have found it to be worth while — without painful consequences, etc., this favorable evaluation makes a difference in the felt quality of our liking: "Even in the midst of direct enjoyment, there is a sense of validity, of authorization, which intensifies the enjoyment." — *The Quest for Certainty* (New York: Minton, Balch, 1929), p. 267.

Do you find this to be true in your own experience? Can you give examples? If it is true of aesthetic experience, do you think that this gain in enjoyment is the result of aesthetic or nonaesthetic factors? Might it not be due to moral factors, e.g., the realization that appreciating the work will not cause us future pain, or social factors, e.g., the fact that other people also think highly of the work? When would favorable evaluation enhance valuing for *aesthetic* reasons?

2. Are there any specific works of art of which you would say, from your own experience, "I like it but I know it isn't good" or "I know it's good but I don't like it"? In each case, what are your reasons for saying this?

3. Are there any works of art which have been "ruined" for you by critical analysis? Was this because criticism showed up the flaws in the work or for some other reason?

4. In what sense, if any, do you think that aesthetic experience is "critical"? Do you think that the experience is most valuable precisely when the percipient is being "critical"?

5. "The problem (of criticism) is not one of analysis of the whole into elements but one of realizing aspects of the whole." — Morris, *The Aesthetic Process,* p. 156.
   What, precisely, is the distinction which is being drawn here? What do you take to be the significance of this distinction for the theory and practice of criticism?

15

The Meaning and Confirmation of the Value-Judgment

The aesthetic value-judgment is of the form, "*x* is aesthetically good (or bad)." Thus, "Botticelli's 'Birth of Venus' is beautiful," "*War and Peace is the greatest of novels*," "The poems of Edgar Guest are sentimental."

The purposes of evaluation were discussed in the previous chapter. Now we must examine the value-judgment itself. Even such a simple and spontaneous assertion as "That's nice!" raises serious questions for philosophical analysis. If we can answer these questions, we can clarify our beliefs concerning the evaluation of art, and we can make our specific judgments more circumspect and sound.

The very first question, of course, is that of the *meaning* of the value-judgment. Let us be clear that the issue is not the meaning of the specific value-predicates, e.g., "beautiful," "ugly," "sublime," etc. The distinctions between these terms were discussed earlier (Chapter 11). Rather, no matter which predicate we use, what exactly are we asserting in the value-judgment? If we are, quite simply, ascribing value to the work, then why do people so often say that something is "beautiful *to me*"? Is its value a property of the work, like any other property, such as size? Why, then, this reference to the spectator, if the judgment is about the work? Shall we go so far as to agree with the opinion of much common sense, after it has become tinged with sophistication — that "beauty is in the eye of the beholder"?

What, precisely, *is* the relation between aesthetic value, the work, and the percipient? If we are not clear about this, then, in the most literal sense, we do not know what we are talking about when we make value-judgments.

We voice the judgment as though it were a truth. We say "the work *is* —" as though we were describing a fact about things. As we saw in the previous chapter, judgments are used as tools of social persuasion, to induce others to share our likings and, perhaps, to change theirs. But our judgment will be accredited by others only if it is capable of being shown to be true, i.e., it must be confirmable. Confirmation, however, depends upon meaning. *How* we test the judgment's truth, what evidence we look for, what reasons we give in support of it — all these depend on what we mean by the judgment. If the judgment is about the work, and that alone, then we will look to the work for confirmation; if it is about the percipient, then we must go to quite another area for evidence.

But there is an even more basic question. Can there be *any* confirmation at all for an aesthetic value-judgment? Of course, the judgment is, verbally, a declarative statement. But is it like "Canada is north of the United States"? Or like "The sum of the angles of a triangle is equal to the sum of two right angles"? Can it be established by empirical evidence, like the former? The value-judgment is just that — a judgment of *value*. Can the existence of values be demonstrated by *facts?* Think of the sort of claim that is often made by motion picture advertisers — "This movie cost four million dollars to produce." Does it follow from this fact that the movie is *good?* All too many cinema "epics" show that it does not. What kind of evidence, then, *can* support the value-judgment?

Where there is factual evidence, as in the proposition about Canada, or reasoning, as in the proposition about triangles, we expect, and we get, *agreement.* All concerned accept the proposition. But not only is disagreement about art notorious (how often have you wrangled with a friend over the merits of some novel or moving picture or piece of music). There are some people who take disagreement so much for granted that they consider "agreement" quite meaningless, where talk about art is concerned. For there can be a "meeting of minds" only where *reasons* can be given for different viewpoints. Reasons show that some views are sound, others indefensible. In the evaluation of art, however, we have nothing but personal opinions. No *reasons* can be given. No reasons *need* be given. Each man's opinion is, as far as it goes, final, decisive, unarguable.

Which brings us to the next large problem of this chapter, viz., the meaning of "good taste" and "bad taste." In ordinary discourse, the vulgar retort, "Who sez?!" expresses skepticism of some assertion. In the evaluation of art, the question has particular pertinence. Most people refuse to believe that one man's opinion about art is as good as that of anybody else. Therefore, when a man makes an aesthetic judgment, they want to know with what authority, if any, he speaks. But you see what questions this belief involves: What is the meaning of "good taste"? *Is* there any tenable distinction between "good taste" and "bad taste"? And, related to these, does it make any sense to speak of the "improvement" or "education" of taste?

So once you start thinking critically about the simple-sounding judgment, "*x* is aesthetically valuable," you run into a whole cluster of problems: what does the judgment mean?; how, if at all, can it be confirmed?; how, if at all, can value-disagreements be overcome?; are some judgments more authoritative than others?

These are questions that, in one form or another, have probably occurred to you before. Perhaps you did not think of them in such general terms. More likely you were involved in disagreement about some *specific* work of art. But if you trace out the implications of such disagreement, you get involved in the questions just stated. This chapter will show how these questions are answered, systematically and critically, by opposing theories.

The theories to be studied are *objectivism, subjectivism,* and *objective relativism.*

1. OBJECTIVISM

We have noted that the value-judgment speaks of the work of art alone. It makes no reference to the spectator or, indeed, to anything else except the work. It ascribes value to the work as though beauty were something "out there," in some things and not in others.

Objectivism grounds its theory on this conviction of common sense. It takes value to be inherent in the work. Aesthetic value is "objective" or "absolute" (this theory is sometimes called "absolutism"). These terms are highly ambiguous, but they can be given a fairly precise meaning in this context. Any property of a thing is "objective" or "absolute" when it is *nonrelational,* i.e., when this property exists in the object, independently of the existence of any other object. Such a property differs from that of being "to the left of," or being "cousin of," or being "startling." An object can be described by these predicates only if there is something else, which is to the right of, or a cousin, or somebody being startled. Aesthetic value, by contrast, exists and its nature continues to be what it is, independently of anything else.

Objectivism does not commend itself solely because we use language this way. The theory also rests on the common empirical fact that some objects, because they are beautiful or graceful in themselves, seem to force us to look at them. Aesthetic value "presents itself . . . with compelling power." [1] We feel as though we are discovering something which was

[1] Greene, *op. cit.,* p. 5.

there all the time. We "open our eyes to beauty," but the beauty was there while our eyes were shut.

C. E. M. Joad states the central thesis of objectivism by saying that "If . . . the object possesses the quality of being beautiful, nothing that happens in or to any mind that may be apprehending the object can possibly affect its beauty." [2] He puts the same thesis dramatically: Suppose that the Sistine Madonna of Raphael continues to exist when the last human being dies out. "Has any alteration occurred in the picture? Has it experienced any change? . . . The only change that has occurred is that it has ceased to be appreciated. Does it therefore automatically cease to be beautiful?" [3] Joad then appeals to common sense, to "the undoubted fact that we all of us do think that it is better that an uncontemplated Madonna should exist than an uncontemplated cesspool." [4]

Such an appeal to common sense is always hazardous in philosophy. Common sense is not a unitary body of beliefs which are held in common by all. What we call "common sense" harbors a great many different and even logically inconsistent beliefs. So in the present case. Many people, who would not willingly admit that they have any less "common sense" than Joad, do *not* think that the "uncontemplated Madonna" is better than the "uncontemplated cesspool." "If nobody is around to look," they would say, "what difference would it make? Why talk about 'better' or 'worse' at all?" All nonobjectivist philosophers appeal to *this* strain in common sense. One of them says that "[An] object could have no kind of value . . . if nothing else than this object existed." [5] Another voices the conviction that values can only be understood in relation to what human beings feel: "What could by no possibility ever be an instrument for bringing any satisfaction to anybody, is absolutely without value." [6]

Joad calls his "Madonna-cesspool" example "a cogent argument." [7] But is it an *argument* at all? I do not mean by this, "Is it a *good* argument?" We have just seen that not everybody accepts it. Rather, is it an argument, in the sense that it offers evidence and reasoning to establish a conclusion which is in dispute? Is the issue between Joad and the nonobjectivists one of evidence? All parties accept the (hypothetical) facts — the Sistine Madonna exists when no human beings exist to contemplate it. The dispute is over the question whether this object is "beautiful." But surely this is just a dispute over whether we will *call* the Raphael Madonna "beautiful" or not. Whether we call it one or the other, depends on how we decide to

[2] C. E. M. Joad, "The Objectivity of Beauty," in Vivas and Krieger, *op. cit.*, p. 469. Reprinted by permission of the Oxford University Press.
[3] *Ibid.*, p. 470.
[4] *Ibid.*, p. 470.
[5] Lee, *op. cit.*, p. 73.
[6] Lewis, *op. cit.*, p. 387.
[7] *Op. cit.*, p. 471.

define "aesthetic value." It is not like the question whether a certain drug will cure some disease or whether a mathematical proof is logically valid. Neither factual evidence nor deductive reasoning can settle matters between Joad and his opponents. They could go on interminably (perhaps until, as on Joad's hypothesis, they cease to exist, like everybody else), shouting, "It is beautiful!" — "It isn't!" without any chance of resolving their dispute.

In other words, given the definition of "aesthetic value" as an objective or absolute property, the definition, *in and of itself*, cannot be argued about. Like all definitions, it is only a starting point. We must see what follows from it in the whole theory of objectivism. What does it imply for the methods of confirming the value-judgment, for the meaning of "good taste," for the possibility of settling disagreements about art? This is where the genuine issues come in. We can test the theory for its logical consistency and for the empirical evidence which is supposed to support it. We can set it against the enterprise of evaluation and criticism, as this has been carried on historically, to see whether the theory makes sense of these activities and provides a sound basis for criticism. The "Madonna-cesspool" dispute is hollow. (But how often have you engaged in comparable disputes?) Once it is out of the way, we get down to the real problems.

Let me now, therefore, set out the major theses of objectivism. All of these are corollaries of the objectivistic conception of "aesthetic value": (1) The value-judgment can be confirmed or disconfirmed. The judgment is true when the property which it ascribes to the work is actually present in the work. (2) Therefore, when two people disagree about the value of a specific work, only one of them can be right. The one who is wrong is attributing a property to the work which it does not in fact possess. (3) "Good taste" is the capacity to apprehend the property of aesthetic value, when it occurs in an object. A man has "bad taste" when he lacks this capacity. (4) Therefore, some aesthetic judgments are authoritative, others are not.

Now THERE IS ONE FACT which is invariably cited to disprove objectivism. You can probably guess what it is. It is the fact that men do *not* agree about the goodness or badness of works of art. If beauty is "out there" in the object, then why do we not all find it there? If value-judgments can be decisively confirmed, how is it that men continue to cling to opposing judgments? In fact, we disagree about nothing so much as art.

This line of argument is often thought to be a quick and decisive refutation of objectivism. Actually, as the following analysis will show, the facts of agreement and disagreement are highly complicated. Even more important, what these facts *prove*, for or against objectivism, is not straightforwardly clear.

THERE ARE SOME OBJECTIVISTS who try to deny the fact of disagreement. They must, of course, admit that people often make opposing judgments. Yet they hold that "in time" or "in the long run," disagreements tend to fall away and opinions converge on each other. There are many examples of artists, popular in their own day, who have been relegated to limbo with the passing of time. The greats, however, survive. "There is overwhelming agreement . . . that Bach's *B-minor Mass* is one of the greatest, if not the greatest, work ever composed, and that Tolstoi's *War and Peace* is the best novel ever written." [8]

This appeal to posterity raises certain crucial questions, however. For one thing, how long is "the long run"? At what point in the history of an artist's reputation can we say that a consensus of opinion has been arrived at? Doubtless we can find a period in which critical opinion about certain works is fairly settled or even close to unanimous. But a later historical period may also agree about the same works, except that its judgment is completely *opposed* to that of the earlier age. Indeed, the reputations of most and probably all works tend to fluctuate in this way. "From A.D. 400 to 1000 Euripides seems to have driven Aeschylus and Sophocles out of the field. In 1840 he was a botcher and bungler: to-day [1929] he stands, so far as we can judge, among the dozen greatest poets of the world." [9] Again, the Augustans took Dryden and Pope to be supreme; the nineteenth century considered their work prosy and lifeless; in our own time, their reputation is once more on the upswing. Now at which curve in the cycle are we to find the "consensus of history"? If we choose the judgment of one age over another, what keeps our choice from being completely arbitrary? We are then certainly not appealing to *all* posterity.

Moreover, it is not even true, of course, that there is always common agreement in any one age. More than one reader will probably dissent from the judgments on Bach and Tolstoy quoted above. "Wilenski and Fry in their books on French painting entirely ignore [Millet's] art while Mather considers it the 'most significant work of the century'." [10]

More important, even when two different ages "agree," in the sense that their judgments on a certain work are favorable, they may admire the work *for different reasons*. Indeed, this is almost always the case. Different ages "look for" different things in the work and therefore "read" it and evaluate it in highly diverse ways. Shakespeare's *Hamlet* has been well thought of, for at least most of the three and a half centuries since it was written. However, it has been read and performed as a swashbuckling melodrama, the study of an introspective, Romantic hero, a commentary

---

[8] Carroll C. Pratt, "The Stability of Aesthetic Judgments," *Journal of Aesthetics and Art Criticism*, XV (1956), 7–8.

[9] E. E. Kellett, *The Whirligig of Taste* (London: Hogarth Press, 1929), p. 150.

[10] Heyl, *op. cit.*, p. 97.

on the social order, a Freudian drama, and so on. Similarly, Professor Boas has shown in detail that there have been radically different interpretations of the famous "Mona Lisa" since the sixteenth century. At first it was esteemed for its lifelikeness;[11] in the nineteenth century, however, it became the vague, enigmatic depiction of "the eternal feminine."[12] Does the favorable evaluation of *Hamlet* or the "Mona Lisa" over the centuries lend support to objectivism? Can we say that later centuries were *agreeing*, if they interpreted these works in such profoundly different ways?

These questions give a new turn to our discussion. We are now led away from the *factual* issues of the history of taste to *analytic* problems: What is the *meaning* of "agreement" and "disagreement"? Unless we can get clear about these meanings, it is pointless just to cite historical facts. For we will not know what these facts prove about agreement and disagreement, and therefore what their bearing is on the truth or falsity of objectivism.

WHEN, THEREFORE, DO TWO VALUE-JUDGMENTS disagree with each other? Presumably when one says, "work of art *x* is good," and the other says, "work of art *x* is bad." But we have just noted that the work may be interpreted and therefore apprehended aesthetically in different ways. As a result, it is evaluated on different grounds. The subject of both judgments seems to be the same, "work of art *x*." But this phrase refers to highly dissimilar aesthetic objects. Then are the two judgments really in disagreement?

In general, two propositions disagree with each other when they cannot both be true. But in the present case, they speak of the "same" object in different respects, or of different properties of the same object. They may then both be true. Hence they are not really disagreeing. Surely there is no real disagreement when A says, "The table is brown," and B says, "No, it is wooden." This is obvious enough. Yet when the same sort of thing occurs in talk about art, it is not obvious at all, because the speakers fail to make clear how they are interpreting the work and how they are judging it. "One listener may be impressed by the gorgeous rhythms and melodies of Gershwin while another is depressed by the stodgy and unimaginative use of the bass and the sameness of style."[13] The former listener therefore judges Gershwin favorably, the latter judges him unfavorably. Can they not both be right, in different respects?

Consider an even more obvious case in which disagreement is purely verbal. Suppose A means by "*x* is good" simply "I like it" and B means by "*x* is bad" simply "I don't like it." Are they contradicting each other? Obviously both assertions can be true.

Joad calls attention to an especially important distinction in value-judgments, viz., the distinction between "what is good and what we like."[14]

---

11 Cf. above, p. 111.   12 *Op. cit.*, p. 224.
13 Pratt, *op. cit.*, p. 9.   14 *Op. cit.*, p. 464.

This corresponds, respectively, to the distinction between critical "evaluation" and "valuing" in the previous chapter.[15] A judgment of "what we like" is merely a report of our feelings during the aesthetic experience — whether we were pleased or displeased, etc. A judgment of "what is good" does not just report our immediate response. It results from thoughtful reflection upon and analysis of the work. Such analysis may show deficiencies in the work which we did not see during our spontaneous "liking" of the work. Therefore, when A is valuing and B is evaluating critically, the meanings of their apparently conflicting judgments and the grounds on which they are made, are utterly different. Here again, there is no real disagreement.

Therefore, we cannot tell merely from the linguistic utterances, "x is good" and "x is bad," whether there is genuine disagreement. We have to go beyond the words of the judgment to see what the phrase, "the work of art," refers to, and what claim is being made about it. Notice that this is also true when the judgments seem to be *agreeing* with each other, i.e., when both A and B say "x is good." If they have interpreted the work in radically different ways, or if A is only reporting a "liking" while B is offering a reasoned evaluation, then they are not really in agreement.

Hence the mere fact that two different historical periods call a work "good" proves nothing by itself, and, unless their judgments are examined further, this fact cannot be used as evidence on behalf of objectivism. And the mere fact that one period calls the work "good" whereas another calls it "bad" proves just as little by itself, and, without further analysis, this fact cannot be used as evidence *against* objectivism.

Now, SUPPOSE THAT THE OBJECTIVIST wants to use the facts of historical agreement as ammunition for his theory. He must show that the agreement is genuine. He must therefore show that critics of different periods are talking about the *same* objective property of aesthetic value. But the opponents of objectivism doubt that he can do this. They turn the facts of history of taste against the objectivist.

They argue in this way: If so many *different* values are found in *Hamlet* or the "Mona Lisa," can we justifiably say that there is any *one* value-property? Must not "aesthetic value" be a big, loose, all-encompassing concept in order to accommodate all the values that different periods find in the work? Indeed, does not "aesthetic value" become simply a name for the fact that different ages *do* take aesthetic satisfaction in the work? But if so, the objectivist must give up his theory. For in the first place, "aesthetic value" no longer denotes some specific property "in" the work.

[15] Cf. above, pp. 372 ff.

And in the second place, whether aesthetic value exists now comes to depend upon the facts of aesthetic experience, which is just what the objectivist wanted to deny originally.

We cannot tell how strong this argument is, until we see the case that objectivism makes for itself. What *is* the property of aesthetic value, according to objectivism? All that the theory has told us thus far is that value is "objective" or "absolute." This *characterizes* aesthetic value, but it does not describe the specific nature of the property itself. Until objectivism gives us such a description, the appeal to historical judgment will prove little or nothing. We must therefore look ahead to the next section, in which the theory is presented in detail.

There is, however, one further thing that we should see about the history of taste. Suppose that we find *real* disagreement about a work of art. In other words, A and B have the same interpretation of the work, they both make reasoned evaluations of it, they use the same criteria of evaluation — and yet A concludes "*x* is good" and B concludes "*x* is bad." As when a critic writes, "I think the novel is a failure for precisely the reason that many critics seem to like it most." [16] Or when "The very qualities in Manet that attracted Daumier, repelled Courbet." [17] Does such disagreement refute objectivism?

Not necessarily. For it is still wholly possible that one of the opposing critics has failed to see the value-property that is *there* in the work. It does not follow logically from "A does not find aesthetic value in *x*" that "there is no aesthetic value in *x*." This argument, used by the objectivist to save his theory, is, as a matter of logic, completely sound.

What is more, the objectivist can continue to use this argument no matter how much real disagreement we find. We might find, as in the old Latin saying, that there are "as many opinions as there are men." Still the objectivist could insist — and rightly so — that this does not disprove his theory. No matter how much men may differ, aesthetic value remains "objectively" within the work. If you understand this, then you will not be surprised to learn that Joad, the objectivist, freely admits that "[The] consensus of opinion among experts . . . is non-existent. . . . Tastes change, and the consensus of one generation, in so far as it exists, is often diametrically opposed to that of another." [18]

However, the objectivist's argument is a two-edged sword. For he is really saying that empirical facts — the actual judgments that men have passed on art — do not weaken his theory. But if the theory is not weakened by the facts of disagreement, neither can it be *strengthened* by the facts of *agreement*. If objectivism appeals to empirical evidence at all, then it must accept *all* the evidence, both positive (agreement) and

[16] Quoted in Heyl, *op. cit.*, p. 98.
[17] Quoted in Heyl, *op. cit.*, p. 98, n. 8.   [18] *Op. cit.*, p. 466.

negative (disagreement). No genuinely empirical theory can accept *just* the positive evidence and try to explain away the negative evidence.

But now, if historical evidence does not count, what reason do we have to think that there is *any* "objective" value-property in art? And how could we ever *know* that it exists? Again, we must not jump to the conclusion that objectivism has been "refuted." Rather, we must again ask the objectivist to spell out his theory.

To SUM UP: Whether objectivism is true or false cannot be decided by the facts of the history of taste. Examination of these facts always drives us back to the really basic questions, "What *is* the property of aesthetic value and how can we know it?" The facts of disagreement may create a presumption or suspicion that there really is no objective property there at all. But this cannot be any more than a suspicion unless we examine the objectivist's answers to our questions.

Often, in philosophy, you have to spend a lot of time going through evidence and unraveling arguments, only to show, in the end, that they do not settle the original question. We have had to do this with agreement and disagreement because people so often think that objectivism stands or falls upon these facts. I have tried to show that these facts are, upon inspection, complicated and mixed, and that they are not decisive, one way or the other. The vital tests for objectivism are: (1) can it describe clearly the property of aesthetic value, so that (2) it can tell when this property is being correctly apprehended?

In the long history of objectivism, there have been several different conceptions of the aesthetic value-property. These theories are of two kinds, chiefly: (1) theories which deny that "aesthetic value" can be defined; (2) theories which hold that "aesthetic value" can be defined and identify it with some describable property of the work, usually a formal property.

(1a) AESTHETIC VALUE IS OBJECTIVE; those objects which possess it call aesthetic attention to themselves; when they do, we find value *in* the object. But as to defining "aesthetic value" — that cannot be done. We know it well enough when we find it. However, we cannot "put it into words." Aesthetic value is like nothing else in the world; hence it defies conceptual description. It is something which is grasped as a whole or not at all; hence it cannot be analyzed.

Such a property, if it is to be known at all, can be known only by *intuition*. This term is widely used, both in philosophy and outside of it, e.g., "woman's intuition." It connotes direct awareness, as in the sensory awareness of a taste or odor. When the mystic "intuits" God, he describes his experience in sensory terms. So the Psalmist says, "O taste and see that the Lord is good." Therefore, the object of intuition is not known by reasoning or inference. When the scientist or the detective infers that, such-and-such being the case, a certain event that he cannot observe is probably the cause, he has arrived at his conclusion by "reasoning it out." But when the woman in love or the race track better "intuit" that something is the case — that the man really loves her or that a certain horse will win in the fourth race — they, unlike the scientist or the detective, can give no reasons for their belief. Often they will say that they "just feel it," though many times they will also say that they "just *know* it." Finally, intuition generally claims certainty. It carries with it a feeling of self-assurance which excludes the possibility that it can be mistaken. Taking sensory experience again as the model: when I smell a certain odor, I cannot be mistaken about how it smells. I may use the wrong words to describe it; I may not even know which words to use; I may be wrong in thinking that the odor comes from one place rather than another. Yet the odor has just the quality which I sense it as having and it would be absurd of you to say that my sensation is "incorrect."

The intuitionist objectivists (if we may dub them with such an ugly-sounding name) want to describe how aesthetic experience feels. The value of the work is something that is grasped directly; we do not reason it out or infer to it. And when we perceive the value-property, we cannot doubt its existence.

Moreover, the intuitionist objectivists want to put evaluation on a firm cognitive basis. The positive value-judgment is true when the work actually possesses the value-property; the negative judgment is true when it does not. We can know decisively whether the judgment is true or false by inspecting the work. Hence, when two people disagree, one of them is wrong because he either fails to intuit the property which is in the work or because he thinks he apprehends a property which is not, in fact, in the work. The man of "good taste" is one who has the capacity to discern the aesthetic value-property.

WHEN WE TURN TO THE CRITICISM of intuitionism, the first question is the question that has always been put to the intuitionist in any area of experience — aesthetic, moral, religious, amatory, or whatever — "What if intuitions conflict with each other?" Suppose that A and B both believe that beauty is a unique, indefinable property, and suppose that they both apprehend work of art x aesthetically, but A judges that "x is beautiful" and B judges that "x is ugly." How could this disagreement be resolved? Intuitionism, by definition, does not permit any reasons to be offered on behalf of either judgment. The intuition claims to be self-certifying. There is no court of appeal beyond it. Hence intuitionism estops the whole process of discussion, analysis, and appeal to evidence, by which we usually try to adjudicate value-disagreements.

The intuitionist might reply that that judgment is correct which is made by the man of "good taste." But this is, clearly, question-begging. For "good taste" is defined as "the capacity to discern beauty" and it is just the existence or nonexistence of beauty which is in question. Whether it is A or whether it is B who possesses "good taste," cannot be decided until we know whether the work does or does not possess beauty. Unless the theory can give us *independent* criteria which will enable us to recognize "good taste," the whole issue of "good taste" and "bad taste" will be stalemated just as badly as the issue of conflicting judgments.

This is the odd paradox in intuitionism: It starts out to be an extreme kind of objectivism. Yet it turns into "subjectivism." There is no way to determine the validity of the value-judgment; hence, it is impossible to decide when one judgment is "superior to" or "more authoritative than" another.

A might, of course, say that B is "value-blind." But B might then retort that A is "seeing things." From then on the epithets can get progressively nastier — "insensitive," "vulgar," etc. In the absence of evidence and reasoning, name-calling can terminate a dispute, even if it does not settle it. Indeed, intuitionism lends itself to this sort of thing because of intuition's pretensions to certainty. The man who is persuaded of his unquestionable rightness will not readily tolerate disagreement. That is why intuitionism, in all areas, has so often led to authoritarianism, i.e., setting up some person or institution whose decisions are enforced by suppressing all dissent. Art has had its "dictators," too, whether they were individual critics or "Academies."

Thus intuitionism leads us fairly quickly into a blind alley. The theory tries to preserve the common sense convictions that aesthetic judgments are either true or false, and that some men speak with greater authority on art than others. However, it almost immediately gives rise to irrationalism of various kinds. Worst of all, it provides no basis for critical analysis. Thus there is no way to disclose the value of the work to those who have not yet seen it.

But even if the foregoing criticisms are sound, note that they do not, in one respect, *disprove* the theory. It *may* still be true that aesthetic value is an irreducible, objective property and it *may* be that some men have the capacity to discern it, while others do not. But if the theory is stated in this way, as simply a possibility, then it is a very different theory and it is making a much weaker claim. Anything is *possible*, except what is logically self-contradictory. Once you say only that intuitionism *may* be true, you have withdrawn the theory from the reach of evidence, either for or against it.

So it is a desperate last refuge to say that intuitionist objectivism has not been "refuted." The critic of the theory will concede this. But this will not keep him from arriving at his conclusion, viz., that we have no reason to think that the theory is true.

(1b) THE PREVIOUS THEORY moves in a small circle. It says that beauty is just what it is, though we cannot say what it is. Either the percipient recognizes it or he does not. There can be no reason-giving.

A contemporary objectivist, Professor Vivas, sees the shortcomings of the intuitionist theory. On this theory, he says, value becomes "altogether fortuitous and miraculous, to be apprehended only by those who do so accidentally and forever closed to those who do not." [19] Art criticism is possible, however, only if it can appeal to properties of the work which are "available for public inspection." [20] Only so, furthermore, can we escape from purely "subjective" judgments which are based upon personal and accidental associations.

Therefore Vivas, although he too believes that value is objective, wants to be able to say more about it than the intuitionist can. Consequently he insists that aesthetic value "depends" on the "discriminable structure" [21] of the work. This structure can be analyzed and discussed as much as any objective property of things. The structure is not the *same* as aesthetic value, but the latter would not exist and would not be what it is, were it not for the structure. We can point to the "architecture" of a Bach fugue and say that the work is beautiful *because of* its form.

Professor Vivas' theory is a modern version of one kind of objectivism, which has been widely held throughout the history of criticism. As in intuitionism, beauty remains "just beauty," something indefinable and unanalyzable. However, there are certain properties which always occur along with beauty, and which are present only when beauty is present. These properties are, therefore, infallible indications of the existence of beauty. Pointing them out proves the value-judgment decisively. It follows, of course, that value-disagreement can be settled. We will call this the "accompanying-properties" theory.

In the history of this theory, the properties which accompany beauty have usually been taken to be formal properties of one kind or another. Thus art has been evaluated by "rules" for "composition" in painting, "proportion" in sculpture and architecture, "unity" in music.

THIS THEORY is clearly superior to intuitionist objectivism, for the reasons given by Vivas. And it has been accepted, even if unconsciously, by many critics in the history of art. Yet it has difficulties of its own.

---

[19] Eliseo Vivas, "The Objective Basis of Criticism," in *Creation and Discovery* (New York: Noonday Press, 1955), p. 195.
[20] *Ibid.*, p. 198.
[21] *Ibid.*, p. 195.

The initial question is, of course, "*Which* properties are the concomitants of beauty?" There are two kinds of answers.

The first is to define these properties very precisely and specifically. Thus, in the history of sculpture, "canons" of proportion have been laid down. These establish with mathematical precision the "proper" ratios between the various parts of the human anatomy. These ratios are the accompanying properties of beauty in sculpture. The sculpted figure must embody these ratios, if it is to be beautiful. Hence, the goodness or badness of the sculpture can be ascertained decisively.

But there is a clear objection to this approach. Suppose some sculptor violates the canons of proportion, not because of ineptitude or ignorance, but quite deliberately. Suppose that he thereby achieves formal proportions and a distinctive expressive effect, which are aesthetically satisfying. If his work is judged strictly by the canons, it must be condemned. What is worse, those who look at sculpture, using these canons as a standard of perception, will be systematically incapable of appreciating the value of the work.[22]

How were these canons arrived at in the first place? They did not arise simply from a knowledge of human anatomy. That in itself would not be enough to determine what is good and bad in the artistic representation of the body. Rather, the canons were derived from examination of specific works of sculpture. The proportions found in those works which were aesthetically pleasing were set up as the "proper" or "ideal" proportions. However, these were works created by particular artists, working at certain periods in history. When new movements in art develop, and the goals of art change, the sculptor's methods and techniques will also change. The old canons are no longer adequate as criteria of value. They fail to explain how aesthetic delight can be taken in the new sculpture.

The upholders of the old order can, of course, claim that the new sculpture is not "*really*" beautiful." But the evidence of aesthetic experience counts for more than traditionalism. The objectivists implicitly concede this, for in time the old canons are given up. The old ratios are *not* present in all good works of art.

It is most unlikely that we can find any set of specific properties which always occur along with beauty. Works of art are too diverse and complicated. Considering the history of taste, and the great number of artistic traditions and styles, we can even say that it is impossible, for all practical purposes, to find any such properties.

Many objectivists therefore give another kind of answer to the question, "Which properties always accompany beauty?" Instead of citing specific properties, they answer in general and abstract terms. They will say, e.g., that all and only those works which possess "organic unity" are beautiful.

22 Cf. below, pp. 445 ff.

Organic unity, as we have seen,[23] is not a specific property, like the mathematical ratios between the parts of a work. It is more like a *kind* of property, of which there are specific instances. Organic unity can be achieved in many different ways, by radically dissimilar works.

Thus, to go on with the previous example, there can be *many* canons of proportion. The old canons are valid for the periods and styles from which they were originally derived. Then, when a new style of sculpture arises, which depicts the body with different proportions, new canons can be developed. The constant factor, organic unity, requires that whatever proportions are employed, all the parts of the work must contribute to the value of the whole. If the new anatomical proportions fulfill this requirement, then the work can be shown to be good.

This theory is still a kind of objectivism. The new proportions are just as much "there" in the work, as the old proportions were in the earlier works. And this theory is obviously much more catholic and workable than the previous one. It can be applied in practical criticism to good advantage. Indeed, it has been used widely, in the history of art criticism. The critic does not try to tell what beauty *is*; that is a hopeless task. But he can apply general rules, to explain why the work is beautiful. Because these rules *are* general, he can respect the differences between individual works. He does not demand that the work must fit into preconceived molds, as the previous theory does.

But throughout our discussion of the "accompanying-properties" theory, one major question has been latent. It must now be raised.

The "accompanying properties" are not *identical* with beauty. The anatomical proportioning in the sculpture is not the same as the beauty of the sculpture. Nor does "organic unity" mean what "aesthetic value" means. The whole point of the theory is that the "accompanying properties" are only *indications* of aesthetic value. Value itself is indefinable and unanalyzable.

But we can say that *a* always accompanies *b* only if we can recognize *b* whenever it occurs. If beauty is "just beauty," as the theory holds, how can we know it? Only by intuition. And then we fall prey once again to all the notorious difficulties of intuitionism. If A finds work of art *x* valuable, in his aesthetic experience, and B does not, then it will do no good to say that the work does or does not possess certain properties. For whether these properties are accompaniments of beauty must remain uncertain so long as we are uncertain whether the work possesses beauty.

Here again, it is not the mere fact of disagreement which is the central problem. The real issue is whether and how we can know that value is present in the work. If we can show decisively that the work possesses aesthetic value, it would not matter how many people passed negative judgment upon it. Their judgments would be demonstrably wrong.

[23] Cf. above, pp. 230–233.

The "accompanying-properties" theory tries to demonstrate the existence of beauty, which pure intuitionism can only point to. But insofar as the "accompanying-properties" theory itself rests upon intuition, it cannot succeed. It would, if it could establish a rigorous, logical relationship between the "accompanying properties" and "just beauty." It would have to show conclusively that "work x is beautiful," and it must then show that this is true if and only if "work x possesses properties p, q, r." But if the theory cannot establish the first proposition, the second proposition has no point.

At this point, some readers may propose that the "accompanying-properties" theory should simply disown its family relationship to intuitionism. Why should it be burdened with the mysteries of intuition and the dilemmas into which intuition leads? But if we give up intuition, how will we know which works are beautiful? Which works will we look to, to find the properties on which value "depends"? Why, those which give aesthetic enjoyment to the audience. Instead of appealing to the "miraculous" property of "just beauty," as Vivas calls it,[24] let us appeal to the empirical evidence of what people like and dislike in aesthetic experience.

Using aesthetic response as the starting point, we can then examine the work to see which properties in it are responsible for our delight and satisfaction. In this way, as Vivas says, we can distinguish between value-judgments which are based upon accidental, personal associations in the percipient, and those which rest upon discriminating perception of what is genuinely in the work. Hence we can distinguish between good and bad reasons for aesthetic judgments and we can show that one man's judgment is better than another. We will lose the supposed "certainty" of intuition — just "seeing" the property of beauty — but that is no great loss. As Vivas says, "Infallibility is not possible but it is not necessary either." [25] We will still have what all objectivism wants — "the objective justification of . . . taste." [26]

This theory arises because of the inadequacies of the earlier ones. But it must now face this question: Is this theory still a theory of objectivism? Let us remind ourselves. What is "objectivism"? It is the view that aesthetic value exists in the work independently of any relations between the work and the spectator. But now this view has been given up. The properties on which aesthetic value "depends" are objective, but value itself is attributed to those works which give us aesthetic satisfaction. Hence "value" is now conceived of in *relational* terms.[27]

Once you do this, you must face the fact that there are *many different* valuings of the "same" work of art. We saw this earlier in *Hamlet* and the

[24] Cf. above, p. 400.
[25] *Op. cit.*, p. 200.
[26] *Ibid.*, p. 203.
[27] I do not imply that Professor Vivas would accept the view which has just been sketched, as it stands.

"Mona Lisa." Hence there will be many different interpretations of and judgments upon the work. There will not be just the one and only one correct interpretation, just the one and only one true judgment, that objectivism, in its most extreme form, insists upon.

It does not really matter, of course, what *label* we give this new theory. We might call it "modified objectivism" (though we have just seen that the basic doctrine of objectivism, i.e., its nonrelational conception of value, has now dropped out); we might call it "relativism," since it resembles the theory of that name, to be studied later; we might also call it "jabberwocky." No, it is not the label that is important. (Notice, though, that the names which are given to controversial theories often become colored by emotion. "Relativist" and "absolutist" are not emotionally neutral terms; they are frequently used as epithets.) What *is* important is that you should see why extreme objectivism is often given up in favor of such a theory.

LET ME THEREFORE give a brief summary of our analysis.

Objectivism begins by making evaluation simple and clear-cut. Aesthetic value is known intuitively and therefore infallibly; the value-judgment can be shown decisively to be true or false. The "accompanying-properties" theory tries to make evaluation more than just a matter of "either you see it or you don't." It tries to escape from the hopeless subjectivity of intuitions. It seeks an objective basis for criticism in artistic properties which can be observed and discussed publicly. Yet insofar as it still presupposes the intuition of beauty, the theory fails. Hence it turns to aesthetic like and dislike for its starting point. But then it conceives of value relationally, and it can hardly be said to be a theory of objectivism any longer.

To sum up the summing-up: We started with common sense, i.e., value-judgments are about the beauty which is in the object; they are demonstrably true or false; the judgments of some men are demonstrably better than those of others. But when we try to justify these beliefs, we encounter serious, perhaps fatal, objections. So we seem forced to move to the opposite pole and now we locate aesthetic value in felt experience. But then evaluation becomes far more complicated, for there are a whole host of interpretations and judgments. And unless we can show that some of these are "truer" or more "valid" than others, we may have to give up our common sense beliefs altogether.

This is the "dialectic," i.e., the movement of ideas, in the theory of evaluation. As we try to do justice to some evidence, our ideas develop flaws (e.g., the obscurity of "intuition"), or they fail to account for other evidence (e.g., the breakdown of traditional canons). Therefore the dialectic must go on. It is like a debate among opposing theories. There are still other theories to be discussed. If the student is to understand what we do when we judge a work of art, he must try to understand each of these theories.

What theory he will accept as his own, he must decide for himself, at the close of this chapter. But he will have the right to any one theory only if he can appreciate the strengths and weaknesses of all of them.

(2) THERE IS ONE FURTHER VERSION of objectivism. Unlike theories (1a) and (1b), this theory holds that "aesthetic value" *can* be defined. We can say more about beauty than simply that "you'll know it when you see it." We can tell what it is. Since it is publicly observable, we do not have to use intuition. The judgment, "*x* is beautiful," is demonstrably true if *x* possesses the property of beauty. Hence disagreements concerning art can be resolved.

Since this theory gives a definition of "aesthetic value," we will call it the "definist" theory. Usually "value" has been defined as a formal property of some kind. Indeed, this school of objectivism has often held that beauty *consists in* just those aspects of the work which theory (1b) considers "accompanying properties," e.g., fixed ratios between the sections of a musical composition or the parts of a painting, "organic unity," etc. Again, rules or canons can be set up to determine the presence or absence of value.

If this theory is valid, it provides the most objective basis possible for evaluation. I pointed out a moment ago that theories of evaluation oscillate between the "objective" pole — the properties of the work of art — and the "subjective" pole — the aesthetic responses of the audience. Theory (2) is far out toward the objective pole. Thus it avoids getting involved in the troublesome facts of aesthetic response, i.e., its variability from person to person, its "subjectivity," etc. Since we can define and therefore describe aesthetic value, anyone at all can recognize it.

The most obvious way to keep clear of aesthetic response is to say that beauty can be known without having aesthetic experience at all. To apprehend beauty does not require an unusual attitude of perception; nor do we have to feel pleasure or emotional excitement. Aesthetic value can be apprehended just by detached examination of the work. It can be known in the same way that we know that this apple is a good apple of its kind. We do not have to like the apple or want to eat it. Yet we can all agree on the criteria of a good apple — texture, firmness, etc. — and we can therefore agree on this apple's goodness or badness. Thus the definist theory becomes a kind of "marks-giving."

THIS IS COMPLETE OBJECTIVITY in evaluation. But whenever a theory moves to a dialectical extreme, it will be challenged from the opposite pole. Suppose we *do* examine the structure of the work and give it certain marks. What does that have to do with what people actually feel in aesthetic experience?

Could a work score high, according to the criteria of evaluation, and yet be dull and uninteresting? This is certainly a logical possibility. For "beauty," on this theory, does not refer to the qualities of the work when it is being apprehended aesthetically. Indeed, complete disparity between a work's high marks and its aesthetic interest is more than a logical possibility. It occurs often, in the history of criticism. When a certain style of art became highly traditionalized, its characteristic features were taken to be definitive of beauty. Much art was produced in an attempt to emulate these models. Yet because these works were imitative and unoriginal, they were dull and lifeless. They did not excite aesthetic interest, not even in the marks-givers. But the marks-givers could ignore this, since, for them, aesthetic value has nothing to do with aesthetic experience.

Now, of course, theory (2) is not "refuted" by the fact that high marks and aesthetic interest do not always go together. Those who hold this theory can still hold that the beauty is recognizably "there" in the work, no matter what people may feel. But, as we saw earlier, this kind of argument is purely definitional. It is simply another way of saying that "beauty" has been defined without any reference to aesthetic experience. The man who criticizes theory (2) does not wish to hear the definition repeated. It is precisely the usefulness of this kind of definition that he is challenging. For, he argues, what is the use of talking about the beauty of the object, unless we thereby explain what people actually feel in aesthetic experience, and unless we can thereby get others to enjoy what they have not enjoyed before? Beauty, on the definist theory, is a cold, objective thing, which can be known mechanically. That is not what we are concerned about when we evaluate and criticize art.

DEFINIST THEORY can meet this challenge only by moving closer to the subjective pole. Professor Joad does this. He defines "beauty" as the reproduction of certain "patterns or structures of reality." (He has a metaphysical meaning for this concept which it would take us too far afield to discuss.) However, Joad then adds that this property of beauty "arouses a certain kind of emotion in us." [28] As always, when aesthetic experience is brought into the picture, the fact that different people have different experiences must be reckoned with. Joad does not try to dismiss this fact.[29] He argues, however, that it does not destroy his view: "[The] different estimates of the value or beauty of a picture that may be advanced no more imply that the picture has no aesthetic value in its own right, than the varying guesses that may be made as to the temperature of a room prove that the room has not a temperature which is independent of and unaffected by the guesses." [30] As we have already seen, this rebuttal is, logically, sound enough. Beauty *may* continue to exist, untouched, no mat-

[28] *Op. cit.*, p. 473. [29] Cf. above, p. 396. [30] *Op. cit.*, pp. 473–474.

ter how much people disagree. But then the perennial question arises (do you see how the analyses of the various schools of objectivism tend to fall into a similar pattern?): How do you *know* whether the work possesses beauty?

Joad gives a frank and candid answer. He does not take refuge in intuition, authoritarianism, or undefined "good taste." He holds that some value-judgments are more correct than others. But, he goes on to say, "it is impossible to know with certainty which of the conflicting judgments is in fact nearer to the truth." [31] It follows that we cannot "decide with certainty who is a person of good taste and who is not." [32]

In making these admissions, Joad is a great deal more honest than many traditional objectivists, who either did not face up to the problem of how we can know beauty or else tried to weasel out of it. Yet Joad's very honesty gives the game away. It does no good to say that the beauty either is or is not there, and that one judgment is therefore sounder than another, unless there are clear ways of deciding intelligently for one or the other. Unless the theory can distinguish true knowledge of beauty from error and delusion, it cannot serve as a basis for evaluation and criticism. Joad likens the beauty of the work to the temperature of a room, because the existence of either one is not affected by the guesses that people make about it. But you see, of course, where the analogy breaks down. We can *know* which guess about the temperature is right. We have thermometers. By Joad's own admission, we have no thermometers for measuring aesthetic value.

Set Joad's theory alongside the "marks-giving" theory and this painful paradox arises: what we *can* know, i.e., the wholly objective, formal properties of the work, does not necessarily have anything to do with what we are interested in, i.e., aesthetic experience and the evaluation based upon it; what we can *not* know is what we are most interested in, i.e., the relation between objective beauty and aesthetic enjoyment. Either, then, mechanical marks-giving, but what is the use of that? Or else beauty *does* cause us aesthetic delight, but we can never tell whether beauty is actually present in the work, so we have no way of telling which percipients are actually responding to beauty and which are not.

Once more, it *may* be that beauty, as defined by Joad, exists independently of our perception. But unless the definist theory can set forth clearly the conditions under which beauty can be known, we have no reason to believe in this form of objectivism either. As Osborne neatly puts it: "[It] is no different to say that beauty is an objective property but we cannot know it and to say that we cannot know whether beauty is objective." [33]

---

[31] *Ibid.*, p. 474; cf., also, p. 475.   [32] *Ibid.*, p. 474.
[33] H. Osborne, *Theory of Beauty* (New York: Philosophical Library, 1953), p. 75.

THUS FAR, the analysis has shown the implications of definist theory, i.e., starting with a definition of "aesthetic value," certain consequences have been shown to follow. But there is a more central criticism of the theory, viz., to challenge the very attempt to define "beauty." Can we identify aesthetic value with any specific property or group of properties, as definist theory attempts to do?

There are reasons to think that we cannot.

First, because works of art are so profoundly different from each other. Take into account the diversity of artistic media and of the formal structures which can be created within them; then consider the infinite range of styles and methods in the history of art. Can we reasonably expect to find any properties which are common to all aesthetically valuable objects, and only to them? Not likely. The fact that traditional definitions have met with only partial acceptance and have so often broken down is strong presumptive evidence against the success of any definition.

Unless he restricts aesthetic value to a small area of art, the definist must try to take account of the enormous diversity of works of art. He will therefore be forced to define "aesthetic value" in terms of some highly abstract notion such as "unity" or "harmony." But "unity" or "harmony" is more like a *synonym* for "value" than a definition of it. It does not tell us what beauty *is*. It does not spell out the properties which make up beauty. It is simply a term of positive appraisal, like saying that the work is "good."

Yet even if the definist pays the price of narrowness, and identifies beauty with some specific formal property, his definition is open to another kind of criticism. The formal structure of the work is only *one* element of the work. There is also the matter, expression, and often the subject matter, as well. When we say that a work is "beautiful," we are referring to *all* of these in reciprocal interaction with each other. It is the *total* work that we are judging.[34] No definition in terms of form alone can explain the meaning of "beauty."[35]

But there is something else in the common meaning of "beauty" that no purely objectivist definition takes account of. "Beautiful" is often used like "pleasing" or "surprising" to refer to the spectator's response. It is not like "symmetrical" or "Petrarchan sonnet," terms which do not refer to felt response. Indeed, some philosophers would hold that the only thing that beautiful objects have in common is that people feel delight or enjoyment in perceiving them. At this point, the objectivist conception of value is given up altogether.

EACH OF THE OBJECTIVISTIC THEORIES — intuitionism, the "accompanying-properties" theory, the definist theory — begins with common sense and

[34] Cf. above, chaps. 9–10, pp. 382 ff.
[35] Cf. above, p. 271.

each tries to justify it. Objectivism rests upon what all or nearly all of us believe, viz., that aesthetic judgments can be shown to be true or false, that the judgments of some men are more authoritative than those of others, that there is a real difference between "good taste" and "bad taste." But each of the objectivistic theories has great difficulty in articulating these beliefs so that they will be clear and workable.

Should we then give up these beliefs altogether? The next major theory proposes just that.

2. SUBJECTIVISM

Not that this theory is completely divorced from common sense. As we have noted, common sense believes a great many different things. For the most part, it is probably objectivistic. Yet common sense also believes that "Beauty is in the eye of the beholder," that the value of a work of art cannot be *proved* — "Either you like it or you don't" — and therefore that "It's all a matter of taste." But "taste," in this colloquial saying, does not mean what objectivism means by "good taste," i.e., a faculty of superior discrimination which gives authority to aesthetic judgments. Rather taste is now, simply, habitual preference, i.e., what one generally likes or dislikes. If a man happens not to like a given painting or a certain composer, you cannot show that he *ought* to. If such common sense were literate enough to know Latin, it would quote the old phrase, *de gustibus non est disputandum* ("there is no arguing about tastes").

There has been a widespread reaction against objectivism or absolutism of all kinds in our own time. Cultural anthropology has shown that there are almost as many moral codes as there are societies. Belief in a "universal" or "absolute" morality has been severely weakened as a result. The same is true of political and religious absolutism. But absolutism has also declined because of its own theoretical weaknesses. In morals, as in aesthetics, many have concluded that it is unable to justify its beliefs. It is noteworthy that the two thinkers whom we studied in the previous section, Vivas and Joad, are much more modest in their claims than traditional objectivists. These modern objectivists see the force of the criticisms which have been directed against their view; hence they realize it when their theory leads into blind alleys and they admit its shortcomings. Finally, absolutism or objectivism stands for an "aristocratic" way of life. It gives rise to an *élite*, which dominates those who lack superior endowments. But a society such as ours has little patience with such an aristocracy. It would be downright "un-American" for you to tell me what I *ought* to like in art or almost anything else.

Professor C. J. Ducasse has worked out "a declaration of independence in matters of taste in art." [36] He thinks that we have been too long intimidated by critics who wrapped themselves in the mantle of objectivism. He speaks up on behalf of laymen "who in general are deplorably humble and easily awed." [37] There is no reason to be "awed" by those who profess to tell us what is "really beautiful." "[There] is a realm where each individual is absolute monarch, though of himself alone, and that is the realm of aesthetic values." [38]

This sentiment will probably commend itself to many readers. Yet it has been said that those who "overtly profess" such a view "do not really believe it in the sense of being able to accept its full implications." [39] Can we "really believe" that anybody's judgment of a work of art is just as good as anybody else's? Does the opinion of the rank amateur count for as much as the reasoned evaluation of a man who has had long experience in the arts and has developed great aesthetic sensitivity? Is *de gustibus* the last word in aesthetic evaluation?

Well, Professor Ducasse "really believes" all these things. He is the most thoroughgoing exponent of *subjectivism* in recent aesthetics.[40] And, as we shall now see, he argues for it persuasively.

"THIS WORK IS BEAUTIFUL" sounds as though it were simply ascribing a property to the object. Objectivism, as we have seen, takes seriously the language of the judgment. For Ducasse, however, the judgment refers primarily to the *experience* which the spectator has, when he apprehends the work aesthetically. He says "This work is beautiful," when he has felt pleasure ("ugly," if his feelings have been unpleasant).[41]

This is the keystone of subjectivism. When we say that an object has aesthetic value, we are reporting our feelings. We are not, as in the various versions of objectivism, pointing to objective properties. Hence, Ducasse can simply by-pass the vexing problems that objectivism gets involved in. He does not have to decide whether "beauty," standing for an objective property, can be defined, and, if it can be, which properties are identical with beauty. And the problem of how we can know whether the value-judgment is true, can be solved handily:

---

36 *Art, the Critics, and You*, p. 10.   37 *Ibid.*, p. 118.

38 *Philosophy of Art*, p. 288.

39 Osborne, *Theory of Beauty*, p. 82.

40 Ducasse demurs at the use of "subjectivism" to describe his theory (cf. *Philosophy of Art*, p. 284; *Art, the Critics, and You*, pp. 90–91), though he uses the word at other places (cf. *Philosophy of Art*, p. 293). However, his total theory makes it clear, I think, that his concessions to an objectivistic way of talking are purely nominal. His views are of the kind which have usually been called "subjectivistic," and, in any event, any word will do to mark off this theory from objectivism and objective relativism.

41 *Philosophy of Art*, p. 234. I omit reference to Ducasse's description of beauty as a "capacity."

That a given railroad bridge is a good bridge can be proved or disproved by running over it such trains as we wish it to carry, and observing whether or not it does carry them. But there is no similar test by which the beauty of a landscape could be proved or disproved. Judgments of beauty . . . have to do with the relation of the object judged to the individual's own pleasure experience, of which he himself is the sole possible observer and judge.[42]

Either I feel pleasure or I do not. The judgment reports my feelings. I alone can know what they are. Hence I am the "final and infallible judge." [43]

Now there is no longer any problem of disagreement about values. Of course, different people are constituted differently. Hence where A feels pleasure in apprehending x, B does not. But we do not have to decide which one is "right." Beauty is not an objective property. It varies with the spectator. "[An] object which one person properly calls beautiful will with equal propriety be not so judged by another." [44]

The reader might grant what is, after all, the obvious fact that judgments vary from person to person and even with the same person at different times. Still, if you have any objectivism in you, you might want to take issue with Ducasse. You might want to argue that though people assert different judgments, the real question remains, "But is the work really beautiful?"

Ducasse draws an analogy with "the taste of pineapple": "Some persons like it, and others dislike it; but it would be absurd to say that it is *really* good, although some dislike it, or *really* bad, although some like it." [45] You see, Ducasse has undercut the whole issue of evaluation, as the objectivist understands it. Evaluation is now wholly a matter of what one likes or dislikes. No further questions can arise.

But are not some people more sensitive and discriminating aesthetically than others? To which Ducasse replies:

> There are connoisseurs of beauty . . . but their judgments of beauty are "binding" on no one. Indeed it is hard to see what could possibly be meant by "binding" in such a connection, unless it were an obligation on others to lie . . . concerning the aesthetic feelings which in fact they have or do not have. . . . There is, of course, such a thing as good taste, and bad taste. But good taste, I submit, means either my taste, or the taste of people who are to my taste, or the taste of people to whose taste I want to be.[46] . . . Tastes can be neither proved nor refuted, but only "called names," i.e., praised or reviled.[47]

---

42 *Ibid.*, p. 286.
43 *Ibid.*, p. 268.
44 *Ibid.*, p. 284.
45 *Art, the Critics, and You*, p. 120. Italics in original.
46 *Philosophy of Art*, p. 285.
47 *Ibid.*, p. 291.

But do we not sometimes give objective reasons in support of our judgments? We demonstrate the beauty of the painting as the objectivists would have us do, viz., by appealing to "principles" or canons of composition, etc. Ducasse's rejoinder is that such rules simply describe those properties of art-objects which most people happen to like. Hence, they are valid only when they *"predict to us* that we shall feel aesthetic pleasure here, and aesthetic pain there." [48] If, however, they fail to describe what I actually like or dislike, they are not "binding" upon me. And I have no obligation to accept the judgments which they are used to support.

A critic of subjectivism charges that it cannot answer the question, "[Why] is it that certain works of art continue throughout the centuries to be highly praised and thus receive an established reputation?" [49] (You will remember that some objectivists cite this fact in defence of their theory.) Ducasse gives a characteristically straightforward reply. The appeals to historical consensus "prove nothing whatever, except that beauty is found in the object . . . by such as do find it there." [50] Agreement simply shows that some people, since they are "built" the same way, take pleasure in the same thing.[51] But it "cannot possibly prove the object's beauty to those who do not perceive any in it." [52]

Finally, we usually place great faith in those who have extensive knowledge of art and specialized training in artistic techniques. We think that they speak of art with greater authority than the amateur. But Ducasse, as you might expect, is suspicious of these people. He holds that knowledge about art "is indispensable to persons of one class, namely, those who desire to be able to *talk* about works of art in a manner that will be intelligible to those who are similarly equipped, and impressive to the humble who are not." [53] Specialized knowledge, however, is often fatal to aesthetic enjoyment. For then one becomes interested in problems of technique, etc., and thus one loses the capacity for aesthetic contemplation.

But even when knowledge about art makes a difference to aesthetic experience itself, Ducasse holds to his central thesis: the spectator now likes what he did not like before; but his judgment and taste have not become "better" than anybody else's. *"There is . . . no such thing as authoritative opinion concerning the beauty of a given object."* [54]

THE OPPONENTS OF SUBJECTIVISM agree that the theory cannot be "refuted." [55] For what would a "refutation" be? Is it a demonstration that the theory is logically self-contradictory? But given Ducasse's analysis of the

[48] *Ibid.*, p. 292. Italics in original.   [49] Heyl, *op. cit.*, p. 123.
[50] *Philosophy of Art*, p. 289; cf., also, p. 304.
[51] *Ibid.*, p. 286.   [52] *Ibid.*, p. 289.
[53] *Ibid.*, p. 225. Italics in original.
[54] *Ibid.*, p. 284. Italics in original.
[55] Cf. Weitz, *op. cit.*, pp. 193, 194; Joad, *op. cit.*, p. 465.

meaning of the aesthetic judgment, and what it implies for the confirmation of the judgment, the theory is logically consistent. If the judgment makes no claim other than that the speaker has had certain feelings, it cannot legislate for or be "binding" upon anyone else. Besides, do we *want* to refute Ducasse's theory? It is an engaging, jaunty theory, with its free-swinging "I'm-as-good-as-anybody-else" refrain. It cuts down to size the snobbism and affectation that are so prevalent in art criticism and talk about art.

Yet if the theory cannot be refuted in the above sense, still it can be criticized. Granted that Ducasse is logically consistent. A theory of aesthetic evaluation is not a purely formal, deductive system, like a mathematical system. Logical consistency is not the only test. A theory of evaluation is intended to explain the activities which we carry on in the name of judgment and criticism. It is accountable to the facts of our experience. I want to argue that subjectivism exaggerates the importance of some facts and ignores the importance of others. I want to argue that the theory is too narrow and one-sided.

LET US BEGIN BY ADMITTING that the percipient is the "final and infallible judge" of whether he has felt pleasure. (Some philosophers would want to challenge Ducasse even at this point. Are we always sure whether we have experienced pleasure? Might not the aesthetic experience be such a complicated and subtle mixture of feelings that we cannot quite decide whether we "really enjoyed" it? But there are other, larger issues to discuss, so we will simply waive this question.) We have no occasion to challenge the judge's "infallibility." Not because we cannot do so, since he alone knows what feelings he had, but rather because it is not his feelings that we chiefly want to find out about when we evaluate art. As it stands, his report of his feelings is simply and solely a "brute fact." Unless he is a good friend, we are not greatly interested in whether he felt pleasure or displeasure.

The spectator's autobiographical report is only a starting point. We want to go beyond it. *Why* has he felt pleasure or displeasure?

Then we find facts like this: Richards, in *Practical Criticism*, from which I have already quoted,[56] cites the responses of students to a poem which begins,

> A Health, a ringing health, unto the king
> Of all our hearts today!

One student, in defending his judgment of the poem, wrote: "Nobody worships the King, and patriotic verse tends to be insincere."[57] Another wrote: "As a staunch royalist . . . I had thought after reading the first line

---

[56] Cf. above, pp. 55–57.   [57] *Op. cit.*, p. 120.

to enjoy this little poem." [58]   And another: " 'King' associates itself in my mind with Tyranny, an impossible subject for poetry." [59]

Now, it is understandable enough that British students will think of "the King" more readily than, say, Americans will. But in the poem "king" is not capitalized; he is described as "the king/ Of all our hearts"; there is not the remotest allusion to monarchy or "tyranny" throughout the rest of the poem. (In fact, the poem is a birthday tribute to the novelist, George Meredith.) What has happened is that these three students have simply misread the words of the poem. Having misconstrued its literal meaning, they then adopted attitudes which were inappropriate for appreciation of the poem, and they therefore "looked for" the wrong things in the poem.

Each of these students felt pleasure or displeasure. That is just a not very interesting fact. But does their reading do justice to what is in the poem? Is their experience a reliable index of the poem's value? Are we prepared to accept their evaluations?

Here is another example, the poem whose first stanza reads:

> Softly, in the dusk, a woman is singing to me;
> Taking me back down the vista of years, till I see
> A child sitting under the piano, in the boom of tingling strings
> And pressing the small, poised feet of a mother who smiles as she sings.

One student says that the effect of the poem is impaired since it is doubtful "that 'tinkling' strings can boom." [60]   Perhaps so, but the word in the poem is not "tinkling." Another student describes his associations: "This poem unfortunately associates itself with jazz, and 'coal black mammies' thumping the old piano down in Dixie. This association condemns it." [61]   Still another student believes that the poet is describing his visit to a concert. Professor Richards comments: "A reader who can think the woman is singing — 'softly, in the dusk' — on a concert platform has not managed to approach very closely to the poem." Richards concludes that this student's negative criticisms of the poem "are less binding for that reason." [62]

I have not quoted from these students so that you and I can have a condescending feeling of superiority toward people who read poems so badly. All of us, at one time or another, have doubtless been guilty of misreadings which were at least equally egregious. I am, rather, trying to cite evidence for Richards' conclusion that some judgments are "less binding" than others and to show that we can give reasons for saying this. Richards' word "binding" is precisely the word used by Ducasse when he *denies* that any one judgment is more "binding" than any other. Generalize Richards'

[58] *Ibid.*, p. 121.   [59] *Ibid.*, p. 121.   [60] *Ibid.*, p. 106.
[61] *Ibid.*, p. 108.   [62] *Ibid.*, p. 113.

conclusion to evaluation of all the arts and then the issue is joined with Ducasse.

Richards sums up his findings by detailing the many ways in which readers can misconstrue the poem and therefore fail to appreciate it. Thus he says that "The rapidity with which many readers leap to a conviction as to a poem's general intention, and the ease with which this assumption can distort their whole reading, is one of the most interesting features in the protocols." [63] Often the reader will approach the poem with fixed ideas, e.g., "that lines *must* not run over, that sonnets *must* have a definite division, that strict descriptive accuracy *must* be achieved." [64] These "presuppositions" cripple aesthetic perception. "By blinding the reader to what else is in the poem . . . he *forces* his predilection . . . upon the poem — rejecting, comparatively unread, poems that will not allow it." [65]

These are only some of the ways in which the reader can go wrong. He may approach the work "unsympathetically" because he is a "staunch royalist" or for a host of other reasons. He may lack sufficient familiarity with the work to understand its "general intention." The formal structure may be too complicated or too subtle for him to grasp. He may not have the knowledge which is required to understand the work's symbolism.

In each of these cases we can *show* that and how he went wrong. We do not condemn his perception of the work because of dogmatism or snobbery. We make our case by calling attention to objective properties of the work which can be observed by all. It may be as simple as pointing out that "king" is not capitalized and that the poem speaks of "the king/ Of all our hearts," not the King of England. But we have seen that the total reading of a poem can turn on just such simple matters. In most cases, of course, the analysis of the work would have to be far more complicated and detailed. In any event, we can *show* that some interpretations of a work of art are distorted, irrelevant, or short-sighted. The value-judgments which are based upon these experiences are not reliable judgments of the work's goodness or badness.

Thus we begin with the judgment, "x is beautiful" = "I have felt pleasure in apprehending x," but we do not stop there. We go on to test the soundness of the judgment. Now, Ducasse recognizes that people try to defend their judgments. He holds, however, that the "reasons" which they give simply describe which objects please or displease them.[66] But here again subjectivism is open to question.

I would like to put the criticism in this way: Ducasse ignores the distinction between *causes* and *reasons*. A cause is some psychological occurrence which leads the percipient to like or dislike the work and therefore to judge

[63] *Ibid.*, p. 206.   [64] *Ibid.*, p. 296. Italics in original.
[65] *Ibid.*, p. 300. Italics in original.
[66] *Philosophy of Art*, pp. 290–291.

it favorably or unfavorably. A reason is something which *justifies* his liking or dislike and therefore *supports* his judgment of the work's value. Causes are not always reasons.

Whatever experience a man has, there will be causes for it. However crude and superficial some aesthetic experience is, it can be explained causally, e.g., misreading, lack of familiarity, preoccupation with oneself, etc. "Cause" is a large and promiscuous category. "Reasons" are much more limited. In morality, similarly, there are causes for all actions, but reasons only for those which are ethically justified. We ask a man who performs an act of needless cruelty, "Why did you do that?" and he replies, "Because I was angry." That was the *cause* of his action. But, as we say to him, "That's no *reason* for acting that way."

Consider the reader who misunderstands the words of the poem, therefore takes the poem to be saying something wholly different from what it really is saying, and then feels aesthetic displeasure. He tries to uphold his judgment by saying that the poem has such-and-such properties, which he — mistakenly — attributes to it. These properties displease him. But he is then only describing the *causes* of his negative judgment. Citing such-and-such properties is not a *reason* for the negative judgment, because these properties are not genuine properties of the work. The judge is, as Ducasse says, describing the sort of thing which he dislikes. He is telling us why he had the experience which he had. But he is not *justifying* his judgment upon the work.

Ducasse uses "reason" so broadly that he destroys the crucial distinction between causes and reasons. Therefore he destroys the possibility of reasongiving. The whole area of aesthetic evaluation becomes, as Ducasse says, a state of "anarchy." [67] There is no way to distinguish what is sound from what is unsound, what is justified from what is unjustified.

For Ducasse, the be-all and end-all is just what each person feels. But, as Santayana argues, this is not enough:

> Mere taste is apt to be bad taste, since it regards nothing but a chance feeling. . . . Chance feeling needs to fortify itself with reasons and to find its level in the great world. When it has added fitness to its sincerity . . . it will have acquired a right to live.[68]

Judgments lack "fitness" when the work has been misinterpreted or when the percipient does not possess aesthetic sympathy. They gain "fitness" only when the judge can show that he has seen and responded to what is genuinely within the work.

Ducasse generally speaks of "connoisseurs" scornfully. He is, you will remember, the spokesman for the aesthetic "layman." Hence he makes out

[67] *Ibid.*, p. 288.
[68] *Reason in Art*, p. 207.

"connoisseurs" to be pretentious people who use highfalutin talk about art to impress the layman. At several places, however, Ducasse recognizes that some people *do* possess greater aesthetic sensitivity than others. Thus he points out that those who do not respond to the formal structure of music "simply *do not hear the music;* they hear only musical elements." [69] Surely this implies that some people — those who "do hear the music" — are better judges of aesthetic value than others? How then can Ducasse say that "there is no such thing as authoritative opinion concerning the beauty of a given object"? [70]

Ducasse never seems to face up to this. On his analysis of "opinion concerning beauty," i.e., a report of what one has felt, only the speaker's opinion can be "authoritative," as we have seen. But it is just this analysis of the value-judgment which is now being challenged. Ducasse cannot simply restate his basic thesis. He must give us an *argument* to support it. His argument appears to be that even when connoisseurs see more deeply into the work, their judgments are not "binding" on anyone else. And they are not "binding" because they "cannot possibly prove the object's beauty to those who do not perceive any in it." [71]

This is essentially the argument that I used earlier to criticize "marks-giving." [72] But in the present case, the connoisseur is not simply a marks-giver. He is not simply ticking off the properties of the work mechanically. On Ducasse's own showing, the connoisseur has had an aesthetic experience and his perception has been acute. If a man can defend his judgment by pointing to properties in the work which he has perceived and responded to, then he gives us reasons for accepting his judgment. Men of wide experience and trained discrimination make such judgments. Their opinions are therefore "authoritative."

Still, Ducasse insists that *other* people do not take pleasure in the same works. This is, of course, true. But from this "brute fact," Ducasse infers that the connoisseur's judgment is not "binding" upon them. There seems to be an ambiguity here in the word, "binding." Well-founded judgments are "binding" upon us in the sense that we should accept any assertion which is supported by strong reasons. They are *not* "binding" upon us in the sense that we must ourselves have the same experience as the judge. Perhaps we have some other, but still legitimate interpretation of the work. Or perhaps we are not capable of viewing the work in the same way, because our senses are not sufficiently acute or because our emotional sympathies are limited. How many of us can look raptly at a single vase for several hours and enjoy it, as Roger Fry did? Very few, doubtless. His acute powers of discrimination enabled him to relish at great length the contours and

---

[69] *Philosophy of Art,* p. 230. Italics in original. Cf., also, pp. 278–279.
[70] Cf. above, p. 412.   [71] Cf. above, p. 412.
[72] Cf. above, pp. 405–406.

texture of the vase. Being a skilful critic, he could describe his experience. Even if we do not or cannot share his experience, are we prepared to say that his judgment of the vase's beauty is no more "binding" than that of the insensitive amateur?

Indeed, we often *do* accept evaluations which do not describe our own experience. And we are not then simply lying about our feelings or kowtowing to authority, as Ducasse has it.[73] This is an important fact which Ducasse overlooks. We may fail to take pleasure in the object and still say that it is aesthetically good. We understand the causes of our failure to respond. We have some incapacity, some personal idiosyncrasy, some bias which keeps us from appreciating the work. (I think that I could appreciate the painting of Paul Klee if I had more of a sense of humor.) Then, although we have had feelings of displeasure, we do not say, "The work is ugly." We do not take our immediate feelings to be final and decisive, as Ducasse has it. We recognize the difference between mere like or dislike and thoughtful evaluation.

Sometimes our whole temperamental make-up keeps us from appreciating the work. To those who know the writings of both E. M. Forster and James Joyce, it will be easily understandable why Forster, as he tells us, does not like Joyce's *Ulysses*. The world depicted by Joyce is teeming, vulgar, and sprawling, crowded with common, often uninhibited people. Forster has shown himself to be, in his novels and criticism, a man of fastidious refinement and gentility, perhaps a little overrefined, possibly even a little bloodless. Forster cannot readily respond to Joyce. Yet he recognizes his own limitations and sees beyond them. He is therefore able to acknowledge value in the work which he does not feel:

> The more I read Joyce the more I am compelled to recognize his genius. I never can appreciate him; I suppose I should never try. But reading him, I become more humble.

Let me state this criticism of Ducasse in this way: It is a fact of aesthetic evaluation that we can and do meaningfully say, "*x* is good, but I don't like it." Indeed, I would add, it is one of the hallmarks of the good critic that he can say this. For then he recognizes the distinction between spontaneous feeling and reasoned judgment. But on Ducasse's theory, one cannot meaningfully say this, since to say "*x* is good" is to say no more and no less than "I like it."

After all is said and done, of course, there always remains the sort of person who will not relinquish the privilege, granted to him by Ducasse, of being "absolute monarch, though of himself alone, [in] the realm of aesthetic values." He will not accept any judgments which do not tally with what he

[73] Cf. above, p. 411.

418

likes and dislikes. His motto usually is "I may not know anything about art, but I know what I like." (The painter Whistler, so the story goes, once overheard a lady say this in a London art gallery, whereupon he commented sourly, "Yes, madam, so does a cow.") It is no great achievement to "know what one likes," when this simply means "to *like* what one likes." As we have seen throughout our discussion of Ducasse, the percipient *is* the "infallible judge" of that. But his judgment will carry weight only if he "knows something about art," and if what he "knows" enters into and makes a difference to aesthetic perception. Then the judge can give reasons to support his opinion. Often it is the most naïve and undiscriminating person who is most dogmatic about his beliefs. Such a person will stubbornly refuse to admit that another's opinion is better than his, even in the face of evidence that the other has seen into the work with greater experience, knowledge, and discrimination.

Ducasse still champions the "layman":

> A person's taste . . . may be indeed more *sensitive* than that of another, in the objective sense that he is able to get pleasure or displeasure from differences in the object that, to the other person, make no difference. But the latter will then call the other "oversophisticated," "effete," "precious." [74]

Yet what does this name-calling prove? Ducasse himself admits — what is an incontestable fact — that some percipients are more discriminating than others. Some opinions about the value of a work of art are therefore better than those of others. This can be demonstrated by analysis of the objective properties of the work. Despite all this, the self-satisfied layman will cling to his narrow, uninformed opinions and call the sensitive person names. What does this prove except that, to coin a phrase, "it's a free country"?

Indeed Ducasse, reacting against snobbism and authoritarianism in art, wants to preserve the freedom to be "honest, vigorous, and unashamed" [75] in our aesthetic opinions. But is freedom still freedom which is worthy of the name, when "anything goes," when, as Ducasse himself says of his theory, we are in a state of "anarchy"?

3. OBJECTIVE RELATIVISM

The dialectic has moved between the objective and subjective poles of evaluation.

If you go wholly to the objective pole, and try to judge the work "in itself," you ignore aesthetic experience altogether. Applying certain criteria of value, you can make "true" judgments about the work. But this is

---

[74] *Art, the Critics, and You*, p. 121. Italics in original.
[75] *Philosophy of Art*, p. 305.

simply mechanical "marks-giving." And it often has little relation to what people actually feel during aesthetic contemplation. Or, if the objectivist does appeal to experience to confirm the judgment, he holds that only one intuition of the work can be "correct," or else, like Joad, he ends up in scepticism.

As we have seen, the theoretical difficulties of this view are great. Hence the next movement of the dialectic is to the subjective pole. Now everything depends upon what people actually feel during their aesthetic experience. Indeed, this is all that evaluation is — a description of what we like or dislike. But, on the theory of subjectivism, all value-judgments carry equal weight, one can no longer give reasons in support of a judgment, and "good taste" becomes simply personal preference or social snobbery.

The theory of *objective relativism* tries to avoid going to either extreme. It tries to steer a middle course between "the mythical absolute values of the objectivist and the irresponsible preferences of the subjectivist." [76] The objective relativist believes that he can take account of and explain more of the data of evaluation, than either of the opposing theories can.

He draws upon the insights of both of the other theories. Yet he denies that his theory is simply a patchwork of borrowed ideas. He contends that relativism (I will use this term occasionally in place of "objective relativism") "is a distinctive position which differs radically from subjectivism and absolutism." [77] Indeed, if relativism is simply an adding together of the other theories, it would be hopeless from the start. For the basic theses of objectivism and subjectivism are logically incompatible with each other. Any view which attempted to synthesize them would be internally inconsistent, and therefore fatally weak.

You may decide, after studying relativism, that the theory escapes this fate. Even so, any theory which tries to mediate between philosophical extremes courts the danger that it will *not* be a "distinctive position." Such a theory is often inherently unstable. It seems to oscillate between one extreme and the other. It moves to one pole when it tries to meet one kind of difficulty and then to the other when it tries to solve another kind of problem. As you read this section, you may find yourself saying, at one time, "Isn't relativism simply objectivism in different words?," and, at another time, "Isn't this just a pretentious kind of subjectivism?"

Moreover, relativism, like most philosophical compromises, is more complicated than the previous theories. It tries to be more catholic and inclusive than either objectivism or subjectivism, which it considers too narrow. The two other theories "take the easy way out." They oversimplify evaluation. Objectivism makes it simply "marks-giving" or intuition; for subjectivism, it is simply what anybody happens to feel. Relativism, by contrast,

---

[76] Heyl, *New Bearings*, p. 125.
[77] Bernard C. Heyl, "Relativism Again," in Vivas and Krieger, *op. cit.*, p. 445.

has a complicated machinery of concepts. The relativist claims that we need all these concepts, in order to do justice to the data of evaluation and criticism.

OBJECTIVE RELATIVISM begins where objectivism begins, i.e., with the common sense conviction that the value-judgment refers to the object, not the speaker. But the relativist, like the subjectivist, thinks that value is never "absolute," i.e., unrelated to human experience. So although we predicate value of the work, we cannot test the judgment merely by objective examination of the work. It must be tested by the evidence of aesthetic experience. The relativist then appeals to aesthetic response. Do people actually like the work which is said to be "good"? But he wishes to escape the "anarchy" of subjectivism. He wants to be able to show that some experiences count for more than others in judging the work, and that there is a real distinction between "good taste" and "bad taste."

Given its objectives, the theory of relativism must be, as I have noted, fairly complicated. Professor C. I. Lewis has recently set out its concepts in great detail.

To begin with, Lewis distinguishes between the value which is a property of the object and the value which is a feeling in the aesthetic percipient. Thus his theory makes room for both objective and subjective factors. An experience which is good in the very having of it (whether we call it "pleasing," "satisfying," or whatever),[78] is an experience of "*intrinsic* value." Nothing but immediate experience can be intrinsically good. No object "has strictly intrinsic value." [79] Things are good or bad only if they cause joy or dissatisfaction in our experience. When intrinsic value is felt, directly and immediately, in perceiving an object, that object possesses "*inherent* value." All aesthetic objects possess inherent value.[80]

This brings us to the definition of "aesthetic value" which is distinctive of objective relativism. Aesthetic value is neither an "absolute" property nor an immediate feeling. It is that property of objects which is a "potentiality" or "capacity" for causing experiences of intrinsic value.[81] Aesthetic value is a *relational* property. The definition refers to aesthetic experience. Aesthetic value is, therefore, one of those properties which belong to a thing because of what it does in interaction with a human organism. Bread is "nutritious" because of its effects upon the body; cyanide is "poisonous" for the same reason. Bread is not nutritious, nor is cyanide poisonous, "in itself."

But this does not mean that the property exists only when the object is

---

[78] *Op. cit.*, pp. 403 ff.
[79] *Ibid.*, p. 387; cf. p. 407.
[80] *Ibid.*, pp. 391–392, 432–434.
[81] *Ibid.*, p. 458.

actually in contact with a human being. The piece of bread is "nutritious" even when it is not being eaten and is therefore nourishing nobody. This is the whole point of the notion of "potentiality" or "capacity": the bread *would* nourish if it were eaten. Similarly, the aesthetic object *would* create aesthetic delight if someone were to behold it.[82] The potentiality remains within the object even when it is not being experienced. The chemical properties of the bread, in virtue of which it nourishes, the formal, etc., properties of the work of art, in virtue of which it gives aesthetic delight — these properties are "in" the object.

In this respect, relativism is close to objectivism. There *is* a stable object with enduring properties. These properties can be examined and known publicly. Therefore it can be justifiably said of the students quoted from Richards' *Practical Criticism* that they have "misinterpreted" or "misunderstood" the work.

However, the only evidence that the work possesses the potentiality of value is that it *actually* creates felt goodness in somebody's aesthetic experience. In Lewis' terms, the only evidence for "inherent value" is "intrinsic value." But suppose — what is certainly true — that the same work creates different responses in different people. Does the experience of each percipient count equally in determining the value of the work? If work x creates pleasure in A, but displeasure in B, does it or does it not possess "inherent value"? What *is* the evidence, if any, that the work possesses the "potentiality" of value? What can keep us from concluding *de gustibus . . . ?*

Lewis, however, "does not intend to put evaluations which the fool makes in his folly on a par with those of the sage in his wisdom." [83] He therefore distinguishes different kinds of value-judgment:

(1) The autobiographical report of the speaker's feelings during the aesthetic experience, e.g., "I liked that." This, of course, is the judgment which is central to Ducasse's theory. Like Ducasse, Lewis holds that the speaker cannot be mistaken in making this judgment (unless, possibly, he uses the wrong words to describe his feelings).[84] But whereas Ducasse limits all evaluation to this report of feelings, Lewis calls attention to

(2) another kind of judgment, the "most important and most frequent type of evaluation." [85] This is the judgment which ascribes value to the object. It does not say "I like it," but rather "It is beautiful." Since beauty is a potentiality for stimulating the experience of intrinsic value, this judgment makes an empirical *prediction*. It predicts that if other spectators apprehend the work aesthetically, *then* they will feel aesthetic delight. This prediction, like any other empirical prediction, can be found to be

---

[82] *Ibid.*, p. 389.
[83] *Ibid.*, p. 397.
[84] *Ibid.*, pp. 374–375, 377, 407.
[85] *Ibid.*, p. 375.

wrong. Hence, unlike (1), this judgment is not infallible. Lewis calls such a judgment "non-terminating,"[86] since there is no limit to the number of experiences which can confirm it. It can be supported by a great deal of evidence, i.e., when a large number of spectators fulfill the prediction in their experience, but the judgment never achieves certainty. There is always the possibility that it will be falsified by *further* evidence.

Here relativism parts company with objectivism. Most objectivists (but not all, e.g., Vivas) claim certainty for the value-judgment. Its truth can be known once-for-all by intuition or "marks-giving." Or, if he does not think that certainty can be achieved, the objectivist clings to it as an ideal. Lewis, however, makes the process of testing the judgment indefinitely open-ended. Certainty is neither theoretically nor practically possible. Aesthetic judgment, like all empirical knowledge, can never be more than probable.

But now, what of the problem of different responses to the same work? Lewis' answer is this: the autobiographical report (1) is not always reliable evidence for the truth of the value-judgment (2). "[On] first hearing a piece of music . . . we cannot be mistaken about our present enjoyment of it, or felt indifference or distaste; but any conclusion we draw from that about this musical composition . . . as a continuing source of possible enjoyments or dissatisfactions, may later prove to be in error."[87]

A man looks at an object and sees it as red. It really "looks" red to him. But sometimes the object is not *"really"* red." It only *seemed* to be red because the man is color-blind, or because the lighting conditions were poor, and so on.[88] If he claims that it is "really red," his judgment will be falsified by the experience of other spectators, with better eyesight, under normal lighting conditions, etc. So too in aesthetic perception. "We may momentarily like a picture because it is hung in a poor light which obscures its bad drawing or its crude colors."[89] Or the spectator may have some personal idiosyncrasy which distorts his perception. Again, the autobiographical report will not provide a sound basis for the value-judgment. We can give reasons for saying that the picture is *"really"* bad." We "refer to observable physical properties of the painting on the one hand and to general principles of pictorial art on the other."[90] Also we take account of "the capacities of apprehension shared by humans generally."[91] By taking account of both the objective and subjective conditions of perception, we can make a better prediction of the effect of the picture upon future spectators, than can be made by the man who has seen the picture in a bad light or in some highly idiosyncratic way.

---

[86] *Ibid.*, pp. 375–376. Lewis' category of "terminating judgment" is omitted from this exposition.

[87] *Ibid.*, p. 410; cf., also, p. 457.   [88] *Ibid.*, p. 392, n. 4.   [89] *Ibid.*, p. 410.

[90] *Ibid.*, p. 411.   [91] *Ibid.*, p. 416.

Sometimes such a person can *himself* "compensate for" [92] his peculiarities or disabilities. Just as the color-blind man who knows that he is color-blind can make the appropriate adjustments when he sees a traffic light, so the aesthetic spectator can distinguish between his personal response and the inherent value of the work. He can say meaningfully, "I don't like this but it is good." The last half of his statement, the "non-terminating" judgment, can then be a reliable prediction that *others* will like the work.

PROFESSOR B. C. HEYL aso uses the concepts of objective relativism, but he applies them more specifically to the problems of evaluating art. Hence we will consider his views, to supplement those of Lewis.

On the theory of relativism, as we have seen, aesthetic value is a *relational* property. An object can be said to have value only because of its inter- action with the spectator. But once we introduce a spectator, values become highly variable. They are, Heyl says, "significantly dependent upon one's culture and environment, upon one's temperament and experience." [93] Therefore one and the same work of art will be interpreted in different ways. And different standards or criteria will be used to evaluate it.

Whereas Lewis slights this important fact of art criticism, Heyl empha- sizes it. And he tries to make room for it, in the theory of relativism.

Heyl, unlike the objectivist, does not wish to say that one and only one standard is legitimate, and therefore that one and only one judgment is correct. "[Differing] though equally sensitive persons will respond to music in differing ways and . . . therefore more than a single critical attitude is justified." [94] The history of art criticism discloses *many* evaluations of a single work, arising out of different cultural perspectives, different bodies of knowledge about the work, different approaches to the work, etc. "[Rela- tivism] accepts the rich variety of critical processes." [95] It is sheer dogma- tism to say that just one standard is the proper one.[96] "[There] exist a number of conflicting yet genuinely superior artistic principles which have been evolved as a result of sensitive and trained experience, reflective inquiry, and cultural equipment. Between such principles definitive judg- ment cannot justly be made." [97]

Any single judgment is "binding" upon others only if they resemble the critic in their makeup. They must share with him "fundamental similarities in their temperament, education, and environment." [98] Therefore, critical judgments are, in general, binding only upon those who live in the same

[92] *Ibid.*, pp. 420–422.   [93] "Relativism Again," p. 440.

[94] *New Bearings*, p. 140.

[95] Bernard C. Heyl, "The Critic's Reasons," *Journal of Aesthetics and Art Criticism,* XVI (1957), 178.

[96] Bernard Heyl, "The Absolutism of F. R. Leavis," *Journal of Aesthetics and Art Criticism*, XIII (1954), 249–255.

[97] *New Bearings*, pp. 135–136; cf., also, "Relativism Again," p. 443.   [98] *Ibid.*, p. 137.

cultural period. However, the critic must tolerantly respect those who do *not* resemble him and therefore make different judgments.

But Heyl, unlike the subjectivist, does not hold that *all* judgments are *equally* valid. Like Lewis, Heyl does not think that mere liking or disliking is enough for evaluation. There must also be thoughtful analysis of and reflection upon the work. And only certain individuals can make authoritative judgments of the work.

There are certain attributes which one must possess in order to be a *qualified* critic. These include (1) "a natural sensitiveness to the aims of the artist and to the qualities of the works he is judging," [99] (2) wide experience in the arts, (3) extensive historical and other knowledge about art, (4) the ability to take account of his personal eccentricities and their influence upon his judgment, and (5) "a critical system which will present a satisfactory theoretical basis for artistic evaluations." [100] In all of these respects, there is room for the education and cultivation of taste. "Good taste" is not, as Ducasse would have it, simply a matter of arbitrary personal preference. It can be shown empirically that a man either does or does not possess the attributes just enumerated.

At the objective pole, some judgments are more valid than others because they are more *relevant* to the work being judged. We must not apply value-criteria which miss the point of what the work is trying to do, aesthetically. The man who judges an "abstract" or "nonobjective" painting in terms of literal resemblance to ordinary experience, is using an inappropriate criterion. Similarly, "To appraise the merits of Chinese art on the basis of western criteria, or to appraise the merits of western art on the basis of Chinese criteria, would be indeed unwise." [101]

Therefore, Heyl insists, relativism "emphatically does *not* imply that one criterion is as good as the next." [102] The relativist critic can endorse many different standards, even though they are opposed to each other. But "the competent critic . . . may pronounce *definitive* judgment upon those *inferior* ones which depend upon crude and untrained experience, hasty intuitions, and cultural ignorance. . . . If the relativist assumes . . . that there are a number of better kinds of people, he also assumes that some minds are finer than others — more intelligent, subtle, sensitive, orderly." [103]

RELATIVISM tries to escape the blind alleys of objectivism and the "anarchy" of subjectivism. The relativist believes that his theory is stable and balanced. It relates value and evaluation to what people actually experience in their aesthetic moments. Yet it tries to preserve the common sense belief that some judges speak with greater authority than others.

[99] *Ibid.*, p. 92.   [100] *Ibid.*, p. 93.   [101] *Ibid.*, p. 147.
[102] *Ibid.*, p. 143. Italics in original.   [103] *Ibid.*, p. 143. Italics in original.

The strength of relativism is clearly shown in its treatment of value-disagreement.

The well-known fact that different individuals and ages have varying opinions of the same work — this fact is not explained away or swept under the rug. Rather, as Heyl says, the relativist "accepts" it. But he tries to make sense of disagreement. The basic definition of "aesthetic value" emphasizes the importance of the spectator. Since there are differences in training, cultural background, and so on, among different spectators, they will interpret the same work differently. They "set" themselves to respond in different ways. Depending upon the interpretation, the emphases in the work will fall at different places, the symbols will have different meanings, or, for some interpretations, there will be no symbolic meaning in the work at all, and so on.

Hence, a great deal that seems to be "disagreement" really is not disagreement at all. For often the interpretations are so different that the judges are speaking of genuinely *different* works. Or they are calling attention to different aspects of the work.[104] Relativism always forces us to go beyond the mere verbal utterance, "*x* is beautiful," or "*x* is not beautiful." The critic must always make clear his interpretation of the work and therefore his standards of evaluation.

The interpretation is legitimate when it is relevant to what is genuinely within the work. It must be coherent; it must not ignore salient features of the work; it must be sympathetic to the aesthetic purpose of the work. If the untrained amateur could put into words his approach to the work, as he cannot always do, we would understand why his judgment has no authority. For he would make it clear that he "misses" a great deal in the work and that he has failed to grasp its aesthetic import. Emotional shallowness, lack of familiarity with the work, ignorance — all of these may lead the amateur to render a verdict which is different from that of the trained and sensitive person. But they are "disagreeing" only verbally, for they "see" and therefore judge different things.

Relativism puts disagreement on an empirical basis. Resolving disagreement is a matter of evidence. We test the legitimacy of an interpretation by examining the work. And we test the qualifications of the judge by Heyl's criteria. We do not praise a man as a "good critic" simply because we happen to like what he likes. Whether he is, or is not, qualified is, as the eighteenth-century philosopher Hume put it, a "[question] of fact, not of sentiment." [105]

When the dispute is between an uninformed and undiscriminating person, and one who is experienced and perceptive, the former can be shown

---

104 Cf. above, pp. 394–395.
105 David Hume, "Of the Standard of Taste," in *Essays: Moral, Political, Literary,* ed. Green and Grose (London: Longmans, Green, 1898), I, 279.

"in fact" to be an inferior judge. If he is honest, he will often say, "Oh! I didn't see that," or "I need more time to learn about the work." This is how the "education of taste" begins. But when the dispute is between two percipients of roughly comparable experience, sensory acuteness, etc., settling the issue is more complicated. It must first be established that they are both interpreting and judging the work in the same way. Even then, there may be less disagreement than might appear. Again, the appeal is to empirical evidence. Has A noticed this detail which makes a difference to the expressive significance of the work? Has B seen how an image is repeated here? The analysis of the work is a long and difficult affair. Works of art are enormously rich and complex. We do wrong to think that there is any easy way to decide the dispute. But there *are* the objective properties of the work to appeal to. A can get B to "see what he has not seen before," and B can do as much for A. In this way they can come together in their judgments. It is a clear fact of our experience that attitudes and judgments *can* be altered by examination of what is in the work.

But what of the kind of "disagreement" in which A and B have *different* interpretations of the work? Even here, the gap between them can be narrowed. In some cases, at least, the two interpretations can be *combined* into a single, coherent "reading" of the work. This new interpretation will be richer than the original ones. It will draw upon more of the work. Thus, appreciation of the "music" of a poem may be enhanced by appreciation of the poem's "truth." Or the plastic values of a painting may be "fused" with the values of its representational subject matter.

Often, however, this will not be possible. Two or more interpretations may be so radically different from each other that they cannot be combined in a single experience. Each interpretation requires certain perceptual "sets" toward the work; it calls attention to some features of the work, but not to others; it finds in the work a certain "tone" or mood. In all these respects, two interpretations may be opposed to each other. Such interpretations make wholly different demands upon the spectator and they disclose utterly different values in the work.

Franz Kafka's novel, *The Castle*, is a highly elusive and "ambiguous" work. It has no clear and straightforward meaning. Each particular episode in the plot is concrete and realistic. Yet the significance of the total work is not easy to pin down. *The Castle* has been subjected to a host of interpretations. Kafka has been described by different critics as "the tragically enduring seeker after truth; the mistaken upholder of a false religious attitude; the unwitting revealer of the folly of all forms of mysticism; and the conscious satirist of such beliefs." [106] Now one cannot put together all of these "readings" into a single perception of the work. They are antithetical to each other. We can read Kafka as a painfully honest and

[106] Ronald Gray, *Kafka's Castle* (Cambridge University Press, 1956), pp. 10–11.

sincere spokesman for human aspiration; or we can read him as a satirist. But how can we read him as *both*? The expressive "tone" of the work is completely different in each case; the significance which we attach to the events of the plot is correspondingly different. Our felt responses will therefore be different.

At this point, we come to what is probably the most important insight in relativism. For relativism teaches us that we should not ask "But which is *the* true interpretation of the novel?" Works of art are infinitely complex. They are, to use Boas' word, "multivalent," [107] i.e., they possess many different values. Any interpretation is sound if it gives the percipient a coherent grasp of what is objectively in the work. Some interpretations, we just noted, take in more of the work than others. Some yield richer fruits in aesthetic values than others. Often, however, two sound interpretations are pretty much on a par. If so, we should not look for the one-and-only-one "correct" interpretation. The search is futile and it often ends up in dogmatism. Instead of trying to resist a plurality of interpretations, we should profit from them. By "reading" the work in different ways at different times, we can find diverse values in it.

The good critic will make clear his interpretation, and therefore his reasons for evaluating the work as he does. However, he will also respect other interpretations if they are informed, discriminating, and unified. You see this most often in music criticism. For there the critic is usually judging *performances* of works of art. Therefore he meets a plurality of "readings" and he must recognize that each of these may be valid "in its own way." Thus a distinguished contemporary music critic says of one pianist's performance,

> . . . while I do not share [his] conception of the [later] movements — I feel them to be easy-going and relaxed, which he does not — I enjoyed the superb things he made of them in accordance with his own conception, especially the verve, the strength, the humor that he put into the last movement.[108]

Thus, in various ways, objective relativism narrows down value-disagreement and shows how it can be overcome. But sometimes, after critical analysis and reason-giving have done all that they can do, there still remains bedrock disagreement. A and B share the same interpretation of the work, they have approximately the same degree of familiarity with it, etc., etc., and still they disagree. A says, "But don't you see such-and-such in the

[107] Cf. George Boas, *A Primer for Critics* (Johns Hopkins Press, 1937), p. 44; *Wingless Pegasus*, p. 63. However, Boas uses the word to refer to both the aesthetic and extrinsic values of the work.

[108] B. H. Haggin, *Music in the Nation* (New York: William Sloane Associates, 1949), p. 157.

work?" and B replies, "Yes, I see that. But (he may say this either sorrow-fully or with conviction) I *still* don't like it."

This kind of disagreement probably occurs far less often than we think. Far more frequently, disagreement takes the forms we have just discussed — the judges differ in their sensory acuteness and familiarity with the work, one has more historical knowledge than another, they are using different interpretations, and so on. Still, there are fundamental differences of temperament and personality among human beings, and this will sometimes lead to insuperable disagreement. If B "still doesn't like it," he can respect A's judgment because it is grounded on the facts of the work, because it uses relevant standards of evaluation, etc. Often B will understand what there is about himself that keeps him from enjoying the work. Perhaps he has some "blind spot" or emotional incapacity. If he has self-knowledge, he will know this; if he is honest, he will admit it; and if he is reasonable, he will acknowledge the soundness of a value-judgment which does not re-flect his own feelings, but which *does* give a thoughtful and well-founded estimate of the value of the work of art.

No man can be completely catholic in his tastes. We respond to some things but not to others. The emotional capacities and "turn of mind" which enable us to respond to one kind of art, keep us from appreciating another kind. Indeed, we should be highly suspicious of the man who "likes everything." The odds are that he is insensitive to the unique nature of each particular work; hence, all works are pretty much the same to him. Such a man has bad taste, or perhaps it is more accurate to say that he has "no taste." For taste is the capacity to discriminate what is within the work. When, however, men have the taste required to appreciate one style or school of art, they must often pay the price of being insensitive to other styles. As Santayana says, "If our appreciation were less general, it might be more real." [109]

The fact that different men respond to different things has no earth-shaking implications for evaluation. It does not lead us into critical "an-archy." On objective relativism, the value of a work can only be appreciated by those who have the appropriate qualifications for perception. If A has the qualifications for appreciating work x, and B has them for y, no grave theoretical issue is raised. Relevant interpretations of the work of art are made by both A and B, and each can give reasons for his evaluation. A problem is raised only if we think we have to decide whether A or B is "right." But for objective relativism, as we have seen, this is a pseudo-problem.

The critic, Hazlitt, puts it well:

[The] dispute between the admirers of Homer and Virgil has never been

[109] *The Sense of Beauty,* p. 35.

settled, and never will: for there will always be minds to whom the excellences of Virgil will be more congenial, and therefore more objects of admiration and delight than those of Homer, and *vice versa*. Both are right in preferring what suits them best, the delicacy and selectness of the one, or the fulness and majestic flow of the other. . . . Both are right in what they admire, both are wrong in condemning the others for what they admire. . . . We cannot . . . force opposite excellences into a union by all the intolerance in the world.[110]

THROUGHOUT THIS DISCUSSION of disagreement, I have been applying the theory of objective relativism. In my opinion, this theory handles the facts of disagreement better than either objectivism or subjectivism can. It puts disagreement on an empirical basis; it shows how disagreement can be overcome, when it can be; it generates a spirit of tolerance and humility in art criticism, where they have too often been in short supply.

But throughout the discussion, I have *presupposed* the basic concepts of relativism. I have presupposed the relativist definition of "aesthetic value" and its corollaries — reason-giving and the meaning of "qualified critic." However, it is just these basic concepts which must now be challenged. The opponents of relativism contend that there are serious logical weaknesses in these concepts. They argue that these concepts, once they are analyzed critically, turn out to be vague or question-begging. Therefore, the theory is much less cogent than it seems to be at first.

Our analysis of relativism will also summarize most of the major issues in this chapter, and it will show the basic points of opposition between the three theories which we have studied.

(1) THE MOST FUNDAMENTAL CONCEPT in relativism is "potentiality." "Aesthetic value" is defined as "the potentiality or capacity of an object to create a certain kind of aesthetic response in the qualified spectator." We have seen why relativism uses this definition. It wants to stick to the common sense belief that value is "in" the object. Yet it does not want to make value "absolute," as objectivism does, and therefore unknowable. So although value is "in" the work, and continues to exist when it is not experienced, it is defined in terms of aesthetic response. The work *would* be enjoyed *if* someone (with the proper qualifications of perception) were to contemplate it.

But does the notion of "potentiality" really explain anything? If aesthetic value is a potentiality, is it a genuine property of an object? When we say that an object has some property, e.g., "This desk is wooden," we usually mean that there is something fairly stable and enduring which is part of the

---

[110] "On Criticism," in *The Complete Works of William Hazlitt*, ed. Howe (London: J. M. Dent, 1931), VIII, 222–223.

object. But is the same true when we say that "This work has (the potentiality of) aesthetic value"? The only evidence we have of "potentiality" is "actuality," i.e., that the work actually pleases someone. Do we attribute potentiality to the work whenever *any* aesthetic experience is had? Lewis says that we do: "If one should experience delight in the presence of some artistic monstrosity, the enjoyment . . . would prove — if one choose so to put it — that the object experienced had that much of genuine goodness." [111] Hence, no matter what experience the percipient has, no matter how undiscriminating or distorted his perception may be, it provides *some* evidence for saying that the object has value-potentiality.

But what does Lewis mean except that the object *caused* a certain experience? What is added by saying that the object had the "potentiality" to do this? When the relativist says this, it sounds as though he were describing a permanent property of the work. But he is really just describing an episode in the history of the work, i.e., at some particular time, somebody had a certain experience in the face of it. Relativists are fond of comparing "This work is beautiful" to "This bread is nourishing." Suppose a loaf of bread is used to hit somebody over the head with, or to hold down a pile of papers. Would we say that bread had the "potentiality" to be a weapon or a paperweight? This sounds extremely odd. Similarly, if the work cited by Lewis really *is*, as he says, an "artistic monstrosity," then do we want to say that it has the "potentiality" of value? The meaning of "potentiality" has now become so big and inclusive that it seems to have *no* meaning any more.

The relativist apparently wants to eat his cake and have it too. He wants to speak of a "property *in* the object." And yet he wants to bring in aesthetic response too, as evidence — the only possible evidence — that the property exists. But there are many different responses; and if each one is evidence for the property, all sorts of properties will have to be ascribed to the object. Thus it is difficult to see how we can still talk about "*the* property" or, indeed, about any *property* at all.

Indeed, the same work can often arouse completely *opposite* responses. It may create delight in A and disgust in B. If we then attribute to it the "potentiality" for doing both, are we not ascribing *contradictory* properties to the work? Look again at the sentence just quoted from Lewis. The work in question is an "artistic monstrosity." Yet, because somebody has enjoyed it, it "has that much of genuine goodness." How can a work of art be both "monstrous" and "genuinely good"?

Thus the concept of "potentiality" runs into trouble. At this point, an offer of assistance comes to the relativist from unexpected quarters. Both the objectivist and the subjectivist are willing to help him out! Each one says the same thing to the relativist: "I will show you the way out of your

[111] *Op. cit.*, p. 433.

difficulties. Of course, all that you have to do is to give up your theory and come over to *my* side." The objectivist urges the relativist to stop talking about "potentiality" and to talk, rather, about properties which are *really* objective, i.e., which are not defined in terms of subjective response. The subjectivist urges the relativist to stop deceiving himself with talk about "potentiality" and to admit that "*x* is beautiful" means nothing more than "I have felt pleasure while looking at *x*." Then there will be no problem about the work cited by Lewis.

In other words, the relativist is invited to give up the middle ground and to move either to the objective or the subjective pole.

(2) THE RELATIVIST will doubtless thank his opponents for their generosity. But he will decline the invitation to commit suicide. He holds that his critic has misunderstood the meaning of "potentiality."

When we ascribe value to an aesthetic object, we are not merely saying that it has aroused a certain response in a given spectator. We are making a prediction of the kind of response which it will create in future spectators. Lewis goes on to say, just after the sentence I have quoted, that "any single experience" may be an unsound basis for judging "the potentialities of [the object] for further experience or for experience in general." [112] That judgment will be verified or falsified in the responses of other people.

The objectivist and the subjectivist, who were so friendly just a minute ago, now go back on the attack. The relativist is trying to save his theory. They challenge his defense.

The objectivist denies that we are making a prediction when we assert the value-judgment. When we say "*x* is beautiful," are we thinking ahead to what other people will feel? Surely not. We are saying, rather, that we have found value embodied in the object. Moreover, what *is* the prediction, exactly, that the relativist is talking about? Lewis speaks of the work's "potentiality for experience in general." How many people, over how long a period of time, are needed to test the judgment? Lewis himself calls the judgment "non-terminating," because the possible confirmations are limitless. When, if ever, can it be said that the judgment has or has not been confirmed?

Therefore, the objectivist concludes, relativism does not give a faithful analysis of what we *mean* when we make the value-judgment. And the prediction that it speaks of is hopelessly broad and indeterminate.

Ducasse, the subjectivist, takes a different line: "[Supposing] we should . . . discover some widespread agreements and thereby be enabled to formulate some probable predictions. I then ask, what of it? What exactly will this prove concerning the aesthetic merits of the objects judged?" [113]

[112] *Ibid.*, p. 433.
[113] *Philosophy of Art*, p. 287.

(3) THE RELATIVIST HAS A READY REPLY: "This will prove everything that we need to know, and everything that we can ever know, about the value of an aesthetic object. What else can prove the aesthetic value-judgment but the evidence of common aesthetic experience? When we say that a work is beautiful, we are not attributing to it some mysterious 'absolute' property, which it is supposed to possess no matter what people feel, when they look at the work. Certainly Ducasse, the subjectivist, will agree to this. And yet the value-judgment says *more* than simply that one man has had certain feelings. The judgment describes the worth of the object to human beings generally. If they find it good, as men have long found Giotto and Beethoven good, then the judgment is proved (within limits of probability). What else do we want to say about aesthetic value? What else *can* we say?"

Whereupon the objectivist and the subjectivist once again unite against the common enemy and they exclaim in unison, "Nose-counting!" The objectivist holds that whether a thing has value cannot be decided by taking a poll. For Joad, aesthetic value remains inherent in the object no matter what "guesses" people make.[114] The subjectivist has a very different conception of aesthetic value. But he too believes that nothing is settled by making successful predictions. All that this shows is that many people are constituted alike, and that when we know this, we can anticipate how they will respond. This does not "prove" anything to those who have a different sort of temperament and therefore respond differently.

(4) THE RELATIVIST REPLIES: "No, it is not just a matter of 'nose-counting' or (to use a more polite phrase) the evidence of shared aesthetic experience. To be sure, that evidence is indispensable. For are we not speaking of aesthetic value and therefore of human interest and delight? But there is something more that proves the value-judgment. We can give *reasons* in support of the judgment. That is why we analyze the work critically. We can show what there is about it that creates the experience of felt value. As Lewis says, when we support the evaluation of a painting, we 'refer to observable physical properties of the painting on the one hand and to general principles of pictorial art on the other.'[115] The charge of 'nose-counting' would be legitimate only if relativism considered the subjective side of aesthetic experience and nothing else. But it does not."

All right, then. The relativist examines the "observable properties" of the work and he appeals to "general principles of pictorial art." If the work fails to measure up to these principles, it is bad. But Ducasse will again ask the same question, "What of it?" What are these "principles"?

---

114 Cf. above, p. 406.
115 *Op. cit.*, p. 411.

They have no inherent sanctity or force. They are simply generalized descriptions of what some people happen to like, e.g., some people prefer "balance" to a lack of balance in painting. Indeed, Lewis says as much. For just after the sentence which I have quoted, he says:

> But if one who is untutored in art should challenge the principles of criticism . . . and persist in asking *why* these objective characteristics of the painting make it a poor picture, then the critic must eventually be driven to . . . the [rude] observation, "Apparently your color-perception is faulty: those who are expert in such matters, as well as most other people, do not find that combination and arrangement of colors pleasing." [116]

The subjectivist will use this passage as ammunition for his attack. Relativism tries to give "reasons." But, in the last analysis, the only "reason" that can be given to the dissenter is, "Well, *other* people like this." Once again, what is this but just plain "nose-counting"? The relativist tried to appeal to the objective side of the aesthetic transaction to save himself. What the relativist calls "objective," however, turns out to be nothing but a generalization of a great many "subjective" responses. If large numbers of people did not happen to enjoy these "observable properties" of the painting, critical analysis and all the rest would prove nothing. In any event, it still proves nothing to those who happen to have different responses.

At this point, the subjectivist gives voice to a suspicion which has been building up in him. He says to the relativist: "It has become increasingly clear to me that you and I should not be fighting at all. For are you really saying anything different from what I have been saying? Isn't your theory simply subjectivism? Strip away all the high-sounding talk about 'potentiality,' 'prediction,' and 'principles.' Then aren't you just saying that people like what they like and that aesthetic value is where you find it? You and I can make common cause against the objectivist. We both agree on the basic thesis that 'aesthetic value' must be defined in relation to what human beings actually feel. Why do you have to obscure this agreement by bringing 'objective' factors into evaluation (which turn out to be highly 'subjective')? Why don't you admit that '*x* is beautiful' means 'I take aesthetic delight in *x*'? Then you can get rid of the complicated problem of confirming the judgment. You will not have to appeal to the experiences of an indefinite number of people in an endless period of time. The judgment is confirmed and confirmed decisively by the man who makes it."

(5) A FAINT-HEARTED RELATIVIST might succumb to this proposal and go over to the subjectivist camp. But most relativists will not. They will

[116] *Ibid.*, pp. 411–412. Italics in original.

reply to the subjectivist: "As you point out, we agree on one basic thesis. This sets us both off from the objectivist. However, the rest of your theory is completely unacceptable to me. You believe that the value-judgment is nothing but a report of personal feelings. Therefore any judgment is as good as any other and 'good taste' loses its meaning. This, clearly, won't do. We do not, in fact, give equal weight to all judgments when we evaluate a work of art. Some people are not qualified to judge. They are ignorant of the work, or they have little familiarity with it, or they lack the discrimination which is needed to perceive its subtleties. Other men have the attributes of the good critic listed by Heyl,[117] and they speak with authority about the work. We all know who these men are and we learn from them. 'Good taste' is therefore meaningful. It is absurd to think that *de gustibus* is the last word about tastes. I cannot admit that the person who likes the dime-store novel, and nothing but the dime-store novel, is on a par with the man who reads Shakespeare discerningly and responds to it feelingly.

"You have accused me several times of resorting to 'nose-counting.' But Lewis makes it clear that relativism is not committed to 'nose-counting':

> [There] are those who are especially to be relied upon for judgment, because they have a greater breadth of pertinent experience, and perhaps some higher degree of the requisite powers of discernment. . . . Their judgment may stand as against any number of contrary votes gathered indiscriminately, because it is something objective which is judged, and not something relative to the particular and perhaps undiscerning experience.[118]

This is a strong argument, perhaps the strongest that the relativist can offer. But here is the rebuttal to this argument, as stated by Joad:

> The expert, we shall say, is the man who recognizes what is good and likes it; he is, in other words, the sort of person who prefers (x) to (y). Thus in attempting to escape from the impasse of complete subjectivism by the appeal to experts, we find ourselves completing a vicious circle. The argument now runs as follows. By what criterion are we to judge (x) to be superior to (y)? Answer, by the consensus of opinion among persons of good taste, who unanimously prefer (x). By what characteristics are we to recognize these experts whose judgment is to be trusted to establish the superiority of (x)? Answer, they may be known by the fact of their universal preference for (x).[119]

(6) SOME RELATIVISTS never seem to face up to this criticism. Perhaps it is just as well, for it may be that no satisfactory reply is possible in terms of their theory. Perhaps Joad's objection can be met only by mov-

---

[117] Cf. above, p. 425.
[118] *Op. cit.,* p. 460.
[119] *Op. cit.,* p. 467.

ing toward objectivism or subjectivism. Professor Heyl recognizes the problem. But he makes this candid statement: "[Since] the relativist cannot define with finality the competent, cultured, sensitive or expert critic, his position is, to a degree, unavoidably imprecise." [120]

Let us, however, give the last word to the relativist. Then you can decide whether he escapes successfully from Joad's criticism.

The relativist says to Joad: "You charge me with being guilty of a vicious circle. But you draw the circle much too narrowly and thereby misrepresent my theory. I do not hold that a man is, as you say, an 'expert,' simply because he 'prefers' some works to others. It is not enough just to *like* Shakespeare, Beethoven, and Michelangelo — all the 'safe,' universally respected artists. A man has 'good taste' only if he prefers these works for good *reasons*. If he happens to like them, but he is uninformed about them, or he is blind to a great deal that is contained in these works, then he lacks good reasons. This, after all, is what I have been saying all along — mere liking is not enough. When I call A. C. Bradley a great Shakespearean critic, I mean much, much more than that he 'prefers' Shakespeare. It is far more important that Bradley discusses Shakespeare's characters with great psychological insight; he calls attention to subtle thematic and formal relations within the plays; he describes acutely the emotional and intellectual profundity of the plays; and so on. These analyses *justify* his 'preference' for Shakespeare.

"Similarly, a man does not forfeit the title of 'expert' simply because he happens to dislike works which are generally considered good. Some eminent critics have delivered themselves of minority, even 'lunatic fringe' opinions, e.g., Dr. Johnson's criticism of 'Lycidas,' Hanslick's condemnation of Wagner, T. S. Eliot's judgment that *Hamlet* is a 'failure.' We should not reject these judgments out of hand. (The very fact that we listen to them seriously shows the tribute we pay to men of aesthetic sensitivity). We should see what reasons these critics give for their conclusions; we must see whether these reasons are appropriate to the aesthetic character of the work or whether they are irrelevant to it. We may decide, as most later critics have done, that Johnson's reasons are unjustified because he is reading the poem incorrectly and making the wrong demands upon it. Even so, though Johnson, like Aristotle, nods occasionally, he remains a great critic. The point is, as Lewis says, that 'it is something objective which is judged.' We can examine the work to decide whether the critic's perception has been discriminating, informed, sympathetic, etc.

"Now, *of course*, we can conclude that a critic like Johnson has 'made a mistake' only by drawing upon the analyses of *other* critics. But there is no vicious circle here either. How can human beings learn about aes-

[120] "Relativism Again," p. 445.

thetic value except by pooling the insights of aesthetic response and analysis? Nobody has a pipeline to 'The Truth.' And nobody is an infallible oracle. Like all knowledge, our knowledge of art and of critics develops slowly and progressively. It consists of objective analyses of the work, the interpretations and judgments made by different critics, and the aesthetic responses of human beings over a long period of time. There is nothing quick and simple about the process (as both the objectivists and subjectivists mistakenly make it out to be). Out of this fund of fact, opinion, and feeling, emerges well-founded judgment of the work. At the same time, and in the same way, we come to recognize the 'expert.' What the critic says in defending his evaluation reveals his capacities. He shows himself to be a man of great emotional range, wide knowledge, experience in the arts, etc.

"When a critic gets us to see what we had not seen before in the work of art, we have evidence of the objectivity and discrimination of his perception. But the surest proof that 'good taste' is not simply what we happen to like, is this: we often admire a critic's analysis, his reasoned judgment, and his capacities for aesthetic appreciation, even when we happen not to like the same works that he does."

Is THE RELATIVIST'S REPLY a good one? Perhaps it evades Joad's argument. Perhaps it begs the question. Clearly, the dialectic between the relativist and his opponents could go on indefinitely. Indeed it *has*. The problems of evaluation and taste are discussed throughout Western thought.

But we can stop here. The reader has now seen the central issues in the theory of evaluation. The reasoning is involved and the evidence is complicated. There is some plausibility in each of the three major theories. The reader will therefore see that the problems of this chapter are not to be solved hastily or simply. Any man who tries to "solve" them glibly or with a simple-sounding formula thereby proves that he has not really understood the problems at all.

BIBLIOGRAPHY

* Heyl, *New Bearings in Esthetics and Art Criticism*. Part II.
* Rader, *A Modern Book of Esthetics*. Pp. 480–503.
* Vivas and Krieger, *The Problems of Aesthetics*. Pp. 430–479.
* Weitz, *Problems in Aesthetics*. Pp. 683–696.
  Ducasse, *Philosophy of Art*. Chaps. XIV–XV.
  Gotshalk, *Art and the Social Order*. Chap. VIII.
  Heyl, Bernard, "The Absolutism of F. R. Leavis," *Journal of Aesthetics and Art Criticism*, Vol. XIII (Dec., 1954), 249–255.
  Hume, David. "Of the Standard of Taste," in *Essays: Moral, Political, Liter-*

ary, ed. Green and Grose. London: Longmans, Green, 1898. I, 266–284.

Hungerland, Helmut, "Perception, Interpretation, and Evaluation," *Journal of Aesthetics and Art Criticism*, Vol. X (March, 1952), 223–241.

Lee, *Perception and Aesthetic Value*. Chaps. V–VI.

Lewis, *Analysis of Knowledge and Valuation*. Chaps. XII–XV.

Pepper, Stephen C. *The Work of Art*. Indiana University Press, 1955.

Santayana, George. *Reason in Art*. New York: Scribners, 1946. Chap. X.

Vivas, Eliseo. "The Objective Basis of Criticism," in *Creation and Discovery*. New York: Noonday Press, 1955. Pp. 191-206.

QUESTIONS

1. Why does objectivism emphasize *formal* properties, either in defining "aesthetic value" or in the "accompanying-properties" theory? Are formal properties more stable and less variable than the other elements of the work of art?

2. How do you think Ducasse would reply to the criticisms of his theory which are made in this chapter? How strong do you think these criticisms are?

3. Are some predicates, e.g., "attractive," "pleasant," less objectivistic in meaning than "beautiful"? Discuss.
   Analyze each of the following statements, by showing to what extent they designate objective properties, and to what extent they manifest personal responses:

   "This is square."   "The situation is hopeful."
   "This is red."   "The situation is tense."
   "This action is unjust."   "This is beautiful."

4. Liking or satisfaction is often the *cause* of an aesthetic value-judgment. Could "I like it" ever be a *reason* for the judgment? If so, under what circumstances?

5. "Relativism has been called, to be sure, a disguised form of subjectivism; but the charge is ill-founded." — Heyl, "The Critic's Reasons," 174. Discuss.

6. "[When] one says one admires Renoir for his opulent line, one thinks one has explained why Renoir is admirable; but suppose an opulent line disgusts someone?" — Boas, *A Primer for Critics*, p. 146.
   What do you take to be the significance of this question for evaluation and criticism?

7. Which of the theories of evaluation discussed in this chapter seems to you to be most sound? Or do you think that there is some other theory which is more cogent than these? Defend your answer.

8. " 'Good taste' is not so much a matter of *what* one likes as *how* one likes." Discuss.

9. Find two reviews of the same moving picture, book, play, concert, or exhibition of paintings in newspapers, magazines, etc. Compare them with regard to the following questions: (1) What reasons are given in support of the value-judgment? (2) Do the reviews disagree with each other? If so, in what sense of "disagreement"? (3) Is one reviewer's judgment more "authoritative" than that of the other?

10. Why can we generally "agree to disagree" about aesthetic values whereas we frequently cannot do so in politics and ethics? What implications does this have for aesthetic evaluation as a social process?

PART VI

The Criticism of Art

16

Kinds of Criticism

Thus far we have spoken of just one function of criticism, the "judicial" or "evaluative," i.e., finding reasons to support the value-judgment. But criticism has other functions.

It tries to *explain* or *clarify* the work of art. The critic may explain to the reader who does not know the Scotch language, the meaning of the dialect words in Robert Burns' love poetry; he may explain the historical allusions in a novel; he may interpret the meanings of symbols; he may trace out the formal structure and show its expressive significance; he may, through his "appreciation" of the work,[1] describe the effect which it should have on the percipient. To clarify the meaning and structure of the work is unquestionably one of the chief purposes of criticism. Indeed, as we shall see, some recent critics consider it even more important than evaluation. I will call this the "interpretive" function of criticism.

We need interpretive criticism because of the nature of art itself. Almost any work of art worth talking about is highly complex. Its formal structure is often subtle and complicated; it is generally rich in expressive overtones. Once we have learned to appreciate the work, we see its great clarity, and its impact upon us is direct. But we must first have extensive familiarity with the work.[2] And even then, our own efforts may not be enough. We must enlist the aid of critics.[3] Otherwise, the work will be obscure and incomprehensible, and we will be unable to respond to it.

[1] Cf. above, p. 385.   [2] Cf. above, chap. 3, sec. 2.   [3] Cf. above, p. 245.

The distinguished contemporary critic, R. P. Blackmur, argues that interpretive criticism is particularly necessary in our own time. Literature is by no means the only art which draws upon the activities and concerns of "life" in its subject matter, but it does so to a greater extent than any of the other arts. In our age, Blackmur points out, this creates a grave problem for the reader. "[The] burden of descriptive and historical knowledge is greater than any man or groups of men can encompass." [4] Hence the reader may lack the knowledge which the artist presupposes. Moreover, we no longer live in a stable and unified culture, in which beliefs and values are shared by the artist and his audience. "The audience is able to bring less to the work of art than under the conditions of the old culture, and the artist is required to bring more." [5] It is difficult to comprehend not only the obviously "ambiguous" works of literature, but also those which seem to be "readily accessible." "Shaw is as difficult as Joyce, Mann as Kafka, if you really look into them." [6]

Hence the "burden for critics" is "to make bridges between the society and the arts." [7] The critic must explain "*what gets into the arts* . . . those forces that operate in the arts which are greater than ourselves and come from beyond or under ourselves." [8]

How IS INTERPRETIVE CRITICISM related to judicial criticism?

They are, clearly, *different* from each other. One *explains* the work, the other *judges* it. Moreover, judicial criticism *presupposes* interpretive criticism. As Professor Greene puts it, "The question, What is it worth? presupposes the question, What is it?" [9]

However, the relation between judicial and interpretive criticism is not quite so simple. These two critical functions blend with and influence each other. The distinction we have drawn between them should not blind us to the realities of what critics actually do. It would be a caricature of critical procedure to say that the critic first answers the question "What is it?" and then goes on to "What is it worth?"

Interpretation is not carried on in an airtight compartment. It very readily spills over into evaluation. When we tell what the work "is," we are telling, either directly or by implication, what it is like, as an aesthetic object. Therefore we are describing the kind of value which it has for the spectator, and the degree of such value. Relatively little interpretive criticism is "value-free." Most of the words which we use to describe "what it is" have connotations of "what it is worth." Suppose we describe a piece of music as "light," or, at the other extreme, "profound." Or sup-

[4] R. P. Blackmur, "A Burden for Critics," from *The Lion and the Honeycomb* (New York: Harcourt, Brace, 1955), p. 202. Copyright, 1948, by Richard P. Blackmur. Reprinted by permission of Harcourt, Brace and Company, Inc., and of Methuen & Co. Ltd.
[5] *Ibid.*, p. 206. [6] *Ibid.*, p. 205. [7] *Ibid.*, p. 206.
[8] *Ibid.*, pp. 210–211. Italics in original. [9] *Op. cit.*, p. 371.

pose a critic says, "This work is not tragedy; it is simply melodrama." Such words "describe," but they are also implicitly evaluative.

That is why many critics do not give an explicit, formal evaluation of the work. They do not have to. What they say about the work conveys the critic's opinion much more precisely than the judgment, "This is beautiful," can do. The eminent critic, Matthew Arnold, says that the chief concern of the critic is to disseminate knowledge. Evaluation, Arnold says, may "pass along with it — but insensibly and in the second place . . . as a sort of companion and clue, not as an abstract lawgiver." [10]

Conversely, the critic's sense of values will usually influence his interpretations. He approaches the work with beliefs about what he should "get out of" art of this kind; these beliefs determine what he will look for in the work, and therefore how he will "read" it. His temperamental and emotional leanings lead him to see things in the work which another critic tends to ignore or interpret in another way.

The work of art is charged with values. Hence, when we talk about it, factual and evaluative matters run together. Almost any piece of critical writing shows this. Nevertheless, the distinction between judicial and interpretive criticism is an important one. Though they go together, they have very different purposes. We will see, later in this chapter, the confusions which result when the distinction is ignored.

EVALUATION AND INTERPRETATION can be carried on in many different ways. In this chapter, we shall study some of the major kinds of criticism. Each of them uses distinctive methods. They call attention to different aspects of art. Some emphasize the origins of the work, e.g., the process of creation, the society in which the artist lived; other kinds of criticism are chiefly concerned with the effects of the work upon the percipient; still others try to concentrate wholly on the intrinsic structure of the work.

We can learn from each kind of criticism. But we must demand that each should have workable criteria of evaluation, and that it should be illuminating, in its interpretation of the work of art.

1. CRITICISM BY "RULES"

To evaluate the work of art requires *criteria* of value. If the critic is not content simply to report his feelings, he must examine the properties of the work. He can defend his evaluation, however, only if he can show how, and in what degree, these properties make the work good. Thus he must

[10] "The Function of Criticism at the Present Time," in *Essays Literary and Critical* (London: Dent, n.d.), p. 24.

have a standard by which to recognize and measure artistic goodness. The criterion might be — to take examples which we have already studied — "verisimilitude," "moral nobility," "emotional power." Without such a standard, he cannot support his judgment; without it, we cannot understand why he has made the judgment.

In general, these criteria show whether the work is a good one "of its kind." They measure value, not only in the specific work, but also in other works which resemble it. We think that when a play is called a "tragedy" or a "comedy," it must have certain formal and expressive properties, which are characteristic of that literary form. When an artist makes a sculpture for some social purpose, such as the commemoration of a historic event, his work should draw upon social tradition, it should be readily appreciated by all members of the community, and so on. Similarly, there are criteria for a "well-constructed" sonata or fugue.

But in the criticism of a specific work, all will depend on how these criteria are applied. If they are applied unintelligently, judicial criticism will be unsound and interpretive criticism will go wrong.

THE "NEOCLASSICAL" CRITICISM of the sixteenth, seventeenth, and eighteenth centuries was, to a great extent, traditionalized and formalized. As its name indicates, neoclassicism took the art of Graeco-Roman antiquity to be the "model" for all art, both in literature and the visual arts. The leaders of this movement, notably Boileau (1636–1711), drew up highly detailed codes for the evaluation of art. These criteria were thought to be universally valid, largely because they had the authority of Aristotle and Horace behind them. Hence, neoclassicism discouraged novelty and experimentation in art.[11]

The neoclassical critics classified works of literature and painting into kinds or *genres*, e.g., in poetry, the Pastoral, the Elegy, the Sonnet. Fixed "rules" were set down, measuring the goodness of works of a certain kind. In the first place, the differences between the *genres* must be respected. A work must be "pure," in the sense that it has unity of tone and style. It should not mix literary forms. Then there are rules for each specific *genre*. Thus one neoclassical critic stipulates that the "heroic poem" must be animated by the Christian religion, "the hero must be a pious and moral . . . character," the events must be "noble and stately." [12] This is, of course, an example of the "ideal"-imitation theory.[13] Neoclassicism also held to the "essence"-imitation theory.[14] Hence the rules

---

[11] Cf. above, p. 159.

[12] George Saintsbury, *A History of Criticism and Literary Taste in Europe* (Edinburgh: Blackwood, 1902), II, 90–91.

[13] Cf. above, chap. 5, sec. 3.

[14] Cf. above, chap. 5, sec. 2.

that all fictional personages should be of a well-defined "type," that they should act consistently according to this type, and that they should not display unusual or idiosyncratic behavior.

Probably the best-known of the neoclassical rules were the three "dramatic unities." These were stated by Castelvetro (1570). Drawing upon the authority of Aristotle, he held that there must be unity of time and place in the drama, i.e., the scene of the drama must not be moved from one place to another, and the time in which the action occurs must be continuous. In other words, these rules prohibit Act II from taking place, as in a modern play, "Five Years Later," or in a locale completely removed from that of Act I. If the unities of time and place are respected, then, according to Castelvetro, unity of action will follow necessarily. For the events of the play will have to be continuous and related. These unities — time, place, action — dominated much of European drama for over two centuries.

It is worth noting that the "three unities," supposedly derived from Aristotle, are not to be found in Aristotle. He emphasizes only one of them, unity of action, which Castelvetro considers subordinate. Aristotle, as we have seen, insists that there must be a tightly knit connection between the events of the play, leading up to the climax.[15] He speaks of time in only one passage, and then only briefly: "Tragedy endeavors, as far as possible, to confine itself to a single revolution of the sun."[16] Aristotle never mentions unity of place.

BUT IT IS NOT AS HISTORY that the rules concern us. We want to see what sort of art criticism results when these rules are applied. For this purpose it is instructive to consider, first, a neoclassical critic of relatively little eminence. For a poor critic reveals the weaknesses of a critical system more clearly than one whose intelligence and sensitivity overcome these weaknesses. Our critic is indeed a poor one; he has been called "the worst critic that ever lived."[17]

Thomas Rymer, who wrote in the late seventeenth century, attempted to ground his criticism on Aristotle's *Poetics*. He speaks of "the greatest English poets . . . unhappy . . . through their ignorance or negligence of these fundamental Rules and Laws of Aristotle."[18] Rymer uses these rules, as he understands them, to criticize Shakespeare. Thus he applies the rule of psychological "type," the neoclassical version of Aristotle's "universal," to *Othello*. He condemns the play utterly, because this rule is violated throughout. Thus Shakespeare makes out Iago to be a liar.

[15] Cf. above, pp. 67 ff., 117 ff.
[16] *Op. cit.*, V, p. 8.
[17] Cf. Saintsbury, *op. cit.*, p. 391; cf., also, p. 397.
[18] Quoted in Nahm, "Introduction" to Aristotle, *op. cit.*, p. x.

But this is not "true to type," for Iago is a soldier, and soldiers are always "open-hearted, frank, plain-dealing." Similarly, Desdemona could never love a black man, Othello could never become a Venetian general, and so on. Moreover, Shakespeare violates the rule of "purity of *genre*," because he introduces "comic relief" into the middle of tragedy. And he is, clearly, no respecter of the "dramatic unities," e.g., the action skips about from one locale to another. For all these reasons, Rymer concludes that Shakespeare, in writing tragedy, "appears quite out of his element; his brains are turned; he raves and rambles without any coherence." [19] (Rymer's criticism is to be found in *A Short View of Tragedy,* a title which one might stop to think about.)

We must turn to other, greater figures in neoclassical criticism, to see what is wrong with Rymer.

John Dryden wrote this note on the flyleaf of a book by Rymer: "It is not enough that Aristotle has said so, for Aristotle drew his models of tragedy from Sophocles and Euripides: and, if he had seen ours, might have changed his mind." Why is this such an acute remark? Partly, because it is a protest against authoritarianism in criticism — "it is not enough etc." Such a protest had great point, in an age which sought to justify its value-criteria by appealing to antiquity. More important, however, Dryden sees that the Aristotelian criteria have only limited validity. They cannot be justifiably applied to modern tragedy. Dryden is here implying that the critic must recognize the distinctive nature of the work of art, before he applies his rules. The criteria of evaluation must be relevant to the work.

Dryden's great successor, Alexander Pope, develops this argument in his *Essay on Criticism* (1711). Pope is, to a great extent, in the mainstream of neoclassical criticism. He takes "Nature" [20] to be

the source, and test, and end of art.

He believes in

Those rules of old discover'd, not devised.

And yet, Pope insists that the rules must not be obeyed blindly and inflexibly. They can even be violated, on occasion.

The rules can be broken when, as a result of doing so, the work

gains the heart, and all its end at once attains.

[19] Quoted in Saintsbury, *op. cit.,* p. 396.
[20] Cf. above, pp. 121 ff.

Rymer judges the work without considering its effect upon the reader. But for Pope, it is the aesthetic "end" of the work that is important. The work has achieved its purpose when "rapture warms the mind." Moreover, Rymer, in applying the rules of "type," "unity," etc., is judging only *parts* of the work. And he is considering the parts — characterization, form, etc. — in isolation. The goodness or badness of the parts can only be judged intelligently, however, when we understand how they function within the total work.[21] Thus Pope says that we must consider

> the joint force and full result of all.

But Rymer's most fatal shortcoming is, probably, his lack of aesthetic "sympathy."[22] He does not try to appreciate the play for what it is. He does not make an effort to accept it and respond to it as a distinctive work of art. He blinds himself to its values. He tries to force the work into the preconceived image of the rules, and condemns it for failing to fit. Whereas Pope insists that we must read sympathetically. Or, as he puts it, we must read the poem

> with the same spirit that its author writ.

Thus a modern critic says of Desdemona's marriage to Othello, which Rymer condemns: "It is not out of character, it is only extremely unusual and strange. But it was meant to be so."[23]

Pope reminds us of what Rymer has forgotten. The work must be read and evaluated aesthetically. That is why Pope emphasizes the aesthetic effect or "end"; that is why he insists upon the *whole* work — for aesthetic perception grasps the work as a unity, it does not analyze into parts; that is why he urges critics always to consider the artist's purpose.

Later in the eighteenth century, Dr. Johnson makes a detailed and powerful indictment of criticism by rules. Like Pope, he is himself still within the neoclassical tradition.[24] But Johnson exposes the abuses of neoclassicism so effectively that the tradition is dealt a fatal blow. In the latter part of the century it is clearly on the decline.

Most important of all, Johnson distinguishes, clearly and concisely, "that which is established because it is right, from that which is right only because it is established."[25] What *justifies* the rules, which dictate to the artist and his work? Traditionally, they had been considered eternally

[21] Cf. above, pp. 382 ff.
[22] Cf. above, p. 36.
[23] Bradley, *Shakespearean Tragedy*, p. 71.
[24] Cf. above, pp. 121 ff.
[25] *Rambler*, no. 156, in *Johnson, Prose and Poetry*, p. 247.

valid. But this endows them with an authority which they do not possess. "The rules hitherto received . . . will be found, upon examination, the arbitrary edicts of legislators, authorised only by themselves . . . and then, by a law which idleness and timidity were too willing to obey, prohibited new experiments of wit." [26] You see that Johnson not only challenges the rules; he condemns them, for stifling innovation in art.

We have seen how Rymer invoked the rules, in his criticism of Shakespeare's tragedies. Johnson, however, offers a powerful rebuttal.

Like Pope, he appeals to the aesthetic effect of the work. Shakespeare "never fails to attain his purpose; as he commands, we laugh or mourn, or sit silent with quiet expectation." [27] Like Pope, also, Johnson insists that the critic must consider what the artist is trying to do. "When Shakespeare's plan is understood, most of the criticisms of Rhymer and Voltaire vanish away." [28] The rules are seen to be silly and irrelevant. "To the unities of time and place he [Shakespeare] has shown no regard." [29] But if the unities are to be used for aesthetic evaluation, we must remember what aesthetic perception is like. The spectator realizes that the play is "make-believe." He knows that he must imagine himself to be in Egypt. And "[surely] he that imagines this may imagine more." [30] The change of dramatic "place" is therefore no fault, because it does not impair aesthetic interest. Similarly, in the case of time: "he who can multiply three Hours into twelve or twenty-four, might image with equal Ease a greater Number." [31] One of the unities *is* in Shakespeare, and that is precisely the unity which Aristotle insisted upon: "one event is concatenated with another, and the conclusion follows by easy consequence." [32] Nor is Shakespeare to be condemned for mixing tragedy and comedy. The mingling of "joy and sorrow" is "natural" in human existence [33] and, again, it enhances the dramatic effectiveness of the plays.

WHAT CONCLUSIONS CAN WE DRAW from this discussion?

Not, surely, that critics should do away with rules altogether. We must have criteria of goodness and badness if we are going to evaluate art at all. Nor is it the point of our discussion that the rules of neoclassicism are simply senseless. If they were, they would not have dominated criticism for so long. Rather, each of them has some point. The "dramatic unities" emphasize the importance of dramatic concentration and intensity. The spectator's interest is often dispersed, when there are many changes in time and place, and when the events of the play are unrelated to each other. The rule of "purity of *genre*" reminds us that the mingling

[26] *Rambler*, no. 158, in Samuel Johnson, *The Rambler* (London: Bohn, 1850), p. 273.
[27] "Preface to *Shakespeare*," in *Johnson, Prose and Poetry*, p. 495.
[28] *Ibid.*, p. 496.   [29] *Ibid.*, p. 501.
[30] *Ibid.*, p. 502.   [31] *Rambler*, no. 156, *op. cit.*, p. 246.
[32] "Preface to *Shakespeare*," *op. cit.*, p. 500.   [33] Cf. above, p. 129.

of many styles and moods frequently creates incoherence in the work. Finally, the rule of psychological "type" is derived from the "essence"-theory, one of the most acute and important theories of art.

No, what is wrong with Rymer-criticism is not simply that it uses rules, or that it uses the rules of neoclassicism. What is wrong with the rules is that they are applied blindly and mechanically. Therefore the critic is systematically unable to appreciate the value of the work and his criticism, both judicial and interpretive, is completely wide of the mark.

Pope and Johnson do not use these words, but they make it clear that the criteria must be *aesthetically relevant*. Before he can judge the work, the critic must have a sense of what the work is trying to achieve in the experience of the reader. Unless the critic understands and respects the "end" of the work, he will misinterpret and misjudge the "means."

It follows that criticism should always begin with felt aesthetic response. Perhaps we should say of Rymer, not that his aesthetic perception was faulty, but that he simply did not perceive the play aesthetically, at all. If he had, he might have felt the work's power, and he might have been more hesitant about applying his rules. The aesthetic "end," which must govern the whole critical process, can only be disclosed to aesthetic perception.

Rymer was so self-assured, in making his blundering judgments, because he thought that he had the authority of tradition behind him. So there is another moral here for criticism, viz., the critic should be on the alert for novelty in art, and he should be prepared to give up traditional criteria when they are not well-adapted for judging new and different works. This is a corollary of the principle that we must always respect the aesthetic uniqueness of each work. Much of our aesthetic experience is a tension between tradition and novelty. Poor Rymer was tradition-ridden. All of us, however, build up habits of perception, as a result of our encounters with art over a long period of time.[34] These habits should not be rigid and inflexible. "Nearly all good poetry is disconcerting, for a moment at least, when we first see it for what it is. Some dear habit has to be abandoned if we are to follow it."[35] The critic's judgment will be aesthetically relevant only if he will give up the old criteria, when necessary. The mind and tastes of the good critic are plastic and adaptive.

2. CONTEXTUAL CRITICISM

The "context" of the work of art includes the circumstances in which the work originated, its effects upon society, and, in general, all of the relations and interactions of the work with other things, apart from its

[34] Cf. above, pp. 380–382. [35] Richards, *Practical Criticism*, p. 254.

aesthetic life. Aesthetic perception focuses upon the work itself, taken in isolation. However, the work, considered nonaesthetically, exists in a context. It was created by a human being, who had certain psychological traits. He lived in a society whose institutions and values necessarily affected his thinking and being. He had political, economic, and racial loyalties. Moreover, once the work has been published or displayed, it has effects upon personal and social life. As Plato and Tolstoy emphasize, it has moral influence; it can be used for purposes of social reform; it can alter the thinking and attitudes of its audience.

Contextual criticism is that kind of criticism which explores the historical, social, and psychological context of art.

IN ONE FORM OR ANOTHER, this kind of criticism is almost as old as art criticism itself. Some works of art are clearly social products, for they embody the symbols and beliefs of the artist's culture, and they reflect the characteristics of his race. Since the Greeks, such works have been studied in their relation to society. The biography of the artist, at least in the visual arts and literature, is a subject of interest as far back as the sixteenth century.[36] The historical analysis of literature is to be found at the beginning of the eighteenth century.[37]

But never has contextual criticism been carried on so intensively and so successfully, as in the past one hundred years. Indeed, the rise and growth of contextual criticism is probably the most striking development in the history of criticism since the middle of the nineteenth century. Using new concepts and techniques of analysis, the contextualists have produced a vast body of knowledge about art. They have turned their methods on classical as well as contemporary art, and they have brought to light previously unheard-of facts. In the past, art has often been considered the product of "madness" or "inspiration";[38] hence it was thought to defy factual investigation. The contextual critics take art to be one empirical phenomenon among others. It can be studied as physical events or human history or economic activity can be studied. The successes of their research prove the soundness of their claim. The contextual criticism of the last one hundred years is a major intellectual achievement in its own right.

I CAN INDICATE only briefly the major causes of the rise and development of contextual criticism.

One of the most deep-seated and influential ideas of nineteenth-century thought is that of the context itself, i.e., a thing cannot be understood in

---

36 Cf. René Wellek and Austin Warren, *Theory of Literature* (New York: Harcourt, Brace, 1949), pp. 67 ff.

37 Cf. Edmund Wilson, "The Historical Interpretation of Literature," in *The Intent of the Critic*, pp. 43–45.

38 Cf. above, p. 95.

isolation, but only by examining its causes, consequences, and interrelations. This pregnant idea stimulates inquiry in many fields, including art criticism. The century is, to a great extent, historically minded, and many of its leading thinkers and scientists approach their data genetically, i.e., in terms of its origins.

There is a more specific cause of contextualism within art criticism itself. Many nineteenth-century thinkers wanted to make criticism "scientific." On the one hand, they were impressed by the preciseness and certainty of the natural sciences. The movement known as "positivism" celebrated science as the highest achievement of the human mind. On the other hand, they were appalled by the apparently hopeless subjectivity of critical judgments and the endless disagreement among critics. If art could be studied scientifically, i.e., contextually, perhaps evaluation could also become scientific at last.

At the same time an intellectual development was taking place which gave promise of fulfilling this ambition. The social sciences, notably sociology, cultural anthropology, economics, and psychology, were on the rise. They were exploring personal behavior and society scientifically, sometimes with startling success. They examined phenomena, such as mental processes, which were thought to be mysterious, and others, such as religion as a social institution, which were thought to be taboo. Why could not art be studied in the same way?

These motives to contextual criticism are still very much alive today. Contemporary scholars are carrying on the work which was envisioned a century ago.

In this section, we will study some of the major schools of contextual criticism.

KARL MARX is the father of one particular school of contextual criticism. But his thought is a major force in the development of contextual criticism generally. For Marx is one of the leading figures in the movement to study scientifically all institutions in society, including art.

Society, for Marx, is not a heterogeneous collection of institutions — government, education, family life, religion, art, etc. All of these have in common a certain set of values or "ideology." It is no coincidence that a certain kind of family organization is found in the same culture along with a certain form of government and judicial system. These activities fall into a clear, intelligible pattern, according to Marx, because they all reflect the ideology of the time.

The ideology, in its turn, can be studied causally. The most basic institution in society is the economic. The system of ownership of the means of production and exchange is the source of the ideology and it influences all other institutions. Hence the Marxist theory is called "economic determinism." Marx held that once the dynamics of economic activity are understood, the structure of society can be understood, and the course of social change can be predicted.

How, precisely, the economic factor is related to the other aspects of a society, according to Marx, is a difficult question of interpretation, which we cannot enter into. If Marx held that the economic factor is the sole and sufficient cause for other institutions being as they are, then his theory is clearly untenable. This view is a vast oversimplification, and there is no evidence to support it. It is important for us to see why this view is mistaken in the case of fine art, though the same criticisms would hold in discussing government, family life, etc.

Primarily, art is influenced by forces in society *other than* the economic. The moral ideas of the period, its whole "world-view" or outlook on life, the level of culture and taste, the prevailing religious beliefs — these, and many other elements, may leave their imprint upon the artist and therefore upon his works. But more important, the work of art is as it is, largely because of factors which are *peculiar to* the realm of fine art. Fine art, as such, would not exist without a medium, forms, and techniques. These have no counterpart outside of art. They have a life and significance of their own to the artist. They set limits to his creative activity and they also suggest the course it should take.[39] They are altered or discarded in response to *artistic* needs. We cannot understand the history of art unless we understand the peculiarly artistic reasons for the evolution of different styles and conventions.

For these reasons, more moderate Marxists repudiate "the absurd claim that Marx considered works of art to be the direct reflexion of material and economic causes."[40] They hold, rather, that the economic factor is one of many causes that influence art. However, they describe the economic factor as the "final," "decisive," or "ultimate" cause.[41] Here their theory becomes critically vague, since they fail to explain the meanings of these terms. Since we are not chiefly concerned with social theory, however, we can turn to the specific application of Marxism to fine art.

Each critical outlook has its own particular insight into art. Marxism helps us to see that "the art work lives in a world of society."[42] Society affects art in two ways chiefly, according to Marxism.

Primarily, the artist is stimulated to create by the vital social issues of his time. Marx held that all societies are divided into classes, along economic lines. There is incessant struggle between those who control economic wealth and those who do not. Their conflict creates tensions in

[39] Cf. above, pp. 103 ff., chap. 9.
[40] Ralph Fox, "Marxism and Literature," in Schorer, Miles, McKenzie, eds., *Criticism* (New York: Harcourt, Brace, 1948), p. 136.
[41] *Ibid.*, p. 135.
[42] Christopher Caudwell, "English Poets," in *Criticism*, p. 129.

all areas of life. It leads to political and legal changes and social unrest. It leads also to the making of art. The artist, like any member of society, is involved. He may either associate himself with the forces of economic protest, or he may be a spokesman for the old order. In either event, his work originates in and is given direction by the social dynamics of his time.

But economic forces are not simply extrinsic to the work. They enter into the art-object itself. "Art works are always composed of objects that have a social reference. [Words, notes, forms] have emotional associations which are social." [43] The artist's subject matter — the characters, settings, events, etc. — and the symbols which he uses, reflect the ideology of this time. The ideas and attitudes which he expresses place him on one side or the other of the class struggle. So all of the elements of the work show the influence of society.

How sound is this theory as a basis for art criticism?

The first part of it, which describes the motives to creation, is not a basis for criticism at all. What impels the artist to create is outside the work of art itself. It might be involvement in the class struggle; it might also be the desire to make money or to woo and win lady fair. This is a question for the psychology of artistic creation or for the autobiography of the artist.

If we consider it simply as a theory of creation, there certainly is *some* truth in the Marxist view. It is clear that some artists have been animated by feelings of social protest. But were the injustices which they condemned always basically economic? They were in some cases, such as the "proletarian" novels of the Thirties. In far more cases, however, the artist did not conceive of social issues in purely economic terms. Therefore, the Marxist tries to show that social problems, in all these instances, were rooted in economic struggle. It is highly questionable whether this can be shown, but Marxist critics have attempted it, in their analyses of traditional artists.

The late nineteenth-century dramatist, Henrik Ibsen, dedicated himself avowedly to social reform. He said: "No man is ever free of responsibility for the society to which he belongs, or without a share in its guilt." In a number of his plays, e.g., *Brand, The Enemy of the People, The Wild Duck,* his characters extol the integrity and perseverance of the individual, even when he stands out against society. The Marxists therefore hold that Ibsen was motivated by the conflict of "petty bourgeois" individualism against large-scale capitalism.[44] Notice that this is a hypothesis about the underlying sources of social tension. It does not describe the

---

[43] *Ibid.,* p. 129.
[44] Angel Flores, ed., *Ibsen* (New York: Critics Group, 1937), *passim.*

social problem as the artist himself understood it. Moreover, even if this hypothesis were sound, it would not explain Ibsen's motives in writing *other* plays. Indeed, it is difficult to see how the theory could account for most instances of artistic creation, unless its key term, "economic," became so broad and vague that the theory lost all precise meaning.

The more important aspect of Marxism, for our purposes, is, as I have noted, its theory of the work of art itself. Can this theory aid criticism? The answer is, in my opinion, the same for Marxism and all other schools of contextual criticism, viz., if describing the origins of the work can help explain, in Blackmur's phrase, "what gets into" [45] the work, then the answer is "Yes." Genetic criticism can assist the aesthetic critic, so long as it is aesthetically relevant. If it can be shown that economic and social issues are present within the body of the work, and therefore make a difference to its aesthetic import, then Marxist criticism should certainly be used. Again, the economic conception of "social" is almost certainly too narrow. But a strict Marxist analysis will help to elucidate some works. And a broader view of social structure and social change can be used to analyze many others. It is relevant to Titian's paintings to describe contemporary Venetian aristocracy; some of the novels of Dickens, Hardy, and Dreiser take their rise from the social and economic injustices of their time. Marxist criticism has been one of the prime movers in developing this kind of approach to art. It helped to inspire such pioneer studies as Parrington's social-political analysis of American literature.

But the Marxists have exaggerated the importance and value of their approach. What is a fruitful idea, when used judiciously, has grown into "fanatic falsification." [46] "[Every] formula of knowledge must fall the moment too much weight is laid upon it." [47] What are the limitations of Marxist criticism?

Most obviously, there are many works of art for which social-economic categories of analysis are *not* relevant. We can say, rightly, that Haydn wrote many symphonies for his aristocratic patron. But this fact is extrinsic to the music. We might even want to say — though here the ice is much thinner — that Haydn's music "reflects" the charm and refinement of aristocratic society. If, however, we want to say anything more precise and detailed about the music, we shall have to begin speaking in *musical* terms. Then we must describe the orchestra that the symphonies are scored for, Haydn's use of the sonata form, the humor and delicacy which are expressed in the music.

"Pure" music is only the most obvious example. There are works in

---

[45] Cf. above, p. 442.
[46] R. P. Blackmur, "A Critic's Job of Work," in *The Double Agent* (New York: Arrow Editions, 1935), p. 278.
[47] *Ibid.*, p. 270.

all the arts which elude the concepts of Marxist criticism. If the Marxist recognizes the limitations of his approach, he will grant this. Some Marxists, however, try to apply their system even to these works. Then, one of two things generally follows.

The critic passes negative judgment upon the work. It is condemned for being "empty." The most damning word in Marxist criticism is "formalist." It is applied to those "pure" works which are lacking in social significance. The rejection of subject matter, as in abstract painting and sculpture, "destroys art itself." [48] But here the Marxist is guilty of "methodolatry," i.e., his methods of research, which ought to be tools for arriving at a conclusion, are allowed to dictate the conclusion. Whereas his social-economic concepts should be given up, in the face of "pure" art, they become, instead, rigid and inflexible. What cannot be treated by these concepts is condemned. The work is not considered and judged for what it is.

If the critic does not condemn the work outright, he must attempt to analyze it. However his contextual concepts are not well adapted to explain the intrinsic structure of the work. Therefore the Marxist critic often expands their meanings. But then his criticism blurs the distinction between two kinds of data — the contextual and the aesthetic — and it is endlessly confusing. For example, contemporary atonal music is often said by Russian critics to be "bourgeois." Now this term has a relatively well-defined meaning in Marx' economic theory. A man or an economic system can be meaningfully described as "bourgeois." But it is literally nonsense to say that a kind of music is "bourgeois." All that can be meant by this is that such music is composed and played in countries which have systems of bourgeois capitalism. This is only a contextual fact *about* the music. It does not tell us what is *within* the music. "Bourgeois" is as useless for artistic analysis as any other aesthetically irrelevant concept.

What is wrong with Marxism here is the inherent weakness of all contextual criticism, i.e., the basic concepts are necessarily too narrow for the purposes of art criticism.

The contextualist, by his very nature, is concerned with what lies outside of the work of art, e.g., the economic structure of society. He can talk about this in historical, social, psychological, etc., terms. When he turns to the work itself, he uses the same terms. Hence, he can only talk about those elements of the work which are derived from or resemble "life." The Marxist critic emphasizes the subject matter of the work, and the "ideas" which it expresses. These can be discussed in social-economic language. But what the Marxist calls, disparagingly, the "formalist" elements

[48] Nikolai Bukharin, "Poetry and Society," in Vivas and Krieger, *op. cit.*, p. 511.

in the work cannot be discussed in this language. His apparatus of criticism is therefore fatally limited.

Moreover, once social injustice or class struggle "get into" the work as its "content," they are not independent elements. The "content" interacts with the "form." The social issue or "idea" is not the same within the work as it is outside the work. It is transformed by the sensory "body" and structure. It has a different significance. Hence, even in judging artistic "content," which is the only thing that the contextualist can talk about at all, his categories, taken straight from economic or social theory, are not adequate.

These are serious limitations in Marxist and in all contextual criticism. Nevertheless, when social themes *are* part of the "content," the Marxist can often provide us with helpful interpretations of the work. But even here, some Marxists are guilty of "fanatic falsification," though of a different sort. They claim that their interpretation is the *only* legitimate interpretation of the work. But no critic, of whatever school, can make this claim. The facts of art and the history of taste belie him. Works of art are multivalent, there are too many sound interpretations of a single work,[49] ever to justify the "one-and-only-one-meaning" claim.

Moreover, even when interpretive criticism has done its job, the critic still has another function to perform. As Edmund Wilson says:

> The problems of comparative value remain after we have investigated . . . the Marxist economic factor and the racial and geographic factors. No matter how thorough and complete our explanations of works of literature may be . . . we must be ready to try to estimate the relative degrees of success attained by the products of the various periods and the various personalities. . . . We shall not otherwise write literary criticism at all, but merely social or political history as reflected in literary texts.[50]

The Marxists, however, do not stop with interpretive criticism. They also engage in *judicial* criticism.

Indeed, the concepts which they use to describe the context of art, become transformed into criteria for judging art. The Marxists hold, as we have seen, that works of art originate in and reflect the class struggle. This is, whether true or false, an issue of *fact*. The Marxists also hold, moreover, that a work is *good* when it voices the protest of the lower class in society and furthers its revolutionary development. The work is bad when it allies itself with the ruling class.

But this will not do as a basis for judicial criticism. "Promoting revolutionary feeling" is not an *aesthetic* concept. The Marxist, like Plato

---

[49] Cf. above, pp. 424–428.
[50] *Op. cit.*, p. 57.

and Tolstoy,[51] ignores or rejects the value of art "for its own sake."[52] His evaluation is *moral*, not aesthetic.

The painting which has been produced in the Soviet Union dramatizes the difference between moral-political and aesthetic values. It is somewhat melodramatic, lifelike "imitation" of the heroes and events of the Russian Revolution. Such painting probably has social and propagandistic effects which the Marxist approves. Aesthetically it is just about as bad as the historical paintings in our own state capitals.

The use of factual, interpretive concepts, e.g., "social awareness," for evaluation, is another error which is found in a great deal of contextual criticism. We will encounter it again. This mistake, with the lopsided value-judgments which it leads to, has, more than anything else, made art critics in our time suspicious of contextualism.

In actual practice, Marxist criticism is not always guilty of the bald error which I have just described. Often, social facts, interpretive criticism, aesthetic evaluation, and moral evaluation are run together. The Marxist critique of Ibsen can again serve as an example.

As we have seen, the origins of the plays are located in the conflict between the "petty bourgeoisie" and large-scale capitalism. Within some of the plays, individualism is an important theme. To the extent that Ibsen's plays preach social revolt, they are applauded by the Marxist. Ultimately, however, Ibsen fails, according to the Marxist. For although the artist condemns the society of his time, he does not propose the Marxist alternative to it, viz., proletarian revolution. This too is explained contextually by the Marxists. They argue that no true proletarian class had emerged in Norway, at the time that Ibsen wrote. But this social-moral evaluation also has an aesthetic side to it. Like some non-Marxist critics, the Marxists contend that many of Ibsen's symbols are vague and unintelligible. This is a weakness in the aesthetic effectiveness of his plays. If this criticism can be shown to be sound, and if it is supported by the evidence of aesthetic experience, then it is, of course, aesthetically relevant. Again, however, the Marxist does not speak of "purely" aesthetic matters. He holds that Ibsen's symbolism illustrates the artist's "blurred and indefinite" social thinking.[53]

YOU WILL SEE that there are two things that must be kept in mind, while reading Marxist or most other contextual criticism. First, you must be careful to distinguish *genetic* facts, i.e., the origins of the work, *interpretation*, i.e., explaining what is within the work, and *evaluation*. You will have to draw these distinctions yourself, since the critic usually does not.

[51] Cf. above, pp. 340 ff.
[52] Cf. Caudwell, *op. cit.*, pp. 129 ff.
[53] Cf. Flores, *op. cit.*, pp. 36–37, 39–40, 74.

Second, you should always be aware of the *limitations* of the contextual approach. What *else* is in the work, that cannot be explained in social terms? Does the critic treat social themes as though they were independent elements within the work, thereby ignoring their interrelations to the other elements? Has the critic's social bias led him into misreading, e.g., does the very vagueness of the symbolism in *Peer Gynt enhance* its aesthetic value?

THE FRENCH CRITIC Hippolyte Taine, a contemporary of Marx, did even more than Marx to popularize the social approach to art. Taine is not, like Marx, a major figure in social science. But he studied the phenomenon of art as a social process much more thoroughly and systematically than Marx. And the very boldness of his claim — that art is a direct and predictable outgrowth of social forces — stirred the imagination even of those who held that Taine had failed to prove his case.

Taine, like many men in the middle of the nineteenth century, was enormously impressed by the spectacular successes of science. He sought the same degree of certainty in the study of history. He therefore took natural science for his model. The arts, philosophy, science, government — indeed, all major social institutions — are causally determined to be what they are, just as much as physical events. "There are similarly connected data in the moral as in the physical world, as rigorously bound together." [54] If we had precise, even quantitative knowledge of the causes of social change, "we might deduce from them as from a formula the characteristics of future civilisation." [55]

Literature, too, must be studied deterministically, i.e., we must learn the causes which bring it about and dictate the form which it takes. Like Marx, Taine places art in a social setting. It is not something mysterious, "a mere individual play of imagination, the isolated caprice of an excited brain." [56]

It arises out of and reflects "certain general traits, certain characteristics of the intellect and the heart" [57] which are common to the society in which the artist lives. If we can find the causes of these "traits," we can explain how and why different societies have each brought forth a distinctive body of literature. Now we come to Taine's famous trinity — "race," "surroundings," and "epoch." These three are, he holds, the sole and exclusive causes of all literary, and indeed of all social achievements. [58]

"Race" refers to "innate and hereditary dispositions." [59] There are clear

[54] H. A. Taine, "Introduction" to *History of English Literature,* trans. Van Laun (London: Chatto and Windus, 1877), I, 31.
[55] *Ibid.,* p. 25; cf., also, pp. 23–24.
[56] *Ibid.,* p. 1.
[57] *Ibid.,* p. 13.
[58] *Ibid.,* p. 25.
[59] *Ibid.,* p. 17.

racial differences between peoples, "some brave and intelligent, some timid and dependent," [60] etc. "Surroundings" [*milieu*] is a large, omnibus category. It includes climate; thus Taine says that the characteristic differences between the German and Latin races are largely due to the fact that the former lived "in cold moist lands, deep in rugged marshy forests or on the shores of a wild ocean," the latter "within the loveliest landscapes, on a bright and pleasant sea-coast." [61] But "surroundings" also refers to the influence of other societies, social pressures, wars, etc. The "epoch" is the particular historical period. In his *History of English Literature*, Taine says that he "endeavoured to define these primary springs, to exhibit their gradual effects, to explain how they have ended by bringing to light great . . . literary works." [62]

Probably no one nowadays believes that Taine succeeded in this attempt. Taine has had lasting influence, because of his methodical exploration of the social origins of art. But, like most intellectual pioneers, he was overly ambitious. Taine did not demonstrate a rigid, causal relation between his causal trinity and the works of English literature.

He seems to do so, at places in the *History*. But this is because he describes the literary work too patly, and thereby makes it resemble what he had "predicted," on the basis of "race, surroundings, epoch." Taine often has to ignore the distinctive characteristics of the individual artist, in order to draw him as a representative of his age. The writer then turns out to be "a composite figure . . . a colourless abstraction." [63]

But it is precisely the individuality of the artist which sets him apart, and which makes him worthy of study in the first place. Taine, like all others who have tried to explain artistic genius by means of its origins, failed: [64]

> La Fontaine and Racine were both born in Champagne, within a few leagues and within a few years of each other, in exactly the same social stratum. The one wrote mocking and cynical fables, the other tragedies of fatal passion. And of the thousands of Champenois whose "race, *milieu*, and time" were the same as theirs, not one can compare with either of them.[65]

Indeed, at one place in the *History*, a crucial place, for here he is discussing the greatest of English authors, Taine almost seems to give up his theory. For he says of Shakespeare that "all came from within — I mean

[60] *Ibid.*, p. 17.
[61] *Ibid.*, p. 19.
[62] *Ibid.*, p. 36.
[63] Martin Turnell, "Literary Criticism in France," in *Critiques and Essays in Criticism*, ed. Stallman (New York: Ronald, 1949), p. 426.
[64] Cf. above, chap. 4, sec. 3.
[65] Albert Guérard, *Literature and Society* (Boston: Lothrop, Lee, and Shepard, 1935), p. 135.

from his soul and his genius; circumstances and the externals contributed but slightly to his development." [66]

OTHER ERRORS IN TAINE'S APPROACH are less obvious. It is doubly important to expose them, however, because they survive in our own thinking and speech. How often we say that some artist "reflects his society." So Taine had spoken of the novel as a "mirror" of its age. Thus a duality is set up — the age, with its attitudes and values, on the one hand, the work of art, a product and "mirror" of the age, on the other.

Professor Boas shows acutely that this way of thinking is confused from the start:

> [That] the age is something different from its manifestations is superstition. . . . Works of art are not expressions of an age; they help make up the age. . . . Take away the novels of Dickens, the poetry of Tennyson, pre-Raphael-ite and academic painting, the sculpture of Woolner and Thornycroft, con-tinue the process until all the aesthetic produce of the time is annihilated, and what is left of the Victorian Age? Its philosophy, science, politics, and eco-nomics. But even assuming that these were not influenced by the art of the period — which is contrary to fact — the age would be unrecognizable with-out its works of art. The same remark holds good of any age. For an age is the intertwining of all the activities of human beings living during the period involved.[67]

There is a further error in thinking of art as the "mirror" of its time. From the standpoint of art criticism, this error is even more serious. For it consists in ignoring the uniqueness of fine art.

We have to remind ourselves again that the whole "mirror"-analogy is misleading.[68] A mirror simply duplicates the objects reflected in it. They remain in the mirror image what they are outside of it — fat men, wooden tables, etc. The same is not true of social beliefs and values when they "get into" the work of art. There they are embodied in the sensory medium of art and structured by artistic form. They are dramatized by concrete personages who live a life of their own within the work. As a result, the beliefs and values of the artist's society acquire meaning and expressive power which they lack outside of art. The social belief is not now in its usual habitat, i.e., everyday personal and institutional behavior. It is in a different and unique context — that of art. It is, therefore, neces-sarily different. The work is not like a "mirror." It is more like a web or — I will use the old metaphor — an organism, i.e., a unique organization of interrelated elements.

[66] *History of English Literature,* trans. Van Laun (London: Chatto and Windus, 1877), II, 50.
[67] *Primer for Critics,* p. 49.
[68] Cf. above, pp. 112 ff.

If we forget this, and conceive of art as a "reflection" of society, we will consider only the "real life" elements in the work and study these in abstraction from the total work. It is true of Taine, as it is of Marx,[69] that his approach lends itself to this. Then we are using the work as a historical document, like a constitution or a political pamphlet. There is nothing wrong with this, of course, if our interest is sociological. But it is a fatal mistake if we want to understand the work *aesthetically*. One modern critic has protested that the historical approach "dissolves literature into its history. Are the scholars studying literature, or are they not? That is the question." [70]

The moral is the same as before: We can and ought to use social-genetic knowledge, when it helps us to understand what "gets into" the work. But contextual criticism ought to be just that — a help. It should not be permitted to swamp or distort aesthetic evaluation.

There is one final error in Taine which is also present in the Marxists and many other contextualists, viz., factual-contextual concepts are converted into criteria of evaluation.

Taine's whole effort was to show how art is representative of its society. He also holds, however, that a work is *better* when it is clearly representative of its time: "The more a book represents . . . the mode of being of a whole nation and a whole age," Taine says, "the higher is its place in literature." [71] He also makes the odd assertion that works of literature are "instructive" to the historian "because they are beautiful." [72] Surely, however, there is no clear correlation between the degree to which the work "reflects" its society and its "beauty." Frequently, mediocre and uninspired works are closest to the mainstream of social custom and belief. The great artist, because of his imaginative daring and vision, often transcends the values of his own time. Social typicality cannot be a criterion of aesthetic value.

IN MARX AND TAINE, the emphasis falls on society. The individual artist is considered essentially as a resultant of social conditioning. Another kind of contextual criticism pays much greater attention to the psychology of the individual.

This critical movement also gained momentum during the middle of the nineteenth century. Its growth was stimulated by the great critic, Sainte-Beuve, among others. Sainte-Beuve was not a rigid determinist, like Taine. He held, however, that if we could gain knowledge about the artist's life, the chief influences upon him, etc., we could gain a proper understanding

---

[69] Cf. above, pp. 455–456.
[70] Tate, *op. cit.*, p. 10.
[71] *Op. cit.*, I, 35.
[72] *Ibid.*, p. 34.

of his work and we would therefore avoid reading irrelevancies into it or losing its true meaning.

However, the central figure in the development of the psychological approach was, of course, Freud, whose theory of the genesis of artistic creation we have already discussed.[73]

Freud's thinking has stimulated an incalculable number of psychological and psychoanalytic studies in the arts.[74] The Freudians have either used the work of art as a document which, upon analysis, reveals unconscious psychological forces in the artist's personality; or they have brought to bear upon the work what is known or conjectured about the psychological make-up of the artist. The former approach is clearly of interest only to psychology. The latter approach has often been extremely fruitful in interpretive criticism, particularly when the symbolism of the work is ambiguous or elusive. Indeed, the greatest contribution of Freudianism, probably, is that it has shown the richness of symbolic overtones in many works, and the latent, concealed meanings from which they spring. Freudianism has been able to show this by showing the origins of these symbols in the psychological needs and drives of the artist.

I will give some examples of psychological analysis in a moment. Before doing so, let me note that Freudianism is subject to precisely the same limitations and abuses as the other schools of contextual criticism which we have studied. Because it is a theory of psychology, not an aesthetic theory, it is best equipped to deal with those elements of the work which are of psychological significance. It emphasizes subject matter, theme, symbol, "idea," all the elements of the work which draw upon psychological events outside of art, and which can be treated by the concepts of psychology. By the same token, it is relatively ill equipped to deal with artistic form, medium, style, technique, all the elements which are peculiar to the realm of art. From this it follows that Freudianism, like other kinds of contextualism, is not adequate for judicial criticism. Since it treats primarily of artistic "content," which is only part of the aesthetic object, it cannot make a comprehensive judgment of the work's aesthetic value. Moreover, some Freudians, like Taine and the Marxists, have used factual, explanatory notions for evaluative purposes. One critic, who is not Freudian but who uses a psychological approach, "slights *Macbeth* as uninteresting because it is least related to what he conceives to be Shakespeare's personality." [75] Once again we see how the contextual tail can wag the aesthetic dog.

The psychological critic, like any critic, must respect the intrinsic sig-

[73] Cf. above, pp. 89 ff.
[74] Cf., e.g., Frederick J. Hoffman, *Freudianism and the Literary Mind* (Louisiana State University Press, 1945); Otto Rank, *Art and Artist*, trans. Atkinson (New York: Knopf, 1932).
[75] Wellek and Warren, *op. cit.*, p. 71.

nificance of fine art. He should not make the mistake of letting his psychological interests blind him to the aesthetic goodness of the work. If he does, then his criticism, for all its up-to-date talk and sophistication, is simply Rymer-criticism, i.e., he is, by virtue of his approach, systematically incapable of seeing the work for what it is. Hence his judgment is not to be trusted. It is, as we have seen, an instance of "the genetic fallacy,"[76] to try to equate the art-object with the psychological forces that were at work in the artist.

But if the critic takes care not to "dissolve" art into psychology, we can learn much from him. We should not go to the opposite extreme, which says that the personality of the artist has nothing whatever to do with the work.[77] Let me show how, specifically, psychological knowledge can help in interpretive criticism.

THE WORKS OF ART are the novels of Franz Kafka, *The Trial* and *The Castle*. These are almost perfect specimens of the kind of art that Freudianism has helped to make us sensitive to, viz., highly symbolistic works in which, as in a dream, each specific event is concrete or even prosaic, and yet the totality of these events is irrational and mysterious. (Kafka knew Freud's theories and it is not unlikely that he wrote with them in mind. In appraising the significance of Freud, we should also note the incalculable effect which he has had upon the *artists* themselves, both in literature and painting.) I will not, however, cite a specific Freudian analysis. Rather, I want to show how the biography of the artist can be used to illuminate these works.

Only the most unintelligent reader will take seriously any "summary" of *The Trial* and *The Castle*. (The really intelligent reader will read the books themselves, if he has not yet done so.) However, I must say something about the plot of each in order to explain their difficulty.

The protagonist in *The Trial* is put under arrest one morning. He is not informed of the charges against him; he is not imprisoned; he is not brought to trial. Indeed, he himself makes every effort to meet and confront his accusers. But he is never able to do so. At the end, his executioners come for him. He accompanies them willingly enough. He is stabbed to death and dies, as he says, "like a dog!"

The protagonist in *The Castle* (in both novels, he has no last name except for the initial K) believes that he has been requested by the authorities in the Castle to accept employment as a surveyor. He journeys to their city and tries to contact them. The Castle is high above the city, however, and it is inaccessible. His attempts to meet with his superiors are, as in *The Trial*, almost completely futile. As in *The Trial*, his whole experience is

[76] Cf. above, pp. 88 ff., 162 ff.
[77] Cf. above, p. 58, n. 35.

one of nightmarish ineffectuality and frustration. He does not give up. He continues his efforts to speak to those in the Castle. He continues to fail, however, and he dies without having succeeded.

Well, the usual plaint — "What does it *mean?*" — is in order. The life of the artist can, I think, help. The salient psychological data comes, in this case, not from a contextual critic, but from the artist himself.

Kafka's famous "Letter to his Father" is a lacerating personal document. With painful honesty and great acuteness, Kafka, now middle-aged, describes his relations with his father since childhood. What is of most interest to us is that he says, at one point, "My writing was all about you." [78]

Kafka draws a profile of his father — open, vigorous, bluff — and of himself, withdrawn and ineffectual. The father, being what he is, makes demands which his son cannot fulfill. As a father, Kafka says, "you have been too strong for me." [79] Hence the great fear which his father instilled in him.[80] And because Kafka recognizes his filial obligations, his failures create in him "a boundless sense of guilt." [81]

Kafka describes in detail the "only . . . episode in the early years of which I have a direct memory":

> Once in the night I kept on whimpering for water, not, I am certain, because I was thirsty, but probably partly to be annoying, partly to amuse myself. After several vigorous threats had failed to have any effect, you took me out of bed, carried me out onto the *pavlatche* [the balcony above the inner court-yard] and left me there alone for a while in my nightshirt, outside the shut door. . . . I dare say I was quite obedient afterwards . . . but it did me inner harm. What was for me a matter of course, that senseless asking for water, and the extraordinary terror of being carried outside were two things that I . . . could never properly connect with each other. Even years afterwards I suffered from the tormenting fancy that the huge man, my father, the ultimate authority, would come almost for no reason at all and take me out of bed in the night and carry me out onto the *pavlatche,* and that therefore I was such a mere nothing for him.[82]

The father, then, was endlessly powerful,[83] but his power was unreasonable,[84] and he exercised it in inexplicable ways.

Can this "real life" factual data which lies outside of Kafka's novels be of help in interpreting them? It can, I believe, give us a starting point, at

[78] Franz Kafka, *Dearest Father,* trans. Kaiser and Wilkins (New York: Schocken, 1954), p. 177.
[79] *Ibid.*, p. 140.
[80] *Ibid.*, p. 138.
[81] *Ibid.*, p. 170; cf., also, pp. 150, 157, 161.
[82] *Ibid.*, pp. 142–143.
[83] *Ibid.*, p. 147.
[84] *Ibid.*, p. 145.

least. One who is utterly bewildered upon first reading Kafka (and that probably includes most people), will not disdain this.

Let us conceive of the authorities in *The Trial* and *The Castle* on the model of the father, as described by Kafka. Then the novels express certain truths about social authority. On the one hand, the institutions which exercise authority over human beings are irrational. There is no rightful basis for their authority. And they wield power unreasonably. Even the law, which tries to be so exact and formal and which is hedged about with pompous self-righteousness, is ultimately absurd.

Yet there is far more in Kafka than just a critique of social institutions, a theme which is also found in many other works of art.[85] More important is the response of human beings to their institutions. They do not turn their back upon authority, even though it is hopelessly incomprehensible. Consider the father-son relationship. The son's emotions are deeply and inalienably involved in his father. Nothing that the father does, no matter how outrageous and tyrannical, can alter this. The son cannot break away from the father. The surest proof of this is that he feels guilt when he is unable to live up to his father's demands. Otherwise he would feel indifference or rebelliousness. Using this relationship as a model, let us say that the authority of his institutions is vital to a man's existence. He would not escape from it, even if he could. Despite the irrationality of authority, man remains committed to it. He endures its frustrations and willingly accepts its judgment. The guilt which he feels is the measure of his commitment. And he shows his guilt by his willingness to die "like a dog!"

How can this interpretation make the novels more meaningful and more valuable?

Nothing in the novels is more perplexing, upon first reading, than K's persistence in trying to seek out the court and the castle. A sufficiently discouraged reader might put the sobersides question (*The Trial*), "The court is leaving him alone; why doesn't he leave the court alone?"; or (*The Castle*), "Why doesn't he just forget about the men in the castle, since they seem never to have heard of him?" But if we use Kafka's autobiographical data, the question collapses. K. cannot sever the bonds which tie him to his superiors. The "judges" are remote, but they are not impersonal. His emotions and values are bound up in them. His pursuit of them is the mark of his involvement. What seems silly and incomprehensible, at first reading, is now seen as an act of dedication and loyalty.

Once aesthetic perception is directed in this way, other aspects of the work are illuminated. One of the most rewarding things in Kafka is the rich, expressive texture which runs through the works. But expression arises from subject matter and theme, and colors them in turn. The reader who is bewildered by "meaning" will miss the heavy, nightmarish tone that hangs

[85] Cf. above, p. 329.

465

over *The Trial*. The expressive tone emerges from the hopelessness of K's predicament, but the reader must understand the peculiarity of that predicament, which is more than merely an endless pursuit. Oddly enough, however, the very same theme often gives rise to humor, particularly in *The Castle*. Indeed, K. is involved in a classic comic situation, viz., the incongruity of a man trying to do what is clearly impossible, being defeated, and coming back for more; or, close to the same thing, Bergson's "mechanical" and "repetitive" behavior.[86] But again, once we understand the profound seriousness of K's predicament, Kafka's comedy will be more than just comedy. It now becomes macabre and sardonic, and it is edged with pain.

Can all of *The Trial* and *The Castle* be interpreted in terms of the "Letter to his Father," or is Kafka's childhood only a clue to certain phases of the novels? If we keep in mind the distinction between the origins of a work of art and its intrinsic significance, then the latter is far more probable. The novel is not simply a transcript of the author's early experiences. There is no point-for-point correlation between the "Letter" and the details of plot and characterization in the novels. If we tried to force the novel to fit the pattern of the "Letter," we would lose a great deal that is in the novel, and we would almost certainly distort a good deal more. For example, Kafka's account of his childhood describes his almost unrelieved fear and guilt. There is certainly "nothing funny" about the night on the *pavlatche*. Yet, as we have seen, there is comedy of a kind in the novels. In both *The Trial* and *The Castle*, K. is twitted for his inability to "take a joke." (Incidentally, Kafka himself found *The Trial* uproariously funny.) Once again, we are reminded that the work of art has a life and significance of its own.

Even if the interpretation of the novels on the model of the father-son relationship is used to carry us only part of the way, still, like any hypothesis in interpretive criticism, it must be tested. Does the interpretation satisfy the criteria of aesthetic "relevance"?[87] Does it tie in to the events and characters of the work and clarify them? Does it help to give a coherent structure to the whole? Can it be absorbed into aesthetic perception, so that it makes a felt difference in aesthetic experience? Or is it merely a schematic theory, suggested by Kafka, but useless for the purpose of reading Kafka? If so, it falls prey to the perennial danger of contextual criticism, viz., subordinating literature to psychology and social theory. Moreover, I have only sketched the interpretation. There are many questions which we need not pursue here, but which would have to be met in any full-dress discussion. Which institutions precisely are symbolized by the court and the castle? Do they stand for a church, or for a moral ideal, or

[86] Cf. above, pp. 298, 293–294.
[87] Cf. above, chap. 2, sec. 5.

for all institutions, or simply for the family relationship itself? Or do we have to decide this? Is it more faithful to Kafka to leave the symbolism elusive and indeterminate?

Finally, even if this interpretation should prove to be coherent and helpful, I would not for a single instant claim that it is the *only* possible interpretation. All works of art worth talking about are multivalent, and Kafka, because of his conspicuous ambiguity, is one of the best examples of this. I have already cited the great number of divergent interpretations of *The Castle*.[88]

THE PSYCHOLOGICAL APPROACH to art, then, draws upon the life of the artist. But it can do more than this. It can bring to bear upon the work what psychology has learned of human motivation and personality. In this way, too, it can clarify the behavior of characters in drama and the novel, symbols in literature and painting, etc. In this kind of psychological criticism there is not necessarily any reference to the biography of the artist.

Such criticism has been applied to what is without much question the single most widely — and hotly — discussed problem in all interpretive criticism, viz., "the Hamlet problem."

The literature of *Hamlet* criticism is endless. Almost every conceivable interpretation of the play has been put forward. Often these interpretations are completely opposed to each other, and some of them are very fanciful indeed. Among other things, the critics have been intrigued by Hamlet's "madness." Is he really mad or is he only feigning madness? One wag, after having read through a good deal of *Hamlet* criticism, asked, "Are *Hamlet*'s critics mad or are they only making believe?"

This question need not be answered here, fortunately, since it is not my purpose to give an exhaustive survey of *Hamlet* criticism. (Nor will I so much as mention the question, "Who *wrote Hamlet?*") Rather I want to show how "the Hamlet problem" is treated by Freudian criticism. This will be the most detailed illustration, in the present section, of how contextual criticism can serve the interests of interpretive criticism.

Our discussion of *Hamlet* has another purpose. We have, several times now, wrestled with the questions, "Can we ever say that one interpretation of a work is 'better' or 'more legitimate' than another? And if so, when?" [89] We will now see how several conflicting interpretations can be tested, as we try to fit them to the inner facts of the work.

WHAT I HAVE CALLED "the Hamlet problem" is really a cluster of several problems. Central to them all, however, is the question, "Why does Hamlet delay?" The Ghost tells him, early in the play, that his uncle, Claudius, has murdered his father. Hamlet's first response is,

[88] Cf. above, p. 427.   [89] Cf. above, pp. 259 ff., 425 ff.

O my prophetic soul! mine uncle! (I, v),

so it may be that he suspected Claudius even earlier. Yet he does not fulfill his promise to the Ghost to avenge his father, and he seems even to put it off on numerous occasions.

The simplest interpretation, probably, is that which "reads" the play in terms of the conventions of dramatic literature at the time that Shakespeare wrote (note that this is yet another kind of contextual criticism). *Hamlet* is seen as one of the "revenge plays" which were a standard dramatic *genre* of the period. There is a common plot structure in these plays. They begin with a crime, usually murder; the duty of vengeance is imposed on the next of kin, who must identify the murderer; he meets and overcomes various obstacles before he can carry out his duty; at the end, both the venger and his victim are usually slain; the victim must suffer perpetual torment in the afterlife for his sins.

If *Hamlet* is such a play, then its hero is a resolute, courageous young man who is fully prepared to kill his uncle. Why, then, does he permit four months to elapse, during which he does nothing, between the visitation of the Ghost and the arrival of the players at court? On this interpretation, Hamlet must make sure that the Ghost is not a delusion or an evil spirit:

. . . the devil hath power
To assume a pleasing shape (II, ii).

As one critic says,

. . . he does not flinch from [his duty]. He pauses only so long as is justly necessary to resolve all reasonable doubt of the reality of the obligation. He will not act rashly, but with judgment.[90]

Claudius' reaction to the play within the play persuades Hamlet of his guilt. Killing Claudius is now clearly justified. However, Hamlet cannot do so because the king is continuously surrounded by his guards. Hamlet finds him unguarded only once during the play, and that is precisely when Claudius is at his prayers (III, iii). If Hamlet were to kill him now, Claudius would not suffer the damnation decreed by the "revenge play."

There are other, related interpretations, according to which Hamlet's delay is due solely to the obstacles which he has to overcome. The obstacles, however, are less obvious than in the theory just described. For example, it is argued that justice would not be served unless the Danish citizenry understood the reasons for the slaying of Claudius. The act of

[90] Robert Gray (1891), in Claude Williamson, *Readings on the Character of Hamlet* (London: George Allen & Unwin, 1950), p. 177.

revenge would be self-defeating if Hamlet's countrymen took it to be an unscrupulous act motivated by the prince's own desire for the crown.

These interpretations, like the interpretations of any work of art, must square with the details of the play. They must organize "what happens in *Hamlet*" into a coherent whole. The greatest stumbling block to the interpretations just described is what Hamlet himself says about his delay.

The soliloquies in Shakespeare's plays, generally, must be accepted at face value. There is no intent to deceive or confuse the audience (though the speaker himself may be confused or mistaken in what he believes).[91] Hamlet, in his famous soliloquies, does not attribute the delay to tactical obstacles, such as the king's guards. Over and over again he berates *himself* for the delay, as he would not if the difficulties were purely external.

> . . . I,
> A dull and muddy-mettled rascal, peak,
> Like John-a-dreams, unpregnant of my cause (II, ii).

When he does speak of causes outside himself, such as the possibility that he has been duped by the Ghost, it appears to be afterthought and rationalization.

The above interpretations must, somehow, take account of the soliloquies. Some critics hold that the soliloquies are not essential either to the plot or to the character of Hamlet. They are used by Shakespeare simply for their poetic quality. A somewhat more ingenious explanation is that the soliloquies are simply devices for delaying the murder, so that the spectator's interest will be sustained and prolonged. Such dramatic devices are customary in the "revenge play."

Neither explanation is wholly satisfactory. In different ways, they trivialize the soliloquies. On the first explanation, indeed, Hamlet's speeches are a conspicuous weakness in the formal structure of the play. They are excrescences which do not fit coherently into the entire work. On the second explanation, they serve only a secondary dramatic purpose. They are not of prime interest in themselves, or as revelations of Hamlet's character.

We are justified in rejecting any interpretation which lessens the value of the work, if there is another which enhances its value. The soliloquies will be most interesting to us if they can be shown to be in close interaction with everything else in the play. Then they would both arise out of and color the events of the plot, and, by revealing Hamlet's character, they would increase the psychological interest of the play and enrich its expressive content. We must therefore look for explanations of the soliloquies other than those just given.

More generally, all interpretations which use the model of the "revenge

[91] Cf. above, p. 328.

play" seem to be inadequate. *Hamlet* loses the stature of tragedy and becomes melodrama. Such an interpretation is not faithful to the feelings which the play arouses in us. The play seems more complex and deeper than that. Moreover, what is, in recent times at least, the focus of interest in the play, i.e., Hamlet's character, is of minimal importance on these interpretations. They make him out to be courageous and vigorous, but a man with essentially a simple personality. However, even before Hamlet learns about the Ghost, his opening speech and his first soliloquy testify to a highly sensitive and introspective character.

On the "revenge play" approach, *Hamlet* is an exciting, blood-and-thunder play, but not much more. Moreover, the soliloquies, in their length and substance, are incongruous with this kind of play, so that *Hamlet* seems also to be something of a patchwork. It has been conjectured, indeed, that the play as we know it is the product of several authors, Shakespeare, Thomas Kyd, perhaps others.

So we look ahead to another interpretation. We want one which will take account of all the details in the play, give a coherent "reading" of the whole, and deepen the aesthetic interest of the work.

Whereas the first interpretation minimizes the importance of Hamlet's character, Coleridge makes the entire play pivot around it. The delay is due, not to external causes, but to Hamlet's own nature. He does not vacillate because he is a coward. Rather, in him "we see a great, an almost enormous, intellectual activity, and a proportionate aversion to real action." [92] Hamlet loses himself in "thinking too precisely on the event" (IV, iv), and therefore lacks the capacity for doing. He "delays action till action is of no use, and dies the victim of mere circumstance and accident." [93]

Coleridge clearly overcomes the objections to the first interpretation. He takes account of and, indeed, emphasizes the highly introspective character of the soliloquies. Hamlet now becomes a far more complicated and interesting personality. He falls into the classic pattern of the tragic hero, for one "particular fault" (I, iv) prevents him from meeting the challenge of circumstance. Because of the protagonist's central importance in *Hamlet*, the play becomes much more unified, formally and expressively, than on the first interpretation. Overall, it regains its stature as a tragedy.

However, the Coleridgean interpretation cannot be fitted to *all* the evidence of the play. It makes out Hamlet to be excessively "contemplative" and therefore slow to take action. At many places in the plot, however, Hamlet is anything but that. He is not only brave and resolute, as Coleridge says; he is also *rash*. In I, iv, when the Ghost beckons to Hamlet, his friends try to keep him from following it. The prudent Horatio cautions

[92] Williamson, *op. cit.*, p. 32.
[93] *Ibid.*, p. 33.

What if it tempt you toward the flood, my lord?

But Hamlet shouts

> ... unhand me, gentlemen; —
> By heaven, I'll make a ghost of him that lets [hinders] me,

and he dashes after the Ghost. In III, iv, upon hearing Polonius behind the curtain, he draws instantly and kills him. The Queen describes this as a "rash and bloody deed." In IV, vi, he shows himself to have been a man of swashbuckling action in abandoning the ship bearing him to England. In V, ii, he describes his quick-witted, decisive action in contriving the death of Rosencrantz and Guildenstern. In V, i, he does not hesitate to accept Laertes' challenge to fight in the name and memory of Ophelia. Hence the Coleridgean interpretation appears to be only partially valid.

Just here the Freudian interpretation begins. It is set forth by Ernest Jones in *Hamlet and Oedipus*, which is probably the best-known Freudian study in recent contextual criticism.

For Jones, as for Coleridge, the cause of the delay must be found within Hamlet himself. But, as we have just seen, Hamlet does not usually procrastinate when action is called for. Why does he do so in *this* instance, i.e., killing his uncle? As late as IV, iv, Hamlet does not know the answer:

> ... I do not know
> Why yet I live to say, *This thing's to do;*
> Sith I have cause, and will, and strength, and means
> To do't.

Thus Hamlet is, according to Jones, "a strong man tortured by some mysterious inhibition." [94]

Some critics are willing to give up and say that the play is essentially a mystery. Jones, however, finds that Hamlet falls into the pattern of neurotic behavior studied by Freud and his followers.

> [Whenever] a person cannot bring himself to do something that every conscious consideration tells him he should do ... it is always because there is some hidden reason why a part of him doesn't want to do it; this reason he will not own to himself and is only dimly if at all aware of. That is exactly the case with Hamlet.[95]

Since Hamlet's delay is due to unconscious forces, Jones believes that psychoanalytic theory can be applied.

[94] Ernest Jones, *Hamlet and Oedipus* (Garden City: Doubleday, 1955), p. 39.
[95] *Ibid.*, p. 60.

Jones sees in Hamlet the workings of the "Oedipus complex," i.e., Hamlet, as a child, had a strong erotic attachment to his mother and therefore "secretly" desired the death of his rival, his father. With maturity, these desires are necessarily "repressed." [96] However,

> The long repressed desire to take his father's place in his mother's affections is stimulated to unconscious activity by the sight of someone usurping this place exactly as he himself had once longed to do. More, this someone was a member of the same family, so that the actual usurpation further resembled the imaginary one in being incestuous.[97]

Thus the man whom Hamlet is sworn to kill is the very man who has enacted Hamlet's own deepest desires. The act of vengeance is therefore surrounded by guilty feelings which obscure moral duty and paralyze action. "By refusing to abandon his own incestuous wishes he perpetuates the sin and so must endure the stings of torturing conscience. And yet killing his mother's husband would be equivalent to committing the original sin itself, which would if anything be even more guilty." [98]

The evidence which would have to be examined, in order to test the validity of this interpretation, is exceedingly complicated. We would not only have to decide how well this interpretation fits the details of the play; the soundness of the whole psychological theory, on which the interpretation is based, is also in question. We can certainly say, however, that Jones' theory is, at the very least, a plausible one; at the most, a fair case can be made for saying that it is the best answer yet given to "the Hamlet problem." It overcomes the objections to the "revenge play" and Coleridgean interpretations. It makes the soliloquies coherent with the rest of the play. It may account for the play's enduring appeal. And it seems to be supported, among other things, by the fact that, as one critic ingenuously puts it, "Hamlet seems quite a bit concerned with his mother's sex life."

Jones uses his theory to analyze not only the work of art, but also the artist. He contends that Hamlet's conflict reflects a similar conflict which took place in the man, Shakespeare.[99] This theory is extremely speculative. And since we are interested in art, not psychology, we need not go into it. However, it is worth noting that Jones says of the work of art and the artist's personality, that "to increase our knowledge of either automatically deepens our understanding of the other." [100] That word, "automatically," is highly questionable. It shows us, not for the first time in this section, how the contextualist overstates his case and how he can thereby mislead

[96] *Ibid.*, pp. 78, 90–91.
[97] *Ibid.*, pp. 93–94.
[98] *Ibid.*, pp. 102–103.
[99] *Ibid.*, chap. VI.
[100] *Ibid.*, p. 14.

his readers. Much of the artist's personality never "gets into" the work at all. What is finally included in the work depends largely on such factors as the limitations of the medium and the interplay of elements in the work, which becomes intrinsically absorbing to the artist. Neither can we "automatically" infer from the work to the artist. Such inference, as we have seen, is generally very hazardous and often downright mistaken.

In our age, when talk about psychology is so much in the air, it is easy to fall into the error of considering the work simply a "reflection" of the artist's personality. When it is true at all to say this about a work of art, it is, as I argued earlier, only a partial truth. There is always more to the work than that. And we must remind ourselves that works of art can often be appreciated and criticized aesthetically, without saying a single word about the artist. Psychological documents are doubtless often fascinating, and works of art can sometimes be treated as psychological documents. But it would be a profound and cruelly expensive mistake to think of them as *nothing but* that, and thereby to blind ourselves to their intrinsic nature and value as objects of aesthetic perception.

THROUGHOUT OUR DISCUSSION, it has been necessary to caution against the exaggeration and abuse of contextual criticism. But it would be an error to close this section on a negative note. What the contextualists have taught us about art is of incalculable value. We now see more clearly than ever before in art criticism, how much of the artist and his society "gets into" the work of art. The work therefore has much greater human significance to the spectator. It is richer in meaning and expressive force.

Much of the best contextual criticism does not belong to any of the schools we have discussed. A contextualist need not be a partisan Marxist or Freudian. He can combine psychology and psychoanalysis, history, sociology, and other disciplines. Often these will all be required to explain a complex and subtle symbol or a myth which was traditional in the artist's society.

There is only one painting by Titian, the "Allegory of Prudence" (see Plate 27), which carries a "motto" on it. Translated from the Latin, it reads: "from the [experience of the] past, the present acts prudently, lest it spoil future action." [101] There are three faces depicted in the painting, one of an old man, turned to the left, one of a middle-aged man, in the center, the third, of a young man, turned to the right. The distinguished critic Erwin Panofsky traces back this symbol of the motto into medieval and Renaissance art. He shows that the faces stand for the past, the present, and the future respectively. But the painting also depicts a wolf, on the

[101] Erwin Panofsky, "Titian's *Allegory of Prudence:* A Postscript," in *Meaning in the Visual Arts* (Garden City: Doubleday, 1955), p. 149.

473

left, a lion, in the center, and a dog, on the right. Panofsky finds the origin of this symbolism in Egyptian religion, and shows that its meaning is the same as that of the three human heads. "What could have caused the greatest of all painters to combine two heterogeneous motifs apparently saying the same thing? In other words, what was the purpose of Titian's picture?" [102]

Further research is required. Now the critic investigates the life of the artist and other paintings by him. Panofsky is thus able to reveal something that previous generations had not seen, viz., that the face of the old man is that of Titian himself. The middle-aged man is his son; the youth is his "adopted" grandson. The painting is not simply allegorical. It is a personal testament by the artist. But "it is doubtful whether this human document would have fully revealed to us the beauty and appropriateness of its diction had we not had the patience to decode its obscure vocabulary." [103]

Again we see that interpretive criticism and judicial criticism are closely related. With Panofsky's "decoding," the work speaks to us more clearly and powerfully, as a "human document."

FINALLY, contextualism has had a subtle but powerful effect on all artistic evaluation.

Contextualism shows us that the creation of art is not wholly a matter of individual "inspiration." Art is one social activity among others. Anthropologists have studied the art of a culture as they study its family structure. They have made us more sympathetic to primitive art and the art of other societies by bringing such art to the attention of the West. As our tastes have become more catholic, our standards of judgment have become more flexible. In earlier ages, critics in the visual arts held that Greek or High Renaissance art "were the norms for judging all art." [104] Now critics are more prepared to believe that "Perfect art is possible in any subject matter or style." [105]

Moreover, the approach of contextualism to Western art itself has also stimulated more catholic and tolerant evaluation of art. Once we learn the origins of a thing and the influences which have molded it, we are less inclined to consider it "eternally" or "absolutely" valid. When we understand its natural history, we also understand its limitations. It has value within the particular situation in which it arose, not in *all* situations. This is true of a political institution, such as monarchy, and of a moral code. It is also true of art. Contextualism has placed art in its natural setting. Fine art is not a "spiritual mystery." It arises in the circumstances of human living and it answers to human needs. Furthermore, the origins of art are infinitely

---

[102] *Ibid.*, p. 165.   [103] *Ibid.*, p. 168.
[104] Meyer Shapiro, "Style," in *Anthropology Today*, ed. Kroeber (University of Chicago Press, 1953), p. 291.   [105] *Ibid.*, p. 291.

various. Insofar as they make the work what it is intrinsically, they create different values in the art-objects of different periods and cultures. We now see that different kinds of art can all be valuable "in their own way." In a word, contextualism has made us more relativistic.

3. IMPRESSIONIST CRITICISM

The contextualists of the mid-nineteenth century wanted to be, above all, "scientific." Art criticism was to become as objective and precise as the physical sciences.

By the close of the nineteenth century, there was a strong reaction against this kind of criticism. The reaction was due to several causes.

Primarily, the movement of "Art for art's sake" was proclaiming the aesthetic "isolation" and "self-containedness" of fine art.[106] The contextualist showed the interrelations of the work to other things and often blurred or ignored its aesthetic values. "Art for art's sake" necessarily, therefore, moved in the opposite direction from contextualism. Moreover, by the end of the century, contextualism, or at least the most widely publicized variety of contextualism, seemed to have failed. The determinists, like Marx and especially Taine, had drawn elaborate blueprints for the complete, genetic "explanation" of art. But the blueprints remained just that. Art and the artist could not be explained simply as the resultants of psychological and social forces. Genius could not be explained like gravity.

Furthermore, those who led the revolt against contextualism were strongly influenced by emotionalist theory. Oscar Wilde said, "Art is a passion." [107] The critic's emotions are necessarily aroused. Hence, objectivity, even if it were desirable, is not possible:

Objective criticism has no more existence than objective art, and all those who deceive themselves into the belief that they put anything but their own personalities into their work are dupes of the most fallacious of illusions. The truth is that we can never get outside ourselves.[108]

Finally, the new movement was suspicious of all critical "rules," contextual, neoclassical, or whatever. Rules are too rigid and formal for the "subjective" critic responding to the "passionate" work. Art cannot be judged by rules.[109]

---

[106] Cf. above, pp. 352 ff.
[107] "The Critic as Artist," in *Portable Oscar Wilde*, p. 117.
[108] Anatole France, *On Life and Letters*, 1st series, trans. Evans (New York: John Lane, 1911), pp. vii–viii.
[109] Cf. above, pp. 382 ff.

The critic therefore has no use for history, psychology, and so on, and he frees himself from rules. All that the critic requires is "a certain kind of temperament, the power of being deeply moved by the presence of physical objects." [110]

WHAT, THEN, DOES THE CRITIC actually do? In the famous statement of Anatole France, "[the] good critic is he who relates the adventures of his own soul among masterpieces." [111] He records and describes the ideas, images, moods, and emotions which are aroused in him by the work of art. This conception of criticism is set forth, at the turn of the century, by France, in the criticism of literature, Wilde and Pater, in the criticism of literature and the visual arts, and by the composer Debussy in music criticism. The latter says: "To render one's impressions is better than to criticize, and all technical analysis is doomed to futility." [112]

The "impressionists" react against "objective criticism" with a vengeance. Both in contextual criticism and criticism by rules, attention is on the object. But for the impressionist, the central questions are:

> What is this song or picture, this engaging personality presented in life or in a book, to *me*? What effect does it really produce on me? Does it give me pleasure? and if so, what sort or degree of pleasure? [113]

Moreover, the critic can give free rein to his imagination and emotions, while looking at the work. His criticism need not be limited to what is in the work: "All books in general, and even the most admirable, seem to me infinitely less precious for what they contain than for what he who reads them puts into them." [114]

The critic can enjoy such freedom because impressionism rejects the usual functions of criticism. It is not the job of the critic primarily to pass judgment on the work or to explain it to the reader. Art criticism has *no* purpose beyond itself. Like art, "[it] is . . . its own reason for existing." [115] Hence it is not a defect in the critic if he fails to describe accurately what is contained in the work. Wilde asks: "Who cares whether Mr. Ruskin's views on Turner are sound or not? What does it matter?" Wilde considers the criticism as a work of art in its own right. He eulogizes Ruskin's "mighty and majestic prose . . . so fervid and so fiery-coloured in its noble eloquence, so rich in its elaborate, symphonic music." [116]

---

[110] Pater, "Preface" to *The Renaissance*, p. xxvii.   [111] *Op. cit.*, p. vii.
[112] Quoted in Max Graf, *Composer and Critic* (New York: Norton, 1946), p. 291.
[113] Pater, *op. cit.*, p. xxvi. Italics in original.
[114] Anatole France, *On Life and Letters*, 2nd series, trans. Evans (New York: John Lane, 1914), pp. xi–xii. Cf., also, Wilde, *op. cit.*, p. 87.
[115] Wilde, *op. cit.*, p. 82.   [116] *Ibid.*, p. 84.

IMPRESSIONIST CRITICISM did not start with the impressionists. The writings of many earlier critics were, to some extent at least, descriptions of the critic's own responses. And France is probably right in insisting that the personal element cannot be kept out of art criticism. Complete impersonality is often found in "marks-giving," [117] which is usually a mechanical and sterile kind of criticism. Virtually all the great critics have a distinctively personal touch.

But though there is some impressionism in most critics, it is doubtful that impressionism, in itself, is a sound basis for criticism. Impressionist critiques are often of literary interest in their own right. However, if we ask for something more than this, impressionism will usually fail us.

Impressionism sets no limits to the critic's discourse. He can talk about anything and everything. If we seek an interpretation of what is in the work, it will be only a lucky coincidence if we get it from him. Similarly, we cannot expect a reasoned evaluation of the work.

The bane of impressionism is its aesthetic irrelevance. Impressionist criticism often has little or nothing to do with the inherent structure and value of the work. Irrelevance is, of course, a perennial danger for *all* criticism, and no single kind of criticism has foolproof protection against it. We have seen this to be true both in neoclassical and contextual criticism. However, impressionism is the only kind of criticism which deliberately invites irrelevance, and, as in Wilde, even welcomes it.

Rymer was guilty of irrelevance because he applied the neoclassical rules heavy-handedly and unimaginatively. Yet these rules are, after all, relevant to some works at least.[118] A more intelligent critic than Rymer, even if he were not first-rate, could reasonably be expected to tell us something about the work, by judicious use of the rules. Impressionism, however, eschews all rules. It can therefore easily turn into sheer emotional outpouring. These effusions are often of no value whatever, either literary or critical.

Indeed, there are indications that the leading impressionists themselves did not believe in complete, unrestrained impressionism. Wilde grants the importance of historical scholarship and detailed analysis of the work. [119] He also says that the critic can share the very emotions which are expressed in the work.[120] Finally, he says that by "fine scholarship and fastidious rejection," [121] the critic can determine the value of the superior work and distinguish it from lesser works. In these passages, Wilde turns back toward the work itself, its interpretation and evaluation.

Even more important, the leaders of the impressionist movement are not complete impressionists in their critical *practice*. Wilde, France, Pater,

[117] Cf. above, pp. 405–406.
[118] Cf. above, pp. 448–449.
[119] *Op. cit.*, p. 91.
[120] *Ibid.*, pp. 100–101.
[121] *Ibid.*, p. 107.

Lemaître, in their critiques of specific works, do more than simply record their personal feelings. They also explain the structure and expressive character of the work. Their "objective" insights are usually mingled with their "impressions." Yet the insights are there all the same, and they are often interpretive criticism at its best. They keep the critique from falling into loose, undisciplined reverie.

Although complete impressionism cannot do the work which we require of the critic, a certain amount of it can benefit both him and us. Perhaps the best thing that it can do is to instill in the reader the critic's own *enthusiasm* for the work. If his enthusiasm becomes infectious, we will almost certainly have a better understanding of the work's value. Mere enthusiasm, however, is not enough. The critic must explain what he is enthusiastic *about,* and *why.*

4. INTENTIONALIST CRITICISM

Wilde asked, rhetorically, "Who . . . cares whether Mr. Pater has put into the portrait of Mona Lisa something that Leonardo never dreamed of?" [122] The opponents of impressionism took him seriously. *They* cared. They said of the impressionist: "We shall not begrudge this exquisite soul the pleasure of his sensations." But they were quick to "point out that . . . interest has been shifted from the work of art." [123] Paradoxically, the same charge was brought against "the school of Taine," [124] in other respects so much opposed to the impressionists, which had shifted interest from art to history and sociology. Hence, early in this century, an attempt is made to restore attention to the work of art.

The best way to do so is, precisely, to "care" about the artist's purpose. The central critical question now becomes: "What has the poet tried to do, and how has he fulfilled his intention?" [125]

Intentionalist criticism cannot be restricted, historically, to the reaction against impressionism. It crops up recurrently in the history of criticism. It is found throughout the nineteenth century, as a corollary of the Romantic emphasis upon the personality and "genius" of the artist. [126] We have already seen it suggested in Pope and Johnson, in the eighteenth century. [127] And it is very much alive at the present time. One recent author writes: "To me it seems that the highest type of response to music . . . puts us

---

[122] *Ibid.,* p. 84.
[123] J. E. Spingarn, "The New Criticism," in *Creative Criticism* (New York: Harcourt, Brace, 1931), p. 6.
[124] *Ibid.,* p. 35.
[125] *Ibid.,* p. 18.
[126] Cf. above, pp. 158 ff.
[127] Cf. above, pp. 447–448.

most thoroughly in *rapport* with the intentions of the composer." [128] You have unquestionably encountered intentionalism in books about art, courses in the arts, etc.

Intentionalism is always a plea for aesthetic "sympathy." It cautions against approaching the work in a "spirit," as Pope says, alien to that of the artist. Thereby it keeps us from looking for the wrong things in the work. Considered in this way, intentionalism is a healthy idea for *any* kind of criticism.

BUT EVERYTHING DEPENDS on what we *mean* by "intention." The term has several different meanings which are often confused in our talk about art. The confusion is disastrous. For, on one meaning of the term, "intention" is *not* a sound and workable basis for criticism.

In this sense, "intention" is a *psychological* term. It refers to something that went on in the mind of the artist. It is the conception which he has, prior to and during creation, of the finished work of art which he wants to produce. The intention is, in other words, the goal of his activity, as he imagines it. This "psychological intention," as I will call it, is therefore something which lies outside the work of art itself. (Since intentionalism, in this sense, is concerned with one of the origins of the work, it can be considered a species of contextual criticism.)

There are strong objections to using "psychological intention" either to interpret or evaluate the work of art.

First, there is a "practical" problem, but not a trivial one, by any means. It is the difficulty, often the impossibility, of knowing what the intention *is*. The intention is something in the artist's private experience. Unless he describes it, in letters, conversation, or autobiography, it is known only to him. Therefore the criterion of intention could not be applied to the vast majority of works of art. Further, even when the artist has described his intention, his account may suffer from all the usual evils of artists talking about artistic creation, e.g., rationalization, conscious deception, unconscious self-deception.[129]

Moreover, it is almost always a mistake to speak of "*the* intention" of the artist, as though he had a fixed, unitary conception of the work from first to last during creation. The creative process, as we have seen, is not usually a direct, uninterrupted movement toward the artist's goal. It involves experimentation, revision, tracing out new "leads" suggested by the medium, and so on.[130] Therefore the artist's intention *changes* as he proceeds. Often the artist has *many* intentions. Which of them shall we use for criticizing the work?

[128] Chandler, *op. cit.*, p. 232.
[129] Cf. above, p. 94.
[130] Cf. above, pp. 99 ff.

However, let us even suppose that the artist has a clear, fixed intention throughout and that we know what it is. Still, the intention is something external to the work. It is at least logically possible that the intention does not explain what is within the work itself. The intention may not be realized in the work because the artist is unable to control his medium or because he chooses an inappropriate subject matter or for other reasons. Intention would then be irrelevant to interpretive criticism.

Nor can we judge the *value* of the work in terms of the artist's success or failure in fulfilling his intention. He may have failed, and yet the work is aesthetically valuable, in its own right. Or he may have succeeded, but if the intention was silly or banal, the work will be aesthetically trivial.

Finally, even if he succeeded, his intention is not necessarily either the only or even the best way of interpreting the work. Once the work has been brought into being, it has an independent life of its own. It is interpreted in many different ways by various critics and in successive generations. They may find values in the work which are completely unlike those which the artist intended; indeed, considering the multivalence which criticism has found in most works of art, this is almost always true. Moreover, later interpretations may make the work a *better* one than the artist conceived of:

> Debussy, listening to his String Quartet being tried out for the first time, said to the musicians, "You play the third movement twice as fast as I thought it should go." Then he paused a moment to enjoy the disturbance he had created and added, "But it's so much better your way!" [131]

For all these reasons, "psychological intention" is a weak and misleading critical concept. Therefore, another meaning of "intention" has been proposed: "The poet's real 'intention' is to be found, not in one or another of the various ambitions that flit through his mind, but in the actual work of art which he creates. His poem is his 'intention.' " [132] However, if the "intention" just *is* the work of art, there seems to be little point in using the word any more. Moreover, it is somewhat misleading to speak of "intention" in this sense, since the word usually refers to a state of mind, which is something quite different from a work of art.

There is, however, still another meaning of the term. Let us now speak of the "aesthetic intention." This is a metaphoric way of referring to the total effect that the work is supposed to have on the aesthetic percipient. The percipient's response is, of course, something different from the work itself, just as the artist's "psychological intention" is. Unlike "psychological

---

[131] Charles Munch, *I Am A Conductor*, trans. Burkat (New York: Oxford University Press, 1955), p. 52.
[132] "The Growth of a Literary Myth," in Spingarn, *op. cit.*, p. 167.

480

intention," however, "aesthetic intention" focuses our interest on the work as an *aesthetic* object. And it is a wholesome corrective to Rymer-criticism. It induces the critic to ask, "What is this work trying to achieve, as an aesthetic vehicle?" This keeps him from applying value-criteria which are irrelevant to the import of the work. The concept of "aesthetic intention" thereby heightens respect for the uniqueness of the work, and this is as indispensable in art criticism as it is in aesthetic appreciation.

With the "aesthetic intention" in mind, the critic can then ask the second intentionalist question, "*How* is the effect achieved?" This will lead to an examination of the intrinsic structure of the work. The concept of "aesthetic intention" is sometimes most useful when the critic judges that the work *fails* in its intention. There may be clear indications within the work of the sort of effect that it is trying to achieve. Perhaps the effect is supposed to be "big" or "epic," perhaps the work is "trying to be" profound. But, as we say, the work "doesn't come off." Instead of being profound, it is only pretentious; instead of being emotionally powerful, it is sentimental. Again, analysis of the elements of the work will be called for.

Now that the distinction between "psychological intention" and "aesthetic intention" has been drawn, it should be noted that the former *can* sometimes be aesthetically relevant. If the "psychological intention" has been realized within the work, so that it affects the work's intrinsic nature, it can be used profitably by the critic. The artist's account can clarify certain elements within the work and also the "aesthetic intention" of the whole. This has often been true in contemporary art, when the style or symbolism of the work made it, initially, inaccessible to its audience.

The guiding principle for the use of "psychological intention" in criticism is the same as for all other contextual facts — it must help to explain what is demonstrably *in* the work and thereby illuminate the nature and value of the aesthetic object.

5. INTRINSIC CRITICISM

We come now to the most important critical movement of this century. It is the movement in literary criticism known as "The New Criticism."

A phrase of Matthew Arnold's can be taken as its motto: "To see the object in itself as it really is." The New Critics attempt to concentrate solely upon the *intrinsic* nature of the work. By the same token, they shun what lies "outside" the work. "Emphasis should be kept on the poem as a poem." [133]

[133] Brooks and Warren, *op. cit.*, p. xv.

It would be as accurate as such a generalization can be, to say that the New Criticism repudiates each of the kinds of criticism which we have studied thus far.

Many leaders of this movement have condemned contextualist criticism bitterly.[134] They charge it with diverting attention away from "the poem as a poem" to biography, sociology, history, and so on. The emotional outpourings of the impressionist are condemned for the same reason, except that impressionism diverts attention to the critic himself.

The New Critics are extremely patient, careful, sophisticated, in their analyses; their work is, in the best sense of the word, "professional." It is not difficult to understand why they scorn impressionism, which seems to them to be undisciplined and diffuse. But even if it were not, they would still reject impressionism, because it stresses the *effects* of the work upon the reader. The New Critics, in general, avoid speaking of the emotions aroused by the work. John Crowe Ransom (who, incidentally, gave "The New Criticism" its name) says that the critic should "attend to the poetic object and let the feelings take care of themselves." [135] Just as the effects of the work are ignored, so are the origins. Intentionalism is also repudiated.[136]

In some respects, therefore, the New Criticism has greater affinity to the "objective" criticism of the seventeenth and eighteenth centuries than to more recent kinds of criticism. Attention is focused upon the work, and the critic tries to remain impersonal. However, the New Criticism does not accept criticism by rules either. For one thing, the New Critics are much more interested in interpretive criticism than judicial criticism. You can go through a great deal of their writings without finding a single explicit value-judgment. They seek primarily to explain and clarify the work. Insofar as evaluation does occur, it is not by the application of rules. The New Critics, who know the history of criticism, are suspicious of rules. They devote themselves to analysis of specific works and let the evaluation arise out of their interpretation. As Leavis says, "My whole effort [is] to work in terms of concrete judgments and particular analyses." Hence he has little use for "principles and abstractly formulable norms." [137]

All "intrinsic" criticism respects the uniqueness of the particular work. Like aesthetic perception itself, it sees what is distinctive about the work, what sets it off from "similar" works. Criticism by rules, however, presupposes that works can be classified into "kinds" and are therefore subject to the criteria which measure goodness in each "kind." The New

---

[134] Cf. above, p. 461.

[135] "Criticism as Pure Speculation," in *The Intent of the Critic*, pp. 96–97.

[136] Cf. W. K. Wimsatt, jr., and M. C. Beardsley, "The Intentional Fallacy," *Sewanee Review*, LIV (1946), 468–488.

[137] *Op. cit.*, p. 215.

Critics, with their flair for the individuality of each work, doubt the legitimacy of such classification. The criteria of value must be adapted, often improvised, for the specific work in question. As Ransom puts it: "Each poem is a new poem, and each analysis is probably the occasion of a new extension of theory in order to cope with it." [138] (It is worth noting that the New Critics usually work with single poems or novels, whereas contextual criticism tends to lump together all works by a single author or of the same period.)

So rules, like context, intention, and the critic's "impressions," are rejected. Showing what the New Criticism is *not*, helps to explain what it *is*. We must now, however, study its techniques and objectives more directly.

THE NEW CRITICISM is a movement in literary criticism. However, it has striking resemblances to an earlier movement in the criticism of music and the visual arts, viz., formalism.

Hanslick, we have seen, proclaimed the intrinsic significance of music. He spoke scornfully of those who used music as a stimulus to emotions and then measured the value of the composition by the intensity of their emotions.[139] For these people, as we said earlier, "a good cigar or a warm bath" is as valuable as a symphony.[140] Nor need the critic take account of the life of the composer or the time in which he lived.[141] Music consists in the elements of the medium, "sound and motion," "forming . . . a complete and self-subsistent whole." [142] When Bell and Fry attempted to educate taste to appreciate "pure" painting, they took music as their model.[143] They, too, found the value of art in the distinctive elements of the medium — line, mass, plane, etc., in painting and sculpture — interacting with each other in a unique formal structure. They use such words as "rhythm," "harmony," "tension," to describe these formal relations.

It is no accident that we find references to Hanslick and Fry in the literature of the New Criticism,[144] for their conception of art is largely similar to that of the New Critics. Ransom draws an analogy between a poem and the formal design of the visual arts.[145] Cleanth Brooks says that a poem is "a pattern of resolutions and balances and harmonizations." [146] Notice these words — "resolution" and "harmonization" are taken from the vocabulary of music, "balance" from the visual arts. The

---

[138] Quoted in R. W. Stallman, "The New Critics," in Stallman, *op. cit.*, p. 496.
[139] Cf. above, p. 183.   [140] Cf. above, p. 143.
[141] Cf. *The Beautiful in Music*, pp. 99–103.
[142] *Ibid.*, p. 68.   [143] Cf. above, pp. 142–143.
[144] Cf. W. K. Wimsatt, jr., and M. C. Beardsley, "The Affective Fallacy," *Sewanee Review*, LVII (1949), 30; Stallman, *op. cit.*, p. 498.
[145] *Op. cit.*, p. 123.   [146] *Op. cit.*, p. 203.

poem is a formal pattern, which contains inner forces and tensions and which unifies them into a self-contained whole.

As in Hanslick and Fry, the emphasis is on the artistic medium. Thus the New Critics set right the error of the contextualists, who think chiefly of the "ideas" or "themes" that come from outside of art, and who therefore ignore the medium in which they are embodied that is peculiar to art.[147] The literary medium is language, with its explicit meanings, associations, imaginative and emotional overtones, traditional and cultural significance, ordered by such formal devices as rhythm, in all literature, and rhyme and meter, in poetry. (The influence of the formalists is also to be seen in recent analyses of form and rhythm in the novel and drama, an area which is now being explored as never before in literary criticism.[148] Form and rhythm had previously been studied chiefly as they occur in poetry.)

Words, however, *mean*. Just here it would seem that music and "pure painting" break down as models. Hanslick and Fry, after all, held that these arts are "self-contained" precisely because they do not refer beyond themselves to "life." Literature (except for nonsense poetry) can hardly avoid such reference. Bell, you remember, said that literature is not a "pure art" for just this reason.[149] Can we treat the novel or poem simply as a formal pattern? Must we not take account of "content" as well as "form," and will this not involve us again in the categories of contextualism?

These questions have agitated a great deal of discussion among the New Critics, particularly with regard to the value of "truth" in art and the nature of aesthetic "belief."[150] It would be a mistake to say that they have arrived at any single answer. Many of them, however, hold and indeed insist that poetry embodies "knowledge" and is therefore a cognitive structure.[151] But though there certainly is "meaning" in literature, it is peculiar to the specific work of art and cannot be stated or expressed in any other form. The "meaning" is expressed, qualified, shaded, by the interaction of images, ideas, emphases, and tensions within the structure of the work. That is why it is a "heresy" to paraphrase it in straightforward prose.[152]

T. S. Eliot said in a famous passage: "The 'greatness' of literature cannot be determined solely by literary standards; though we must remember that whether it is literature or not can be determined only by literary

---

[147] Cf. above, pp. 452, 455–456, 460, 462.
[148] Cf. above, pp. 245–246.
[149] Cf. above, p. 142.
[150] Cf. above, chap. 12.
[151] Cf., e.g., Tate, *op. cit.*, p. 9; John Crowe Ransom, *The New Criticism* (Norfolk: New Directions, 1941); Wimsatt and Beardsley, "The Affective Fallacy," pp. 46, 48, 52.
[152] Cf. above, p. 325.

standards." [153] You see how Eliot faces both ways. The uniqueness of the artistic medium, and its importance, are insisted upon, in the manner of the formalists; yet the connection of literature with "life," and therefore the importance of its moral profundity, "truth," philosophical coherence, and the like, are also recognized. The same duality is to be found in many of the New Critics.

Now WHAT, EXACTLY, is the job of the critic, according to the New Criticism? We would doubtless get different answers from those who have been called "New Critics." Blackmur's statement is probably as good a brief answer as we can find. The critic must "concentrate maximum attention upon the work which the words and the motions of the words — and by motions I mean all the technical devices of literature — perform upon each other." [154] (Notice the similarity to Hanslick's description of music, "sound and motion.") The "words" — "the critic is [an] explicator of meanings." [155] He must make clear the literal meaning, but more important, he must trace the nuances and overtones of meaning which the words have acquired, either in ordinary communication or in special kinds of discourse. The analysis need not be "merely verbal," for it may lead to discussion of cultural symbolism and other contextual relations of words. "The motions" — meter, rhythm, imagery, expressive "tone," metaphor, irony, and so on. And how they "perform upon each other" — the rich and subtle meanings which the words take on, in their interaction with each other.

When you see our age referred to as an "age of criticism" (sometimes there is an implied comparison with a "creative age"), it is usually the New Criticism that is being referred to. For its achievement has been so extraordinary that the movement must necessarily loom large in our time. Never before in the history of criticism has there been so much systematic, close textual and formal analysis of literature carried on by critics of the first rank. The progenitors of the New Criticism are Eliot and Richards in the twenties; Brooks, Ransom, Leavis, and Tate are only a few of the later critics.

I WOULD LIKE TO GIVE specific examples of their work. Their critiques, however, by their very nature, do not lend themselves to summarization. They are too closely knit. Many of these critiques seem to be as compact and tightly woven as the "organic" works of art which they study! An outline could hardly do justice to their subtlety and richness of detail.

---

[153] "Religion and Literature," in *Essays Ancient and Modern* (New York: Harcourt, Brace, 1936), p. 92.
[154] R. P. Blackmur, "The Enabling Act of Criticism," in Stallman, *op. cit.*, p. 417.
[155] Wimsatt and Beardsley, "The Affective Fallacy," p. 48.

The artistic interpretations of the contextualist critics, by contrast, can be outlined comparatively easily.

Undoubtedly the best thing that the student can do is to read in the New Critics themselves.[156] As a second-best, I will refer, in brief, to the analysis of Robert Frost's "After Apple-Picking" by Brooks and Warren.

The first eight lines of the poem are as follows:

> My long two-pointed ladder's sticking through a tree
> Toward heaven still,
> And there's a barrel that I didn't fill
> Beside it, and there may be two or three
> Apples I didn't pick upon some bough.
> But I am done with apple-picking now.
> Essence of winter sleep is on the night,
> The scent of apples: I am drowsing off.[157]

These lines and those that follow describe the activity of apple-picking and the weariness of the narrator who now begins to think of sleep. On one interpretation, the poem is descriptive and narrative. But it is characteristic of the New Criticism that it finds "more" in the work. Close analysis of the "words and their motions" discloses new "symbolic overtones" [158] in the superficially simple poem.

Brooks and Warren say of lines seven and eight:

> . . . the word *essence* comes strangely into the poem. It is not the kind of everyday, ordinary word characteristic of the vocabulary of the previous part of the poem. [This word] most readily brings in the notion of some sort of perfume . . . but it also involves the philosophical meaning of something permanent and eternal. . . . The word scent (as contrasted with synonyms such as odor or smell) supports the first idea in essence, but the other meanings are there, too, with their philosophical weighting. The scent of apples is a valuable perfume . . . but it is also to be associated in some significant way with the "winter sleep." [159]

The analysis pursues this suggestion. The "winter sleep" opposes rest and reward to labor and waking life. "After Apple-Picking" now takes on a deeper, even a "philosophical" meaning.

---

[156] Cf., e.g., Brooks and Warren, *Understanding Poetry*; Brooks, *The Well Wrought Urn*; Stallman. *Critiques and Essays in Criticism*; Ray B. West, jr., ed., *Essays in Modern Literary Criticism* (New York: Rinehart, 1956).

[157] Lines from "After Apple-Picking" from *Complete Poems of Robert Frost*. Copyright, 1930, 1949, by Henry Holt and Company, Inc. By permission of the publishers. P. 88.

[158] *Op. cit.,* p. 389.   [159] *Ibid.,* p. 390. Italics in original.

To go one step further, we may say that the contrast is between the actual and the ideal. Now we can look back at the very beginning of the poem and see that what appeared to be but a casual, literal detail — the ladder sticking through a tree — initiates this line of meaning. The ladder is pointing "Toward heaven still." It points, not toward the sky . . . but toward *heaven*, the place of man's rewards, the home of his aspirations.[160]

There is further verbal explication, along with analysis of the meter (again, it is not possible to present here all the detail of the critique). Finally, the "root-idea" of the poem is worked out: man's ideals must be grounded in the realities of ordinary existence and should not try to deny them.[161]

You see how far this is from a simple narrative about picking apples. Most readers would probably never suspect the presence of this "root-idea" in the poem. Is the interpretation given by Brooks and Warren aesthetically relevant, or is it simply a fanciful hypothesis? The answer can only be found by asking the usual questions: Does the interpretation draw upon what is demonstrably contained within the work? Is it coherent? Can it be taken over into aesthetic perception, where it will control the reader's "set" and expectations toward the work and guide his attention, so that there is a difference in the felt quality of his experience?

THE NEW CRITICISM, like other kinds of criticism, has "the defects of its virtues." It has turned critical interest back toward the work itself, which had been all but forgotten by some earlier critics. It has corrected the exaggerations and abuses of contextualism, impressionism, and intentionalism. Yet some of the New Critics have reacted so strongly against their predecessors that they have fallen into exactly opposite mistakes.

For one thing, they have sometimes dismissed contextual knowledge altogether, as though it were never more than irrelevant psychology, history, etc. This is just as wrong-headed as thinking that art is *nothing but* psychology or history. It impoverishes criticism needlessly. The critic can and should use whatever can help him. Since the artist's biography, the concerns of his society, the myths of his culture, *sometimes*, at least, "get into" his work, interpretive criticism can hardly proceed without knowledge of them.

The emphasis of the New Critics is upon the formal pattern of the work. But the form is what it is because of its interaction with everything else in the work. The work is unified by playing upon the historical meanings of a single word or concept; the unfolding of a cultural symbol affects the imagery. Formal analysis cannot then be "merely formal." It must consider the historical and social referents of words and

---

[160] *Ibid.*, p. 391. Italics in original.   [161] *Ibid.*, pp. 394–395.

symbols, and it must therefore become contextualistic, to some extent. (It is, unfortunately, true that a few of the New Critics have deprived themselves of the help of psychology, social history, etc., because their fear that "scientism" is going to dominate our culture has made them resentful of all science.[162] But this is simply irrational.) It is note-worthy that Brooks and Warren, in the second edition of their widely influential textbook, *Understanding Poetry*, concede that questions of his-tory and biography were not treated sufficiently in the first edition and they set about to rectify the mistake.[163]

No critics are more *ingenious* than the New Critics. They have shown their ingenuity in finding new "levels of meaning" in the work and in tracing the multifarious overtones of a single word. You can see this even in my brief account of the analysis of "After Apple-Picking." Their subtlety has brought to light hitherto unsuspected values in works of liter-ature. But this "virtue," too, has its "defects." Sometimes the critic is so intent on working out some "symbolic meaning" that the critique becomes an end in itself. The critic is so absorbed in the idea suggested by the novel or play that he loses contact with the work itself. His critique then consists largely of his own reflections. In these cases, the New Criticism is guilty of irrelevance just as much as any contextualist or impressionist criticism. Or, related to this, the critic's explication of some detail may remain relevant to the work, but he becomes so absorbed in it that he fails to relate the detail to the significance of the work as a whole. He does not then give us a coherent interpretation of the work.

There is, finally, a "defect" which is less easily detected because it oc-curs in the critic's basic presuppositions. The New Critics, we have noted, tend to avoid explicit value-judgments. Yet some of them pre-suppose a theory of evaluation which must be questioned.

Their constant concern is with "the work itself." That is why they have no use for the impressionist, who becomes absorbed in his own emo-tions. His autobiographical report "is neither anything which can be re-futed nor anything which it is possible for the objective critic to take into account. The purely affective report is either too physiological or it is too vague." [164] The "objective critic" therefore says little or nothing about the effect of the work upon the reader. As we have seen, he busies him-self with the structure of meanings which is intrinsic to the poem.

The New Critics have been taken to task for this:

The value of literature surely lies in its actual or potential effect on read-ers — admittedly, on experienced and sensitive readers. . . . To deny this is

162 Cf. above, pp. 310–311.
163 *Op. cit.*, p. xxi.
164 Wimsatt and Beardsley, "The Affective Fallacy," p. 45.

to fall into the . . . fallacy of believing that a work of art fulfils its purpose and achieves its value simply by *being*.[165]

The implications of this "fallacy" are important.

What happens, in some of the New Critics, is that their preoccupation with "the work itself" leads them to become *objectivists*.[166] Or, to say the same thing in another way, their disdain for impressionism leads them to reject relativism. Their method of criticism — intrinsic, structural analysis — lends itself to the view that literary goodness is intrinsic and non-relational. Often, in these critics, the objectivism is unvoiced and it may even be unconscious. Sometimes, however, they say explicitly that they are trying to escape from "the morass of relativism, of impressionism." [167]

We have already discussed the shortcomings of objectivism. However it is worth seeing what form they take in the New Criticism.

The basic thesis of objectivism is that value is inherent in the object apart from any spectator. Those of the New Critics who are also objectivists assume that, once the structure of the work is laid bare, the value of the work is established. The value-judgment, whether it is stated or only suggested, does not have to be tested further.

The New Critics often call themselves *aesthetic* critics. They mean by this that they stick to the intrinsic structure of the work. But take "aesthetic" to refer to the relation between disinterested attention and the work. Then, does formal analysis always describe and explain the value of the work in aesthetic experience? Only if we assume what the objectivist critic often seems to assume, viz., that the aesthetic experience is simply a living-through of the critical analysis. He must assume that the experience is a transcript, in perception and emotion, of what the critique describes, analytically and conceptually. The meanings which have been unearthed by the critic will be felt values to the reader.

But this assumption is unsound. It claims too much for criticism and, like all objectivism, it pays too little attention to aesthetic experience. There are crucial differences between these two activities.[168] The critical analysis, in itself, cannot guarantee the aesthetic goodness of the work. The details which are spelled out in analysis may not cohere into a unified aesthetic object. And what the critic describes as the significance of the whole may not "come off" in aesthetic immediacy. An elaborate pattern of meanings, which is clear to the critic, may be confused or turgid to the percipient; symbolic overtones that are important to the critic may

---

[165] David Daiches, "The 'New Criticism': Some Qualifications," in *Literary Essays* (New York: Philosophical Library, 1957), p. 173. Italics in original.
[166] Cf. above, pp. 397–409.
[167] Theodore Spencer, "The Central Problem in Literary Criticism," *College English*, 4 (1942), 160–161. Cf., also, Brooks, *op. cit.*, Appendix 1.
[168] Cf. above, pp. 377 ff.

have little or no impact upon the reader. This shows, not that the reader is insensitive — I am assuming the qualified and discriminating percipient — but that there is a world of difference between a work, when it is studied piecemeal and discursively, and the same work, when it is grasped as an aesthetic unity.

As relativism insists, the aesthetic value-judgment must be tested in aesthetic experience. A judgment which sounds plausible, as part of a critique, may not tally at all with aesthetic response.

The objectivists among the New Critics, like earlier objectivists, can, and sometimes do claim that the work is valuable irrespective of felt response, or that the value can be apprehended only by those who possess "good taste." But to justify these claims, they would have to develop their theory of evaluation systematically. We saw in the previous chapter the problems that they have to face. They must defend the definition of "value" in the former claim and show that the latter claim is not guilty of question-begging.

Objectivism, since it takes value to be a nonrelational property, has held traditionally that one and only one evaluation of the work is correct. Some of the New Critics often seem to imply the same thing. They appear to deny the legitimacy of any other interpretation or the validity of any other value-judgment. This aspect of objectivism is especially painful when it occurs in their writings. For the New Critics, perhaps more than any other in the history of criticism, have shown how rich and complex a work of art can be. By their learning, patience, and subtlety, they have re-interpreted works which earlier generations had neglected, and they have revealed new and deeper meanings in long familiar works. They, more than anyone else, should know that many legitimate interpretations are always possible.

Objectivism has been responsible for needless weaknesses in some of the New Criticism. To be an *objective* critic you do not have to be an *objectivist*. What is the important meaning of "objective" as applied to criticism? The real force of the term is that it excludes both aesthetically irrelevant knowledge, such as we find in some contextualists, and undisciplined emotional outpouring, as in some of the impressionists. A critic can perfectly well be objective in this sense, and also be a relativist. Such a critic concentrates upon what is intrinsic to the work. He brings in contextual knowledge only when it is relevant, and he does not confuse his immediate response with evaluation. But he judges the work always in relation to what people feel when they look at it as an intrinsic object. And he knows, and indeed insists, that other interpretations and evaluations of the work are at least equally valid.

ONE FINAL WORD, to guard against a possible misunderstanding. This chapter has distinguished various kinds of criticism, each with its own presuppositions, methods, and purposes. But it would be a mistake to think that critics can be classified, simply and solely, under just one of these headings. Most critical writings are a mixture of one or more critical kinds. Even the most "objective" or "formalistic" critic usually gives us his personal reactions to the work, and all but the most uninhibited impressionist interprets the work itself, even if only indirectly. Indeed, there would be no logical inconsistency in combining all five of the critical kinds in a single critique, even though such a promiscuous mixture would probably seem odd and incoherent. But though most critics use a number of methods, they generally favor one kind or another.

The good critic will, nonetheless, adapt his techniques and value-criteria to the particular work he is studying. He will therefore use different kinds of criticism in different cases. He will also consider the audience he is writing for, the level of its taste and its familiarity with a work of this style or *genre*.

BIBLIOGRAPHY

* Rader, *A Modern Book of Esthetics*. Pp. 132–179, 527–571.
* Schorer, Miles, McKenzie, eds. *Criticism*. New York: Harcourt, Brace, 1948.
* Venturi, Lionello. *History of Art Criticism*, trans. Marriott. New York: Dutton, 1936.
* Vivas and Krieger, *The Problems of Aesthetics*. Pp. 414–430, 498–514.
* Weitz, *Problems in Aesthetics*. Pp. 275–305, 360–379, 660–682.
  Demuth, Norman, ed. *An Anthology of Musical Criticism*. London: Eyre and Spottiswoode, 1947.
  Fry, *Transformations*.
  Graf, Max. *Composer and Critic*. New York: Norton, 1946.
  Hauser, Arnold. *The Social History of Art*. New York: Vintage, 1958. 4 vols.
  Osborne, *Aesthetics and Criticism*.
  Panofsky, Erwin. *Meaning in the Visual Arts*. Garden City: Doubleday, 1955.
  Stallman, Robert W., ed. *Critiques and Essays in Criticism*. New York: Ronald, 1949.
  Stauffer, Donald A., ed. *The Intent of the Critic*. Princeton University Press, 1941.
  Sullivan, J. W. N. *Beethoven*. New York: Mentor, 1953.
  Wellek, René, and Warren, Austin. *Theory of Literature*. New York: Harcourt, Brace, 1949.
  Wimsatt, W. K., jr., and Brooks, Cleanth. *Literary Criticism: A Short History*. New York: Knopf, 1957.

QUESTIONS

1. Analyze carefully some critiques of specific works in the sources listed in the Bibliography. What kinds of criticism do they exemplify? Does the critic use

more than one of the approaches described in this chapter? How is his interpretation of the work related to his judgment of its value?

2. "[If] we consider this special spiritual activity of art we find it no doubt open at times to influences from life, but in the main self-contained — we find the rhythmic sequences of change determined much more by its own internal forces — and by the readjustment within it, of its own elements — than by external forces." — Fry, *Vision and Design*, p. 9.
   Analyze the soundness of this view by examining the account of some major historical change in art, as described by Hauser, in the work cited in the Bibliography.

3. Study some of the interpretations of *Hamlet* in the work by Williamson, cited earlier (cf. above, p. 468, n. 90). Are there any which seem to you to be more adequate than those discussed in this chapter? How do you determine the "adequacy" of an interpretation?

4. Sullivan, in the work cited in the Bibliography, says that "the Eroica symphony is an amazingly realized and co-ordinated expression of [Beethoven's] spiritual experiences" (p. 76). Study Sullivan's exposition of this thesis. What does he mean by "expression"? What evidence does he have for this view? Does he argue from the facts of the composer's life to the nature of the music, or conversely? How strong is his argument?

5. Look at the reproduction of Titian's "Allegory of Prudence" (Plate 27). Does Panofsky's contexual critique (cf. above, pp. 473–474) enhance the aesthetic value of the work? If so, how?

6. Read France's critical essays in "On Life and Letters" (cf. above, p. 475, n. 108, p. 476, n. 114). Are they completely impressionistic? Do they have any "objective" validity?

7. The "psychological intention" has been defined as the artist's conception of the work which he wants to create (cf. above, p. 479). His intention, in another sense, might be to make money, arouse his audience to the existence of certain social evils, win fame, etc. Could the intention in this sense ever be aesthetically relevant? If so, how? Can you give specific examples?

8. Which of the theories of art studied earlier (chaps. 5–8) is, in your judgment, most closely related to each of the kinds of criticism studied in this chapter? Explain your answer.

9. For each of the kinds of criticism studied in this chapter, cite some specific works of art which, in your judgment, can be treated more fruitfully by this kind of criticism than by any other. Explain your answer in each case.

17

The Educative Function
of Criticism

At the beginning of his now classic *Shakespearean Tragedy*, A. C. Bradley describes the purposes of his critique. Here Bradley shows himself to be, not merely a critic, but also a critic who is thoughtfully concerned about the methods and functions of criticism. To this extent, he is a philosopher of art criticism.

Bradley has one goal above all:

> Nothing will be said of Shakespeare's place in the history either of English literature or of the drama in general. . . . I shall leave untouched, or merely glanced at, questions regarding his life and character, the development of his genius and art, the genuineness, sources, texts, inter-relations of his various works. . . . Our one object will be what . . . may be called dramatic appreciation; to increase our understanding and enjoyment of these works as dramas.[1]

Thus Bradley shuns various kinds of contextual criticism. His studies of the tragedies are, for the most part, intrinsic criticism. As he recognizes, this involves analysis of the plays. But analysis can also be justified by the purpose of criticism:

[1] *Op. cit.*, p. 1.

493

[The] dissecting processes . . . are still, and are meant to be, nothing but means to an end. When they have finished their work (it can only be finished for the time) they give place to the end, which is that same imaginative reading . . . of the drama from which they set out, but a reading now enriched by the products of analysis, and therefore far more adequate and enjoyable.[2]

Art criticism is sometimes interpretive and sometimes judicial. These critical functions are important in themselves. But, in all areas of value, the chief reason for analysis and evaluation is to enrich our future value-experience.[3] So the chief function of art criticism is to make aesthetic experience better than it would otherwise be, to make it, as Bradley says, "more adequate and enjoyable." What is gained in human enjoyment is the ultimate, and the best possible justification for criticism.

Criticism makes aesthetic experience better by making aesthetic perception more discriminating. It enables us to see what we had not seen before. We can now discern and therefore respond to all that is richly contained within the work. Criticism calls our attention to the sparkle or charm of the sensory matter, the subtlety of form and the way in which its formal structure unifies the work, the meaning of symbols, and the expressive mood of the entire work. Criticism gives us a sense of the work's "aesthetic intention," so that we do not make illegitimate demands upon it. Criticism also develops aesthetic "sympathy" by breaking down the prejudices and confusions which get in the way of appreciation. It explains the artistic conventions and social beliefs of the artist's time. It relates the work of art to the great world and shows its relevance to our own experience.

In these and many other ways, criticism is *educative*. It teaches, but it does not simply impart knowledge. Directly or indirectly, it instructs perception, thought, feeling, and imagination, so that they can all lean toward the work of art sympathetically and knowingly.

Thus the critic performs an indispensable function in our aesthetic lives. He is the seer and guide. It has been said that the great artist must create the audience for his works, but he rarely does so without the great critic. The critic directs perception to the values of new and unfamiliar art and thereby encourages its acceptance. Many artists have achieved fame largely because of the educative activity of the critic. Ruskin performed this service for the painter Turner, the late Olin Downes for Sibelius, the critic-editor Robert Bridges for the poet G. M. Hopkins. Probably the best example is that which we have already studied, i.e., the achievement of Roger Fry, in educating an entire generation to appreciate Post-Impressionist painting and sculpture.

---

[2] *Ibid.*, p. 2.
[3] Cf. above, pp. 373 ff.

IN THE LAST CHAPTER, we studied some of the major kinds of criticism. All of them can be educative, in different ways. I want to show this for each kind of criticism in turn.

Criticism by rules begins by classifying the work in a certain *genre*. This in itself can be aesthetically educative. To call a poem a "lyric" or an "elegy" already gives us a sense of its aesthetic intention. It helps us to "set" ourselves appropriately as we begin to read. We expect a certain expressive "tone," and, when the work is highly traditionalized, we are in a position to understand its stylistic and formal conventions. Moreover, the application of rules to the work picks out salient details in it. Our perception can become more discriminating as a result. Then the evaluation which results from judging by the rules has the same educative function as all evaluation, viz., it tells us the kind and degree of value we can expect to find in the work. This too influences our aesthetic "set." Criticism by rules tells us both what the object "is" and "what it is worth." [4]

Contextual criticism, we have seen, is strongest in dealing with subject matter, symbol, conceptual theme — all the elements which point beyond the work to "life" — weakest in dealing with the "purely" artistic elements of medium and form. If we take it at its best — as we should take all criticism — contextual criticism can be invaluable. For some works, indeed, which make historical or social references, or whose symbolism is unclear, contextual criticism is absolutely indispensable. It does a large part of the job of interpretive criticism. The knowledge which it discloses helps toward a coherent "reading" of the work. But neither the knowledge nor the interpretation can be educative if it remains detached from aesthetic experience. The knowledge must be absorbed into the "equipment" with which the percipient meets the work. "Ideal aesthetic knowledge, absolutely ready response, would bury the whole system of discriminations in our nerves and our habits." [5] Further, the interpretation which the contextualist helps to build must be translated into our perception. The aesthetic spectator has to "structure" the work as it unfolds before him — he must distinguish what is of primary importance from that which is only secondary, he must decide how the parts are interrelated and where the climax falls, etc. The artist, of course, gives leads to the spectator. But a work can be interpreted in different ways, as we have seen more than once. The artist cannot dictate rigidly how the work shall be apprehended. Ultimately the viewer or listener must do the job of active, creative perception. The contextualist critic cannot do it for him, but he can contribute much.

The contribution of the impressionist is quite different. He deliberately shuns contextual knowledge and he gives no formal interpretation. And yet — unless his "impressions" are wildly irrelevant — his critique can also

---

[4] Cf. above, p. 442.   [5] Prall, *Aesthetic Analysis*, pp. 57-58.

be educative. His moods, images, and thoughts, as he describes them, can suggest the richness of the work. By indirection, they call attention to the properties of the work which have stimulated them. The impressionist also educates when he, so to speak, makes impressionists of *us*, i.e., when he encourages us to approach the work with a fertile imagination. Too many of us are intimidated or inhibited by works of art. We hesitate to think any thoughts or feel any emotions other than the "proper" ones that we have read or heard about. The impressionist can make our perception more supple, inventive, and alive. Finally, and best of all, the impressionist often infects us with his own enthusiasm for the work. Perhaps more than any other kind of critic, his writing has zest and gusto. It has the interest of any intense, personal statement. Other kinds of criticism often seem to be lifeless by contrast. They may analyze carefully and judge scrupulously, but the whole business seems mechanical and prosaic. When we have finished reading the critique, we still have no interest in looking at the work for ourselves. The impressionist often stimulates such interest. We approach the work, after having read him, not only sympathetically, but eagerly. The measure of the critic's success is the spontaneity and delight of our experience.

"Psychological intention" can be educative for some, though not all, works of art. When the critic asks, and can answer, the question, "What was the artist trying to do?" he makes us more sympathetic to the work. The question is especially pertinent when the work is in a radically new style or form. People have an unfortunate tendency to dismiss such works offhand. "Psychological intention" gets us to understand the artist's purpose, and this is the first step in seeing that what he has achieved may be worth while. "Aesthetic intention" is, of course, educative under any circumstances. We must have some sense of what the work is "trying to do" if we are to look at and respond to it appropriately. But since "aesthetic intention" refers to immediacies of experience, it is not readily described. It generally eludes conceptual description. Hence the critic must often resort to suggestive, metaphoric language to convey the intention. Many of the best critics have excelled in this kind of writing. James Agate says of Tchaikovsky's Fifth Symphony that it is "drenched with self-pity." "But," he goes on, "I like listening to it just as I like looking at a fuchsia drenched with rain."

Finally, intrinsic criticism, such as the New Criticism, is clearly educative because it guides perception to what is hidden beneath the surface of the work. By disclosing the meanings embodied in the work, it makes our experience more subtle and, as Bradley says, "more adequate."

THUS EACH KIND OF CRITICISM is educative, in its own way. But "the common reader," the person who takes some interest in art and wants to increase his interest, must do his job, too. Criticism by itself is never enough. It is no substitute for direct aesthetic awareness. We traduce criticism and we rob ourselves of enjoyment if we forget this. Sometimes people gain information from the critic, but they fail to work this information into their discrimination of the work. They are satisfied just to be able to talk plausibly about the work. Sometimes they read the critic's account of his own experience, but they make no attempt to experience the work for themselves. Criticism is educative, ultimately, only in its end product — felt aesthetic experience. Criticism can be educative, therefore, only when the percipient makes the effort of aesthetic attention and sympathy.

T. S. Eliot is probably the foremost critic of our time. But he speaks for the enlightened "common reader" here:

> So the critic to whom I am most grateful is the one who can make me look at something I have never looked at before, or looked at only with eyes clouded by prejudice, set me face to face with it and then leave me alone with it. From that point, I must rely upon my own sensibility, intelligence, and capacity for wisdom.[6]

JUST AS no one kind of criticism has a monopoly on educative usefulness, neither is any kind of criticism foolproof against being *anti*-educative. Any critical method, instead of sharpening discrimination and encouraging interest, can have just the opposite effect.

Criticism by rules can, in various ways, blur the uniqueness of the work of art. By classifying works into *genres*, such criticism stresses the similarities of the work to other works, rather than its differences. There is a real danger that the critic will, therefore, overlook what is distinctive about *this* work. His reader will, accordingly, perceive the work as a stereotype. His responses will be the mechanical, habitual ones developed by other works in this *genre;* he will fail to see the work as a fresh and unique object. Moreover, the application of rules places greater weight upon the parts of the work than upon the whole. Unless the critic's judgment is balanced by attention to the whole, he will, indeed, "murder to dissect." He will fail to show how the parts contribute to what Pope calls "the full result of all." His reader will have knowledge of details, and evaluations of each of them, but aesthetic appreciation requires, above all, a sense of the whole. Only so can the percipient "set" himself to respond appropriately. And only so can he interpret each detail, and give it its place in a coherent unity.

The danger in using contextual criticism is obvious. It is pointed up in

[6] T. S. Eliot, "The Frontiers of Criticism," in *On Poetry and Poets* (London: Faber and Faber, 1957), p. 117.

the writings of many of the contextualists. It is, of course, that the critic will give us knowledge *about* the work and nothing more. Such critics fail to show — sometimes they seem not to care — how this knowledge is relevant to the interpretation and appreciation of the work. The unwary reader learns the contextual facts and thinks that this is enough. But he may then use the work simply to pick out elements which illustrate these facts — "This is where the composer's love affair went sour," and so on. Since many of the contextual facts have no aesthetic relevance whatever, he often spends his time looking for things in the work that simply are not there. Contextual criticism is profoundly antieducative when it results in diverting attention from the art-object to its context.

The impressionist critic can also divert attention from the work of art. If his writing is exciting or attractive, as it often is, the reader takes the critique to be an end in itself and loses sight of the work. If the critique is simply a wild flight of fancy, as it sometimes is, he learns nothing of the intrinsic properties of the work. Moreover, even when the critique is aesthetically relevant, it is usually one-sided. The impressionist excels in giving an evocative description of the work's total quality or "flavor." But he tends to be weak on details. Hence the critique does not increase our discrimination. One who is under the influence of an impressionist critic often experiences a vague, generalized mood, in the face of the work, but he fails to see the details which would make his emotions more varied and more specific.

"Psychological intention" is part of the context of the art-object. Criticism in terms of it is therefore subject to the same perils which we have just noted in contextual criticism generally.

It would seem, however, that intrinsic criticism would have to be educative. For it confines itself to what is within the work, and it makes the work more significant to us. Yet even when all of its analysis of meaning remains "inside" the work — as it does not always do, in the New Criticism — such criticism can still be antieducative, though in a rather subtle way.

The ingenious and imaginative critic can, as we have seen, find many different overtones of meaning within the work. An expert critic will be able to demonstrate how each of these is grounded in the words of the poem or drama. Still, his detailed exposition of meanings may be *too* complex to be of help in aesthetic perception. The percipient is unable to assimilate all of these meanings into his experience. Once again, we must remind ourselves that the aesthetic experience is signally different from the critical experience. We can comprehend each of the meanings which are spelled out piecemeal by the critic. But these meanings cannot always be worked into the aesthetic object. The rhythm of aesthetic perception is brisk and urgent, by contrast to the pace of analysis. The rhythm will be slowed down or collapse altogether, if the reader attempts to distinguish each of the meanings disclosed by the critic. As Ransom says, in criticizing one of the New Critics, the "movement of the poem" must "come off faster"[7] than the critic allows it to do. Aesthetic attention attempts to grasp an object in its immediacy. The work which is weighted down with a vast superstructure of interpretation is too lumpy and complex to be grasped. It is unable to make a direct, immediate impact.

Consider the student taking a course in literature, in which the instructor and the textbook use the methods of the New Criticism. After a short while he comes to see how superficial his earlier reading of the poem or novel was. He missed the deeper levels of meaning, the "more" which the New Criticism always finds in literature. And yet, just because he was not aware of the complexity of the work when he first read it, he could seize it as a concrete unity, and, in some degree, feel its imaginative and emotional excitement. After he has studied critiques of the work, he is far better informed than before. Yet all of the meanings which he has learned cannot be absorbed into the aesthetic body of the work. All too often, therefore, his reading of the novel becomes a process of *recognizing* the meanings, one after the other. The work therefore loses its vitality and excitement.

Thus, it is not enough for the criticism to be "relevant" simply in the sense that the critique sticks to what is in the work. To be educative, it must also be "relevant" in the sense that what is learned can enter into and intensify aesthetic experience.[8] Criticism is anything but educative when it disperses aesthetic interest and transforms it into a cognitive exercise.

What follows from this, I need hardly say, is not that there should be *no* explication of meanings at all. That would be silly, for it would deprive us of all the educative gains of intrinsic criticism. The moral is, rather, that the critic should always bear in mind the aesthetic experience which his reader is going to have. The critic must remember the salient differences between analysis and aesthetic perception. And he must therefore remember the needs and limitations of aesthetic perception. Consequently, he must himself set limits to his explication. He should try to make perception more intelligent and informed; but he should not so overload it that it cannot function at all.

We can generalize this conclusion to apply to all kinds of criticism. We have found that they can all be antieducative in different ways. There is no infallible remedy for this. But criticism is more likely to be educative when the critic seeks always to honor his responsibility to his read-

---

[7] *The New Criticism*, p. 123.
[8] Cf. above, pp. 58–59.

er's future aesthetic experience. All the errors of criticism which we have just discussed result from forgetting this. The critic becomes absorbed in himself, or infatuated with his methods, or he is really more interested in scholarship than the enjoyment of art. A critic can assist and guide the spectator only if he remembers what aesthetic awareness is like, how it proceeds and what it seeks. Whatever his methods, the critic must ultimately bring about "formation in the receptive mind of a whole condition of feeling and awareness," [9] a "condition" which will enable the percipient to respond to the work of art acutely and intensely.

AESTHETIC EXPERIENCE comes first, in importance and value. It is the goal or end of criticism. Criticism is an aid and a means, not an end in itself.

From this follow some further guiding principles for criticism.

The critic must always recognize that his interpretation and value-judgment must be tested in aesthetic experience. They do not prove themselves. They are proved when the interpretation can be used fruitfully within aesthetic awareness, and when the judgment tallies with the goodness that people actually feel in their encounter with the work. Hence there is no room for finality or infallibilism in art criticism. A critique is, or should be, a hypothesis, not a dogmatic verdict.

Since it is a hypothesis, it is always subject to revision. The critic, like the rest of us, must keep going back to the work. Unless he holds to his pet interpretation inflexibly, he will almost inevitably change it, as he discriminates details which he had not seen before and gains new insights. If you will look back at the passage quoted from Bradley at the beginning of this chapter, you will find him saying of critical analysis that "it can only be finished for the time." The critic who forgets this pays the price of narrow and short-sighted criticism.

Moreover, the critic should choose his methods and value-criteria in the light of aesthetic experience. He must adapt his procedures to the nature of the aesthetic object. Old standards often will not be relevant in judging new and different works. As an aesthetic percipient, he must make every effort to see what is good in the work; as a critic, he must select or, often, devise techniques of analysis which explain the work's goodness. Hence the critic's methods and criteria must be flexible, not rigid. And they should be varied, not limited, in order to take account of the endless diversity of works of art.

The critic who recognizes the richness of works of art will also recognize that many interpretations of a work, not his alone, are legitimate. Accordingly, many value-judgments are sound. Different observers find different values in the work. Aesthetic experience is the goal. Any in-

---

[9] Richards, *Practical Criticism*, p. 333.

terpretation which is relevant and coherent, and which abets genuine aesthetic experience, must be respected. For this reason, too, dogmatism is unjustified in criticism.

But there is another reason, the final reason, for humility in criticism. Works of art are inexhaustibly rich. There is no limit to what they will give to those who approach them with disinterested love and sympathy. No single interpretation can capture and distill the aesthetic goodness of the work, not even the partial goodness which it has on this interpretation alone. Neither can a whole host of interpretations ever sum up all of the values which the work may disclose. No amount of critical talk suffices. The critic who respects the precious uniqueness of the work knows and will gladly admit that there is more still to be said. There will always be more to be said. And no matter how much we say about the work of art, "at the hypothetical limit of attention and interest there will always remain, quite untouched, the thing itself." [10]

[10] Blackmur, "A Critic's Job of Work," p. 276.

BIBLIOGRAPHY

Eliot, T. S., "The Frontiers of Criticism," in *On Poetry and Poets*. London: Faber and Faber, 1957. Pp. 103–118.
French, ed., *Music and Criticism*.
Isenberg, Arnold, "Critical Communication," in *Aesthetics and Language*, ed. Elton. New York: Philosophical Library, 1954. Pp. 131–146.
Richards, *Practical Criticism*.

QUESTIONS

1. "Analysis is an indispensable procedure, but the analysis of a given piece is valueless to anyone who does not have some previous knowledge of the work." — Virgil Thomson, "The Art of Judging Music," in French, *op. cit.*, p. 111. Do you think that this is true? If so, why?
2. In what ways can criticism be of help to the creative artist? Can you find any specific instances in which the artist acknowledges such help?
3. "A good critic keeps his criticism from becoming either instinctive or vicarious." — Blackmur, "A Critic's Job of Work," *op. cit.*, p. 277. What do you think Blackmur means by "instinctive" and "vicarious" here?

PLATE 1. VAN GOGH: *The Yellow Chair*, BY
COURTESY OF THE TRUSTEES OF THE TATE GALLERY.

PLATE 2. SHAHN: *Handball*, COLLECTION MUSEUM OF MODERN ART, MRS. JOHN D. ROCKEFELLER, JR., FUND.

PLATE 3. GÉRICAULT: *The Raft of the Medusa*, LOUVRE.

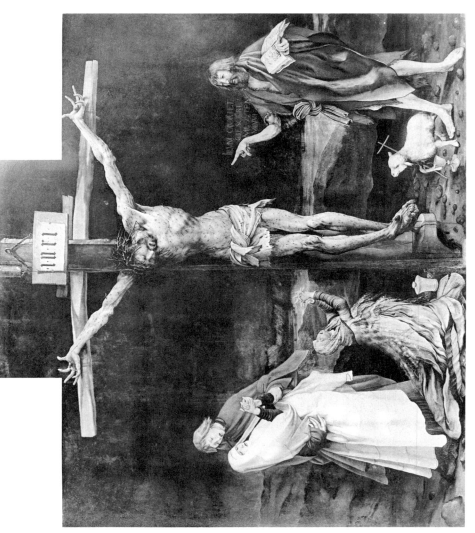

PLATE 4: GRÜNEWALD: *Crucifixion*, THE ISENHEIM ALTARPIECE, BILDARCHIV FOTO MARBURG.

PLATE 5. PERUGINO: *Crucifixion*, SANTA MARIA MADDALENA, FLORENCE, PHOTO FROM ALINARI.

PLATE 6. CORREGGIO: *Jupiter and Antiope*, LOUVRE.

PLATE 7. SEURAT: *Sunday Afternoon on the Island of La Grande Jatte*, COURTESY OF THE ART INSTITUTE OF CHICAGO.

PLATE 8. VAN GOGH: *The Starry Night*, COLLECTION MUSEUM OF MODERN ART, ACQUIRED THROUGH THE LILLIE P. BLISS BEQUEST.

PLATE 9. CÉZANNE: *The Quarry Called Bibemus*, FROM ERLE LORAN, *Cézanne's Composition*, UNIVERSITY OF CALIFORNIA PRESS, 1943.

PLATE 10. *Photograph of the same motif by Erle Loran*, FROM ERLE LORAN, *Cézanne's Composition*, UNIVERSITY OF CALIFORNIA PRESS, 1943.

PLATE 11. MODIGLIANI: *Jeanne Hébuterne*, COLLECTION MR. AND MRS. SIDNEY BRODY.

PLATE 13. CHALFANT: *After the Hunt*, FROM ALFRED FRANKENSTEIN, *After the Hunt*, UNIVERSITY OF CALIFORNIA PRESS, 1953.

PLATE 12. HARNETT: *After the Hunt*, THE MILDRED ANNA WILLIAMS COLLECTION, CALIFORNIA PALACE OF THE LEGION OF HONOR, SAN FRANCISCO.

PLATE 14. KOLLWITZ: *The Parents*, WOODCUT, 1923, COLLECTION OF ERICH COHN.

PLATE 15. SAINT-GAUDENS: *Grief*, ROCK CREEK CEMETERY.

PLATE 16. HOGARTH: *He Revels,* FROM *Works of Hogarth,* GEORGE BARRIE, 1900, VOL. 3.

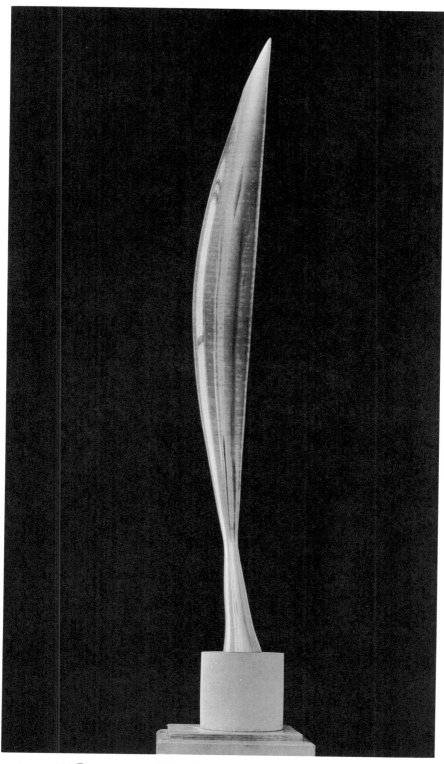

PLATE 17. BRANCUSI: *Bird in Space*, COLLECTION MUSEUM OF MODERN ART.

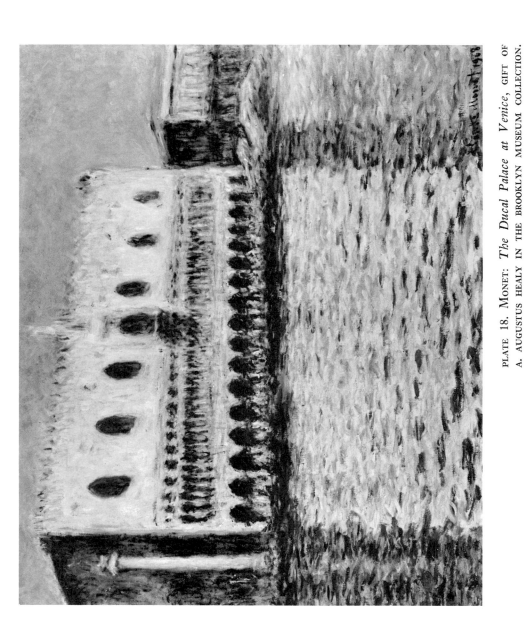

PLATE 18. MONET: *The Ducal Palace at Venice*, GIFT OF
A. AUGUSTUS HEALY IN THE BROOKLYN MUSEUM COLLECTION.

PLATE 19.   CÉZANNE: *The Card Players*, COLLECTION STEPHEN C. CLARK.

Plate 20. PICASSO: *Les Demoiselles d'Avignon,* 1907, COLLECTION MUSEUM
OF MODERN ART, ACQUIRED THROUGH THE LILLIE P. BLISS BEQUEST.

PLATE 21. MONDRIAN: *Composition in White, Black, and Red*,
COLLECTION MUSEUM OF MODERN ART, GIFT OF THE ADVISORY COMMITTEE.

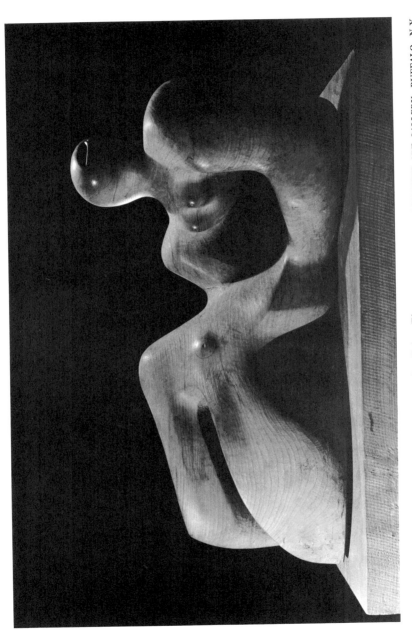

PLATE 22. Moore: *Reclining Figure*, COURTESY OF ALBRIGHT ART GALLERY, BUFFALO, N.Y.

PLATE 23. GIOTTO: *Death of St. Francis*, SANTA CROCE, FLORENCE, PHOTO FROM ALINARI.

PLATE 24. GOYA: *Accident in the Arena at Madrid*, FROM GOYA'S ETCHINGS.

PLATE 25. MOHOLY-NAGY: *Composition*, THE SOLOMON R. GUGGENHEIM MUSEUM.

PLATE 26. PICASSO: *Glass of Beer, or Portrait of Jaime Sabartes*, MOSCOW MUSEUM OF WESTERN ART.

PLATE 27. TITIAN: *Allegory of Prudence*, PRIVATE COLLECTION.

Index

its affinity to formalism, 483–485; the methods of, 485–487; the limitations of, 487–490; the educative function of, 496, 498–499
Nietzsche, F., 95

Objective relativism: the basic theses of, 421–425; its analysis of value-disagreement, 425–430; criticism of, 430–437
Objectivism: the basic theses of, 390–392; and critical disagreement, 392–397; intuitionist objectivism, 397–400; "accompanying-properties" objectivism, 400–404; definist objectivism, 405–408; contrasted with relativism, 432–437; in "The New Criticism," 488–490
Oedipus Rex, 74–75, 288
Osborne, H., 133, 381, 407, 410

Panofsky, E., 473–474
Parker, De Witt H., 205, 230, 235, 236, 282–284, 381–382
Parkhurst, H. H., 240
Pater, Walter, 142, 353, 476–478
Pepper, Stephen C., 44, 76–77, 156, 219, 276–277, 282
Perry, R. B.: on art and morality, 359–361
Philosophy: the critical function of, 3–7
Philosophy of criticism: its relation to aesthetics, 371–372; the problems of, 388–390
Picasso, 99, 137, 234, 261, 357
Plato: 46, 95, 159, 224, 233, 291, 303–304; on imitation, 110–114, 116; on art and morality, 340 ff.
Plotinus, 224
Pope, Alexander, 393, 446–448, 478–479, 497
Porter, Katherine Anne, 91–92
Portnoy, J., 172n.
Post-Impressionism: in the visual arts, 136–138
Poussin, 141

Prall, D. W.: 34, 220, 353, 495; theory of "surface," 61–63; on artistic media, 225–226
Pratt, Carroll C., 393, 394
Psychology: experimental aesthetics, 11–13, 54–55, 77–81; and criticism, 461–473

Rader, M., 150n.
Rank, Otto, 462n.
Ransom, John Crowe, 186, 190, **482**, 483, 484n., 485, 499
Raphael, 238–239
Raynal, M., 135n., 137
Recurrence: 234, 239; with variation, 234, 239
Reid, L. A., 281, 306
Rembrandt, 127, 141, 151–152
Renoir, 223
Respighi, O., 251
Reynolds, Joshua: 202; "essence"-theory, 121–128; "ideal"-theory, 128–132
Rhythm: 234–235; in the visual arts, 70–72
Ribot, T., 98, 108
Richards, I. A.: 55–57, 64, 331, 333, 413–415, 449, 485, 500; on artistic "truth," 310–315
Rodin, A., 137
Romanticism: the origins and development of, 158–161
Rouault, G., 329
Rymer, Thomas, **445–449**

Sabartés, J., 261
Saint-Gaudens, A., 125
Sainte-Beuve, C. A., 461–462
Saintsbury, G., 121n., 128, 161n., **444–445**, 446n.
Santayana, George: 38, 48, 92, 220, 244, 277, 278, 282, 326, 354–355, 371, 374, 416, 429; on expression, 251 ff.
Schoen, Max, 97n.
Schopenhauer, A., 43
Shakespeare: 88, 95, 112, 121, 123, **129–**